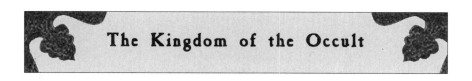

The Kingdom of the Occult

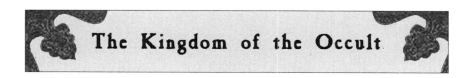

The Kingdom of the Occult

WALTER MARTIN

JILL MARTIN RISCHE

KURT VAN GORDEN

THOMAS NELSON
Since 1798

NASHVILLE   DALLAS   MEXICO CITY   RIO DE JANEIRO

Published in Nashville, Tennessee, by Thomas Nelson. Thomas Nelson is a trademark of Thomas Nelson, Inc.

Thomas Nelson, Inc. titles may be purchased in bulk for educational, business, fund-raising, or sales promotional use. For information, please e-mail SpecialMarkets@ThomasNelson.com.

Unless otherwise noted, Scripture quotations are taken from THE NEW KING JAMES VERSION. © 1982 by Thomas Nelson, Inc. Used by permission. All rights reserved.

Scripture quotations marked NIV are from HOLY BIBLE: NEW INTERNATIONAL VERSION®. © 1973, 1978, 1984 by International Bible Society. Used by permission of Zondervan Publishing House. All rights reserved.

Scripture quotations marked KJV are from KING JAMES VERSION.

Scripture quotations marked NASB are from NEW AMERICAN STANDARD BIBLE®. © The Lockman Foundation 1960, 1962, 1963, 1968, 1971, 1972, 1973, 1975, 1977. Used by permission.

Scripture quotations marked NRSV are from NEW REVISED STANDARD VERSION of the Bible. © 1989 by the Division of Christian Education of the National Council of the Churches of Christ in the U.S.A. All rights reserved.

ISBN-13: 978-1-4185-1644-4
ISBN : 1-4185-1644-9

Printed in the United States of America

13 — 12 11 10 9

Dedication

To Darlene Martin, with love. Thank you for trusting me with something very dear—the legacy of Walter Martin. I never could have done it without you.

And to Carol Rische, a mother-in-law who gave me a mother's love and taught me how to be content. Absent from the body and at home with her Lord. We miss you, Mom.

"Her children rise up and call her blessed" (Prov. 31:28).

—JILL MARTIN RISCHE

To my wife, Cindy, who abounded in patience and love throughout this project.

And to the entire Martin family, whose love for God's truth is never ending. When Dr. Martin officiated our wedding in 1980, he blessed my wife and me with a blessing that continues today. A hearty thanks to the Martin family for inviting me into this project, and for their love, prayers, and support for our mission work among the cults and occult all of these years.

"And whatever you do, do it heartily,
as to the Lord and not to men" (Col. 3:23).

—KURT VAN GORDEN

Contents

Acknowledgments

This book could not have been written without the love and support of my husband, Kevin, and our children, Christina and Justin. I would also like to thank everyone who sent us Walter Martin tapes—your kindness means so much; Kathleen Rasmussen—for your excellent work transcribing my father's tapes—you were a vital part of our team; Steve Laube, whose wisdom made a difference; my mother, Elaine Stein, for her constant encouragement; my sister and dearest friend, Elaine Martin—you brighten all our lives; my sister-in-law, Lynn Friedman, for the counseling ideas (and all those fun Fridays); Rick and Ronaele Wolf, for loving us—you have a special place in my heart; Jan Loewen and her daughter, Amanda, for your friendship and love—you are a gift to us; and Rhonda Hogan and Jennifer Stair, for their kindness.

—Jill Martin Rische

I would like to acknowledge Steve Laube, who did a masterful job as our agent, and the hardest worker on my behalf, my wife, Cindy, who as the codirector of our missions assisted in keeping our work balanced, and proofread chapter after chapter, providing helpful suggestions. Mark, our son, also did a great job proofreading the manuscript chapters. I love you all.

Finally, I would like to thank my late friend and mentor Dr. Walter R. Martin, who taught me the skills of research and initiated our mission work among the cults. His biblical apologetic answers still stand today because truth is impenetrable by error.

—Kurt Van Gorden

Introduction

Years ago, I remember my father pacing the foyer of our home, leafing through a notebook of references on the occult. It had always been in the back of his mind to write a companion volume to *The Kingdom of the Cults*, but something always prevented him from beginning the new project.

Looking back, I can see that God had other plans.

When my husband, Kevin, and I began Walter Martin Ministries in 1998, we talked about the things we hoped to accomplish, and *The Kingdom of the Occult* was at the top of our list. I never thought I would be the one to do it; I just felt it should be done. And then one day our friend (and intrepid agent) Steve Laube brought up the pressing need for a book on the occult, and this time I knew God's plan for *The Kingdom of the Occult* included me. Kurt Van Gorden, my father's gifted researcher and longtime family friend, seemed the perfect fit for a coauthor, and this journey began. I can honestly say it has been an extraordinary one in so many ways. I never thought that working on a book about the occult would be the experience of a lifetime, but that is exactly what it has become. During the past year, one verse made all the difference in my life and in Kurt's life as well: "The joy of the LORD is your strength" (Neh. 8:10).

In the midst of all the evil things that needed to be read and evaluated, the presence of the Holy Spirit constantly protected us. Each time we sat down to write, we prayed for God's protection, and every single time, He answered us. Surrounded by books on Witchcraft, Satanism, and demon possession, our hearts would be filled with joy that Jesus defeated Satan and every dark aspect of the occult on the Cross. There was joy in the fact that He is greater than anything that might come against us, and peace in knowing He loves us and called us to His work. The Word of God and the power of the Holy Spirit strengthened and encouraged us in a way we had never experienced before. It has been a wonderful year, and we hope the sense of overwhelming joy and victory we felt each day in writing this book shines through on every page.

Although my father is with the Lord, the ministry he had on earth as a representative of the gospel of Jesus Christ lives on. The wisdom of God is, of course, eternal. Our physical lives may end in this world, but that does not mean God is finished using our walk and our witness for His glory. My father always intended to write *The Kingdom of the Occult*, and now—in thought and word—he has done so. The deed belongs to God.

The occult deserves a healthy respect, but it is nothing any Christian need fear. It is the ultimate enemy in power and purpose, but Jesus faced the worst it had to offer . . . victoriously. We are the winners—we are the chosen children of God. And as His beloved children, we must be ready not only to proclaim the gospel, but to *defend* it. And that is exactly what my father, Kurt and I have done in this book.

The Kingdom of the Occult is the product of a unique blend of ideas. My father's work on the occult provided the foundation that Kurt and I built upon. We edited transcripts from his lectures and sections of his writing, adding our chapters, comments, and critiques where necessary. Whenever possible, his words remain verbatim—changes or additions were made only to include subject matter my father rarely taught or to facilitate the flow of the manuscript. The meaning behind his words was carefully preserved and, in all new material, his position clearly expressed. Many of the case studies in this book reflect my father's experiences in dealing with the occult, and they are invaluable learning tools for those fighting against the world of the occult.

In 1978, Walter Martin had this to say about the defense of the faith:

Today, the Christian Church is not on the advance, she is in retreat. The reason she is in retreat is because the world threatens her. About us on every side are people trying to poke holes in Scripture instead of proclaiming Scripture. We are attacked by philosophers, psychologists, and psychiatrists; by the whole massive front of evil, no matter what garb it takes. The idea is to push back the Christian Church. And there is only one way that you can resist such force: "Not by might nor by power, but by my Spirit, Says the Lord of hosts" (Zechariah 4:6). It is a grounding in the Word of God, it is a fullness in the Spirit and life, it is the realization that if we are going to be more than conquerors for Christ, then we must have our priorities ordered and we must get *into* the Scriptures and get *out* with the answers. . . .

When you are talking with people in the occult, remember that they are flesh and blood human beings, not supernatural caricatures. They have needs and wants—they are people who will bleed if you stick them with a pin or cry if a loved one dies. They did not abdicate their citizenship in the human race because they were taken captive by the devil. You must be able to identify with them. You have to realize, "There but for the grace of God, go I." It is terribly important to understand that they are people of value and worth to God, and all the blasphemy, the anger, and the awful things they may say to you and *about* Christ they say in ignorance—exactly like the apostle Paul, who called himself the least of all the apostles who obtained mercy because he did what he did in ignorance.

You and I are the commissioned and ordained servants of the King of Kings. He gave us the opportunity to obtain that knowledge. He gave us the power of the Spirit. He gave us access to His Word. He challenged us to become more than conquerors. He opened the fields unto harvest.

Will you not hear the voice of the Lord of the Vineyard? See these fields of the cults and the occult, and reach out to them in the name of Jesus.[1]

Our battle is not against flesh and blood, but against ancient powers and principalities (Eph. 6:12). It takes the Word of God, His beloved Son, and the awesome power of His Holy Spirit to defeat them.

In the end, *The Kingdom of the Occult* is about the magnificent power of God and its triumph over evil—the proof of what my father always used to say: "Cheer up! I've got good news for you: I've read the end of the book, and *we win!*"

Jill Martin Rische
Kurt Van Gorden
September 15, 2007

---

1. Martin, *Evangelizing People in the Cults and Occult,* CD/audiotape (Anaheim, CA: Melodyland Christian Center, August, 1978).

I pray also that the eyes of your heart may be enlightened in order that you may know the hope to which he has called you, the riches of his glorious inheritance in the saints, and his incomparably great power for us who believe.

—EPHESIANS 1:18–19 NIV

Quick Facts about the Kingdom of the Occult

- The word *occult* comes from the Latin word *occultus,* meaning hidden or secret things.[2]

- God defines the *occult* as having its origin with Satan, the devil.

- Satan is a proud spirit-being, a personality created in another dimension by the all-powerful Being, the God of creation.

- Occultism often denies the Trinity, the deity of Christ, His atonement on the Cross for our sins, and His bodily resurrection, but it may also promote a blend of Christian and occult beliefs.

---

2. *University of Notre Dame Latin Dictionary and Grammar Aid Online,* s.v. "occult," http://catholic-archives.nd.edu/cgi-bin/lookup.pl?stem=occulo&ending= (accessed September 25, 2006).

1

The Kingdom of the Occult

I t is a sad and frightening fact that people are fascinated with the secret or "occult" things that God has condemned (Deut. 18:9–12). One cannot see a movie like *Harry Potter* or read *The Exorcist*, which presents Satan unvarnished and portrays the truth about demonic possession in terms everyone can understand, without being plunged into the core of the occult. Today there is a tremendous fascination with the mysterious and the unknown. The great scholar C. S. Lewis wrote, "There are two equal and opposite errors into which our race can fall about the devils. One is to disbelieve in their existence. The other is to believe, and to feel an excessive and unhealthy interest in them. They themselves are equally pleased by both errors, and hail a materialist or a magician with the same delight."[1]

The modern age is strong proof of this unhealthy fascination. People are attracted to evil and captivated by it. They are vulnerable to temptation because of a growing revolt against science and technology that, for all their efforts, cannot meet man's spiritual hunger. People are asking, "If science and technology are supposed to produce all the good things, why haven't they accomplished it?" Instead, there is a continuous degradation of personality. People are not treated as human beings anymore but as computer data, numbers assigned from womb to tomb.

Today, a terrible spiritual vacuum exists in which people are forced to live because they turned from the living God and tried to fill the resulting emptiness with physical pleasure. Man crowds into this vacuum all the moral and ethical values attached to the material world. Again and again people protest, "There's got to be something more than this, because we're not satisfied." Satisfaction has not come through the dollar sign. Satisfaction has not come through the pill. Satisfaction has not come through economic aggrandizement or political conquests

---

1. C. S. Lewis, *The Screwtape Letters* (New York: HarperCollins, 1961, copyright restored 1996 C. S. Lewis Pte. Ltd.), preface.

or military supremacy. Lost in a spiritual void, the human heart searches for some kind of reality apart from God and His Word, and discovers the occult reality from another dimension.

Today, the kingdom of the occult encompasses the globe like a spiderweb of immense proportions, its overall membership estimated in the hundreds of millions.[2] It is the purpose of this book to investigate this dimension of darkness and to examine its influence in America and throughout the world. It is also our aim to familiarize readers with the refreshing truths of the Gospel of Christ that they may see the great heritage that is ours in the Christian faith and be challenged to live and to witness more effectively for the Savior.[3]

Our approach to the subject is threefold: (1) *historical analysis* of key facts connected with the rise of the occult, (2) *theological evaluation* of the occult's major teachings, and (3) *apologetic contrast* from the viewpoint of biblical theology, with an emphasis upon exegesis and doctrine.[4] A study of the occult is a serious business. Its teachings represent a growing spiritual force in the world today, a force intent on turning people away from established Christian churches and the historic teachings of the Bible.

THE DIMENSION OF DARKNESS

The Bible is a dimensional book in the sense that a dimension is a realm of reality, sometimes imperceptible, but nonetheless genuine. Human beings live in a dimension subject to the five senses, and they tend to make the mistake of believing that anything beyond the realm of those senses simply is not there. To accept such reasoning would be a fatal mistake from a biblical perspective.

Even as people live in the dimension of earth, so the Bible says there is another dimension of heaven, where God reigns as Sovereign. This second dimension of heaven, or the throne of God Himself, is more real than human senses can perceive; it is a dimension that was bridged when God chose to become man in the person

---

2. *The Association of Religion Data Archives Online*, s.v. "International Data," http://www.thearda.com/internationalData/countries/Country_234_2.asp (data collected by World Christian Encyclopedia and World Christian Trends), http://worldchristiandatabase.org/wed// (accessed September 26, 2006).

3. Walter Martin, ed. Ravi Zacharias, *The Kingdom of the Cults*, rev., upd., exp. ed. (Grand Rapids: Bethany House, 2003), 23.

4. Adapted from Martin, *The Kingdom of the Cults*, 18.

of Jesus Christ. Because of Him, mankind now has access to a realm of infinite power, indescribable love, and cosmic justice.

The third dimension is one of spiritual darkness, controlled by Satan and his hosts. The Bible describes it as hell, or the alienation of the spiritual nature of man from fellowship with his Creator. It belongs to the "prince of the power of the air, the spirit who now works in the sons of disobedience" (Eph. 2:2). This dimension is portrayed in Ephesians 6:10–12, where the warning is given that it is the domain of the forces of incalculable wickedness, presided over by the one whom the Bible designates as "the ruler of this world" and "the god of this age" (John 14:30; 2 Cor. 4:4). This domain is described variously in the Bible as "outer darkness" (Matt. 8:12; 22:13; 25:30), "fire" (Matt. 5:22; 13:42; 18:8, 9; 25:41; Mark 9:22–49), "suffering" (Jude 7), consciousness of separation from God, and fear of others suffering the same (Luke 16:19–31), "prison" (1 Peter 3:19), and, metaphorically, a vast lake of molten sulfur, from which there is no deliverance (Rev. 19:20; 20:10, 14, 15; 21:8).

Perhaps this dimension is best described in terms of the condition of its occupants, who are portrayed as "wandering stars for whom is reserved the blackness of darkness forever" (Jude 13).[5] The apostle Peter indicated that some of the fallen angels were already chained in the darkness of hell, awaiting judgment: "God did not spare the angels who sinned, but cast them down to hell and delivered them into chains of darkness, to be reserved for judgment" (2 Peter 2:4). It is possible, then, that hell may be one dimension with many levels, some restrictive and some not, since Satan and an unknown number of his demons are still free to roam the earth.[6]

---

5. These three realms are enumerated only for distinction, not biblical order.
6. Albert Barnes analyzes the possible structure of hell: "[Cast them down to hell]—Greek *tartaroosas*—'thrusting them down to Tartarus.' The word here used occurs nowhere else in the New Testament, though it is common in the Classical writers. It is a verb formed from [Tartaros], Tartarus, which in Greek mythology was the lower part, or abyss of Hades, Hadees, where the shades of the wicked were supposed to be imprisoned and tormented, and corresponded to the Jewish word Geenna—'Gehenna.' It was regarded, commonly, as beneath the earth; as entered through the grave; as dark, dismal, gloomy; and as a place of punishment. Compare the notes at Job 10:21–22, and Matt 5:22. The word here is one that properly refers to a place of punishment, since the whole argument relates to that, and since it cannot be pretended that the 'angels that sinned' were removed to a place of happiness on account of their transgression. It must also refer to punishment in some other world than this, for there is no evidence that THIS world is made a place of punishment for fallen angels. [And delivered them into chains of darkness]
cont'd on next page

Biblical theology teaches us that Jesus Christ came into the world to deliver men from this darkness, because originally hell was prepared *not for man* but for Satan and his followers. They go there by divine decree, while man is the only creation that chooses it freely. This is clearly derived from Jesus' words: "Then He will also say to those on the left hand, 'Depart from Me, you cursed, into the everlasting fire prepared for the devil and his angels'" (Matt. 25:41). Whatever hell's dimension may be, one thing is absolutely certain: if it required the death of the most perfect Being who ever lived to deliver us from it, then it is to be avoided at all costs.

It is against this domain of darkness that the Christian is in mortal combat, and not against mere flesh and blood. This dimension is the unopened door with its handle on *our side* in the dimension of earth. It is with the tools of the occult that men open this door, and through it proceeds the power of awesome evil. There is no force on earth that can overpower Satan except Jesus, who is head of all principalities and powers, and the Church, which is His body (Col. 1:15–20; Eph. 6:12).[7]

SATAN—YESTERDAY AND TODAY

Down through history, Satan's public awareness has ranged from fascinating to revolting, and as far back as scholars can reach into the study of religion they find some kind of concept or image of him (although his name often varies). The Chaldeans and Babylonians, for example, produced numerous caricatures and portrayals of Satan. Resh Lakish comments in the Babylonian Talmud that "Satan, the evil prompter, and the Angel of Death are all one."[8] However, the clearest picture

---

6. (cont'd): 'Where darkness lies like chains upon them'—Robinson, Lexicon. The meaning seems to be, that they are confined in that dark prisonhouse AS IF by chains. We are not to suppose that spirits are literally bound; but it was common to bind or fetter prisoners who were in dungeons, and the representation here is taken from that fact. This representation that the mass of fallen angels are confined in 'Tartarus,' or in hell, is not inconsistent with the representations which elsewhere occur that their leader is permitted to roam the earth, and that even many of those spirits are allowed to tempt men. It may be still true that the mass are confined within the limits of their dark abode; and it may even be true also that Satan and those who are permitted to roam the earth are under bondage, and are permitted to range only within certain bounds, and that they are so secured that they will be brought to trial at the last day." *Barnes' Notes,* Biblesoft.
7. There are several other ways to open a door to Satan's domain besides the occult. Rebellion, which is like Witchcraft, stubbornness, which is like idolatry (1 Sam. 15:23), and just outright sin. Dr. Martin used to say, "Had the Devil never existed, there is enough residual evil within man to send him to hell without the Devil's aid."
8. *Babylonion Talmud: Tractate Baba Bathra Online,* s.v. "Folio 16a v. 4," http://www.come-and-hear.com/bababathra/bababathra_16.html (accessed August 20, 2007).

of Satan, alias the Devil, the adversary, Abaddon, Belial, or Beelzebub ("Baal-Zebub," from 2 Kings 1:2)—appears in the New Testament. It is important to understand the clear, biblical picture of the nature of Satan in order to grasp the power of the occult.

According to Ezekiel 28, Satan, called the "king of Tyre" was once a beautiful, created being; a marvelous messenger of light. Satan's original name, Lucifer, means *light bearer*, and he occupied a position of tremendous privilege and responsibility in the kingdom of heaven. Today, many popular teachers state that Satan was "the most beautiful" of God's creations, but this is a claim that cannot be proven, since *beautiful* is the only description given. The Bible reveals that Lucifer was hurled from his high position in heaven. He was, quite literally, driven out by Michael the archangel, who fought against him until the power of God prevailed (Rev. 12:7–9).[9]

In the account by the prophet Isaiah, Lucifer revolted against the throne of God because he wanted to be like the Most High God, thereby falling from his place of glory through his pride (14:12–21). Jesus said, "I saw Satan fall like lightning from heaven" (Luke 10:18), which, for Christians, removes all doubt of Satan's existence and fall. Though he lost the radiance and splendor that was reflected from the throne of the Lord, and with which he was anointed because of his exalted position, Lucifer (at this point renamed Satan) threw the whole force of his own being and of his partners in angelic rebellion into a great cosmic war intended to disrupt God's divine plan and win for himself either terms of armistice with the Creator or else, ultimate triumph.

Satan's strategy evidently depended on the fallacious premise that because he had not been annihilated by divine wrath, God was incapable of such an action and was therefore neither infinite nor omnipotent.[10] There is no delusion like self-delusion, and Satan became self-deceived. Satan's decision to pursue his own prideful goals, rather than the will of the Creator, caused him to wield the vast

---

9. Satan was the real force behind the king of Tyre, who became his puppet king. Also, the popularity of the inaccurate teaching that Satan was "the most beautiful" of God's creations is evident in the number of search engine hits it receives, but it has no biblical basis.

10. Some may argue that we do not know Satan's reasoning, except for Isaiah's disclosure of his prideful thoughts, but this does not necessarily mean that he thought God was *not* almighty. Instead, he may have thought of himself as coequal. Satan, in destroying humanity, may not think that he can *still* ascend God's throne or beat Him in battle. He may just be fighting to destroy as many of God's creatures as possible before going down in the end.

power and authority at his command in spiritual warfare against the throne of the Eternal.

In the third chapter of Genesis, Satan tempts Eve to sin through the same avenue of pride that paved the way for his own downfall eons earlier. Although his handiwork was well-known in the universe at large (already disrupted by sin and its consequences), Satan had not yet succeeded in penetrating the garden of Eden and subjecting this part of God's creation to his sphere of influence and power. But with the fall of Eve and Adam, Satan accomplished this goal, too, though not without incurring the divine prophecy that the physical seed of the people he had led to spiritual rebellion and physical destruction would someday crush him and bring about his ultimate destruction (Gen. 3:15). As the last Adam, Jesus Christ accomplished this triumph through His death and resurrection.

SATAN'S TRIUMPH

Satan triumphed in Eden. Man was expelled from the garden and separated from fellowship with his Creator, a fact that no doubt added fuel to Satan's theory that the Creator was not almighty, since He could have prevented the fall of man even as He could have prevented the fall of angels. Ignoring the biblical truth that true love is based on freedom of choice (John 3:16) and that God had displayed this kind of love in creating angels and men with this capacity, Satan plunged on to disrupt the entire human race and to interfere with the will of his Creator.

Throughout Scripture, we find Satan repeatedly attempting to thwart the divine will. It was the power of Satan that energized the priests of the demon gods of Egypt, who opposed Moses as he sought to deliver Israel, and it was Satan who imitated the miracles of God to confuse Pharaoh, something he will also do through the great coming Antichrist (Ex. 7:11–12; 2 Thess. 2:9–12).

In the book of Job, Satan accused, attacked, and tempted the righteous Job. Satan told God that Job would curse Him to His face, and he argued for the end of the divine power that protected Job and his family. Satan hoped to strengthen his argument that God would lose out to him whenever man was faced with a free choice. But Job proved Satan wrong, for he maintained his spiritual integrity. Job's experience reveals much about the devil's methods and nature. For example, Satan inspired Herod to murder children in an attempt to destroy the infant Jesus (Matt. 2:16), and he influenced Judas to betray the Son of God (John 13:27). The Lord

Jesus Christ, however, invaded Satan's kingdom and successfully bound him during his earthly ministry: He encountered him on the Mount of Temptation and exerted divine authority by defeating him on the Cross (Luke 4:1–13).

Christ gave His apostles power over demons and the capacity to resist the devil, though He did not hesitate to describe Satan as "the ruler of this world" (John 14:30). The apostle Paul called Satan "the god of this age" (2 Cor. 4:4), and he urged the Church to "put on the whole armor of God" (Eph. 6:11–18). Other apostles wrote that we must resist the devil (James 4:7; 1 Peter 5:9).

THE TRUE SATAN

We must try our best to avoid thinking of Satan in terms of historic caricatures. He does not wear a red suit, nor does he possess a beard, horns, or leering smile as he is so frequently depicted at Halloween. The cloven hoof is a symbol of Satan, as are the goat's head and the inverted cross, but they are only imaginative figures assigned to him. Satan does not smell of sulfur, he does not possess a pointed tail, and he is in no way connected with the flames of hell. Based on what we can learn from the Bible, he has not yet been near any flames of that nature, and he has no desire to be.

Satan is not a *he* as we understand male or female; Satan is, according to the Bible, a personality independent of gender. Satan is a proud spirit, a personality created in another dimension by an all-powerful Being, the God of creation. He was created to serve the Lord, but he was given free will. He chose to exercise his will against the sovereignty of God, and he fell from his first position of glory when he uttered that terrible pronouncement, "I will be like the Most High" (Isa. 14:14). "I . . . I . . . I" is Satan's constant egotistical affirmation.

In *Paradise Lost,* the poet John Milton portrayed Satan as somewhat of a hero. Many media outlets, in discussing exorcism, have emphasized the power of Satan so that he makes Jesus Christ seem pallid by comparison. But nothing could be farther from the truth. Though Satan's power is enormous, and though he exercised that power in Eden to usher in sin and death, he was nevertheless encountered and defeated by the last Adam, Jesus Christ (Rom. 5:14–15).

In John 14:30, Jesus said He had defeated Satan, but Satan was to remain powerful and capable of great authority for a time. The brilliant twentieth-century preacher Donald Grey Barnhouse once observed, "The ruler of this world has come and has found *plenty* in us."[11] Satan's activity is well-known throughout the world. If we recall the Nazi concentration camps of Dachau, Auschwitz, Belsen, Buchenwald, or *The Gulag Archipelago* of Aleksandr Solzhenitsyn, then we are aware that Satan's activity is not "corporate evil" but *personal* violence, deceit, and hatred.

When men deal with Satan, they are not dealing with an illusion or a projection of human evil; they are dealing with a real entity who was totally and absolutely routed by Jesus Christ. The finality of Satan's defeat will come when he is cast into a lake of fire and sulfur, a place that the Bible describes as *eternity without God*.[12] There Satan and all who followed him, acknowledging him as their god by refusing to recognize the true God and His Son, Jesus Christ, will then find eternal judgment a terrifying reality.

CASE STUDY

Walter Martin

I cannot help but think, when we talk about occultism, just how deadly it can become. I was giving a series of lectures in New York some time ago, and a minister and his wife came to me with an incredible story. He began by saying, "Walter, I want to tell you something because I know you'll believe me. If I tell other people, they'll just write me off."

This took me a bit by surprise and I answered, "Well, after twenty years of seeing all the things I've seen, yes, I think I might just believe you. What happened to you?"

He gave the following account:

We come from a family of Spiritists. Everyone in our family practiced mediumship and held séances. I was born again and escaped, but my sister was still in it. She practiced with the Ouija board and went through the whole routine. I was so concerned about her that

---

11. Walter Martin, *Doctrine of the Demons*, CD/Audio, www.waltermartin.com.
12. See Jesus' illustration of this in Mark 9:44, 46, 48.

one night I went over to her home. On the way there, I said to my wife, "Tonight is the night we face her with this."

We arrived and went inside, and she was sitting there with a Ouija board on the table in front of her. I warned her, "I've come here to show you this thing is devilish." She just laughed at me.

I sat down across from her, and the two of us started a dialogue with the Ouija board. (Parker Brothers manufactures the "game" *Ouija* by the thousands.) And as I sat there in that room, an eerie feeling came over me. I started to ask questions of the Ouija board—and it answered me.

The first question I asked of this "force" was, "Who are you?"

The force spelled out the word, "S-P-I-R-I-T."

"What is your name?" It refused to give it.

"Were you there when the resurrection of Christ took place?"

The answer came on the board, "Yes."

"What did you experience?"

"F-E-A-R."

It was then I began to get very concerned. I asked, "What do you feel toward me?"

"H-A-T-E."

"What do you think of the Bible?" It spelled out a four-letter obscenity.

At that point, I decided to break off contact with the Ouija board. So I stood up from the table, took my Bible, and said, "I'll have no more to do with this. It's devilish." And I threw my Bible into the center of the Ouija board.

At that moment, the board levitated off the table and flipped the Bible into the air with such force that it flew across the room and hit the wall. My sister and my wife screamed.

As I stood there looking at it, something smashed me in my stomach and knocked me to the floor. I was doubled over—breathless—with my head between my knees, and the only thing I could gasp was, "Jesus, Jesus, Jesus. Help!"

My sister said, "Really, you've gone too far now. You're not going to try to fool me anymore."

But I was lying on the floor in such a convincing position that my wife and sister came over to help me. When we pulled up my shirt, there was a red welt the size of a fist over my solar plexus! At that juncture, my sister recognized that I had been hit—*but by nothing visible in that room*. The next thing I knew, we were all having a prayer meeting. My sister came out of the occult to Christ, and the Ouija board was splintered and burned.

"I never would have believed this, Walt, unless I lived through it," he finished. "What do you think hit me?"

"Well, read the book of Acts," I said. "The seven sons of Sceva probably had the same question. Remember how they tried to cast out demons? What happened? The demon said, 'Jesus I know, and I know about Paul, but who are you? Then the man who had the evil spirit jumped on them and overpowered them all. He gave them such a beating that they ran out of the house naked and bleeding'" (Acts 19:15–16 NIV).

"I've learned my lesson," he replied. "I leave the Ouija boards and all of this to the Holy Spirit. I don't bother with it anymore."

These are not innocent things. They are dangerous things that must be faced by believers in Christ. The people who play with Ouija boards and think it is cute; the people who try to levitate tables, read tarot cards, tea leaves, and their palms; the people who try to find out whether they are Gemini, Virgo or Scorpio, and what the paper said today about what tomorrow will be—these are the people who are flirting with the kingdom of the occult. And it is *dangerous*, because it reaches out to another dimension and endangers the soul. You do not have to go to Africa to find demons. Africa, South America, the dark continents of the world—none are darker than America.[13]

13. Martin, *Doctrine of the Demons,* CD/Audio, www.waltermartin.com.

SCRIPTURAL RESPONSE

In Acts 13, the apostles Paul and Barnabas had been sent forth by the Holy Spirit. Passing through the city of Paphos, they encountered a sorcerer (occultist), a false prophet who called himself Bar-Jesus or "Son of Jesus":

> Now when they had gone through the island to Paphos, they found a certain sorcerer, a false prophet, a Jew whose name was Bar-Jesus, who was with the proconsul, Sergius Paulus, an intelligent man. This man called for Barnabas and Saul and sought to hear the word of God. But Elymas the sorcerer (for so his name is translated) withstood them, seeking to turn the proconsul away from the faith. Then Saul, who also is called Paul, filled with the Holy Spirit, looked intently at him and said, "O full of all deceit and all fraud, you son of the devil, you enemy of all righteousness, will you not cease perverting the straight ways of the Lord? And now, indeed, the hand of the Lord is upon you, and you shall be blind, not seeing the sun for a time." And immediately a dark mist fell on him, and he went around seeking someone to lead him by the hand. Then the proconsul believed, when he saw what had been done, being astonished at the teaching of the Lord. (vv. 6–12)

A number of interesting things emerge from this encounter that reveal the unchanging attitude of God toward all forms of occultic practices and those who are involved in them. The word *sorcerer* is derived from the Greek word *mavgo*, meaning *seer* or *sorcerer*.[14] Bar-Jesus' primary goal was to divert Sergius Paulus, governor of the island, from the Christian faith. When Paul addressed Bar-Jesus, it should be noted that Paul was "filled with the Holy Spirit," and so it was actually the Holy Spirit who spoke in condemnation of the occultist and occult practices in general. The words of the Spirit are definitive, compelling, and judgmental. He accused the occultist of fraud and of being filled with all deceit, and termed him a son of Satan and an enemy of all that is right. He accused him of perverting the path or the way of the Lord, which is termed *right* in contrast to his *wrong*. Then

---

14. *The KJV New Testament Greek Lexicon Online,* s.v. "mavgo," http://bible.crosswalk.com/Lexicons/Greek/grk.cgi?number=3097&version=kjv (accessed August 20, 2007).

he followed this assessment with swift judgment (blindness). As a result of that judgment by the Holy Spirit, salvation came to Sergius Paulus because he saw the power of the Lord and was convinced of the truth of the teaching of Paul and Barnabas.

God's Truth

A closer examination of this encounter in Acts 13 reveals precisely what occult practitioners, knowingly or unknowingly, truly are:

1. They are in league with Satan and possess certain supernatural powers.
2. They are false prophets.
3. They seek to influence people politically and ecclesiastically, particularly those in positions of power (vv. 6–7).
4. They attempt to prevent those who are seeking to hear the Word of God from learning it by opposing those who preach it (v. 8).
5. They deliberately attempt to divert prospective converts from the faith as their ultimate goal (v. 8).

In contrast to this, the judgment of the Holy Spirit is explicit:

1. He calls such attempts and practices "full of all kinds of deceit and trickery" (v. 10 NIV).
2. He designates occultism and the occult as having its origin with the devil, by calling Bar-Jesus "son of the devil" (v. 10).
3. He unmasks the occultists' tactics and declares them to be enemies of all that is righteous. He calls them perverters of the ways of the Lord, which are designated as "straight," or right (v. 10).

If this were not sufficient, the Spirit then struck the occultist (a medium) blind and used this judgment to convince Sergius Paulus, the seeker after truth, that the gospel of Jesus Christ is the truth and that the way of occultism leads to destruction.

God's attitude toward occultism and occult practices has not altered. Neither has His attitude altered toward those who teach such practices, and those who persist in pursuing them for their own ends.

Satan's Lies

The occult seduces the unwary with its offer of limited knowledge of the future and supposed control over the lives of others.[15] It promises power. If someone involved in the occult can provide secret information to an individual that only he knows, and then predict something that does indeed occur, then the occultist has secured power over the other person through fear.

The occult holds out the promise of love, but it is not the divine, unconditional love of God (*agape*) as described in Scripture. Rather, it is psychosexual love (*eros*), which explains why many of those who are in the world of the occult are immoral, recognizing only a standard of authority established by their own reasoning.[16]

The occult offers a small degree of certainty in a world of uncertainty. Moving outside the realm of established religion, it promises things that the Church forbids. It provides a sense of belonging, so desperately needed by people who reject God's love in Jesus Christ, and accept substitutes rather than regeneration in the image of God through faith in the Lord Jesus Christ. At its heart it is egocentric: the occultist seeks first his own ends and then the ends of others. It provides no exit from the realities of life and the problem of sin, but is merely a satanic diversion that frequently masks itself in Christian terminology. That is why we often see Spiritist churches deny the Trinity, the deity of Christ, His atonement on the Cross for our sins, and His bodily resurrection, yet still use Christian terminology, quote the Bible, and sing hymns (altered to fit their theological system). They have the *form* of Christian unity, as did the sorcerer in the book of Acts, but they are devoid of the saving, historic gospel (2 Tim. 3:5). It should come as no surprise to us that Satan, who created "another Jesus . . . a different spirit . . . and a different gospel" (2 Cor. 11:4), should introduce under the guise of Christianity practices that seem to follow a biblical pattern but culminate in eternal spiritual death.

---

15. Deuteronomy 13:1–2 tells us that sometimes occultists will give a sign or wonder that actually "comes to pass." The Lord God allows this to "test" our hearts to see if we will follow false gods (Deut. 13:5). True knowledge is fed to the occultist by Satan.
16. For more information on the difference between *eros* and *agape* love, see Anders Nygren, *Agape and Eros,* trans. Philip S. Watson (New York: Harper and Row, 1969).

CONCLUSION

It is only necessary to read Deuteronomy 18:9–14 to learn that God considered Canaanite occult practices "abominations" worthy of capital punishment:

> When you come into the land which the LORD your God is giving you, you shall not learn to follow the abominations of those nations. There shall not be found among you anyone who makes his son or his daughter pass through the fire, or one who practices witchcraft, or a soothsayer, or one who interprets omens, or a sorcerer, or one who conjures spells, or a medium, or a spiritist, or one who calls up the dead. For all who do these things are an abomination to the LORD, and because of these abominations the LORD your God drives them out from before you. You shall be blameless before the LORD your God. For these nations which you will dispossess listened to soothsayers and diviners; but as for you, the LORD your God has not appointed such for you.

In these verses, God has given an index of occultic practices. Additional passages, such as Isaiah 47:12–15 and the book of Daniel, where astrology and other such practices are condemned by God in the strongest terms, prove that the Lord did not change His mind; He is still diametrically opposed to all occultism.

The divine edict "I am the LORD, I do not change" (Mal. 3:6) extends also to the New Testament revelation. In Acts 19:19, those who heard the word of the Lord and believed it brought all the tools of the occult in their possession to the feet of the apostles, and burned them because such practices were accursed. The practice of Witchcraft is specifically mentioned and strongly condemned in the Old and the New Testaments (Ex. 22:18; Lev. 19:31; Deut. 18:9–14; 1 Sam. 28:7–19; Gal. 5:20). God recognized what men had failed to recognize: knowledge of the future is in *His* hand, and any attempt to obtain from the hand of demons what has been denied by the will of the Divine is an experiment fraught with peril and dangers undreamed of by the human soul.

The world of the occult is to be avoided by believers in Christ because we are the temples of the Holy Spirit (1 Cor. 6:19). We are to avoid *participation* in the activities of this dark dimension while, at the same time, standing firmly against it to "contend earnestly for the faith which was once for all delivered to the saints"

(Jude 3). Christians are urged to put on the full armor of God to do warfare in the spiritual dimension, confident that if we resist the devil, he will flee. Remember, "He who is in you is greater than he who is in the world" (1 John 4:4), a reference to the strength of God's power against Satan and all his hosts, whether spiritual or corporeal (Eph. 6:11; James 4:7).

The Church of Jesus Christ must stand and fight against the evil of the occult because she has been commanded to do so, and because she possesses the power to do so. Christ has risen from the dead and is triumphant over all the forces arrayed against Him; it was impossible that death should hold Him who alone is designated in Scripture "Prince of life" (Acts 3:15). The "great High Priest" of the Christian church rebuked Satan on earth and defeated him on the Cross to redeem the sons of men (Heb. 4:14; Luke 4). The King of eternity disdained occultic practices, for they originate with Satan, and those who practice them are indeed fools who rush in where the angels fear to tread (Jude 9).

The revolt against reason and logic today has brought on the drug culture and a yearning for some sense of security. It has brought on the absorption with alcohol, drugs, sex, and now the absorption with death that is rapidly replacing sex in Western culture. This revolt against reason and logic has produced an irrational faith and an irrational way of life—fertile ground for the seeds of the occult.

In direct opposition to these false, satanic doctrines are the good, sound doctrines of Scripture that are taught by Christ and ordained by the apostles. These doctrines alone are pure and true since their origin is God Himself, who adjures us through the Holy Spirit to continue in the things we have learned from His Word and to study to show ourselves approved, faithful handlers of the Word of truth (2 Tim. 2:15).

RECOMMENDED RESOURCES

1. Barnhouse, Donald Grey. *The Invisible War.* Grand Rapids: Zondervan, 1965.
2. Lewis, C. S. *The Screwtape Letters.* New York: HarperCollins, 2001.
3. Martin, Walter. *Spiritual Warfare.* CD/audiotape, Walter Martin Ministries, www.waltermartin.com.
4. Mather, George and Larry Nichols. *Dictionary of Cults, Sects, Religions and the Occult.* Grand Rapids: Zondervan, 2005.

Quick Facts About the Occult Revolution

- Occultists define the occult as truth; a deeper, more profound truth than the visible facts science provides.

- The occult is built upon one word: experience.

- Experience is not subject to divine authority.

- Death is not a violent result of sin, it has no sting, and it is neither friend nor enemy.

2

The Occult Revolution

The moment Lucifer fell from heaven and became Satan, the world of the occult was born. The occult or "secret knowledge" born of rebellion took root and grew strong, nurtured in oral and written tradition that passed on secret rituals, spells, and incantations from one generation to the next.[1] Ancient man built his cities in peace and destroyed them in war, leaving behind clear and consistent evidence of worship in carved images, stone altars, temples, and tombs.[2] Although the nature of worship and its origin have always been subjects of debate, the evidence is clear that from time immemorial, humans acknowledged the existence of supernatural power and *worshiped.*

There are compelling messages in the crumbling parchments and well-worn tablets of the ancients; their words and actions echo from the past, bringing with them the power to teach by example. The details of their everyday lives, pieced together from the remains of their cities, are a primary source of knowledge. In the ruins of so many lands like Italy, Egypt, and Israel, the worship history of the ancient world is written.

THE OCCULT IN ANTIQUITY

The first humans in the book of Genesis were monotheistic, just as God's true faith has been through the ages.[3] Genesis 1:27 reveals plainly the intimate nature of the

---

1. John G. Gager, *Curse Tablets and Binding Spells from the Ancient World,* (New York: Oxford, 1992) 7.
2. Mitchell Dahood, "Are the Ebla Tablets Relevant to Biblical Research?" *Biblical Archaeological Society Archives,* http://members.bib-arch.org/nph-proxy.pl/000000A/http/www.basarchive.org/bswbSearch.asp=efPubID=3dBSBA&Volume=3d6&Issue=3d5&ArticleD=3d6&UserID=3d0& (accessed July 22, 2006).
3. For a recent study on early monotheism, see Norman L. Geisler, "Primitive Monotheism," *Christian Apologetics Journal* 1, no. 1, (1998): 1–5. Here, Geisler argues for early monotheism from biblical history, archaeological discoveries (Ebla Tablets), anthropological studies, and philosophy to conclude that "there is early evidence to believe that Monotheism was the first religion."

relationship between one God, the Creator, and man, His creation: "So God created man in His own image; in the image of God He created him; male and female He created them." And after the flood had eliminated every human being except Noah and his family, "Then God spoke to Noah and to his sons with him, saying: 'And as for Me, behold, I establish My covenant with you and with your descendants after you'" (Gen. 9:8–9). The biblical record portrays a personal relationship between God and early man; a close emotional and spiritual bond of communication and worship.

William F. Albright, one of the world's great archaeologists, confirms the credibility of the biblical record as legitimate historical evidence in *The Archaeology of Palestine*. "Discovery after discovery has established the accuracy of innumerable details, and has brought increased recognition to the Bible as a source of history."[4] Although the historical and theological debate of ancient monotheism versus polytheism is far from settled in some academic circles, the fact that ancient man left significant evidence of monotheistic beliefs cannot be discounted. Brian Brown, in his detailed work *The Wisdom of the Egyptians*, observes, "Wherever we can trace back polytheism to its earliest stages we find that it results from combinations of monotheism."[5] As a direct result of modern scientific evaluation of ancient evidence, the deviation of monotheism into polytheism has now become more accepted by scholars.

It is clear from the biblical record that Adam and Eve worshiped one God, and that the occult played a role in man's descent into polytheism early in Israel's history.[6] In the book of Exodus (c. 1400 BC), Moses wrote, "You shall not permit a sorceress to live" (22:18).[7] And again in Leviticus 19:31, "Give no regard to mediums and familiar spirits; do not seek after them, to be defiled by them: I am the LORD your God."[8]

4. W. F. Albright, *The Archaeology of Palestine* (Baltimore: Penguin, 1960), 127–128.
5. Brian Brown, *The Wisdom of the Egyptians* (New York: Brentano's, 1923) chap. 2, 43, http://www.sacred-texts.com/egy/woe/index.htm (accessed August 21, 2007).
6. See Merrill F. Unger, *Biblical Demonology: A Study of Spiritual Forces at Work Today* (Grand Rapids: Kregel, 1994), 9–20.
7. Tradition places the actual Exodus at 1446 BC, but some scholars argue for an earlier date.
8. See also Leviticus 19:26–31; 20:26–27, and Deuteronomy 18:10–12. Leviticus (1440–1400 BC). The Dead Sea Scrolls contain portions of the last chapters of Leviticus written in Palaeo-Hebrew (or Canaanite), which was used to indicate Moses' authorship; use of this script dates to 6th–4th centuries BC. For more information see Golb, Norman. *The Origins of the Dead Sea Scrolls: The Search for the Secret of Qumran*, 95–104.

In Romans 1:18–32, the apostle Paul details the deviation of man's worship from God-inspired to a demonically inspired, polytheistic worship of beasts, fowl, and insects. He informs us that mankind's spiritual descent into false religions worldwide resulted from suppressing God's "truth in unrighteousness" (v. 18). The key element in Romans is that God "gave them up to uncleanness" (v. 24), which was followed by their creature worship. This "uncleanness" is a vast, all-inclusive area that embraces such base practices as animism, Paganism, and varied occult rituals. In discussing prehistoric occult activities among ancient civilizations, Old Testament scholar Merrill Unger notes that "traffic in the realm of evil spirits goes back in most ancient times to the antediluvian world . . . The earliest history of Egypt, Mesopotamia, and the Graeco-Roman world is replete with examples of cultivation of the demoniacal arts."[9]

In Paul's continued theme, fallen man was carried away through "the lusts of their hearts, to dishonor their bodies among themselves" (Rom. 1:24). At first glance, this indicates sexual perversion, but it is important to note the plural "lusts," which does not limit the lusts to sexuality and could represent all forms of dishonoring the body. These "lusts" were often found in occult rituals and the ancient Paganism that embraced it, sexual perversion being central to many Pagan rites, which harmonizes with the "vile passions" found in verse 26.[10] Paul's conclusion is that man, left to his own devices, never ascends to God on his own, but descends into the basest religious forms, including secret and hidden practices that are passed from one initiate to another.

Great Britain's Stonehenge (3100 BC) and the lesser-known but more complex Avebury (2400 BC), detail Neolithic devotion to different types of Pagan worship and interest in occult knowledge.[11] The Etruscan civilization reached its zenith in western and central Italy sometime around 500 BC, but the remnants of its culture remain a powerful illustration of the apostle Paul's point.[12] Although the relics of these ancient societies are few, and the complete truth of their histories lost to time, what remains is enough to testify to the influence of the occult on their religion and and culture.

---

9. Unger, *Biblical Demonology*, 158.
10. Details of these rites can be found in Michael Grant, *Eros in Pompeii: The Secret Rooms of the National Museum of Naples* (New York: Scribner, 1981).
11. Stonehenge, "About Stonehenge," http://www.stonehenge.co.uk/about.htm (accessed July 18, 2006).
12. For more information see Michael Grant, *The Etruscans* (New York: Scribner, 1981).

The Etruscans embraced the supernatural. In their book, *A History of Pagan Europe*, modern Pagan leaders Prudence Jones and Nigel Pennick point out, "The Etruscan religion was not simply a religion of practice and precedent, in the more usual Pagan style, but also a revealed religion, whose sacred writings gave detailed instructions for the practice of ceremonies and concerning the nature of the divine powers."[13] Detailed archaeological evidence discovered in Etruscan tombs points to the acknowledged power of this divine revelation. The doctrine of the Etruscans was outlined in three sacred books. "These were the books of divination (by entrails); the books of interpretation of omens (especially lightning); and the books of rituals."[14] Fatalism also played a key role in everyday life, with individuals choosing not to fight against the end of things or against death itself.

To the Etruscans, science and the sacred were inextricably intertwined. Etruscan kings were also high priests, professionally trained in what would be the equivalent of modern-day colleges. It was a blend that would dismay the politicians of today: the ultimate intermingling of church and state. Everything appeared to be determined by divination in Etruscan society, to the point where even the Romans who followed after them preferred to dismiss such minute analysis as simple superstition. Eventually, the worship of Etruscan deities such as the chief god, Voltumna, and Tinia and Uni was diluted by the great social force of war and the inevitable change it brought. The Roman war machine had formed and was growing at an ever-increasing pace.[15]

Roman religion began as a general belief in the supernatural. It grew in the hearts of simple villagers and spread as a result of an ever-expanding populace. As the people increased, the gods multiplied to meet their needs. In this era of proliferating deities, universal sacrifices were made by worshipers to whatever anonymous god or goddess might be in charge of a particular field or grove. As Rome expanded and its influence grew, its deities developed more specific identities, until there were thirty-three names, gathered from inscriptions on a series of imperial tablets.[16] Mars, the god of war; Vesta, the goddess of inner life—all had a purpose and a following. Centuries passed, and with their passing, the worship of multiple

---

13. Prudence Jones and Nigel Pennick, *A History of Pagan Europe* (London: Routledge, 1995), 26.
14. Ibid.
15. Ibid., 26–7.
16. Ibid., 36.

gods and the "secret knowledge" so much a part of it grew and became an intrinsic part of Roman life.

The Renaissance or "rebirth" arrived in Europe at the start of the fourteenth century, focusing new light and attention on these ancient secrets. Although most scholars maintained that ancient Paganism died out and was in essence reborn at a later date, Jones and Pennick disagree, pointing out that the European native religious tradition (much like the Native American tradition in North America) never ceased to exist in Europe. They claim that just as other religions retained their basic beliefs and authentic traditions, the European religious heritage survived the centuries to resurface unscathed in the modern world. "This tradition is presented as having been superseded first by Christianity and Islam and, more recently, by post-Christian humanism. . . . On the contrary, it has continued to exist and even to flourish more or less openly up to the present day, when it is undergoing a new restoration."[17]

Although widespread evidence for this position is lacking, Jones and Pennick could find solid historical evidence supporting their position in the early letters of Bishop Winchester to Saint Boniface. In 723–24 AD he wrote to encourage Boniface in his conversion of the "heathen" and to give instructions on how to defend the faith against their beliefs. "Whence or by whom or when was the first god or goddess begotten? Do they believe that gods and goddesses still beget other gods and goddesses? If they do not, when did they cease and why? If they do, the number of gods must be infinite. In such a case, who is the most powerful among these different gods? Surely no mortal man can know. Yet man must take care not to offend this god who is more powerful than the rest."[18] The bishop's comments confirm the survival and strength of the Pagan gods and goddesses, and their prevailing influence on the people.

The power of the occult is nothing new and certainly nothing secret. Its influence spans the centuries and continues into the modern world. The apostle Paul's example in Romans is precisely what we find today in the kingdom of the occult.

---

17. Ibid., 261.
18. *Medieval Sourcebook,* s.v., "The Correspondence of St. Boniface," http://www.fordham.edu/halsall/basis/boniface-letters.html (accessed February 11, 2005).

THE OCCULT TODAY

To the astute observer, there can be no doubt that our postmodern Western world is in the midst of a violent revolt against reason and logic. People are acting contrary to reason, and their behavior patterns have no relationship to logic. The great horror of the Charles Manson Family cult killings were exactly that: a total irrationality. The Manson Family cult was convicted of the August 8, 1969, murders of actress Sharon Tate, her unborn baby, and her four houseguests, in addition to the August 10, 1969, murders of Leno and Rosemary LaBianca. One cult member, Charles "Tex" Watson, claimed just prior to entering the Tate home, "I am the devil here, to do the devil's work."[19] What was the meaning behind these killings? What was derived from it?

The Church of Satan, founded in 1966 by Anton Szandor LaVey, was created for one purpose alone: to worship a corporate evil known as Satan.[20] From his 1976 interview with LaVey, journalist John Godwin painted a detailed portrait of both the man and his motives:

LaVey made a good entrance. He is a massive six-footer in his early forties, dressed completely in black, wearing a clerical collar and a silver pentagram medallion around his neck. His skull is clean-shaven, Tartar fashion, and he sports a black chin beard à la Ivan the Terrible.

He has a forceful, calm voice, a surprisingly amiable laugh, and a patiently cautious way of answering questions he must have heard several hundred times before.

"How do we visualize Satan? Purely symbolically, as the all-pervasive force. The only true God, in fact."

---

19. Other murders were eventually attributed to the Manson Family cult. From the transcript of Prosecutor Vincent Bugliosi's closing argument in *State of California vs Charles Manson, et al.*, January 21, 1971. Text available at http://www.law.umkc.edu/faculty/projects/ftrials/manson/mansonsummation.html (accessed July 15, 2006).
20. Born Howard Stanton Levey in Chicago, Illinois, April 11, 1930. This according to Levey's daughter, Zeena Schreck, who confirmed the birth name through Levey's birth certificate. http://www.churchofsatan.org/aslv.html (accessed July 15, 2006). The Church of Satan's official history gives LaVey's purpose in founding the cult as "the first organized church in modern times promulgating a religious philosophy championing Satan as the symbol of personal freedom and individualism." See http://www.churchofsatan.com/home.html (accessed May 30, 2006).

"Well, then whose adversary is he?"

LaVey smiled. "The adversary of all man-made spiritual religions. To all that we consider the contemptible crutches man has had to invent. We totally reject the concept of there being an antithesis to God. He is God."[21]

It is clear in LaVey's response to Godwin that segments of our Western culture have embraced an irrational mood. After all, if God truly exists as Creator of the universe and Sovereign of all things, who would want second best? Who needs the devil if you are logical and rational? In the midst of this revolt against reason and logic, there has arisen an irrational faith, and the occult fits neatly into it; it is unscientific and metaphysical, and certainly does not follow the four formal laws of logic. It appeals to many who are unwilling to understand or accept the great issues of time and eternity.

Today, undeniable evidence of the occult explosion pervades every aspect of society. American journalist Nat Freedland observed this phenomenon in the late 1960s and, after investigating it, became convinced of its power and was eventually drawn into the occult itself. Freedland wrote, "No modern, post industrial society has ever experienced anything like this occult explosion."[22]

Why is there such a tremendous development in the field of occultism? What is the powerful force driving it? The easy answer is "the devil is behind it," but in this case, the easy answer also happens to be the truth: the devil *is* behind it. The Scripture says he is "the god of this age" and "the prince of the power of the air" (2 Cor. 4:4, Eph. 2:2). Today, in the United States and in our foreign mission fields, millions of people are involved in the kingdom of the cults, but there are *hundreds* of millions of people involved in the occult revolution; numbers so high they cannot accurately be counted.[23]

---

21. John Godwin, *Occult America* (New York: Doubleday, 1972), 241–249. Interview available online at http://www.churchofsatan.com/Pages/LaVeyOccultAmerica.html (accessed May 9, 2006).
22. Nat Freedland, *The Occult Explosion: From Matic to ESP—The People Who Made the New Occultism* (New York: G. P. Putnam's Sons, 1972), 14.
23. Two reasons that the number is difficult to fix is that there is an overlapping of cults with the occult, and no one has attempted a worldwide poll or statistic on occult practitioners. See, however, the ensuing paragraph on the 2005 Gallup Poll statistics on American belief in occultic practices.

David Moore, a writer for the Gallup Organization, analyzes the American interest in the occult: "A recent Gallup survey shows that just about three in four Americans hold some paranormal belief—in at least one of the following: extra sensory perception (ESP), haunted houses, ghosts, mental telepathy, clairvoyance, astrology, communicating with the dead, Witches, reincarnation, and channeling."[24] According to Gallup, this 2005 poll shows "little change" from the original poll four years earlier (2001). With the population of the United States hovering around 300 million people, these believers would account for approximately 225 million Americans. In view of these statistics, the number of adherents worldwide must be astronomical. This does not indicate that those who believe in it also practice it, but belief is generally the first step toward practice.

Unfortunately, it is increasingly common today that people investigate psychic phenomena, explore ESP and clairvoyance, and probe astrology in order to discover what might happen tomorrow. Tremendous progress has been made in Parapsychology and in the study and analysis of psychic phenomena that, fifty years ago, scholars would have found absurd.[25] Duke University once led the nation in developing a department of study for Parapsychology, but today there are at least twenty scholarly journals, many from universities, devoted to studying the paranormal and Parapsychology. In our modern world, it has achieved pseudoscientific validation through media programs that give the audience precisely what they wish to see; some of it genuine, some questionable. This peculiar combination of fantasy and reality piques people's interest, and they may go on to embrace psychics, ESP, and Parapsychology because of it.[26]

The SciFi channel, in its paranormal program *Ghosthunters,* opens the door to the dangerous world of demonic activity through the popular format of reality TV. Viewers need only sit back and watch demons knock over chairs, punch investigators, or whisper blurred comments through the modern Ouija board, a digital tape

24. David W. Moore, "Three in Four Americans Believe in Paranormal," Gallup, June 16, 2005, http://www.gallup.com/poll/16915/Three-Four-Americans-Believe-Paranormal.aspx (accessed June 2, 2008).

25. Duke University developed a department of study for Parapsychology, the Rhine Research Center, in 1935.

26. Although the world of the occult is a reality, it rarely performs for television cameras. Facts, storytelling and circumstantial evidence can be manipulated and combined with educated guesses to make anything appear plausible.

recorder. This practice, known as *electronic voice phenomena* or *EVP*, poses an even greater threat than the well-known and often mocked Ouija board; at the touch of a button, demons step into our world and speak. The Travel Channel, the National Geographic Channel, and numerous others offer programs on haunted sites and taboo rituals steeped in the occult. This media coverage has given status to the occult and to the power of Witchcraft.

Several schools now offer courses on the occult. A growing interest in sorcery and Witchcraft generated by the Harry Potter stories has prompted an Australian university to launch a special course open to the public. "The 12-week course at Adelaide University will explore the Witchdoctors of Africa, shamans from the Amazon and Zambezi valleys, Witches from the 16th century and others who practise [*sic*] magic rituals."[27]

Interest in Witchcraft is increasing at an enormous rate in the United States and abroad.[28] Its growing influence can been seen through such television shows as *Charmed* and *Buffy the Vampire Slayer*, movies such as *The Witches of Eastwick* and *The Craft*, and books such as the Harry Potter series. There is reality in the world of Witches. People have experienced Witchcraft, and they are testifying to the truth of that experience. Because of this, people are drawn to Witchcraft in increasing numbers so that it has become very much in vogue.

It is important to note that many experiences are real in the sense that something happened, but these same experiences are not valid as a standard for truth. Real experiences may contradict truth, as in an optical phenomenon. A mirage in the desert or on a road surface is such an example. The "water" of a mirage can be photographed and seen by multiple people, but in reality there is no water; it was only heat wave refraction on the hot sand or road surface. The experience was real, but the truth was quite different. So it is with many facets of the occult. People have real experiences, but the truth of these experiences reveals a source that is an enemy of God and His people. The ultimate test of truth for the Christian is to examine all experience by God's Word. In addressing this puzzle of experience versus truth, Christian scholar Os Guinness noted, "It is equally plain that the Bible affirms that

27. BBC News, "Potter prompts course in witchcraft," February 18, 2002, http://news.bbc.co.uk/1/hi/education/1827166.stm (accessed May 15, 2006).
28. Michael Jordan, *Witches: An Encyclopedia of Paganism and Magic* (London: Kyle Cathie Limited, 1996), 11.

the reality of the occult does not give it legitimacy. The Old and New Testaments are united in rejecting it as wrong, but real."[29]

As a result of this insidious media barrage, millions of people have accepted some aspect of the occult as valid. Spiritual defenses have been and continue to be undermined and weakened, until it is now quite common to find Protestant and Catholic people reading horoscopes more religiously than their Bibles and replacing their prayer lives with yoga relaxation techniques. The *International Herald Tribune* recently documented this worldwide resurgence of occult belief in its article "Meanwhile: Europe's love of the occult," in which author Michael Johnson shows percentage increases in Europeans' love of the occult and ponders the prevailing attitude of irrationality. "Stop trying to figure out the world. The occult can do it for you. . . . Palmistry, the crystal ball and astrology have never been so popular."[30]

The attitude that "everyone is doing it" fosters a false sense of acceptance and unity with others. As the occult vocabulary invades the everyday language of society, the terms raise less concern and find a resting place in the minds of the unwary.

Today, the Church must be wise enough to read the signs of the times, and clever enough to comprehend what is going on, so that we may recognize the vocabulary and methods of the occult, and deal with the issues facing us.

WITCHCRAFT AND THE OCCULT

The word *occult* is derived from the Latin word *occultus,* meaning "hidden or secret things." When someone discusses the occult, he or she is referring to the hidden or secret things involving some form of religion, and something connected to the metaphysical. A Witch is a male or a female who utilizes occult powers for what that person considers to be good or evil ends. Witchcraft is often confused by the media with Satanism, yet most practicing Witches worship divinity in nature (expressed as gods and goddesses) rather than Satan.[31] The Covenant of the Goddess, which claims to be "one of the largest and oldest Wiccan organizations,"

---

29. Os Guinness, *The Dust of Death: The Sixties Counterculture and How It Changed America Forever* (Downer's Grove, IL: IVP, 1973) 310.

30. Michael Johnson, "Meanwhile: Europe's love of the occult," *International Herald Tribune,* August 15, 2007, http://www.iht.com/articles/2007/08/15/opinion/edjohnson.php (accessed June 2, 2008).

31. There are exceptions to this, where some practitioners merge Witchcraft with Satanism, but the overall picture of modern Witchcraft is nature worship.

defines *Witchcraft* as "an earth religion—a re-linking (re-ligio) with the life-force of nature, both on this planet and in the stars and space beyond."[32]

Some Witches choose the label *white Witch* or *black Witch,* depending upon their purpose in employing their powers, although this distinction is not as common as it once was. Similarly, the incorrect designation of Witches as female and wizards as male still finds its way into books, films, and television programs. *Man, Myth and Magic,* an authoritative encyclopedia on the occult, explains that "both male and female members of Wicca are known as Witches, although the cult is mainly matriarchal."[33]

Even though Christians see both as corrupt branches of the same tree, in recent years, Witches have begun to distance themselves from Satanists. Both claim to have a different worldview and do not agree on many issues.[34] According to *Witches: An Encyclopedia of Paganism and Magic,* "An important point should perhaps be clarified here: those who practice diabolism are not Witches. The devil is a peculiarly Christian individual and the doctrine of Witchcraft rejects the Christian god. Thus, all Witches distance themselves from Satanism and the diabolical arts championed by such bizarre characters as Anton Szandor LaVey and the infinitely more sinister Charles Manson."[35]

But Anton LaVey's public comments on Witchcraft, made in the 1970s, seem to portray a cultural perspective of Witchcraft *before* its deliberate detour away from the appearance of evil. The Church of Satan founder, and black Witchcraft practitioner, completely rejected the concept of "white Witches," stating categorically, "White Witches are no more than a by product of Christianity, or they wouldn't have to call themselves white Witches in the first place. I don't think white Witches have the courage of their convictions."[36] Ironically, modern Witches blame

32. Covenant of the Goddess, "Basic Philosophy," http://www.cog.org/wicca/about.html#PHIL (accessed August 21, 2007).
33. Frank Smyth, "Modern Witchcraft" in *Man, Myth and Magic: An Illustrated Encyclopedia of the Supernatural,* ed. Richard Cavendish (New York: Marshall Cavendish, 1970), 14:1866.
34. Josh McDowell and Don Stewart, *The Occult: The Authority of the Believer Over the Powers of Darkness* (San Bernardino, CA: Here's Life Publishers, 1992), 199.
35. Jordan, *Witches: An Encyclopedia of Paganism and Magic,* 15.
36. John Fritscher (aka Jack Fritscher), "Straight from the Witch's Mouth: An Interview with Anton Szandor LaVey, High Priest and Founder of The Church of Satan," http://www.jackfritscher.com/Non-Fiction/Witchcraft/Straight%20Witches%20Mouth.html (accessed June 4, 2006).

Christians for the devil, and Satanists blame Christians for the Witches. However, LaVey's position that there is no such thing as a white Witch seems to find support in history. Jeffrey Burton Russell, a professor of history, points out that this perspective on white Witchcraft is largely the "creation of modern writers, mainly occultist, and seldom appears in the history of world magic."[37]

Definitions aside, all Witchcraft reaches for occult power, and none of it can rightfully or logically lay claim to God as the source of that power. The Christian reason for rejection of both white and black Witchcraft is its opposition to God's Word (Deut. 18:9–12). In order to battle effectively in the spiritual realm, Christians must purge their minds of the cartoon images of good Witches and bad Witches, such as those found in L. Frank Baum's *Wizard of Oz*, with the pointed hat, shiny shoes, and broomsticks. They must set aside the adventure of J. K. Rowling's Harry Potter and think of Witches as real individuals lost in a dark, spiritual world carefully crafted over thousands of years by Satan and his angels—desperate souls, absorbed by the hidden or secret mysteries of the occult.

This insidious power supersedes all rational barriers and purposefully withstands the test of time. In the 1970s, a small, twenty-five-cent booklet called *Everyday Witchcraft: Love Magic, Charms, Spells, Fortune-telling* pointed the way to the occult, and though out of print, is still listed thirty-five years later on Amazon.com.[38] Inside, it reveals the secret to Witchcraft: "Though you needn't be a Witch to practice Witchcraft, there are some Witchy things you must do if you are to summon occult powers."[39] This is the opening salvo: the summoning of occult powers. It goes on to warn, "Various malign influences are always loose in the atmosphere. No matter what you do or don't do, one day these forces may decide to focus on you or your family. However, when you start practicing Witchcraft the chances of drawing the attention of these mischief makers increases greatly."[40] This booklet, put out by a secular publishing house, informs people that they can summon occult powers, but if they do, *watch out*, because malign forces

37. Jeffrey Burton Russell, *Witchcraft in the Middle Ages* (New York: Cornell University Press, 1972), 6.
38. See http://www.amazon.com/Everyday-witchcraft-fortune-telling-everything/dp/B00072ODZ4/ref=sr_1_1?ie=UTF8&s=books&qid=1212417852&sr=1-1.
39. Delphine C. Lyons, *Everyday Witchcraft: Love Magic, Charms and Spells, Fortune-telling: Everything You Need to Know to Enjoy Occult Power!* (New York: Dell, 1972), 4.
40. Ibid., 14.

inhabit the universe, and if someone chooses to open the door, only God knows what may come through the other side.

The technology-driven world of the twenty-first century has produced a cluttered, confusing showcase of occult paraphernalia. Gone are the tiny, dark occult bookshops of yesterday, and in their place stand the megamall book chains, Pagan websites, and worldwide online auctions—each one devoting huge space to Witchcraft, reincarnation, paranormal experiences, and psychic healing. All these irrational, parlor-game occult practices that amused people in the early twentieth century are today taken very seriously by millions of believers.

For the first time in history, the doorway to the occult has been left permanently ajar on a global scale, luring the unsuspecting—twenty-four hours a day— to the dimension of darkness. The kids who play with Ouija boards and think it is fun; the teenagers who try to levitate tables and read tarot cards, tea leaves, and their palms; and the parents who identify themselves as Virgo or Scorpio and believe what today's paper says about *tomorrow* are people flirting with the kingdom of the occult, and it is perilous, because it reaches out to another dimension and endangers the soul.

SPIRITISM

In recent years, the number of people involved in Spiritism has climbed into the hundreds of millions.[41] Those who believe profess many different religions: Witchcraft, Paganism, Voodoo, and New Age ideology all teach that the dead can be reached through various means. Theosophy and Eastern religions paste a veneer of respectability over what is nothing more than the influence of demons in psychic phenomena. Now more than ever, the influence of those attempting communication with the dead pervades modern culture. People have embraced an Eastern type of cultic Christianity, lightly sprayed with biblical terminology.

One of the best examples of this is Dr. Marcus Bach, the famous liberal theologian who instituted an investigation into psychic phenomena during the 1960s, an

---

41. Statistics for occult practitioners can only be broadly assessed due to the solitary nature of many believers and the assimilation of occult knowledge into traditional or indigenous religions. For a review of statistics based on various researchers and writers, see Adherents, http://www.adherents.com/Na/Na_617.html. See also Worldwide Religious News (WWRN) (Search Occult), http://www.wwrn.org/.

investigation originally motivated by skepticism.[42] Bach attended many Spiritist séances during his detailed exploration of occult phenomena, with the aim of examining them under the most exhaustive test conditions. The ultimate skeptic, Bach tested every experience. If floating trumpets appeared, he ran his hands up, down, and around them. If ghostly materializations occurred, he touched them. One night, as he was preparing to leave a séance, something unique occurred:

> I was making minute mental notations of all that was happening—the hovering, swaying motion of the "spirits," the rhythm of life, like the rise and fall of a tide, as many as four speaking simultaneously in whispered voices, excited, hurried persuasive. Suddenly the galaxy of spirits melted away. For a long still moment nothing happened. Then the swirling ectoplasmic effluvia glowed from the floor and quickly took on the form of a girl. Before the figure was complete, it spoke.
>
> "Marc, dear—Marc, dear—Marc, dear."
>
> Those who know me well call me Marc; those who know me better call me Marc, dear, so I knew this must be a "familiar spirit!" I got up and walked over until there was a space of less than four feet between us. "Yes?" I said. "Who are you?"
>
> The answer was fraught with disappointment. "Don't you know me?"
>
> I did not. I had no idea who this might be. I had really been too absorbed to think very much about personal contact with the spirits. . . . Nor did I propose to offer any hint of whom I thought she *might represent*. No leads, I determined.
>
> "I do not know you. Who are you?"
>
> "Paula," came the answer.
>
> The name and soft manner in which it was uttered brought the sudden

---

42. There is little doubt that charlatans exist in the world of the Spiritists but not everything is a trick. There is also a hardcore, deep, spiritual evil that can be found in Spiritism; it exists and it is real. Harry Houdini, the celebrated illusionist-magician, investigated Spiritism, and he was perfectly right when he said that he could duplicate many of their experiences. His exposé revealed the deceptive tricks employed by the tricksters and hucksters in the world of noises, rapping, tapping, and apparitions at the séances. After years of investigating séances, he found none that convinced him of its reality. See Harry Houdini and Joseph Dunninger, *Magic and Mystery: Incredible Psychic Investigations of Houdini and Dunninger* (New York: Weathervane, 1967).

unfolding of a forgotten drama. Twenty years ago my sister Paula had died at the age of twenty-three. Her child Janette had died shortly before. These deaths had been among the deep sorrows of our family, but time and travel reduce the past into forgetfulness. No medium or spirit had plucked this name out of my mind because I wasn't thinking of Paula. I had not thought of her even once during the séance.

I looked at the presence before me closely.

"How do I look?" she asked.

"You look fine," I replied.

"The right height?" she whispered. "Do you think I should be taller?"

"No. You are about the height I remember."

"I wanted to do a good job," she told me earnestly. "Do I look all right?"

"Yes," I assured her, recalling that one theory of materialization is that the spirit "takes" the ectoplasm and fashions according to its memory the human form which clothed it on earth.

. . . Did this form and these features resemble Paula? I must admit they did. Very much. The outline of the figure was recognizable and convincing. It was like a "false front," a flat, two-dimensional body with the semblance of arms clothed in a shadowy gray-white film. The face, though typically mask-like, was strikingly reminiscent. There was an illusion of long blond hair. I cannot say whether the voice was Paula's or not. After twenty years I would not remember. Just now, however, it was Paula returned.

But why shouldn't it be? I asked myself as I stood there. The Spiritists at Chesterfield knew I was coming. If, as some people say, they have a well-laid system of espionage they could easily have traced my family and got Paula's description. If this was someone "dressed up," play-acting, if this was a marionette using the voice of a ventriloquist, naturally it would be constructed as to represent Paula. This thought haunted me more than the presence. I wished I could convince myself some way. The impulse to reach out and touch the figure became stronger. I moved closer. I moved slightly to one side so that the red light would strike the spirit's face more directly. We were about three feet apart now. Paula was talking about life in the spirit world. I was asking hasty questions: Have you seen Jesus? What is heaven like? What about the element of time? Can you be everywhere at once? Are terms like Methodist, Reformed, Presbyterian, Catholic ever used where you are?

Her voice seemed to laugh. She answered, "No, no," to all questions save the one about heaven. It was like speaking to a living person secretly, clandestinely, knowing that time was running out. Her features seemed to become clearer. Perhaps it was my mind playing tricks.

And then a thought came to me. "Paula," I said, "do you remember the catechism we learned at home?"

"Of course!"

"Paula, do you remember the first question in that catechism?"

"I remember."

"What was it?" I asked almost fearfully.

The answer came at once. "'What is your chief comfort in life and in death?'"

"Go on," I urged.

"'That I, with body and soul, both in life and in death am not my own—'" She interrupted herself. "Here where we are the words have a greater meaning!"

Then quickly, breathlessly, she told me that serving God means personal development. Life on the spirit plane is an evolvement. Like the breaking of a chrysalis. Like the ascent in a spiral. Like the growth of moral affection to higher and higher "heavens." Several times she interrupted herself with "Do you understand? Is that clear?" as if she felt her message was vital, all-absorbing. Death, she insisted, was not a violent result of sin. It had no sting. It was neither friend nor enemy. It was part of the divine purpose, a purpose without beginning or end.

The whispering grew fainter. "I can stay no longer. I must go now."

"Paula, one more thing. Can you put your arms around me?"

"I'll give you a kiss," she said. "Come closer."

"You come close to me." I wanted her to come nearer the red light. She did. There was now scarcely a foot between us. Her face was luminous, seemingly transparent, and without depth.

I leaned forward and lowered my head. The web-like texture of ecto-

plasmic arms encircled my neck. Something soft and flaxen brushed my
forehead. Then Paula vanished—into the floor, it seemed.

I walked back to my chair and sat down. . . . The séance was ended.[43]

Dr. Marcus Bach began his study of Spiritism as a skeptic and ended it as a convert to its reality. He has done us a great service by going where no Christian can
go—into the lair of the demons—and returning with something enormously
revealing: death is not a violent result of sin, it has no sting, and it is neither friend
nor enemy. This information is a direct contradiction of divine revelation: "O
Death, where is your sting? O Hades, where is your victory?" (1 Cor. 15:55). The
apostle Paul taught the direct opposite of that spoken by Dr. Bach's ghostly visitor:
"For the wages of sin is death, but the gift of God is eternal life in Christ Jesus our
Lord" (Rom. 6:23).

When Spiritism becomes rampant and horoscopes can be found in newspapers
and magazines around the world, when courses on Witchcraft and Paganism are
easily available in colleges, when self-help books teaching spells and fortune-telling
to adults and children can be bought at neighborhood retailers, then the Church
must awaken to the fact that the kingdom of the occult is real and powerful, and
its sights are set on human souls.

CASE STUDY

Walter Martin

I was a guest speaker a few years ago at a church in Newport Beach,
California. After the service was over, the pastor asked if I would meet with
a young girl who had some serious problems in her life—problems they
believed were directly related to her involvement in psychic phenomenon,
possibly related to prior mission field activities. The pastor described some
of her experiences to me, including ones that had taken place with a
Christian psychologist present.

---

43. Marcus Bach, *They Have Found a Faith* (Indianapolis: The Bobbs-Merrill Company, 1946),
117–21.

"Walter," he said, "it appears to me that we are dealing with Satan."

I agreed to meet with her, and as we pulled into the parking lot of the motel where I was staying, I suddenly felt we should pray. We bowed our heads and started praying, and it was a good thing that we did. You see, parked next to us was a car, and inside of it was the young lady we had come to see. The moment we started praying, she became semicatatonic, and strange sounds began coming out of her. Her eyes were glassy, and she told us later she could hear everything we were saying and see everything we were doing, but she couldn't move. *She could not move out of that automobile.* She was bound to the seat. After we finished praying, I went over to see her and there she was, sitting in the seat making very strange noises.

I looked at her and said, "If you get out of the car and come with us, they will leave you alone, and you will be free. But you must come!"

She made a herculean effort to get off that seat, but she couldn't do it. Two men had to lift her out of the car and carry her across the lawn to the room. The moment we entered that room, she made it almost impossible for *four* grown men to hold her down. I had never seen such power in one human being. It exploded so fast, and the violence and sounds that accompanied were so amazing that I said to the pastor, "Now we know what we're dealing with, and I think we'll be here for quite a while."

Three hours later, we knew this girl was full of demons, and it was not the first century; it was the twentieth century! This was a girl who had lived a Christian life on the surface but was *never a Christian*—a girl who played the game but never believed it—a girl who had taught Sunday school while she worshiped Satan, and finally was taken over by him. She had all the form and all the appearance: the perfect tare in the wheat field.

Four men held her down while we prayed for her. Whenever I said, "In the name of the Lord Jesus Christ, come out!" her body leaped, twisted, and jerked all over the bed. Her mouth smiled in a funny, twisted way, and she said, "We can outlast you."

But we weren't about to be outlasted.

This went on for three hours, and every once in a while she would groan, and one demon would leave. After that, she would sit up and say, "I feel fine. I feel so much better. Let's go."

The psychologist, who was not a believer in demon possession until he walked into that room, was now a *firm* believer. It changed the course of his whole practice. He told me, "I would never have believed this without seeing it. I believe."

I knew he believed because one time, during the course of the evening, she said, "I feel all right now, but I'm tired. I think I'll go home." And as she tried to get out of the bed, he said, "Oh, no you don't!" as he grabbed her and pulled her back. The moment she was in the bed she growled and writhed; it took four of us to hold her down again.

The switch from normalcy to possession was instantaneous. A terrible presence invaded the room and remained there the entire time. At the end of three hours, we asked her to pray, but she couldn't say the name of Christ. It stuck in her throat. The muscles in her neck knotted up, and the veins in her forehead protruded. She couldn't open her mouth and say "Jesus" for a full five minutes. We prayed for her; we knew if she could pray to Him she would be delivered. We told her to pray and ask God for forgiveness for praying to Satan and to "Renounce Satan and all his works."

She said, "I can't do it! I can't do it!"

"Renounce him in the name of the Lord Jesus."

She finally cried out, "Jesus, forgive me!" She renounced Satan and all of his works, even though it took her at least half an hour to be able to say it.

Three hours later, a totally different girl got up off that bed, hugged her husband, and walked out the door. She told us later that she knew the demons had been there all these years, but she was afraid of them. They'd threatened to kill her if she ever told anyone about them. She was part of a Christian church—a professing Christian—but not a believer. The church kept watch over this woman and her family after these events occurred, and I understand from them that she's a brand-new wife and mother, and they have a brand-new family.[44]

How did this happen? It began in the Far East and continued in America; she reached out to the occult. She knew the second most powerful force in the universe was satanic. She was discouraged and downtrodden,

---

44. For more information on demon possession and exorcism, see chapter 14.

and she didn't get her prayers answered by God. So what did she do? She reached out into the world of the occult and gave herself to Satan. She turned the handle on the door and opened it, and that's what came in.

This is what we find today: people in the world of the occult endorsing Christianity. They go along with the surface of the gospel, but in their hearts, they do not believe it.

THE OCCULT AND THE CHURCH

Christians must become aware of the dangers of occult infiltration into the Church itself, and they must be able to spot its presence. From bishop to layman, no one is safe from its subtle temptation:

The classic example would be the late Episcopalian bishop, James Pike, who . . . began to consult mediums, including the famous Arthur Ford, in an attempt to contact the spirit of his dead son. Pike became a firm believer in the life after death from his occult involvement rather than from biblical doctrine and took many people with him to the dark world of the occult. When the Church "waters down" the gospel of Christ, the door to occultic practice swings wide open.[45]

Another case in point is that of the Lutheran Church in America, who mailed a piece of literature to their Sunday school superintendents in an effort to persuade them to buy a kit called "Mystery Trip." The "Mystery Trip" contained six posters, a Delphic Fortune Caster game, incense, tarot cards, a cassette on how to understand and practice occultism, a leader's guide, and a reprint of an article on occultism from *Reader's Digest*.[46] It was a complete kit on do-it-yourself occultism sent out *not* by the local occult society, but by the Lutheran Church, in a dangerously misguided attempt to help young people understand the occult.

Christians open themselves to the world of the occult when they consult astrology charts, play with Ouija boards, visit palm readers, or engage in contemplative prayer that directs them to withdraw into silence and "open" their spirits to what-

45. McDowell and Stewart, *The Occult*, 20.
46. An example of "Mystery Trip" is in Walter Martin's personal library.

ever may come along. It is never possible to open the door to the soul with impunity. Someone will get hurt, and it will most likely be you. Taking quiet time to dwell on the power, glory, and love of God is biblical; chanting the name of Jesus by rote, setting up icons to worship, and walking labyrinths while focused on self-awareness are not. An elaborately crafted maze of chairs, prayer stations, wood or greenery (labyrinths), and the meditation that accompanies such will not guarantee you access to the wisdom of God, and it has never been a requirement. Jesus said, "Come to Me, all you who labor and are heavy laden, and I will give you rest" (Matt. 11:28). The Bible teaches that the path to God is simple, not complex.

The infiltration of the occult into the Church today has been cleverly planned and well executed, not only by its visible proponents but by its *invisible* ones. The Bible emphasizes that the enemy Christians face is not flesh and blood, so it is safe to assume that the power behind this movement originates with the prince of the powers of the air.

The Emerging or Emergent Church movement began with foundational questions such as *Who is God?* and *What is our purpose here?* It flourished by incorporating some questionable worship practices historically associated with Catholic mysticism, then wandered into the realm of the occult by actively dismantling biblical authority. Over the last decade, its confusing message has spread through evangelical denominations at a rapid pace. Protestants, dissatisfied with the average church service, went looking for something "new" and ventured, in some cases, into the realm of the secret or hidden things—the world of the occult.

In the Emerging Church, chanting, prayer stations, and rituals supplant simplicity in worship. It is one thing to kneel and fervently pray, and quite another to mindlessly chant the name of Jesus over and over again. The Scripture teaches that God is our Father, and Jesus, our Brother. Is it necessary or even logical to repeat the name of your earthly father and brother over and over again? What is the purpose of doing so with your heavenly Father? Jesus told people exactly how to pray, and He did not mention mantras, prayers stations, or labyrinths:

And when you pray, do not use vain repetitions as the heathen do. For they think that they will be heard for their many words. Therefore do not be like them. For your Father knows the things you have need of before you ask Him. In this manner, therefore, pray:

Our Father in heaven,
Hallowed be Your name.
Your kingdom come.
Your will be done
On earth as it is in heaven.
Give us this day our daily bread.
And forgive us our debts,
As we forgive our debtors.
And do not lead us into temptation,
But deliver us from the evil one.
For Yours is the kingdom and the power and the glory forever. Amen.
(Matt. 6:7–13)

There is great power in the Lord's Prayer; Jesus would never have instructed us to follow it if it were not necessary on a daily basis. In the spiritual battles Christians face every day, the constant prayer of "deliver us from evil" is desperately needed. Signs of the occult revolution are everywhere today—even within the Church—and it can no longer be successfully ignored.

Several key teachings reveal the infiltration of aberrant ideas into local church bodies:

- *Personal experience is emphasized over the ultimate authority of Scripture.* Candles, incense, prayer stations, mantras, yoga, labyrinths, and icons are used in conjunction with biblical teaching.

- *Key biblical doctrines are reinterpreted.* The book of Revelation, for example, might be presented as "fulfilled" and Israel's biblical significance diminished or dismissed.

- *The modern Church becomes the new "Israel."* In this view, also known as replacement theology, God has abandoned Israel for his adopted children, a twisting of biblical theology that the apostle Paul refuted. "For if the firstfruit is holy, the lump is also holy; and if the root is holy, so are the branches. And if some of the branches were broken off, and you, being a wild olive tree, were grafted in among them, and with them became a partaker of the root and fatness of the olive tree, do not boast against the branches . . . And they also, if they do not continue in unbelief, will be grafted in, for God is able to graft them in again" (Rom. 11:16–18, 23). God never withdrew His love from Israel; He never withdrew His promise that some would believe.

- *Tolerance of all faiths is promoted at the expense of doctrinal integrity.* Defending the Christian faith as the only true means of salvation is characterized as "unloving" and "intolerant."

- *Spiritual maturity is ignored in favor of emotional experiences.* Personal time with Jesus is overlooked in favor of prescribed ceremonies and sacraments.

Skeptics may attempt to write off the occult penetration into every area of modern society as absurd, but the millions of dollars spent promoting the occult year after year cannot be dismissed. Someone is listening, someone is reading, and someone is asking questions.

Reasons for Revolt

Why would human beings, created in the image of God, turn to anything created and fostered by the devil? First and foremost, the lure of the occult is the direct result of a revolt against science and technology, and against the age in which we live. People are tired of testing and validating truth by the empirical method. In their revolt against this system, they are looking for something *outside* of our known reality.

Second, there is a rebellion against materialism. In an affluent and materialistic society, young people turn to drugs, alcohol, and sex to escape it. They rebel in multiple ways because they reject a society that displays so *little* concern for so many. Instead, they pursue a new reality to fill the vacuum of the soul, and Satan stands ready to supply that reality.

Third, there is a rejection of religion in general. Many people believe it is responsible for the world's problems, and they turn away from Christianity in particular because the Church is in an age of apostasy. It is in a state of corruption, rejecting the historic truths yet preserving the outward appearances—the form—of godliness, without the power intrinsic within the structure (2 Tim. 3:5). The revolt is against religion and its connection to the whole world order. Surprisingly enough, many of the attacks that occur against Christianity in the midst of this revolt do not come from philosophers or scientists; the most devastating attacks originate from behind the pulpit and from theological seminaries. The slings and arrows against the faith come from those who should be out preaching the gospel and defending the faith; the shepherds set to watch the sheep. It is a sad but irrefutable fact that the worst enemies of the faith are often those commissioned to proclaim it.

This threat must be very carefully understood: the Christian Church is divided between orthodoxy and anarchy. It is divided between the conservative theologians who seek to defend the faith, and the liberal theologians who demythologize most of the substance of the Christian gospel and then remythologize it all over again, retaining only its moral and ethical values. Added to the mix are the *death of God* theologians, who work diligently to bury the substance of the Christian gospel and preserve the embalmed corpse, which is the church, so that it can continue to pay salaries they have not yet begun to earn. Then there are the *neoorthodox* theologians, who want part of the substance of the gospel and part of the form of the gospel, with no real commitment to the authority of either.

It is a time of anarchy within the Church, when the defense of the faith, as commanded in Jude 3, has been sacrificed upon the altar of compromise by church leaders more interested in methodology than in biblical obedience. This compromise is promoted in the guise of a "new" evangelistic approach that confuses the majority and promotes the media image of Christians as "tolerant." Perhaps the best recent example of this is the "Evening of Friendship" held on November 14, 2004 in Salt Lake City, Utah, where Christian leaders worshiped with Mormons in their Tabernacle, despite the fact that this cult is intent on the destruction of orthodox Christianity.[47] In the midst of this chaos, is it any wonder that people are confused? Alliances like this demonstrate just how far the Church has strayed from the example of Jesus Christ. Between modern theologians and seminaries, and the feeble attempts of the Church to "relate" to those bent on destroying it, it is easy to see why the visitor in the pew wants nothing to do with Christianity.

---

47. For more details, see Carrie A. Moore, "Evangelical preaches at Salt Lake Tabernacle," *Deseret Morning News*, November 15, 2004, http://deseretnews.com/dn/view/0,1249,595105580,00.html.

A divided Church has been rejected—yet here, in this terrible rejection, lies one of the greatest opportunities of evangelical Christianity. The Church must present something to the world that it desperately needs: an undivided Christ and an unchanged gospel, a vital and dynamic witness, a living Redeemer who can transform the lives of men, women, and young people because He is *alive*, and He has the power to do it. That is the response to the rejection of a church divided.

Finally, another reason for the modern occult revolution lies in the human heart's fascination with the mysterious and the unknown. People are reaching out, trying to find something that will give them assurance in a world that appears to have gone mad, a world that embraces the new morality, a world that tolerates situation ethics, and a world that revels in rebellion. They need to believe that they are not inanimate cogs in a great big wheel, with no purpose or goals for existence. They crave certainty in an uncertain age, and occultism offers them this tantalizing lure: *Come into the world of the occult and find what the Church cannot offer: secrets and mysteries to meet the needs of the day.*

SCRIPTURAL RESPONSE

In the face of all of this, the Christian Church must learn the biblical position and take definitive action. The approach is threefold: examine the many facets of occultism, explore what the Bible has to say on the subject, and evaluate how best to convey biblical truth to the world.

The world of the occult is built upon one word: *experience.* It is not built upon revealed authority. Therefore, the Christian must test all experience by divine authority. The purpose of this book is not to tear people apart or to attack them. The Bible instructs Christians to "test everything; hold fast [cleave tenaciously] to what is good" (1 Thess. 5:21 NRSV). The apostle Paul reminds us to "test everything" no matter what it appears to be. In Acts 16 and 17, he gave the glorious truth of the gospel to the Bereans, and after they heard the gospel of Christ—the *Charisma*, the message of redemption—they took the revelation of God Himself, examined Old Testament Scriptures, and compared what Paul said with what the Scriptures said. When they saw that it was in perfect accord, *then* they believed the gospel. The Scripture says they were nobler than those at Thessalonica because they searched the Scriptures (Acts 17:11).

What does the Bible have to say about the occult? What does it say about the information Marcus Bach received—the doctrine of demons—from a demon who looked exactly liked his sister? Bach's experience is paralleled in 1 Samuel 28:6–19:

And when Saul inquired of the LORD, the LORD did not answer him, either by dreams or by Urim or by the prophets.

Then Saul said to his servants, "Find me a woman who is a medium, that I may go to her and inquire of her." And his servants said to him, "In fact, there is a woman who is a medium at En Dor." So Saul disguised himself and put on other clothes, and he went, and two men with him; and they came to the woman by night. And he said, "Please conduct a séance for me, and bring up for me the one I shall name to you." Then the woman said to him, "Look, you know what Saul has done, how he has cut off the mediums and the spiritists from the land. Why then do you lay a snare for my life, to cause me to die?" And Saul swore to her by the LORD, saying, "As the LORD lives, no punishment shall come upon you for this thing." Then the woman said, "Whom shall I bring up for you?" And he said, "Bring up Samuel for me." When the woman saw Samuel, she cried out with a loud voice. And the woman spoke to Saul, saying, "Why have you deceived me? For you are Saul!" And the king said to her, "Do not be afraid. What did you see?" And the woman said to Saul, "I saw a spirit ascending out of the earth." So he said to her, "What is his form?" And she said, "An old man is coming up, and he is covered with a mantle." And Saul perceived that it was Samuel, and he stooped with his face to the ground and bowed down.

Now Samuel said to Saul, "Why have you disturbed me by bringing me up?" And Saul answered, "I am deeply distressed; for the Philistines make war against me, and God has departed from me and does not answer me anymore, neither by prophets nor by dreams. Therefore I have called you, that you may reveal to me what I should do." Then Samuel said: "So why do you ask me, seeing the LORD has departed from you and has become your enemy? And the LORD has done for Himself as He spoke by me. For the LORD has torn the kingdom out of your hand and given it to your neighbor, David. Because you did not obey the voice of the LORD nor execute His fierce wrath upon Amalek, therefore the LORD has done this thing to you this day. Moreover the LORD will also deliver Israel with you into the hand of the Philistines. And tomorrow you and your sons will be with me. The LORD will also deliver the army of Israel into the hand of the Philistines."

What a contradiction! Here is a king practicing Spiritism—violating the Word of God—and he swears *by God* to give protection to a woman who is possessed by a demon. This demonstrates how far men can fall from divine grace when they turn away from the presence of God. The Spiritists are quick to say, here, that the medium at Endor materialized Samuel, but she did not. She planned to material-ize something Saul could *believe* was Samuel; only the text indicates that she got the shock of her life. The prophet Samuel actually appeared by divine intervention; he predicted cosmic judgment, and the séance ended in destruction. This is the only séance ever recorded in the Bible, and God interrupted it. He ended it with a pro-nouncement of judgment.

It is important to note at this point that there is no such name as "Witch" in the Bible; that translation is used in King James English. The word used here is "medium," someone governed by another spirit. This medium, or *Witch*, inter-ceded with the dead. She had a familiar spirit, a demon, and it was the function of her demon to imitate whoever the woman requested, just as a demon imitated Bach's sister. But this time, something happened that was not on schedule.

Mediums attempt to interpret and predict the future; all occult forums are attempting to predict the future. What is the goal of all these things? First, they want to control life and the circumstances of life. Second, they promise people healing for bodies and for minds. Third, they promise aphrodisiacs, secrets of love that can only be uncovered by occult phenomena. Occultism is heavily laden with psychosexual implications, and those involved in it are usually involved in immorality. Fourth, they are constantly seeking future knowledge; always trying to lift up the curtain of eternity to see what God is going to do.

This is the objective of all Spiritists: to penetrate by psychic phenomena another dimension of reality—and other dimensions of reality *do* exist. There is a dimension known as the throne of God and a dimension known as hell. Ephesians 2:2 describes a dimension known as the domain of "the prince of the power of the air," the god of this age. And finally, humans inhabit a space-time continuum, so there are four dimensions that God has revealed. Do not dismiss the fact that there are other dimensions of reality: just because our senses cannot perceive them immediately does not mean that they do not exist. The Bible says that Jesus Christ did not ascend through the substratosphere, the ionosphere, and outer space into the heavens—all one great space-time continuum that is part of the material dimension. Jesus Christ ascended *through* the heavenlies; the dimension opened, and He passed *through* it into the very throne of God Himself. Stephen saw Him with heaven open, standing at the right hand of God, a figure descriptive of authority and power.

The lesson to be learned from Saul's sin is that the psychic world is a world populated by the forces of darkness, not by Uncle Harry, Aunt Edith, Cousin Willy, and all the people one may hope to summon in a séance. They cannot be reached. A great gulf exists between this dimension and whatever dimension they are in, be it heaven or hell; Luke 16 reveals its presence. People will never penetrate beyond the next dimension, and that dimension is *hostile* to this one. It is controlled by the person Jesus Christ said is the ruler of this age, so stay out of it! Once the door opens, Satan and his power will come through.

In Genesis 40:7–8, we find one of the most potent statements in the Bible regarding this. Joseph was one of God's children and a prophet, and he had something to say about God that is quite interesting: "So he asked Pharaoh's officers who were with him in the custody of his lord's house, saying, 'Why do you look so sad today?' And they said to him, 'We each have had a dream, and there is no interpreter of it.' So Joseph said to them, 'Do not interpretations belong to God? Tell them to me, please.'"

What was the prophet saying? *Go to God for the answers!* Do not seek answers from any source but the Divine, or they will be the wrong answers, and if they supply accurate information, it is to endorse a *wrong* path. Satan will give something good so that evil will come of it.

Interpretation belongs to God. In Isaiah 8:19, the children of Israel were having exactly the same problem, and God gave them an answer: "And when they say to you, 'Seek those who are mediums and wizards, who whisper and mutter,' should not a people seek their God? Should they seek the dead on behalf of the living?" God will reveal what people need to know; seek the answers from *Him*. Remember, all of these things lie in His hand. Should people seek from those who are possessed by demons? No, seek from God. If any reliable knowledge is going to come to you at all, it is going to come from Him, not from other sources. He warned Israel: *stay away from them.*

God was so determined to communicate this that He commanded in Exodus 22:18, "You shall not permit a sorceress to live." That was the dictum laid down in the law of Israel: they were to execute a medium. "And the person who turns to mediums and familiar spirits, to prostitute himself with them, I will set My face against that person and cut him off from his people. . . . A man or a woman who is a medium, or who has familiar spirits, shall surely be put to death; they shall stone them with stones. Their blood shall be upon them" (Lev. 20:6, 27).

The Holy Spirit gives additional warnings in Isaiah 47:13–14, and again in Daniel 1:17–20:

> As for these four young men, God gave them knowledge and skill in all literature and wisdom; and Daniel had understanding in all visions and dreams. Now at the end of the days, when the king had said that they should be brought in, the chief of the eunuchs brought them in before Nebuchadnezzar. Then the king interviewed them, and among them all none was found like Daniel, Hananiah, Mishael, and Azariah; therefore they served before the king. And in all matters of wisdom and understanding about which the king examined them, he found them ten times better than all the magicians and astrologers who were in all his realm.

They had *ten times as much knowledge* as all of the astrologers, soothsayers, and occultists in the king's entire realm. The Spirit of the living God was in them.

And finally, in Daniel 2:27–28, we see a marvelous picture of how God dealt with these things. "Daniel answered in the presence of the king, and said, 'The secret which the king has demanded, the wise men, the astrologers, the magicians, and the soothsayers cannot declare to the king. But there is a God in heaven who reveals secrets, and He has made known to King Nebuchadnezzar what will be in the latter days.'" The wise men, the magicians, and the soothsayers fail, but there is a God in heaven who makes known dreams and visions; He is the one to whom interpretations belong.

CONCLUSION

An entire mission field of souls involved in the cults and the occult lies at the doorstep of the Church. Christians must study the principles of these things in order to utilize them against a supernatural enemy bent on their destruction. There are millions of people who have yet to be reached with the gospel of Jesus Christ. They are souls for whom He died. God requires the Church to learn these things—not to pound people over the head with the knowledge gained, but so that Christians will be moved with compassion for the lost and go out and bring them to the Lord Jesus.

God did not send His Son into the world to judge the world, but that the world through Him might be saved (John 3:17; 12:47). If the Church of Jesus Christ does not reach the Spiritist, the Satanist, or the Mormon, who will? Some Christians may never have the opportunity to travel across the oceans to meet an Aborigine or Zulu, but Aborigines and Zulus are all over the landscape in the United States. They just wear different labels, such as Witch, Pagan, or Unitarian Universalist—whatever it may be.

Scripture tells us in Isaiah 47:13 that God wants us to learn something:

> You are wearied in the multitude of your counsels;
> let now the astrologers, the stargazers,
> and the monthly prognosticators
> stand up and save you
> from what shall come upon you.
> Behold, they shall be as stubble,
> the fire shall burn them;
> they shall not deliver themselves
> from the power of the flame;
> it shall not be a coal to be warmed by,
> nor a fire to sit before!

The people who want to uncover the future cannot see that God has planned their destruction. That is how helpless they are; they cannot save themselves. How will they save anyone else?

Never forget that the world of occultism is the world of demonism. A devil is not under every chair or behind every lamppost, but rest assured, Satan exists. You meet him in many forms, but the most common form is the world of psychic phenomena. He is there, and he is always trying to convince and control people by showing them extraordinary things.

There is another Jesus, another spirit, and another gospel (2 Cor. 11:3–4). They are counterfeit; do not be fooled by them. The Jesus of the Spiritists is an advanced medium; the Jesus of the Witches is a super Witch; and the Jesus of Theosophists is the reincarnation of the world's soul. But the Jesus of the Bible is the Lord God Jehovah in human form, and that is what separates God's children forever from the kingdom of the occult. Learn about the other Jesus, and do not be led astray by him. It may sound like the real thing, but it is not. When these people say, "I believe in Jesus," look them straight in the eye and ask, "Which one?" It has a terribly disarming effect upon them.

Who is Jesus? Which spirit is at work? What is the gospel being preached? Is it grace alone through faith? Jesus answered people's questions. Paul answered people's questions. The apostles answered people's questions. And today, those who are successful in carrying forth the ministry of the gospel are still in the business of answering questions. That is part of the challenge of the kingdom of the occult.

RECOMMENDED RESOURCES

1. Albright, William F. *The Archaeology of Palestine.* Baltimore: Penguin, 1960.
2. Gordon, Cyrus H. *The Common Background of Greek and Hebrew Civilizations.* New York: Norton, 1965.
3. Martin, Walter. *The Baptism of Boldness.* CD/audiotape, Walter Martin Ministries, www.waltermartin.com.

Quick Facts About the Doctrine of the Demons

- Satan promotes a doctrine that represents itself as pure religion and as truth.

- This doctrine teaches that Jesus Christ is not God in human flesh. Jesus was perfect humanity; Christ was the God idea in Him.

- Jesus is one of many equally good ways. He is an aspect of the truth; he is a fragment of the life.

- Secret knowledge of the future exists outside of God, and should be pursued.

- There are supernatural beings other than God, and they can be contacted and controlled.

3

The Doctrine of the Demons

S olomon's ancient proverb "There is nothing new under the sun" (Eccl. 1:9) has proven particularly relevant when applied to man's fascination with the occult and his dabbling in the demonic activity that characterizes it. According to the earliest biblical manuscripts, demons were present in ancient times, and they are present today. A wealth of historical evidence supports the biblical position, providing details of the physical descriptions and distinctive personalities of countless demons in every known culture. Professor J. Den Boeft, in his commentary *Calcidius on Demons,* notes, "The belief in the existence and the activity of demons played a large role in the life of late Antiquity, both in practical everyday religion and in the theoretical reflections of philosophy and theology. The religious and philosophical views show a great variety reaching from simple faith to very elaborate demonological systems."[1]

Scholars throughout history have disputed the cultural meaning of the word *demon,* arguing it refers to good spirits as well as bad, but the Bible is clear in its definition. Demons are never referred to as anything other than evil supernatural beings. The Old Testament uses the Hebrew word *sheediym* to describe spiritual beings that are both rational and malignant: "they sacrificed to demons" (Deut. 32:17).[2] *Adam Clarke's Commentary* analyzes the biblical translations of the word "demon":

> The Septuagint *ethusan* [and] *daimoniois,* they sacrificed to demons: the Vulgate copies the Septuagint: the Arabic has *sheeateen,* the plural of

---

1. J. den Boeft, *Calcidius on Demons* (Leiden: E. J. Brill, 1977), 1.
2. *Ethusan* NT:2380 (Strongs Number); *daimoniois* NT:1140. "The original word sheediym has been variously understood. The Syriac, Chaldee, Targums of Jerusalem and Jonathan, and the Samaritan, retain the original word. . . . the Vulgate, Septuagint, Arabic, Persic, Coptic, and Anglo-Saxon, have devils or demons. The Anglo-Saxon has devils. *Lasheediym,* OT:7700; *shed*

cont'd on next page

Sheetan, Satan, by which the rebellious angels appear to be intended, as the word comes from the root *shatana*, he was obstinate, proud, refractory. . . . And it is likely that these fallen spirits, having utterly lost the empire at which they aimed, got themselves worshipped under various forms and names in different places.[3]

The word *demon* is derived from the Greek word *daimónion*, meaning an evil spirit or spirits, comparable in meaning to *pneúmati toó akathártoo*, meaning unclean spirit.[4] This definition is supported by multiple examples throughout the Bible and one unique encounter Jesus had with a demon in Luke 9:42, where He intentionally linked the word *demon* to the definition of *unclean spirit*. "And as he was still coming, the demon threw him down and convulsed him. Then Jesus rebuked the unclean spirit, healed the child, and gave him back to his father." Jesus Christ equated "demon" with "unclean spirit," and this is the foundation for the Christian interpretation of the Greek. The Bible is as much an historical work as a theological one, and its eyewitness testimony must be weighed in the balance; it cannot be dismissed.[5] Although theologians and historians may dispute the Greek cultural interpretation of the word, the clear biblical interpretation in meaning and context is that there are powerful, malignant spirit-beings bent on the destruction of human beings.

It is apparent from the historical record that the ancient world recognized the existence of evil and acknowledged the manifestation of it through demonic activity. From India's bloody goddess Kali to Sumeria's Ishtar, from the Ammonites' god Molech to the Greeks' Harpies and Gorgons, history is replete with the names, faces, and exploits of the demonic realm. The voice of Moses echoes from the distant past,

---

2. (Cont'd) (shade); from OT:7736; a doemon (as malignant): *ruwach* from OT:7306; wind; by resemblance breath, i.e. a sensible (or even violent) exhalation; figuratively, life, anger, unsubstantiality; by extension, a region of the sky; by resemblance spirit, but only of a rational being (including its expression and functions)." (*Adam Clarke's Commentary on the Bible* [CD-rom, 1996], *Interlinear Transliterated Bible* [Biblesoft, 1994], and *New Exhaustive Strong's Numbers and Concordance with Expanded Greek-Hebrew Dictionary* [Biblesoft and International Bible Translators, 2003]).
3. *Adam Clarke's Commentary.*
4. John 8:49—demon = NT:1140 (Strong's Number); daimonion, neuter of a derivative of NT:1142 (*Interlinear Transliterated Bible*).
5. For an interesting review of biblical archaeological evidence, see G. P. Hugenberger, *Evidences for the Historicity of the Bible*, Park Street Church, http://images.acswebnetworks.com/1/934/Historicity_of_Bible.pdf (accessed June 2, 2008).

revealing the common practice of ancient demon worship and Israel's participation in it: "They sacrificed to demons, not to God, to gods they did not know, to new gods, new arrivals that your fathers did not fear" (Deut. 32:17). And King David's in Psalm 106:37–38, "They even sacrificed their sons and their daughters to demons, and shed innocent blood, the blood of their sons and daughters, whom they sacrificed to the idols of Canaan; and the land was polluted with blood."

Rome exemplified the Pagan practice of demon worship, displaying at the peak of its power temples, murals, writings, and graffiti detailing the influence of the demonic. Nowhere is this more apparent than in the ruins of the doomed city of Pompeii. Historian Michael Grant sheds a great deal of light on the immersion of Roman culture in the worship of multiple deities, especially their involvement in what was called the *Mystery religions*, cults that often included drunkenness and orgies. Although the worship of Jupiter and Vesta drew many followers, it was the Mystery religions like those of Bacchus (Dionysus) and Isis—with all their implied darkness and perversion—that captivated the empire. "There were somewhat formal cults of a national and civic character. But what engaged the emotions of the Pompeians far more deeply, as with millions of inhabitants of the Empire, were the Mystery religions. For they promised salvation in the after-life to their initiates and were only, much later, prevented by Christianity from completing what might have been a total take-over of the ancient world."[6]

The Middle Ages brought a revival in knowledge of the demonic realm and its interaction with people. The Renaissance is remembered for its genius and beauty, but it included a much darker side than the historical picture of *enlightenment* created by Michelangelo and others. Conjuring demons became so common a practice during this time that the self-proclaimed magicians and sorcerers who summoned them began recording demonic names, powers, and physical descriptions.[7] The Church tried to combat the conjurors with countless books and treaties on how to deal with sorcerers, Witches, and magicians, but the public interest remained strong. Inevitably, the conflict between the Church and those involved in the "dark arts" intensified, culminating in some of the cruelest Witchcraft trials in history. Hundreds of years later, this spirit of hysteria reasserted itself once more in Europe and America, producing the same terrible results.

---

6. Grant, *Eros in Pompeii*, 51.
7. J. S. Forsyth, *Demonologia or, Natural Knowledge Revealed* (London: A. K. Newman, 1831), 315.

From ancient times to modern, the presence of evil has left its mark on the hearts, minds, and history of humanity. Demons are real, and they are powerful. If people ignore them, they do so at their own peril.

DEMONOLOGY

The apostle Paul reveals the truth about demonic strategy in 1 Timothy 4:1, and his words have great meaning for today. "Now the Spirit expressly says that in latter times some will depart from the faith, giving heed to deceiving spirits and doctrines of demons." The Greek word here for "depart" is *aposteésontaí,* meaning to slide back from; "giving heed to deceiving spirits," or wandering spirits; and *didaskalíais daimoníoon,* meaning the teaching of the demons. *Didaskalíais daimoníoon* are two words that appear together only once in the New Testament, and this appearance should arrest the attention of every Christian who takes the New Testament seriously. Here, the apostle Paul, with one stroke of his pen under the inspiration of the Holy Spirit, reveals that there is such a thing as the teaching of the demons; there is something that *originates* with Satan that represents itself as pure religion and as truth.[8]

In today's world, some people feel it is politically incorrect or even embarrassing to acknowledge the genuine, and truly important, study of demons in the Old and the New Testaments. But anyone who has knowledge of occultism or the kingdom of the cults knows immediately how foolish this is: demons are not little individuals running around with pointed tales and pitchforks, copies and caricatures of the devil that he loves to see the world make, particularly on Halloween. Demons are malignant beings that are simply *other dimensional;* they live in a dimension other than this, but they are capable of entering it.

As we saw in chapter 1, Scripture teaches the reality of other dimensions. There is the dimension of heaven, the throne of God. The Lord Jesus Christ ascended—in Greek *dieleeluthóta toús ouranoús,* meaning "passed into the heavens" (Acts 1:9; Eph. 4:10)—through dimensions, into the heaven of heavens, the throne of God (Heb. 4:14).

Then there is another dimension mentioned in Scripture that is under the control of the prince of the power of the air, and beyond that dimension is the throne

---

8. *Interlinear Transliterated Bible,* Biblesoft.

of God. The Bible teaches that if it were not for the direct intervention of God the Holy Spirit, the Church would be overcome by the power of Satan. "For the mystery of lawlessness is already at work; only He who now restrains will do so until He is taken out of the way" (2 Thess. 2:7). God permits evil to go on, and He restrains it as He goes, until the restraint is lifted. When that happens, the Scripture teaches that all hell will break loose in the dimension of earth, but it is the Spirit that restrains now. That is why John exults in 1 John 4:4, "He who is in you is greater than he who is in the world." Christians are protected by the person, the presence, and the power of the Holy Spirit.

EVIDENCE FOR DEMONS

Exactly what evidence is there in the New Testament for demons? The best examples are found in the experiences of Jesus Christ. When He encountered Satan, He did not encounter the corporate evil within man, He did not encounter philosophic abstraction, and He was not simply using personification to speak of evil. When Jesus encountered the devil, He had a dialogue with him. Now, in this dialogue, Christ was either schizophrenic, which the New Testament flatly rejects, or He was speaking with *another* dimensional being, and in His conversation with him, Satan revealed something. "Then the devil, taking Him up on a high mountain, showed Him all the kingdoms of the world in a moment of time. And the devil said to Him, 'All this authority I will give You, and their glory; for this has been delivered to me, and I give it to whomever I wish. Therefore, if You will worship before me, all will be Yours'" (Luke 4:5–7). This is what the devil desires: *worship*.

Demons are quite literally Satan's children; fallen angels or spirits who followed Lucifer in his rebellion against the throne of God. They worship the devil, not God. When Christ encountered demons early in His ministry, He dealt with them, and they confessed something about Him. "Let us alone! What have we to do with You, Jesus of Nazareth? Did You come to destroy us? I know who You are—the Holy One of God!" (Mark 1:24) When Christ encountered demons, He expelled them.

The New Testament teaches a personal satanic being. It teaches that there are evil beings or spirit-beings that control individuals. They are capable of creating illness, mental and physical; they are capable of binding people; they can create all forms of symptoms in human life, and unrecognized, they will wreak awful destruction. There is not a devil behind every lamppost and under every seat, but it is very foolish to assume there are none at all. This is precisely what the world has assumed, and it explains its present condition. This great force is loose; people try to give it other names, but they will not succeed.

CASE STUDY

Sir Arthur Conan Doyle; Wales, 1920
This is the account of the wanderings of a Spiritist, geographical and speculative. . . .

There was one memorable night when I walked forth with my head throbbing and my whole frame quivering from the villa of Mr. Southeray at Merthyr. Behind me the brazen glare of Dowlais ironworks lit up the sky, and in front twinkled the many lights of the Welsh town. For two hours my wife and I had sat within listening to the whispering voices of the dead, voices which are so full of earnest life, and of desperate endeavours to pierce the barrier of our dull senses. They had quivered and wavered around us, giving us pet names, sweet sacred things, the intimate talk of the olden time. Graceful lights, signs of spirit power had hovered over us in the darkness. It was a different and a wonderful world. Now with those voices still haunting our memories we had slipped out into the twinkling cottage windows. As I looked down on it all I grasped my wife's hand in the darkness and I cried aloud, "My God, if they only knew—if they could only know!" Perhaps in that cry, wrung from my very soul, lay the inception of my voyage to the other side of the world. The wish to serve was strong upon us both. God had given us wonderful signs, and they were surely not for ourselves alone. . . .

Here is a bit of authentic teaching from the other side which bears upon the question. I take it from the remarkable record of Mr. Miller of Belfast, whose dialogues with his son after the death of the latter seem to me to be as certainly true as any case which has come to my notice. On asking the young soldier some question about the exact position of Christ in religion he modestly protested that such a subject was above his head, and asked leave to bring his

higher guide to answer the question. Using a fresh voice and in a
new and more weighty manner the medium then said:

"I wish to answer your question. Jesus the Christ is the proper
designation. Jesus was perfect humanity. Christ was the God idea in
Him. Jesus, on account of His purity, manifested in the highest
degree the psychic powers which resulted in His miracles. Jesus
never preached the blood of the lamb. The disciples after His ascension forgot the message in admiration of the man. The Christ is in
every human being, and so are the psychic forces which were used
by Jesus. If the same attention were given to spiritual development
which you give to the comfort and growth of your material bodies
your progress in spiritual life would be rapid and would be characterized by the same works as were performed by Jesus. The one
essential thing for all on earth to strive after is a fuller knowledge
and growth in spiritual living."

I think that the phrase, "In their admiration of the man they
forgot His message," is as pregnant a one as I ever heard.

Australia, 1920

Social gaieties are somewhat out of key with my present train of
thought, and I was more in my element next evening at a meeting
of the Rescue Circle under Mr. Tozer. . . [9] The circle sits round with
prayer and hymns while Mr. Love falls into a trance state. . . . He
is then controlled by the Chinaman Quong, who is a person of
such standing and wisdom in the other world that other lower spirits have to obey him. The light is dim, but even so the characteristics of this Chinaman get across very clearly, the rolling head, the
sidelong, humorous glance, the sly smile, the hands crossed and
buried in what should be the voluminous folds of a mandarin's
gown. He greets the company in somewhat laboured English and
says he has many who would be the better for our ministrations.

---

9. A rescue circle was a Spiritist meeting or séance for the purpose of helping confused, departed
souls on the 'other side' by leading them toward the light.

"Send them along, please!" says Mr. Tozer. The medium suddenly sits straight and his whole face changes into an austere harshness.

"What is this ribald nonsense?" he cries.

"Who are you, friend?" says Tozer.

"My name is Mathew Barret. I testified in my life to the Lamb and to Him crucified. I ask again: What is this ribald nonsense?"

"It is not nonsense, friend. We are here to help you and to teach you that you are held down and punished for your narrow ideas, and that you cannot progress until they are more charitable."

"What I preached in life I still believe."

"Tell us, friend, did you find it on the other side as you had preached?"

"What do you mean?"

"Well, did you, for example, see Christ?"

There was an embarrassed silence. "No, I have not."

"Then, bethink you, friend, that there may be truth in what we teach."

"It is against all that I have preached."

A moment later the Chinaman was back with his rolling head and his wise smile. "He good man—stupid man. He learn in time. Plenty time before him."

There were many others, most of whom returned thanks for the benefit derived from previous meetings. "You've helped us quite a lot," they said. Between each the old Chinese sage made comments upon the various cases, a kindly, wise old soul, with just a touch of mischievous humour running through him. We had an exhibition of the useless apostolic gift of tongues during the evening, for two of the ladies present broke out into what I was informed was the Maori language, keeping up a long and loud conversation. I was not able to check it, but it was certainly a coherent language of some sort. In all of this there was nothing which one could take

10. Arthur Conan Doyle, *Wanderings of a Spiritualist,* (New York: George H. Doran, 1921), 13, 16, 26, 137–139.

hold of and quote as absolutely and finally evidential, and yet the total effect was most convincing. I have been in touch with some Rescue Circles, however, where the identity of the "patients" as we call them, was absolutely traced."[10]

It has always been possible to communicate with demons, but it is a communication expressly forbidden by God. Sir Arthur Conan Doyle and his wife ignored the biblical warning to "test the spirits" (1 John 4:1) and spent the rest of their lives promoting the doctrine of the demons.

DEMONIC DOCTRINE

God reveals in Acts 16 exactly how the doctrine of the demons works. It is detailed and quite thorough. It is not a theologian's pipe dream; it is a New Testament revelation. The pity is it is not preached on very often, primarily because it can be a difficult subject, but Christians ought to face it. Nothing is ever solved by running from it, only by facing it in the power of Christ's resurrection.

In Acts 16:16–18, the apostle Paul was carrying on a glorious ministry of evangelism. As he was preaching and carrying on this wonderful ministry, it was inevitable that Satan would make his appearance, and he did:

Now it happened, as we went to prayer, that a certain slave girl possessed with a spirit of divination met us, who brought her masters much profit by fortune-telling. This girl followed Paul and us, and cried out, saying, "These men are the servants of the Most High God, who proclaim to us the way of salvation." And this she did for many days. But Paul, greatly annoyed, turned and said to the spirit, "I command you in the name of Jesus Christ to come out of her." And he came out that very hour.

The spirit of divination associated with this girl, *puthon* in the Greek, is directly linked in translation to an area in Greece known as Delphi, where the Oracle or Pythia answered wealthy pilgrims' questions about their futures (fortune-telling).[11]

---

11. NT:4436 (Strongs number) Puthon. *New Exhaustive Strong's Numbers and Concordance with Expanded Greek-Hebrew Dictionary.*

"Having a spirit of Python, or of Apollo. Pytho was, according to fable, a huge ser-pent, that had an oracle at Mount Parnassus, famous for predicting future events; Apollo slew this serpent, and hence, he was called Pythius, and became celebrated as the foreteller of future events; and all those, who either could or pretended to predict future events, were influenced by the spirit of Apollo Pythius."[12] This slave girl possessed a spirit of divination associated with the Delphic spirit, and through her powers she brought much gain to the people who utilized her services.

It is important to note here that *she* followed Paul. Satan is quite pious; he clothes all forms of deviltry in the most pious terminology. Here, he announced to the world: "Paul is a servant of the Most High God. They are showing you a way of salvation." The King James Bible translates "*the* way of salvation" but in the Greek, the definite article "the" is not in the text. The Greek says it is "*a* way of sal-vation." Satan does not recommend Jesus Christ's gospel; he distorts it. Under no circumstances will Satan acknowledge that Jesus Christ is eternal God, the incar-nate way, truth, and life. Instead, Satan presents Jesus as one of many equally good ways; he is an aspect of the truth; he is a fragment of the life. This young girl walk-ing behind Paul cried out "these men are servants," but she was not doing the talk-ing. She did not say this to them once or twice; she shouted it for "many days." Finally, Paul became annoyed, and he said to the *spirit* in the girl (not to the girl), "I command you in the name of Jesus Christ to come out of her." The demon came out in the same hour, and when her masters saw that all their hope of profit was gone, they became angry (v. 19).

The Holy Spirit is very bad for the demonic business of divination. This is why occultism fears the presence of the Spirit. They do not fear other spirits, but they do fear Christians who are filled with the Holy Spirit. They want no part of Spirit-filled Christians, who have power from God to overcome them. Some Christians are afraid of demons, and they do not need to be. It is demons who are afraid of Christians. They are afraid because "He who is in you is greater than he who is in the world" (1 John 4:4). The Church should not be afraid of the doctrines of the demons or of the demons themselves. Instead, let *them* be warned to be afraid of the Church, for it is the Church that represents Jesus Christ, and against *it* the gates of hell will not pre-

---

12. *Adam Clarke's Commentary.* For more information on the Delphic Oracle, see Rachael Kohn, The Ark (Radio National), January 9, 2005, http://www.abc.net.au/m/relig/ark/stories/s1266794.htm.

vail (Matt. 16:18). That is Christ's promise, and they know it. Therefore, Christians mistakenly back up from something they could march into victoriously, with the Cross before them, bringing deliverance to the souls of those imprisoned.

Jesus Is "A Way"

Christ as *a way* is one of the first planks in the platform of the doctrines of demons. Jesus is *a* way, but not *the* way (John 14:6). The Spiritists say he is the greatest medium. The Baha'i say he is one of nine great world prophetic manifestations of deity. The Jehovah's Witnesses say he is a superangel named Michael. The Mormons say he is one God in a pantheon of divinities, but the record of Scripture is that He is indeed the Lord God Jehovah Himself in human form, and *this* they cannot face. That is why when Paul turned to the girl and said, "I command you in the name of Jesus Christ," the spirit came out of her. No power is capable of resisting the Lord Jesus.

It is vital to ask questions, to probe the theology of others. Some people may label Christians who do this "intolerant," but it is a method born of concern, and the Church must be *desperately* concerned. For where men have turned from the living God, they have opened themselves to the doctrine of the demons, and within them the powers of darkness move. These forces are here, and they are real.

Pursue Secret Knowledge

One of the doctrines of the demons teaches that people can obtain information from sources other than God and that this secret knowledge is reliable. But God warns that this knowledge will lead people astray and into great spiritual darkness. The person who wants to interpret the future *apart* from God is a person who would lead you away from the Lord your God, and that person is dangerous. It does not matter who he is or whether she wears a cross around her neck; crosses are cheap, and pious talk is cheap. It is possible for someone to be baptized in the church, teach Sunday school, marry a Christian, and live a pseudo-Christian life, but in reality be filled with every kind of unclean spirit if he or she has never been to the Cross. There are people like this in churches around the world. Is it any wonder that the Church is ineffective? The majority of Christians have little discernment. The apostle Paul teaches that one of the great gifts of God's Spirit is the "discerning of the spirits" (1 Cor. 12:10). Christians must learn to be discerning. God has not left us in darkness.

Explore Powers Other Than God

This is the third plank in the doctrine of the demons: explore or play with supernatural powers *other* than God. One of the most successful demonic strategies is *absorption*—playing with something you cannot control. This absorption with occult power turns people away from the One who controls all things, in whose hands the Church must commit itself as witnesses and servants of Jesus Christ. The devil is engaged in trying to get people absorbed with the future and the powers involved in revealing it. Acts 16:16–19 paints the picture of a possessed girl absorbed in forecasting the future, and it is clear (based on the great wealth she produced) that *many* people were fascinated by it.

In Genesis 40:8, a great deal of light is shed on this dangerous deception. Joseph, a prophet of God, was given this illumination from the Holy Spirit after Pharaoh's chief butler and chief baker came to him and said, "We each have had a dream, and there is no interpreter of it." Joseph answered them, "Do not interpretations belong to God?" This is what the Creator, Lord of heaven and earth, has to say on the subject of divination: the future belongs to Him—do not play with it.

Isaiah 45:11 is another telling passage. The prophet spells out here, in very clear terms, exactly what God wants people to know regarding the pursuit of secret knowledge apart from God. "Ask Me of things to come concerning My sons; and concerning the work of My hands, you command Me." God is saying, *Talk to Me about it! Do not talk to the crystal balls or the bearded prophets; do not talk to the people who read palms or tea leaves; do not talk to the people who claim to know secret things.* And then He gives His credentials: "I have made the earth, and created man on it. I—My hands—stretched out the heavens, and all their host I have commanded. I have raised him up in righteousness, and I will direct all his ways" (vv. 12–13). God ends with the promise that Israel shall be saved by God "with an everlasting salvation" (v. 17).

What is God's answer to people who spend their days trying to find out the future? *Talk to Me about it if you truly want answers. I have them, and if I choose not to give them to you, it is better that you do not know them.* If people knew everything the future held right now, maybe they would stay away from home tonight; maybe they would turn away from the person next to them or a member of their family; maybe life would not be bearable anymore. That is why the Lord has placed these things within His own providence.

Equate the Truth with Mythology

In 2 Timothy 4:3–4, the fourth plank in the doctrine of the demons is revealed. The apostle Paul was speaking to the Church concerning God's expectations of His children and the nature of the end times. He described what the world was going to be like then, and told the Church what to expect. These are powerful words, in that Paul obviously intended that the Church not only be edified by them, but that they *pass them on* to others and prayerfully meditate on them. Paul said that at the consummation of time, certain things are going to happen: "For the time will come when they will not endure sound doctrine, but according to their own desires, because they have itching ears, they will heap up for themselves teachers; and they will turn their ears away from the truth, and be turned aside to fables."

This is exactly what has happened today—people hearing only what they wish to hear: soft lights, soft music, and even softer sermons characterize our age. The word "fables" here is *muthos*, the Greek word for fiction or mythology. One of the reigning schools of Protestant theology today is Rudolf Bultmann's school of *demythologization*. He examined the Bible and removed all the "myths" out of the Old Testament and all the "myths" out of the New Testament, and when he finished, he did not have much of either one left, so he *remythologized* the whole book. Bultmann gave us a world with a remythologized New Testament: a Cross transformed into a myth that must be interpreted to gain some kind of esoteric meaning for today.[13]

In his second letter to Timothy, Paul warned the Church to watch out for exactly this. He spoke of the great deterioration that would take place morally, ethically, and spiritually toward the end of the age. The apostle went out of his way to say that these are men who preserve an outward form of religion but are a standing denial of its power. This teaching of the demons or of evil spirits will dominate the consummation of time.

The doctrine of the demons equates the truth with mythology, and it surrounds the Church today on every side. Who is at the forefront of this onslaught? It is the theologians and church seminaries. The very places that should be giving the truth, now promote the deadliest of lies. Their Bible is mythology: fables and legends that

---

13. For more information on Rudolf Bultmann's demythologization of the Bible, see Philip Edgcumbe Hughes, "Scripture and Myth: An Examination of Rudolf Bultmann's Plea for Demythologization," http://www.biblicalstudies.org.uk/article_myth_hughes.html.

must be reconstructed to meet the needs of our age. The truth has been equated with mythology.

Deny Jesus Christ

What is the primary doctrine of the demons? It is this: the denial that Jesus Christ is truly God in human flesh. First John 4:2–3 warns, "By this you know the Spirit of God: Every spirit that confesses that Jesus Christ has come in the flesh is of God, and every spirit that does not confess that Jesus Christ has come in the flesh is not of God. And this is the spirit of the Antichrist, which you have heard was coming, and is now already in the world." Whoever denies that Jesus is Christ is anti-Christ. Whoever denies that Jesus Christ has come in the flesh is not of God. People involved in the cults or the occult will call Jesus anything but the *one*, eternal Lord.

This is the core of Christianity: Jesus Christ is Lord to the glory of God the Father, and every tongue shall confess it one day. John 1 blends beautifully with 1 John 4 on this most important of subjects. The same man who wrote both of them was saying exactly the same thing: "The Word became flesh and dwelt among us" (John 1:14) and "Every spirit that does not confess that Jesus Christ has come in the flesh is not of God" (1 John 4:3). This is the prime attack of Satan; he must under-cut the person of the Master. He dares not allow the worship of the Lord Jesus, because he seeks worship for himself. Remember Satan's words to Christ in Matthew 4:9: "All these things I will give You if You will fall down and worship me."

THE JESUS OF THE BIBLE

In 2 Corinthians 11:3–4, Paul emphasized that there is another Jesus—a counter-feit Jesus, not the real Jesus. He is a Jesus who resembles the Christ of the Bible, but he is not God in human form. The Jesus of the Mormons or the Jehovah's Witnesses and the Jesus of the occult is not the Jesus of the Bible. Today, anyone can say the name of Jesus, so it is critical that the Church ask, "Jesus who?" The only true, New Testament response is Jesus Christ, God the Son, second Person of the Holy Trinity, God in human form. Any other definition is meant to deceive and to sustain the teaching of the demons. The Lord Jesus warned of this in Mark 13:6, when He said that at the end of the ages there would be those coming in His name, claiming to be Christ, and this is exactly what has happened.

Moses warned against false prophets as far back as Deuteronomy 13. Jesus warned, "Beware of false prophets, who come to you in sheep's clothing, but inwardly they are ravenous wolves. You will know them by their fruits" (Matt. 7:15–16). Someday they will stand before Him and say, "Lord, Lord, have we not prophesied in Your name, cast out demons in Your name, and done many wonders in Your name?" and Christ will turn to them and say, "I never knew you; depart from Me, you who practice lawlessness!" (vv. 22–23).

There is always power in the name of Jesus, but the question must be asked, who is using this power, and for what purpose? Is it for God's glory, or for selfish ends? Remember the words of the apostle Paul: "Some indeed preach Christ even from envy and strife, and some also from goodwill: The former preach Christ from selfish ambition, not sincerely, supposing to add affliction to my chains; but the latter out of love, knowing that I am appointed for the defense of the gospel. What then? Only that in every way, whether in pretense or in truth, Christ is preached; and in this I rejoice, yes, and will rejoice" (Phil. 1:15–18).

The important thing is that the good news gets out; God will judge the motives of the people who preach it. *Be on guard against deception.* Miracle or no miracle, whatever leads people away from God is the doctrine of the demons. Remember, a miracle in and of itself means nothing. It is intended to bring someone to a deeper adoration of God, and a commitment to the service of the Lord Jesus. If it commands someone to do something that is forbidden by Holy Scripture, it is not of God and must be rejected, for the Scripture says Satan appears as the angel of light (2 Cor. 11:14).

CONCLUSION

The Church of Jesus Christ has a grave responsibility. We must render an account to God. There is such a thing as the doctrine of the demons; it is a challenge to the Church that must be met. Never forget the words of Jude 3: "Beloved, while I was very diligent to write to you concerning our common salvation, I found it necessary to write to you exhorting you to contend earnestly for the faith which was once for all delivered to the saints." Put up a good fight for the faith! The Greek word *epagonizomai* means to put up a stiff resistance for the faith; to struggle; to compete for a prize.[14] This is the responsibility of the Church, and it is one we cannot get away from.

---

14. "To struggle for"; NT:1864 from NT:1909 and NT:75; *New Exhaustive Strong's Numbers.*

If someone attacks Christianity, God commands a response. The Church cannot sit still, smile benevolently, and quote John 3:16. We must give answers. "Be diligent to present yourself approved to God, a worker who does not need to be ashamed, rightly dividing the word of truth" (2 Tim. 2:15). This is what Christians are called to do—*study*. No one gets any information by osmosis; God requires His people to study His Word.

Paul spoke his mind clearly in 2 Timothy 4:1–2, when he said, "I charge you therefore before God and the Lord Jesus Christ, who will judge the living and the dead at His appearing and His kingdom: Preach the word! Be ready in season and out of season. Convince, rebuke, exhort, with all longsuffering and teaching." For the time will come when people will not put up with wholesome teaching; they will follow their own desires and gather a crowd of teachers around them to "tickle their ears" (see verse 4). They will close their ears to the truth and turn away to mythology.

The Church must face hardship, work to spread the gospel, and do all the duties of its calling, so we can say, along with the apostle Paul, "I have fought the good fight, I have finished the race, I have kept the faith" (2 Tim. 4:7). That must be the testimony of every Christian: the great race, the course, and the faith. Fight the good fight of faith. The weapons of our warfare are not carnal; they are spiritual (2 Cor. 10:4). "Put on the whole armor of God, that you may be able to stand against the wiles of the devil" (Eph. 6:11).

This is the challenge of the age in which we live. The challenge is here—the time is now.

RECOMMENDED RESOURCES

1. Bruce, F. F. *The New Testament Documents: Are They Reliable?* Grand Rapids: Eerdmans, 2003.

2. Gromacki, Robert G. *New Testament Survey.* Grand Rapids: Baker, 1974.

3. Kaiser, Jr., Walter C. *The Old Testament Documents: Are They Reliable and Relevant?* Downers Grove, IL: InterVarsity, 2001.

4. Kitchen Kenneth A. *The Bible in Its World. The Bible and Archaeology Today.* Grand Rapids: Eerdmans, 2006.

5. Martin, Walter. *Evil and Human Suffering.* CD/audiotape, Walter Martin Ministries, www.waltermartin.com.

Quick Facts About Ancient Paganism

- Ancient Paganism teaches the existence of one Supreme Being: multiple gods exist under the authority of this one Being (henotheism); demons exist separately from these gods.

- Jesus is one powerful god among many gods.

- Modern Paganism believes in the divine principle, male and female; many gods may or may not exist within this principle.

- Jesus was a good man who exhibited the divinity present in all humanity.

- Nature is a manifestation of divinity, not a "fallen" creation of deity.[1]

- Humanity's basic nature is good; salvation may or may not be needed, but reparation for bad behavior can be achieved through good deeds.

---

1. Jones and Pennick, *A History of Pagan Europe*, 2.

4

Ancient Paganism

In order to understand the faiths of today, we must carefully explore the faiths of yesterday. The roots of Pagan religions run deep and strong in the history of mankind, influencing almost every aspect of human society. These faiths are legion, and it would be impossible to examine all with any shred of accuracy within the limited scope of this work. In view of this fact, the civilizations of Greece, Rome, Egypt, and Persia have been chosen based on their global influence, both ancient and modern, as well as their involvement in the occult.

Archaeological evidence reveals that man has always worshiped, always reached to a power he considered greater than human power—a power outside himself. The ruins of the world stand as monuments to these ceremonies, and ancient writings provide valuable details supporting the fact that religious faith is an integral part of man's history, uniquely rooted in realities both inside and outside himself: his *spiritual nature,* as evidenced by words and deeds, and the *physical existence* of the Divine, as evidenced by revelation and eyewitness testimony.[2]

In support of the biblical record, Wilhelm Schmidt maintained that all ancient cultures throughout the world originally contained the belief in a Supreme Being. He details the progression of ancient religious beliefs in his *Origin and Growth of Religion:*

- The Supreme Being is generally acknowledged as creator and called *Father* in every primitive culture where He is addressed. He lives somewhere above the earth.

- He is a being, so his physical form cannot be accurately represented. He is described as *invisible, like the wind, or like fire.*

---

2. For more detailed information on these civilizations, including personal stories of life in the ancient world, see Fordham University's *Internet Ancient History Sourcebook,* http://www.fordham.edu/HALSALL/ANCIENT/asbook07.html.

- He is eternal: He existed before any other being, and He will not die.

- He is all powerful and all knowing.

- He is good, and all good comes from Him, including moral law. He is unalterably righteous.

- He despises evil, and it must be kept far from Him.

- He is the just Judge. Human beings are separated from Him by past offenses, and they abandoned Him for lesser, more accessible gods; yet primitive religions retain His memory as the Sky-God.[3]

Schmidt argued for a universal Sky-God among many cultures, but only within Scripture do we see God's full identity revealed. The Bible also explains the serious nature of the offenses mankind committed so long ago. Human beings were created to fellowship with their Creator: to walk with God. The vast sum of human history portrays man's need to worship—to commune with the Father—and in his rejection of God, man deprived himself of this basic need, creating a spiritual void of immense proportions. Into this void came Satan. He actively instigated the separation of God and man; his one intention, "I will be like the Most High" (Isa. 14:14). He sought to gain the worship of God's most beloved creation: human beings, and in that gain, to destroy them. Idolatry was his goal, and he was brilliantly successful at it.

History details the progression of mankind's rebellion against the Father, his fateful choice to follow his own wisdom and that offered by anything or anyone other than God. From the first revolt in the garden of Eden, man wandered from the worship of the one true God, Elohiym.[4] The result of this rebellion was Paganism, with its inherent idolatry.

The story of Jacob and Rachel is the first time the word *idols* is used in the Bible, and it reveals the early descent of man into Paganism. The book of Genesis, written by Moses about 1450 BC, places Paganism far back into the realm of the

---

3. Adapted from Wilhelm Schmidt, *The Origin and Growth of Religion: Facts and Theories* (New York: Cooper Square, 1972), 264–273.

4. Genesis 1:1 OT:430 plural of OT:433; gods in the ordinary sense; but specifically used (in the plural thus, especially with the article) of the supreme God. (*New Exhaustive Strong's Numbers and Concordance*).

ancients. According to Genesis 31:19, "Laban had gone to shear his sheep, and Rachel had stolen the household idols that were her father's." The importance of these family gods can be seen in the risk Rachel took in stealing them. Her father, Laban, was so enraged at Jacob's decampment and assumed theft that he pursued Jacob relentlessly for seven days until he caught up with him:

> And Laban said to Jacob: "What have you done, that you have stolen away unknown to me, and carried away my daughters like captives taken with the sword? Why did you flee away secretly, and steal away from me, and not tell me; for I might have sent you away with joy and songs, with timbrel and harp? And you did not allow me to kiss my sons and my daughters. Now you have done foolishly in so doing. It is in my power to do you harm, but the God of your father spoke to me last night, saying, 'Be careful that you speak to Jacob neither good nor bad.' And now you have surely gone because you greatly long for your father's house, but why did you steal my gods?"
>
> Then Jacob answered and said to Laban, "Because I was afraid, for I said, 'Perhaps you would take your daughters from me by force.' With whomever you find your gods, do not let him live. In the presence of our brethren, identify what I have of yours and take it with you." For Jacob did not know that Rachel had stolen them.
>
> And Laban went into Jacob's tent, into Leah's tent, and into the two maids' tents, but he did not find them. Then he went out of Leah's tent and entered Rachel's tent. Now Rachel had taken the household idols, put them in the camel's saddle, and sat on them. And Laban searched all about the tent but did not find them. And she said to her father, "Let it not displease my lord that I cannot rise before you, for the manner of women is with me." And he searched but did not find the household idols. (Genesis 31:26–35).

Not only did Rachel steal these gods, but she risked her life to keep them, a clear indication of the importance of idol worship in ancient times, and her participation in it.

HISTORY OVERVIEW

3800–3000 BC[5]	Village settlements develop into cities; first year of Jewish calendar (3760); first phonetic writing (3500); Western Europe is Neolithic; Sumerian city-states; Semitic tribes settle Assyria; evidence of astronomy in Egypt, Babylon, India, China
3000–2000 BC	Earliest known alphabet (Sumerian) developed (3100) —evolves into cuneiform (2600); Gilgamesh epic; Pharaohs begin to rule Egypt (3100); Stonehenge and Avebury built in Great Britain (2900); King Khufu (Cheops) finishes the Great Pyramid at Giza (2680); Phoenicians settle on coasts of Lebanon/Syria; Minoan Civilization in Crete (2000–1500); Hinduism develops; Hammurabi, king of Babylon, writes code (2250)
2000–1500 BC	Abraham born (2000–1800); rise of the Assyrian Empire— cities of Ashur and Nineveh; Hittites use hieroglyphs (1500); Israelite Exodus from Egypt (1400–1300); Mycenaeans conquer Minoans (1400); Phoenician alphabet—precursor to Greek alphabet—develops and spreads (1100)
1500–1000 BC	Akhenaton reveals monotheistic religion in Egypt (Amarna Period, 1350); son Tutankhamen returns to Egypt's earlier gods; Greeks destroy Troy (1250); Oracle at Delphi begins (1200)

---

5. All dates are Circa. Authorities disagree on (and cannot substantiate) many dates, so the intent here is to provide a general historical framework. See "Context of Ancient Israelite Religion" (ca. 2000–539 BCE), Jewish Virtual Library, http://www.jewishvirtuallibrary.org/jsource/History/context.html; "The Iliad," Internet Classics Archive at http://classics.mit.edu/; and "Timelines of Art History: The world (BC/BCE)," Art History Web site, http://www.art-and-archaeology.com/timelines/t10001.html for more details.

    The term *BC* (Before Christ) dates history from the birth of Christ and *AD* (Latin Anno Domini—year of our Lord). The exact date of His birth is not known, however, and this leaves the accuracy of historical dating in question by +/- 10 years. The system BCE (Before the Common Era) and CE (Common Era) dates history by counting back from the existing year (ex. 2008). Recently, the debate on this has become heated, with some claiming a total erasure of Christ from the historical timeline if the BCE system remains in use. The opposite side contends that the BC dating is Christian in nature and excludes those who are not Christian. However, it is indisputable that altering the dating system is historical revisionism.

1000–800 BC	Solomon succeeds King David, builds Jerusalem temple (975); after Solomon's death, kingdom divided into Israel and Judah; Jews begin to record Old Testament books of Bible (oral tradition preserved Jewish beliefs for hundreds of years); Greeks develop forerunner of modern alphabet (800)
900–700 BC	Prophets Amos, Hosea, Isaiah; Homer's *Iliad* and the *Odyssey* (800); first recorded Olympic games (776); Assyrians conquer the kingdom of Israel (722–721)
700–500 BC	King Hezekiah of Judah and the prophet Isaiah successfully resist the Assyrian siege of Jerusalem (716); end of Assyrian Empire (616)—Nineveh destroyed by Chaldeans (Neo-Babylonians) and Medes (612); founding of Byzantium by Greeks (660); Celtic druids influence tribal rule in Great Britain (600); building of the Acropolis in Athens
600–500 BC	Prophets Jeremiah and Ezekiel (600–580); Lao Tzu, Chinese philosopher and founder of Taoism (550); Babylonian king Nebuchadnezzar destroys Jerusalem (587–586); Babylonian captivity of the Jews; Cyrus the Great of Persia conquers Babylon, frees the Jews (539); democracy develops in Athens; Confucius (500) develops philosophy in China; Buddha (300) founds Buddhism in India[6]
500–400 BC	Prophets Ezra, Nehemiah, and Malachi (450); Greeks defeat Persians—development of Classical Greece; birth of the Roman Empire; Xerxes I, king of Persia (485)
400–300 BC	Alexander the Great (356–323) conquers Persia and Jerusalem, invades India, dies in Babylon; Socrates executed (399); Plato writes dialogues; philosopher Aristotle born (384)

---

6. See Heinz Bechert, ed., *Dating the Historical Buddha* (Göttingen, Germany: Vandenhoeck and Ruprecht, 1991; 1992), vols. I and II, for a recent revision of the long held 560 BC dates for Buddha's life.

300–151 BC	Beginning of Roman world domination; Jewish scholars translate Hebrew Bible, or *Tanach*, into Greek in Alexandria, Egypt—it takes the name *Septuagint* or LXX, referring to the number of men responsible for the translation (250); Qumran (200)
100–51 BC AD 50–1	Julius Caesar (100–44); Roman general Pompey conquers Jerusalem (63); Cleopatra on Egyptian throne Herod is Roman governor of Judea (37); Caesar murdered (44); Caesar's nephew, Octavian, defeats Mark Antony and Cleopatra (31) and rules Roman Empire as Emperor Augustus; birth of Christ (3 BC–6 AD)

Definition

Paganism can be defined from the Christian perspective as the worship of many gods (polytheism) other than the God of creation as revealed in the Bible. The word *Pagan* is derived from the Latin term *Paganus,* meaning rural or rustic (*pagus* meaning a village or country district), but its actual meaning can differ based on language, culture, and context.[7]

The early Church referred to itself as "soldiers of Christ" and to those who were not as *Paganus* or *civilians.*[8] According to the etymology of the word *Paganus,* however, this term was generally a neutral classification. "It was once thought its meaning of 'non-Christian, heathen' developed because the ancient idolatrous religion persisted in the rural districts long after Christianity had been generally accepted in the towns and cities of the Roman Empire. While it may indeed be true that the older Roman religions lingered in remote hamlets, this is not the word's true origin."[9]

---

7. University of Notre Dame Latin Dictionary and Grammar Aid, s.v. "Paganus," http://catholic.archives.nd.edu/dgi-bin/lookup.pl?stem=Paganus&ending= (accessed 9/20/06).
8. See Ephesians 6 for the apostle Paul's reference to the Church as soldiers and James J. O'Donnell's article "Paganus" at http://www9.georgetown.edu/faculty/jod/paganus.html, for an in-depth commentary on the origin and usage of the term *Paganus.*
9. The Institute for Etymological Research and Education, "Words to the Wise," Take Our Word for It, http://www.takeourword.com/TOW143half/page2.html (accessed 9/20/06).

Historian Ronald Hutton points out the modern reassessment of the meaning of *Pagan* in academic circles, noting Pierre Chuvin's position that it more than likely referred to the people who simply followed the faith of the *pagus*, "the local unit of government; that is, the rooted or old, religion."[10] The Hebrew uses the word *nokriy*, meaning "strange" or "different" (anyone outside the accepted society norm), and it is translated *Pagan* in the New King James Version.[11]

In their text, *A History of Pagan Europe*, Pagan leaders Prudence Jones and Nigel Pennick narrowly define *Paganism* as a nature-worshiping spiritual tradition.[12] They maintain that this definition is rooted in antiquity but do not offer historical evidence that such roots exist.[13] Based on this assumption, they characterize Pagan religions as having the following characteristics:

> *Polytheism*—a plurality of divine beings which may or may not be avatars . . . or other aspects of an underlying unity/duality/trinity/et cetera
>
> *Nature as a Theophany*—a manifestation of divinity, not as a 'fallen' creation of the latter.
>
> *The Female Divine Principle*—called the Goddess, as well as, or instead of the male divine principle, the God.[14]

What is clear throughout history is that Paganism stands as the antithesis to Christianity. While Pagans worship many gods, Christians worship only one.[15] Where Pagans chant spells and worship the divine in nature, Christians pray to and worship the *Creator* of nature.[16] Pagans view the evil in the world as something outside themselves. They are generally the victims of it. Christians view the evil in this world as twofold: within them and outside of them.[17] Ancient Pagans acknowledged a supreme God, but they worshiped whatever lesser gods they believed could

---

10. Ronald Hutton, *The Triumph of the Moon: A History of Modern Pagan Witchcraft*, (New York: Oxford, 2001), 4.

11. "Foreign, or (concretely) a foreigner, or (abstractly) heathendom; OT:5236 from OT:5234" *New Exhaustive Strong's Numbers*.

12. Jones and Pennick. *A History of Pagan Europe*, 2.

13. Ibid.

14. Ibid.

15. Belief in one God or monotheism is seen in Mark 12:29; 1 Corinthians 8:5–6; Galatians 4:8; and James 2:19.

16. Matt. 4:10; John 4:23–24; 1 Timothy 2:8.

17. 2 Cor. 1:12; Gal. 6:14; Eph. 2:2; Col. 2:20; 1 John 2:16.

help them the most. They practiced magic (manipulating supernatural powers), which often employed the use of binding spells and curse tablets, in an attempt to influence their lives and the lives of others for better or worse.[18]

From the seeds of rebellion against God, occult power was born, and Paganism—fostered by Satan and his demons—lives and thrives on this power. The worship of multiple gods and goddesses reigned supreme in the ancient world for thousands of years; divinities too numerous to count dominated lore, culture, and ceremony, their varied names and faces scattered throughout nations and kingdoms. Professor Georg Luck, in his compilation of ancient writings *Arcana Mundi: Magic and the Occult in the Greek and Roman Worlds*, comments, "Ancient history shows us a succession of great empires—Egypt, Persia, Athens, Macedonia, Rome—and each of these had its Pantheon of divine powers. As one culture conquered another, it took over some of its gods, usually the ones that could be identified with a native deity, or the ones suitable to become at least the attendants, the courtiers as it were, of native deities."[19] Humans may have called them gods, but the God of the Bible revealed their true identities as *demons*:

> They provoked Him to jealousy with foreign gods;
>> With abominations they provoked Him to anger.
> They sacrificed to demons, not to God,
>> To gods they did not know,
>> To new gods, new arrivals
>> That your fathers did not fear. (Deut 32:16–17)

ANCIENT PAGANISM

Ancient Paganism is defined by its writings, and they are to be found everywhere, in almost every culture known to man. One large group of these writings that reveal the sheer number of gods and goddesses—and man's relationship to them—are preserved in the curse tablets and binding spells of the ancient world. Long ignored by scholars, and now the object of intense scrutiny due to the groundbreaking work

---

18. Georg Luck, *Arcana Mundi: Magic and the Occult in the Greek and Roman Worlds,* (Baltimore: John Hopkins University Press, 1985), 191.
19. Ibid., 6.

of scholars such as Georg Luck and John Gager, this strange collection of bits of parchment, wood, stone, metal, and precious gems excavated from ancient cities, opens thousands of tiny windows into worlds long gone.

Curse tablets and binding spells are personal, full of the details of everyday life. Names, places, deities: all can be found in them. These valuable glimpses into the lives of peoples and cultures long dead reveal the power of polytheism and its hold on ancient man. John G. Gager in *Curse Tablets and Binding Spells from the Ancient World*, makes this observation about man's early religious beliefs and attitudes:

> It is necessary to keep in mind three fundamental characteristics of the "spiritual universe" of ancient Mediterranean culture: first, the cosmos literally teemed, at every level and in every location, with supernatural beings; second, although ancient theoreticians sometimes tried to sort these beings into clear and distinct categories, most people were less certain about where to draw the lines between gods, *daimones*, planets, stars, angels, cherubim, and the like; and third, the spirit or soul of dead persons, especially of those who had died prematurely or by violence, roamed about in a restless and vengeful mood near their buried body.[20]

A glimpse into the ancient world via curse tablets reveals a deep belief in the supernatural:

> Greece/Asia Minor—First Century BC (Small lead tablet)
>
> I, Antigonê, make a dedication to Demeter, Kore, Pluto, and all the gods and goddesses with Demeter. If I have given poison/spells to Asclapiadas or contemplated in my soul doing anything evil to him; or if I have called a woman from the temple, offering her a mina and a half for her to remove him from among the living, (if so) may Antigonê, having been struck by a fever, go up to Demeter and make confession, and may she not find Demeter merciful but instead suffer great torments. If anyone has spoken to Asclapiadas against me or brought forward the woman, by offering her copper coins . . . (*back*) Let it be permissible for me (presum-

---

20. Gager, *Curse Tablets and Binding Spells*, 12.

ably in company with the target of the spell) to go to the same bath, under
the same roof, or to the same table.[21]

And another:

I hand over to Demeter and Kore and the gods with Demeter those who
attacked and flogged me and put me in bonds and accused me. . . . But as
for me, let me be blameless. . . .[22]

Another example of man's belief in multiple gods is the Great Magical Papyrus
of Paris. This papyrus, Egyptian in origin, dates to 100–150 AD and was to be performed as part of an exorcism:

The protective charm you must write on a tin tablet: [magic words] and
hang it on the patient. This is the object of fear for every daemon and
frightens him. Stand facing him and exorcise him. The formula of exorcism
is the following: "I conjure you by the God of the Hebrews, Jesus [magic
words], you who appear in fire, you who are in the midst of land and snow
and fog, Tannetis, let your angel descend, the pitiless one, and let him arrest
the daemon that flies around this creature shaped by God in his holy paradise, for I pray to the holy god through Ammon [magic words]. I conjure
you [magic words], I conjure you by him who appeared to Osrael [=Israel]
in a pillar of light and a cloud by night and who has saved his people from
Pharaoh and has brought upon Pharaoh the ten plagues because he would
not listen. I conjure you, every daemonic spirit, to tell me who you are; I
conjure you by the seal that Solomon put upon the tongue of Jeremiah, and
he spoke. So you speak, too, and tell me what kind of a daemon you are,
one in heaven or one in the air or one on the ground or one underground
or one in the underworld, or a Ebusaen or a Chersaeon or a Pharisee.
Speak, whatever you are, for I conjure you by God the light-bringer, the
invincible one, the one who knows what is in the heart of every living crea-

---

21. Ibid., 189
22. Ibid., 190.

ture, the one who created the race of men from dust, who brings [them] out of uncertain [places], who gathers the clouds, sending down rain upon the earth, and blesses its fruit and is blessed by every heavenly power of angels and archangels. I conjure you by the great god Sabaôth, who stopped the river Jordan and divided the Red Sea through which Israel marched, making it passable. For I conjure you by him who revealed the hundred and forty tongues and distributed them according to his own command. I conjure you by him who burned down the stiff-necked giants with his beams of fire, who praises the heaven of heavens. I conjure you by him who put mountains around the sea [or?] a wall of sand and told it not to overflow, and the deep obeyed. Thus must you also obey, every daemonic spirit, for I conjure you by him who has moved the four winds together from holy eternities, by the heavenlike, sealike, cloudlike [god], the fire-bringer, the invincible. I conjure you by him who is in Jerusalem, the pure [city], for whom and near whom the unextinguishable fire burns forever and ever, with his holy name [magic words], before whom trembles the hellfire, and flames leap up all around, and iron explodes, and whom every mountain fears from the depth of its foundations. I conjure you, every daemonic spirit, by him who looks down on earth and makes its foundations tremble and has created the universe from a state of nonbeing into a state of being."[23]

Most scholars consider this writing to be older in *idea* than its approximate date of writing. The author is thought to be a scholar; perhaps a physician, magician, or possibly all three. It is clear from this window into antiquity that the author did not hesitate to combine elements of Christianity and Judaism with the Egyptian worship of Ammon and other gods. When dealing with a demon, the prevailing attitude appeared to be "Better safe than sorry." What is most interesting to the Christian is that the dominant power reflected here is that of Jesus and the great God Sabaoth: a military name for Jehovah.[24] Magicians did not hesitate to incorporate any deity, provided they would facilitate the magic. Dr. Gideon Bohak

23. Luck, *Arcana Mundi*, 191.
24. For more information on this name, see NT 4519, *New Exhaustive Strong's Numbers.*

explains that scholars have yet to agree upon a universal definition of the term *magic*: "What one society may label 'magic,' another would label 'religion,' and another 'science,' so that by choosing one label we are implicitly choosing sides."[25]

The essence of magic may be a mystery to some, but the Bible reveals that the purpose of magical arts is to *hunt souls*:

> Therefore thus says the Lord GOD: "Behold, I am against your magic charms by which you hunt souls there like birds. I will tear them from your arms, and let the souls go, the souls you hunt like birds. I will also tear off your veils and deliver My people out of your hand, and they shall no longer be as prey in your hand. Then you shall know that I am the LORD." (Ezek. 13:20–21)

Paganism penetrated every society where mankind sought to worship. It presented many faces, but its motive was consistent: a relentless attack upon the Creator. This campaign was not just man's imagination reacting to actual events of life (*myth creation*), its origin went much deeper. Pagan thought and Pagan practice grew from the heart of man—a heart in fierce rebellion against God.

GRECO-ROMAN WORLD

The history of Greece spans a period of at least six thousand years, while the Roman Empire evolved from the Etruscans approximately 500 BC.[26] Classical Greece is perhaps the most revered, thanks to brilliant philosophers such as Socrates and Plato, legendary writers such as Aeschylus and Homer, and Pythagoras, the father of mathematics. The Minoans and Mycenaeans preceded the Classical Greeks but left little information about their civilizations other than pottery, clay figures, a few bronze artifacts, and various ruins. There is some evidence of altars in the caves of Crete, and it is thought that both the Minoans and Mycenaeans (who conquered them) worshiped bulls and offered sacrifices to them.

---

25. Gideon Bohak, "Traditions of Magic in Late Antiquity," University of Michigan Library, n.d. http://www.lib.umich.edu/pap/exhibits/magic/ (accessed October 3, 2006).
26. The Etruscans were also polytheistic, worshiping gods such as their chief god Voltumna; Tinia; and Uni.

Greek Timeline

2900–2000 BC	Early Bronze Age; widespread polytheism; no single Scripture; worship of fertility goddess (from Neolithic culture)
2000–1400 BC	Minoan Age; worship of the Bull (possibly Mithras); evidence of Goddess worship (Snake goddess); Mystery religions emerge (1800)
1500–1100 BC	Mycenaean Age; warlike culture dominates more peaceful Minoans; Trojan War (1200)
1100–750 BC	The Dark Ages; development of the Greek alphabet; Greek mythology recorded; Oracle at Delphi; Greek city-states grow (800); Greek colonies present in Italy (750); Homer writes *Iliad* and *Odyssey* (700); Monarchy overthrown and replaced with archons—Greek city-states and their rulers (680)
750–480 BC	Archaic Period; Messenia (region in southwest Greece) conquered by Spartans; Dracon's legal system reforms (625); coin currency introduced (600); birth of Pythagoras (580)
480–336 BC	Classical Period; Dionysus festivals influence Greek theatre; democracy develops in Athens; Greek/Persian Wars (490 and 480–479); Parthenon and the Acropolis begun (449); Herodotus, Greek historian, writes *The Histories* (430); Socrates' trial (299); Plato (386); Aristotle (384); Alexander the Great of Macedonia defeats the Persians (333)
336–146 BC	Hellenistic Period; first Roman victories over Greece (200)

The vast amount of information available today pertaining to the culturally rich civilization of Greece requires a more specialized focus and analysis. Occult knowledge permeated many aspects of ancient Greek and Roman society, but nowhere was it more evident than in the Mystery religions that consumed the interest of the Greek populace and nearly succeeded in enveloping the entire Roman Empire. A close examination of the use of secret ceremonies, sacrifices, oracles, curse tablets, binding spells, and magic—all interwoven with the myths of the gods—reveals their significance in the Greco-Roman world.

The ancient world surrounding the Mediterranean Sea was a very small place geographically, but its influence on human culture spanned the centuries. Israel, Turkey, Italy, Egypt, and Greece all encircle the Mediterranean like diamonds on a vast necklace. Viewed through the eyes of geography alone, it is easy to see why the ancient world is called the birthplace of civilization and the greatest melting pot of all time.

Today, a tourist can catch a ferry from Italy and arrive in Greece eight hours later; Haifa, Israel, is approximately 150 miles from Cyprus; and Istanbul, Turkey, is separated from Athens, Greece, by a mere 350 miles. It is a very small world, indeed. As the American culture infiltrates and influences today's world, so the power of Greece and Rome penetrated to every corner of ancient civilization. This saturation enveloped all areas of human endeavor, including art, music, philosophy,

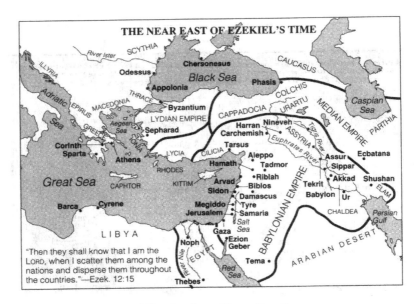

The Ancient Near East[27]

---

27. *Nelson's Complete Book of Bible Maps and Charts: Old and New Testaments* (Nashville: Thomas Nelson, 1993), 232.

and religion. Eventually, Greece and Rome became inextricably intertwined in history—their cultures merged, and their gods blended. Both empires shared state religions, philosophies, and what came to be known as the Mystery religions, due to a veil of secrecy carefully woven by powerful proponents.

THE RATIONAL VERSUS THE IRRATIONAL

In the history of the world, Greece has always been viewed as the seat of rationalism. Aristotle, Socrates, Plato, and other Greek philosophers impacted both ancient and modern worlds with their teachings, but it is important to note that these teachings represented a *part* of Greek culture, not the whole.

To view a culture through the single lens of rationalism is to discount the power of the irrational in the lives of a complicated people. It would be as if, a thousand years from now, the world judged Germany through the eyes of Karl Marx or Friedrich Nietzsche alone. Ancient Greeks were committed to the logic of the mind, but this belief fluctuated in popularity, its ebb and flow similar to that of the ocean tides.

E. R. Dodds, in his work *The Greeks and the Irrational,* suggests that the early Greeks' belief in the irrational or supernatural phenomena was an important influence in the growth and development of Greek culture. It affected the way ancient people viewed their world and reflected the widespread faith in supernatural beings, and the fear and respect they had for the powers held by these beings.[28] This clear, historical record of Greek reverence for the supernatural is difficult to dispute, and it must be weighed against the facts of rationalism to produce a balanced picture of the ancient Greek people. John Gager agrees with Dodds's assessment of ancient Greek society, pointing out that "as the testimony of the curse tablets clearly reveals, the confusion of political and legal affairs generated a need on the part of many to call upon higher powers to sustain their cause . . . the use of curse tablets was by no means limited to 'unlettered and superstitious' members of the lower classes. In classical Greece as in imperial Rome, their power was accepted and employed by all, including the wealthy and powerful Athenian aristocrats cited on numerous Greek tablets."[29]

---

28. E. R. Dodds, *The Greeks and the Irrational* (Berkeley: University of California Press, 2004), 136.
29. Gager, *Curse Tablets and Binding Spells,* 119.

THE MYSTERIES

The Mystery religions were thought to have developed in Greece in approximately 1800 BC, although it is Egyptian religion that some scholars believe influenced Greece considerably in the centuries before Alexander. This belief is upheld by Plutarch (46–122 AD), a famous Greek philosopher and priest of Apollo at Delphi:

> Indeed all men have Isis and know her and the Gods of her company; for though they learned, not long ago, to call some of them by names known to the Egyptians, still they knew and honoured the power of each of them from the beginning . . . Not different Gods for different peoples, not Barbarian and Greek, not southern and northern; but just as sun and moon and earth and sea are common to all, though different to one Providence that also directs powers ordained to serve under her for all purposes, have different honours and titles been given according to their laws by different nations.[30]

Citizens belonged to one of three different levels within the two major Mystery religions known as the Eleusinian and Orphic Mysteries. Greek citizens of every social level aspired to reach one of the higher levels in either of these Mysteries. They were characterized by secret ceremonies and animal sacrifices; those called the "greater Mysteries" were related to the harvest season (September or October), and the membership in them was exclusive. The rites of the lesser Mysteries took place late in winter and were open to almost anyone. The worship of Dionysus fell into the category of the "greater Mysteries"; it began in the rural districts of Greece, eventually making its way to the cities, where the Orphic Mysteries embraced it. Today, Dionysus is still hailed as a "Savior myth" that preceded Jesus Christ. Paganism uses the Savior myth (or Christ myth) argument to reinforce the mistaken belief that Christianity is nothing more than a copycat religion when it was, and still is, unique. The myth of Dionysus never had anything in common with the truth of Jesus Christ. "The cult of Dionysus was tied to wine-making and involved plays and phallic processions. Beginning in the rural areas, it was later incorporated into city life in Athens, and the Orphic Mysteries then added a new mysticism to

---

30. W. M. Flinders Petrie, *Personal Religion in Egypt Before Christianity,* 2nd ed. (London: Harper & Brothers, 1912), 121–123.

the worship of Dionysus, who became the god who is destroyed, who disappears, who relinquishes life and then is born again."[31]

The oracle of Delphi held great religious and political power in ancient Greece. Pilgrims from all over Greece and beyond would march for days up a steep mountain trail, simply to consult her. It was a time-consuming and expensive endeavor, costing ten days' wages, and as such it became a luxury available only to the rich. Today, scientific exploration of the temple area at Delphi has upheld the ancient descriptions of its unique location above a volcanic fissure.[32] A guild of women served Apollo in the temple at Delphi, but only one was selected to be his "voice," and she was called the *Pythia*.[33] The Pythia sat inside a cave, perched on a high stool or chair inside a fissure (or chamber) in the earth. Modern explorers have now confirmed the fact that ethylene gas leaks from cracks in the floor of this fissure and that it is a blend of dangerous chemicals that would have influenced the Pythia's state of mind, leaving her vulnerable to outside influences and shortening her life. The ancient Greek historian Plutarch (c.100 AD), made it clear that the gas alone did not cause the trance of the Pythia; many other people smelled it and thought its scent was "sweet," but it did not cause them to slip into a trance.[34]

Dr. John Hale, an archaeologist studying the ruins of Delphi, confirms the accuracy of the historical descriptions of the Pythia and her role in ancient society. "I've been working . . . with colleagues in geology and chemistry and toxicology, I think we can say that the conditions at Delphi very much vindicate the ancient sources."[35]

Polytheism dominated the civilizations of Greece and Rome, where the public and private worship of many different gods was an intrinsic part of everyday life. When Rome conquered Greece, it assimilated many of the Greek gods into its pantheon of gods.

---

31. Elliott Shaw, gen. ed, "Greco-Roman Religion," Overview of World Religions Web page, PHILTAR (University of Cumbria), http://philtar.ucsm.ac.uk/encyclopedia/europe/grecorom.html (accessed August 26, 2007).
32 The picture of a famous painting entitled *Priestess of Delphi* by John Collier (1891) is available at Wikimedia, http://commons.wikimedia.org/wiki/Image:John_Collier_-_Priestess_of_Delphi.jpg (accessed August 26, 2006).
33. It is thought that a member of this guild or perhaps even the Pythia herself was the woman the apostle Paul rebuked in Acts 16.
34. John Hale, interview by Rachael Kohn, "The Delphic Oracle," *The Ark* (ABC Radio International, August 8, 2004), http://www.abc.net.au/rn/relig/ark/stories/s1266794.htm (accessed September 7, 2006).
35. Ibid. This is a fascinating, detailed interview.

GREEK AND ROMAN GODS

Greek Name	Roman Name	Other Name	Symbol	Dist. Feature	Animal	Sphere of Influence	Place (not exclusive)
Aphrodite	Venus	Cypria	Cupids	Wings	Doves	Love, Sex	Cyprus
Apollo	———	Phoebus	Bow, Laurel, Wreath, Lyre, Halo	Long hair, No beard	———	Music, Medicine, Archery, Prophecy, Sun	*Delos, Delphi*
Ares	Mars	———	Armor, Arms	Beard *or* No Beard	———	War in bad sense	Thrace
Artemis	Diana	Phoebe	Crescent, Bow (Early Modern Period)	Short hunting dress	Deer	Hunting, Young girls, Wilderness	Arcadia, Brauron
Athena	Minerva	Pallas	Helmet, Spear, Armor, Olive Tree	Severe beauty	Owl	Wisdom, Ordered battle, Cities, Weaving, Carpentry	Athens
Demeter	Ceres	———	Wheat, Torch	———	———	Grain, Fertility, Agriculture	Eleusis
Dionysus	Bacchus	Nykterios	Vine	———	———	Wine, Fertility	Not exclusive
Hades	Pluto	Dis	Crown	———	———	Underworld	Not exclusive
Hekate (daughter of Demeter)	Hecate	Triple goddess	A torch in each hand	Three women back to back	———	Birth, Fertility, Death	Not exclusive
Hera	Juno	———	———	———	Cow	Marriage	Argus
Pan ——	———	———	———	Half goat ——	———	Flocks, pastures fields, and forests	Arcadia
Poseidon	Neptune	———	Trident	Beard	Horse, Sea creatures	Sea, Earthquake	Not exclusive

Cont'd on next page

Greek Name	Roman Name	Other Name	Symbol	Dist. Feature	Animal	Sphere of Influence	Place (not exclusive)
Zeus	Jupiter	Jove	Thunderbolt	Beard	Eagle, Bull	Sky Weather, Kings, Justice	Olympia[36]

ROME

The world of Rome, especially around the time of the birth of Christ, had much in common with the world of today. Civilizations from the four corners of the world came together and melded into the Roman Empire, producing an army of awesome proportions and a dazzling array of deities. This impressive pantheon flourished under a tolerant religious attitude that encouraged exploration and exploitation.

In many respects, the Roman Empire appears much like modern-day America. "This was an age in which materialism, moneymaking, vulgarity, and often total disregard for the accepted canons of morality were combined with genuine religious belief."[37] The Roman people searched for some sanity in a world of constant war, fierce political backbiting, and the pessimistic mumbling of Stoic Greek philosophers preaching "reabsorption" into the cosmos.[38] State religions dedicated to the worship of Jupiter, Juno, Minerva, and other gods (belonging to the original thirty-three-deity pantheon established by the Romans before the inclusion of foreign gods) ruled Rome, but the patriotic feelings they engendered were not enough for the average Roman citizen. Historian Michael Grant observes that ancient man needed beliefs that could "satisfy his ever-deepening conviction that the terror and

---

36 Adapted from a chart by Dr. Lawrence Kim, University of Texas, available at http://www.utexas.edu/courses/larrymyth/thegods.html (accessed October 3, 2006). Dr. Kim notes that this chart is not comprehensive and that places associated with the gods are extremely selective. Some of Artemis/Diana's items, such as her crescent moon, are assigned to her in times well after antiquity, in the early modern period and beyond, so they do not necessarily represent Greek and Roman depictions of the goddess.

37. Michael Grant, *The World of Rome* (New York: World, 1960), 184.

38. "According to the Stoics, the active principal of the world is the Logos, the subtle fire which everywhere orders motion. They taught polyonmy, that is, that the various names of the gods are but different titles of the One God." (Schmidt, *The Origin and Growth of Religion,* 19).

power of Death the Ravisher could be overcome . . . and that life, after all, had some meaning."[39]

The Romans viewed their state gods in an emotionless way. Each god had a specific task to fulfill, and it was that task that mattered (and its impact on daily life), not the personality of a particular god or goddess. The worship of deities coincided with basic human needs, such as crops and the seasons associated with them, fertility, and winemaking. The idea of a personal relationship with a god was virtually unknown:

> Roman religion was essentially state controlled religion, families maintaining household shrines dedicated to fertility and plenty, but the individual citizen playing no part in the religious ritual of the state which was carried out by pontiffs, augurs, and flamens (special priests). This extended until, with the exception of the Capitoline Triad of Jupiter, Juno, and Minerva, the state cult gave way to the cult of the emperor. Imperial deification began after the assassination of Julius Caesar in 44 BCE when the Roman Senate proclaimed him as a god and the deification of strong emperors continued, though most preferred to rule under the aegis of a greater deity than themselves, the most popular being Sol Invictus, the Unconquered Sun.[40]

ROMAN TIMELINE

3000—1000 BC	Bronze Age—small settlements, possibly influenced by Nordic culture
1000—500 BC	Etruscan civilization develops—polytheism dominates with its sacrifices, readings of entrails, and fatalism
510—300 BC	Rome conquers Etruscan kings; Rome conquers Italy

Cont'd on next page

---

39. Grant, *The World of Rome*, 185.
40. http://philtar.ucsm.ac.uk/encyclopedia/europe/grecorom.html.

299—100 BC	Civil wars; Punic (Carthaginian) Wars; Rome conquers Greece and Spain (130); names of Roman/Greek gods begin to be used interchangeably
100 BC—0	Mystery religions flourish (Mithras, Isis, and Dionysus); Augustus becomes first Roman Emperor. Pompeii is destroyed.
0—400 AD	Steady expansion of Roman Empire; Christianity enters Rome, likely related to the influence of the apostle Paul (beheaded by Nero approximately 64 AD)[41]; Peter crucified upside down; Nero persecutes Christians (60); Jerusalem destroyed (135); Justin Martyr (150); Clement of Alexandria (180); continued persecution of Christians (303–305); Constantine becomes emperor (312), sees vision in the sky of the chi-rho sign (first two Greek letters of the word "Christ")—and places it on every shield in his army (313) with the order "Conquer in this sign"; Christianity becomes only government-sanctioned religion. Constantine sends his mother, Queen Helena, to research and mark key Christian sites (stable in Bethlehem, Golgotha, Jesus' tomb); Constantine convenes the Council of Nicaea (325); Eusebius (300)
410—540	Goths sack Rome (410); East/West emperors dethroned; Roman Empire falls (455); Byzantium conquers Italy

Like Greece, it was the Mystery religions that gradually began to gain power in the Roman Empire. Heavily influenced by the Greek Mysteries, they assumed the names and characteristics of the Greek pantheon of gods. In the Mysteries, the individuals actually did play a role, and religion transitioned from the impersonal to the personal. It was this transformation that produced an overwhelming emo-

---

41. Early church tradition states that Paul and Peter were martyred by Nero. Their names were located in Roman cemeteries. See Clement, *The Persecution Under Nero*, and Eusebius, *Chronicon* 2.211; *Hist. eccl.* 2.25. Available at Early Christian Writings, http://www.earlychristianwritings.com/1clement.html, and Christian Classics Ethereal Library, http://www.ccel.org/ccel/schaff/npnf201.toc.html.

tional response. The Roman people craved something more than its state gods and religions could supply, a fact supported by the ruins of one of its most popular resort cities—Pompeii. Michael Grant explains the far-reaching influence of the Mystery Religions in Pompeii and throughout the entire Roman Empire. "They promised salvation in the after-life to their initiates and were only, much later, prevented by Christianity from completing . . . a total take-over of the ancient world."[42] If Christianity truly had been nothing more than a copycat religion, logic dictates it would have had little or no effect on the Mysteries, since they were in essence one and the same. It was because Christianity offered something completely different to the ancient world that it eventually triumphed over the Pagan Mystery religions.

THE MYSTERIES

Although they are most often associated with Greece and Rome, ancient Greek historian Herodotus (430 BC) wrote that they originated in Egypt: "The daughters of Danaus brought them from Egypt, and taught them to the Pelasgic women"[43] These Mystery religions associated with the earth goddess Ceres (Demeter, Isis), the god Bacchus (Dionysus, Osiris), Mithras, and others capitalized on widespread discontent by incorporating "irrational ecstasy" with just the right amount of pageantry.[44] In these cults, followers devoted themselves to the *mystery* of one deity, who then became a savior for them, helping them endure their everyday life and promising them a blissful afterlife. They eventually developed into substantial cult movements that brought chaos and dismay to the temples of Jupiter, Mars, Vesta, and other state-sponsored gods and goddesses. Although they lacked the political clout of state religions, the sense of freedom the Mysteries offered lured many away from the private worship of Jupiter and Vesta. And where private hearts wandered, treasuries often followed.

Seasons, such as spring (fertility) and autumn (harvest), depended on the benevolence of various deities who had to be appeased in order to bless their fol-

---

42. Grant, *Eros in Pompeii*, 51.

43. The Greek historian Herodotus came to be called the "Father of History" because of his detailed records on the ancient world. (The Internet Classics Archive, "The History of Herodotus," http://classics.mit.edu/Herodotus/history.2.ii.html [accessed February 18, 2008]).

44. Grant, *Eros in Pompeii*, 51.

lowers. The worship of the goddess Ceres often included the god Dionysus as well. During these rites, the priest and priestesses performed an X-rated miracle play or drama that reinacted the marriage of the Corn Maiden Proserpina (the Greek's Persephone) to Pluto, the god of the underworld.[45] This became a constant reminder of mortality; the imminent loss of something young and beautiful at the hands of the god of death. Michael Grant notes that this ceremony was originally linked to the blessing of the corn—its fertilization and growth—beginning as an integral part of the cycle of seasonal life and retaining that level of importance throughout its development. Initiates into this cult were ranked in one of two tiers: the highest tier given the name "The Beholders." It was their duty to carry (and so, behold) sacred objects in a procession. A "sacrament" of mint and barley water was also taken to ensure the blessings of the deities in charge of the afterlife.

If Ceres represented a combination of womanly serenity and passion, the worship of Bacchus/Dionysus offered an exploration of the untamed, animal elements of human nature. A wall painting in the cult room of a Patrician family in Pompeii (c. 50 BC) shows secret initiation rites into the Mysteries that included "reading from a sacred text, purification, the flagellation of the initiate with ecstatic dancing, the revealing of the sacred phallus, and . . . a mystical marriage to the god.[46] Members of this cult lost themselves in the pleasures of the flesh and achieved, at least for a brief time, some escape from the world around them.

Throughout history, the worship of Bacchus has kept much of its original mystery, revealing only glimpses into the darkness it seemed to cultivate—a darkness rife with drunken partying, secret perversions, and the power of the occult. "From the first century B.C. there is a tantalizing, sinister glimpse of their rites, mixed with myth, on the wall paintings of the Villa Item at Pompeii."[47] One painting shows a demonic-type of female with wings and boots; another shows a young girl hiding her head in an older woman's lap, as if afraid or threatened; another painting depicts violent initiation rites. The cult of Bacchus had a long history of violence and wild sexual orgies, its excesses prompting the Roman Senate to forbid the celebrations completely in 186 BC. It apparently did not improve with age, as the

45. See Herodotus, "Accounts of Personal Religion," c. 430 BCE–300 CE," Ancient History Sourcebook http://www.fordham.edu/halsall/ancient/personalrelig.html (accessed February 18, 2008).
46. Hellenic Communication Service, "Roman Shipwrecks," http://www.helleniccomserve.com/mccannlecture6.html (accessed October 6, 2006).
47. Michael Grant, Eros in Pompeii, 51.

wall paintings of Pompeii confirm beyond doubt. If Ceres represented passion, then the worship of Bacchus undoubtedly represented chaos.

In the days of the Roman Empire, people searched for peace in a dangerous world where peace of any kind simply did not exist. The great Roman historian Tacitus (115 AD) revealed:

> I am entering upon the history of a period, rich in disasters, gloomy with wars, rent with seditions, nay, savage in its very hours of peace. Four Emperors perished by the sword; there were three civil wars; there were more with foreigners—and some had both characters at once . . . Rome was wasted by fires, its oldest temples burnt, the very Capitol set in flames by Roman hands. There was defilement of sacred rites; adulteries in high places; the sea crowded with exiles; island rocks drenched with murder. Yet wilder was the frenzy in Rome; nobility, wealth, the refusal of office, its acceptance—everything was a crime, and virtue the surest ruin. Nor were the rewards of informers less odious than their deeds; one found his spoils in a priesthood or a consulate; another in a provincial governorship; another behind the throne; and all was one delirium of hate and terror; slaves were bribed to betray their masters, freedmen their patrons. He who had no foe was destroyed by his friend.[48]

The Mystery religions enticed their followers with offers of secret knowledge and fulfillment. Religious rites involving sacrifices, sexual immorality, psychic reading of animal entrails, oracles, and predictions reveal the influence and power of the occult in the ancient world. When the growth of Christianity finally began to outpace the Mysteries, the creative Roman mind-set encouraged many to embrace both the Mystery religions *and* Christianity–a "pick and choose" strategy still prevalent today. "We hear of Alexandrians who worshipped both Jesus and Sarapis, and the new conception of motherhood in representations of the Virgin Mary sometimes recalls effigies of Isis."[49] The early Christians battled the priests of Cybele, fighting to

---

48. Tacitus, *Histories,* bk. I, Internet Classics Archive, http://classics.mit.edu/Tacitus/histories.1.i.html (accessed August 28, 2007).
49. Grant, *The World of Rome*, 207.

emphasize the unique blood atonement of Jesus Christ whenever Pagan priests equated it with the ritual slaughter of a bull carried out in Cybele worship.

EGYPT

A land of mystery and magic, Egypt has captivated the imaginations of millions throughout the centuries, and the modern world has shown itself to be equally as fascinated with everything Egyptian. Blockbuster movies such as *The Mummy* and *The Scorpion King* attest to the continued popularity of Egyptian culture. Cable television offers never-ending specials on the excavation of Egyptian tombs and temples, CT scans of mummies, and speculation on the Egyptian method of building pyramids. But there is a much darker side to Egyptian culture, and it is reflected in countless histories on the subject.

EGYPTIAN TIMETABLE

Archaic	3100–2800 BC	Polytheism; Pharaoh Menes
Old Kingdom	2650–2150 BC	Pharaohs Imhotep, Khufu; development of papyrus; astronomy; Egyptian myths develop (Osiris and Isis dominate)
Middle Kingdom	2130–1640 BC	Pharaohs Amenemhet I, II, III; character alphabet develops (2000)
New Kingdom	1550–1050 BC	Akhenaton reveals monotheistic religion in Egypt; son Tutankhamen returns to Egypt's earlier gods; Tutankhamun, Nefertiti, Ramses II, III

Third Intermediate and Late Period I	1059–517 BC	Cyrus the Great conquers Mediterranean coast— Egypt/Greece alliance defeated but Egypt not invaded (549)
Persian Period I	515–425 BC	Persian influence on all things Egyptian; Darius, Xerxes, Artaxerxes; evidence of Egyptian religious influence on Greeks (Herodotus 430)
Persian Period II	340–330 BC	Darius III, Artaxerxes III
Greco-Roman Period	330–30 BC	Augustus Caesar, Alexander, Ptolemy I[50]

As far back as the historical record reaches, Egypt worshiped many gods. Thousands of books have been written detailing the names, duties, and influence of these deities on everyday Egyptian life and on the lives of those who lived nearby. Ancient cultures in the Mesopotamian basin did not exist in a vacuum; trade and conquest were great motivators, and Egypt actively participated in both. An intermingling of thoughts, ideas, and beliefs permeated all areas of life: the arts, architecture, philosophy, and religion.

Evidence of this blending can be found in the curse tablets and binding spells translated and analyzed by John Gager. "On a geographical scale, our tablets range from Britain to North Africa, from Mesopotamia to Spain. Behind this mix lies a conscious intention on our part to undermine the confidence with which cultural, geographical, and chronological labels are applied to ancient text and traditions, as if they represented clear, distinct, and nonoverlapping categories."[51] History shows a pattern of influence that spread from country to country, people to people. The Egyptian gods have much in common with the gods worshiped by Greece and Rome.

---

50. This timeline is meant as a brief overview of a long and complicated Egyptian history; dates are always approximate. See http://www.touregypt.net/ehistory.htm for a more detailed timeline.

PAGAN GODS OF EGYPT

Name	Responsibility	Form or Sacred Animal
Aker	Earth-god • Helper of the dead	Two lion heads
Amon	Wind-god • God of Thebes • Helper of the pious	Human (ram and goose sacred)
Anubis	Glorifier of the dead	Jackal-headed, black-skinned
Apis	Ensures fertility	Bull
Aton	Sun-god	
Atum	Primordial creature-god	Serpent-human
Bes	Protection at birth • Dispenser of virility	Group of demons
Edjo	Goddess of Delta/Lower Egypt	Uraeus serpent
Geb	Earth-god • Consort of Nut • Begetter of Osiris	Human
Hathor	Sky-goddess • Goddess of love, dance, alcohol	Cow
Heket	Primordial goddess	Frog
Horus	Sky-god	Falcon
Isis	Goddess of healing • Daughter of Geb • Consort/sister of Osiris • Mother of Horus	Human

51. Gager, *Curse Tablets and Binding Spells*, 7.

Khepri	Primordial god • Rising Sun	Scarabaeus
Khnum	Giver of the Nile • Creator of mankind	Human with ram's head
Khons	Moon-god	Human
Maat	Justice • Daughter of Ra	Human
Meskhenet	Goddess protector of newborns and of destiny	
Min	God of virility and reproduction	
Mut	"Eye of the sun," consort of Amon	Vulture or human
Nekhbet	Goddess of Upper Egypt	
Nut	Sky-goddess • Consort of Geb • Mother of Osiris and Seth • Mother of heavenly bodies	
Osiris	Dead pharaohs • Ruler of dead, life, vegetation	
Ptah	Creator-god • Lord of artisans	
Ra	God of sun, earth, and sky • Father of Meat • National god	Human with Falcon head
Sekhmet	Goddess of war and sickness	Human with lion head
Selket	Guardian of life • Protector of dead	Scorpion
Seshat	Goddess of writing and books	
Seth	God of chaos, desert and storm, crops • Brother of Osiris	

Shu	God of air, bearer of heaven	
Sobek	Creator-god	Crocodile
Sothis	God of Nile floodwaters	
Thermuthis	Goddess of fertility and harvest; fate	Serpent
Thoth	God of wisdom, moon, chronology • Messenger of gods	Ibis or baboon
Thoueris	Goddess of fertility and women in labor	Hippopotamus[52]

The history of Egypt is rich in detail. It is a brilliant civilization with many accomplishments in human culture: science, architecture, medicine, art, and so much more. What is not so well-known, however, is the extent of the blending of beliefs that occurred between the Egyptian, Greek, and Roman religions.

GREEK, ROMAN, EGYPTIAN DEITIES

Greek Name	Roman Name	Egyptian Name
Apollo	Apollo	Horus
Dionysus	Bacchus	Osiris[53]
Demeter	Ceres	Isis
Zeus	Jupiter	Amun[54]
Typhon (son of Hera)	——	Typhon

52. *Nelson's Complete Book of Bible Maps & Charts.*
53. Herodotus confirms that ancient Egyptians believed the Greek god Bacchus was Osiris. "For the Egyptians do not all worship the same gods, excepting Isis and Osiris, the latter of whom they say is the Grecian Bacchus" (Herodotus, *The Histories,* vol. 2, Internet Classics Archive [accessed February 18, 2008]).
54. "The Egyptian name for Jupiter is Amun" (Ibid.)

Herodotus points out that both Pan and Hercules originally belonged to the Egyptian pantheon of gods.[55] Egyptologist William Petrie confirms this intercultural blending of gods in his *Personal Religion in Egypt Before Christianity.* Details of the religious education received by Plutarch from an Egyptian tutor, Ammonios (66 AD), document the Egyptian schools of theology as only a contemporary source can. Petrie estimates that these religious beliefs were commonly accepted for many years prior to the date of Plutarch's text. "His information must be taken as that of the official priesthoods and state religion, rather than that of the more speculative and eclectic sects. As an initiate of the Osirian and Dionysiac Mysteries, and in high office at the Apollo ritual at Delphi, he resembles a philosophic clergyman of an Established Church, with great regard for his own knowledge and beliefs, rather than a theological free-lance trying to build up a new system or to discredit old faiths.[56] As the student of an Egyptian tutor, Plutarch's assessment of Egyptian religion is invaluable.

Central to Egyptian theology was the belief that *logos* or rational knowledge (rational part of the soul) breathed life into man. Without this *logos,* there was no true existence. With the breath of *logos,* man came to understand life and the gods who controlled it.

The Pharaohs of Egypt were considered the sons of Amen (Amun or Amon), and this linked them to divinity. But beyond this common stereotype of king as god, Plutarch offers sharp insight into the various schools of religious thought operating in ancient Egypt. He examines Egyptian religion by perspective, presenting "eight theories on the origin and nature of the gods."[57]

Heroic—During the rule of Alexander the Great (350 BC), "Euhemerus the Messenian, who of himself composing the counter-pleas of a baseless science of myths unworthy of any credit, flooded the civilized world with sheer atheism, listing . . . all those who are looked on as gods, into names of generals and admirals and kings, who existed in bygone days."

Daimonic—A theory that Plutarch preferred: the heroes of the past were gods who had once been demons (good or bad spirits). Myths "are passions neither of gods nor of men, but of mighty daimons who have been born more manful than men, far surpassing us in the strength of their nature, yet not having the divine

---

55. Ibid.
56. Petrie, *Personal Religion in Egypt,* 108.
57. Ibid., 114–23.

unmixed and pure, but proportioned with the nature of soul and sense of body, susceptible of pleasure and pain and all the passions."

Physical—Petrie comments that some believed that the earth, sea, and sky (all elements) were physically different gods. "The death of Osiris was in Athyr when the Nile sinks. Typhon conquering Osiris was the sea invading the Nile valley, shown by the shells and salt left there; and Horus subduing Typhon was strong rain swelling the river."

Cosmic—Petrie notes this theory was probably a result of the influence of India. "It was an outcome of the Physical theory, as it adopted Osiris as the moist and Typhon as the fiery principle. Hence the sun became Typhon, and the moon Osiris. The twenty-eight years of life or reign of Osiris were the days of the month; the burial of Osiris in a coffin hewn out of a tree-trunk was in a crescent-shaped coffin; the tearing him into fourteen parts referred to the days of the waning moon. . . . Osiris consorting with Isis is the moon below the earth."

Dualist—Adopted from Persia, "from two opposite principles, and two antagonistic powers—the one leading to the right and on the straight, the other upsetting and undoing—both life has been made mixed, and this Kosmos irregular and variable and susceptible of changes of every kind. For if nothing has been naturally brought into existence without a cause, and *Good* cannot furnish cause of Bad, the nature of Bad as well as Good must have a genesis. . . . Zoroaster, then, called the one Oromazes and the other Areimanios, and further announced that the one resemble light . . . and the other darkness and ignorance, while that between the two was Mithrïs; wherefore the Persians call Mithrïs the Mediator."

Allegorical—According to Petrie, Plutarch preferred this system above all others. "For Isis is the feminine part of Nature and that which is capable of receiving the whole of genesis; in virtue of which she has been called 'Nurse' and 'All-receiving' by Plato, and by the multitude, 'She of myriad names,' through her being transformed by logos, and receiving all forms and ideas." But Petrie went on to comment, "The system is merely a mass of introspective ideas of the vaguest kind, without any probability that such thoughts had ever induced mankind to believe in and worship such gods."

Seasonal—A theory condemned by Plutarch. "We shall get our hands on the dull crowd, who take pleasure in associating the ideas about these gods either with changes of the atmosphere according to the seasons, or with the generation of corn and sowings and ploughings, and in saying that Osiris is buried when the sown corn is hidden by the earth, and comes to life and shows himself again when it begins to sprout. For which cause also they say that Isis on feeling she is pregnant ties an amulet around her on the sixth of Paophi, and that Harpocrates is brought forth about winter solstice, imperfect and infant in the things that sprout too early. For which cause they offer him first-fruits of growing lentils, and the keep the days of thanks for safe delivery after the spring equinox. For they love to hear these things and believe them, drawing conviction from things immediately at hand and customary."

Animal—Petrie states Plutarch's reaction to several facets of this theory: (1) "First view, 'that the gods out of fear of Typhon changed themselves into these animals,' which he laughs at, saying that it "beats any juggling or story-telling." (2) Next the view "that all the souls of the dead that persist have their rebirth into these animals only," which he says is "equally incredible."

Plutarch's final conclusion on this is mankind "not paying honor to these (the animals) but through them to the Divine."[58]

There were different schools of thought in Egypt, just as there are today, and this diversity influenced the growth and development of different religious cults.

OSIRIS, ISIS, DIONYSUS, AND ZEUS

Brother and sister, husband and wife—ruler of the underworld and queen of heaven—Osiris and Isis ruled the myths of Egypt. It is thought that Isis and Osiris appeared sometime in Egypt's Fifth Dynasty (2500–2300 BC), Osiris as the chief god of the afterlife, and Isis as mother. Both gods were represented by some aspect of agriculture, and elements of their myths can be found in multiple cultures throughout the ancient world. This points once again to the importance of geography in the early history of religions. The civilized world was a miniaturized version of today's world; imagine New York, Boston, Atlanta, New Orleans, Chicago, and Los Angeles all located within the state of California, each just a few hours from the other—easily accessible by ship or camel. Trade routes on land and sea guaranteed the spread of individual beliefs, and conquerors such as Alexander the Great and the Roman emperors drove the spread of knowledge at a frenzied pace.

---

58. Adapted from Ibid.

The myth of Osiris centers on his murder by his brother Set, and his eventual resurrection through the help of Isis. Both the rituals of Osiris and Dionysus are linked to wine, and it is probable that the Greeks saw many similarities between their Dionysus and the story of Osiris (death, dismemberment, resurrection). Osiris and Dionysus represented rebirth and the promise of something eternal. It is also thought that Zeus and Osiris were blended at some point, due to the spread of the cult of Isis. "The diffusion of Isidism among the Greeks led to the identification of the ancient Greek god Zeus with Osiris, and of the ancient Greek god Apollon with Horus, with Isis being rather conceived as identical to Hera. The central name of Isis was preserved in personal god-bearing names (Isidorus), whereas the real meaning of Diodorus was 'given as gift by Osiris/Zeus', and Apollodorus signifies that the bearer was 'given as gift by Horus/Apollon.'"[59]

In the earliest worship of Isis, she was known as the goddess of fertility, magic, and motherhood. Her nature was dual: maternal and malicious (whereas in later myths she is usually represented as benevolent only). Goddess of a thousand names, Isis is often associated with pictures of the corn harvest or holding her child as she prepares to nurse him. As a matriarchal goddess, her blessing was often asked upon marriages. Later history of Isis worship (100 AD) details an evolution of sensuality in her myth and rituals, especially during the time of the Roman Empire. Promiscuity related to the Isis Mystery religion became so prevalent and depraved throughout the Roman Empire that it was eventually banned approximately 250 AD. History supports the fact that Osiris and Isis were enormously popular, their worship spreading from Egypt to Greece, Rome, and beyond:

> The spread of the worship of Isis outside of Egypt began even before its conquest by the Greeks and later the Romans. As early as the fifth century BCE, the Greek historian and ethnographer Herodotus described the worship of Isis in Egypt, at Cyrene, Bubastis, Sais, and Memphis. In his *Histories* Herodotus claims that Isis is Demeter in the Greek language (2.59.156), and that the "mysteries" known as Thesmophoria in Greece, which celebrated the goddess Demeter, had their origin in the worship of

---

59. Muhammad Shamsaddin Megalommatis, "Yemen and the Bab el Mandeb Straits According to the 'Periplus of the Red Sea,'" Buzzle, http://www.buzzle.com/editorials/8-6-2005-7432.asp (accessed October 8, 2006).

Isis at Sais. In mainland Greece, Isis was also being worshipped in Piraeus, the port of Athens, by Egyptian merchants as early as the fifth century BCE (Turcan 1996, 81). By the beginning of the second century BCE, the worship of Isis, with or without her associated deities—Sarapis, Horus, and her assistant the jackal-headed god Anubis—was known throughout the Hellenistic world, from Sicily to the shores of the Black Sea."[60]

Without a doubt, the spread of religions influenced the melting pot that was the ancient Greco-Roman world. As Plutarch phrased it, "Indeed all men have Isis and know her and the Gods of her company; for though they learned, not long ago, to call some of them by names known to the Egyptians, still they knew and honoured the power of each of them from the beginning."[61] Merchants carried their beliefs wherever they traded, like busy bees spreading pollen. With the advent of Alexander the Great, Greek religion and thought spread throughout the cultures of the ancient world (Hellenistic era). Rome's tolerance in openly welcoming most foreign gods led to the growth of the Mystery religions and the empire's fascination with them. Multiple altars to various deities filled ancient temples as people sought to appease all the gods.

The power of the *individual* is seen throughout history. Individuals appropriated gods from one land and introduced them into another; transplanting them from one locale to the next in the course of everyday life. Sometimes the names remained the same; sometimes they did not. The historical record reveals that from the earliest and most primitive cultures on earth, a common knowledge existed of a Supreme Being, and this common knowledge became diluted into a polytheistic worldview. [62]

PERSIA

Persia is known in the modern world as Iran. It is a country rich in history, conquering and being conquered down through the centuries by empires such as Assyria, Babylonia, and Greece.

60. Gail Corrington Streete, "An Isis Aretalogy from Kyme in Asia Minor, First Century B.C.E.," in Richard Valantasis, ed., *Religions of Late Antiquity in Practice* (Princeton: Princeton University Press, 2000), 369.
61. Petrie, *Personal Religion in Egypt,* 121.
62. Schmidt, *The Origin and Growth of Religion,* 262.

PERSIAN TIMELINE

5000–2300 BC	Polytheism dominates. It is similar to the polytheism found in India (Vedic) and includes three identical names for deities: Ahura Mazda (supreme god), Daïva, and Mithra; Ur, capital of Sumer, develops—the home of Abraham.
2000–1800 BC	Abraham leaves Mesopotamia for Canaan, now modern-day Israel.
1900–1600 BC	Mesopotamia is divided into rival states, Babylonia in the south, Assyria to the north
1700–1600 BC	Babylonia's King Hammurabi writes a code of law (1750); prophet Zarathustra (1200, Greek-Zoroaster) emphasizes the importance of Ahura Mazda, and teaches the reality of the struggle between good and evil (dualism); polytheism is still practiced[63]
850–730 BC	Assyrian records first mention Arabs, nomads who herd sheep and goats in the deserts of the Arabian Peninsula south of Mesopotamia; Assyrian Empire expands from the Persian Gulf to Egypt and Asia Minor, including Mesopotamia and today's Israel
580 BC	Under King Nebuchadnezzar, Babylonians take Syria from Egypt and conquer Judea; Babylonians destroy the First Temple in Jerusalem and take the Israelites into slavery; Cyrus the Great (590–529 BC) conquers Mesopotamian coast and Asia Minor, defeats

---

63. Some modern followers of Zoroaster claim his teachings date from 6000 BC, but there is little historical or archaeological evidence to support this.

	Greek/Egyptian alliance; unification of Medians and Persian Empires (Medes and Persians 560 BC)
530 BC	Persia conquers Babylon and sends the Jews back to rebuild Jerusalem and the second temple
330 BC	Alexander the Great conquers Persia and creates a commercial center in Babylon
160 BC–110 AD	Roman armies add Persian territories to their expanding empire
215–630 AD	A new Persian Empire rises with Mesopotamia at its core; Pagans, Christians, Jews, and Buddhists worship alongside Zoroastrians, whose ancient religion is the official faith
570 AD	Islam's founder, Muhammad, is born; teaches there is only one god; Jesus is a prophet and also the Messiah, but salvation can be found only in the Qu'ran [64]

Unlike the Romans and Egyptians, the kings of Persia did not consider themselves gods. Instead, they acted as representatives of their supreme god, Ahura Mazda. The history of Persian religion can be divided into three distinct eras: first, the polytheistic worship of Ahura Mazda, lesser deities such as Mithra, and the elements (air, water, fire, and earth); second, the advent of Zoroaster's dualism; and finally, the rise of Islam, which eventually replaced Zoroastrianism.[65]

---

64. Timeline adapted from "The History of Iraq," *Seattle Times,* http://seattletimes.nwsource.com/news/nation-world/usiraq/timeline/ (accessed October 10, 2006). For references to Jesus as Messiah in the Koran, see Sura 3:45; 4:157, 171. "It is interesting to compare Jesus and Muhammad according to the Qur'an:

  Jesus did miracles (Sura 3:49; 5:110), but Muhammad did not (Sura 13:8: 'thou art a warner [of coming divine judgment] only'; also 6:37; 6:109; 17:59 and 17:90–93).

  Jesus was sinless (Sura 3:46), but Muhammad sinned and needed forgiveness (Sura 40:55; 'ask forgiveness of they sin'; 42:5: 'ask forgiveness for those on the Earth'; 47:19; 'ask forgiveness for thy sin'; 48:2: 'that Allah may forgive thee of thy sin').

  Jesus was called 'the Messiah' and was even born of a virgin (3:45–57)! Yet Muhammad is supposed to be the greatest of the prophets." (Martin, chap. 16, "Islam," in *Kingdom of the Cults*).

65. Timeline dates can only be considered approximate, as not much is known of Zoroaster's life.

The people of Persia, also known as Aryans (Indo-Europeans) acknowledged a supreme god (Mazdaism) before Zoroaster's time, but they also worshiped many lesser deities, such as Spenta and Mainyu. Ahura Mazda was considered the Creator and the greatest of the gods, but in practice the ancient Persians worshiped many gods, including Mithra (god of war). Herodotus characterized the Persian religion as simplistic, a worship of many gods and at times, nature itself—wind, fire, water, earth, and sky.

These, I know, are the sorts of nomoi [rituals] which are observed in Persia; they do not regard it as proper to dedicate statues or temples or altars, but consider it folly to do so; I suppose it is because they do not think that the gods have the shape of men, as the Greeks do. It nomos to go up onto the highest mountains and sacrifice to Zeus, calling the whole circle of the heavens Zeus; and they sacrifice to the sun and the moon and the earth and fire and water and the winds. Originally, these were the only gods to whom they sacrificed, but they later learnt from the Assyrians and Arabians to sacrifice to Ourania; the Assyrians call Aphrodite Melitta, the Arabians Alilat, the Persians Mitra. This is the form which sacrifices to the gods whom I have mentioned takes among the Persians: they do not build an altar or light a fire when they intend to sacrifice, nor do they use libations, or flute music or garlands or barley-meal; but when a man wishes to sacrifice to any of the gods he takes the victim to an open place and calls upon the god, after garlanding his tiara, usually with myrtle. It is not possible to ask for benefits for the single individual actually sacrificing, but he prays for success for all the Persians and for the King; for he is himself included in all the Persians. When he has cut up the victims into joints and cooked the flesh, he puts it all on a prepared bed of green stuff, as soft as possible, usually clover. When he has made his arrangements, a Magos standing by sings a hymn to the gods, which they say is an account of their coming into being; for it is not the custom to sacrifice without a Magos. Then after waiting a short time the sacrificer takes the flesh away and does what he wishes with it.[66]

---

66. Herodotus, *Histories*, vol. 1; Michael Crawford and David Whitehead, *Archaic and Classical Greece: A Collection of Ancient Stories* (Cambridge: Cambridge University Press, 1983), 201.

The worship of everything as divine eventually led to depravity, and it was upon this scene that the prophet Zarathustra came, teaching that some things were not worthy of worship; he called the people back to the true teachings of Ahura Mazda (Mazdaism). According to the modern Zoroastrians, these teachings were ancient, and Zoroaster's purpose was to *remind* people of them.[67]

Scholars continue to debate the origin of Persian dualism (good against evil), some pointing to the similarity in the names of three of India's gods (Ahura Mazda, Daïva, and Mithra), while others argue that these gods represent polar opposite meanings in each culture, and so could not be identical. For example, Daïva is honored in India; Davaï (used in the plural) are despised in Persia. There is some evidence, however, of a Babylonian influence on dualism:

> There is a clear and historically logical origin of Persian dualism, and it is strange that it has been overlooked by many in their search. It lies close at hand. It is the Babylonian myth of the struggle between Merodach and the Dragon, between the God of intelligence and the Tiamat monster of the chaos deep. There are many points of resemblance, and even of identity, between the Babylonian and the Zoroastrian dualistic conceptions. In the creation tablets, Tiamat . . . is personified as the Power that rules over the primeval chaos and darkness. . . . Marduk, as the selected representative of order and light, advances to meet her.[68]

The question of the evolution of dualism has never been answered to anyone's complete satisfaction, but the similarity of ideas (Babylonia) and names (India) points once again to the dynamic of a geographical melting pot. In assessing the ancient religion of Persia before the birth of Zoroaster, Mary Boyce concludes that the similarities between it and the new religion taught by Zoroaster are evident, "as if the second were in many respects a natural development of the first, without any break in continuity."[69]

---

67. "Traditional Zoroastrianism: Tenets of the Religion," http://tenets.zoroastrianism.com/ (accessed October 13, 2006).
68. Henry Goodwin Smith, "Persian Dualism," *The American Journal of Theology* 8, no. 23 (1904): 487–501, http://links.jstor.org/sici?sici=1550-3283%28190407%298%3A3%3C487%3APD%3Ew.0.CO%3B2-Y (accessed October 7, 2006).
69. Mary Boyce, "On Mithra's Part in Zoroastrianism," *Bulletin of the School of Oriental and African Studies* 32, no. 1 (1969): 11, http://links.jstor.org/sici?sici=0041-977X%281969%2932%3A1%3C10%3AOMPIZ%3E2.0.CO%3B2-A (accessed October 7, 2006).

THE TEACHINGS OF ZOROASTER

1. Ahura Mazda is the one uncreated Creator of all, but some lesser gods are still worthy of worship.

2. Many gods of Persia are corrupt and so cannot be true gods. They are not worthy of worship.

3. All beings are divided into two classes (dualism): those who belong to Ahura Mazda (the All Wise), and those controlled by Anro Mainyus (the Destroying Mind), the source of all evil. "When man does Good he adds to the weight of Good on the balance scales of life; and when he does bad things he adds to the weight of the Evil forces on the balance scales."[70]

4. Zoroaster is the greatest of all prophets: "The creator Ahura Mazda spoke to Zarathushtra thus: 'O Zarathushtra! I have created no one better than you in the world, and I shall likewise not create one better after you are gone. You are my chosen one, and I have made this world apparent on account of you. And all these people and monarchs whom I have created have always maintained the hope that I should create you in their days, so that they should accept the religion, and their souls should attain to the supreme heaven.'"[71]

5. Human beings are caught in the struggle between good and evil. There are serious consequences for choices made.

6. Free will determines the choice between good and evil, as taught by the Avesta/Gathas (scripture).[72]

7. Righteousness leads to happiness, and impurity to unhappiness.

8. Gods and men all have a guardian spirit (not the soul). Mithra, Rashnu, and Sraosha determine Judgment at Chinvat-bridge ("Bridge of the Judge") in the afterlife. "There is to be a Day of Judgment and that is close at hand. On that Day of days the Wise Lord [Ahura Mazda] will triumph over the

70. Morris Katz, *The Journey* (Victoria, BC: Trafford Publishing, 2004), 40.
71. "What is Zoroastrianism?" Avesta—Zoroastrian Archives, http://www.avesta.org/zfa1.html (accessed October 14, 2006). (SD81.3)
72. S. A. Nigosian, *The Zoroastrian Faith: Tradition and Modern Research* (Montreal: McGill-Queens University Press, 1993), 23.

evil spirit Angra Manyu. All the dead will come to life again and the good souls and the bad souls will be tried. They will be passed through a flow of molten metal. The good will pass through as if the molten metal is warm milk. They will not be harmed. But the evil ones will burn everlastingly.[73]

MODERN ZOROASTRIANISM

1. All scriptures are sacred (the Gathas, Yashts, and the Vendidad). They are prayed in the fire temples, before the Sacred Fire to further righteousness and fight evil.

2. All fire temples and rituals of the Yasna are sacred.

3. All creatures of Ahura Mazda are worthy of worship.

4. Exposure to the elements (Dakhma-nashini) is the only method of corpse-destruction for a Zarathushtri.

5. Marrying, Zarathushtri man or woman, to a Zarathushtri only is commanded in the Vendidad, to preserve the spiritual strength of the Aryan Mazdayasni religion, and the ethnic identity of the Zarathushtri Aryans.

6. The righteous of every religion go to heaven, all religions are equal, and it is folly to convert. God has given us birth in our respective religions, to adore him in them, and not to mistrust His Judgement (sic) and rebel and go over to another faith. For, each faith leads ultimately to god. Followers of Zoroaster do not convert other people, but they rely on *marriage within* and *increased child birth* to increase their numbers.

7. Ahura Mazda sends the Saoshyant to the earth to defeat evil and further righteousness (Ashoi). The Zarathushtri religion was the first to proclaim that Ahura Mazda will send the Saoshyant, born of a virgin, and many other religions took on this belief.

8. When the Saoshyant (Savior) comes, the final spiritual battle between the forces of good and evil will commence, resulting in the utter destruction of evil. Ristakhiz, the ressurection (sic) of the dead will take place—the dead will rise, by the Will of Ahura Mazda. The world will be purged by molten

---

73. Katz, *The Journey*, 41–42.

metal, in which the righteous will wade as if through warm milk, and the evil will be scalded. The Final Judgement of all souls will commence, at the hands of Ahura Mazda the Judge (Davar), and all sinners punished, then forgiven, and humanity made immortal and free from hunger, thirst, poverty, old age, disease, and death. The World will be made perfect once again, as it was before the onslaught of the evil one.[74]

Mithra

Once considered the chief rival of Christianity in the second century AD, the worship of the god Mithra also appears to have crossed the boundaries of geography. Mithraism has roots in many different cultures: cave paintings in Crete detail what appears to be the worship of Mithra by ancestors of the Greeks, the ancient Minoans, and Mycenaeans; ancient Persia lists Mithra in their pantheon of gods; and 50 AD saw the advent of Mithras worship in Rome. Mithras, the god of war, drew the loyalty of the Roman legions. It was a Mystery religion, open only to men. Justin Martyr (150 AD) revealed how the Pagan Mystery cult of Mithras in Rome copied sacred Christian rites and perverted them:

For the apostles, in the memoirs composed by them, which are called gospels, have thus delivered unto us what was enjoined upon them; that Jesus took bread, and when He had given thanks, said, "This do ye in remembrance of Me, this is My body;" and that, after the same manner, having taken the cup and given thanks, He said, "This is My blood;" and gave it to them alone. Which the wicked devils have imitated in the mysteries of Mithras, commanding the same thing to be done. For, that bread and a cup of water are placed with certain incantations in the mystic rites of one who is being initiated, you either know or can learn.[75]

In Persia, Mithra was a god who took bloody revenge on the enemies of the Persian people. India worshiped him as a god of fidelity and friendship. The

---

74. Adapted from "Traditional Zoroastrianism: Tenets of the Religion," http://tenets.zoroastrianism.com/ (accessed October 13, 2006).
75. Justin Martyr, *Apology I* (Christian Classics Ethereal Library, 2007), 66, http://www.ccel.org/fathers2/ ANF-01/anf01-46.htm#P3935_744654 (accessed October 14, 2006).

Roman religious myth presented him as a savior god, who died and was resurrected, offering salvation to those who believe in him.

THE SAVIOR MYTH[76]

Osiris, Dionysus, Mithra—the "rising saviors" of the Pagan world—became formidable rivals of Christianity during the second century (100–195 AD), but the counterfeit promise of the savior myth was a threat the early Christian church met and skillfully refuted. The eyewitness testimony of the apostles to the person and teaching of Jesus Christ provided a rock-solid foundation for the defense of the Christian faith in the face of rampant Pagan license. Today, one eyewitness alone can send a defendant to his death in the American system of justice, and yet the biblical record—full of eyewitness accounts and strongly supported by archaeological finds—is a primary source repeatedly dismissed by skeptics opposed to the message of Christianity. Still, the fact remains that the historical Jesus *did* exist based on the irrefutable testimony of his disciples and other credible historical sources, and He had nothing in common with the Pagan saviors.

Historian Hans Kippenberg calls into question the so-called similarity of these Pagan "rising saviors" to Jesus Christ, arguing that they had no relation to Him even as an archetype, since most of them died and did not rise again. "Recent research has made it likely that an interpretation of these gods [rising saviors] as representing death and rebirth is untenable for the simple reason that the majority of them died without returning. They were at best rescued from complete annihilation. So they are certainly not the ancestors of Jesus Christ."[77] Unfortunately, Christians today regularly encounter a resurrected form of this argument that challenges the very existence of Jesus Christ without offering a single primary source to support its claim.

The most troubling aspect of this argument is a curious story pattern that seems to repeat itself through the centuries: a son of god is born (sometimes of a virgin), murdered by an evil enemy, and resurrected to become the savior of the world. These apparent similarities were the foundation for a Pagan assault against the validity of Christianity in the ancient world, and they are still used for the same

---

76. Also known as the *Christ myth*.
77. Hans G. Kippenberg, "Comparing Ancient Religions," *Numen* 39, no. 2 (1992): 221.

purpose today. The argument usually goes something like this: The Pagans had the story first; therefore, Christians must have borrowed from ancient Pagan religions. Christianity, then, is nothing more than a copycat religion full of stolen Pagan theology reinterpreted to fit a Christian agenda. If all of these events can be found in Pagan myths centuries before Christianity—a child conceived by a virgin, murdered, and resurrected—then Christ more than likely never existed (or at best, mythological legends were built around him after his death to deify him). So, in essence, Jesus was the product of myth and imagination (mythicism).

Similarities to the Christian religion seem to abound in various cultures whose gods reputedly:

- were born of a virgin on or near December 25

- were born in a cave

- acquired twelve disciples

- suffered a terrible death at the hands of an enemy

- descended into the underworld or hell and were eventually resurrected

- promised an end to suffering followed by eternal happiness

- were called Deliverer or Savior by their followers

In the past, these claims have caused confusion among Christians and non-Christians alike, largely due to the fact that primary source material on this subject was difficult to access. In reality, however, *rising saviors* from multiple cultures seldom have much in common. Their general stories may seem parallel at first, but ironically, "the devil is in the details." Plutarch, in his assessment of the origins and natures of ancient gods noted:

> Of all gods who are not ingenerable and indestructible, the bodies lie buried with the priests when they have done their work, and have service rendered them, while their souls shine in heaven as stars; the soul of Isis is call Kuôn (Dog star) by the Greeks, but Sothis by the Egyptians, that of Horus is œriÿn, and that of Typhon (Set) Arktos (the Great Bear). . . . But those alone who inhabit the Thebaid . . . believe that no God is subject to

death, and that he whom they themselves call Knïf is ingenerable and immortal" (xxi, 2, 3). The same idea appears in Lucian (*Jup. Trag.*) where the tomb of Zeus in Crete is instanced as showing that even he died. The grade of gods thus subject to death is that which has been definitely created, and may therefore perish, not being eternal. And this was connected with the older theory of daimons, and souls being transformed from them into men or gods; for "Isis and Osiris being changed through virtue from good daimons into gods (as afterwards were Herakles and Dionysos) possess the dignity of gods and diamons at one and the same time.[78]

Isis, Osiris, Dionysos—all were just "good daimons" elevated to the rank of gods. Zeus, the great Greek god of legend, died and stayed dead, as his grave in Crete confirms. The closer the lens of history comes to the details of the rising saviors, the less they look like the one and only Savior.

In refuting the Savior myth, it is important first to separate the problem of the historical Jesus from the problem of Pagan saviors. Jesus is a historical person: the gospel of John (c. 90 AD) details the earliest eyewitness account of His life. This ancient document is credible and offers more proof of authenticity than other respected manuscripts, such as Homer's *Iliad* (800 BC) or the Buddhist scriptures, recorded more than eight hundred years *after* the death of Buddha. In addition to John's account, there are the eyewitness testimonies of Matthew, Mark and James. Flavius Josephus (c. 37 AD) also refers to the death of James, the brother of Jesus:

> Festus was now dead, and Albinus was but upon the road; so he assembled the sanhedrim of judges, and brought before them the brother of Jesus, who was called Christ, whose name was James, and some others, [or, some of his companions]; and when he had formed an accusation against them as breakers of the law, he delivered them to be stoned: but as for those who

---

78. From Plutarch xxvii, 3, as quoted by Petrie. Petrie observed, "The nature of gods was considered to vary greatly" (*Personal Religion in Egypt,* 111–12). For more information on this, see Plutarch's *What is God?* Available online at FullBooks, http://www.fullbooks.com/The-Complete-Works-Volume-3-Essays-and2.html.

seemed the most equitable of the citizens, and such as were the most uneasy at the breach of the laws, they disliked what was done. [79]

The Roman historian Tacitus (c. 110 AD) provides perhaps the single most important proof of the historical Jesus, outside of the New Testament:

> But all human efforts, all the lavish gifts of the emperor, and the propitiations of the gods, did not banish the sinister belief that the conflagration [burning of Rome] was the result of an order [by Nero]. Consequently, to get rid of the report, *Nero fixed the guilt and inflicted the most exquisite tortures on a class hated for their abominations, called Christians by the populace. Christus, from whom the name had its origin, suffered the extreme penalty during the reign of Tiberius at the hands of one of our procurators, Pontius Pilatus,* and a most mischievous superstition, thus checked for the moment, again broke out not only in Judaea, the first source of the evil, but even in Rome, where all things hideous and shameful from every part of the world find their centre and become popular.
>
> Accordingly, an arrest was first made of all who pleaded guilty; then, upon their information, an immense multitude was convicted, not so much of the crime of firing the city, because of the hatred of mankind. Mockery of every sort was added to their deaths. Covered with the skins of beasts, they were torn by dogs and perished, or were nailed to crosses, or were doomed to the flames and burnt, to serve as a nightly illumination, when daylight had expired.
>
> Nero offered his gardens for the spectacle, and was exhibiting a show in the circus, while he mingled with the people in the dress of a charioteer or stood aloft on a car. Hence, even for criminals who deserved extreme and exemplary punishment, there arose a feeling of compassion; for it was not, as it seemed, for the public good, but to glut one man's cruelty, that they were being destroyed.[80]

---

79. Flavius Josephus, *Antiquities,* 20, chap. 9, available online at Christian Classics Ethereal Library, http://www.ccel.org/j/josephus/works/ant-20-htm.

80. Emphasis added. Nero hoped the public would blame the Christians for the burning of Rome (Tacitus, Annals [ca. AD 110], Book 15.44, available online at University of Texas, http://www.utexas.edu/courses/ancientfilmCC304/lecture30/christians.pdf [accessed August 26, 2007]).

The historical Jesus is real and certainly defendable. Once this argument is separated, the Savior myth can be refuted by pointing to the following facts:

1. The *rising saviors,* when examined individually, have virtually nothing in common. Any similarities between them and Jesus Christ usually prove to be part myth, part imagination. "There is now what amounts to a scholarly consensus against the appropriateness of the concept [of dying and rising gods]. Those who still think differently are looked upon as residual members of an almost extinct species . . . The category of dying and rising deities as propagated by [Sir James] Frazer can no longer be upheld."[81]

2. Human beings, whatever their cultural differences, are the same in nature the world over. Historical investigation supports the fact that most primitive human beings believed in one Supreme Being, immortal, existing from eternity.[82] This being is above lesser gods and is common to thousands of cultures. It is neither a great phenomenon nor a result of theft that saviors abound throughout the ancient world or that Christianity centers around *the* Savior, Jesus Christ.

3. The Mediterranean Basin is a small geographical area, and Neolithic cultures shared contact and exchanged cultural elements through this contact (8000 BC).[83] Trader caravans and ships spread knowledge between cultures for millennia. "The international character of the East Mediterranean culture is reflected by the intrusion of Canaanite gods into the Egyptian pantheon during the Empire Period. Astarte and Anath appear in the Contendings of Horus and Seth."[84]

81. Tryggve N. D. Mettinger, *The Riddle of Resurrection: "Dying and Rising Gods" in the Ancient Near East* (Philadelphia: Coronet Books, 2001), 7, 41.
82. Schmidt, *The Origin and Growth of Religion,* 176.
83. For more information on this see W. Creighton Gabel, "European Secondary Neolithic Cultures: A Study of Prehistoric Culture Contact," *The Journal of the Royal Anthropological Institute of Great Britain and Ireland* 88, no. 1 (1958), available at http://links.jstor.org/sici?sici=0307-3114%2819580801%2F06%2988%3A1%3C97%3AESNCAS%3Es.0.co%3B2-2 (accessed October 8, 2006). See also http://archaeology.huji.ac.il/golan/.
84. Cyrus H. Gordon, *The Common Background of Greek and Hebrew Civilizations* (New York: Norton, 1965), 127. See also "The Contendings of Horus and Seth," http://touregypt.net/contendingshorus-seth.htm. Approximate date for Contendings of Horus and Seth is during the time of Ramses V (1150 BC).

4. Wars and weather extremes influenced cultural development. Joseph ruled Egypt (1520 BC), and Jacob migrated to Egypt because of famine approximately 1500 BC. The Israelites conquered Canaan (1300 BC).

5. The influence of ancient Judaism is evident throughout different cultures.[85] Monotheism and the prophecies of a Savior, born of a virgin, sacrificed for sins, and resurrected can be found throughout the Old Testament documents. The first book of the Old Testament, Genesis, was recorded approximately 1446 BC (oral tradition likely preserving it for countless years prior to that date), and the entire Old Testament was translated into Greek around 250 BC, making it available in the common language of the Hellenistic empire that extended to the ends of the known world. Since the Old Testament prophesied of the virgin-born Messiah, it is not surprising that the story spread before Christ's first advent. An Egyptian papyrus dated to 340 BC reveals, "Who is the author of Re-birth? The Son of God, the One Man, by God's Will."[86] And from another source, dated to approximately the same time, "The Lord and maker of all . . . from himself made the second God, the Visible . . . whom he loved as his Son." Although not in agreement with Christian doctrine as to the nature of the Son, these two writings predate Christianity and point to what can be considered a common knowledge. Old Testament history (both oral and written) provides a basis for the existence of mutual knowledge, since the cultural and religious practices of neighboring and distant nations is referenced several times by different authors.

In light of these historical facts, the Savior myth can be seen as a common belief emerging from the similar nature of human beings, a diffusion of knowledge from a central base—the Middle East, and the direct result of the distortion of biblical prophecy. Common knowledge produced generally similar stories whose details were invariably different. James Frazier's The Golden Bough (1900) provided a wealth of ammunition to Pagans and anti-Christians alike, all based on what modern scholars now consider to be poor

---

85. For more information see Tony Fahey, "Max Weber's Ancient Judaism," *American Journal of Sociology* 88, no. 1 (1982): 62–87, available at http://links.jstor.org/sici?sici=0002-9602%28198207% 2988%3AI%3C62%3AMWAJ%3E2.0CO%3B2-3 (accessed October 8, 2006).

86. Petrie, *Personal Religion in Egypt,* 114–23.

scholarship. Historian of religions Jonathan Z. Smith contends that the myth of the dying/rising god as portrayed by Frazier and others is pure fantasy, a product of wishful thinking unsupported by historical evidence.[87]

A close examination of the identities of the *rising saviors* strongly supports Smith's conclusion.

Refuting the Savior Myth

Name	Myth	Truth
Osiris	Son of Geb and Nut (the earth and sky); torn into pieces and scattered by brother Set; Isis (sister and wife) gathers pieces, gives them to Egyptian embalmers, and Osiris is resurrected.[88]	Osiris was a good daimon (demon)—a created being elevated to the rank of god; not born of a virgin; one of many gods, not God incarnate; not sacrificed for the sins of the world; no unconditional love for all people; once resurrected, becomes god of the underworld, implying a spiritual resurrection, not a physical one; no offer of eternal salvation by grace.
Dionysus/ Bacchus	Conceived by the goddess Demeter/Persephone, fathered by Zeus/Jupiter; placed in Semele's womb (descendant of Poseidon) until Semele is burned to death by Zeus	Conceived by a goddess, not born of a mortal virgin; one of many gods, not God incarnate; not sacrificed for the sins of the world; no uncon-

---

87. For more information see Jonathan Z. Smith, "Dying and Rising Gods," *Encyclopedia of Religion* (New York: MacMillan, 2005); and *Drudgery Divine: On the Comparison of Early Christianities and the Religions of Late Antiquity* (Chicago: University of Chicago Press, 1990).
88. Petrie, *Personal Religion in Egypt*, 111, 132.

Name	Myth	Truth
	and the baby saved by Hermes, sown into Zeus's thigh, and born for a second time.[89]	ditional love for all people; resurrected only as a baby, not as a man; no offer of eternal salvation by grace.
Mithra	Born from a rock as an adult before the earth was created; shepherds witnessed his birth (before humans were created); possibly an angel, he is a lesser god than Ahura Mazda in the Persian pantheon; Mithra killed a bull from some part of the moon, and the blood of the bull brought the life of creation to the universe; during the battle the dog, scorpion (or a raven), and snake helped him to succeed; he became an unconquerable god and friend to soldiers in Roman mythology (Mithras).[90]	Not born of a mortal virgin; he is a lesser god and one of many gods, not God incarnate; not sacrificed for the sins of the world; no unconditional love for all people; not resurrected; no offer of eternal salvation by grace.
Adonis/ Tammuz (Babylonian or Sumerian deity)	Born in the same cave of Bethlehem where Jesus was later born; nature god (fertility, corn/plants); he was a shepherd responsible for the lamb's milk; called a healer, he saved people	Not born of a mortal virgin; one of many gods, not God incarnate; killed to steal his sheep, not sacrificed for the sins of the world; no uncondit- ional love for all people;

89. Grand Valley State University, "Greek History and the Gods," http://faculty.gvsu.edu/websterm/Greekhistory&gods.htm (accessed August 27, 2007).

90. Franz Cumont, chap. 4 in *The Mysteries of Mithra* (Internet Sacred Texts Archives, 2006), http://www.sacred-texts.com/cla/mom/index.htm (accessed August 31, 2007).

Name	Myth	Truth
	from death; married to Inanna, he was killed by robbers from the underworld, who took his sheep; Inanna and demons brought him back from the underworld.[91]	resurrected by demonic power; no offer of eternal salvation by grace.
Attis (Phrygian Deity)	Born of Nana, daughter of the river god Sangarius and the goddess Cybele, who transformed herself into the male god Agdistis and impregnated Nana; condemned to death upon birth (December 25) by his grandfather, he is left by a river to die, but is rescued by a shepherd; he eventually emasculates himself for his betrayal of Cybele with herself (Agdistis) and dies; Cybele resurrects him three days later and proclaims him her daughter and her lover. He is called the good shepherd and savior of humanity.[92]	Born of a river deity, not a mortal virgin; killed himself by emasculation because of sexual betrayal, not sinless incarnate Deity sacrificed for the sins of the world; no unconditional love for all people; resurrected as a woman, not a man, to become daughter and lover to her mother, no offer of eternal salvation by grace.

91. The Jewish Encyclopedia contends that "Adonis-Tammuz, however, was a solar deity; the thunder-god is not believed to have died, and why a lament should have been instituted over him and should have become typical of mourning is one of the unsolved riddles in the way of the interpretation now generally favored" (http://www.jewishencyclopedia.com/view.jsp?letter=H&artid=31 [accessed August 27, 2007]). See also Donald A. Mackenzie, *Myths of Babylonia and Assyria* (Project Gutenberg, 2005), http://www.gutenberg.org/files/16653/16653-h/16653-h.htm (accessed September 11, 2007).

92. For more information, see Giovanni Casadio, "The Failing Male God: Emasculation, Death and Other Accidents in the Ancient Mediterranean World," *Numen* 50, no. 3 (2003): 231–68.

Other so-called *rising saviors*, such as Baal, bear little or no resemblance to Jesus Christ. According to eminent archaeologist Cyrus H. Gordon in his translation of the Ugaritic texts, Baal was one of a pantheon of gods, very similar in nature and personality to the Greek pantheon. He was not born of a mortal virgin, and he did not suffer and die for the sins of the world: he suffered as a direct result of his constant fights with another god, Mot (death). He was resurrected multiple times in conjunction with seasonal fertility rights, copulated with a heifer before one of his deaths, and produced a tauromorphic (bull-shaped) son. Despite his repeated resurrections, he remained Mot's eternal slave.[93]

Hercules, Asclepius, Horus—all the details of their mythical lives differ markedly from the historical life of Jesus; not one is identical. A close examination of the myth of Gautama Buddha, said to have been "born of a virgin," also reveals serious flaws. The birth itself is marked by "remarkable manifestations of nature," and the child Buddha stands and walks immediately after birth, saying, "Among all creatures I am the most excellent, for I am about to destroy and extirpate the roots of sorrow caused by the universal evil of birth and death."[94] The myth of Buddha far outpaces the facts of his life as the son of a chieftain in Nepal. There is no historical evidence whatsoever for a virgin birth or any other parallel to the life of Jesus Christ.

Krishna is another hat tossed into the *rising savior* ring by those who paint Christianity as a derivative of Hinduism. The usual claim is that Krishna was crucified, died, and resurrected twelve hundred years before Christ. But it is interesting to note that unlike Jesus, Krishna was not even an historical person, he was the eighth incarnation (or avatar) of the Hindu god Vishnu.[95] Dr. Edwin Bryant, pro-

---

93. Gordon, *The Common Background of Greek and Hebrew Civilizations*, 201.

94. John Fenton, "Biographical Myths; Illustrated from the Lives of Buddha and Muhammad," *The Folk-Lore Record* 3, no. 1 (1880): 26–39, available at http://links.jstor.org/sisi?sici=17441994%281880%0293%3A1%3C26%3ABMIFTL%3E2.0.CO%3B2-P (accessed August 28, 2007). The historical record: Gautama Buddha, founder of the Buddhist religion, was the son of Suddhodana, a chieftain reigning over a district near the Himalayas in what is known today as the country of Nepal. At an early age, Siddhartha Gautama, his true name, observed the many contradictions and problems of life; he abandoned his wife and son when he felt he could no longer endure the life of a rich nobleman, and became a wandering ascetic in search of the truth about life. For more information, see Martin, "Buddhism," in *Kingdom of the Cults*.

95. M. M. Ninan, *Hinduism: What Really Happened in India*, 2nd ed. (San Jose: Global Publishers, 2004), available at "India: A Christian Heresy," http://www.scribd.com/doc/416127/Hinduism-A-Christian-Heresy (accessed May 16, 2008). Many argue that Krishna was a historical figure, but there is scant evidence to support this.

fessor of Hinduism at Rutgers University, in a recent response to Christian apologist Mike Licona, answered the Krishna crucifixion claim with "That is absolute and complete nonsense. There is absolutely no mention anywhere [in the Bhagavata-Purana (life of Krishna)] which alludes to a crucifixion." Bryant went on to say, "Krishna was killed by an arrow from a hunter who accidentally shot him in the heel. He died and ascended. It was not a resurrection."[96]

Pagan websites scattered across the Internet attack Christianity using the worn and discredited tactic of the rising savior. Rarely, if ever, do they cite any primary sources for these claims. There are many other savior-gods from cultures worldwide, but an examination of their myths using primary source documentation always reveals the differences between Jesus Christ and myths. Jesus is not a copycat savior: He is *the* Savior, the fulfillment of ancient prophecy. Christianity was not a copycat religion; it was and is a fulfillment of Judaism. It was a reminder of and a return to the prophetic truth as proclaimed in Judaic writings for centuries. It is not impossible that in the corruption of monotheism into polytheism, these prophecies and truths (known by human beings and by fallen supernatural beings) were assimilated, reinterpreted, and appropriated.

There is one Supreme God; He created and loves all people; sin separated man from Him; He sent the Savior of the world, Jesus Christ, as a sacrifice to remove the barrier of sin; He conquered death and gave life eternal to all who believe. Jesus is a fulfillment of prophecy.

Messianic Prophecies	Old Testament (Tanakh)	New Testament Fulfillment
Messiah will be: A descendent of Eve who will defeat Satan	Gen. 3:15	Gal. 4:4
A descendant of Abraham	Gen. 12:3; 18:18	Acts 3:25–26
A descendant of Judah	Gen. 49:10	Matt. 1:2 and Luke 3:33

96. Mike Licona, "A Refutation of Acharya S's Book, The Christ Conspiracy" (TruthQuest Publishers, 2001) on the Risen Jesus Web site, http://www.risen-jesus.com/index.php?option=content& task=view&id=22 (accessed August 27, 2007).

Messianic Prophecies	Old Testament (Tanakh)	New Testament Fulfillment
God incarnate	Ex. 3:13–14; Deut. 18:15–16; Isa. 9:6	John 4:26; 5:45–47; 8:58
Born of a virgin; the Son of God	Isa. 7:14; Ps. 2:7	Matt. 1:18; 3:17; Mark 1:11; Luke 3:22
Born in Bethlehem	Micah 5:2	Matt. 2:1
Riding a donkey	Zech. 9:9	Matt. 21:2
Betrayed by a friend	Ps. 41:9	John 13:18, 21
Crucified; pierced through hands and feet (no bones broken)	Ps. 22; 34:20	Matt. 27:34–50; John 19:17–36; Luke 23:33; 24:36–39
Stripped of his clothes (lots cast); crucified with criminals	Ps. 22:18	Matt. 27:35, 38; Mark 15:24, 27; Luke 23:34; John 19:23–24
Given gall (vinegar) to drink	Ps. 69:21	Matt. 27:34; Mark 15:23; John 19:29–30
Raised from the dead	Ps. 16:10–11; 49:15	Matt. 28:5–9; Mark 16:6; Luke 24:4–7; John 20:11–16; Acts 1:3; 2:32
In heaven (ascended)	Ps. 22:18	Matt. 27:35, 38; Mark 15:24, 27; Luke 24:51[97]

97. This is only a brief listing of Messianic prophecies. Hundreds of biblical verses support Jesus Christ as the one and only Messiah. For more information, see: "324 Messianic Prophecies" (Hope of Israel Web site), http://www.hopeofisrael.net/index.php?option=com_content&task=view&id=49&Itemid=27.

Ralph Woodrow

In my earlier Christian experience I came across literature that directly connected Ancient Paganism with Christianity. While the Roman Catholic Church was usually the target of such literature, it seemed also that other churches were contaminated by customs and beliefs apparently rooted in Paganism. Alexander Hislop (1807–1862) who wrote *The Two Babylons* (New York: Loizeaux Bros, 1943), with its alarming subtitle, *Papal Worship Proved to be the Worship of Nimrod and His Wife*, was the textbook on which much of this teaching was based. With his voluminous notes and references, I assumed, as did many others, that his claims were factual.

As a young 1960s evangelist, I preached on the mixture of Paganism with Christianity and eventually wrote a book, *Babylon Mystery Religion* (1966), based on Hislop's theories. The demand for a book connecting Ancient Paganism to Catholicism pushed my publication into the hundreds of thousands and it was translated into several foreign language editions.

Only occasionally did I receive a critical letter about my book. One person who caught my attention was a high school history teacher who showed me solid evidence that Hislop was not a reliable historian. This caused me to carefully, and prayerfully, go back through Hislop's work. As I did this, it became clear that Hislop's "history" was often only an arbitrary piecing together of Pagan mythological stories.

Finding similarities, and ignoring differences, Hislop taught that Pagan gods like Adonis, Apollo, Bacchus, Cupid, Dagon, Hercules, Janus, Mars, Mithra, Moloch, Orion, Osiris, Pluto, Saturn, Vulcan, Zoraster, and many more, were all rooted in Nimrod! He did the same with Pagan goddesses like Aphrodite, Artemis, Astarte, Aurora, Bellona, Ceres, Diana, Easter, Irene, Iris, Juno, Mylitta, Proserpine, Rhea, Venus, and Vesta, he claimed, were all rooted in Semiramis, who Hislop insisted was Nimrod's wife.

By piecing together bits and pieces of stories about these various gods and goddesses, Hislop claimed that Nimrod was a big, ugly, deformed black man. His wife, Semiramis, was a most beautiful white woman with blond hair and blue eyes, a backslider, inventor of soprano singing, the originator of priestly celibacy, the first to whom the unbloody mass was offered! This is not factual history—it is more like tabloid sensationalism.

When I researched the articles on "Nimrod" and "Semiramis" in various encyclopedias, nothing was said of them being husband and wife, and quite to the contrary, they apparently did not live in the same century! My continued research through the rare books found on Hislop's footnotes showed that in a number of cases the quotations, in their context, did not match his claims.

I realized that similarity does not prove common identity and that many claims made about the Pagan origins of Catholicism are unconnected. For this reason I pulled *Babylon Mystery Religion* out of print and wrote *The Babylon Connection?* (1997) to examine Hislop's faulty conclusions.

Finding similarities in Ancient Paganism, when there is no tangible or logical connection, proves nothing. We would have to eliminate common biblical practices because Pagans practiced the same, like kneeling in prayer, water baptism, raising hands in worship, taking off shoes on holy ground, a holy mountain, a holy place in a temple, offering sacrifices without blemish, a sacred ark, city of refuge, bringing forth water from a rock, laws written on stone, fire appearing on a person's head, horses of fire, the offering of first fruits, tithes, the fish symbol, the cross symbol, Easter sunrise service, the Christmas tree, et cetera. Claims that imply "all these things started in Babylon" are not only divisive and fruitless, they are untrue.

To all my brothers and sisters in Christ who feel that finding Babylonian origins for present-day customs or practices is of great importance, my advice is to move cautiously, lest we major on minors. If there are things in our lives or churches that are indeed Pagan or displeasing to the Lord, they should be dealt with, of course. But in attempting to defuse the confusion of Babylon, we must guard against confusing the issue by creating a new "Babylon" of our own making.

Scriptural Response

The legacy of Ancient Paganism lives on in the modern world. A simple search engine on the Internet will point to the cyberspace temple doors of Isis, Bacchus,

Cybele, Osiris, Zeus, Mithras, Ahura Mazda, and many other Pagan gods. Ancient idols pilfered from archaeological sites inevitably arrive on the Internet auction site eBay. A small statuette of Baal can be seen in living color on computer screens all over the world, and purchased for three hundred dollars at the touch of a button. University libraries offer volumes of spells, curses, healing potions, demon summoning, and other forbidden knowledge. The events that occurred so many thousands of years in the past retain their awesome power to influence lives today.

It is important to remember, in light of Paganism's pattern of reshaping truth (as in *rising saviors*), that the purpose of Pagan religions is to imitate. The point of imitation is deception—to lead people away from God (Deut. 13).

Why are people attracted to the Pagan religions of yesterday?

- Pagan religions are unknown and exciting.

- Pagan religions are mysterious and appeal to people's carnal nature.

- Pagan religions are a display of power outside of the human capacity to control it.

- Pagan religions are a substitute for hearing the voice of God.

- Pagan religions are a spiritual narcotic.[98]

Narcotics affect the brain and the central nervous system. And what effect do narcotics have? They give a feeling of well-being. They create hallucinations and generally tend to remove the subject from reality. That is the product of a normal narcotic phenomenon, and that is precisely what happens in the realm of the spirit. The moment people accept Pagan religion and the occult power that energizes it, they accept a substitute for reality in the dimension of the spirit. It is a narcotic that numbs the spiritual nature and makes it insensitive to the reality of God, so that it does not hear the voice of God; it hears other voices. And the hallucinations people have are not mental; they are spiritual. That is why they are able to believe that the Bible is borrowed Pagan ideology, when it is in truth the Word of God. When someone is

---

98. The term "spiritual narcotic" is used by Christian scholars to illustrate man's spiritual lethargy. See Samuel A. Meier, "Money," in *Baker's Evangelical Dictionary of Biblical Theology* (Grand Rapids: Baker Publishing Group, 1996).

under the influence of a spiritual narcotic, he or she is incapable of rational spiritual judgment. The power of the occult lies in the irrational—never in the rational.

How can Christians succeed in this eternal battle of good and evil? Scripture gives specific instructions on spiritual warfare to the Church of Jesus Christ:

> Finally, my brethren, be strong in the Lord and in the power of His might. Put on the whole armor of God, that you may be able to stand against the wiles of the devil. For we do not wrestle against flesh and blood, but against principalities, against powers, against the rulers of the darkness of this age, against spiritual hosts of wickedness in the heavenly places. Therefore take up the whole armor of God, that you may be able to withstand in the evil day, and having done all, to stand.
>
> Stand therefore, having girded your waist with truth, having put on the breastplate of righteousness, and having shod your feet with the preparation of the gospel of peace; above all, taking the shield of faith with which you will be able to quench all the fiery darts of the wicked one. And take the helmet of salvation, and the sword of the Spirit, which is the word of God; praying always with all prayer and supplication in the Spirit, being watchful to this end with all perseverance and supplication for all the saints. (Eph. 6:10–18)

Today, the world overflows with generations of people overcome by a spiritual narcotic—denied, by their own choice, of an encounter with the Holy Spirit, when they could be lifted to the height of heights into fellowship with the living God. But the good news is this: the Holy Spirit empowers Christians to lead those lost in the dominion of the occult to this transforming fellowship. "Be diligent to present yourself approved to God, a worker who does not need to be ashamed, rightly dividing the word of truth" (2 Tim. 2:15).

Knowledge of deceptive occult theology is knowledge that will transform, and together with the living power of the Word of God, it will tear down strongholds:

THE OCCULT VS CHRISTIANITY

Concepts of . . .	The Occult	Christianity
Man	Basically good; inherently divine; part of God	Created in God's image but also has sinful nature (Gen. 1:26; Isa. 59:2; Rom. 3:23)
God	Supreme Being— Creator God; various lesser gods; nature; divine principle (male or female	Personal living God; sovereign ruler of the universe; only living true God (Isa. 44:24–26; 45:5–7)
Earth	Sacred; living organism; has consciousness; assisted by earth spirits; worthy of worship	Created by God for His own purposes to ultimately glorify Him; not divine or worthy of worship (Col. 1:16; Rev. 4:11)
Salvation	By performance of good works; all will eventually be purified; no need for salvation	By grace, through faith in Jesus Christ—His death and resurrection to pay for sins, and give eternal life (John 3:16; 1 Cor. 15:20–26; Eph. 2:4–8)
Evil	Present outside of man; gods are responsible for it and tempt humans to choose it; human beings are victims of it.	Evil is rebellion against God's will through man's sinful nature and through Satan (Prov. 8:13; Matt. 15:19; John 3:19–20; 8:44; 1 John 3:8)

THE OCCULT VS CHRISTIANITY (CONT'D)

Concepts of . . .	The Occult	Christianity
Jesus Christ	One of many powerful gods; an enlightened teacher, a human able to perfectly express the divinity present in all human beings	The second person of the Trinity; God's only begotten Son (same nature as God); the promised Messiah; the God-Man who perfectly obeyed the Father, enabling Him to be the sacrifice for all sin by His death and shedding of blood on the Cross; the only mediator between God and man (John 4:25–26; Acts 4:12; Rom. 5:9–19; 8:1; 1 Tim. 2:5; Heb. 2:14; 1 John 5:11–12)[99]

CONCLUSION

History, by its very nature, is so much more than an analytical regurgitation of facts and faces. It teems with the triumphs and failures of the human soul; it portrays horror, bitter injustice, loyalty, and deep, abiding love; and it can powerfully persuade the hearts and minds of people—even to the point where one might actually change the world.

Throughout history, Paganism has worked to corrupt the true monotheism of the living God, deriding early Christianity by suggesting it was nothing more than a copycat religion comprised of stolen elements from the Pagan religions that preceded it. But historical facts continue to prove repeatedly that Christianity is unique—and Jesus Christ is the only Savior.

In several very important aspects, Christianity stood apart from every known religion in the Roman Empire:

- Christianity welcomed the poor and sick, and took care of them.

---

99. Martin, *The Kingdom of the Cults,* 115.

- Christianity not only talked about the power of Jesus Christ; Christians demonstrated it: many people were healed and countless demons cast out on a regular basis. They were forced to submit—in front of witnesses—to the name of Jesus.

- Christianity promised salvation from eternal punishment, through the death and resurrection of Jesus Christ, to everyone who believed: rich or poor, slave or free. "This transcendent doctrine of redemptive suffering— of life given to man originally, lost by man, and restored to him by the Redemption—was a concept unknown to the Pagan Mysteries."[100]

- Christianity offered the revolutionary doctrine of unconditional love. The concept of selfless love—love that extended to all human beings, regardless of gender, age, social status, or race—was a doctrine completely unknown in the Roman Empire. It was a revolutionary idea: a love that embraced everyone, even those rejected by society.

- Christianity promised eternal life in an everlasting paradise with God. It promised not only a new heaven but a new earth, a type of eternal life that had never before been available, and Christ was the only one who could provide it. "The Savior, too, was no created being endowed with human shape as intermediary between God and man, but God himself incarnate in man."[101]

Jesus Christ offered something to the world that it simply could not find anywhere else—love, redemption, resurrection, and eternal life in a paradise far beyond anything it could ever imagine.

There is one eternal God, one Son, one Savior, one Hope. The Church of Jesus Christ possesses a rich spiritual and historical heritage that all the Pagan rhetoric ever recorded cannot destroy, "And because you are sons, God has sent forth the Spirit of His Son into your hearts, crying out, "Abba, Father!" Therefore you are no longer a slave but a son, and if a son, then an heir of God through Christ" (Gal. 4:6–7).

---

100. Grant, *The World of Rome,* 209.
101. Ibid.

Recommended Resources

1. Gordon, Cyrus H. *The Common Background of Greek and Hebrew Civilizations.* New York: Norton, 1965.

2. Herodotus, *The History of Herodotus,* Internet Classics Archive, http://classics.mit.edu/Herodotus/history.html.

3. Hoffmeier, James K., ed. and Alan R. Millard, ed., *The Future of Biblical Archaeology: Reassessing Methodologies and Assumptions.* Grand Rapids: Eerdmans, 2004.

4. Kaiser, Jr., Walter C. A. *History of Israel from the Bronze Age Through the Jewish Wars.* Nashville: Broadman & Holman, 1998.

5. Schmidt, Wilhelm. *The Origin and Growth of Religion.* New York: Cooper Square, 1972.

6. Mettinger, Tryggve N. D. *The Riddle of Resurrection: Dying and Rising Gods in the Ancient Near East.* Coniectanea Biblica, Old Testament Series 50. Stockholm: Almqvist & Wiksell, 2001.

Quick Facts About Kabbalah

- Kabbalah is known as the secret Torah; historically, it is Jewish mysticism.

- Kabbalah denies the deity of Jesus Christ, the virgin birth, and His atonement and bodily resurrection.

- Salvation is not necessary; all mistakes are atoned for through Kabbalah study or reincarnation.

- Hermetic Qabalah is an occult system of magic based on a different interpretation of the Hebrew Bible.

- Hollywood Kabbalah combines Judaic Kabbalah with some Hermetic Qabalah, and New Age ideas and methods.

5

Kabbalah

Kabbalah is not something easily defined; in fact, its beliefs often defy description. Contrary to popular thought, it is not a single book, nor is it a single belief system. Perhaps the best description of Kabbalah is based on its historical roots, which place it firmly in the realm of Jewish mysticism (spirituality).

The Tanakh is the Hebrew Bible, and the first five books of it are known as the Torah or Pentateuch. Simply put, the Tanakh is the Divine revelation of G-d to His people, and Kabbalah is the occult, or *secret* interpretation of this revelation. Just as there is a public written Torah, there is also a hidden version that came to be known as the secret Torah, passed down through the centuries through oral tradition and recorded in writing for the first time during the twelfth century. This tradition teaches the meaning behind the written words—the *inner* Torah—contemplating aspects of God and the nature of man, as well as the truth about creation and other key questions of life. But the heart of Kabbalah, the driving force behind all Kabbalistic teaching down through the centuries, is the quest for secret supernatural power: the belief that it is possible for people to access the power of God and use it to transform themselves and the world around them.

Kabbalah encompasses such a wide variety of themes and individuals that it is only possible to scratch its complex surface in this assessment. As Christianity is divided into many sects, so the followers of Kabbalah are divided into numerous factions. The actual spelling of the word *Kabbalah* varies and is determined by the scholar or sect describing it. Some groups define Kabbalah as Jewish mysticism, others as a scientific method—devoid of religious or philosophical overtones—intended to discover God's nature and purposes. Judaic Kabbalah, or secret Torah, is the philosophy of the Torah—also referred to as the "wisdom of the Torah" or the "hidden science"—and as such, its fundamental nature is the focus of endless debate. If philosophers can be depended upon for one thing, it is the persistent refutation of opposing viewpoints. Such is the case with the Kabbalists, who spend time in three main pursuits: studying Kabbalah, arguing Kabbalah interpretation, and informing opposing camps that they are not true Kabbalists. In this respect, they have much in common with the Pharisees and Sadducees of Jesus' time, who routinely disputed everything.

In today's confusing world of Kabbalah, three categories best define the largest segments of this esoteric movement: Judaic Kabbalah, Hermetic Qabalah, and Hollywood Kabbalah. All claim an "authentic" teaching lineage in their leaders, and all agree that it is mandatory for Kabbalah to be taught since it is a hidden science, and as such cannot be learned without someone who is trained to teach it correctly.

Kabbalists as a whole also agree on one basic approach to Torah: it should always be interpreted as *metaphor*. According to Kabbalists, Moses was the author of Torah, and he never intended for it to be taken literally. This method also applies to the rest of the Hebrew Bible; all is symbolism, imagery, and allegory. The wisdom of Kabbalah was written about events and ideas from the world above, not the physical world known as the world below (earth). Only by studying it correctly can one hope to ponder the mystery of godliness, for it is not possible for God to know man or for man to know God on this earth; he can only know what God is *not*. Kabbalist Rav Michael Laitman of Bnei Baruch, a nonprofit organization teaching a modern version of the "wisdom of Kabbalah," defines its *essence* this way:

> Kabbalah has been shrouded in mystery for thousands of years. And it's called the hidden science for three reasons: One, in the past, Kabbalists taught only a few worthy, highly developed people from each generation who already possessed certain inner qualities not developed in humanity as a whole until recently, and these inner qualities allowed them to understand and use it correctly. So, in the first place it was purposely hidden by the Kabbalists themselves. Two: all Kabbalistic books are written in a way that uses words that seem to talk about people and things, but in fact not a single word in any Kabalistic book is talking about the physical world, and if you don't learn how to read these books from a Kabbalist in the authentic teaching lineage, you simply can't understand them. It doesn't matter how bright you are, all you're going to end up with is a product of your imagination, and nothing else. And three, Kabbalah reveals the purpose and the

nature of this system that we call life, and unless a person has a powerfully real and serious need to ask this very question, they can't hear the answer, not even if it's shouted at them.[1]

Kabbalists assert the authority of antiquity for these teachings, claiming they can be traced to Abraham himself: "The wisdom of Kabbalah is the most ancient of all wisdoms. It goes back to the time of Abraham, the Patriarch, in the eighteenth century BC, thirty-eight hundred years ago. Abraham the Patriarch was an ordinary Bedouin tribesman in Babylon who discovered the existence of godliness, a reality outside of this world."[2] Unfortunately for the followers of Kabbalah, there is no historical or archaeological evidence to date in support of this argument. According to Kabbalists, Abraham discovered godliness but not God, since God is *transcendent* in the sense that He cannot be close to man and still be God. Humans can only know *about* Him, and even this knowing is subject to man's perceptions and may not even be reality.

This is not the historical God of Judaism, and it is certainly not the nature of God as revealed in the Torah; it is a reinterpretation of the God of the Bible that can be traced to the time of Alexander the Great and the relocation of the Jews to Alexandria (c. 330 BC), and later to Simon the sorcerer of Acts 8. During Alexander's rule, some Jewish leaders, influenced by the Greek world around them, redefined their view of God. The Torah reveals a God who is very close to man or *immanent*; He can also be *eminent*—far beyond man in nature and power but not ever prevented by these from being close to man.[3] The God some Jews embraced in Alexandria and in the centuries that followed was far removed from man.[4] He became *the* Creative Force—an It—unknowable and certainly unreachable, and therefore man needed to formulate a method of knowing Him.

1. Michael Laitman, "What is the essence of Kabbalah?" Kabbalah TV, http://www.kab.tv/eng/?item=137 (accessed May 14, 2007).
2. Michael Laitman, "Great Kabbalists Throughout History," Kabbalah TV, http://www.kab.tv/eng/?item=137 (accessed May 14, 2007).
3. Christian theology agrees with the *immanent* and *eminent* God—Acts 17:28 and 1 Timothy 6:16.
4. *Transcendence* as used among Christian theologians does not mean the same thing. In Christian theology, it describes God's nature beyond created things, without denying his personal nature. Greek philosophers described an impersonal god who transcends nature, while Christian revelation demonstrates a God who is personal and transcendent. Dr. Norman Geisler states, "The God who is prior to all things He created, and who is upholding all things, is also above all things, is transcendent. The apostle affirmed that there is 'one God and Father of all, who is over all and through all and in all' (Ephesians 4:6)." Norman Geisler, *Systematic Theology*, vol. 2. (Minneapolis: Bethany House, 2003).

This system was more than likely influenced directly by the philosophy of Plato and his *doctrine of recollection*, based on Socrates' question: How can man ever learn what he does not know? "Do you see what a captious argument you are introducing—that, forsooth, a man cannot inquire either about what he knows or about whit he does not know? For he cannot inquire about what he knows, because he knows it, and in that case is in no need of inquiry; nor again can he inquire about what he does not know, since he does not know about what he is to inquire."[5]

In order for humans to reach the knowledge they needed to learn, it was necessary for the mind to access divine knowledge already present within each human being—knowledge gained from a soul's previous life. This previous existence would eventually become known as *reincarnation*.

The world of Alexandria was a melting pot of religions and philosophies, exposing leading Jewish scholars to Socrates, Plato, and Pythagoras, as well as the writings of Hermes Trismegistus, and Gnosticism—a legacy carried on by the sorcerer Simon Magus—the same Simon the apostle Peter rebuked in Acts 8:20–23. Hippolytus, the Roman Bishop and historian (c. 170 AD), reveals details of the true identity of Simon Magus in his *Philosophumena*:

> It seems, then, expedient likewise to explain now the opinions of Simon, a native of Gitta, a village of Samaria; and we shall also prove that his successors, taking a starting-point from him, have endeavoured (to establish) similar opinions under a change of name. This Simon being an adept in sorceries, both making a mockery of many, partly according to the art of Thrasymedes, in the manner in which we have explained above, and partly also by the assistance of demons perpetrating his villany, attempted to deify himself. (But) the man was a (mere) cheat, and full of folly, and the apostles reproved him in the Acts. . . . .
>
> And Simon denominates *the originating principle of the universe an indefinite power*, expressing himself thus: "This is the treatise of a revelation of (the) voice and name (recognisable) by means of intellectual apprehension of the Great Indefinite Power. Wherefore it will be sealed, (and) kept secret, (and) hid, (and) will repose in the habitation, at the foundation of

---

5. Tufts University, s.v. "Meno: Socrates," Perseus http://www.perseus.tufts.edu/cgi-bin/ptext?lookup =plat.+meno+80e.

which lies the root of all things." And he asserts that this man who is born of blood is (the aforesaid) habitation, and that in him resides an indefinite power, which he affirms to be the root of the universe.[6]

The continued survival of these ideas is perhaps best seen in the arguments of first-century Gnostic, Valentinus, and in the endurance of the Hermes Trismegistus Gnostic tradition:

GNOSTIC HERMES

Valentinus and his followers distinguished three classes of man,
hylics, psychics and pneumatics and opposed spiritual, intuitive, to
"psychic," that is logic and discursive and heavenly:
Adam received a spiritual germ that was sowed
by Sophia stealthily into his soul . . .
in order that the bone, his logic and heavenly
soul, not be empty, but full of spiritual marrow.

Thus Adam could beget three different types of man, materialists, true believers and spiritual people:
From Adam three natures were born,
first
the *irrational,* to which Cain belonged;
secondly
the *rational* and righteous;
thirdly
the *intuitive* type, men like Seth.[7]

This focus on the "universe" and the abstract mysteries of it formed the heart of Gnosticism that endured throughout the centuries. The writings of Hermes Trismegistus resurfaced in Europe during the twelfth century and influenced many

---

6. Hippolytus, "Simon's Forced Interpretation of Scripture; Plagiarizes from Heraclitus and Aristotle; Simon's System of Sensible and Intelligible Existences" (chap. 4), in *Philosophumena,* bk. 6, http://www.philosophumena.com/book_vi.htm, emphasis in original. In this work, Hippolytus (c. 170–236 AD) discusses the allegories inherent in the system of thought put forth by Magus.

7. Gilles Quispel, "Hermes Trismegistus and the Origins of Gnosticism," *Vigiliae Christianae* 46, no. 1 (1992): 4. *Excerpta ex Theodoto* 53, 2–5, and *Excerpta* 54, 1, http://www.jstor.org/pss/1583880.

schools of thought. "The most important revival of ideas and motifs akin to Gnostic thinking in Jewish literature is attested in the writings of early Kabbalah. G. Scholem was the first to interpret central teachings of the Book *Bahir* as repercussions of ancient Gnosticism: for the first time in Jewish sources, God is theosophically described not merely as a heavenly king but with a pleroma of hypostatized potencies and a cosmic tree as the totality of his powers."[8] This mélange of ideas could very well have produced a symbolic and obscure interpretation of the Torah that, combined with the writings of the Greek philosopher Philo, would eventually form the foundation of Kabbalah.[9]

KABBALAH BASICS

The study of Kabbalah is meant to answer the most confusing questions of life, such as *Who or what am I?* and *What is my purpose in life?* The answers to these questions cannot be achieved individually. Only a careful, supervised education may provide the truth behind the mystery. Students of Kabbalah must be instructed by rabbis who were taught by preceding rabbis in the *correct* teaching lineage—very much like an apprenticeship; not just any rabbi may teach Kabbalah.

Kabbalists assert that any explanation of Kabbalah teachings outside of those offered by the correct teaching lineage is oversimplification and thus suspect. However, this is a criticism that can be applied to all areas of study, whether it be religion, philosophy, science, or the arts, and therefore, just as it is possible for a scholar of history to assess and make general, accurate observations of historical religious development, it is possible to observe and assess Kabbalah based on the writings of respected teachers.

Judaic Kabbalah

The initiate venturing for the first time into the realm of Jewish mysticism and philosophy will not find a single text entitled *Kabbalah*.[10] Instead, students study various commentaries representative of different schools of thought on the Torah, written by respected Kabbalists down through the centuries. Just as the Torah has commentaries such as the *Talmud* (*Mishna and Gemara*) written on it, the "wis-

8. Wouter J. Hanegraaff, ed., et al., *Dictionary of Gnosis and Western Esotericism* (Leiden, the Netherlands: Brill, 2006), 637.
9. Hanegraaff, *Dictionary of Gnosis and Western Esotericism*, 1–19.
10. Also spelled Cabala.

dom" or tradition of Kabbalah also produced many interpretations after it was first transcribed in the twelfth century.

It is important to note here that a key difference between conservative Judaic Kabbalah, Christian, Hermetic, and Hollywood Kabbalah is the approach to the authority of the Talmud in the interpretation of the *Zohar*. Medieval scholars taught that a mature knowledge of the Talmud cannot be divorced from the study of the *Zohar*, and if it is, that study is worthless. Many modern rabbis concur with this teaching method:

> Anyone who opens a page of the Zohar, or any Kabbalistic book, sees that kabbalah is inextricably bound up in the Jewish tradition. In kabbalah (real kabbalah, that is) ritual practices are given cosmic meaning. The Talmud is quoted on each page of the Zohar; authority is granted to the Zohar because it is attributed to Rav Simeon Bar Yochai, a talmudic rabbi. Kabbalah, for the uninitiated, is a Hebrew word—that ought to provide a clue. To teach it as a universal "technology" of salvation is a travesty of tradition and a spiritual sham.[11]

Some modern schools of Kabbalah discourage followers from serious Talmudic study. Students are told they are not even ready to read Torah until they are able to understand it, and this understanding can only be achieved through studying select rabbis' *opinions* of it. The authority of the Torah and Talmud becomes secondary to modern interpretation. "Only if a person knows how to explain all of the words that he reads is it permissible for him to read and study Torah. Otherwise, he will understand all of the books of the Torah as if they were stories about historical events. Generally, the term 'Torah' is related to the books, which were written by special kabbalists, and carry within them the concealed Upper Light."[12] Conservative Jewish scholars, however, strongly advocate the study of the Torah and the Talmud before ever embarking on the teachings of Kabbalah.

The most popular and respected of Kabbalistic works is the *Zohar*, written by

---

11. Rabbi David Wolpe, "False Promises in Berg's 'Becoming,'" *Jewish Journal*, http://www.jewishjournal.com/home/preview.php?id=13394 (2004), (accessed June 1, 2007).
12. Bnei Baruch World Center for Kabbalah Studies, "To Our Students," Kabbalah.info, http://www.kabbalah.info/engkab/lesson05.htm (accessed May 16, 2007). See also http://www.kabbalah.info/.

Moses de Leon (c. 1250) but attributed by him to Simeon ben Yohai (170–200 AD).[13] This conclusion regarding authorship was first drawn by Gershom Scholem, a scholar and Kabbalist, who meticulously researched and assessed the evidence of the *Zohar*'s authorship in hopes of proving the existence of an older manuscript written by Simeon ben Yohai.

But the truth behind the *Zohar*'s origins turned out to be the opposite of what Scholem had anticipated finding: "In regard to this question all I can say is that after making a close study of Moses de Leon's writings and their relation to the *Midrash Ha-Neelam* and the components of the *Zohar*, I have come to the conclusion that they were all written by the same man."[14] The dispute over authorship is still ongoing, but regardless of its source, many Kabbalists affirm that the *Zohar is Kabbalah*. Although predated by the *Sefer Yetzirah* (Book of Creation, c. 800) and the *Sefer Bahir* (Book of Brilliance, c. 1100), which first explained the *Ten Sefirot* in detail, the *Zohar* is by far the most prominent today.[15] Moses de Leon focused on allegorical interpretation of the Torah in his writings, rather than formulating a systematic, analytical method of interpretation, which resulted in a commentary so rich in imagery and confusing symbolism that it required multiple commentaries down through the centuries to explain it.[16]

The *Zohar* is a difficult read for some people and incomprehensible for most, since it is written in what is called the "language of the branches," a philosophical language rather than a cultural one such as English or Spanish. For example, the majority of both Jews and Christians would agree that Genesis 1 reveals actual physical details of the creation. Kabbalists would say that in the language of the branches, Genesis 1 has nothing to do with creation at all. Kabbalah focuses on the interconnectedness of the world above with the world below, and the language of the branches is key to understanding who God is and what His purposes for this world might be. This is the secret Torah.

Judaic Kabbalah focuses on the historical teachings of the *Zohar*, *Sefer Yetzirah*,

---

13. Gershom Scholem, *Major Trends in Jewish Mysticism* (New York: Shocken, 1961), 187–93. Scholem concluded that Moses de Leon likely named the revered Simeon ben Yohai as the author of the *Zohar* in order to sell more copies of his book.

14. Scholem, *Major Trends in Jewish Mysticism*, 187–93.

15. *Stanford Encyclopedia of Philosophy*, http://plato.standford.edu/entries/israeli/ (accessed July 17, 2008).

16. Gershom Scholem, *Major Trends in Jewish Mysticism*, 158.

and *Sefer Bahir*, interpreted in turn by the commentaries of rabbis in the correct teaching lineage. A modern-day proponent of Judaic Kabbalah is the Bnei Baruch World Center for Kabbalah Studies, founded by Rav Michael Laitman, PhD. Dr. Laitman offers everything Kabbalah on his website, Kabbalah.info, including video teachings and study courses. He is the disciple of Rabbi Baruch Ashlag, son of Rabbi Yehuda Ashlag, who is the author of the *Sulam* commentary on the book of *Zohar*.

Bnei Baruch defines the language of the branches in this way: "The wisdom is no more and no less than a sequence of roots which hang down by way of cause and effect in fixed, determined rules, weaving into a single, exalted goal described as: 'the revelation of His Godliness to His creatures in this world.' Which means that there is an upper force, and then there are governing forces that descend from this upper force and bring about our existence in this world."[17] Bnei Baruch bases its teaching on the method of Rabbi Yehuda Ashlag, who taught, "Just as a person cannot function properly in this world without having knowledge of it, so also the soul cannot function properly in the upper world without knowledge of it. The wisdom of Kabbalah provides you with this knowledge."[18]

Ein Sof

The God of the Kabbalists is *transcendent*, meaning He cannot know man and still be God. This idea probably took root and developed among the Alexandrian Jews (c. 330 BC), who struggled with their theological identity in the philosophical world of Greece. During the reign of Alexander the Great, more Jews lived in Alexandria than in Jerusalem, and although they believed their Scripture was superior to Greek philosophy, some were not immune to its influence. Gradually, over a period of several hundred years, a second method of scriptural interpretation evolved due to the influence of Plato, Philo, and other philosophers; it substituted the literal meaning of Torah for symbolic imagery and came to be known as the allegorical method of interpretation. This method of interpretation touched every aspect of Torah, including the nature of God, and its influence is clearly seen today.

---

17. Jehudah Ashlag "What is the Essence of Kabbalah?" Kabbalah TV, http://www.kab.tv/eng/?item=137 (accessed May 14, 2007).
18. Bnei Baruch Kabbalah Education & Research Institute, "About Bnei Baruch," http://www.kabbalah. info/engkab/abouteng.htm.

According to Kabbalists, there was always *Ein Sof* (meaning without end, or infinite); God as *It*, not *He*. This impersonal divine force splintered at creation and now inhabits everything. God is literally in all things, so He cannot be described, He has no limitations, and He only intermingles with the universe through the channels of the *Ten Sefirot*.

The Ten Sefirot *or* Tree of Life

The known qualities of God are usually represented by a diagram called the *Ten Sefirot* (also spelled *Sephiroth*) or *Tree of Life*, but this diagram can vary depending upon which rabbi or school of thought is using it. It is sometimes depicted as an upside-down tree (roots pointing upwards, branches pointing toward the lower world or earth). What is not so well-known, however is that Simon Magus (c. 67 AD), the sorcerer of Acts 8:9, used the same tree analogy to describe the nature of God. According to Hippolytus:

> Now Simon, both foolishly and knavishly paraphrasing the law of Moses, makes his statements (in the manner following): For when Moses asserts that "God is a burning and consuming fire," taking what is said by Moses not in its correct sense, he affirms that fire is the originating principle of the universe. . . . (Simon) employs the terms secret and manifest; it may, (I say, in general,) be affirmed that the fire, (I mean) the super-celestial (fire), is a treasure, as it were a large tree, just such a one as in a dream was seen by Nabuchodonosor, out of which all flesh is nourished. And the manifest portion of the fire he regards as the stem, the branches, the leaves, (and) the external rind which overlaps them. All these (appendages), he says, of the Great Tree being kindled, are made to disappear by reason of the blaze of the all-devouring fire. The fruit, however, of the tree, when it is fully grown, and has received its own form, is deposited in a granary, not (flung) into the fire. For, he says, the fruit has been produced for the purpose of being laid in the storehouse, whereas the chaff that it may be delivered over to the fire. (Now the chaff) is stem, (and is) generated not for its own sake, but for that of the fruit. . . .[19]

---

19. Hippolytus, *Philosophumena*, chap. 4.

The Tree of Life—the Sefirot—of the Kabbalah appears to have been an image that Simon Magus was quite familiar with, a philosophy full of metaphors used to describe God and the power emanating from Him.

Kabbalah teaches that the Ten Sefirot reveal certain aspects of God's nature and plan, detailing how His power emanates into the world below:

These Sefirot correspond to qualities of G-d.[20] They consist of, in descending order, Keter (the crown), Chokhmah (wisdom), Binah (intuition, understanding), Chesed (mercy) or Gedulah (greatness), Gevurah (strength), Tiferet (glory), Netzach (victory), Hod (majesty), Yesod (foundation) and Malkut (sovereignty). The middle five qualities are mentioned explicitly and in order at 1 Chronicles 29:11: Yours, O L-rd, is the greatness (gedulah), the strength (gevurah), the glory (tiferet), the power (netzach), and the splendor (hod). I have seen this passage translated in widely varying ways, but the Hebrew corresponds to the names of the Sefirot in order.[21]

The names, order and definitions of the Sefirot have changed throughout history. Gershom Scholem defines the Sefirot as "spheres, whole realms of divinity, which underlie the world of our sense data and which are present and active in all that exists."[22] The Sefirot are equally divided into feminine aspects of God and male

20. The spelling of God as G-d is explained by Rabbi Jeffrey Wolfson Godwasser: "God's name is treated with unusual care in Jewish tradition. The divine name, YHWH (spelled with the Hebrew letters yud, hey, vav, hey) is never pronounced. Traditionally, Jews read the word 'Adonai' (often translated as 'the Lord') whenever reading God's holiest name in Torah or in prayer. However, 'Adonai' is not God's name. Among some traditional Jews, speaking even the word 'Adonai' is avoided outside of worship or study. This 'stand-in' for God's name is itself replaced by 'Ha-Shem' ('The Name'). The practice also has been extended to other Hebrew words associated with God. For example, the Hebrew word 'Elohim,' which means 'God' (the title, not God's name), is pronounced 'Elokim' outside of prayer and study.

In recent years, some Jews have carried the practice even further by abstaining from writing the English word 'God' and substituting the spelling, 'G-d' or 'Gd.' However, there is no prohibition in Jewish law from writing 'God' in any language other than Hebrew." (About.com, "Why Do Some Jews Spell God 'G-d'?" Ask the Rabbi, http://judaism.about.com/od/reformjudaismfa1/f/god_spelling.htm.)

21. Tracey Rich, "Kabbalah and Jewish Mysticism," Judaism 101, http://www.jewfaq.org/kabbalah.htm (accessed May 21, 2007).

22. Scholem, *Major Trends*, 11.

aspects of God. In Kabbalah, each quality of God (also known as a *vessel*) of the Ten Sefirot is studied in order to determine its effect on life and how best to utilize its power. These qualities do not change the nature of God as *one* God; they simply describe man's perception of God.

According to Kabbalah, there are some qualities of God that can be known (the Ten Sefirot) and some that cannot be known (the Ein Sof—infinite qualities). The Ten Sefirot correspond to the known characteristics of God or the Godhead, and through these emanations, God radiates to the world. These vessels are connected to the universe in ways that God cannot be connected, with the result that every action in the lower world vibrates through the Ten Sefirot and in some way affects the universe, the upper world, and God. Man acts—God *reacts*. Judaic Kabbalists devote themselves primarily to the study of the *Zohar* and other commentaries on the Ten Sefirot. Rabbi Pinchas Giller explains the Kabbalah's interpretation of biblical truth as it relates to the Patriarchs: Abraham, Isaac and Jacob:

> Each patriarch's spouse complements his sefirotic identity. Therefore, just as Abraham is the paradigm of Hesed, so Sarah is the paradigm of Din. She is a judgment specialist. When she hears Abraham discussing her having a child with the angels, she laughs bitterly and says, "How can I have a child when my husband is so old?" When Abraham palms her off as his sister to Pharaoh and Avimelekh, she goes along without protest or interaction. According to a tradition in the Midrash, when she hears that Abraham has taken Isaac up to the mountain to be sacrificed, she dies immediately of a broken heart, not being able to imagine any divine intervention or mercy. Hence, Sarah is clearly the paradigm of Din.
>
> Rebekah, Isaac's spouse, is the paradigm of Hesed, just as Isaac is the paradigm of Din. In every situation, she is outgoing and interactive. At the well, when she is first spotted by Abraham's servant Eliezer, she is peripatetic; running to and fro, washing his feet, watering the camels; she is like a giving spring of Hesed herself. Similarly, as she prepares to help Jacob steal the blessing from Esau, she slaughters the goats, skins them, prepares them as a meal. In every way she is an energetic font of activity as opposed to Isaac's imploded Din and passivity.
>
> Jacob is more complex and so his spousal relationships are more com-

plex. Rachel, his apparent true love and erotic ideal, is the paradigm of
Malkhut. Yet Leah, the apparently despised first wife, is indicative of something higher, for she is the paradigm of Binah, the next sefirah up, which is
a transformative, intuitive feminine wisdom. So it is that Jacob's relationship with Leah is not devoid of spiritual qualities, but they are tucked away
in the higher realms of the sefirotic tree, and therefore difficult or impossible for an outsider to understand.[23]

The following Sefirot diagram is based on the teachings of Rav Isaac Luria (b.
1534), the *Ari* or "the holy lion," possibly the most revered rabbi in the history of
Kabbalah:[24]

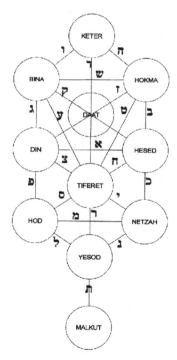

---

23. Rabbi Pinchas Giller, "God in Kabbalah," in Rabbi Bradley Shavit Artson and Deborah Silver, ed.,
    Walking with God (Bel Air, CA: American Jewish University, 2007), http://www.ajula.edu/content/
    html/other/god.unit%207.pdf, 11.
24. Diagram by Dr. Bryan Griffith Dobbs, 1999. See http://www.kheper.net/topics/Kabbalah/Ari-
    tree.html.

The first of the Ten Sefirot is the Crown (in Hebrew, *Keter*). . . .

Wisdom and Intelligence are the second and third of the Ten Sefirot. They are parallel emanations from the Crown or first Sefirah. . . . The first three Sefirot form a triad constituting the world as a manifestation of the Divine Thought. The remaining seven Sefirot likewise fall into triads. The Divine Thought is the source whence emanate two opposing principles, one active or masculine, the other passive or feminine. The former is Mercy (*esed*), the latter is Justice (*Din*). From the union of these two there results Beauty (*Tifêrêth*). The logical connections between these three principles, as they stand in the *Zohar*, are extremely difficult to fathom. . . .

The third triad are: Victory (*Neza*), Glory (*Hod*), and Foundation (*Yesod*). The first of these is the masculine active principle. The second is the feminine passive principle, while the third is the effect of their combination. What aspect of a God-saturated world do these three Sefirot point to? The *Zohar* tells us, as follows: "Extension, variety [or multiplication], and force are gathered together in them; and all forces that come out, come out from them, and it is for this reason that they are called Hosts [*i.e.* armies or forces]. They are [the two fore-mentioned Sefirot] Victory and Glory" (iii. 296). The allusion is obviously to the physical, dynamic aspect of the universe, the ceaseless, developing world with its multiplicity and variety of forces, changes and movements. From their coalescence comes the ninth Sefirah, Foundation. Rightly so; for it is the endless, changeless ebb and flow of the world's forces that, in the last resort, guarantees the stability of the world and builds up its 'foundation.' It creates the reproductive power of nature, endows it with, as it were, a generative organ from which all things proceed, and upon which all things finally depend.

The last of the Sefirot is Royalty (*Malkut*). Its function is not very apparent, and its existence may be due to the desire on the part of the Kabbalists to make up the number ten—a number which looms largely in the Old Testament literature, as well as in the theology of the Talmud, Midrashim, and Philo. Generally speaking, this tenth Sefirah indicates the abiding truth of the harmonious co-operation of all the Sefirot, thus making the universe in its orderliness and in its symmetry a true and exact manifestation of the Divine Mind—an *'Olam Azilut, i.e.* a world of emanation, as the Kabbalists themselves style it.[25]

Isaac the Blind

Rabbi Isaac Luria, known as the *Ari*, is revered as the rabbi who transformed the study of Kabbalah by revealing the doctrine of *Shevirat haKelim* or "shattering of the vessels" (a vessel is one of the Sefirot). Rav Luria was a student of Moses Cordovero (b. 1522), a rabbi teaching in the small community of Safed, located by the Sea of Galilee. Cordovero is perhaps best known for the development of the concept of the Ten Sefirot and for his comprehensive compilation of Kabbalistic knowledge in his work *The Pomegranate Orchard.* Rav Luria assimilated many of his teacher's ideas and incorporated them into his writings, a process that contributed significantly to the growth and development of Kabbalah.

Rav Luria, a recluse from Provence who recounted frequent visits by Elijah the prophet and other deceased luminaries, taught his students it was possible to communicate with the righteous dead. It was through this communion with Elijah that Rav Luria received revelations on the true essence of Kabbalah that would transform and empower it.

Rav Luria's doctrine of the "shattering of the vessels" states that at some point in time, God chose to create, and during this act of creation He poured light into all of the Sefirot vessels until the Godhead shattered, scattering points or sparks of light throughout the universe. The *tikkun olam* (repairing or perfecting the world) doctrine reveals that all things in this lower world contain a spark of the divine light—a light that longs to return to its original state of unity. At the consummation of time, through the efforts of Kabbalists and the process of reincarnation, the divine light will be gathered together once more.

Key Principles of Lurianic Kabbalah

According to a newer translation of Rav Luria's work, *Kabbalah of Creation,* by Eliahu Klein, the foundation of Luria's Kabbalah is based on five key elements:

---

25. J. Abelson, *Jewish Mysticism* (New York: Dover, 2001), 150–52. Also available online at Sacred-Texts.com, http://www.sacred-texts.com/jud/jm/jm11.htm. See also Rutgers University, "Kabbalah in English," http://remus.rutgers.edu/~woj/arcana/kabbalah.html.

1. The cosmic emanations of existence: Emanation, Creation, Formation, and Action.

2. The different qualities of light as they manifest through cosmic dimensions. The ten *sefirot* (cosmic energy centers): Crown, Wisdom/Intuition, Love, Strength, Beauty, Endurance, Praise, the Base (Foundation), and Sovereignty (kingship—royalty—nobility—stewardship).

3. How the cosmic dimensions and the qualities of light correspond to each other and to the development of the cosmic bodies: the thirty-two pathways (the number of intersections of the above ten centers) of the Tree of Life.

4. Five Cosmic Archetypes, which include the Ancient One; the Great Macro Face, which includes the union of the Great Father and Great Mother principle embedded within creation; the Divine miniature male (Little Face) and the Divine miniature female (Feminine).

5. How do these energies, lights, pathways, and Divine entities work together to create a living reality map that interfaces with reality as we know it? This is the subject matter for all Lurianic texts.[26]

The world of Kabbalah is a complicated one, offering a mystical, all-knowing yet unknowable, impersonal God—a God far different from the God of Abraham, Isaac, and Jacob. It relies upon the symbolic commentaries of *men* for truth instead of upon the factual, written Word of God.

Hermetic Qabalah

Both the spelling of the word *Kabbalah,* and its intrinsic meaning, change considerably when used in conjunction with its magical interpretation. Where Judaic Kabbalah uses the Ten Sefirot to describe the knowable aspects of God in an effort to understand the *Ein Sof*—the nature of God, Hermetic Qabalah uses the Ten Sefirot as a magical tool to progress from ordinary reality to *Ein Sof,* the inexpressible *infinite* divine. Visualization techniques, such as the one used by Kala Trobe in her New Age/magic/occult-oriented Qabalah work, *Magic of Qabalah,* are a com-

---

26. Isaac ben Solomon Luria, *Kabbalah of Creation: The Mysticism of Isaac Luria, Founder of Modern Kabbalah,* trans. Eliahu Klein (Berkeley, CA: Atlantic Books, 2005), xliv, emphasis in original.

mon method for accessing this "magic" or Occult power. Trobe encourages her
readers to draw upon the power of *black* light (as opposed to Kabbalah's implied
white light). She then leads them in imagining the "intoxication" of revenge and
the thrill of manipulating people to do their will.[27]

Hermetic Qabalah has a long and complex history, tracing its roots back to
Gnostic and Neoplatonist writings, and possibly to an actual figure known as
Hermes Trismegistus. The teaching of Trismegistus, considered by some to be an
historical personage and the father of Hermetic magic, can be traced to the
Hellenistic era, encompassing the rule of Alexander the Great and influencing religion and philosophy in the Roman Empire; the ideas and practices of Greece significantly impacted various cultures. There is, however, a convincing argument by
some that its source is actually Egyptian and Gnostic.[28] John Michael Greer, the
Grand Archdruid of the Ancient Order of Druids in America, points out, "The
Hermetic philosophy was seen as a primordial wisdom tradition, identified with
the 'Wisdom of the Egyptians' mentioned in *Exodus* and lauded in Platonic dialogues such as the *Timaeus*."[29]

Whatever its origin, the philosophy of Hermes Trismegistus was written in
many texts (the exact number of which is unknown) and divided into two main
parts: the philosophy of occult science, and writings on philosophy. Both
attempted to explain a worldview rooted in the philosophy of Plato, which eventually reemerged in the early Church as a blend of philosophy and mysticism.[30]

In essence, this religious mysticism or Neoplatonism focused on the influence of
fate on human existence and the twin or dual nature of reality: the physical plane (a
lower form of existence) and the divine reality (a higher form). The higher reality is
linked to intelligence, transforming God into nonpersonal intellect. The lower level
is physical, subject to fate, and thus considered inferior to the higher reality.

27. Trobe, *Magic of Qabalah*, 137.
28. See John Michael Greer, "An Introduction to the *Corpus Hermeticum*," http://www.sacred-texts.com/chr/herm/h-intro.htm (accessed September 4, 2007); Miriam Lichtheim, *Ancient Egyptian Literature*, vol. 1–2 (Berkeley: University of California Press, 1975); Jean-Pierre Mahé, "Hermes Trismegistos" in *The Encyclopedia of Religion*, vol. 6 (New York: Macmillan, 1987); and G. R. S. Mead, trans., "Poemandres, the Shepherd of Men," http://www.sacred-texts.com/chr/herm/hermes1.htm.
29. Greer, "An Introduction to the *Corpus Hermeticum*."
30. The word *Neoplatonism* is a relatively modern term (mid-nineteenth century) created to describe an ancient philosophy. It is used to differentiate between Plato's philosophy and the religion/philosophy blend that developed in Rome and Greece after his death.

Humans, as part of the physical realm, are separated from this ultimate intellect but can ascend through the different levels by magical means and reincarnation, eventually reuniting with the ultimate intelligence in the higher reality. The link between Kabbalah/Qabalah and Neoplatonism is best seen in descriptions of God's nature and imagery of the levels of the cosmos.[31] What is clear is that, somehow, the Torah of the Hellenistic Jews became intertwined with Plato's philosophy, melding into a syncretistic set of mystical beliefs. These beliefs evolved in several different philosophical directions, one of which is the magic-oriented teachings of Qabalah:

> In Hermetic, magickal, Qabalah in contrast, the ten sefirot ("sephiroth") pertain to ten aspects of what could be called the astral or magical world. . . . They are identified with ten grades of magical initiation, the seven planets of traditional astrology (with the lowest sefirah, Malkhut, representing the Earth, and the two highest the fixed stars and the sphere of God) and with a numerological analysis of the numbers one to ten. The twenty-two paths which link the ten sefirot are identified with one of the twenty-two Hebrew letters and twenty-two Major Arcana tarot trumps). Thus, not only each sefirah has a particular archetypal meaning, but each path as well, making thirty-two archetypes altogether. By the proper means therefore it is possible to invoke any of these fundamental essences.[32]

Hermetic Qabalah employs many tools of the occult, such as tarot cards, astrology and numerology, relying upon this information to accomplish good and thus move upward in the realm of the Ten Sefirot. Where Judaic Kabbalah relies upon the study of the text of the Torah and its commentaries to progress in the knowledge of God, Hermetic Qabalah emphasizes magic and magical tools as the primary way to unite with the Godhead.

---

31. Plotinus (c. 220 AD), was a Greek philosopher considered to be the founder of Neoplatonism. He blended the philosophy of Plato with more religious or mystical elements. An analysis of his writings reveals many similarities to the philosophy of Kabbalah. "The world," Plotinus writes, "is only an image of the spiritual world. . . ." See *Select Works of Plotinus* and Joan F. Adkins, "Neoplatonism in Marvell's 'On a Drop of Dew' and 'The Garden,' *The Bulletin of the Rocky Mountain Language Association*, Vol. 28, No. 4 (Dec., 1974), p. 77.
32. M. Alan Kazlev, "Qabalah and Kabbalah," the Hermetic Qabalah Web site, http://www.kheper.net/topics/Hermeticism/Qabalah.htm (accessed May 23, 2007).

Qabalah obsession, study, and practice in the late nineteenth century became the catalyst for the formation and growth of modern Witchcraft, Wicca, and innumerable versions of occult theology. Its principles and methods are incorporated into the magic rituals of Witchcraft and Satanism today.

CHRISTIAN CABALA

The Renaissance saw the birth of yet another version of Kabbalah—this time labeled *Christian Cabala*—a misnomer of eternal proportions. Thought to have originated with the Spaniard Ramon Lull (c. 1230), it is believed that it moved into Europe through the migration of Jewish converts to Christianity. These converts reinterpreted Kabbalistic doctrines from a distinctly Christian perspective, linking Jesus Christ, His atonement, and His resurrection to the Ten Sefirot. Jewish leaders from the Middle Ages clear down through the nineteenth century were outraged by the theft of secret Jewish mysticism, but powerless to stop it. "Its messianic undertones raised hackles, and in the rationalist world of the nineteenth century, many Jewish scholars were plainly embarrassed by this irrational literature."[33]

Christian Cabala differed from Judaic Kabbalah in its analysis of the Tree of Life and the nature of God. Cabalists taught that Jesus Christ, by His atonement and resurrection, replaced the Ten Sefirot as a means of reaching the Ein Sof, who was the immanent deity (close to man), not the transcendent God of Judaic Kabbalah (unknowable). Professor William Varner notes that new meanings were then assigned to the diagram of the Ten Sefirot, which were divided into two segments: three upper and seven lower. The Cabalists connected the last seven sefirot to the lower or earthly world.

---

33. Harvey J. Hames, *Exotericism and Esotericism in Thirteenth Century Kabbalah*, Ben Gurion University http://www.esoteric.msu.edu/VolumeVI/KabbalahHames.htm (accessed May 24, 2007).

THE THREE UPPER SEFIROT IN CHRISTIAN CABALA

Keter: Crown	Represents the *Father*, the name of God, *Ehyeh* ("I am"), was also assigned to this sefira by Paul Ricci.[34]
Hokma: Wisdom	Represents the *Son*, the second person of the Trinity; divine name *Yah(hy)* assigned to this sefira by Ricci; "the masculine sefirot on this side of the schema also served to underscore the identification of *chochmah* as the Son."[35]
Binah: Intelligence or Understanding	Represents the *Holy Spirit of God*. "*Elohim* was assigned to this sefira and emphasized the feminine characteristics of that side of the schema. Thus, the upper three form a triad answering to the Holy Trinity. This use of the upper triad of the sefirotic tree to teach the Trinity was a common denominator among all Christian interpreters of the Cabala."[36]

The esoteric nature of the Ten Sefirot itself left it vulnerable to widespread reinterpretation. This is perhaps the reason medieval rabbis eventually forbade any instruction in it until the age of forty.

The Christian Cabala movement coalesced during the fifteenth century around the figures of Giovanni Pico della Mirandola (b. 1463) and Johann Reuchlin (b. 1455). Mirandola, who became known as Pico, enthusiastically and single-mindedly used Cabala in an effort to support the deity of Jesus Christ. The Church fiercely opposed his endeavors, resulting in debates so heated that they triggered intense interest within European scholarly circles. Pico arranged to have many of the original Cabalistic texts translated into Latin, and his interpretation of the Ten Sefirot would have far-reaching effects on the development of Christian Cabala. "Their focus on 'Divine Names,' practical or magical kabbalah, and the synthesis

---

34. William Varner, "The Christian Use of Jewish Numerology," The Master's Seminary Journal, 52, http://www.tms.edu/tmsj/tmsj8c.pdf (accessed May 24, 2007).
35. Varner, "The Christian Use of Jewish Numerology."
36. Varner, "The Christian Use of Jewish Numerology."

of Christian doctrine with kabalistic philosophy and speculation, became the zeitgeist of the era."[37]

The work of Johann Reuchlin, a devotee of Pico, in his *De Arte Cabalistica* (c. 1517), incorporated Pico's ideas but focused mainly on the names of God and their significance pertaining to the deity of Jesus Christ. According to William Varner:

> Human history, Reuchlin argued, divides into three periods. In the first, a natural period, God revealed Himself to the Patriarchs through the three-lettered name of "Shaddai" (ydv, +*sdy*). In the period of the Torah, He revealed Himself to Moses through the four-lettered name of the Tetragrammaton (hwhy, *yhwh*). In the period of redemption He revealed Himself through five letters: the Tetragrammaton with the addition of the letter *shin*, thus spelling "Yehoshuah" (hvwhy, *yhw+sh*) or "Jesus." Thus Reuchlin's arrangement was able to combine the Jewish belief in three ages (that of the Chaos, that of the Torah, and that of the Messiah) with the tripartite Christian division of a reign of the Father, a reign of the Son, and a reign of the Holy Spirit. [38]

The seventeenth and eighteenth centuries saw the influence of Christian Cabala grow and spread across Europe at a rapid pace. Pico's Latin translations, Reuchlin's logical arguments combined with the influence of Paul Ricci, piqued interest in Christian Cabala within the Jewish community, culminating in the conversion of many Jews:

> During the sixteenth and early seventeenth centuries a wave of conversions to Christianity induced by the Cabala took place among the Jews. . . . Ricci unified the scattered dogmas of the Christian Cabala into an internally consistent system. Elaborate exegetical devices, however, as well as number and letter permutations did not appear in his work. Ricci's system proceeded from Adam's original innocence and knowledge of all ten sefirot, through the Fall and its consequence, the loss of knowledge of the three highest sefirot, to the

---

37. Mark Stavish, "Kabbalah and the Hermetic Tradition," Hermetic.com, http://www.hermetic.com/stavish/essays/kabbalah-hermetic.html (accessed May 24, 2007).
38. Varner, "The Christian Use of Jewish Numerology," 50.

conversion and redemption of man at the second advent of Jesus. The Christian interpretation of Cabala reached its apex of theological sophistication in the writings of Ricci.

Although many other Christians wrote about the Cabala, continuing to the eighteenth century, these three "founders"—Pico, Reuchlin, and Ricci—laid the groundwork for all later Christological speculation on the Cabala.[39]

The teachings of Christian Cabala eventually arrived in Germany and England by way of immigration. Not long after this, the emerging fascination with alchemy and the birth of Theosophy and Rosicrucianism merged with the Hermetic into a formidable, if confusing, magical philosophy.[40]

KABBALAH/CABALA JOINT METHODS OF TORAH INTERPRETATION

Names of God	Some Kabbalists ascribe power to the names of God found both in the Torah and outside the Torah. It is possible for this power to be accessed by man and used by him (much like a magical formula) to accomplish human purposes.
Notarikon	Hebrew letters have a dual purpose: literary and mathematical. This method analyzes the numerical value and placement of letters in verses of the Torah in order to discover a deeper meaning within the text. The letters can be used to produce an acronym (e.g., Cabalists claim the word *amen* is the result of the biblical names of

39. William Varner, "The Christian Use of Jewish Numerology," *The Master's Seminary Journal,* 50, http://www.tms.edu/tmsj/tmsj8c.pdf (accessed May 24, 2007).

40. Alchemy was approached from two different perspectives: The first focused on examining chemical reactions and eventually evolved into the science of chemistry; the second perspective focused on the magical properties of metals in order to turn them into gold and/or discover a method of immortality. This was an occult-influenced alchemy that is still practiced today. For more information, see John H. Lienhard, "No. 76: About Alchemists," the Engines of Our Ingenuity Web site, http://www.uh.edu/engines/epi76.htm; and University of Illinois, "From Alchemy to Chemistry: Five Hundred Years of Rare and Interesting Books," http://www.scs.uiuc.edu/~mainzv/exhibit/.

	God—Adonai Melekh Na'amon, meaning "Lord, faithful King") [41]
Temura	Some Kabbalists practiced different systems of Torah *letter substitution*, much as a child's code would use *A* for *Z* or *B* for *Y*.
Gematria	Another method of Torah interpretation (and one whose Jewish origin some historians discount) analyzes the numeric value of words and compares the sum of each word with its matching counterpart. Lurianic Kabbalah (based on the teachings of Rav Isaac Luria) creates complex numerical formulas that produce "Divine energies that generate cosmic sustenance for all dimensions."[42] Supernatural power is accessed through meditation on these divine names. "According to Reuchlin, the Cabalists constantly experimented with the divine name *YHVH* (**hwhy**) to produce all kinds of secret 'truths.'"[43]

Hollywood Kabbalah

A world phenomenon born of a rock star's need for inner peace, Hollywood Kabbalah began as the philosophical creation of former insurance salesman Shraga Feivel Gruberger, who left his wife and eight children, married his ex-secretary, Karen, and changed his name to Philip Berg. As part of this new beginning, Rabbi Berg did what many rabbis had done before him: he took the essence of traditional Kabbalah and combined it with his thoughts and ideas, producing a New Age version of Kabbalah embraced by Hollywood stars and millions of their fans, and contemptuously dismissed by Jewish leaders across the globe.[44] According to Orthodox

---

41. Israel Regardie, *The Tree of Life: a Study in Magic* (York Beah, ME: Weiser, 2000), 435.
42. Luria, *Kabbalah of Creation*, 46. For more information on Gematria, see *Encyclopedia Judaica* (Philadelphia: Coronet Books, 1994).
43. Varner, "The Christian Use of Jewish Numerology," 53.
44. Robert Eshman, "Center of Controversy," *Jewish Journal* (February 14, 1997), available online at rickross.com, http://www.rickross.com/reference/kabbalah/kabbalah10.html, (accessed May 29, 2007). According to Eshman, Berg's Kabbalah Learning Center (now known as simply the Kabbalah Centre) has also been denounced by the Orthodox rabbinical councils of Queens and Toronto, and by Jerusalem's highest rabbinical court.

Rabbi and Cabala teacher Yitzchok Adlerstein, chairman of Jewish law and ethics at Loyola Law School in Los Angeles, "What the Kabbalah Centre is, is equal parts of nonmystical and traditional Jewish wisdom and one part snake oil and hokum."[45]

The Bergs and their two sons, Michael and Yehuda, now run the Kabbalah Centre in Los Angeles, California (kabbalah.com), along with fifty centers worldwide—a marketing jackpot of blessed water, red string, and baby sheets with Hebrew lettering. John Lawrence Reynolds in his book, *Secret Societies*, observes the modernization and marketing of ancient mysticism:

> Berg and his staff, which included Karen's sons Yehuda and Michael, proved to be brilliant marketers. After serving for two millennia as a mystical solution to the deepest questions of spiritual life, Kabbalah was transformed into a supermarket of pious accoutrements, a Wal-Mart of fashion-of-the-day spiritual trinkets and treatises. By 2005, more than twenty books and CDs . . . had been cranked out. With titles like *God Wears Lipstick,* and a twenty-two-volume version of the Zohar, the collection represented at best a successful marketing exploitation of gullible dilettantes and at worst a mockery of an ancient tradition.[46]

Marketing extravaganza or mystical solution, there is no doubt that Philip Berg's followers revere him—even to the point where they believe he can bring the dead to life.[47] Now virtually worshiped as "the Rav" by thousands of students, Berg is a multimillion-dollar success with the power to influence the world. "His followers have been promised that Kabbalah can find their lost children, cure their illnesses, replenish their pocketbooks, and bring them true love." [48] It is no wonder,

45. Joseph Berger, "A Jewish Madonna? Is That a Mystery?" *New York Times,* June 18, 2004, http://query .nytimes.com/gst/fullpage.html?res=9D07E1D71639F93BA25755C0A9629C8B63&sec=&spon= &pagewanted=2 (accessed June 4, 2008).

46. John Lawrence Reynolds, *Secret Societies: Inside the World's Most Notorious Organizations* (New York: Arcade Publishing, 2006), 134.

47. Mim Udovitch, "The Kabbalah Chronicles: Inside Hollywood's Hottest Cult," *Radar* magazine, June 17, 2005, http://radarmagazine.com/web-only/the-kabbalah-chronicles/2005/06/inside-hollywoods-hottest-cult.php (accessed May 26, 2007).

48. Udovitch, "The Kabbalah Chronicles."

then, that Philip Berg's new version of Kabbalah has spread through Hollywood society like a spiritual virus, infecting celebrities such as Madonna, Gwyneth Paltrow, Demi Moore, Ashton Kutcher, Elizabeth Taylor, Roseanne Barr, and many other high-profile, entertainment-industry personalities.[49]

For his teaching authority (essential for credibility in Kabbalah), Rav Berg claims the blessing of the now-deceased Israeli Rabbis Ashlag and Brandwein (his first wife was Brandwein's niece, Rivkah), but Rabbi Ashlag's grandson and Rabbi Brandwein's son have publicly denied any transfer of rabbinical authority between Berg, Ashlag, and Brandwein.

"There isn't a shred of truth in his claim," says Rabbi Ashlag's grandson with anger. "They are degrading the Zohar."[50]

Rabbi Brandwein's close associate, Baruch Horenchik, went on to say, "He is far removed from Rabbi Brandwein. He is a zero. The Rabbi [Brandwein] never acknowledged him."[51]

The Bergs tried to answer this criticism publicly by sending the online magazine *Radar* copies of correspondence (in Hebrew) between Berg and Brandwein, but *Radar's* examination of the English translations of these letters paints a different picture from the one Philip Berg portrays as fact. The Kabbalah Centre disseminates the information that Rabbi Brandwein acknowledged Philip Berg as his heir, a claim of immense importance in Kabbalah, for historically, without the blessing from a student's rabbi, a student could never inherit legitimate teaching authority. But according to *Radar* magazine, this supposed blessing from Brandwein to Berg is vague and certainly questionable. "The position he [Brandwein] blesses Berg for accepting is most likely an administrative post in America."[52] Brandwein went on

49. The Bergs' Kabbalah Centre works with Madonna via Raising Malawi—a corporation feeding and clothing the poor children of this African country, then raising them on the foundation of Berg's Hollywood Kabbalah. See www.raisingmalawi.org.
50. Aynat Fishbein, "The Cabal of the Kabbalah Centre Exposed: New Relations," *Tel Aviv* magazine, September 1994, rickross.com, http://www.rickross.com/reference/kabbalah/Kabbalah1.html. See also Nadya Labi, "What Profits the Kabbalah?" *Time*, November 24, 1997.
51. Fishbein, "The Cabal of the Kabbalah Centre Exposed."
52. Udovitch, "The Kabbalah Chronicles."

to state that "only Jews can receive" the wisdom of Kabbalah—the traditional Jewish position that Philip Berg and the Kabbalah Centre reject.[53]

In addition to Berg's disputed teaching authority and a doctorate whose source is difficult to trace, there is the constant barrage of spiritual literature flowing from the Centre, whose authorship and intent is unclear. *Radar* notes that literature produced by the Centre is similar to other popular spiritual works and aimed at specific groups of people. "According to an internal marketing memo obtained by *Radar*, the target audience for *True Prosperity*, by Yehuda Berg, is 'Christian, Bible Belt.'"[54] The Kabbalah Centre's response to this was that the Bergs and the Centre would not have authorized such a memo.

David Rowan, in his article "Secrets of a Celebrity Sect," describes an even darker side to Philip Berg's Kabbalah Centres, noting that former Kabbalah followers and their relatives experienced high-pressure sales techniques and personal threats that included a warning that their children "might fall ill unless they donated money; and . . . 'dark forces' would bring them personal tragedy if they ever left."[55] Most disturbing of all, however, is the teaching that people are responsible for all things that happen to them—good or bad—a belief central to Philip Berg's theology.[56] This unbiblical and cruel line of reasoning is reflected in the strange songs that children (products of the Kabbalah Centre's *Spirituality for Kids* classes) sing during Jewish holiday celebrations, such as those conducted on Purim. According to Yossi Halevi of the *Jewish World Review*, Gloria Gaynor's pop megahit "I Will Survive" received a theological makeover courtesy of the Kabbalah Centre:

(Sung to the tune of "I Will Survive")

I was living life alone
with no Zohar in sight

53. Udovitch, "The Kabbalah Chronicles."
54. Udovitch, "The Kabbalah Chronicles."
55. David Rowan, "Secrets of a Celebrity Sect," *Evening Standard*, April 6, 2008, http://www.thisis london.co.uk/news/article-1446749-details/Secrets+of+a+celebrity+sect/article.do, (accessed May 22, 2008).
56. Philip Berg, *Immortality: The Inevitability of Eternal Life* (Los Angeles: Kabbalah Centre, 2000), 205, 225.

Weren't we the ones who brought
all this chaos to our lives. . . .[57]

Jewish Journal reporter David Rowan confirms Berg's teaching that people are responsible for their own pain and suffering, "The centre has also caused outrage by claiming that Jews died in the Holocaust because they had failed to read the Zohar."[58]

A close examination of Philip Berg's theology as set forth in his little-known but most enlightening book, *Immortality*, reveals one of the most important things Rav Berg is trying to achieve in this world—*immortality*; he is working on defeating death—first and foremost, his own.[59] Rav Berg teaches that each of the seventy-two Hebrew names of G-d provides access to the divine light and has supernatural power to change lives.

A Centre teacher chanted before a crowd at a recent meeting, "The technology of the name is going into the stem cells, stimulating the immune system, reducing cellular blockage, back to the condition of receiving light."[60] The Centre teaches that simply looking at the names or chanting them can cause actual cell structure to change. Immortality and the defeat of Satan (chaos) is possible for all to accomplish if they follow Philip Berg's Kabbalah, or as the Centre calls it, "technology for the soul."[61] This "technology" also includes scanning the *Zohar* with your fingertips in order to magically gain something from it; it's not necessary to read *Zohar* to benefit from it.[62] *New York Times* reporter and former Kabbalah Centre student Daphne Merkin investigated Philip Berg's Kabbalah Centre and summed it up as "hokum, a brilliantly shrewd commercial enterprise, playing on the existentially orphaned state . . . of many people today."[63]

57. Yossi Klein Halevi, "Hollywood Goes Kabbalah," *Jewish World Review*, April 30, 2004, http://www.jewishworldview.com/0404/kabbalah_centre.php3 (accessed May 31, 2008).
58. John Sweeney, "Kabbalah Leader's Holocaust 'Slur,'" BBC News, January 9, 2005, http://news.bbc.co.uk/2/hi/in_depth/4158287.stm (accessed May 31, 2008); and Rowan, "Secrets of a Celebrity Sect."
59. Halevi, "Hollywood Goes Kabbalah."
60. Halevi, "Hollywood Goes Kabbalah."
61. Halevi, "Hollywood Goes Kabbalah." See also Daphne Merkin, "In Search of the Skeptical, Hopeful, Mystical Jew That Could Be Me," *New York Times*, April 13, 2008, http://www.nytimes.com/2008/04/13/magazine/13kabbalah-t.html?pagewanted=2&ei=5070&em&en=24423b111f7cd552&ex=1208404800 (accessed June 4, 2008).
62. Merkin, "In Search of the Skeptical, Hopeful, Mystical Jew That Could Be Me."
62. Merkin, "In Search of the Skeptical, Hopeful, Mystical Jew That Could Be Me."

And finally, there is Rabbi Yitzhak Kaduri's warning about Philip Berg to be considered. Kaduri was a Kabbalist rabbi so revered in modern Israel that a simple comment from him is credited with handing the presidency of Israel to Moshe Katsav. "Katsav won a shocking victory after Kaduri said he had a 'vision' that Katsav was favored by the heavens."[64] Rabbi Kaduri pronounced, in language impossible to misinterpret, that Kabbalah is only to be studied by "Jewish men who have completed full study of the Talmud" and that any follower of Berg "is endangering his soul."[65]

Nevertheless, "The Rav" has managed to sell his ideas and products to millions—with the help of his Hollywood friends. When confronted by reporter Dina Rabinovitch on the questionable character behind her Kabbalah beliefs, Madonna told her legions of fans to listen to the message Berg preached and *disregard the messenger*—an answer so illogical that Rabinovitch kept reviewing her notes to make sure Madonna had said it.[66]

Madonna encourages millions of people to accept the message of a man who cannot even prove that he *is* who he says he is—a respected Kabbalist rabbi endowed with teaching authority from a revered line of rabbis.[67] It is like telling a surgeon's patients they must only believe the best of him and allow him to operate—even if he cannot produce his diplomas—or like promoting the showman Professor Harold Hill (from the great musical *The Music Man*), who passed out instruments to all the children, with instructions to use the "Think System"—just "think" the music and it will happen.

Berg apparently wants his students to "think" Kabbalah, and the power and energy will come to them. And, in the end, he may not be so far off the mark, for what the philosophy of Berg cannot supply, the kingdom of the occult stands ready and willing to provide. Berg's teaching method contains a well-known hallmark of the occult: the constant mantra of *open your heart* and *reach for the light*. The only catch

64. Israel Insider staff and partners, "Kabbalist Rabbi Yitzhak Kaduri Dies in Jerusalem," *Israel Insider*, http://web.israelinsider.com/Articles/Culture/7665.htm, January 28, 2006 (accessed May 29, 2007).
65. Eshman, "Center of Controversy." According to Eshman, Berg's Kabbalah Learning Center (now known as simply the Kabbalah Centre) has also been denounced by the Orthodox rabbinical councils of Queens and Toronto, and by Jerusalem's highest rabbinical court.
66. Dina Rabinovitch, "Fallen Idol," *Guardian*, June 22, 2005.
67. Abby Ellin, with special reporting by Adam J. Sacks, "The String That Binds: The Kabbalah Centre Wants Your Heart—And Your Money," *Village Voice*, August 3, 2004, http://www.villagevoice.com/news/0432,ellin,55816.1.html (accessed May 31, 2008).

is that what may come to the Kabbalah searcher is not the light of Yahweh Elohim, but the false light of Lucifer, son of the morning. It is real, but it is far from *right.*

Many people caught in the web of Hollywood Kabbalah maintain that they were drawn to it by its ecumenical nature: a convert can remain a Buddhist or Catholic and still practice Kabbalah.[68] But Philip Berg's new idea of religious tolerance directly contradicts other Kabbalist leaders, including the revered Rabbi Yitzhak Kaduri, who flatly refused to see Madonna on her pilgrimage to Israel. "I don't know her, I don't know of her and I won't see her," Kaduri said, reiterating his position that women and non-Jews should not be taught Kabbalah.[69]

The Hollywood Kabbalah of Rav Berg and his family is a study in contrasts: New Age ideas and thoughts intertwined with the mysticism and tradition of the *Zohar.* Sweeping the globe at an alarming rate, it has now set its sights on the little country of Malawi and the children of the world. The Kabbalah Centre's Spirituality for Kids (SFK) curriculum is being taught to the children in orphanages Madonna built in Malawi and in the Kabbalah Centre's global kids summer camp program, Kids Creating Peace. The intent seems clear: reach as many children as possible, and you create an army of future Kabbalists—a force to be reckoned with. In view of the Bergs' track record, it is an alarming agenda.

Even more disturbing, though, are the personal stories of misuse and abuse so easily found in the history of the Bergs and their Kabbalah Centers.[70] Hollywood celebrities may be protected by their financial assets, but ordinary people feel the power of the cult like influence the Bergs exert. There is no shortage of eyewitness testimony.[71] In this respect, and several others, Hollywood Kabbalah appears to be following the controlling lead of another group that is often accused of being a glamorized moneymaker: Scientology.[72]

The Bergs' appropriation of the word *Kabbalah* infuriates many in the Jewish community, but as with other cultic structures, a healthy measure of fear protects

68. Rabinovitch, "Fallen Idol."
69. "Faith, or Fad?" *The Age,* August 12, 2007, http://www.theage.com.au/articles/2004/08/12/1092102573533.htmlrickross.com, http://www.rickross.com/reference/kabbalah/kabbalah92.html (accessed May 30, 2007).
70. Ellin, "The String That Binds." See also Fishbein, "The Cabal of the Kabbalah Centre Exposed: New Relations," *Tel Aviv Magazine,* September 1994, rickross.com, http://rickross.com/reference/kabbalah/Kabbalah1.html (accessed May 29, 2007).
71. Ellin, "The String That Binds."
72. Richard Behar, "The Thriving Cult of Greed and Power," *Time Magazine,* May 6, 1991.

Hollywood Kabbalah from the censure it would most likely receive without its rich funding and entertainment prestige. A frightening example of this is the experience of Rabbi Abraham Union in 1992. Rabbi Union made the mistake of actively trying to warn the Jewish community about the actions and influence of the Bergs' Los Angeles Kabbalah Learning Centre. He suggested the Rabbinical Council of California send a letter critical of the Kabbalah Centre to all Southern California Rabbis. The next day, Rabbi Union found a severed sheep's head on the doorstep of the Rabbinical Council of California. "Several young men appeared at his home that evening and asked, in Hebrew, "Did you get our message?"[73]

Union said that he was certain the men were from the center. He filed a police report, and detectives visited the Kabbalah Centre. They found no evidence of wrongdoing. Union interpreted the incident as a threat on his life. "Of course, [Rabbi Philip] Berg didn't put it there," he said. "There's no proof anybody from the Kabbalah Centre put it there. But we never sent out the letter." Michael Berg denied any connection between the Kabbalah Centre, the severed sheep's head, and the gang threats.[74]

Although Rav Berg promises the light of Kabbalah to all who pay the hundreds and often thousands of dollars required to learn it, the dark side of the Hollywood Kabbalah sect has been consistently exposed by investigative reporters for more than a decade. It stands in stark contrast to the glitzy image of instant spiritual satisfaction so prevalent in the mainstream media.

CASE STUDY

Raquel Hecker

A woman steps into an unassuming five-story building in midtown Manhattan, strides past a propped-up poster with her image on it, takes an elevator up to the second floor and steps out into a gleaming white chamber with rows of pews decorated in a Greco-Roman motif. In the front of the room, a man leading a service for 200 worshippers glances up from a book.

73. Eshman, "Center of Controversy
74. Eshman, "Center of Controversy."

The entire room inhales at once. One woman's jaw goes slack. Madonna—Esther to her friends here at the Kabbalah Centre—has entered the building.

Back before she was Esther, Madonna was my childhood idol. So naturally I was curious how Kabbalah had inspired her—how she had gone from covering Don McLean to covering the Barry Sisters, as she did this past July, performing at a private party for the head of the Kabbalah Centre, Rabbi Philip Berg. . . .The first time I went to the Kabbalah Centre was for a Friday night Shabbat service. As in any temple, there was an ark, over which stood a sign with the Hebrew name and the astrological symbol of the current month. The place was packed, albeit unevenly. The men were seated throughout the left and center sections, the women squeezed tightly into the right section, except for an empty front row. I slid in there and heard two women by the door whisper and point. Slowly, it dawned on me: I had planted my ***** in the designated celebrity row.

When Madonna walks into the Kabbalah Centre, chairs materialize out of thin air to form a new row in front of the celebrity row. I guess it's seating for those who are famous even among famous people! A bearded man runs over with an electric fan and aims it at Madonna, who is flanked by two thin, attractive women in bad blond wigs. Sitting with one yoga-sculpted leg over the other, Madonna dismisses the man with a wave of her hand and he returns, humbled, to where he was sitting.

The service continues: Rabbis take turns leading prayers, then when they're finished step down off the stage to shake Madonna's hand. The Material Girl herself follows along nonchalantly, mouthing indiscernible nothings to her husband, Guy Ritchie, who's sitting across the room in the men's section. Her daughter, Lourdes, comes over to sit with her mother, then restlessly runs out of the room. Men steal glances at these family interactions, women whisper among themselves. I look too, and I'm both mortified and delighted to learn that if you stare at Madonna for long enough, Madonna will look right back at you.

In the middle of the service, unprompted by the Rabbi, everyone begins to sing, and then shout, a raggedly enthusiastic rendition of L'cah Dodi. When the tempo speeds up, for no apparent reason, everyone shouts in unison, "P'NEI SHABBAT N'KABLAH." The men on the bema hold children in their arms or on their shoulders, and Ritchie, wearing a white Kangol cap as an improvised yarmulke, carries his son, Rocco. The chant continues, and Ritchie and some other men form a sort of conga line, weaving in and out of the room, kids in tow. As they go through the door, the children duck to avoid hitting their heads on the metal frame.

The conga line turns back into the room and the men rush the pulpit along with a few enthusiastic stragglers from the pews. They bang their fists on the stage, chanting, "RABBI SHIMON RABBI." The chant morphs into Rabbi Shimon's full name—Rabbi Shimon bar Yochai—to the tune of "Na Na Hey Hey (Kiss Him Goodbye)." I start to sing along: "Rabbi Shimon/Rabbi Shimon/Rav Shimon bar Yochai." The men pump themselves up until they're red in the face, as though they're rooting for a favorite team. The women gossip among themselves, separated by the aisle from the ruckus.

Rabbi Shimon, the man about whom the men are singing, is said to have written Zohar, the 2nd century mystical document that is now considered Kabbalah's most important text. (These days it also provides the basis for a T-shirt I saw someone wearing at the Centre that reads, I SCANNED ZOHAR WITH ASHTON, a reference to actor and Kabbalah devotee Ashton Kutcher). According to legend, the Aramaic manuscripts were lost for years and discovered by Moses de Leon in the 13th century in a cave in Israel. "Kabbalah," literally "to receive," became an esoteric practice studied only by male Hasidic scholars older than 40, and later, a legitimate element of mainstream Judaism.

Philip Berg (né Feivel Gruberger) is trying to change that. An insurance salesman and Orthodox rabbi from Brooklyn, Berg became involved with Kabbalah when he met the renowned Kabbalist Yehuda Brandwein. He studied with Brandwein in Jerusalem and eventually married Brandwein's niece Rizka. Eight children later, he left her and married Karen Berg, an acquaintance from his days selling insurance. According to Centre literature, she possesses "an extraordinary sixth sense and intuition." She was the one who suggested they start the Kabbalah Centre in Israel in the early '70s, then return to the U.S. in 1981.

When Berg spends Shabbat at the New York Kabbalah Centre, he sits at the head table with Karen on his right and Madonna on his left. On

Madonna's recent Reinvention tour, he personally blessed every stage she danced across. I'm not the only Madonna fan who finds this a little weird: Ritchie reportedly got so sick of one of his wife's Kabbalah advisors during the tour that he threatened to hit him. Ritchie, who in June told the British *Sunday Times* he had "never met a Kabbalist who wasn't a *****" allegedly grabbed the advisor by the scruff of the neck and threatened to "break your face." Madonna pulled her husband away.

When Berg isn't on tour, he conducts services at the New York and Los Angeles Centres and at his home in Queens. He recites the liturgy in the manner of a Las Vegas crooner, pausing after each note and sliding into the next when the mood strikes him. I saw him pause for a full minute one Shabbat in the middle of the blessing over the bread. As I counted off seconds, I heard my stomach grumble. "He doesn't sing the next word unless he really means it," I was told by the woman next to me, a former actress and reiki healer.

Berg's gravitas made enough of an impression on Madonna that she recommended his Centres to Kate Capshaw, Gwyneth Paltrow and Britney Spears, among others. Roseanne lectures at the Centre in L.A. Among the stars seen wearing the Centre's trademark red cotton bracelets around their wrists are Kimora Lee Simmons, Sharon Osbourne, Winona Ryder, David and Victoria Beckham, Sarah Jessica Parker, Diane Keaton, Mick Jagger, Naomi Campbell and Courtney Love. Paris Hilton, Madonna explained in an ABC interview, was brought to the Centre by her parents after they heard about her infamous homemade sex video. Kutcher and Demi Moore, who wore matching his-and-hers baby costumes to the Los Angeles Centre's Purim party in March, are rumored to be planning a Kabbalah wedding in Tel Aviv, according to *MSNBC.com*.

Certainly, Madonna has given Berg's organization a particular sort of credibility. Former presidential candidate Wesley Clarke seemed taken with Kabbalah as he grew interested in Madonna's support; in December of 2003, he gave a speech that included Kabbalah in a list of major world religions such as Christianity, Islam and Judaism. More recently, Lindsay Lohan was reported to be studying in L.A. A source told the tabloid *Globe* that "she thinks it's cool because Madonna and Demi are involved." Britney

Spears, who has expressed her admiration for Madonna in interviews and televised lip-locking, was reportedly planning a Kabbalah-Baptist wedding for the fall. No doubt Madonna was disappointed when it turned out only to be a crabcake/rib fest.

Just as Madonna is followed by celebrities who admire her, those celebrities in turn draw their own admirers. On the Kabbalah Centre web site, a young devotee writes that her interest in the Centre began "the minute I heard that Britney wears the bendel [red bracelet] and that it was also shown in her latest music video, 'Everytime.'"

Back in the '80s, Madonna wannabes only had to dress like her; I should know—I was one. So devoted was my Madonna worship that one night when I was 13 I wore a cross necklace to Hebrew school. (My teacher made me take it off.) At my bat mitzvah, I sang "Material Girl" in lace half-gloves and rubber bracelets.

These days, though, keeping up with Madonna isn't so simple; it's not simply a matter of trading your old black bracelets for new red ones. "I want people to think like me now," Madonna told *20/20* last June. (On the same program, she said that changing her name from Madonna, her mother's name, to that of the Biblical heroine who saved the Jews would separate her from her familial legacy of cancer.) And just how does she think? "When in doubt," she said, "act like God."

After one Shabbat dinner, I share a cab home to Brooklyn with Carmen (not her actual name), a self-proclaimed underemployed writer with frizzy graying hair. Warm and maternal, she launches into a reverie about meditating on the 72 names of God, a Kabbalah Centre ritual. Although the concept of 72 names is a part of traditional Kabbalah, the Centre attributes to it special powers.

"The Hebrew letters have so many layers of meaning," Carmen says. "I mean, numerically they mean things. And they have an energy to them. The first time I meditated on the letters I just felt it so deeply." She hesitates. "I can't explain it. My soul knows it. My brain just isn't there yet."

Her eyes are shining and she's a little drunk. But so am I. "You know, I don't believe what they say on television," she says, referring to gossip about Madonna. "She is not on the celebrity bandwagon. I believe she's really doing it from her heart, sincerely. I will never forget last Sukkot. There she was. It was so wonderful seeing her with her family, standing there in her powder-blue tracksuit under the sukkah. And, you know, I was never that into the music."

Not everyone I met through the Kabbalah Centre feels the same way. I got to know more Kabbalah devotees by volunteering to set up Shabbat dinner, usually as one of 10 women who would meet at the Centre and prepare tables for 200. As we worked, I'd ask the students what drew them to the Centre. Several mentioned Madonna. Each would tell her specific story—an epiphany she had reading one of Berg's books, a serendipitous glimpse of one of the Centre's ads in the paper—then mention Madonna as an afterthought. Few of them gave her sole credit with bringing them around to Kabbalah, but just about everyone mentioned her and most said they had heard about it in the first place because of her. Only one credited her without hesitation. "I saw how much she had transformed because of Kabbalah," she said, "and I thought, well, if it worked for her . . ."

One evening, when I had just reported for duty, another volunteer asked me, "Do you have your tickets yet?"

"Huh?"

"Your Madonna tickets!" she exclaimed. "If you buy them from the Centre they are the best seats! And all the proceeds go to the Spirituality for Kids program!" The royalties from Madonna's children's books go to the same fund, which was used to help purchase the former Atkins headquarters for the Kabbalah Grammar School for Children. According to WABC, Madonna spent a total of $22 million on the school, which will open its doors in 2005—but only to pupils whose parents are both Kabbalists. Spirituality for Kids is Madonna's pet project, and she is more than willing to bankroll the K school. (According to Britain's tabloid *The Sun*, this past September Madonna asked for an itemization of exactly how her money was being spent, the implication being that not all of it was going to the kids.)

During another dinner, I sat awkwardly amidst a group of 20-somethings who were discussing in awed tones a Centre organized trip to Israel. Part of their enthusiasm seemed to come from the presence on the trip of

Madonna herself. She may, they said, have it filmed for the documentary she's making with director Jonas Akerlund, which is being billed as the sequel to *Truth or Dare*. A young gay man explained to me that the trip was very special because it would take place over Rosh Hashanah. He then proceeded to tell me how he found Kabbalah. "I had heard about it in the media and I was looking for a book on it in Barnes & Noble," he said. "I found it in the Jewish section and I left right away—I'm not Jewish." (He's Episcopalian, he told me.) "But then I was back in Barnes & Noble and I was looking in the spirituality section and I turned around and there it was—a book on Kabbalah. So I figured, what the hell?" He can hardly wait to go to Israel. Hugh Jackman was at one point rumored to be joining the pilgrimage as were fashionista Donna Karan and former Donald Trump's ex, Marla Maples. (It was during the trip that Madonna told fellow Kabbalists she "was a bit hesitant to come here [to Israel] because of the terror attacks . . . I realize now it's no more dangerous here than it is in New York.")

After the meal, everyone gathered around the Rav's table and sang songs in Hebrew. A young, pretty woman who was standing on a chair to see over the crowd was wearing the same Kangol cap that Guy Ritchie wore. I wonder if she's searching for Madonna.

Celebrity Kabbalah followers like Elizabeth Taylor get private tutoring in their mansions. "There's no set charge, just donations," said one student. But the typical donation is $200 to $300 an hour, and students can only serve kosher food.

For those of us still awaiting our 15 minutes of fame, there's Zohar class, weekdays at 7 p.m. with about 20 fellow students. The classrooms are set up cabaret style, with about 20 small tables covered with pastel tablecloths, platters of fruit, a pitcher of lemonade and a selection of rocks and shells. A camera in the back of the room broadcasts the class on the Internet. The teacher lectures haltingly, the way Berg chants prayers.

"During the week ahead we will want to bad-mouth others," my teacher told a class one Thursday night. "Miriam got leprosy the second she bad-mouthed Moses." Pause. "What is leprosy?"

No one says anything.

"Leprosy is when on your skin there's a big stain, like barley. Every time you speak lashon hara"—talking about someone behind his back—"you might get one."

There are other lessons, too. "Satan makes us feel like we could put things off," the teacher says. "This week, work on your sense of urgency to do things. For example, 'I want to buy a Zohar, but maybe in two weeks'— then it will never happen!"

The Kabbalah Centre loves its product placement. During Shabbat services, one of the rabbis instructed the congregation to drink $3.80, 1.5 liter bottles of Kabbalah water even as he too drinks from a bottle by his side. According to the Rav, the process of making the Kabbalah water is "more complicated than that of making Coca-Cola."

In the lobby you can buy a single red string that has been blessed at Rachel's tomb in Jerusalem for $8.50, or a yard's worth for $26. I opt for the inexpensive option, which is packaged in a card that says "I love you" on the outside and "But not everyone else does" on the inside. Thesmokinggun.com reported that the U.S. Patent Office rejected the Centre's request for a patent on bendels, so they're not exclusive to the lobby. Next season they'll be sold with a Kabbalah candle at Bergdorfs, Barneys NY and Neiman Marcus.

As I leave class with another student, whom I'll call Jane, we walk past posters advertising a few of the Centre's other classes—"How to Find Your Soulmate," "12 Steps to Everlasting Love"—with stock photos of couples kissing and kids on swings. Jane tells me that she works in public relations and that "it's not very Kabbalistic." We walk past piles of tapes for sale on "Divine Sex" and "Kabbalistic Astrology." Over the speakers, I hear "Ray of Light."

Later, Jane and I are folding napkins into origami shapes to add a French-restaurant feel to the next evening's Shabbat dinner. She tells me her parents were originally Methodist but converted to Catholicism "because they moved to a new house that happened to be closer to the Catholic church." They were baptized, renewed their vows, the whole works. Jane has been fishing for religion since her teens; besides attending Methodist and Catholic churches with her parents, she's gone to Pentacostal [*sic*] and Jehovah's Witness services as well. Out of everything she's tried, she says she likes the Kabbalah Centre best: The principles taught in the classes are easy to apply, especially the notion that when you help others you really help yourself.

The next time I go to the Centre, I see a group of lithe, tan people walking away from the building, cameras hanging from their necks. They're dressed too hip to be tourists and too colorful to be Kabbalists, who favor white. I realize first that they're paparazzi and then that I've just missed Madonna.

"Shabbat shalom!" my friend cries. Raised a good Christian, that's the extent of his Hebrew, and he uses it every chance he gets. He has tickets to the Reinvention Tour in New Jersey, but in the nosebleed seats. In an effort to see Madonna up close, he accompanies me to services one night.

Upstairs, after I've split off into the women's section, it takes me a while to spot him. I'm not used to seeing him in a white yarmulke.

The service begins. I watch the door for Madonna, and I can see him doing the same thing over on the other side.

Nothing.

I know her tour is still in town, so I hold out hope. But, after more nothing, I can see my friend glance over at me, confused.

Madonna doesn't show.

He's disappointed. I can't find a way to tell him that I'm secretly relieved. From the cheap seats, he won't be as disillusioned as I am at how my former idol is no longer the unabashedly confident superwoman I so admired. Plenty of people are still following her, but look what she's following. Maybe once the fad has run its course she will reinvent herself as the wayward Catholic iconoclast I knew and loved.

My friend and I spend the rest of the night at a Chinese restaurant drinking tea, reading fortune cookies, and commiserating about how we missed Madonna over steamed pork buns. [75]

It is perhaps one of the saddest commentaries on humanity that a single individual can long so much for the truth and yet refuse to see it. Madonna rejected

75. Raquel Hecker, "Inside the Kabbalah Center: The Most Star-Studded Scene Since Studio 54," *Heeb* magazine, Issue #7, http://www.heebmagazine.com/articles/view/45. ***** denote expletives.

the Jesus Christ of the Bible, and her eternity now rests on the word of the Bergs, who interpret many of the *Zohar's* stories as actual fact (and base much of their teaching on them), while the testimonies of Moses de Leon's contemporaries tell a far different tale. "It can at least be said that by some of his contemporaries, Moses de Leon was already described as the author of the Zohar."[76] And if Moses de Leon is the author, then all the *Zohar* tales of Simeon ben Yohai and his visits from the prophet Elijah now fall into the realm of fiction.

Hollywood Kabbalah	The Bible
The human soul is the essence of God. Man can become like God.	**There is only one God, and people cannot become like Him.** "Before Me there was no God formed, nor shall there be after Me." (Isa. 43:10)
"I often ask people the meaning of the biblical passage that says that man was created in God's image. There aren't many ways to explain it, except in that simplest form. It means that every one of us is built with the essence of God. Our soul is the essence of God, and that means that every single one of us has the potential to become like God and to heal, to bless, to do almost everything that God can do."[77]—Michael Berg	**Lucifer was exiled from heaven and condemned to eternal punishment for daring to think he could be like God.** "How you are fallen from heaven, O Lucifer, son of the morning! How you are cut down to the ground, you who weakened the nations! For you have said in your heart: 'I will ascend into heaven, I will exalt my throne above the stars of God; I will also sit on the mount of the congregation on the farthest sides of the north; I will ascend above the heights of the clouds, I will be like the Most High.'" (Isa. 14:12–14)

76. Scholem, Major Trends in Jewish Mysticism, 187.
77. Rebecca Phillips, "Kabbalah for Everyone," Beliefnet, interview with Michael Berg (2007), http://www.beliefnet.com/story/158/story_15886_1.html (accessed May 28, 2007).

Hollywood Kabbalah	The Bible
Man can save himself; humans can end death by working together to create a better world. "Kabbalah teaches that we are not waiting for a personal savior to redeem us: It's our job, every single one of us and together as a collective, to bring about a world where maybe even, as God says in the Bible, it will be possible that death will end. And I do believe that's a possibility, as have kabbalists and sages for thousands of years."[78]—Michael Berg	God says man needs a Savior. "I, even I, am the Lord, and besides Me there is no savior." (Isa. 43:11) "All we like sheep have gone astray; we have turned, every one, to his own way; and the Lord has laid on Him the iniquity of us all." (Isa. 53:6) "Joseph, son of David, do not be afraid to take to you Mary your wife, for that which is conceived in her is of the Holy Spirit. And she will bring forth a Son, and you shall call His name Jesus, for He will save His people from their sins." (Matt. 1:20–21) Luke 2:10–12; 1 Cor. 15:21–22 Only God can end death. "I am He who lives, and was dead, and behold, I am alive forevermore. Amen. And I have the keys of Hades and of Death." (Rev. 1:18)
Ego, not sin, is responsible for the pain and suffering in the world. It separates humans from God. Man can defeat it.	Sin, not ego, separates man from God. "Then the Lord God said, "Behold, the man has become like one of Us, to

78. Phillips, "Kabbalah for Everyone."

Hollywood Kabbalah	The Bible
"The ego is the main thing within us that is not God; it is the strongest barrier between ourselves and God. In simple terms, when we break down the ego, we become like God."[79]—Michael Berg	know good and evil. And now, lest he put out his hand and take also of the tree of life, and eat, and live forever"——therefore the Lord God sent him out of the garden of Eden to till the ground from which he was taken. So He drove out the man." (Gen. 3:22–24) "For the wages of sin is death, but the gift of God is eternal life in Christ Jesus our Lord." (Rom. 6:23) **Only Jesus can remove the barrier between God and man.** "And He bore the sin of many, and made intercession for the transgressors." (Isa. 53:12) John 1:29–30; Rom. 8:1–3
Jesus was a prophet and Kabbalist "[Jesus, Buddha, and Mohammed were] Prophets AND Kabbalists, yes."[80]—Yehuda Berg **Jesus is a channel or force.**	**Jesus is the Son of God.** "Therefore the Lord Himself will give you a sign: Behold, the virgin shall conceive and bear a Son, and shall call His name Immanuel." (Isa. 7:14)

79. Phillips, "Kabbalah for Everyone."
80. *USA Today,* "Kabbalah Expert: Yehuda Berg," Talk Today, May 27, 2007, http://cgi1.usatoday.com/mchat/20040526006/tscript.htm (accessed May 30, 2007).
81. *USA Today,* "Kabbalah Expert: Yehuda Berg."

Hollywood Kabbalah	The Bible
"Use Jesus as a catalyst in carrying out the spiritual meaning in the Old Testament."[81]—Yehuda Berg	"Joseph, son of David, do not be afraid to take to you Mary your wife, for that which is conceived in her is of the Holy Spirit. And she will bring forth a Son, and you shall call His name Jesus, for He will save His people from their sins." So all this was done that it might be fulfilled which was spoken by the Lord through the prophet, saying: "Behold, the virgin shall be with child, and bear a Son, and they shall call His name Immanuel," which is translated, "God with us." (Matt. 1:20–23)
Heaven and hell are relative. **The devil is not personal—it is a negative cosmic force.** "We believe in a heaven and a hell however we believe that it can be achieved in this world not just afterwards. We don't call it a devil but we do believe there is a power that creates negativity to bring us down."[82]—Yehuda Berg	**Heaven and hell are physical places where people go *after* death.** *Heaven*—Jesus said, "In my Father's house are many rooms; if it were not so, I would have told you. I am going there to prepare a place for you. And if I go and prepare a place for you, I will come back and take you to be with me that you also may be where I am." (John 14:2–3 NIV) *Hell*—Jesus said, "The rich man also died and was buried. And being in torments in Hades, he lifted up his eyes and saw Abraham afar off, and

82. *USA Today,* "Kabbalah Expert: Yehuda Berg."

Hollywood Kabbalah	The Bible
	Lazarus in his bosom. Then he cried and said, 'Father Abraham, have mercy on me, and send Lazarus that he may dip the tip of his finger in water and cool my tongue; for I am tormented in this flame.'" (Luke 16:22–24) **Satan is Lucifer, an angel of great power who rebelled against God. He is *personal* evil.** Now there was a day when the sons of God came to present themselves before the Lord, and Satan also came among them. And the Lord said to Satan, "From where do you come?" So Satan answered the Lord and said, "From going to and fro on the earth, and from walking back and forth on it." (Job 1:6–7) **Satan works to destroy human beings.** "Be sober, be vigilant; because your adversary the devil walks about like a roaring lion, seeking whom he may devour." (1 Peter 5:8)
The Law of Cause and Effect: **People are responsible for everything that happens to them in life—bad things and good things (e.g., the Jews were responsible for the Holocaust).**	**God controls the circumstances of life—He chooses to bless people, discipline them, or allow evil to affect their lives.** "The word of the Lord came again to

Hollywood Kabbalah	The Bible
"No longer are we to consider our-selves victims. From this point onward we must accept respon-sibility for the rotten stuff that happens in our lives. We must admit that we are the cause."—Yehuda Berg[83]	me, saying: 'Son of man, when a land sins against Me by persistent unfaith-fulness, I will stretch out My hand against it; I will cut off its supply of bread, send famine on it, and cut off man and beast from it.'" (Ezek. 12–14)
"All of the negative traist that you spot in others are merely a reflection of your own negative traits. Only by fixing yourself can you change others."—Yehuda Berg[84]	"So the Lord said to him, 'Who has made man's mouth? Or who makes the mute, the deaf, the seeing, or the blind? Have not I, the Lord?'" (Ex. 4:11)

Job 1:21; John 9:1–4 |
| **Evolving spiritually through the process of reincarnation will eventually connect people to God and transform the world by ending suffering and death.** | **Reincarnation is Hindu theology, the foundation of New Age beliefs. Man is born once, dies once, and is resurrected once to judgment.** |
| "Kabbalah teaches . . . that Adam himself was the repository of all the souls that would ever exist on earth itself. His own sould was thus infinitely divisible. When Adam sinned in Eden his vessel was shattered, and his corpor-eal soul was fragmented into what Kabbalists call "sparks"—each spark as unique as the double helix of DNA that determines the char- | "And as it is appointed for men to die once, but after this the judgment, so Christ was offered once to bear the sins of many." (Heb. 9:27–28)

Jesus Christ gives the only victory over sin and death.

"'Death is swallowed up in victory.' 'O Death, where is your sting? O Hades, |

---

83. Yehuda Berg, *The Power of Kabbalah* (San Diego: Jodere Group, 2002), 220.
84. Berg, *The Power of Kabbalah*, 223.

Hollywood Kabbalah	The Bible
acteristics of each individual. In this way the earth was sown with souls while millions more lay in meta-physical silos waiting to being the begin the cycle of birth, life, death, and rebirth."[85]—Philip Berg	where is your victory?' The sting of death is sin, and the strength of sin is the law. But thanks be to God, who gives us the victory through our Lord Jesus Christ." (1 Cor. 15:54–57)
"One of the things that Kabbalah teaches is that the contemporary world filled with pain and suffering is not the world as it is meant to be. As we continue to evolve spiritually, connecting with our soul and be-coming more like God, we can transform this world. We can end the pain and suffering that we take as a given.	"And the God of peace will crush Satan under your feet shortly." (Rom. 16:20)
"There is another concept that when you first hear it, may sound new, but it appears in the Bible. The Bible says there will come a time when death literally will be swallowed up, meaning there will be an end to death."[86] —Michael Berg	1 Cor. 15:21–22; Rom. 6:23

New Age Themes

The similarities between Kabbalah and New Age ideas are evident and difficult to discount. Both encourage the individual to accept the value of symbolic interpretation in lieu of historical interpretation, and both emphasize the mystical instead of the evidential. Kabbalah places a spark of the divine in everyone and everything; New Age teaches the divinity of all.

85. Philip Berg, *Wheels of a Soul: Reincarnation and Kabbalah* (Los Angeles: Kabbalah, 2005), 43.
86. Phillips, "Kabbalah for Everyone."

"Our being and God's being are one. . . . You are the Self, created from the same spirit that in infinite form is called God."[87] —Deepak Chopra

"Your mind and mine can unite in shining your ego away, releasing the strength of God into everything you think and do."—*A Course in Miracles*[88]

"Jesus was perfect humanity. Christ was the God idea in Him. . . . The Christ is in every human being, and so are the psychic forces which were used by Jesus."—A demon's theology, transcribed during a séance (documented by Sir Arthur Conan Doyle).[89]

Narrowly defined, modern New Age teachings can be linked to the transplantation of Hindu philosophy through the Theosophical Society founded by Helena Blavatsky in the latter part of the nineteenth century in the United States, and to the psychic medium Edgar Cayce, whose prophecies scholars now consider foundational to its birth and development.[90] Madame Blavatsky, as she was known, promoted Spiritism, séances, and basic Hindu philosophy while manifesting a distinct antagonism to biblical Christianity.[91]

In the final conflict between religions, Hinduism and Christianity will offer the only viable options in that Hinduism *absorbs* all religious systems, and Christianity *excludes* all others, maintaining the supremacy of the claims of Jesus Christ.[92]

SCRIPTURAL RESPONSE

One thing is certain in the uncertain world of Kabbalah: it has long been associated with the mystery and power inextricably linked to the world of the occult. And the foundation of the occult is the doctrine of demons.

---

87. Deepak Chopra, *The Path to Love: Spiritual Strategies for Healing* (New York: Three Rivers Press, 1998), 11, 13.

88. Miracle Distribution Center, *A Course in Miracles*, comb. vol. (Glen Ellen, CA: Foundation for Inner Peace, 1987), 64. Often linked to Marianne Williamson, a New Age teacher with ties to Oprah Winfrey. For more information, see Kjos Ministries, http://www.crossroad.to/articles2/007/smith-oprah.htm (accessed June 4, 2008).

89. Arthur Conan Doyle, *Wanderings of a Spiritist* (New York: George H. Doran, 1921), 13, 16, 26.

90. J. Gordon Melton, "Edgar Cayce and Reincarnation: Past Life Readings as Religious Symbology," California Institute of Integral Studies, http://www.ciis.edu/cayce/melton.html (accessed June 1, 2007; page no longer available).

91. Adapted from Martin, *The Kingdom of the Cults*, 408.

92. C. S. Lewis is thought to have commented on this. See Martin, *The Kingdom of the Cults*, 408.

In 1676, Thomas Ady, an English physician and skeptic, wrote and published *The Doctrine of Devils*, in which he recorded for posterity a foundational belief of the Nicolaitans, a group made infamous in God's warning to the Churches in Revelation 2:6, 15: "But you have this in your favor: You hate the practices of the Nicolaitans, which I also hate. . . .Likewise you also have those who hold to the teaching of the Nicolaitans. Repent therefore! Otherwise, I will soon come to you and will fight against them with the sword of my mouth" (NIV). Thomas Ady left one of the few historical notations detailing the close link between the theology of the Nicolaitans and the theology of Kabbalah:

> Christ hath still enemies, and several armies of them that march up to confront him. . . . and with the Nicholaitans they account him but a Quality, an Ignis fatuus [fool's light], a meer illusion, a light within them, which is not much better than an Allegory, or rather worse.[93]

Whether examining Hollywood Kabbalah, Kabbalistic principles, or the teachings behind the New Age, a troubling pattern of theology emerges that can only have been crafted by the same intelligence—a being with one goal—the deception and destruction of mankind.

A brief analysis of some Kabbalah "wisdom" and review of the theology of Edgar Cayce—the medium known as the Sleeping Prophet, who channeled theology, prescribed medical treatments, and healed people, all while in a deep trance—reveals disturbingly similar doctrine. Both Kabbalah theology and Cayce theology teach that God is an impersonal force, a consciousness. Cayce says the Trinity is three-dimensional here on earth; possibly eight-dimensional somewhere else. Kabbalah outlines a ten-dimensional universe through its Ten Sefirot or Tree of Life.

In the world of Edgar Cayce's New Age spirituality, the Lord Jesus Christ is part of a cyclic reincarnation. "First, in the beginning, of course (as Adam or Amilius); then as Enoch, Melchizedek, in the perfection. Then in the earth as Joseph, Joshua,

---

93. Thomas Ady, *The Doctrine of Devils* (Cornell University Library, 1676), http://racerel.library.cornell.edu: 8090/Dienst/UI/1.0/Display/cul.witch/003?abstract=&pages=4 (accessed June 12, 2007).

Jeshua, Jesus."[94] First he was Adam . . . who sinned. This is the old idea that the Christ-consciousness is reincarnated in the new body, and that each one of these persons was actually Christ in another age. Kabbalah labels Jesus a Kabbalist, and as such He was subject to personal reincarnation (not collective). New Age theology, like some forms of Kabbalah, also places its hope in the foundational principle of karma—what goes around comes around—reincarnation and the random power of the "universe" will balance the scales of justice.

This idea of cyclic reincarnation is thousands of years old, dating historically to the Hindu religion as seen in the Wheel of Life. It was this endless cycle of birth, death, and rebirth that eventually drove the Buddha to find another way to live and believe, a pathway to *enlightenment* that would point the way out of the endless cycle of the Hindu Wheel.

Hollywood Kabbalah, Cayce, Hinduism, and Buddhism all deny a need for salvation and rely on reincarnation to resolve "negativity" in mankind, a negativity that cosmically combines and builds, causing bad things to happen to good people. There is no original sin. Kabbalah emphasizes that God is *unknowable* (transcendent), and all life holds a spark of the divine light within it; Cayce and New Age theology teach that God is an impersonal cosmic force and there is a spark of the divine in all things. Both teach human beings can become *like God,* and both Kabbalah and Cayce emphasize that humans are capable of saving themselves and the world from negative forces (never sin).

It is important to note, however, that there was a time when Kabbalah *did* acknowledge original sin and discuss it in detail as evidenced in the *Sefer Yetzirah* and *Sefer Bahir* texts. But in the thirteenth century, Moses de Leon chose a different path from that of his fellow Kabbalists when he decided to either avoid the subject of original sin or ignore it. Gershom Scholem traced modern-day Kabbalah's denial of original sin back to its source—Moses de Leon's *Zohar:*

"I have said that the mystics were deeply concerned with the problem of sin and, especially, with the nature and meaning of Adam's fall, and that this

---

94. Edgar Cayce and Jeffrey Furst, *Edgar Cayce's Story of Jesus* (New York: Berkley, 1976), 73. The question put to Cayce was, "Please list the names of the incarnations of the Christ, as Jesus, indicating where the development of the man Jesus began." Each person consulting Cayce was given a number (ex. this reading was given for person #5749) followed by a second number that indicated how many readings a person had been given. (ex. 5749-14).

problem was amply discussed in Kabbalistic literature. This is true with but one exception, that of the Zohar. Whilst the Kabbalists of Gerona deal at length with this subject, and also some of Moses de Leon's circle seems to display a predilection for it, passages referring to the question of original sin are scanty in the Zohar, and especially in its main parts. Moreover, these passages are written with a restraint which cannot be said to have been exercised by the author in regard to the other fundamental doctrines of the Kabbalah. The meager treatment of the subject in the Zohar is also in sharp contrast with the profusion with which the problem was discussed in the contemporary Kabbalistical work *Ma'arekhet Ha-Elohut,* 'The Order of the God-head.' This reticence is not accidental; it is evident that the author of the Zohar considered the subject as extremely dangerous, as it touched the great question, where and how the unity of God's life has been disturbed and whence comes the breach which is now manifest in the whole universe."[95]

And now it is the *Zohar* that has become the strongest part of the foundation of modern-day Kabbalah.

Reincarnation

The gospel of the second chance, or reincarnation, as it has come to be known, is an ancient theology conceived by man in an attempt to escape the judgment of God. A distorted doctrine of sin replaces biblical truth. In reincarnation, people are perfected and sanctified by progressive cycles of rebirth; therefore, there is no need for positive redemption through faith in the Lord Jesus. Sin is not dealt with once and for all on the Cross, as Hebrews reveals: *Christ has, by one sacrifice, forever sanctified* (10:14). But if there is no sin, there can be no judgment; and without judgment, there is no need for a savior.

This view became widely popular in America during the early twentieth century, due largely to the efforts of Charles and Myrtle Fillmore, who founded the Unity School of Christianity in 1889. In a clever philosophical twist, the Fillmores adapted the unpalatable Hindu form of reincarnation called *transmigration* (humans coming back in a animal form), to one of rebirth only in *human* form. In the process, they set forth a series of reasons why reincarnation was viable:

95. Scholem, *Major Trends in Jewish Mysticism,* 231–32.

1. *There are persons, places, and experiences that people encounter that make them feel as if they have already been there—the recurring experience known as déjà vu.*

People remember seeing a specific scene or talking to a specific person about a particular topic, even though in reality they are experiencing this scene or conversation for the first time. The conclusion inevitably drawn by many is that they *did* actually experience it in another life.

The problem with this scenario is that psychologists confirm that the subconscious mind records everything you see, and almost everything you hear. You record all of these things, although consciously you are not aware of it. Later on, these fragments of information are associated with something similar to it; you connect the two, and immediately an image pops into your conscious mind with the thought, *I have been here before.*[96] There are reasons why you think you think you were there, but in reality, you were not. Déjà vu is one of the most common occurrences in psychological studies.

2. *All men are not born equal in regard to station in life, opportunity, or health. Some people are born blind and deaf; if God is just, He cannot allow these things to happen to innocent people. Reincarnation is the only evidence, then, of God being perfectly just to all men.*

The root of this teaching is essentially an attempt to solve the problem of evil: all the injustices in the world can only be resolved by cyclic reincarnation, which will give everyone a fair shake in the end. But God does not have to embrace reincarnation to be just: He can be perfectly fair without authorizing reincarnation. The Bible teaches that there are people in this world who are what they *are* because God permitted it to be so. It was not a judgment based on their past lives—it happened intentionally for God's own purposes. "Who has made man's mouth? Or who makes the mute, the deaf, the seeing, or the blind? Have not I, the LORD?" (Ex. 4:11)

During His ministry, Jesus revealed an important truth about this to His disciples. "Now as Jesus passed by, He saw a man who was blind from birth. And His disciples asked Him, saying, 'Rabbi, who sinned, this man or his parents, that he was born blind?' Jesus answered, 'Neither this man nor his parents sinned, but that the works of God should be revealed in him'" (John 9:1–3). It was not the man's

---

96. See Walter Martin *Reincarnation* (CD/audiotape), www.waltermartin.com.

fault, and it was not his parents' fault—this man was blind in order that the purpose of God might be accomplished.

God does not have to resort to reincarnation to right the wrongs of the world. The wrongs of the world are not God's fault. Sin came about as rebellion by choice through freedom: first of angels and then of men—the freedom of will and choice. God cannot be held accountable for the fact that free will was exercised. He can only be held accountable for creating the capacity to choose, and that is not a crime. He does not have to adjust it all by reincarnation. He says He intends to adjust it another way, by the gospel of reconciliation, and by the promise (Gen. 22:17). "Shall not the Judge of all the earth do right?" (Gen. 18:25). And finally, "He has appointed a day on which He will judge the world in righteousness by the Man whom He has ordained. He has given assurance of this to all by raising Him from the dead" (Acts 17:31).

3. There are unfinished thoughts and unfinished works in everyone's experience. God would be unjust unless He permitted us the capacity to finally finish everything and to finally bring all things to their conclusion.

The Scripture gives us ample evidence that man ceases functioning as an organism when he dies, and Ecclesiastes 3 reminds us that in that day his thoughts and his works perish. God puts a period at the death of the body to whatever that person accomplished in his or her life, and Scripture says it is given to all men first to die and after this, the judgment (Heb. 9:27). Jesus discussed the inequities of life, the cause and effect of human choice, and the inevitability of death and consequences in His parable of Lazarus and the rich man:

There was a certain rich man who was clothed in purple and fine linen and fared sumptuously every day. But there was a certain beggar named Lazarus, full of sores, who was laid at his gate, desiring to be fed with the crumbs which fell from the rich man's table. Moreover the dogs came and licked his sores. So it was that the beggar died, and was carried by the angels to Abraham's bosom. The rich man also died and was buried. And being in torments in Hades, he lifted up his eyes and saw Abraham afar off, and Lazarus in his bosom.

Then he cried and said, "Father Abraham, have mercy on me, and send

Lazarus that he may dip the tip of his finger in water and cool my tongue; for I am tormented in this flame." But Abraham said, "Son, remember that in your lifetime you received your good things, and likewise Lazarus evil things; but now he is comforted and you are tormented. And besides all this, between us and you there is a great gulf fixed, so that those who want to pass from here to you cannot, nor can those from there pass to us."

Then he said, "I beg you therefore, father, that you would send him to my father's house, for I have five brothers, that he may testify to them, lest they also come to this place of torment." Abraham said to him, "They have Moses and the prophets; let them hear them." And he said, "No, father Abraham; but if one goes to them from the dead, they will repent." But he said to him, "If they do not hear Moses and the prophets, neither will they be persuaded though one rise from the dead." (Luke 16:19–31)

The Bible is clear on life, death, and judgment. The argument of *unfinished business* cannot be sustained, because the evidence does not warrant it.

4. *There are many documented and verified cases of people recounting their previous lives in detail, recorded in the files of reputable professional hypnotists, psychologists, and research organizations. These cases prove reincarnation.*

It is true that some of these cases seem irrefutable; however, the solution to this problem lies with an intelligent, supernatural being that has lived through every age of man. He has lived through all human generations, and he knows minute details of human lives. It would not be difficult for him to inform someone in this generation about something that happened four generations in the past, and then encourage that individual to research the information for accuracy. Eventually, the person would arrive at the mistaken conclusion that he actually lived in that generation, when the truth is that *Satan himself* lived in that generation. He wants people to believe in past lives so they accept reincarnation rather than the Word of God.

This is Satan's precision plan; he makes information available for people to discover, confirm, and declare, "I have lived before!" The biblical fact of evil provides a second, malevolent explanation of reincarnation memories: *Satan* is the one who lived before, and he reveals the information for a purpose.

Is that purpose to produce an evangelical Christian? To create a winner of souls? To send people out into the world to reconcile others to Christ?

No. People involved in reincarnation are not evangelists trying to win the world for God. They do not believe "the wages of sin is death" (Rom. 6:23); they believe the old maxim that says, "If at first you don't succeed, try, try again." Failure in life brings the sentence of karma: continuous, cyclic reincarnation. It is the merciless law that what you sow in your old life, you will repeatedly reap in the new one— in *exact* proportion to the crime or kindness—and reincarnation will continue until perfection is accomplished. This is not biblical theology. This is the consummate con game set up to divert people from the gospel of Christ to the *gospel of the second chance*: reincarnation.

The Personality of God

Both Kabbalah and the New Age movement deny a personal God. He does not have a personality; He is an impersonal force permeating all things. But the Bible says the exact opposite:

- God remembers (Exodus 2:24; Ps. 78:39; Rev. 18:5).

- God speaks (Ex. 3:12; Jer. 21:11; Romans 9:14–15).

- God hears, sees, and creates (Gen. 1; 6:5; 21:17; Ex. 2:24).

- God knows (Ps. 44:21; Luke 16:15; Acts 15:8).

- God is a personal spirit (Isa. 63:10; Luke 10:21; John 4:24).

- God has a will, and He will judge the world (Matt. 6:10; Luke 11:31–32; 2 Cor. 5:10).

Reincarnation and the Bible

Some believers in reincarnation try to argue for reincarnation as a biblical doctrine, using the example of Matthew 11:13–14: "For all the prophets and the law prophesied until John. And if you are willing to receive it, he is Elijah who is to come." But Luke 1:17 clarifies exactly what Jesus meant in these comments: "He will also go before Him in the spirit and power of Elijah, 'to turn the hearts of the fathers to the children,' and the disobedient to the wisdom of the just, to make ready a people prepared for the Lord." John the Baptist was a prophet of God who went forth in the *spirit and power* of Elijah. He was not Elijah reincarnated. John the Baptist himself denied that he was Elijah:

> Now this is the testimony of John, when the Jews sent priests and Levites from Jerusalem to ask him, "Who are you?"
>   He confessed, and did not deny, but confessed, "I am not the Christ."
>   And they asked him, "What then? Are you Elijah?"
>   He said, "I am not."
>   "Are you the Prophet?"
>   And he answered, "No." (John 1:19–21)

And the distinctness between John and Elijah is shown in Matthew 16:13–17:

> When Jesus came into the region of Caesarea Philippi, He asked His disciples, saying, "Who do men say that I, the Son of Man, am?"
>   So they said, "Some say John the Baptist, some Elijah, and others Jeremiah or one of the prophets."
>   He said to them, "But who do you say that I am?"
>   Simon Peter answered and said, "You are the Christ, the Son of the living God."
>   Jesus answered and said to him, "Blessed are you, Simon Bar-Jonah, for flesh and blood has not revealed this to you, but My Father who is in heaven."

These are very difficult points for reincarnation advocates to answer. There is no biblical evidence, positively speaking, for reincarnation. The biblical position against it is that reincarnation maintains an impersonal God; it is against the Christian doctrine of the atonement and has no concept of sin or how to deal with it, and certainly is opposed to the deity of Jesus Christ and His bodily resurrection. Christianity teaches *resurrection,* not reincarnation.

CONCLUSION

Scripture speaks very pointedly on principles that contradict Kabbalah, though the word never appears in the Bible. It answers the core of Kabbalah theology, offering a solution to humanity's problems through reunion with God. Kabbalah is refuted primarily by the fact that Jesus Christ died in our place to repair the heart of man and mend humanity's broken relationship to God.

> God, who at various times and in various ways spoke in time past to the fathers by the prophets, has in these last days spoken to us by His Son, whom He has appointed heir of all things, through whom also He made the worlds; who being the brightness of His glory and the express image of His person, and upholding all things by the word of His power, when He had by Himself purged our sins, sat down at the right hand of the Majesty on high, having become so much better than the angels, as He has by inheritance obtained a more excellent name than they (Heb. 1:1–4).

This is the death knell for Kabbalah, Cayce, and the New Age system of reincarnation and restoration: complete forgiveness of sin through the blood of Jesus Christ.

Kabbalists interpret the Hebrew Bible symbolically, relying on innumerable commentaries of men and the tools of Notarikon, Temura, Gematria, and the names of God. In direct contrast to their dependence on the word of man, the Christian is instructed to rely only upon the Word of God, training to "be . . . thoroughly equipped for every good work" (2 Tim. 3:17). To do that you must rightly interpret, or correctly handle, the word of truth. You must be carried along by the Holy Spirit, consistent with Scripture. You must not deny Holy Scripture because of emotions or because of any subsequent material you may think is important. All materials are subject to what the Bible specifically proclaims. Other commentaries and books may be used to help you understand the Bible, but they are not a *substitute* for it—nor can they judge Scripture. Scripture judges *all* forms of interpretation: interpretational viewpoints do not govern Scripture.

The Bible is a book originating with God but fully utilizing the vocabulary, the culture, the background, and the education of man. So, first, you must look at it as you would any other book in terms of language, geography, culture, and background. Once again, those things do not have the right to change Scripture, but they are valuable to give you a background to understanding Scripture. Second, if you are going to interpret, you should understand that biblical literature has prose and poetry; it has history; it has allegory; it has literal and symbolic language—and you have to know which is which. Otherwise, you find yourself in an absolutely untenable position. Third, if you are going to interpret the Scripture, you should be aware of the historical background, so you don't approach a Bible book as if it were written *today*. You need to examine the Bible in its historical context, and in light of the culture that produced it. Fourth, you must understand the geographical conditions of the biblical text. You must understand the influence of terrain and climate, and how people looked upon these things—what it meant to them. The fifth point is the life setting: what kind of people do we meet in the Bible? You must get under their skin. You must look at the times through their eyes, not through your own.

And finally, Christians have a basic hermeneutical or interpretational position: the Old Testament is *always* to be interpreted in the light of the New Testament—never the reverse. You may not build New Testament theology by quoting Old Testament passages without a link to the New Testament. This is, unfortunately, the root of a great deal of heresy. These are the general principles of biblical interpretation, and every Christian should employ them. We are commanded to rightly interpret God's Word, and to do that, we must use the correct tools.

Anything contrary to Holy Scripture is to be rejected because it is dangerous to the soul, and Kabbalah qualifies as contrary to Scripture. The Bible is to be interpreted using specific tools; it is never acceptable to take the entire biblical record and interpret it as metaphor.

The theology offered by Kabbalah has much in common with the theology of psychic mediums such as Edgar Cayce and Jane Roberts, and it has much in common with New Age teachings. What God makes simple, Satan must always complicate. Do not go to the false prophets and the seers; go to the Word of God, to the Holy Spirit, to the Lord Jesus for answers to the questions of sin, evil, and judgment. The truth of the gospel of the resurrection can be summed up in one simple verse: "For God so loved the world that He gave His only begotten Son, that whoever believes in Him should not perish but have everlasting life" (John 3:16). In direct opposition to this simplicity is the doctrine of Kabbalah:

This interpretation says that the Sephiroth were revealed to Adam in the shape of the Tree of Life and the Tree of Knowledge, i.e. the middle and the last Sefirah; instead of preserving their original unity and thereby unifying the spheres of 'life' and 'knowledge' and bringing salvation to the world, he separated one from the other and set his mind to worship the Shekhinah only without recognizing its union with the other Sephiroth. Thus he interrupted the stream of life which flows from sphere to sphere and brought separation and isolation into the world.

From this time on there has been a mysterious fissure, not indeed in the substance of Divinity but in its life and action. This doctrine has been completely hedged round with reservations, but its basic meaning for all that is clear enough. Its pursuit led to the perception of what the Kabbalists call "The exile of the Shekhinah." Only after the restoration of the original harmony in the act of redemption, when everything shall again occupy the place that it originally had in the divine scheme of things, will "God be one and His name one," in Biblical terms, truly and for all time.

In the present unredeemed and broken state of the world this fissure which prevents the continuous union of God and the Shekhinah is somehow healed or mended by the religious act of Israel: Torah, *mitswoth* [commands] and prayer. Extinction of the stain, restoration of harmony—that is the meaning of the Hebrew word *Tikkun,* which is the term employed by the Kabbalists after the period of the Zohar, for man's task in this world. In the state of redemption, however, "there shall be perfection above and below, and all worlds shall be united in one bond."[97]

Satan confuses; God clarifies. Do not seek answers to the questions of eternity from the mouths of demons. Seek your confirmation from Scripture, and test all revelations by *the* revelation: the Word of God.

God is not transcendent as Kabbalists define it—He is not *unknowable.* The God of the Bible is transcendent in the sense that He exists in all dimensions, but He has revealed Himself as *knowable.* The God of the Torah and of the entire Bible

---

97. Scholem, *Major Trends in Jewish Mysticism,* 232–33. The word *Mitswoth* means *commands.*

is *immanent* (close to man), a loving Father to His cherished children throughout all the ages of mankind.

The Scriptures say that God is not the God of a dimension; God is the God of the cosmos and of *all* dimensions. He is omnipresent. "I am the LORD, I change not" (Mal. 3:6 KJV). So no matter where you go in this universe, no matter what dimensional structures you may encounter, you will meet the living God of creation who is always Father, always Son, and always Holy Spirit. He does not change because dimensional structures change. All things are the outcome of His *personal,* creative power (Heb. 11:3).

Redemption and resurrection are God's answer to sin and the corruption of evil; reincarnation is Satan's response. Jesus Christ is *unique.* He is the firstborn from among the dead. By man came death, and by man came also the resurrection from the dead (1 Cor. 15:21). The apostle Paul puts this into perspective when he tells us that we should not think it an incredible thing that God should resurrect the dead (Acts 26:8).

We are dealing with an all-powerful being—the God of the galaxies—and He can wield sufficient energy not only to resurrect all the corpses of earth, but to re-create a billion earths in any stage of development He chooses, simply by command. The Scriptures say that God commands the things that are not, as if they were (Rom. 4:17). He calls them into existence by His own laws, sustains them, and when He finishes with them, has the power to annihilate them. All authority is His in heaven and in earth.

Humans cannot even begin to conceive of such power. We explore the thermonuclear weapon and marvel at its complexity. How this must amuse the infinite intellect that is almighty God, when He looks at us floating around on a semi-burned-out cinder in our little solar system, ninety-three million miles from a nuclear furnace, a furnace that could explode at any moment and that exudes more energy in a few seconds than all the atomic bombs and hydrogen bombs man has exploded up to the present moment. This rather diminishes our concept of power.

Reality consists of the *enormity* of the God who has the power to raise from the dead and grant eternal life. In light of the reality of the God of creation, is it an incredible thing that God should raise the dead?

The whole record of biblical truth is that God sent Jesus Christ to redeem His children, and He raised Him from among the dead. Jesus is alive today, and because

He lives, we will live also. The resurrection of Christ is the hope that should fill us with joy every day of our lives.

Recommended Resources

1. Kjos, Andy and Berit, Kjos Ministries, www.crossroad.to.

2. Markell, Jan, Olive Tree Ministries, www.olivetreeviews.org.

3. Martin, Walter. *Hermeneutics* (Five Part series) (CD/audiotape), Walter Martin Ministries, www.waltermartin.com.

4. Ross, Rick, Kabbalah Centre and Philip S. Berg, www.rickross.com.

5. Scholem, Gershom. *Kabbalah*. New York: Plume, 1978.

Quick Facts about Eastern Mysticism and the New Age

- Eastern Mysticism and New Age occultism teaches that God is an impersonal force pervading all creation.

- Jesus was a man separated from the Christ; Jesus is the human messenger, and Christ is the cosmic consciousness or the divine spirit essence that rested upon Jesus.

- Human beings are divine within because they are part of God or a higher consciousness.

- The material world is a lower form of the spiritual essence and must be eliminated by raising it to a higher consciousness.

- Physical exercises and spiritual techniques that seek occult power are necessary to become one with the universal Spirit or universal Oneness.

6

Eastern Mysticism and the New Age

In the turbulent decade of the 1970s, an explosion of occult knowledge occurred, saturating the Western world with the potent seeds of a new perspective. A strange blend of nineteenth-century Spiritism, mysticism, and humanism, it took the name the New Age movement and quickly evolved into a bolder, more organized revival of ancient occultism. It was a new title with an ancient goal: the penetration of all areas of culture—political, educational, and religious—with man at the center of the universe.[1]

The New Age agenda was clear and surprisingly unified: a millennium without the biblical God. Christian apologists were the first to note the error of "Self" glorification during the mid-1970s Human Potential movement, which eventually merged into the New Age.[2] Dr. Bryce A. Pettit, a mission specialist for cult and occult adherents, wrote:[3]

> The current interest in the effect NRMs have on missionary activities began in 1958 when Walter Martin, an evangelical critic of the "cults," was asked to be part of the Pastor's Conference Team of World Vision Incorporated. He traveled over 25,000 miles throughout Africa and Asia speaking to thousands of Christian workers and gathering information on the impact NRMs were having on their missionary efforts. Over the next few years he

---

1. See Walter R. Martin's extensive definition in *The New Age Cult* (Minneapolis: Bethany House, 1989), 109–10.
2. See Walter Martin, ed., The New Cults (Santa Ana, CA: Vision House, 1980), where the Human Potential Movement, which later became the New Age, is analyzed in detail: "Deception of the New Cults" (11–35); "EST" (105–42); "Silva Mind Control," (237–67); and "Roy Masters Foundation of Human Understanding" (297–319).
3. Bryce A. Pettit, PhD, was a student of Dr. Martin's at Melodyland School of Theology from 1976 to 1979, and he contributed research on Armstrongism in Walter R. Martin's *Rise of the Cults*, rev. and enlarged ed. (Santa Ana, CA: Vision House Publishers, 1978).

visited other countries and continued to gather information relevant to the threat these groups posed to world missions. His Christian Research Institute became the model for dozens, and eventually hundreds, of other counter-cult organizations worldwide over the next four decades.[4]

American journalist Tom Wolfe coined the satiric term the "Me Decade" in 1976, when he powerfully characterized the demotion of God and the enthronement of man as the sovereign of the universe. This societal change of perspective from God to self brought with it a sense of false enlightenment; mankind could only benefit from abandoning outdated ideas of God and focusing on himself. As Wolfe recalled it, "You had finally focused your attention and your energies on the most fascinating subject on earth: *Me*."[5] Wolfe went on to say that the theology of ancient Gnosticism reappeared in the new movements of the 1960s, which taught that at the center of the human soul, "there exists a spark of the light of God. . . . souls who are clear can find that spark within themselves and unite their souls with God's."[6]

Wolfe's observation agrees with contemporary Christian writers who exposed the error of self-worship. The glorification of mankind through the *Human Potential Movement* of the mid-1970s led to the more religious New Age Movement, as observed by Christian apologists. As the New Age movement gained popularity, the Human Potential cults began waving the same banner of "unity in diversity." Part of this emerging New Age success came through undermining Christianity and destroying God's revelation—the Bible.[7] This was important from their viewpoint, since most of these groups believed that man was in the process of evolving from his current status to yet a higher being. Darwinian evolution was part of their process, and since a large number of evangelical Christians still believed in man as God's special creation, Christianity was seen as a blockade to their movement.

The New Age sought, from the very beginning, to undermine Christianity and

---

4. Bryce A. Pettite, "New Religious Movements and Missions," in *International Journal of Frontier Missions* 15, no. 3 (July 01, 1998): 125–34.

5. Tom Wolfe, *Mauve Gloves & Madmen, Clutter & Vine* (New York: Farrar Straus Giroux, 1976), 143–48.

6. Ibid.

7. Baha'i writer Zaid Lundberg, for example, claims "some scholars of religion think that the New Age Movement has surpassed and outdated Christianity as a belief-system/world-view in the West" (*Lights of Irfan: Papers Presented at the 'Irfan Colloquia and Seminars* [Wilmette, IL: Irfan Colloquia, 2000], 69).

destroy the revelation of God as it is given to us in the Old and the New Testament. It is nothing more than the mythology of the ancient world infused with satanic power; a satanic attempt to manipulate, form, and crystallize events, culminating in the rise of Antichrist—the man of sin—whose authority is after the working of Satan with all power, signs, and lying wonders (see 2 Thessalonians 2:9).

The world of the occult embraces everything from astrology to tarot cards, séances and Ouija boards, fortune-telling, Witchcraft, and Satanism. It encourages attempts to penetrate into a dimension of spiritual reality that God has forbidden; a dimension that holds the realm of the prince of darkness, the god of this age, the ruler of this world (see 2 Corinthians 4:4).

The door opened perceptibly for popularizing occultism in the Western world and merging it with Christianity in 1743, when Emanuel Swedenborg, son of a Swedish Lutheran minister, founded Swedenborgianism.[8] His revelations and visions of the deceased marked a new trend among occultists and mediums, who often relied upon séances for contact with the dead. Swedenborg claimed he had conversations with biblical characters, church fathers, and church reformers, including Moses, Jesus, Paul, Augustine, Luther, and Calvin.[9] Many occult, esoteric, mystic, mind science, and New Age groups relied upon this groundwork for occultic contact with spirits.

Swedenborg's metaphysics shaped the thinking of nineteenth-century New England transcendentalists such as Emerson, Thoreau, Ripley, Holmes, and Alcott, who later influenced Madam Blavatsky of Theosophy, Mary Baker Eddy of Christian Science, the early twentieth-century metaphysical schools, the Fillmores of Unity Church, the Ballards of the Mighty I AM movement, New Thought groups, mind science groups, and New Age groups. Swedenborg's occultism was not necessarily mirrored in each of these groups, but it was certainly copied by Blavatsky, with her visions of the twelve Ascended Masters. Theosophists and members of the I AM cults treasured these spirit contacts. Benjamin Creme and other New Age leaders who claimed telepathic or channeled communication with living and dead spirits followed a similar course.[10]

---

8. For more information on Swedenborgianism, see Appendix C in Martin, *Kingdom of the Cults*, 629–41.
9. Ibid.
10. For further information on the influence of the New England Transcendentalists, see Catherine L. Albanese, "Physic and Metaphysic in Nineteenth-Century America: Medical Sectarians and Religious Healing," *Church History* 55 (1986): 493–94.

Mary Baker Eddy, the founder of Christian Science, competed with the new metaphysic groups for followers. She published this affirmation in 1875: "There is no life, truth, intelligence nor substance in matter. All is infinite Mind and its infinite manifestation, for God is All-in-All."[11] Mrs. Eddy's book *Science and Health with Key to the Scriptures* was one of the first attempts to Christianize some of the underlying traditions found in Eastern philosophies. Although she carefully guarded her writings from sounding too much like Hinduism, she could not avoid the residual traces that remained in her new metaphysics. Eddy taught that the material world has no substance in God's existence, which she called Mind. The material world became an obstacle to understanding true Mind. Her teaching still stands opposed to Christianity, where biblically, the material world exists to glorify God as its Creator (Ps. 19:1; 148:3–4; Rom. 1:20–21).

The Theosophical Society was cofounded by the late-nineteenth-century occultist Helena Petrovna Blavatsky. She became a conduit for ancient occult knowledge after she rejected Christianity and reworked Hindu philosophical concepts into her model religion. Later, Charles and Myrtle Fillmore (Unity Church) and others synthesized mysticism and other avenues of thought for the masses. A large portion of this secret knowledge was canonized in the writings of Alice Bailey, the daughter of an Episcopal minister, who came to the conclusion that Christianity was bankrupt.[12] She redefined the terms of Christianity in the light of Theosophy, Hinduism, and the occult in her twenty-four books that unveiled "The Plan" of the Ascended Masters for world peace. Bailey claimed that a spirit-being named Djwhal Khul, who was a Tibetan mystic, spoke through her as the medium for his voice, which sometimes came through the occult power of automatic writing.[13]

NEW AGE PHILOSOPHY

The essence of New Age philosophy is the unity of the world's religions as diverse paths with the same goal. Under the auspices of tolerance, the New Age conception is that all religions are equally valid—memorialized in their theme of "unity in diver-

---

11. Mary Baker Eddy, *Science and Health with Key to the Scriptures* (Boston: Trustees under the will of Mary Baker Eddy, 1934 [rep. 1975]), 468.
12. Bailey predicted that "Christianity will be in a state of chaotic divisions and upheavals" prior to the arrival of the spiritual Hierarchy of the Ascended Masters. (Alice A. Bailey, *The Externalisation of the Hierarchy* [New York: Lucis Trust, 1943], 573).
13. Alice A. Bailey, *The Unfinished Autobiography* (New York: Lucis Trust, 1951), 164.

sity." It is big enough to embrace all: Buddha, Mohammed, Confucius, Krishna, or Jesus. It merges the faiths of the world and places all of their founders on the same plane for truth and authority.

In New Age beliefs, there are many prophets and no single incarnate redeemer. The law of Karma takes precedence over the atonement of Jesus Christ. Sins are cultural and relative instead of offenses toward a holy God. Reincarnation is freedom for this world, and the resurrection of Christ was spiritual. Hell is not a place of eternal punishment, but it is only a state of mind or negative thought. Universalism is preached, which saves everyone in the end through the doctrine of reincarnation.[14]

The New Age movement is an all-pervasive, all-encircling philosophy, birthed from Theosophy and Hinduism. New Age groups comprise a united syncretistic religion; everything comes together under one philosophy. Their divine absolute principle is not a person; it is not God the Father, Son, and Holy Spirit. The absolute principle is an impersonal entity that inhabits all creation, whether they call it consciousness, energy, vibrations, spirit, force, Mind, Brahma, or the One. Esoteric philosophy does not reject deity within nature; it only refuses to accept any single faith, like Christianity, as the only way of salvation. In contrast to the true God who created man in his image, the New Age philosophy re-created God in man's image and likeness.

The core of New Age theology is the integration of all religions, practices, mythology, superstition, and the occult found in the world. It refuses to bow the knee and worship the biblical God of creation.

The god of the New Age movement is Lucifer, light bearer, adversary, prince of darkness, who moves through religion, politics, and economies with one purpose in mind: integrate, unify, and then destroy. And the destruction is aimed at the church of Jesus Christ. The apostle Peter said, "Be sober, be vigilant; because your adversary the devil walks about like a roaring lion, seeking whom he may devour. Resist him, steadfast in the faith, knowing that the same sufferings are experienced by your brotherhood in the world" (1 Peter 5:8–9).

THE NEW AGE TODAY

The New Age movement has mushroomed throughout the world, particularly in the United States. Cloaked in acceptable and seemingly harmless terms, such as the

---

14. For a thorough analysis of New Age theology, see Martin, *The New Age Cult* and Martin, *The Kingdom of the Cults*, 405.

widespread exercises of yoga and meditation, is the hidden agenda of the occult. When one meditates or practices yoga, the mind is said to be emptied to allow the person to become one with the universe, but this is where the person opens the mind and heart to false spirits that await every opportunity to invade a soul that is normally guarded. Noted German authority on the occult Dr. Kurt Koch states the following about the occultic side of yoga: "This technique of relaxation and these 'emptying exercises,' so highly spoken of by the yogis lead to the inflowing of another spirit—other spirits. The students of yoga did not notice it."[15] Similarly, Dr. Koch, who has compiled volumes of case studies on people involved in the occult, wrote the following about meditation: "My counseling work in East and West has given me insight into the nature and practice of meditation. . . . I am totally opposed to meditation in the Far Eastern pattern. . . . We cannot empty ourselves by means of techniques and postures—then other powers flood in."[16] It is difficult to find any New Ager who does not practice either meditation or yoga, but Dr. Koch's warning is clear: if one empties the mind, it becomes an open vessel for other spirits.

It is important to note what Jesus said concerning spirits, particularly demonic spirits that invade human bodies: "When an unclean spirit goes out of a man, he goes through dry places, seeking rest, and finds none. Then he says, 'I will return to my house from which I came.' And when he comes, he finds it empty, swept, and put in order. Then he goes and takes with him seven other spirits more wicked than himself, and they enter and dwell there; and the last state of that man is worse than the first" (Matt. 12:43–45).

From Jesus we learn, then, that demonic spirits can inhabit human beings. Rather than experiment with the occult and New Age practices, where the person unwittingly opens the soul to demons, it is much better to close the door and refuse participation.

The New Age movement was supported by many people who had no knowledge of its origin and nature.[17] The occult is subtle and can deceive anyone. It points to a new religious emphasis. It envisions one planet, one people, harmonious

15. Kurt E. Koch, *Occult ABC* (Germany: Literature Mission Aglasterhausen, 1978), 257–58.
16. Ibid., 243, 244, 246.
17. Liberal religious leaders such as Marcus Bach and Charles Braden embraced the pulpits of the mind-science cults in the 1950s throughout the 1970s, opening a venue for unassuming Christians to ignorantly follow their lead in believing that all religions are equally valid. See Bach, *They Have Found a Faith*, and Charles Braden, *These Also Believe* (New York: Macmillan, 1949).

peace, prosperity, and hope for the world, which come through the creativity of positive thinking, harmonizing yin and yang forces, awakening the god within, or balancing spiritual energy through occult practices.

What unifies the New Age is the foundational belief that there are many equally valid beliefs and techniques that enlighten and liberate the individual. Not all groups use the same terminology, but they respect one another and focus upon the "unity in diversity" motif. Relativistic thinking and tolerance prevents them from excessively criticizing or comparing alternate beliefs and techniques. The general idea of "whatever works for you" is perfectly acceptable as a path to truth. Therefore, most New Age gurus, teachers, and instructors believe that their technique for liberation of the soul or awakening the sleeping "god within" is good, but they do not deny that other techniques or beliefs may produce similar results.

The chart below outlines occult beliefs and powers that are practiced by several New Age groups. Although these also stand alone as general occult practices, the religious setting of the New Age has breathed new life into old practices.

Occult Belief or Practice	How New Age Groups Use Occult Power
Astrology, Horoscopes, and the Zodiac	Some New Age writers and practitioners incorporate teachings about astrology, horoscopes, and the zodiac into their belief system. This is offered as a means for the stars and planetary systems to guide the subject and is often called Elysian Astrology.
Auras	In the occult, these are colored light emanations that surround people. Some New Age adherents claim special power to see these auras and claim to interpret moods and personal characteristics by defining the colors of light.
Automatic Writing	Some New Age authors claim to have contact with spirits that take over their bodies and write through them. This is a form of mediumship. Writers such as Alice Bailey,

Occult Belief or Practice	How New Age Groups Use Occult Power
	Ruth Montgomery, and Jane Roberts are examples.
Clairaudience	The practice of hearing audible voices that other people do not naturally hear. Many New Agers use this occult practice.
Clairvoyance	This is the practice of seeing things that other people do not naturally see. Usually this comes through dreams, visions, or pre-cognition.
Crystals and Colored Stones	As with occult practitioners, New Agers often believe that energy or vibration qualities exist in certain stones and crystals. These are used for a variety of rituals, including physical healing and meditation.
Divination	This is any means of predicting an unknown event with the aid of physical objects or events that are read or interpreted, such as tarot cards, runes, crystal gazing, omens, scrying, palmistry, and dreams. Curious New Agers and psychics employ these.
Extrasensory Perception (ESP)	The occult experimentation with ESP existed prior to the New Age era. ESP is used by "gifted" New Agers who claim the ability to know things through premonitions that are not common to other people.
Medium	A person who acts as a conduit for communication between the spirits and humanity through a variety of manifestations. This

Occult Belief or Practice	How New Age Groups Use Occult Power
	action is centuries old in the occult and is openly practiced by New Agers.
Numerology	New Agers mimic the occult with numerology by affixing values and meanings to certain numbers in order to interpret them as meaningful signs for past or future events.
Out-of-Body Experiences	Some New Age groups, Theosophy, and Rosicrucians practice out-of-body travel and astral projection.
Parapsychology	Academic study of occult powers and perceived gifted powers of certain individuals began at Drew University in the 1920s. Parapsychology is of great interest to New Agers because it appears to deal with latent powers.
Psychic	A person who acts as a medium and who uses auras, numerology, divination, clairvoyance, clairaudience, oracles, telepathy, or ESP as a means for communicating unknown information to the participant. Although psychics have long existed independent of the New Age movement, they are also found within it.
Psychokinesis and Telekinesis	In the occult, psychokinesis is the belief that gifted people can move physical objects by use of their mental powers. New Agers believe that these powers belong to gifted people.
Pyramidology and pyramid power	Pyramids are believed to have mystical power in their hieroglyphics and structure.

Occult Belief or Practice	How New Age Groups Use Occult Power
	Pyramid Power in the New Age is based upon the idea that the pyramid shape draws power and energy from the universe; therefore, pyramid-shaped objects, such as hats, tents, and crystals, hold special significance in the New Age.
Séance	A session with a medium before one or more people, in which the medium attempts contact with deceased humans, angels, or other spirit-beings, usually directed toward contact with a specific departed person known by the participant.
Spirit Guide	Spirit guides are historically rooted in Mayan occultism. The New Age teaches that spirits, either independent spirit-beings or spirits of the deceased, make contact with the living to assist them through life. These are called spirit-guides.
Telepathy	New Age writers and adherents sometimes claim telepathy as a medium for communication with the living or dead. It is said to be nonverbal communication directly from one mind to another.

The founders of New Age groups have publicly announced through their writings their avowed desire to oppose Christianity. They realize they must suppress Christianity because the two messages are from opposing poles. Their denial is aimed at the Christian God, the Bible, and the Christian message of salvation through Jesus Christ alone. Their opposition to Christianity should cause great concern in light of their powerful influence and its source: a dimension the Bible calls the realm of "the prince of the power of the air, the spirit who now works in the sons of disobedience" (Eph. 2:2).

NEW AGE SYMBOLS

The New Age movement today must be recognized for what it is: the ancient world of the occult presented in new terminology. New Age adherents appropriate the Christian symbol of the cross and use it in ways that have little to do with its true meaning. The traditional shape of the Christian cross is like a lower case *t*, or *crux immissia*, with the top post extending over the crossbeam. This best fits the biblical description of Pilate's accusation and inscription "KING OF THE JEWS," nailed over Jesus' head (Matt. 27:37; Luke 23:38).

Several occultic groups use the cross as a symbol that imitates the Christian tradition while they deny its atoning message. "The message of the cross," Paul wrote, "is the power of God" to the saved (1 Cor. 1:18). The Cross of Christ is not just an external religious symbol in Christianity. It is not a logo or an icon. Without the Savior's blood being spilled for the world's sins and without His declaration "It is finished" (John 19:30), there is no hope of salvation. The cross without Jesus Christ is just a meaningless symbol; it is necessary in Christianity and was predicted twelve hundred years before Christ's crucifixion in Psalm 22.

New Age groups use the Cross, but they strip it of Jesus' saving power. Scientology, Theosophy, Unity Church, the Unification Church, and a host of independent New Age gurus use crosses without Jesus Christ as the true Savior. People are often misled into thinking that the Egyptian ankh symbol, *crux ansata* (handled cross), represents a Christian cross. New Age groups use the ankh symbol frequently. In its appearance, it looks like a Cross at the base, but its top is a circle that is sometimes oblong, teardrop shaped, or perfectly symmetrical. This is the Egyptian symbol for the afterlife or reincarnation and, as such, has nothing to do with Jesus Christ or Christianity. Jesus did not die on an ankh for anyone's sins or for his reincarnation. He bore the sins of mankind and died on Calvary's Cross as the vicarious sacrifice to appease God's wrath.

New Age groups also borrow God's rainbow as a symbol from Genesis 9. They use this symbol for unity in an effort to build a bridge to unite the world. God, after destroying the world by flood in Genesis 7, set a rainbow in the sky as a covenant or promise to man that He would never destroy the world by flood again. New Age groups use the symbol of the rainbow, but they do not know the God behind its promise.

Although the New Age publicly stands against the narrow way of Christianity, they still have a tendency to copy it. They reinterpret the church's sacred symbols, but they despise the meaning that God attached to them. This trend must be recognized for what it is: a counterfeit of Christianity—a millennium without God— a kingdom without the King and a cross minus Christ's atonement. The only resurrection is in the form of reincarnation. They offer an endless chain of saviors and avatars who arrive in the world with the purpose of enlightenment, but none offers a final solution to man's sins as Jesus did.

NEW AGE LEADERS

The following is a synopsis of influential leaders and groups responsible for spreading the message of occult powers through their writings, meetings, and media attention. The popularity of the occult has grown step-by-step so that it is now accepted without criticism, and little attention is paid to its societal influence.

Influential Person, Group, or Teaching	Year	The Popularized Occult Practice
Emanuel Swedenborg and the Church of the New Jerusalem.	1743	Swedenborg, the founder of the Church of the New Jerusalem or Swedenborgianism, communicated with the dead by means of conversations and visions, which is akin to the occult practice of mediumship.
New England Transcendentalists	1836	Ralph Waldo Emerson, George Ripley, and Frederic Hedge, all Unitarians, formed the Transcendental Club of America in 1836 as a protest against Harvard Divinity School. Influenced by Emanuel Swedenborg, they concluded that a universal soul or mind permeates creation and is the source of all knowledge, wisdom, and intuition.
Andrew Jackson Davis	1843	Davis claimed mediumship encounters with the spirit world and successful com-

and Spiritism		munication with Emanuel Swedenborg, who died in 1772. His book, *Principles of Nature* (1847), became authoritative to his followers. In 1908, Spiritism, or the Universal Church of the Master, was founded, which incorporated his teachings.
Margaret and Katie Fox	1848	The Fox sisters are credited with the modern Spiritism movement. The contemporary medium Andrew Jackson Davis (1843) laid the groundwork for séances and mediumship. Similarly, the Fox sisters publicized "table rapping" as a means of communication with the dead. Many self-styled and self-proclaimed mediums followed.
Allan Kardec	1857	Kardec was a French author whose book, *Book of the Spirits* (1857), promoted mediumship, séances, and the transmigration of human souls.
Helena P. Blavatsky, Henry S. Olcott, William Q. Judge, and Theosophy	1875	Blavatsky, Olcott, and Judge founded the Theosophical Society in 1875. Mediumship, clairvoyance, and telepathy are used to channel the wisdom teachings of the twelve Ascended Masters.
Mary Baker Eddy and Christian Science	1875	Eddy was a student of the New England transcendentalists, who were influenced by Swedenborg, whose ideas form the backdrop to her writings. The writings of P. P. Quimby and Franz Mesmer (mesmerism) also shaped her "mind over matter" motif.

Emma Curtis Hopkins and the New Thought Movement	1885	Christian Science produced several independent sects, all intending to improve on mind-science teaching. Hopkins, a student and writer for Mary Baker Eddy, left Christian Science to start the College of Metaphysical Science in Chicago (1885). Her movement, called New Thought, spawned the cloning of meta-physical schools in larger cities. She directly influenced the Fillmores (Unity Church), Nona Brooks (Divine Science), Annie Rix Militz (Home of Truth), and Earnest Holmes (Religious Science). They promote healing through mental science. Most New Thought organizations have merged into the New Age Movement.
Charles and Myrtle Fillmore and the Unity School of Christianity (Unity Church)	1889	The Fillmores were students of E.C. Hopkins, Emerson, transcendentalism, the Bible, and Eastern religions. They founded the Unity School of Christianity (now Unity Church) in 1889 by selecting the best meta-physical principles from their studies. Healing through mental science is practiced and they introduced reincarnation under the "Christian" banner.
Swami Vivekananda	1893	Swami Vivekananda was rocketed to cele-brity status after speaking at the 1893 World Parliament of Religions (Chicago). He lectured for three years in the United States and England, introducing Westerners to Eastern mysticism, various meditation formats, and eventually returned to India to establish a worldwide following.

Annie Besant and Jiddu Krishnamurti	1907	Besant was a clairvoyant medium and Theosophist who led the Theosophy Society (1907–1993). She adopted an Indian boy, Jiddu Kirshnamurti, whom she proclaimed as the new messiah for the world. Krishnamurti left Theosophy in 1929 and abandoned his messianic mission, but he gained a worldwide audience of students through his speaking and writing career. His Eastern mysticism promoted occultic meditation and contact with cosmic energy and the all-pervading Spirit.
Rosicrucianism	1909, 1915	The Order of Rosy Cross is said to predate the modern movement by several centuries. These organizations promote astral projection, meditation, and other occult practices. In the United States, several orders exist. The larger orders in the United States were founded in 1909 (Rosicrucian Fellowship) and in 1915 (Ancient and Mystical Order Rosae Crucis or AMORC).
Rudolf Steiner and the Anthroposophical Society	1912	Steiner left Theosophy to form the Anthoposophical Society (1912) and the Christian Community (1922). Through a clairvoyant vision he believed astral bodies enter the human body around age twelve. He promoted spiritual occult experiences and taught the law of karma and reincarnation.
Alice Bailey	1917	Bailey is a popular occultist among New Age adherents. She promotes several occult mediums for contacts with spirits and the dead, including channeling and telepathy. She founded Lucifer's Trust in 1922 (later

		renamed Lucis Trust), the Arcane School in 1923, and World Goodwill in 1932. Occult meditation is practiced.
Ernest Holmes and Science of Mind (Religious Science)	1927 1927	Holmes main work, *Science of Mind* (1927), became the impetus for founding his church, Religious Science (sometimes called Science of Mind). He was a student of Emerson's works and New Thought.
Guy and Edna Ballard	1930	In 1930, the Ballards founded the Mighty I AM movement, now called the Saint Germain Foundation. Guy Ballard claimed mediumship and spirit channeling for the deceased Saint Germain and other entities. Through these occult means, the I AM movement has revelations from the Great White Brotherhood of the Ascended Masters.
Edgar Cayce and the Association for Research and Enlightenment (A.R.E.)	1931	Edgar Cayce, a medium who is dubbed as the sleeping prophet, is credited for popularizing the occult in books containing his psychic readings. He founded A.R.E. as a religious organization to promote his openly occult teachings.
Paramahansa Yogananda and the Self-Realization Fellowship	1935	Blending basic Hindu philosophy with Western terminology, Yogananda was an Eastern mystic who traveled the United States and lectured to thousands of people in packed arenas. He taught that latent occult powers come through the third eye that exists in the forehead. Yoga and meditation are practiced in the Self-Realization Fellowship.

Zen Buddhism, Eastern Meditation, and Yoga	1960s	Although D. T. Suzuki and Alan Watts popularized Zen Buddhism in their twentieth century writings, it did not surge until Zen centers began emerging in the 1960s. As interest in Eastern philosophy grew among Westerners, a stream of Eastern gurus satisfied the Western appetite by flooding the market with books, lectures, seminars, and centers for Eastern meditation (the most popular was transcendental meditation) and various Yoga practices. Many of these later merged with New Age practices, but their occult nature remained the same.
Human Potential Moement	1970s	A barrage of new teachings, seminars, and techniques were developed in the 1970s that promised to raise man's consciousness and make a better human race. A Course in Miracles, Biorhythms, Dianetics, Erhard Seminar Training (EST, later The Forum), Esalen Institute, Firewalking (Tony Robbins seminars), hypnosis therapy (including past life and age regression), Inner Peace Movement, Lifespring, Primal Screaming, Rebirthing, Sylva Mind Control, and yoga are all examples of the Human Potential movement, much of which was based on occult theories. Most of these groups eventually merged with the New Age.
Elizabeth Clare Prophet and the Church Universal and Triumphant	1974	Springing from the I AM movement (and earlier Theosophy), Mark and Elizabeth Prophet moved into the forefront of the I AM cults. They merged Eastern Mysticism, New Age, occult, meditation,

		and the Ascended Masters into one organization.
New Age Spirituality	mid-1970s	Specific material labeling itself New Age began surfacing in the mid-1970s that was largely based upon a global transformation in the Aquarian Age. The starting date for the Aquarian Age varies (1962, 1997, or 2000); New Age journals, magazines, books, music, lectures, seminars, and churches are devoted to global transformation through self-transformation. Most New Age themes unwittingly offer occult practices within the framework of New Age spirituality.
Benjamin Creme and the Tara Center and Share International	1982	Through the occult method of trance channeling and telepathy, Creme taught that he had contact with a Tibetan who was the world's messiah (or Christ). This he announced in world newspapers on April 25, 1982. Creme's books are popular among New Age adherents.

Satan is the architect of all of New Age spirituality, and he uses people, many of whom are sincere and dedicated. Their intentions are good, but they stand in rebellion against the authority of God and His Word; they have no desire to acknowledge the biblical Christ and plan of salvation. As a result of this rebellion, they reject Christianity and turn to the New Age movement, which instills the teaching that the best understanding of deity is to "know thyself" and to become aware of godhood or the cosmic Christ consciousness within you. In New Age spirituality, you do not look up for a place called heaven; it is a myth. Instead, you look inside yourself and find a sleeping god or a higher consciousness. The peace that you will find is what lies dormant within you, not outside of you.

A major advancement of the New Age agenda, giving worldwide attention to the movement, occurred on April 25, 1982, when Benjamin Creme placed advertisements in seventeen of the world's largest newspapers announcing, "The Christ Is Now Here."[18] Creme, a celebrity among trance-channeling occultists and a student of Theosophy and Alice Bailey, would slip into a trancelike state and begin uttering the message of the Teacher. His book *The Reappearance of the Christ and the Masters of Wisdom* (1980) follows a similar path of contact with the hierarchy of Ascended Masters, as did his Theosophy-related predecessor Alice Bailey, who wrote *The Reappearance of the Christ* (1947).

On May 14, 1982, Creme held a press conference in Los Angeles, California, to announce where the new Christ could be found. To the disappointment of his followers and the jeers of skeptics, Creme only revealed that the Christ or Lord Maitreya could be found in the Pakistani community of London, England. It was left to the journalists of the world to locate him and publicly reveal him.[19] Few journalists accepted the challenge, but the New Age movement took center stage as newspapers, magazine, radio, and television reporters dominated the news with inquiries about its teachings.

The eye of the world was once again on the New Age when thousands of small groups combined to announce the "Harmonic Convergence" set for August 17, 1987. At a specific time on that date, New Agers from all walks of life chanted, meditated, and performed rituals at designated locations around the world, but the most popular places were the so-called mystic ones, like Mount Shasta, California; Sedona, Arizona; Santa Fe, New Mexico; and Stonehenge, England, where it was believed that an energy vortex would harmonize the individual's energy for world transformation.

Mr. Creme's Lord Maitreya did not appear and solve the world's problems. World peace did not result from the Harmonic Convergence, but this did not bother the typical New Age believer. The New Age movement had tremendous resilience in the face of defeat; in spite of these blunders, it continued to grow in popularity. In past decades, Christian books at major book retailers dominated the religious section, but the competing New Age book selection now doubles or triples the number of Christian volumes in many stores.

Moving beyond the sensationalistic, limelight-grabbing era of the 1980s, the

---

18. Two of the seventeen newspapers where Benjamin Creme published "The Christ is Now Here" are the *Los Angeles Times,* April 25, 1982, 31 and the *London Times,* April 25, 1982, 5.
19. Kurt Van Gorden attended the press conference and was able to question Mr. Creme on his writings. See also Martin, *Kingdom of the Cults,* 409.

current New Age leaders are more passive about making overblown claims, since a more critical and sometimes harsh media awaits them. They are pleased that their teachings, tenets, and practices have entered mainstream Western culture. This provides stability for their growth.

Today's New Age representatives are no less occultic in their practices and rituals, but they have smoothly refined themselves in acceptable terms so that meditation, yoga, astrology, tarot cards, palmistry, crystals, healing methods, and other practices are welcomed.[20] There is also a shift among some New Agers away from the "New Age" moniker in favor of a more descriptive identity, such as spirituality or "new spirituality."[21]

NEW AGE TERMINOLOGY

Common key terms used by New Age believers help identify New Age thinking. Often the underlying spiritual background to an article, book, or movie can be detected by knowing these terms.

New Age Term	Explanation of New Age Term
Atlantis and Lemuria	These are lost continents that New Agers believe are real, and they sometimes claim contact with Atlantians (Rudolf Steiner, for example) and Lemurians.
Aquarian Age or the Age of Aquarius	The alignment of certain planets within the constellation Aquarius will result in a New Age and global changes on earth.
Avatar	*Avatar* is a Sanskrit word for a Hindu deity, but in the New Age it could be a spiritual teacher.
Channeling and trance channeling	Channeling is the New Age term for a variety of mediumship practices. Trance channeling is the most popular vehicle, in which a spirit takes over the body of a subject and speaks through it.

20. Current leaders among New Age authors are Deepak Chopra, Wayne Dryer, John Gay, Fritjof Capra, Trish MacGregor, Shakti Gawain, Marianne Williamson, Paulo Coelho, Dick Sutphen, and Sylvia Browne.
21. Larry Nichols, George Mather, and Alvin Schmidt, *Encyclopedic Dictionary of Cults, Sects, and World Religions* (Grand Rapids: Zondervan, 2006), 215.

Chakra	*Chakra* is a Sanskrit word from Hinduism that represents seven energy centers in the human body. New Age practitioners use these in a variety of ways for meditation, healing, and to raise self-consciousness.
Christ	Christ is not Jesus, according to the New Age. The Christ is a cosmic consciousness. Jesus is a human messenger, sometimes called an avatar, who manifested the Christ consciousness. He was only one of many christs or, as some New Age writers claim, everybody is a christ.
Christ Consciousness, Cosmic Consciousness, God Consciousness, Higher Consciousness	In the New Age worldview, a universal Oneness exists that permeates all living beings called cosmic consciousness, Christ consciousness, higher consciousness, divinity, or God consciousness. In some New Age writings, these descriptions take on the meaning of raising the individual's consciousness to a higher level.
Christ Self, God Self, Divine Self	New Age teachings describe mankind as a sleeping god. The inner self is described as a Christ, God, or divine self.
Collective Consciousness	In the New Age worldview, human beings who meditate or harmoniously act together become a moving force in the universe by using their collective consciousness.
Guru	*Guru* is Sanskrit for a Hindu teacher. In New Age thought, it is loosely defined as anyone who gains a following.
Harmony and Balance	The New Age worldview is *pantheistic* (everything or all is God) or *monistic* (all is One). Existence is

New Age Term	Explanation of New Age Term
	viewed in dualistic terms, *yang* and *yin*. When things go wrong in the world, it is due to an imbalance of these forces. When things go wrong for the individual, it is likewise due to an imbalance or lack of harmony between these forces.
Holistic Health	*Holistic* is a general term that encompasses a variety of self-improvements for the mind, body, and soul. It is usually related to teachings about chakras, yoga, and meditation.
Illusion or Maya	The material world to monists and pantheists is not real in the sense that it is a lower form or low vibration of the Higher Existence (God) or the Highest Vibration (Spirit). If all is God or all is One, then what we think is reality is said to be an illusion of Spirit; it is a slow vibration of the same substance which then takes on the illusionary (solid) form. If we speed it up, it would disappear as spirit.
Law of Karma	*Karma* is a Sanskrit word from Hinduism that represents actions or deeds. Reward or punishment in a reincarnated existence resulted from one's actions or deeds in a former life.
Kundalini	Through yoga, a coil of energy is released at the base of the spine, traveling through the charkas and eventually releasing deep self-awareness.
Maitreya, Messiah, Buddha, or Christ	A world savior is expected to arrive at any time, according to New Agers. They use predictions about Jesus Christ, Buddha, the Messiah, and Lord Maitreya, claiming they are one and the same, as proof texts to solidify their claim.

Mantra, Om	A *mantra* is usually a word given to a yoga initiate for meditation that he chants in his mind over and over during meditation. The vibration of the word is said to have power. "Om" is a popular mantra people use.
Meditation	New Age teachers use various forms of meditation to bring self-enlightenment and health and to become one with the universe.
Oneness, Universal Oneness, Monism, Pantheism	The foundation of New Age philosophy is the underlying oneness of all universal existence. Those tending toward monism call it the Universal Oneness. Those tending toward pantheism call it God.
Oracles and Runes	Oracles are used by New Agers to make instant decisions about directions in life or to forecast the future. Runes pulled from a bag, casting sticks, and casting dice or stones are some of the methods used. The way they fall determines the interpretation.
The Plan	*The Plan* is a term used by Theosophists who believe that a Hierarchy of Ascended Masters is about to send a Messiah, Maitreya, Christ, or Buddha, whose followers will unite to usher in the Plan for a New World Order.
Planetary Vision	Collective cooperation will bring world peace and harmony in all aspects of life, from economics to culture.
Rebirthing	Rebirthing is the process where the subject undergoes hypnotic or other forms of memory regression to experience his birth once again. This is supposed to release him from unwanted barriers he currently experiences in life.

New Age Term	Explanation of New Age Term
Reincarnation	Most New Age groups believe in reincarnation instead of the resurrection of the body. Reincarnation memory experiences are often connected with the occult, such as in hypnotic regression, past life experiences, and rebirthing therapy.
Therapeutic Touch, Reiki Healing	Therapeutic touch, or Reiki healing, is a healing method for New Agers in which hands are laid upon the participant for healing. Quite often therapeutic touch is combined with yang and yin theories and stone or crystal energies.
Vibrations or Vibes	Spirit and energy are said to be forms of vibration. The highest vibration is God or the Universal Oneness. Low vibrations of spirit form the illusion of matter. The New Age goal is to rid oneself of matter (illusion) through reincarnation or otherwise so everything can be spirit.
Yang and Yin Polarity	New Agers borrowed this from Eastern philosophy, particularly Taoism (I Ching). This is the view that universal existence is based upon the harmonization and balance of two opposing forces, yang and yin (positive and negative, male and female).
Yoga	*Yoga* is Sanskrit for "union." Its goal in Hinduism is to make the subject one with Brahma. Monists and New Age teachers often modify the description as becoming one with universal Oneness.

CASE STUDY

Walter Martin

This incident took place at the First Baptist Church in Van Nuys, California, in front of more than 40 witnesses, including myself. There can be no doubt that it occurred.

A young lady came to the First Baptist Church one evening, right after I had conducted a series of lectures on the cults and the occult. She was an Indian girl who wandered inside in a deranged state and said to the pastors, "Help me, help me! They won't leave me alone."

At first, the pastors thought she was mentally ill. But the next day, the church secretary called me at my motel 75 miles away and said, "You've got to come back here, quickly!"

I said, "I'm terribly sorry, but I'm tied up in meetings, and besides that, I'm exhausted."

"You've got to help us—you won't believe what's going on here. There's a girl upstairs and four of the pastors are conducting an exorcism, and they don't know what they're doing. I'm going to switch you to a phone on the third floor and you can talk to them. We've been trying to get you all day." So, she transferred me to the education building.

One of the pastors answered immediately, obviously shaken, and said, "Dr Martin! I want you to listen to this." Two seconds later, I thought I'd entered a lunatic asylum. I had never heard such screeches, howls, roars, and cursing in multiple languages flowing over a telephone line in my life.

He got back on the phone and said, "That was *one girl* talking. Can you believe it? There are 40 of us here and we're not saying anything! All the noise you heard is coming from her."

It sounded like a football stadium or a madhouse. I said, "You definitely have a problem."

He answered, "What do we do with her?"

For the next four hours, I conducted an exorcism over the telephone! The pastors would talk to the demons, get back on the phone to tell me what the demons said and then go back in the room and talk to the demons again. Now this may sound crazy to you, but it was very real to those men: Christian gospel preachers.

We found out eventually that she had been into the heart of the New Age movement—associated with a half dozen or more New Age organizational ideas and concepts. It turned out she had 100 demons in her! I told them to get a tape recorder or no one will ever believe it happened. They commanded the demons in the name of Jesus Christ to identify themselves, every single one of them. They actually recorded their names and some of them were very interesting. They were the names and the terms of the world of the occult because she had been into all of these movements. She was spewing out the names of demons associated with actual movements.

Four hours later the Holy Spirit cast the last of the demons out of that girl in the name of Jesus. A pastor called me back and said, "It's over. They're gone! Praise the Lord!"

I said, "Yes, praise the Lord!"

And then he said, "She wants to talk to you,"

She came to the phone and said, "I have been possessed for the last few years. I couldn't help myself, and I didn't know where to turn. I kept going to these cults and to these occultic groups and each time there would be more demons instead of less. I finally decided to come here. I want to thank you for staying on the telephone and helping the ministers. I want to praise and thank God that I have just received Jesus Christ as my Savior. I want you to know I am free. They're gone and I love Jesus! Thank God He set me free."

The terrible danger of the occult is that people expose themselves and their children to it and are unaware of the spiritual pitfalls. When it results in the unleashing of satanic power, as in this case study, then they are totally unprepared to deal with it.

NEW AGE THEOLOGY

Who Is God?

New Age theology does not adhere to the biblical God. It defines God in many ways, if indeed the group acknowledges God at all, since some groups acknowledge only a Universal Oneness. Whether God or the Oneness is spoken of, it is generally an impersonal force that permeates creation. Monism and pantheism are the two foundational philosophies to which New Agers subscribe. Monism is the philosophical idea that all reality, material and spiritual, is One, with no real distinction. In the New Age, this is presented as an impersonal force, or a Universal Oneness, in which is contained all reality. Monists do not necessarily call it god unless it is for sake of convenience. In contrast, pantheists call the universal force a god, which is quite often likened to Brahma in Hinduism.

The material world itself is a lower form of the impersonal force. It is said to be a low vibration of the same thing or the same substance. This substance, when existing at a slow vibration, becomes matter. The only true reality is the spiritual substance, which exists in its purest form at a high vibration. A person must use a New Age technique to attain a high degree of spirituality to become one with the high vibration, hence becoming one with God or One with the One. His New Age practice allows him to correct past mistakes and raise his consciousness. The moment he recognizes his Christ consciousness or higher consciousness, he can pick up the threads of his karma, for example, and discover how to escape the endless cycle of reincarnation.

Who Is Man?

Pantheistic New Agers teach the divinity of man. Mankind is divine because this god is the "life" within man and all living creatures. Some New Age proponents, such as Unity Church, limit the nature of this god to living things but not inanimate objects, like a rock.[22] Other New Agers, such as Benjamin Creme, openly state that a rock is as much god as what humans are. Creme wrote, "You are God. I am God. This microphone is God. This table is God. All is God."[23]

Monistic New Agers acknowledge the impersonal force as a Universal Oneness of everything. They teach that the One is imminent in all creation, animate and inanimate. They acknowledge this as an *unknowable* thing, since it is an impersonal entity.

Certain avatars or messengers have brought knowledge to us to help us become One with the One. When New Agers speak of Jesus Christ, they speak of him as a prophet or one of these avatars. The New Age movement also separates Jesus from the Christ. The Christ is a cosmic consciousness that is also the true divinity of all mankind, so Jesus was not special in being a christ. Jesus, as a man, manifested the Christ and learned how to use his Christ consciousness.

---

22. This view is actually called *panentheism* (pan=all, en=in, theos=god), hence "god is in all" as compared to pantheism "all is god." The difference, for example, is that most pantheists will say that a tree is part of God, but the panentheist will say that God is the life in the tree. Pantheism is promoted by Unity Church writers, as portrayed by Charles Fillmore in *Jesus Christ Heals* (Lee Summit, Missouri: Unity School of Christianity, 1944), 31: "God is the love in everybody and everything. God is love."
23. Benjamin Creme, *The Reappearance of the Christ and the Masters of Wisdom* (North Hollywood, CA: Tara Center, 1980), 116.

Scriptural Response

The New Age cannot subdivide the biblical God into a dualistic yang and yin any more than one can subdivide the nature of God in any other manner. As stated in the opening of the Athanasian Creed, "We worship one God in Trinity, and Trinity in Unity; neither confounding the Persons nor dividing the Substance."[24] God's substance, as eternal Spirit, cannot be divided, and His Persons cannot be confused or confounded.

God cannot be reduced to the substance of created matter (pantheism). Neither can He be reduced to an impersonal force (monism). God is distinct from all created things and, therefore, His essential nature is different from creation. The Bible says that God is invisible Spirit (John 4:24; Col. 1:15). He created all existing things and is therefore not a created thing Himself (Col. 1:16–17; Heb. 1:2, 11:3).

God Is a Personal Being

God is a personal Being, according to Scripture. In Exodus 3:14–15, God answered Moses out of the burning bush and announced His name: "I AM." Looking closely at this, "I" (first person singular) "AM" (verb: to be; a reflective cognizant ego; personality), hence properly translated as "I AM."[25] The distinction between God and humans is clear, since no human can be God and God is not a man, for He said, "I am God, and not man, the Holy One in your midst" (Hos. 11:9). God is distinct from mankind in His nature and Being. Even in the incarnation of Jesus Christ, His deity remained unchanged while He became flesh (Phil. 2:6–8). Isaiah

---

24. Alexander Roberts and James Donaldson, eds., *Ante-Nicene Fathers, Volume 7: Fathers of the Third and Fourth Centuries* (Grand Rapids: Eerdmans, 1996), 563.
25. Exodus 3:14 according to Adam Clarke's Commentary: 'ehyeh (OT:1961) 'asher (OT:834) 'ehayeh (OT:1961). These words have been variously understood. The Vulgate translates EGO SUM QUI SUM, "I am who am." The Septuagint has: Egoo (NT:1473) eimi (NT:1510) ho (NT:3588) Oon (NT:5607). "I am He who exists." The Syriac, the Persic, and the Chaldee preserve the original words without any gloss. The Arabic paraphrases them, "The Eternal," who passes not away; which is the same interpretation given by Abul Farajius, who also preserves the original words, and gives the above as their interpretation. The Targum of Jonathan, and the Jerusalem Targum paraphrase the words thus: "He who spake, and the world was; who spake, and all things existed." As the original words literally signify, "I will be what I will be," some have supposed that God simply designed to inform Moses, that what he had been to his fathers Abraham, Isaac, and Jacob, he would be to him and the Israelites; and that he would perform the promises he had made to his fathers, by giving their descendants the promised land. It is difficult to put a meaning on the words; they seem intended to point out the eternity and self-existence of God. Plato, in his Parmenides, where he treats sublimely of the nature of God, says, "Oud' (NT:3761) ara (NT:686) onoma (NT:3686) estin (NT:2076) autoo (NT:846), nothing can express his nature; therefore no name can be attributed to him."

spoke to the singularity of God's nature: "Before Me there was no God formed, nor shall there be after Me" (Isa. 43:10). This tells us that no man will become a god by awakening the god within himself, since God stands alone in His divinity.

The monistic New Age theory is also challenged by the biblical passages that manifest God's person. God spoke of Himself in Genesis 1:26 with the plural pronouns "us" and "our," showing that He is a loving, caring, personal God, who created mankind. God also has the attributes of a personal Being in that He has a will and mind (Rom. 8:27). He is not a mindless impersonal force.

Even further, God is presented in Scripture as a tripersonal Being, as we saw in the Athenasian Creed: "one God in Trinity, and Trinity in Unity." We see all three persons of God's nature (Father, Son, and the Holy Spirit) in the Great Commission of Christ: "baptizing them in the name of the Father and of the Son and of the Holy Spirit" (Matt. 28:19). We see one God in three Persons.

Man Is Not Divine

Since man is not divine, then his nature must be correctly ascertained. Genesis 1 reveals that man was created in the image and likeness of God. Genesis 3 shows that man did not maintain his status in perfect creation, but he fell into sin through the disobedience of one man (Adam), through whom sin was passed on to all. Romans 5:12 records, "Just as through one man sin entered the world, and death through sin, and thus death spread to all men, because all sinned."

God's image in man may be scarred, marred, battered, and crushed, but it still exists (James 3:9). God reached down to man through the gospel of Jesus Christ to save humanity through Christ's atonement.

Paul continues in Romans 5:17, "For if by the one man's offense death reigned through the one, much more those who receive abundance of grace and of the gift of righteousness will reign in life through the One, Jesus Christ." For the grace of God has appeared for the salvation of all mankind, teaching us to abandon worldly lusts and to look for that blessed hope—the appearing of the glory of the great God and of our Savior, Jesus Christ.

Man, then, is but dust and is not divine: "For dust you are, and to dust you shall return" (Gen. 3:19). Scripture says in Hebrews 9:27, "It is appointed for men to die once, but after this the judgment." Man is a fallen creature and is not divine in his inner nature.

Jesus Is the Christ

The New Age movement teaches that Jesus is not the Christ. The Bible says this is the doctrine from the prince of darkness. In 1 John 2, God tells us that Jesus Christ is the propitiation for our sins. His atonement satisfied God's wrath against our sins, and not for ours only, but for the sins of the whole world (1 John 2:2). The apostle John continued with a test for knowing God. Unlike the New Age, where knowing a god means knowing yourself, John tells us that to know God we must first know Jesus as He truly is. Those who deny that Jesus is the Christ are liars: "Who is a liar but he who denies that Jesus is the Christ? He is antichrist who denies the Father and the Son" (1 John 2:22). If we deny the Son, then we cannot claim to know the Father either (v. 23). John brands the New Age movement's teaching on Christ as a doctrine of the Antichrist.

Jesus is the Christ. He asked His disciples, "Who do men say that I, the Son of Man, am?" And Peter responded, "You are the Christ, the Son of the living God." Jesus blessed him, saying, "Blessed are you, Simon Bar-Jonah, for flesh and blood has not revealed this to you, but My Father, who is in heaven" (Matt. 16:13, 16–17). New Agers are wrong by claiming to be little christs. Jesus alone is *the* Christ. Jesus cannot be separated from the Christ because Jesus is the Christ, the Son of the living God.

Man Is Evil

New Age theology teaches that man is essentially good and that he is evolving into full divinity. This doctrine on man aligns with secular humanism—a belief in direct conflict with Jeremiah 17:9: "The heart is deceitful above all things, and desperately wicked; who can know it?" The heart of man is deceitful above everything and incurably sick. God did not create the Nazi death camps of Dachau, Auschwitz, or Buchenwald—these came from the heart of man.

The first chapter of Romans dispels any illusions about the nature of man. He is not essentially good; he is a fallen creature desperately in need of the new birth, "for all have sinned and fall short of the glory of God." (Rom. 3:23).

The New Age movement denies that sin is rebellion against the law of the eternal God. It wants nothing to do with monotheism or the God of creation, who gave us the Law. It does away with Him and with His Law, and it teaches that man may do what is right in his own eyes: if he happens to do any wrong, he will make up for it in his next reincarnation.

The Bible answers this in explicit terms. In Hebrews 1:3, we are taught that Jesus Christ purged human beings of sin and sat down at the right hand of God. Therefore, mankind is not going to improve upon the Lord Jesus, and individuals cannot pay for their own sins through karmic balance. Jesus paid it all. The old hymn is correct: "Jesus paid it all, all to Him I owe; sin had left a crimson stain, He washed it white as snow."[26]

Reincarnation Does Not Exist

The New Age teaches that there is a physical and a spiritual evolution. In the physical realm, New Agers accept the Darwinian evolutionary hypothesis, and in the spiritual realm, they believe man is evolving to eventual perfection of godhood. The New Age religion teaches salvation by works and by reincarnation. The Bible teaches in Ephesians 2:8–10, "By grace you have been saved through faith, and that not of yourselves; it is the gift of God, not of works, lest anyone should boast."

Reincarnation does not exist, but the bodily resurrection does. Jesus said in John 14:19, "Because I live, you will live also." He promised to raise His children to life eternal at the last day. There will be a resurrection of the just to eternal life with God, and of the unjust to eternal separation from God (Acts 24:15).

The New Age movement believes in Karma and reincarnation; people pay for what they did in previous incarnations (rebirths). But the Bible teaches that if someone comes to Jesus' Cross at Calvary, then Jesus will take his or her sins away. He bore in His own body man's sins on the tree. He entered once into the holiest of all, having obtained eternal redemption for us (Heb. 9:12). There is no reincarnation after death. There only remains judgment (Heb. 9:27).

The Law of God Is the Standard of Righteousness

The basic theology of the New Age denies the law of God as the standard of righteousness, but the epistles of Romans and Galatians teach that the law is holy, righteous, just, and good. Sin is transgression of the law, and all unrighteousness is sin. The New Age wants nothing to do with an absolute standard of righteousness. It is a relativistic theology that has no absolute authority except personal authority.

---

26. Elvina M. Hall, "Jesus Paid It All" (1865).

There Is Only One Savior

The New Age movement believes in multiple saviors and avatars: Buddha, Mohammed, Zoroaster, Confucius, Lao Tzu, and Saint Germain, to name a few. They have many gurus and divine messengers. That is why devout Hindu gurus think they are divine; they are gurus because they are messengers from this unknowable being named Brahma. But the Bible speaks of only *one* messenger. At the end of the ages, God appeared in His Son, Jesus Christ alone, to reconcile the world to Himself by His sacrifice of the Cross (2 Cor. 5:19).

The New Age teaches that there are many paths or ways to God. But Jesus said, "I am the way, the truth, and the life. No one comes to the Father except through Me" (John 14:6). And in Acts 4:12, "Nor is there salvation in any other, for there is no other name under heaven given among men by which we must be saved." The earth is God's creation, and we live in God's universe. Man breathes His air by God's mercy. Man perches precariously on a burned-out cinder with a hot core of nickel, 93 million miles from a large solar furnace that is held in place by a force known as gravity, a force no one really understands. Man spins on the earth at a speed of approximately twenty-five thousand miles per hour in space, and there is no guarantee he will be here in the next microsecond.

Christians, however, may feel quite secure. The Scripture says our Father answers our calls to heaven; He never puts us on hold or takes the receiver off the hook. We can face tomorrow because we know He lives. The universe is held together not by esoteric avatars but by the God of the galaxies and the Creator of all things. Scripture teaches that He entered the world in the form of man. "All things were made through Him, and without Him nothing was made that was made" (John 1:3). In Jesus Christ is light, and the life is the light of men (v. 4). The light goes on shining in the darkness of the New Age movement, and they cannot understand it, but it is still truth.

CONCLUSION

The New Age movement teaches a form of universalism: everyone will gain salvation in the end, regardless of his or her particular way, be it a guru, teacher, savior, or an avatar. New Agers have abandoned biblical theology and rejected the God of the Bible. They hate monotheism and love pantheism and monism. They despise Christianity, and they love esoteric mysticism.

There is an extremely significant passage of Scripture relevant to this study that should be carefully considered. Second Timothy 3:1–5 says, "But know this, that in the last days perilous times will come: For men will be lovers of themselves, lovers of money, boasters, proud, blasphemers, disobedient to parents, unthankful, unholy, unloving, unforgiving, slanderers, without self-control, brutal, despisers of good, traitors, headstrong, haughty, lovers of pleasure rather than lovers of God, having a form of godliness but denying its power. And from such people turn away!" This chapter goes on to describe these various practices and then states, in verses 13–17:

> But evil men and impostors will grow worse and worse, deceiving and being deceived. But you must continue in the things which you have learned and been assured of, knowing from whom you have learned them, and that from childhood you have known the Holy Scriptures, which are able to make you wise for salvation through faith which is in Christ Jesus. All Scripture is given by inspiration of God, and is profitable for doctrine, for reproof, for correction, for instruction in righteousness, that the man of God may be complete, thoroughly equipped for every good work.

Second Timothy 4:1–5 instructs the Church:

> I charge you therefore before God and the Lord Jesus Christ, who will judge the living and the dead at His appearing and His kingdom: Preach the word! Be ready in season and out of season. Convince, rebuke, exhort, with all longsuffering and teaching. For the time will come when they will not endure sound doctrine, but according to their own desires, because they have itching ears, they will heap up for themselves teachers; and they will turn their ears away from the truth, and be turned aside to fables. But you be watchful in all things, endure afflictions, do the work of an evangelist, fulfill your ministry.

This is a sober note of warning. It reveals the world in which we now find ourselves. We live in a world hostile to the gospel of Jesus Christ. It is the last days, and 1 John tells us that we have been in the last days for almost two thousand years. The perilous times will come, and men will turn away—that is the key—they will turn away their hearing from the truth, and the truth will be turned into mythology.

What is the real danger of this on the practical level? First, it can neutralize faith. If people start playing with the tools of the occult and the New Age movement, then they will open themselves up to the power that organizes it, sustains it, and operates through it. They will be vulnerable to the prince of darkness. Therefore, of the occult, God says, *Do not touch these things* (Deut. 18:9–12). If you do, then you will follow in the pathway of the nations that preceded Israel and Canaan. They listened to the New Agers of their day: the soothsayers, the fortune-tellers, and the practitioners of the demon gods of Canaan. The Lord destroyed them and said He would destroy all who follow in their footsteps.

Christians dare not walk in the world of the occult. First, it will neutralize your life and your testimony if you are a Christian. Second, it can expose you to satanic attack, to oppression, and to all forms of evil. If you yield yourself to the servant of sin, its servant you are (John 8:34). If you choose to yield yourself to Christ, then you are yielding to righteousness that ends in life. Third, the danger of the New Age movement and the occult is their essence: they are what they always have been—evil. If you turn the handle of the unopened door of a forbidden dimension, what will come through is satanic power of enormous proportions.

We must love the people who are trapped in the New Age movement, for the sake of Christ at Calvary. We must love them enough to learn the difference between what they believe and what we know is truth; love them enough to test them by the Scriptures and help them hold fast to what is good; love them enough to resist Satan on their behalf; love them enough to pray with them and for them; love them enough to stand up to them and tell them the truth. We must love them for Christ's sake. As the Scripture instructs, "Be diligent to present yourself approved to God, a worker who does not need to be ashamed, rightly dividing the word of truth" (2 Tim. 2:15).

Do not play host to the kingdom of the occult. Do not open your doors, your homes, your children, your churches, or your friendships to this new and increasing form of great spiritual darkness. Instead, be filled with the Holy Spirit, kneel before God with your Bible, and cry out to Him. If the church will cry to the Holy Spirit, seek the power of Christ, dig into the mind of the Word, discipline herself, and bow before Him, then God will equip the church. Put on the whole armor of God, the helmet of salvation, the breastplate of righteousness, and the belt of truth. Have your feet shod with the readiness to preach the Gospel. Take the shield of faith—Jesus is Lord—and the sword of the Spirit, which is the Word of God, and stand, praying always in the spirit (Eph. 6:14–18). If you do this, God has promised that we shall be more than conquerors through Him who loves us (Rom. 8:37).

RECOMMENDED RESOURCES

1. Hull, Bill. Jesus Christ, *Disciplemaker.* Grand Rapids: Baker, 2004.

2. Martin, Walter. *The New Age Cult.* Minneapolis: Bethany House, 1989.

3. Martin, Walter. *Spirit of this Age.* CD/audiotape, Walter Martin Ministries, www.waltermartin.com.

4. Pike, Sarah M. *New Age and Neopagan Religions in America.* New York: Columbia University Press, 2004.

Quick Facts About Psychic Phenomena

- Psychic or paranormal phenomena (its modern label) are genuine experiences that cannot be explained by scientific observation; they are experiences of the body and soul that appeal to the spiritual nature of man.

- These phenomena include Extrasensory perception (ESP) and Psychokinesis (PK).

- There are two forms of the phenomenon called ESP: normal and occult.

- Satan is the power behind occult psychic phenomena; their purpose is to deceive mankind and lead people away from God.

- Hypnotism is not a psychic phenomenon, but it can be used in conjunction with occult tools such as regression therapy and automatic writing.

- Biblical texts, taken out of context, are often used to justify psychic events.

7

Psychic Phenomena

The purpose of all occult psychic phenomena, both ancient and modern, is deception. These phenomena, manifested long ago by the magicians of Egypt who imitated the miracles of God, are meant to duplicate and destroy—as the Antichrist will duplicate the miracles of Jesus in order to deceive and destroy humanity. They do not lead people toward God, but *away* from Him. Psychic phenomena intrigue many people because they involve the strange and the extraordinary, offering secrecy, excitement, and power to a world that loves anything cloaked in mystery.

It is imperative in this study of the subject of psychic phenomena that the scriptural meaning of the term be accurately understood. Paranormal phenomena modern psychics point to in relation to the Bible do not exist. But people who dabble in modern psychic phenomena often attempt to use the Bible against itself; they seek to prove that Scripture sanctions intrusion into this dangerous realm, when it does not.

What exactly are psychic phenomena? *Psychic* simply comes from the Greek word *psuke,* which refers to the soul.[1] *Phenomena* refers to experiences: the things that people see, hear, smell, taste, touch, or comprehend. *Psychic phenomena* (also called *Psi* by interested scholars) are events that cannot be explained by scientific observation. They are experiences of the soul; things that appeal to the spiritual nature of man.

People who are interested in Psi, such as Spiritists, Rosicrucians, and occultists involved in all of the various forms of occultism, argue that the Bible has a vast record of psychic phenomena, and they provide multiple illustrations to support their points. In order to refute these key illustrations (the ones they all seem to agree upon), they must be studied in the contexts of both the Old Testament and

---

1. Breath, i.e. (by implication) spirit, NT:5590, *New Exhaustive Strong's Numbers.*

the New Testament. Individual biblical context is then compared to the teachings of Scripture as a whole, until the correct answer to the question of psychic phenomena in the Bible is at last revealed. It is this final answer that must be effectively communicated to the world.

DEFINITION OF TERMS

People involved in the world of the paranormal point to a litany of terms used to describe their experiences. An examination of some of these terms is helpful, and the biblical perspective on them, essential.

Parapsychology is the study of psychic phenomena including extrasensory perception (ESP) and psychokinesis (PK). *Para* in the Greek means "alongside," and *psychology* means the study of the psyche or the soul or the spiritual facility sometimes known as the mind. *Extrasensory perception* is a term coined by ESP researcher Dr. J. B. Rhine and defined in *Man, Myth, and Magic* as "the reception of information by a person through other means than the senses."[2] It is data received through means other than the customary channels of information.

In any study of Psi phenomena, an important distinction must be made between normal ESP and occult ESP, as both exist in the world today. There are two kinds of phenomena called *extrasensory*, since they extend beyond the natural five senses. Scripture, human experience, and occultic influence distinguish these. The term *normal ESP* can be used to describe experiences many people have had (including most Christians) that are difficult to explain, such as husbands and wives or parents and children, separated by a great distance, suddenly "sensing" that something is wrong. Somehow, they seem to *know* an accident or even a death has occurred, and when the facts are investigated, this knowledge is found to be correct—without any communication between the parties involved. This is *normal ESP*, since it occurs commonly in most people. Normal ESP comes without invitation or seeking.

In contrast, when people deliberately try to access ESP, they trespass willingly into the world of the occult, attempting to acquire power over an unexplainable phenomenon. Quite often, intentional exploration of paranormal power or experiences opens the heart and mind to the occult.

---

2. Cavendish, *Man, Myth and Magic*, 875.

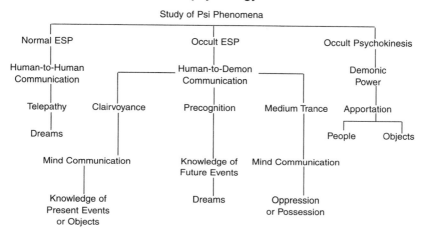

Psychic Phenomena (Psi)
Parapsychology

Study of Psi Phenomena

Normal ESP is the ability to know of an event while it is in process, a telepathic capacity to access information simultaneously present in another person's mind.[3] This normal form of ESP has nothing to do with the occult. It is a latent sense often referred to as a *sixth sense* or *intuition,* more developed in some people but most likely present in all.

The experiments of Princeton researcher Dr. Robert Jahn and his Princeton Engineering Anomalies Research (PEAR) staff appear to support the existence of some type of normal ESP based on lab trials, although his scientific colleagues remain skeptical. "Analyzing data from such trials, the PEAR team concluded that people could alter the behavior of these machines very slightly, changing about 2 or 3 flips out of 10,000."[4]

The key element distinguishing normal ESP from occult ESP is the *source* of the knowledge. Does it originate from a link to a human mind or from a link to

3. Walter Martin held this position based on the ESP studies available during his lifetime. Conclusive scientific proof of these phenomena remains elusive, but Dr. Martin believed there was enough evidence to sustain his conclusions.
4. Benedict Carey, "A Princeton Lab on ESP Plans to Close Its Doors," *New York Times,* February 10, 2007, http://www.nytimes.com/2007/02/10/science/10princeton.html?ex=1328763600&en =2f8f7bdba3ac59fl&ei=5090&partner=rssuserland&emc=rss.

the mind of an interdimensional being, identified biblically as a demon? This is a crucial difference that can be determined through research and confrontation, although not necessarily in that order. A thorough examination of personal spiritual and religious beliefs, daily activities, and individual reputation is enlightening, but not always possible.

At times like this a civil but direct confrontation with the person, using the name of Jesus Christ, will reveal the source of the power. Demons are subject to the name of Jesus; they *must* obey a directive given to them in His name (however reluctantly). This command can be given by nonbelievers, but by doing so they place themselves in a dangerous position, similar to the sons of Sceva in the book of Acts:

> Then some of the itinerant Jewish exorcists took it upon themselves to call the name of the Lord Jesus over those who had evil spirits, saying, "We exorcise you by the Jesus whom Paul preaches." Also there were seven sons of Sceva, a Jewish chief priest, who did so.
>
> And the evil spirit answered and said, "Jesus I know, and Paul I know; but who are you?"
>
> Then the man in whom the evil spirit was leaped on them, overpowered them, and prevailed against them, so that they fled out of that house naked and wounded. (19:13–16).

Normal ESP usually manifests itself in *telepathy*: the ability to access knowledge of an idea or event while it is in process. This knowledge has no connection whatsoever with the occult or with religion. There are numerous cases where people experience knowledge of something happening in a single moment, and they themselves are not present at these events.[5] An individual closely linked to another person's mind—the result of a moment or a lifetime of interaction—may possibly

---

5. These are sometimes called "spontaneous" Psi events. See Carlos S. Alvarado, "Thoughts on the Study of Spontaneous Cases," *Journal of Parapsychology* 115, vol. 66 (2002). Spontaneous intuition, telepathy, or sixth-sense experiences commonly surface with family or friends, like finishing a friend's sentence (exactly what he or she was thinking) or when a person knows something happened to a spouse or child that is miles away. These things, even though difficult to explain, are what we call normal sixth-sense, intuition, telepathy, or normal ESP. It usually occurs even when you are not trying to exercise it, which is unlike those who try to send or receive messages.

receive information related to that person, information accurately transferred from one individual to another.[6] One example of this is the recurring experiences of some people who know when a telephone call is coming or who the telephone call is from, without the aid of caller ID. These people do not have any ties to the occult, yet they seem to have access to information *outside* of their own minds. This could be a normal form of ESP that has nothing to do with the occult.[7]

Occult ESP can be divided into three main categories for the purpose of definition: *clairvoyance, precognition,* and *medium trance. Clairvoyance,* also called *remote viewing,* is the capacity to access knowledge from a source not related to the human mind; this source is always demonic. The information can be linked to an object and/or event located far from the actual physical presence of the person.

Precognition is knowledge of events that have not yet taken place. These projected events may be days, weeks, or months in the future—sometimes even years. The information has nothing to do with human-to-human contact, and everything to do with human-to-demon contact.

A *medium trance* is a direct physical encounter with demonic personalities, usually triggered by attempts to speak to the dead. Demons imitate the bodies and voices of the departed, but Scripture says a great gulf is fixed between the living and the dead (Luke 16:26). No one is permitted to cross this gulf—so who is impersonating lost loved ones? The Bible warns of the power of demonic beings, ancient enemies who use whatever tools they have at their disposal to deceive people—imitating the voices and faces of beloved relatives, and parroting back their words—all for the purpose of luring grieving families and curious spectators ever closer to demonic influence and control.

Although mention of Psi phenomena still elicits groans of disbelief from the scientific community, decades of controlled ESP studies conducted by the PEAR laboratory resulted in enough accurate answers to warrant continued investigation

---

6. An argument against this is that even if we grant that someone had "knowledge" of something, it does not prove that it came from another person's mind. There are equally valid explanations without saying it was transferred *from* a mind *to* a mind. In the 1920–30s, stage performers would do "mental telepathy" acts around America for entertainment. They were discovered to be good guessers who had learned the art of watching subtle body indications, such as eye movement, tensed muscles, or pulsating veins, but they claimed it was an illusion and not any real power.

7. As a word of caution, people seem to remember when a hunch or intuitive thought is correct, but pay less attention to the times when their hunches or intuitive thoughts are wrong.

of the phenomena. According to the *New York Times*, "Several expert panels examined PEAR's methods over the years, looking for irregularities, but did not find sufficient reasons to interrupt the work."[8]

Social psychologist David G. Myers notes the continued interest in the paranormal by a variety of institutions of higher learning. "Five British universities have parapsychology units staffed by PhD graduates of Edinburgh University's parapsychology program. . . . Sweden's Lund University, the Netherlands' Utrecht University, and Australia's University of Adelaide also have added faculty chairs or research units for parapsychology."[9] Interestingly enough, there is not one accredited parapsychology program in America.[10]

The United States military and the CIA investigated Psi phenomena at various intervals throughout the twentieth century, conducting studies under controlled conditions:

> Government-sponsored research in psychic functioning dates back to the early 1970s, when a program was initiated at what was then the Stanford Research Institute, now called SRI International. That program was in existence until 1989. The following year, government sponsorship moved to a program at Science Applications International Corporation (SAIC) under the direction of Dr. Edwin May, who had been employed in the SRI program since the mid 1970s and had been Project Director from 1986 until the close of the program.[11]

The one negative aspect to these studies, however, is the consistent exclusion of the spiritual and religious data necessary to determine the source of the psychic power. The academic prejudice against any information not derived from scientific data remains a barrier of monumental proportions.

---

8. Carey, "A Princeton Lab on ESP Plans to Close Its Doors," 115.
9. David G. Myers, "Is There ESP?" http://www.davidmyers.org/brix?pageID=61. Myers adds, "But other research psychologists and scientists—including 96 percent of the scientists in the U.S. National Academy of Sciences—are skeptical (McConnell, 1991)."
10. "So You Want an Education in Parapsychology" Haunted America Tours, http://www.hauntedamericatours.com/ghosthunting/EDUCATIONINPARAPSYCHOLOGY/.
11. Jessica Utts, "An Assessment of the Evidence for Psychic Functioning," University of California, Davis, http://anson.ucdavis.edu/~utts/air2.html.

Under the cultural label of parapsychology, ESP stands side by side with the equally mysterious phenomenon of psychokinesis (PK). The term *psychokinesis* comes from the Greek word *psyche*, meaning "breath" or "soul," and *kinein*, meaning "to move." Psychokinesis is the capacity to move solid objects by the exertion of mental forces against them or possibly the ability to alter reality. *Psychokinetic energy* is nothing more than demonic power channeled by a medium or someone involved in the occult for the purpose of stimulating faith in occultic phenomena, drawing people further into the world of the occult. The ability to move an object (apportation) is a startling thing, and even more puzzling is the phenomenon of *teleportation*—the physical transference of a human body from one location to another.[12] In India, some religious leaders claim to have teleported from one location to another, but the scientific evidence has yet to be collected.

In 1989, a psychologist and a physicist investigated the phenomenon of psychokinesis and published their findings in the highly respected physics journal *Foundations of Physics*. According to Dean Radin (Princeton Psychology Department) and Roger Nelson (PEAR Lab), "This quantitative literature review agrees with the findings of two earlier reviews, suggesting the existence of some form of consciousness-related anomaly in random physical systems."[13] Radin and Nelson's examination of evidence indicated the statistical probability of some form of psychokinetic power, but these findings have since been disputed by others who maintain that errors exist in the computations.[14]

Defining Psychic Research

ESP and the things connected with it are nothing new. The basic research on Psi phenomena began in the 1880s, not in a scientific laboratory, but with the evaluation of mediums and Spiritistic phenomena. History supports the fact that the roots of ESP in the laboratory lie in the kingdom of the occult.

---

12. Some paranormal researchers distinguish between *apportation*, the movement of objects, and *teleportation*, the movement of human bodies. For the sake of our discussion, we will use apportation in reference to material objects, and teleportation in reference to human bodies.
13. Dean I. Radin and Roger D. Nelson, "Evidence for Consciousness-Related Anomalies in Random Physical Systems," *Foundation of Physics* 19, no. 12 (December 1989): 1499–1514, available at Springerlink, http://www.springerlink.com/content/n0576p6352g84158/.
14. These issues are as hotly debated today as they were decades ago. The scientific community remains skeptical. See I. J. Good, "Where Has the Billion Trillion Gone," *Nature* 389 (October 23, 1997), http://members.cruzio.com/~quanta/review.html, for a review refuting Radin's work.

In 1882, the Society for Psychical Research was founded in London to investigate psychic and Spiritualist claims, and about the same time, the Institute of Metaphysics was formed in France.[15] Soon afterward, the American Society of Psychical Research followed suit (1885). During the late nineteenth and into the early twentieth century, several studies took place in telepathy at Harvard University, Stanford University, and the University of Groningen in the Netherlands that produced interesting results.[16] Harry Price, one of the more famous "ghost hunters" of Great Britain observed:

> The first systematic attempt in Great Britain to examine scientifically the phenomena which we now call psychic was made by a little group of Oxford graduates and undergraduates which went by the name of the Phasmatological Society. This was about 1874. . . . Other attempts at bringing psychic phenomena to the notice of orthodoxy include the one made by Sir William Barrett when, in 1876, he was successful in persuading the British Association at its meeting in Glasgow to permit him to read a paper on thought-transference, even though its publication in printed form was suppressed. Sir William Crookes also tried to interest official science in his experiments with D. D. Home and Florrie Cook, and invited one of the secretaries to the Royal séance: he refused. . . . In spite of the fact that orthodoxy has, in the past, regarded psychics with a certain amount of disapprobation, a few universities have made notable attempts to turn psychical research into a science.[17]

The researchers of the nineteenth century were investigating the psychic phenomena of telepathy, clairvoyance, psychokinesis, and *any* observable fact associated with Spiritism and Spiritistic mediums. These investigations continued into the twentieth century with the research conducted at Duke University by Professor William McDougall, and Joseph and Louisa Rhine (both biologists). According to the Rhine Research Center, J. B. Rhine renamed telepathic and clairvoyant

---

15. During the nineteenth century, the term *Spiritualism* was used to describe psychic beliefs. Today, *Spiritism* is more commonly used.
16. See Harry Price, *Fifty Years of Psychical Research* (New York: Longmans, Green & Co., 1939).
17. Ibid.

medium communication with the dead, calling it extrasensory perception (ESP). "He [Rhine] began experiments to study ESP and, later, psychokinesis (PK), the movement of objects through the will of the mind."[18]

Unfortunately, Dr. Rhine dismissed biblical data in his classification of ESP and thus missed a vital area of information and a fundamental fact: psychic phenomena and the occult have always been inextricably intertwined. Anyone studying the "new science" called *Parapsychology* by Dr. Rhine must acknowledge the historical truth that this "science" came into existence as a result of human attempts to penetrate beyond the grave, proof positive that the past roots of the psychic run deep into the realm of the occult.

OCCULT PSYCHIC PHENOMENA

The moment people venture into the dark side of psychic phenomena, they encounter forces *outside* this dimension; only a psychic force can predict the future—only demonic power manipulates these life-changing experiences. ESP is extremely dangerous when it explores these phenomena.

Levitation

One of the most familiar of these psychic phenomena, and certainly one that has garnered a great deal of attention, is *levitation,* the ability of a solid object to defy the laws of gravity and rise up from the earth with no visible means of support. This has nothing to do with Harry Houdini and the art of illusion. It is not hypnotism. This is the phenomenon of a chair suddenly floating off the floor or a book hovering over a table. Séances occur where individuals—holding hands—feel the table they are sitting at rise off the floor, even though they are not touching it or anything around it. Those involved in a Spiritist séance can see a glass of liquid floating in midair or mediums levitating and moving across the room, and even under test conditions, it defies all known scientific inquiries. The hands of countless skeptics have explored the air beneath these tables, glasses, and chairs, testing for magnetic fields or trickery, yet in many instances, they discovered nothing but empty space. This is levitation in the world of the occult.

---

18. Rhine Research Center, "History," http://www.rhine.org.

These phenomena are real. There have been attempts made to fool the unwary, but this individual fraud does not invalidate the phenomenon as a whole—much as a piece of fake fruit does not prove that all fruit is fake. These are not wild stories cooked up by well-meaning theologians to frighten people back to the study of the Bible. It is something that is genuine, and the people involved experience it frequently.

Apportation

A second term used in the world of the occult is *apportation.* This is the transportation of a solid object from one location to another by a means not visible to observers. It usually refers to the movement of a physical object from one place to another (also referred to as *psychokinesis* or *telekinesis).* This phenomenon is usually difficult for most people to believe, but the former Soviet Union conducted extensive Parapsychology and extrasensory perception (ESP) investigations on the apportation of objects simply because they observed Russian psychics doing these things, and they had no scientific answer for it.[19]

Daniel Dunglas Home (1833–1886) was a young man of Scottish descent who claimed to be the grandson of the tenth Earl of Home (on the wrong side of the blanket). Home was a *physical medium* who was at the center of some remarkable paranormal activity. In his 1863 autobiography, Home—perhaps the most powerful medium in hundreds of years—described the following demonstration of *teleportation* that occurred during one of his séances:

> On the 28th day of February, 1852, while the undersigned were present at the home of Mr. Elmer, Springfield, Mass., for the purpose of making critical experiments in the so-called spiritual manifestations, the following, among other remarkable demonstrations of power, occurred in a room thoroughly illuminated. The table, around which we were seated, was moved by an invisible and unknown agency, with such irresistible force that no one in the circle could hold it. Two men—standing on opposite sides and grasping it at the same time, and in such a manner as to have the great-

---

19. Edwin C. May and Larissa Vilenskaya, "Overview of Current Parapsychology Research in the Former Soviet Union," Laboratories for Fundamental Research, http://222.lfr.org/LFR/cs/Library/Fsu1.pdf.

est possible advantage—could not, by the utmost exercise of their powers, restrain its motion. In spite of their exertions, the table was moved from one to three feet. Mr. Elmer inquired if the spirits could disengage or relax the hold of Mr. Henry Foulds; when suddenly, and in a manner wholly unaccountable by us, Mr. Foulds was seated on the floor, at a distance of several feet from the table, having been moved so gently, and yet so instantaneously, as scarcely to be conscious of the fact. . . .

The undersigned are ready and willing, if required, to make oath to the entire correctness of the foregoing statement."

The original paper was signed by John D. Lord, Rufus Elmer, and nine others, living at Springfield, Mass.[20]

The teleportation of Mr. Foulds occurred in the presence of multiple witnesses. Daniel Home frequently offered to be tested under strict conditions, and the results of these demonstrations of power were consistent and confirmed by many credible observers.[21]

Materialization

A third term that may be a bit more recognizable is *materialization,* also known as *apparition.* This occurs when a spirit-being, or what appears to be the spirit of a departed loved one, actually takes on physical form.[22] This phenomenon often transpires in a room full of people, who then testify to the fact that the figure is solid. In the past, some apparitions even formed with a physician waiting to take the blood pressure and heartbeat! There are affidavits of unbelieving physicians who have been through the experience, and it was very unnerving for them—as it would be an unnerving experience for anyone. Nobel Laureate physiologist Dr. Charles Richet (1850–1935) detailed his experiences in what he termed "metapsychics" in

---

20. D. D. Home, *Incidents In My Life* (New York: Carleton, 1863), 46–47.
21. Although Home was accused of fraud by some throughout his lifetime, it was never proved. His autobiography is quite detailed, supplying dates and locations of séances, names of eyewitnesses, and their personal testimonies describing his ability as a medium and the psychic events directly related to it. Home continually offered to be tested under the most rigorous conditions and was reportedly evaluated by noted scientists such as Sir William Crookes.
22. Materializations are not limited to loved ones; they can be well-known historical figures or unknown individuals.

Thirty Years of Psychical Research. One of his many encounters with a spirit at a séance is particularly enlightening:

> It is therefore established that there was no instrumentation and no theatrical accessories that the medium could use, and that no stranger could enter the room. . . .
>
> The materializations produced were very complete. The phantom of Bien Boa appeared five or six times under satisfactory conditions in the sense that he could not be Marthe [the medium] masquerading in a helmet and sheet. Marthe would have had not only to bring, but also to conceal afterwards, the helmet, the sheet, and the burnous. Also, Marthe and the phantom were both seen at the same time. To pretend that Bien Boa was a doll is more absurd still; he walked and moved, his eyes could be seen looking round, and when he tried to speak his lips moved.
>
> He seemed so much alive that, as we could hear his breathing, I took a flask of baryta* water to see if his breath would show carbon dioxide. The experiment succeeded. I did not lose sight of the flask from the moment I put it into the hands of Bien Boa who seemed to float in the air on the left of the curtain at a height greater than Marthe could have been even if standing up. . . . While he blew into the tube the bubbling could be heard. *. . . A comical incident occurred at this point. When we saw the baryta show white (which incidentally shows that the light was good), we cried "Bravo." Bien Boa then vanished, but reappeared three times, opening and closing the curtain and bowing like an actor who receives applause.*[23]

Richet's scientific account reveals the ability of demons to materialize into solid human forms that walk, talk, move their lips, turn their heads, shift their eyes, and

---

23. Charles Richet and Stanley Debrath, *Thirty Years of Psychical Research* (Whitefish, MO: Kessinger, 2003), 505–6. Emphasis added to indicate footnote. *Explanation of a baryta water experiment is as follows: "Respiration in plant tissues gives rise to carbon dioxide as a waste product. This gas is absorbed by barium hydroxide solution, an alkaline solution known as baryta water. This is then titrated with an acid to find out how much carbon dioxide has accumulated in it. This test allows an estimation of the carbon dioxide output of the plant material to be made." Science and Plants for Schools, "Measuring the production of carbon dioxide (from respiration) with baryta water." http://www-saps.plantsci.cam.ac.uk/osmoweb/baryta.htm.

produce detailed clothing appropriate to the time period of the person they are imitating. These materializations can also involve something called *ectoplasm*. A medium, sitting at a table or in a curtained-off alcove called a "cabinet," will exude a form or substance from the mouth, nose, or body that takes the shape of a so-called departed loved one.[24] Recently, at a séance held by the Haymist Circle in Great Britain, the following manifestation of ectoplasm was demonstrated by a spirit named Timothy:

> Timothy returned and explained to Paul Barker (circle leader) the procedure necessary to be able to show everyone ectoplasm in red light. As Timothy needed to withdraw before the light was switched on, at the appropriate time he would make a knocking sound to indicate Spirit were ready. On hearing the knocks, Paul lit the red lamp to a dim level, and opened the cabinet curtains. As he gradually increased the level of red light, it became clear for everyone to see the ectoplasm that was exuding from David's gagged mouth, spilling down onto his chin and chest. After trying to ensure that all sitters had been able to see this wonderful phenomena, Paul extinguished the light and Timothy spoke, saying that he was now talking to us through the ectoplasm that we had seen being exuded. He withdrew once again, the red light was turned on and as its intensity was slowly increased by Paul, sitters were delighted to see the ectoplasm, this time emanating from David's solar plexus area. A mass of it was across David at hip level, with vibrant folds of this living energy extending down between his legs towards the floor.[25]

This type of phenomenon has been well documented, and the forms of ectoplasm will often match pictures in the family albums of the people present at these séances. Although there have been many fakers of this phenomenon (using chiffon

---

24. A "cabinet" is usually a small section or corner of a room that does not have windows or doors. It was often curtained off to ensure the privacy of the medium.
25. "David Thompson Physical Séance at Jenny's Sanctuary," http://web.archive.org/web/20070105134829/http://www.physicalmediumship.co.uk/seances/Thompson180804.html. This séance took place on August 18, 2004. For more information on medium David Thompson, formerly of the Haymist Circle, see Spiritualist Chatroom, http://spiritualistchatroom.com/documents/docs.cgi?category=archive&item=1041687975.

material as the ectoplasm), the methodical assessment of it by respected scientists such as Dr. Charles Richet and Sir William Crookes is difficult to dispute.

Another famous psychic, Alec Harris (1897–1974), produced multiple materializations throughout a forty-year career. Harris would intentionally separate himself from his audience in a curtained-off alcove in order to concentrate on the spirits and produce physical phenomena.[26] His wife, Louie, described one "circle" or séance in her autobiography, *They Walked Among Us*:

> At last there was movement from the cabinet curtain. The slim, bearded figure of Rohan appeared, standing uncertainly in the aperture before the cabinet. This calm, strong guide always opened our circles with greetings, explanations and advice. It was his habit to come straight out and speak to each sitter in turn, taking his or her hands in his own slender ones. With his deep, soft voice he would welcome each one warmly. . . .
>
> After a pause he came hesitantly forward and commenced his welcoming gesture, taking the hands of each sitter in the front row. . . .
>
> Rohan released my hands and returned to the cabinet. He took hold of the black curtains which hung down to conceal Alec. He parted them, then held one side high above his head to reveal the entranced Alec. Seated in his chair, he was clearly visible to all. Rohan, still holding the curtain, backed away to stand by the window some distance from Alec. It was obvious there were two separate entities before the sitters.
>
> "Can you see the medium clearly?" asked Rohan. "Here am I, standing quite apart from him. Are you sure you can see us both?"
>
> There were excited cries of "Yes" and "Wonderful!" from the sitters. Rohan let the curtain fall back, and came forward to take the hands of those seated in the back row. He always made sure everyone was similarly greeted, that they saw and touched him.[27]

---

26. Harris died in 1974.
27. Louie Harris, *They Walked Among Us* (Psychic Press, 1995), quoted in "Press 'Exposure' Fails," http://www.freewebs.com/afterlife/articles/pressexposure.htm. See also http://www.spirituali-tyvideos.com/watch-video/8RLQ_AyU-Pk/ThePsychicTimes/physical-mediumship-part-two.html for author Alan Crossley's eyewitness acounts of the physical mediumship powers of Helen Duncan and Alec Harris.

In many of these instances, the forms that materialized first as ectoplasm gradually became solid. Witnesses touched skin, clothing, and hair.

There are phony mediums—charlatans—and then there are the real articles.[28] The genuine medium can do this, and do it under test conditions.

Dream Interpretation

Another term of psychic phenomenon is *dream interpretation.* A person might have a dream, and an individual who claims to be psychic offers to interpret the dream. This happens quite regularly in the world of the occult, and people often call it prophecy. The dream interpretation is substantiated by facts present in the person's life, but it is something quite different from prophecy.

The phenomenon of the Internet has raised awareness of and access to thousands of sites promoting dream interpretation. One site, claiming to be "the leading astrology site since 1995!" offers a "Dream Dictionary" for those searching for answers. For example, if someone dreams of flowers, he or she need only consult the Dream Dictionary to discover the hidden meaning behind the dream flowers:

Lilac - Poison, Illness, Death
Daisy - Indecision about feelings
Orchid - Sexuality and sensuality
Rose - Poison, White = purity, Black = death
Lily - Renewal, Springtime, Resurrection
Narcissus - Self-love[29]

Dream communication is as ancient as mankind himself; it is difficult to disprove a phenomenon present in cultures from time immemorial. But when these experiences are used to guide individual choices in life, a discerning individual must question the source behind the information. This source can be God (as revealed in the Bible), it can be the subconscious mind, it can be telepathy, or it can be an evil being.

---

28. It is also possible to have a combination of both, where real demon-possessed psychic have a bag of tricks. Uri Geller and others fit this description.
29. Astrology.com, "Predictions," http://predictions.astrology.com/dd/flowers.html.

Psychic Healing

Psychic phenomena advocates emphasize *healing*—physical, emotional, mental, and spiritual. In the world of the psychic, people spend a lifetime searching desperately for healing.

Edgar Cayce (1877–1945) was the most well-known psychic to offer the lure of psychic healing in modern times. Cayce (pronounced *case-ee*) was called the "sleeping prophet" due to the fact that most of the psychic phenomena associated with him occurred during trances, so that he appeared to be asleep. Cayce frequently "healed" people who approached him for readings:

> The readings make recommendations for a variety of health concerns—from acne, diet, and cancer to arthritis, mental illness, and psoriasis. Nearly every condition that existed between 1901 and 1945—whether it was childbirth, fractures, or vitamin deficiency—is represented in the files of the Cayce material. Interestingly, modern-day researchers have found that many of the recommended treatments, given to specific individuals, seem to be applicable today on a much wider scale. Two notable examples of this are psoriasis and scleroderma. For both of these diseases, the Cayce regimen involved specific diets, chiropractic medicine, and other natural remedies and procedures. In recent years hundreds of people with these two ailments have been helped by following a similar program.
>
> Cayce also saw total health as involving coordination among the physical, mental, and spiritual components of life. Any complete approach to health needed to consider an individual's entire being rather than simply the illness. Because of this concept, it has been said that the beginnings of present-day holistic health started from the readings of Edgar Cayce.[30]

Cayce (with no medical training) gave more than fifteen thousand documented psychic readings for people, some of them for people who lived thousands of miles away from him. During these readings, he diagnosed various diseases and ailments,

---

30. Edgar Cayce's Association for Research and Enlightenment, "About Edgar Cayce: Edward Cayce on . . . Wellness—Health, Healing," http://edgarcayce.org/about_edgarcayce/wellness/wellness_health.asp#.

and on many occasions, he prescribed treatment for his followers that proved to heal their illnesses. His psychic healing methods are continued today through the church he founded in 1931, the Association of Research and Enlightenment (ARE).

William Marrion Branham (1909–1965), was an American psychic healer who traveled from one end of the country to the other, preaching a variety of gospels and laying hands on people in an effort to heal them. Some miraculous healings did occur, all carefully chronicled. When asked in an interview if the Holy Spirit was responsible for the healing, Branham admitted that his "angel" did it.[31] This angel told Branham what to say and do, and when to pray. Eventually, Branham's writings began to reflect this influence, and he ended up denying the Holy Trinity and many other Christian doctrines. "Not one place in the Bible was trinity ever mentioned. . . . It's Catholic error, and you Protestants bow to it."[32]

Psychic surgery is another form of occult healing by which the individual is treated without benefit of anesthesia. The psychic healer appears to reach inside an individual (usually lying flat on a table) and withdraw some type of bloody substance from him or her that is attributed to disease. Psychic surgery, which is sometimes linked to Psi, has been exposed in many cases as a sham that is sometimes deadly because healing rarely takes place. Researcher Martin Gardner reveals that 1970s television star Andy Kaufman visited a psychic surgeon in his final months in a desperate attempt to cure his lung cancer. "He had gone to the Philippines in a sad, futile effort to be cured by a 'psychic surgeon.'"[33] Kaufman's psychic treatment was unsuccessful, and he died on May 16, 1984, at the age of thirty-five.

Although many of these healers often prove to be frauds, this does not automatically discount the reality of psychic surgery. Johanna Michaelson described in

---

31. Koch, *Occult ABC,* 235. According to Billy Paul Branham, William Branham's eldest son, "One night in June of 1947 at Vandalia, Illinois, the Angel of the Lord appeared visibly in the motel room where Brother Branham was staying" (Voice of God Recordings, http://www.branham.org/branhamdefault.asp?home=BillyPaulBranham&LoadPageDetal=BillyPaulBranham.htm). See also David Edwin Harrell Jr., *All Things Are Possible: The Healing and Charismatic Revivals in Modern America* (Bloomington, IN: Indiana University Press, 1979).
32. William Branham, *Conduct, Order, Doctrine of the Church* (Jeffersonville, Indiana: Voice of God Recordings, 1991), 182.
33. Martin Gardner, *The New Age: Notes of a Fringe Watcher* (Buffalo, NY: Prometheus, 1991), 167.

detail her genuine experiences as an assistant to a psychic healer in her book *The Beautiful Side of Evil*. In a recent interview she emphasized, "There is a beautiful side of evil—deceptive, subtle, adorned with all manner of spiritual refinements, but no less from the pit of hell than that which is blatantly satanic."[34] Healing occurs in the world of psychic phenomena, but it is not healing that comes from God.

Psychic Predictions

One famous example of psychic predictions is the "prophet" Nostradamus (1503–1566). Michel de Nostredame was born to a wealthy notary and his wife in Saint-Rémy-de-Provence, France. He showed an interest in medicine at a young age, but his plans to become a doctor were complicated by the plague and his work as an apothecary. By 1550, de Nostredame had become a physician and immersed himself in the world of the occult, gradually building a reputation as an astrologer (although he asked his clients to provide their own birth charts). Eventually, he became known as Nostradamus and authored his first almanac, full of prognostications for that particular year. The almanac proved to be quite successful, eventually enabling Nostradamus to focus specifically on prophecies written in the form of quatrains (four lines per verse) that he organized in groups of one hundred, called *Centuries* (eventually totaling ten volumes). These remain his most famous work, published under the title *The Prophecies*, now a popular occult text.

His reputation as a respected astrologer earned Nostradamus the position of court physician for Charles IX (Catherine de Medici's son), but his true fame came after his death, in the interpretation of his *Centuries*. The prophecies of wars, disasters, and other catastrophes promised by Nostradamus in his quatrains are confusing at best, however, and usually make sense only if interpreted *after* the fact (hindsight clairvoyance). One of his most famous quatrains foretold the death of the French king Henry II—a prediction he used to warn the king:

> The young lion shall overcome the old
> On the field of war in single combat [duelle];

---

34. Ellen Makkai, "Harry the Wiz Is the Wrong Biz," *WorldNet Daily*, November 26, 2001, http://www.wnd.com/news/article.asp?ARTICLE_ID=25446.

He will pierce his eyes in a cage of gold.
This is the first of two loppings, then he dies a cruel death.[35]

Henri II, it would seem, proclaimed a tournament in the Rue St. Antoine,
the site of the Bastille, then in the country, for July 1, 1559, in honour of
the marriage of his daughter Elizabeth of France with Philip II of Spain. He
listed himself as one against all comers. The joust being nearly over and the
sun setting, the Duc de Savoie begged him to quit the running, as his side
was already victorious; but the King wanted to break another lance over it,
and commanded the young Comte de Montgommeri, captain of his Scotch
Guard, to run a tilt in conclusion. He excused himself, but the King
insisted and grew angry. Of course the young man then obeyed, put spurs
to his horse, and struck the King upon the throat, below the vizor. His
lance shivered, and the butt raising the vizor, a splinter wounded the King
above the right eye, cutting several of the veins of the *pia mater*. The King
swooned. He lived on, however, for ten days in terrible agony, as foretold
in the prophecy, *Deux classes une, puis mourir, mort cruelle.* Nostradamus
styles both of them lions, as they both fought under that device. The King
wore a gilt helmet, so that the *cage d'or* was literally fulfilled.[36]

As intriguing as this fulfillment of prophecy seems, not a single quatrain
Nostradamus wrote was interpreted or understood *before* it came to pass. Since
clairvoyance is connected to the occult, and Nostradamus was admittedly involved
in it, it should come as no surprise that some of his predictions might be fulfilled.
His accuracy overall, however, remains a hit-or-miss proposition, the hallmark of
occult prophecy. In contrast, the biblical prophets of God maintained 100 percent
accuracy.

With the advent of the Internet, not only have the interpretations of *The
Prophecies* reached a new peak of creativity, but Nostradamus has acquired several
new quatrains—courtesy of modern writers.

35. Charles A. Ward, *Oracles of Nostradamus: Life of Nostradamus* (Internet Sacred Texts Archive),
   chap. 1, http://www.sacred-texts.com/nos/oonoon05.htm.
36. Ibid.

Poltergeists

The contemporary evidence for psychic activity can be spotted all over the landscape: in homes, libraries, lighthouses, and ships—any earthly place where man dwells—spirits will eventually try to make contact. Poltergeists, also known as familiar spirits, have even infiltrated the realm of television and movie stardom with shows such as the cable SciFi Channel's *Ghost Hunters* and movies such as *Poltergeist.* Their "entertainment" résumé is lengthy and quite successful.[37]

Poltergeists (demons masquerading as humans) are usually imaginative in creating their manifestations: they slam doors, walk up steps, throw objects around a room, moan, cry, touch people, and materialize as dark clouds, red eyes, figures, or colorful moving orbs of light. If they succeed in catching someone's attention, they often speak to the targeted individual audibly or through digital recorders, Ouija boards, or automatic writing, crafting tales of tragedy and woe designed to foster sympathy in the hearts of listeners. In some cases, foul smells or ice-cold temperatures manifest along with other phenomena.

People involved in psychic phenomena refer to these poltergeists as "memory imprints" of dead people searching for peace. Hans Holzer, the famous ghost tracer, observed, "Not all temporary separations of the body and etheric* self include a visit to the next world. Sometimes the liberated self merely hangs around to observe what is being done with the body."[38]

The world persists in its definitions, but the biblical revelation stands: poltergeists are *demons*, not lost human souls caught between this world and the next. They are not ghosts á la Patrick Swayze in the romantic tearjerker *Ghost.* Demons enjoy playing games with human beings, and they have had centuries to perfect their technique.[39] This phenomenon is well-known throughout the world, accepted by millions as fact, and now documented by various media programs. It is authentic.

---

37. Anytime the media is involved in paranormal programs, it is always wise to be suspicious of their results. Some may be legitimate; some may be orchestrated for ratings sake. Independent of obvious television drama, however, there are many reliable accounts of poltergeist experiences from sober-minded people who are not seeking the limelight and have no motive to fabricate their stories.

38. Hans Holzer, *Ghosts: True Encounters with the World Beyond* (New York: Black Dog & Leventhal, 2004), 21. *Etheric* is a New Age term referring to the human "aura" or the energy body, also called the *life force.*

39. See chapter 14, "Demon Possession and Exorcism."

Astral Projection

The psychic phenomenon of *astral projection* occurs when an individual in a state of consciousness claims to leave the physical body and travel long distances, observing other people, recording their actions, and returning to the body to confirm it. Letters, phone calls, and e-mails are all methods of confirmation—detailed proof provided to those "visited."

Robert Bruce and Professor C. E. Lindgren, in their how-to handbook on astral projection, describe the moment when an out-of-body experience (OBE) takes place—as well as its purpose:

> During conscious-exit projection, the real-time body will be vividly aware of the sensation of separating from and leaving its physical body behind. . . . My overall impression is that this process is designed to provide the central animating spirit consciousness with *regular and direct* exposure to the refining and adjusting influences of living karma and universal law, as they exist at vastly higher and more rarefied dimensional levels. This, is how I believe, karma and universal law actually work: the higher subtle bodies filter up and down through the dimensional scale—from the gross physical body to its highest energetic state—whenever the physical body sleeps.[40]

When the mind and heart are opened to these types of occult experiences, a person becomes exposed to malignant spiritual beings waiting to take advantage of any vulnerability. Astral projection may seem harmless on the surface, but its potential impact can be devastating.

ARE PSYCHIC PHENOMENA IN THE BIBLE?

People involved in psychic phenomena often quote the Bible to legitimize their experiences. For example, a passage commonly cited in defense of levitation is the ascension of Jesus in Luke 24:51–53: "Now it came to pass, while He blessed them, that He was parted from them and carried up into heaven. And they worshiped Him, and returned to Jerusalem with great joy, and were continually in the temple

---

40. Robert Bruce and C. E. Lindgren, *Astral Dynamics: A New Approach to Out-of-Body Experiences* (Charlottesville, Virginia: Hampton Roads, 1999), 50–51, emphasis in original.

praising and blessing God." Jesus Christ ascended. The meaning of *ascend* is "to go up"; therefore, some argue that Jesus must have levitated into heaven. Christ was the supreme medium who defied the laws of gravity. Mediums involved with levitation defend it by saying they are simply doing what Jesus did, perfectly in line with the psychic phenomena in the Bible. But a serious flaw in this argument is the key fact that when Jesus *ascended*, he did not float back down to earth. All people who levitate return to the earth 100 percent of the time.

Another example psychics use to support the biblical phenomena of levitation is that of Christ walking upon the water:

> Now in the fourth watch of the night Jesus went to them, walking on the sea. And when the disciples saw Him walking on the sea, they were troubled, saying, "It is a ghost!" And they cried out for fear. But immediately Jesus spoke to them, saying, "Be of good cheer! It is I; do not be afraid." And Peter answered Him and said, "Lord, if it is You, command me to come to You on the water." So He said, "Come." And when Peter had come down out of the boat, he walked on the water to go to Jesus. But when he saw that the wind was boisterous, he was afraid; and beginning to sink he cried out, saying, "Lord, save me!" And immediately Jesus stretched out His hand and caught him, and said to him, "O you of little faith, why did you doubt?" And when they got into the boat, the wind ceased. (Matt. 14:25–32).

The disciples stood in the boat, and Jesus came toward them walking on the water. Psychics argue that it is impossible to walk on water, so in reality, Jesus came to them levitating *over* the water. He commanded Peter to come out of the boat, and Peter came out. It is here, according to the mediums, that Peter lost his faith; he broke the psychic contact with Jesus and could not levitate anymore, and he sank down into the water. The problem with this interpretation is the nature of Jesus Christ; as both man and God, He had the power to walk on the water *He* created if He chose to do so, and that power was easily extended to Peter.

These are classic illustrations of what is termed *biblical psychic phenomena*, and it is necessary to disprove them one by one using a comparison of the scriptural example to the truth behind psychic activity.

Daniel Home, a unique and powerful physical medium, consistently performed various psychic demonstrations—even under test conditions—and many
of the events he initiated were observed by witnesses, including Sir William
Crookes (1832–1919) the famed British scientist responsible for the discovery of
the cathode tube and the advent of X-rays. Crookes was also an acknowledged
authority on the phenomena of Spiritism (an interest originally sparked by skepticism). The following is an eyewitness account of a séance conducted by Daniel
Home:

> Home went into a trance; he walked about the room for some time, arrang-
> ing the light and talking to himself; he then opened the window, drawing
> the curtains, so that we could see nothing but his head; and got outside the
> window. This frightened us, and Lindsay wanted to stop him, but did not.
> Presently, he came back and told us that we had no faith whatever, or we
> would not have been alarmed for his safety. He went into the next room,
> and we saw him pour out from a bottle on the table about half a large wine
> glass of brandy. He brought the glass back with him; then partially cover-
> ing himself with the window curtains, but holding the glass with the
> brandy in it above his head, between us and the window, so that we could
> see it, he was lifted off the floor about four or five feet. While in the air, we
> saw a bright light in the glass; presently, he came down and showed us that
> the glass was empty, by turning it upside down; he also came to us and
> turned it upside down upon our hands; then going back to the window he
> held the glass up, and we heard the liquid drop into it.[41]

In the presence of Viscount Adare, Sir William Crookes, and others, Daniel
Home caused wood blocks to rise from the table; a pencil stood up on its point and
began writing; multiple raps, loud vibrations, and apparitions occurred, along with
consistent events of levitation, apportation, and teleportation. Many people believed he had succeeded in levitating in exactly the same way Jesus Christ "levitated" in the Scripture. Things like this do not happen under normal conditions,

---

41. Viscount Adare, *Experiences in Spiritualism with Mr. D. D. Home* (New York: Arno, 1978), 77.

but Daniel Home was not a normal man; he was a *medium* who derived his energy from a very different source.

Another biblical text misused by the defenders of the occult is Acts 8:39. Scripture reveals that Philip had a discussion with an influential Ethiopian eunuch in which he preached the truth of Jesus Christ from the gospel and then baptized him. After this, the record says, "Now when they came up out of the water, the Spirit of the Lord caught Philip away, so that the eunuch saw him no more; and he went on his way rejoicing. But Philip was found at Azotus" (Acts 8:39–40). The Spirit of the Lord caught up Philip, and the next thing he knew, he was preaching at Azotus. Mediums refer to this as a case of biblical *teleportation*, since Philip moved from one location to another—a solid object moved over a considerable distance. They claim to do exactly the same thing today, but it is not the same event, and God is not the author.

The power of God moved Philip from one place to another so the gospel might be preached to bring people to Christ and so God might be glorified. Objects apported in psychic phenomena imitate the power of God, but the purpose is to lead people *away* from God and deeper into the occult.

Numerous instances of individuals physically moving from one place to another have been recorded by people like J. Stafford Wright in *Man, Mind, and the Spirits* and other investigators of the psychic world, who have compiled extensive case histories. Dr. Kurt Koch recounted this example:

This time I was able to investigate the matter myself. The house in question was also examined by some university men, by the police, by both a Catholic and a Protestant minister, by a government official and by others who were merely drawn through curiosity. Over a period of six weeks 135 objects were reported to have flown through the rooms in an inexplicable manner. Each one of these occasions was carefully noted. At the same time several apports were observed. Once, when the Catholic priest and two other men were in the kitchen a glass ball came flying into the room, and all the doors and windows had been shut! The ball fell at the feet of the priest who picked it up. It felt hot, but it was undamaged. In the ball was a picture of Maria Einsiedel, a Catholic pilgrimage place in Switzerland. The owner of the house exclaimed that the ball had been in the living room, and so the three of them went to investigate. The ball in the living room had disappeared![42]

The combined number of these eyewitness verifications, drawn from the files of the Society for Psychical Research (United Kingdom) and the American Society for Psychical Research, is well into the hundreds, if not more. Verifications from a few sources might be questionable, but when they are reported consistently from different parts of the world, a pattern begins to emerge.

Something is happening. It is a strange thing when reports surface of a mystic in India who stood on a railroad platform, in a crowd of his followers—and suddenly disappeared—only to reappear two hundred miles away at another railroad station, with no train in sight. The reality of this was difficult to disprove when more than fifty people testified that the man stood in one train station one moment, and telegraphed a message (with witnesses) from another train station just a few minutes later. It is not easy to explain away the distance of two hundred miles and two separate groups of witnesses—all of whom cannot be lying—as conjecture and not fact.[43]

Some psychics have indicated that teleportation is quite simple; all it requires is a tremendous concentration of psychic forces. Arthur Ford, a well-known psychic who worked with Bishop James Pike and was responsible for making contact between Pike and his son (who committed suicide), spoke of numerous instances of teleportation that occurred with Pike present.[44]

In 2004, British journalist Emma Heathcote-James published an account of her experiences in exploring the world of psychic phenomena:

> It is a little known fact that for over 100 years we have actually had experimental scientific proof that we all survive the death of our physical bodies, that the living mind separates from the dead brain.

---

42. Kurt Koch, *Between Christ and Satan* (Grand Rapids: Kregel, 1970), 109.

43. Walter Martin, *Psychic Phenomena* (compact disc), Walter Martin Ministries. Available at www.waltermartin.com.

44. For more information on Bishop Pike's occult experiences, see Frank C. Tribbe, comp., ed., *An Arthur Ford Anthology: Writings by and About America's Sensitive of the Century* (Nevada City, CA: Blue Dolphin Publishing, 1999).

There are many credible documented accounts of full and partial mate-rialisations of known deceased people and animals, objects, and sitters being levitated, the apportation of flowers, coins, and other objects, and detailed and specific information coming from the mouths of those who have passed on. Such goings on happen within the branch of physical medi-umship, which is a very rare phenomenon. It has been estimated that only one in 100,000 people has the ability to develop this gift, and it generally takes twenty years or so of disciplined effort to do so.

Physical mediumship producing materialisations is currently the only phenomenon that can be used to provide experimental proof of survival after death. During such physical "séances", or sittings, what I am inter-ested most in is the fact these rare mediums are able to bring the deceased back to Earth in solid form. Everyone present in the room is able to see, touch, speak with, and hold their deceased loved ones. [45]

In cases like this, it is very difficult to dispute the evidence and declare that the teleportation, apportation, or materializations do not occur.

CASE STUDY

Walter Martin

Some time ago, I was preaching at a large camp meeting in New England on the subject of occult phenomena in our day. After one meeting, a lady and her husband came over to talk me. She was visibly shaken, very pale, and she said, "You frightened me very much."

I replied, half jokingly, "Well, if it will keep you away from the occult, I'm happy."

"No, that's not the problem," she said, "I've had an experience I just don't understand, and I need to ask you about it."

"All right, I'm happy to help."

"About five months ago, I had the strangest thing happen to me," she

---

45. Emma Heathcote-James, "From the Author," Campaign for Philosophical Freedom, http://www.cfpf.org.uk/recommended/books/ehj/cfpf-theywalk.pdf, 2.

began. "I was lying in bed—I may have been asleep or I may have been dreaming; I don't know which one—but suddenly I became aware of the fact that my father was desperately ill. He lives in Switzerland, and I could suddenly see the room he was in as clearly as if I were there with him. It was a hospital room, and I could see everything in it. I saw my father in his bed and heard the doctor talking to the nurse."

She went on to describe the things that had taken place during the incident. "When I woke up, I immediately went to the telephone and tried to call my father, but it turned out that he was in the hospital! He'd been taken there for emergency surgery, and his condition was critical. They didn't know whether or not he would live or die. I had no way of knowing that; I knew *nothing* about it."

Her father lived, and she wrote to the hospital staff about her strange experience. "I described the room to them in detail, but the one thing I saw or experienced that didn't make any sense to me was the presence of glass doors behind the bed. I'd never seen anything like that before, and I described it to them as glass doors behind the bed. They wrote back to me and confirmed that everything I had seen, including the position of the furniture in the room, was absolutely accurate, but there were no glass doors behind the bed."

Frustrated and confused, she wrote back to them for more information. "I thought, *There has to be something there,* so I asked them to describe everything in the room." They wrote back again, and described an object behind the bed. It turned out that the glass doors were a portable privacy screen. American hospitals have curtains for privacy, but this Swiss hospital had a folding glass partition, stored behind the bed when not in use. This partition turned out to be the glass doors behind the bed.

This woman had never seen a glass folding screen, so she could only describe it as glass doors. When she explained this in the next letter, it threw everyone including the nurse into a spin, simply because no one three thousand miles away could have known the design of the room, the position of the bed, and the actual clothing the nurse was wearing.

She said, "What is this? It scared me to death."

I told her I would get back to her as soon as possible on this and I did, after verifying her name and reputation. It turned out she was a committed Christian with no connection whatsoever to the occult. I met with her later, and we discussed the phenomena of normal ESP at length, setting her mind at ease.

It is true that humans have the capacity to know an event while it is in the process of occurring, or to know the state of a person/object connected with this event. This knowledge has nothing to do with the occult, which leaves only two possibilities: divine intervention and/or a latent mechanism within the human brain that operates unpredictably during the course of human events.

HYPNOSIS AND THE OCCULT

Does hypnosis have a valid place as far as Christianity is concerned? Is it satanic? Can medical hypnosis be separated from occult hypnosis? And what exactly happens when someone is hypnotized?

The subject of hypnosis is well-known to most people in modern society, but what is not so highly publicized is the fact that a universally agreed-upon definition of it does not exist; its exact nature and mechanism remain a mystery to this day. Sigmund Freud, who pioneered its therapeutic use, described hypnosis as, "A quite peculiar mental state very similar to sleep. . . . Changes occur in it and mental functions are retained during it which are absent in normal sleep."[46]

Barrie St. John, a British hypnotherapist, defines hypnosis as "a natural phenomena best described as deep state of relaxation and concentration, wherein the mind becomes distant and detached from everyday cares and concerns. This state is neither sleep nor unconsciousness but an altered state of awareness, often referred to as the 'hypnotic trance' or 'hypnotic relaxation'. The conscious and analytical part of the mind is safely bypassed allowing access to the unconscious part of the mind whereby you 'let things happen' and react imaginatively to suggestion."[47] Hypnosis has always intrigued people, although it was considered for many years as a simple—if mysterious—parlor game. Eventually, the perception of hypnotism

---

46. Donald Robertson, "Experts Define Hypnosis," UK College of Hypnoses & Hypnotherapy, http://www.ukhypnosis.com/Definitions.htm.
47. Barrie St. John, "A Brief History of Hypnosis," Hypnoshop, http://www.hypnoshop.com/pages/hypnosis-faqs.html.

changed, and people began to think of it as something frightening and a game best avoided.

Dr. Franz Anton Mesmer, a pioneer in the subject of hypnotism, which he initially called "mesmerism" (based on the comments of people who observed his procedures), was forbidden to practice the science in 1784 because it was considered to be devilish, and the results could not be understood by the people of the time. Dr. James Braid, a Scottish physician and surgeon, picked up Mesmer's practices in 1842 and popularized them in the medical profession; he did a fine job of using hypnosis for the treatment of various illnesses, and in the infant science of psychiatry. Sigmund Freud studied hypnosis and at first seemed intrigued by it, but he eventually rejected it as a primary tool on the grounds that it would create more problems than it could solve, so he neglected it in favor of his particular method of psychoanalysis.

The man who truly pioneered the exploration of hypnosis was a physician by the name of James Esdaile, who, while working in India in the 1840s, performed hundreds of major operations using only hypnosis.[48] He did not have anesthesia or painkillers, so he began to use hypnosis in his medical practice.

Medical Hypnosis

Today, hypnosis is recognized by the American Medical Association as a valid branch of medical treatment when it is done by a medical hypnotist or therapist. Hypnosis itself is not related to the occult. In essence, a person who becomes hypnotized is able to concentrate on a specific subject with an intensity that he or she is incapable of repeating under any other circumstance. All of the tremendous focal powers of the mind focus on one specific thing, enabling the individual to accomplish what some in the medical profession have called "semimiracles." People overcome facial twitches, stuttering, shyness—the list is impressively long. This is known as *medical hypnosis.*

How is this accomplished? The human mind operates on more than one level or track, similar to the structure of a modern CD. On each one of these tracks is some level or fragmentation of consciousness. No one fully understands it, because no one fully understands the human psyche or mind. But suppose that the first

---

48. See James Esdaile, *Mesmerism in India* (Honolulu: University Press of the Pacific, 2003).

track is the conscious mind: all the things seen or heard every day. Track 2 is the subconscious or unconscious mind: things absorbed or stored in the memory that people are not aware of on a conscious level. These things can cause enormous problems and complications in an individual's life, particularly if they are unpleasant in nature.

A medical hypnotherapist simply gives the conscious mind a suggestion that acts like a shot of Novocaine, like blocking the nerve in a tooth, so that the message of pain cannot go to the brain. Track 1 in the mind is no longer functioning, and track 2 is now open to penetration. The levels of human consciousness are multiple. Bypassing track 1 allows the hypnotherapist to ascertain the problem in tracks 2 or 3. Some things can be corrected; some cannot.

Hypnotherapy, properly done, can be a great medical boon. In the hands of charlatans and quacks, however—and particularly in the hands of occult practitioners—it is dangerous and can damage or even destroy the mind. It is an instrument for healing or devastation; dependent on the soul who wields it.

Occult Hypnosis

The world of the occult opens the door to the power of demons and the intervention of satanic forces. Hypnosis, in the hands of someone immersed in the occult, becomes a conduit of evil. For example, *regression therapy* became popular in the last half of the twentieth century; encouraging people to search subconsciously for evidence of their past lives. Glenn Ford, a Hollywood star at the time, became involved in hypnotherapy and told his story about regression to a national publication. It made him a firm believer in reincarnation and a devotee of the occultic world. Glenn was a hardcore navy man who did not buy a lot of nonsense; he attended a Presbyterian church for years and even taught Sunday school.

What could possibly have happened to convince a man of Ford's intelligence of the reality of reincarnation? A friend led him into the strange world of the occult through the normal, simple channel of curiosity. Ford submitted to hypnosis at the hand of someone involved in the occult, and was "regressed" back to a level where a new story about a previous existence emerged. He discovered he had been killed in a duel in one of his past lives. A sword penetrated his body, and Ford described the pain under hypnosis. But as real as this sword wound seemed to be, the whole story was nothing but a clever occult farce.

When Glenn Ford awoke, the hypnotist pointed to a birthmark as the exact spot where his wound occurred in a previous incarnation, and Ford believed it after listening to himself speak fluent French on audiotape—a language he had never learned. And it was not modern French. UCLA experts analyzed the tape and determined that Ford was speaking a Parisian dialect common in seventeenth-century France.[49]

After this experience, no one could convince Glenn Ford that he had not been reincarnated. People experience this quite frequently when they enter the world of the occult. It is not uncommon for a person who submits to this occultic phenomenon to experience an encounter with the forces of darkness. Ancient beings, far beyond human control, take possession of them.

Satan is behind the world of reincarnation, and he supplies all the data. He details all the regressions, so it is not surprising when the details check out. He was *there*, after all—he lived through all these ages, and more than likely has case histories on us. It is perfectly possible for him to communicate any information he chooses to the vulnerable through occult hypnosis. It is a minor issue for the prince of darkness to validate details historically when it suits his purposes. These hypnosis sessions do not prove that *you* lived before; they prove that *someone else* lived before, and that individual is using this knowledge to deceive. The Scriptures say that it is given unto man once to die, and after that the *judgment—not* reincarnation (Heb. 9:27).

Another purpose of occultic hypnosis is *psychic communication*. A person undergoes hypnosis and becomes possessed by a spirit in order to communicate information. This is very common in the writings of psychics and in the study of psychic phenomena. Individuals go into a trance, and they have no memory of what took place except for the recording made of it. They speak in other voices, sometimes four and five voices, and they give messages to the people who are present. This is occult hypnosis for the purpose of psychic communication; it often takes place at séances and in other seemingly innocent settings. This is also the case with the use of hypnosis to produce *automatic writing*, a phenomenon by which

---

49. "A New Life for Glenn Ford?" *Paranormal Review*, September 5, 2006, http://paranormalreview.com/News/tabid/59/mid/368/newsid368/25/Default.aspx. For more information see H. N. Banerjee, *Americans Who Have Been Reincarnated* (New York: Macmillan, 1980).

multiple pages of information (sometimes in foreign languages) are produced independent of the conscious mind of the person writing them.

People searching for healing through hypnotherapy make themselves vulnerable to forces over which they can exercise no control. This is the danger of hypnosis in the wrong hands.

Hypnotism is not a game. Christians must recognize that it can be of great benefit in the hands of a trained medical therapist, but hypnosis in the hands of those
who use it for occult parlor games is lethal. Occult hypnosis is an attempt to imitate the power of God and pervert something good. It opens the door to another
dimension and floods the mind and the soul with the forces that Jesus Christ
warned us against—forces controlled by the prince of the powers of the air.

SCRIPTURAL RESPONSE

It is interesting to note that *levitate, apport, materialize, dream analysis, séance,* and
astral projection are all relatively new terms. All of these things, with the exception
of dream interpretation, appear in historical records *after* the Christian era. So the
question remains: what came first? Those involved in the occult would like people
to believe that the Bible proves occultic psychic phenomena, when in reality it
recounts true miraculous phenomena. What follows after these miracles is only
a very cheap imitation. The revelation of God came first, and the demonic imitated it.

Psychics claim the Bible is filled with psychic phenomena such as apportation
and materialization. For example, the argument is made that John the Baptist's
birth was not prophesied by an angel but by a manifestation—a messenger from
the psychic world (see Luke 1:11–13). John the Baptist came into the world after
that proclamation.

In so-called biblical psychic phenomena, psychics assert that the birth of Jesus
Christ was communicated by a materialization—a psychic messenger—who spoke
to Mary (see Luke 1:28–35). They insist these events are angels taking a human
form. In another instance, Abraham encountered three men on the plains of
Mamre (Gen. 18:1–22). The Bible says two of these men went down to Sodom,
and the city was destroyed. Psychics say these two messengers were so-called psychic manifestations or materializations in human form.

Jesus and Levitation

All of these phenomena must be looked at from the biblical perspective. Was Philip's disappearance in Acts 8:39 a case of apportation? When Jesus walked on the water and ascended into heaven, was it actually levitation? Was the angel or messenger who appeared to Zacharias an apparition? As we have seen, the subject of levitation usually includes the example of Jesus walking on the water. The Greek preposition here is *on*—Jesus was *on* the waters. He was not *up* off the water. So, therefore, the argument that Jesus floated over the top of the waves levitating, and that Peter, when he stepped out of the boat, levitated to meet Him is destroyed by the preposition. Jesus stood *on* the water.

Skeptics often argue, "But water will not support your weight!" It will not support yours and it will not support mine, but it will support the weight of Him who created it. "For by Him all things were created that are in heaven and that are on earth, visible and invisible, whether thrones or dominions or principalities or powers. All things were created through Him and for Him. And He is before all things, and in Him all things consist" (Col. 1:16–17), and that includes H_2O. Jesus walked *on* water, and that is not levitation.

Daniel Home levitated; Jesus Christ ascended. What is the difference? There is a great distinction between the two events. First of all, Jesus Christ ascended into heaven as the Son of God. He did not levitate off the earth for the purpose of demonstrating psychic phenomena. "Jesus said . . . 'Do not cling to Me, for I have not yet ascended to My Father; but go to My brethren and say to them, "I am ascending to My Father and your Father, and to My God and your God"'" (John 20:17). He entered into heaven as our great High Priest (Heb. 4:14). Jesus did not levitate; He ascended from one dimension to the other. This is what we read in Luke 24:51: that He ascended *through* the heavenlies: "Now it came to pass, while He blessed them, that He was parted from them and carried up into heaven." When levitation occurs, someone rises up off the earth and floats, but when Jesus ascended, He went *up* and *through*. Daniel Home floated up, around, and down; he did not go into another dimension. Jesus Christ moved through to another dimension, and the Bible says an angel received Him out of their sight. Two young men stood there in white raiment, testifying to His second coming. There is a vast difference between levitation and ascension.

Every person who claims to levitate eventually lands back on solid ground. This is where the resurrection of Jesus is different. He did not levitate. He rose victoriously over death, sin, and the grave. He appeared to His disciples afterward (Luke 24:39), not because He was bound by gravity, but because He was giving them "many infallible proofs" of His resurrection (Acts 1:3). When He later ascended into the air, He went out of their sight and remained at the right hand of the glory of God (Acts 7:56), from where He rules today until His future return to earth. No mere levitation can match Jesus Christ's resurrection and ascension.

Philip and Apportation

God does not levitate. God does not apport, and Philip was not teleported. Philip was removed from Gaza to Azotus by the Spirit of the Lord, placed there for the purpose of preaching the gospel (Acts 8:40). This is not the same as a Spiritistic medium or someone in psychic phenomena insisting, "He moved from this room to another." What was the purpose of going from one room to the other? Was redemption preached? Did a transformation occur? No, the purpose of demonstrating another dimension of reality was to convince people to place their faith in it.

All that Scripture teaches here is that Philip was found at Azotus, but no details were given as to how God did this. Even among evangelical biblical commentators, some see it as a miracle, and others see it as only a description that Philip was found there. In the absence of details, speculative answers must be guarded against. What happened to Philip cannot be duplicated in the occult, since God did not reveal precisely what took place. In view of this, psychic claims of biblical teleportation can only be an attempt at deception—a tool of Satan. We find similar conditions with the best magicians of Pharaoh's court when Moses withstood him. If the magicians could make their trickery or occult powers appear in any form like the true miracles of Moses, then they could at least cast doubt before Pharaoh that Moses was sent of God. Any psychic experience that is hard to explain is a tool of the great deceiver to draw us away from Christ and His truth.

God warned the Jews to beware of this very thing. They were told to watch out for the people who demonstrated extraordinary powers because they would use these powers to lure them away from God:

> If there arises among you a prophet or a dreamer of dreams, and he gives
> you a sign or a wonder, and the sign or the wonder comes to pass, of which

he spoke to you, saying, "Let us go after other gods"—which you have not known—"and let us serve them," you shall not listen to the words of that prophet or that dreamer of dreams, for the LORD your God is testing you to know whether you love the LORD your God with all your heart and with all your soul. (Deut. 13:1–3)

Occult psychic phenomena are certainly signs and wonders; anyone who has ever experienced one knows the truth of that. But God warns that if someone shows you a sign or a wonder and it comes to pass, that person will lead people into the worship of other gods. People engaged in the study of these phenomena are individuals who end up worshiping someone other than the God of the Bible and trusting someone other than Jesus Christ as the Savior of lost souls. The maze of occult phenomena will only lead away from the Cross and into darkness.

Paul and Astral Projection

A claim is also made by some that the apostle Paul left his body, went to heaven, and came back again, and that this is evidence of astral projection. In so-called projection, the astral or spirit body leaves the physical body and goes into the "astral" plane of existence. During this time, the spirit is capable of travel in multiple dimensions, eventually returning to the physical body.

There are actual cases of astral projection, but what is it and how is it accomplished? Do people truly leave their bodies, or are there forces at work that create the illusion and then provide supernatural information to support it? In dealing with the subject of astral projection, people in the occult cite Paul's experience as proof that mankind survives death and the astral body goes on as a type of envelope into the next plane of reality. They are looking for power in their lives right now, and they are looking for the conquest of death.

Paul did not experience astral projection. He explained in 2 Corinthians 12:2–4 exactly what took place when he referred to this experience. "I know a man in Christ who fourteen years ago—whether in the body I do not know, or whether out of the body I do not know, God knows—such a one was caught up to the third heaven. And I know such a man—whether in the body or out of the body I do not know, God knows—how he was caught up into Paradise and heard inexpressible words, which it is not lawful for a man to utter."

Paul simply used a figure of speech here when he said, "My experience with Jesus

Christ was so fantastic, I cannot tell you whether I was on earth or I was in heaven." But there is not a line there that says that Paul experienced astral projection and floated around in some ethereal realm where he could observe mankind. That is all you get with astral projection. But when you have an encounter with the Holy Spirit, you can be lifted to the height of heights, and you are lifted into fellowship with the living God.[50] Another perspective that throws biblical light upon astral projection is the question of whether humans truly leave their bodies. The Bible makes human existence one entity—God breathed life into Adam, who was a lifeless clay form, and he became a living soul (Gen. 2:7). James 2:26 teaches that the "body without the spirit is dead," so it is biblically impossible for the spirit to leave the body without the body *dying*. Adam's body was dead; it had no life until God breathed life-giving spirit into him and he became "living." And, as James says, if the spirit leaves the body, then it is dead. It is safe to conclude, then, that the apostle Paul did not leave his body in some kind of astral projection experience.[51]

The human mind is a wonderful creation of God and is fully capable of experiencing any dream or vision that God allows it to have of heaven or His throne room. But the Bible explicitly links leaving the body with death, so Paul could not have done so without dying.

Jesus and Materialization

People involved in the occult often point to the resurrection of Jesus Christ as proof of materialization. But it is a comparison that falls short on many levels, not the least of which is the fact that Jesus received an entirely new flesh-and-blood body—a body capable of moving through locked doors into a room full of people—without the aid of a sleeping medium (Luke 24:39; John 20:26–28). Jesus' new, glorified body had no need of an ectoplasmic umbilical cord. He could move from place to place at will and eat or drink with whomever He wished (Luke 24:41–43). He promised His disciples that He would one day drink of "the fruit of the vine"

---

50. There is some debate on whether or not Paul had a near-death experience after being stoned and left for dead in Lystra. But since Paul said in 2 Corinthians 12:2 that he doesn't know what happened—only God knows—any discussion remains purely speculative.

51. Some theories on astral projection, such as Robert Monroe's *Phasing* model, argue that out-of-body experiences (OBE) can take place without ever leaving the body. This would be quite difficult to prove under the best of circumstances, however, so its legitimacy in Paul's situation is simply speculation.

again with them in His Father's kingdom (Matt. 26:29). Jesus ascended into heaven with this new body, and He will return in the same way (Acts 1:11). The conjured demons of the mediums may take on the appearance of flesh and blood temporarily, but Jesus became man *permanently*.

Daniel and Materialization

Occult practitioners also cite the story of the angel Gabriel wrestling with Jacob in Genesis 32:24, or the handwriting on the wall in Daniel 5 as examples of *materialization*. But Daniel reveals the answer to materialization, and it is something quite different than occultists would have us believe: "In the same hour the fingers of a man's hand appeared and wrote opposite the lampstand on the plaster of the wall of the king's palace; and the king saw the part of the hand that wrote. Then the king's countenance changed, and his thoughts troubled him, so that the joints of his hips were loosened and his knees knocked against each other" (Dan. 5:5–6).

King Belshazzar made a great feast for a thousand of his lords, and when they were drunk, they all blasphemed God, and despoiled His temple by stealing sacred temple objects and using them. God took a very dim view of this and sent a unique message to the king.

Belshazzar was very disturbed—as anyone would be if a man's hand suddenly appeared in midair and proceeded to write on a wall—so he asked his magicians, the astrologers, and the Chaldeans for the interpretation. He asked the soothsayers for the answer, but no one could help him. The queen remembered Daniel then, and told the king, "Inasmuch as an excellent spirit, knowledge, understanding, interpreting dreams, solving riddles, and explaining enigmas were found in this Daniel, whom the king named Belteshazzar, now let Daniel be called, and he will give the interpretation" (Dan. 5:12).

God revealed the interpretation to Daniel, and it was a very direct explanation: *God has numbered your kingdom and He has finished it. Your kingdom is at an end; it is divided and given to the Medes and the Persians.* That night, Belshazzar was murdered, and it happened exactly as God said it would.

The people who believe the Bible teaches psychic phenomena insist that this hand was a materialization of a human hand from another dimension, and it had to be interpreted by Daniel, who was a medium. But the Bible clearly states, "There is a man in your kingdom in whom is the Spirit of the Holy God. And in the days of your father, light and understanding and wisdom, like the wisdom of the gods, were found in him; and King Nebuchadnezzar your father—your father the king—made him chief of the magicians, astrologers, Chaldeans, and soothsayers" (Dan. 5:11).

Daniel was not a medium; he was a *prophet*, and the Spirit of the living God dwelled in him. Daniel interpreted the message on the wall because the Holy Spirit lived in him; even the Pagans recognized that. The materialization of a human hand was not ectoplasm conjured from a medium. It is *not* an example of materialization. It was a direct act of God (who allowed everyone present to see a human hand writing on the wall), but it was not a case of biblical materialization. Daniel was a man who became a prophet indwelled by the Holy Spirit. He was master of the mediums and magicians—they could not match him.

Angels and Demons

Poltergeists are far more than the "mischievous spirits" that psychics portray them to be. Fallen angels can never be *friendly* spirits, no matter how pleasant and charming they appear; if challenged in the name of Jesus Christ, they inevitably reveal their identity as demonic beings powerful enough to penetrate the dimension of earth. Their purpose is to deceive men and women by use of creative storytelling and parlor tricks, such as vibrating tables, flying pictures, and apparitions—all meant to destroy human lives. The enemy is clever, powerful, and sadistic, and his forces have had centuries to perfect their stories and games.

TWO KINDS OF ANGELS [52]

GOD'S ANGELS	FALLEN ANGELS
Accountable to God (Job 2:1)	Oppose God
Sent by God (Ex. 23:20)	Requested by humans
Respond to God's will (Ps. 91:11)	Respond to rituals (at *their* will)
God chooses which angel (Matt. 18:10)	We choose our favorite angel
Fulfill God's will (Luke 4:10)	Fulfill our will (at first)
Speak in the name of God (Luke 1:28)	Speak like us (if they choose)
Bring awe, respect, fear (Luke 1:11–13)	Appear friendly and natural like us

52. Berit Kjos, *A Twist of Faith*, chap. 8, "Deliver Us from Evil *or* There Is Not Sin or Evil!" on the Kjos Ministries Web site: http://www.crossroad.to/Books/TwistofFaith/8-Evil.htm.

The purpose of psychic phenomena is imitation. They seek to deceive, and those who practice them are reaching out for some type of spiritual reality in order to conquer death. There are Christians who make the claim that believing in Jesus Christ as Savior and Lord gives them the exclusive power to face death without fear. But a good Spiritist faces death without fear too. Many people, lost in the euphoria of psychic phenomena in which they have seen reality in another dimension, face death without fear. They believe they do not die but instead move one step higher to the next plane, and from there to the plane after that, in infinite progression. Coupled with reincarnation, this belief is quite comforting; they do not face judgment and hell.

Belief in psychic phenomena is a substitute for faith in the God of the Bible and in His Son, Jesus Christ. These phenomena can only imitate what faith in God through Christ promises: the conquest of fear and death, and power for living here on this earth. What the Christian obtains as a gift from God through the power of the Holy Spirit, people dabbling in the occult obtain by satanic means. God is not in the least bit interested in participating in occult psychic phenomena.

The Scripture teaches that at the end of the ages, the Church should anticipate the outgrowth of great spiritual darkness. This is a work of the devil, and if Christians remain silent in the middle of an entire generation given over to the pursuit of occult Psi phenomena—a generation making a concerted attempt to take over the Word of God and use its terms to describe satanic phenomena—then today's Christians will bequeath chaos to the Church of tomorrow. A clear delineation must be made; someone must say, "*Here* is God and *there* is Satan."

Christians can be led astray by paranormal phenomena and wander into the kingdom of the occult. By dabbling in the things God warned them to leave alone, they create confused and frustrated lives. An example of this is a story told by a Christian woman about her encounter with the occult. Unable to sleep one night, she was listening to a talk radio program when they announced their latest guest—someone deeply involved in the occult. This guest introduced the topic of astral projection by describing an actual experience of the spirit leaving the body, and suddenly, the woman lying in bed listening—a Christian woman—began to get the oddest feelings and the strangest impulses. She wanted to *leave* her body and experience this projection. The feelings were overwhelming her, but in that moment a quiet voice spoke to her heart and told her quite clearly, *This is not of God.* She listened to that voice and prayed, "Lord Jesus, deliver me from this." Instantly, the feeling left her, and she turned off the radio program.

Christians are not immune to having their minds corrupted. The Bible says that you will not lose your soul, but your mind can be corrupted from the simplicity that is in Christ; you can be deceived and led astray (2 Cor. 11:3).

Jesus Christ walked on the water, He did not levitate. Philip was not teleported, and there is no such thing as apportation in biblical theology. Philip was moved by the Spirit of God from one place to the other, which is much different from moving an ashtray from one room to another or appearing and disappearing in a railway station. And finally, Scripture indicates that when it comes to the interpretation of dreams, God has a corner on the market. If someone wants to know what a dream means, then he or she should pray about it. In fact, we should pray about anything disturbing, because without prayer, it will continue to disturb. It is not necessary to see a psychiatrist or a psychologist or to dabble in dream analysis to find out the meaning of dreams. Genesis 40:8 says, "Do not interpretations [of dreams] belong to God?" The answer is *yes, they do.*

God holds the key to all interpretation. The word *interpret* in Hebrew is *pathar,* which means "to open up."[53] Do not inquire of the wizards or the mediums; ask the Lord for direct information. "And when they say to you, 'Seek those who are mediums and wizards, who whisper and mutter,' should not a people seek their God? Should they seek the dead on behalf of the living?" (Isa. 8:19–20). God is the one who will provide information, and He is willing (up to a point) to give people that assurance.

CONCLUSION

Parapsychology is dangerous when it delves into the areas of clairvoyance, precognition, and medium trance. The moment it enters the realm of the occult, people encounter forces outside this dimension; only a supernatural force can predict the future and cause events to transpire.

Psychokinetic energy, channeled by a medium or someone involved in the occult is for the purpose of stimulating faith in occultic phenomena and generat-

---

53. *Pathar* (paw-thar'); a primitive root; to open up, i.e. (figuratively) interpret (a dream), *New Exhaustive Strong's Numbers and Concordance.*

ing support for occultism. It inspires fear, respect, and fascination. This is one of the great weapons of the prince of darkness: fascination with the mysterious and the unknown.

The purpose of occult psychic phenomena is to imitate. The purpose of imitation is deception—to lead us away from the Lord our God (Deut. 13:5). Why are people attracted to this type of paranormal activity?

- It is the unknown—and exciting.

- It is mystifying and appeals to the carnal nature.

- It is a display of power outside of man's capacity to control it.

- It is a substitute for the voice of God.

- It is a spiritual narcotic.[54]

A pharmaceutical narcotic affects the brain and the central nervous system, producing a feeling of well-being. It creates hallucinations and generally tends to remove the subject from reality. This change is the product of a chemical narcotic phenomenon, and the same effect is precisely what occurs in the realm of the spirit. The moment an individual accepts occult phenomena and believes them implicitly, the phenomena become a substitute for reality in the dimension of the spirit.

The psychic dimension of the occult is a narcotic that anesthetizes man's spiritual nature and makes him insensitive to the reality of God so he does not hear the voice of God—he hears other voices. These hallucinations are not mental; they are spiritual. They enable someone to believe that the Bible is talking about psychic phenomena, when it is not talking about that at all. It deceives the heart into accepting that these phenomena are compatible with Holy Scripture, when they are not. A person under the influence of a chemical narcotic is incapable of rational judgment, and people under the influence of a spiritual narcotic become incapable of rational *spiritual* judgment.

---

54. The term "spiritual narcotic" is used by Christian scholars to illustrate man's spiritual lethargy. See Meier, "Money," *Baker's Evangelical Dictionary.*

The world today encompasses generations of people overcome by a spiritual sedative. Please do not think that the world of psychic phenomena—the world of the materializing spirit, apportation, levitation, or séance—is an illusion. These are real events happening in the world today, and the only answer to them is the historic gospel of Jesus Christ. The only way to deal with them is from the perspective of Scripture. Remember what Jesus told us: "He who is in you is greater than he who is in the world" (1 John 4:4). The Word of God sends the Church out to meet the forces of darkness—to put on the whole armor of God—and *stand*. Do not run. Do not panic. Do not be frightened. Stand firm in the knowledge that the power within the hearts of the children of God causes the kingdom of darkness to tremble. "Above all, taking the shield of faith with which you will be able to quench all the fiery darts of the wicked one. And take the helmet of salvation, and the sword of the Spirit, which is the word of God" (Eph. 6:16–17). Take these and stand against the powers of darkness, and the world of occult psychic phenomena will dissolve in the face of biblical revelation.

The Church must not shy away from the fight. Instead, we must implore God to burn the challenge deep into each and every heart so we may *see* the souls for whom Jesus Christ died—lost and undone—wandering within the domain of the prince of darkness. We must pray for a spirit of love, compassion, and understanding; we must draw from the power of the Holy Spirit and reach out to the lost, trusting God to protect His people from the power of darkness.

RECOMMENDED RESOURCES

1. Koch, Kurt. *Lure of the Occult.* Grand Rapids: Kregel, 1971.

2. McDowell, Josh. *A Ready Defense.* Nashville: Thomas Nelson, 1993.

3. Michaelson, Johanna. *The Beautiful Side of Evil,* Eugene, OR: Harvest House, 2005.

4. Martin, Walter. *Doctrine of the Demons.* CD/audiotape, Walter Martin Ministries, www.waltermartin.com.

QUICK FACTS ABOUT ASTROLOGY

- Astrology is the ancient practice of interpreting the stars and the position of the planets to forecast national destiny, personal character, or personal destiny.

- Historically, astrologers believed in a direct causal connection between heavenly bodies and earth, but some modern astrologers see the link as more spiritual than causal.

- The zodiac has twelve constellations or signs: Aries, Taurus, Gemini, Cancer, Leo, Virgo, Libra, Scorpio, Sagittarius, Capricorn, Aquarius, and Pisces.

- Natal or birth horoscopes are based upon the calculation and charting of the geocentric positions of ten planets, a zodiacal sign, the twelve houses, and the angular aspects of the planets to the time and place of birth on earth.

- Since the 1930s, regular astrology and horoscope columns have appeared in newspapers that use modern interpretation schemes.

- Astrology usurps God's sovereignty and authority, and it is condemned as an abomination in the Old Testament.

8

Astrology

A strology is a serious subject that must be analyzed and assessed in light of its universality and occultic roots.[1] God condemns astrology as an abomination in both the Old and New Testaments. In spite of this, Christians too often treat astrology lightly or dismissively instead of heeding God's warning. Today, millions of people from all walks of life—educated and ignorant—practice this ancient form of occultism.

Astrology is part of a satanic plan to deceive the mind and lead the unsettled soul astray. The apostle Paul tells the Church in 2 Corinthians 2:11 that it is their duty to be aware of Satan's schemes and tricks, and Peter seconds this warning with one of his own. "Be sober, be vigilant; because your adversary the devil walks about like a roaring lion, seeking whom he may devour" (1 Peter 5:8).

The single most popular realm of the occult is astrology, which deceives countless people through daily horoscopes that claim to interpret the affect of the stars and planets on individual lives. Countless New Age teachers repackage astrology by integrating it with their particular teachings in the Aquarian Age (which is named after a zodiacal sign). They adopt pseudoscientific jargon and market their books to millions of followers who eagerly await the next publication.

Astrology merchandisers sell innocent-looking jewelry, charms, and emblems bearing one of the twelve signs of the zodiac (the Greek name for the constellation belt). Members of the countercultural movement of the 1960s became faddish promoters of astrology, hoping for the anticipated Age of Aquarius and world peace in

---

1. A good analysis of astrology can be found in Wouter J. Hanegraaff, Antoine Faivre, Roelof van den Brock, and Jean-Pierre Brach, eds., *Dictionary of Gnosis and Western Esotericism* (Leiden: Brill, 2006), 109–41. Christian apologetic articles can be found in Geoffrey W. Bromiley, ed., *The International Standard Bible Encyclopedia* (Grand Rapids: Eerdmans, 1979), 1:341–44; Walter A. Elwell, ed., *Baker Encyclopedia of the Bible* (Grand Rapids: Baker, 1988), 1:223–25, and Merril C. Tenney, ed., *The Zondervan Pictorial Encyclopedia of the Bible* (Grand Rapids: Zondervan, 1976), 1:392–94.

their lifetime. This promotion fed a marketing frenzy that spawned books, songs, art, and musicals with astrological themes that sold into the millions of copies.[2]

Even in our postmodern age, sales of astrology materials are continually increasing by leaps and bounds. An occultic tsunami has flooded the world with astrological information that circles the globe. Daily newspapers, weekly and monthly magazines, and the ever-present Internet are cashing in on the human desire to know the future from the stars associated with their birth. Popularized astrology flows freely in countries where the Christian gospel struggles for a hearing.

A few professional astrologers like Carrol Righter, Maurice Woodruff, and Jeane Dixon have criticized this popular movement. They minimize the trendy approach and attempt to cast serious horoscopes to authenticate their art.[3] In their view, traditional astrology provides a basis for analysis of the stars that will influence individual lives. Even more critical are the historians of astrology such as Tamsyn Barton, who claimed that the horoscopes popularized in the media today are "quite alien to ancient astrologers."[4]

The contemporary shift between the astrological old school of thought and the new school was due, in part, to the lack of scientific evidence for a causal connection between the planets, stars, and earth. The new school of astrology compensated for the lack of evidence of planetary influence by adopting new interpretations for their practice. *Time* magazine brought the issue forward:

> . . . it was assumed that some kind of emanations issued from heavenly bodies to affect the characters and destinies of men. When scientists found no emanations powerful enough, sophisticated astrologers abandoned causality altogether and eagerly embraced Jung's theory of "synchronicity"—that everything in the universe at any given moment participates through that moment with everything else that shares the same unit of time.[5]

---

2. The countercultural movement seemed ripe for astrology. By 1969, *Time* magazine reported that there were 10,000 full-time and 175,000 part-time astrologers in the United States. See "Astrology: Fad and Phenomena" in *Time*, March 21, 1969, 56.
3. Professional horoscopy is based upon the precise time and location of the subject at birth whereas the popular horoscopy published in the media cannot know this, hence they give extreme generalities and vagueness in their predictions.
4. Barton, *Ancient astrology,* 1.
5. Anonymous, "Astrology: Fad and Phenomena" in *Time*, March 21, 1969, 58.

Natal Astrology and Mundane Astrology

The two most popular branches of predictive astrology are known as *natal astrology* and *mundane astrology*. Natal astrology, also called genethliacal astrology, makes a prediction based on a person's character, present situation or future outlook beginning with a birth date (or a date of conception, for a few minor astrologists). Mundane astrology usually makes a prediction on a larger scale for a national, civil, or political leadership future.

Interest in astrology has waxed and waned throughout modern history, often fading into disuse, except by those on the fringe of society. Resurgence was seen during the twelfth and thirteenth centuries, mainly at the university level and primarily for academic debate and study among philosophers and theologians.[6] It faded once again in the seventeenth century as science advanced the heliocentric Copernican planetary system.[7] On the esoteric level, the Rosicrucians and Theosophists revived interest in the 1890s, but this time it was for the general populace, although their following was small. By the turn of the twentieth century, only a smattering of professional astrologers existed in the West, since most European countries and America had outlawed it in earlier times.[8] Barely twenty years later, however, an astrological revival paved the way for horoscopes to appear in daily newspapers.[9] These popular forms of horoscopes are often contradictory when compared to each other, or they suffer from such deliberate vagueness that they could easily fit anyone from one end of the spectrum to the other.

Although astrology gained a new footing in the twentieth century, it is an age-old problem that was faced by Old Testament patriarchs and the New Testament Church. Astrology and astronomy are both studies of the sidereal universe, but astrology is distinguished from astronomy in that astrology is a form of divination while astronomy is a physical science; the study of outer space and celestial bodies in the universe. Historically, astronomy may have grown from astrology, but it was through the scientific discoveries and mathematical calculations of Johannes

---

6. Wouter J. Hanegraaff, ed., *Dictionary of Gnosis and Western Esotericism*, 123.
7. Wouter J. Hanegraaff, ed., *Dictionary of Gnosis and Western Esotericism*, 131.
8. Wouter J. Hanegraaff, ed., *Dictionary of Gnosis and Western Esotericism*, 136.
9. Richard H. Naylor's horoscope of Princess Margaret was one of the first to capture the public's attention, and it fueled the renewed interest in astrology. Published in the London newspaper *Sunday Express*, August 24, 1930.

Kepler, Nicolaus Copernicus (the father of modern astronomy), Galileo Galilei, and Isaac Newton that the two finally separated.[10] These men of science seriously wounded astrological divination by demonstrating its nonscientific nature.

ANCIENT ASTROLOGY

Ancient astrologers followed diverse methods for predicting, forecasting, and studying the stars, much of which was passed down from generation to generation. Historical evidence traces ancient astrology and the zodiac from Mesopotamia to its neighboring countries. These countries, in turn, synthesized it for their needs and cultural adaptation.

People groups that lacked knowledge of the biblical Creator satisfied their religious cravings by viewing planets and stars as gods and then developing their belief system.[11] What distinguished ancient man in the Bible from others is his singular devotion to a monotheistic God. Israel was surrounded on all sides by people who practiced astrology, which presented a formidable temptation when they strayed from God. The strong biblical injunctions against astrology began with the Mosaic writings of the early Hebrews, who were keenly aware of the astrological systems of their neighboring countries.

The growth of astrology in Mesopotamia, Europe, Africa, India, China, and pre–Columbian America gave rise to general astrological systems that took divergent developmental paths. Current astrological trends are built upon the foundation of six major astrological motifs that incorporate bits and pieces from each other in casting horoscopes and making predictions.

Mesopotamian Astrology

Trade routes and military conquests stretching from the Mediterranean coastal nations to Mesopotamia introduced three centers of astrological thought to one another: Babylonian, Egyptian, and Greek. That ancient man studied and charted stars is evidenced in the biblical book of Job, which portrays a Mesopotamian setting and contains the earliest reference to constellations in the Bible.

---

10. Walter Martin's comment on this agrees with the renowned astronomer Bart J. Bok in *Objections to Astrology*, 23.
11. See, for example, Amos 5:25–6, which speaks about the surrounding nations during Israel's exodus, with their worship of Molech, Sikkuth, Chiun, and the "star of your gods."

Dr. Gleason Archer dates the composition of Job to about 1500 BC, based on informational exchanges between Mesopotamian astrologers and biblical figures.[12] This does not mean that Job or any other biblical figure believed in astrology, but only that they recognized the stars and constellation systems by their commonly designated names (as is still practiced by scholars and scientists). In an informative way, Job mentions God as the creator of the stars Arcturus (*Ursa Major*, Great Bear, or Big Dipper), Orion, Pleiades, and the chambers, or starry skies, of the south (Job 9:9). It is safe to say that Job was expressing awe for God's creative work, which is quite different from the surrounding nations that believed stars radiated power that influenced earthly life. God mentions the same stars and constellations to Job (38:31), with the addition of Arcturus's sons (*Ursa Minor* or Little Dipper) and Mazzaroth (constellations). In this text, God shows that He is the sovereign ruler over the "laws of the heavens" (38:33 NIV), which contradicts Mesopotamian astrology's mystical belief that priests and astrologers assigned divinity to the stars.

It is no surprise, then, that early biblical books spoke of astrology and planetary worship among neighboring nations. Moses, who wrote in approximately 1500 BC, spoke against astrology that would defile Israel before God (like other forms of divination). Indeed, some writers see traces of Chaldean (Babylonian) astrology in Laban's family of Haran, when his daughter Rachel stole images from her father (Gen. 31:9). These images are translated from the Hebrew word *terephim*, which the Persian translators render as "astrolabes." An astrolabe is an ancient instrument or tablet for interpreting the stars.[13] The suggestion by biblical commentators is that Laban and his daughters, who dwelled among the Chaldeans, relied upon astrology.[14] Although Rachel and Leah were the daughters of Laban, they would have conformed to the monotheism found in Abrahamic belief after becoming part of Jacob's household. Even though Abraham came from Ur of the Chaldeans, nothing suggests that he followed anything other than monotheism.

---

12. Archer, *A Survey of Old Testament Introduction*, 464. Walter Martin recommended Gleason Archer's work in Old Testament scholarship. The date of Job has been hotly debated through the years and many equally conservative scholars opt for younger dating, especially the Solomonic period (1,000 BC) and the Babylonian exile (550 BC). See Elwell, *Baker Encyclopedia of the Bible*, 2:1169.

13. Adapted from commentary by Adam Clarke, *Clarke's Commentary* on Genesis 31:19.

14. See Clarke, *Clarke's Commentary*, on Genesis 30:11 where he etymologically traces Leah's son's name, Gad, to a star.

If Babylon set the center stage for early Mesopotamian astrology, then Nineveh was not far behind. King Assurbanipal (mentioned in Ezra 4:10 as King Osnappar) built a library in Nineveh (650 BC) that yielded a voluminous cache containing some seventy tablets of astrological texts in early cuneiform. These tablets also reveal the predominance of astrology over other forms of divination.[15] The Chaldean rule of Babylon in the eighth century BC, through King Merodach-baladan (mentioned in Isaiah 39:1 and 2 Kings 20:12), facilitated the blending of Chaldean astrology with Babylonian concepts.

In the neo-Babylonian empire (c. 614 BC), under King Nebuchadnezzar there is evidence of established schools of astrology (2 Kings 24:1). Here, the biblical figure Daniel and his companions were tested by Nebuchadnezzar against the wisdom of the astrologers: "And in all matters of wisdom and understanding about which the king examined them, he found them ten times better than all the magicians and astrologers who were in all his realm" (Dan.1:20). As indicated in this text, kings in that day kept astrologers close at hand for consultation. In Daniel 2:2, another contest erupts between the Chaldean astrologers and Daniel, where Daniel prevailed once again.

Mesopotamia has produced the oldest archaeological evidences for ancient astrology. The Sumerian records that are inscribed on the Gudea cylinders (c. 2250 BC) provide the "earliest collection of celestial observations and their significance as omens."[16] The Babylonian text *Illumination of Bel* was also "ascribed by the wise men of the time to the period of the great Sargon I, about 2800 BC."[17] Our earliest copy of this comes later, from King Assurbanipal's library at Nineveh.

Mesopotamian omen astrology looked for signs in the skies (solar or lunar eclipses, comets, or meteorites as omens). Omen astrology was usually reserved for nations and kings, a fact not discussed much by modern astrologers. The Assurbanipal library also yielded Sumerian astrological records titled "When Anu and Enlil," so named after the opening line on the tablets.[18] The Sumerian *ziggurats* (stepped towers) have been long thought to be celestial observatories and their

---

15. Barbara Bock, "An Esoteric Babylonian Commentary Revisited," in *The Journal of the American Oriental Society*, Vol. 120 (2000): 615.
16. Hooke, *Babylonian and Assyrian Religion*, 91.
17. Hale, *Beyond the Milky Way*, 17.
18. Taylor, *An Analysis of Celestial Omina in the Light of Mesopotamian Cosmology and Mythos*, 34.

temples had "a special chamber for the astrologers known as *bit tamarti*, 'the house of observation,' where they watched the moon."[19] Mesopotamian astrology and religion centered on worship of a moon god (*Sin*) in contrast to the Egyptian and Greek astrologers, who promoted a sun god.

Omen astrology gradually morphed into a zodiacal theory as new constellations were discovered, named, and tracked. The twelve zodiacal divisions had their origin among the Babylonian astrologers who named the major constellations, although they began with names and images different from today's zodiac. The Babylonian priests defined the twelve zodiacal signs and the zodiacal twelve houses. *Zodiac*, in its Greek origin, means "circle of animals," resulting in these modern constellation signs: Aries the Ram, Taurus the Bull, Gemini the Twins, Cancer the Crab, Leo the Lion, Virgo the Virgin, Libra the Balance, Scorpio the Scorpion, Sagittarius the Archer, Capricorn the Goat, Aquarius the Water Bearer, and Pisces the Fish. From the time of the Babylonian zodiac, with its signs and divisions, which is documented in clay cuneiform tablets about 419 BC, it remains remarkably unchanged among Western astrologers.[20]

From the eighth century BC forward, Babylonian astrology permeated Mesopotamian life and left influential marks upon Egypt, Greece, and northern India. Most early astrological predictions fell in to the ranks of judicial astrology or mundane astrology to forecast the destiny of the nation or king. Mesopotamian astrology blended well with the polytheism, idolatry, and celestial gods of neighboring nations.

Zoroastrian Astrology

Although an accepted link exists between Persian Zoroastrians and Babylon, their distinctive astrology warrants special mention. The Zoroastrian magi are believed by most scholars to be the "wise men" mentioned in Matthew 2:1. While they were star watching, the magi followed His star and found Jesus Christ in Bethlehem. There is nothing present in the New Testament that claims these men were divining astrology to find Christ. As stargazers, they merely saw the star and followed it, believing

19. Hooke, *Babylonian and Assyrian Religion*, 92.
20. Snodgrass, *Signs of the Zodiac: A Reference Guide to Historical, Mythological, and Cultural Associations*, 21.

it had special significance. The magi were part of the priests in Zoroastrianism who added astronomy, astrology, and perhaps magic arts to their practice. These magi in Matthew's gospel are seen delivering gifts to Christ and worshiping Him, which indicates their ascent toward a corrected belief by the time they found Christ.

Zoroastrian priests found conflict between their religion and foreign astrological trends. Zoroaster stood against fatalism and insisted on free will, which stands contrary to theories found in ancient astrology. The fusion of Zoroastrianism and astrology was restricted by their beliefs and reflects the dualism in their theology. They recognized the twelve signs of the zodiac, but they are viewed as good agents working for the good of God in man and earth. Enemy planets that work for darkness run interference with the zodiacal good agents.[21] In this way, the Zoroastrian cosmology stands apart from others in the region.[22]

Egyptian Astrology

Pre-Hellenistic Egyptian astronomy was concerned with the horary table for the rising and setting of various stars. The pyramids exemplified the fact that the ancient Egyptians tracked the sun, moon, and stars. Several aspects of Egyptian cosmology, religious thought, polytheism, and reincarnation are reflected in pyramidal hieroglyphs and architecture. With uncanny precision, they built shafts that coordinated perfectly with particular solar, lunar, or stellar movements. One example is the Queen's Chamber of the Great Pyramid, where "the angle of the rise of the northern shaft from the Queen's Chamber is 39°, and it could have targeted the bowl of the Little Dipper."[23] Other pyramid shafts are said to point to stars to which the spirit or soul of the buried Pharaoh is transferred or embodied after death.

Early Egyptian astrology seems to be rooted in Babylonian zodiacal sources, which integrated well with their sun and planet worship. Some of the zodiacal signs were renamed, or "Egyptianized," to coincide with cultural religious tendencies. Capricorn was renamed the "goat-fish," Cancer was imaged as a scarab, and Aquarius as a Nile god.[24] Against this backdrop, it is no wonder that Egyptian astrology took on its own character.

---

21. Zaehner, The Dawn and Twilight of Zoroastrianism, 206, 238.
22. Most of the Zoroastrian sacred texts were destroyed during the Greek invasion of Persia.
23. Kelley, Exploring Ancient Skies, 262.
24. Hornung, Secret Lore of Egypt, 31.

After the Greek conquest of Egypt through Alexander the Great and the development of the great Alexandrian library (365–323 BC), the Greeks noted that Egyptian astrology was equal to that of the Babylonians. This parallel may have been the byproduct of Egypt's Persian rule from 525 BC to Alexander's conquest in 332 BC, but it is also likely that some information passed along trade routes. Still, this does not diminish Egyptian originality in certain ideas.

Claudius Ptolemy (c. 150 AD), an Egyptian astronomer of Alexandria, introduced a scheme for a geocentric planetary system that remained intact until the heliocentric cosmology of Copernicus in 1543. Some writers debate Ptolemy's Egyptian ethnicity because he wrote in Greek. Yet his advanced education is seen in his writings on astronomy, astrology, music, and geology, and most importantly in the *Tetrabiblos,* his four-book treatise on natal astrology, mundane astrology, and prediction methods. He wrote the earliest known synthesis of Babylonian, Egyptian, and Greek astrology with the coalescence of his Aristotelian worldview. This unified these astrological systems toward a singular cosmology. His work was well respected, and it became the catalyst for many subsequent European works. Greek astrologers used it as the basis for their astrological commentaries and it became the foundational sourcebook for Western astrology as it grew over the centuries.

Greco-Roman Astrology

Ancient Greek astrology is attributed to three possible sources, or perhaps a combination of these. Most scholars say Greek astrology was a refinement of Babylonian astrology. This could be due to colonizing Greeks who lived in Meopotamia as early as the eighth century BC, which created a fertile setting for astrological information exchange and may account for the astrological similarities between these distant nations.[25] It could also be due to Berosus (c. 280 BC), a Babylonian astrologer and historian who was said to have reached the Greek isle of Cos to establish an astrological school, according to Vitruvius, a first-century BC Roman writer.[26] He translated the Babylonian text *Illumination of Bel* into Greek, which adds a new dimension of understanding about how Babylonian traits are found in

25. Wouter J. Hanegraaff, ed., *Dictionary of Gnosis and Western Esotericism,* 111.
26. Dickie, *Magic and Magicians in the Greco-Roman World,* 101.

ancient Greek astrology. Either of these sources can account for the genesis of astrological interest in Greece.

Pythagoras (c. 550 BC) and his followers added their numerology to the zodiacal system in the quest for precise forecasts. Tamsyn Barton wrote, "Their love for numerology led to the notion of offering mathematical values for relationships between bodies in the heavens, as part of a grand scheme in which everything had its number."[27] A Greek contemporary of Ptolemy of Alexandria was Vertius Valens of Antioch, who wrote *Anthologiae* (c. 160 AD). This nine-book work covered natal astrology and gave numerous astrological illustrations. This, together with Ptolemy's work, became the most influential works for the growth of Western astrology.

During the second century, the pre-Nicene Christian apologists actively opposed Egyptian and Greek astrology. Their concern, as Christianity grew from Rome to Alexandria, was that those who practiced astrology would merge it with Christianity. Most of the early Church fathers were well educated, which is why they frequently quoted Pagan sources and boldly refuted them. Early Church leaders like Clement of Alexandria, Tertullian, Lactantius, and Origen spoke out strongly against astrology and made plain its incompatible with Christianity.

Popular acceptance of astrology came late to the Roman Empire. Initially, the Roman Senate condemned astrology and officially forbade the practice in 139 BC. But Dr. Kurt Koch notes, "In a healthy cultural epoch, Cato and Cicero carried on opposition to astrology. When, on the other hand, the first emperors, Augustus and Tiberius, employed astrologers, the germs of decay were already to be seen in the fabric of the Roman Empire. The rising flood of astrology is always a yardstick for the cultural status of the people."[28] Two hundred years later, Firmicus Maternus produced a major Latin work on astrology called *Mathesis* (c. 334 AD). Since it was unlawful to practice astrology, Maternus, who was trained in law, used his skills to write in such a way so as to conceal that he was actually promoting it.[29] His treatise was essentially a Latin version of Hellenistic astrology. And so history reveals that astrology remained a force of some influence—its rise and fall impacting the lives of great and small within the Roman Empire.

---

27. Barton, *Ancient Astrology,* 21.
28. Koch, *Christian Counselling and Occultism,* 97.
29. Barton, *Ancient Astrology,* 80.

Chinese Astrology

As with other ancient civilizations, there was little difference between ancient astronomy and astrology in China.[30] Ancient Chinese astrology developed independently of its Mesopotamian counterpart, perhaps as early as 2000 BC. They divided the *ecliptic* (the path of the sun across the sky) into twelve stations of Jupiter, and each station was further divided two or three times to total twenty-eight uneven parts.[31]

Ho Peng Yoke describes Chinese astrology in terms of traditional judicial or mundane astrology: "Unlike Western astrology, Chinese astrology attempted to tell the destiny of persons holding important positions—from the emperor downwards, and on geographical regions, but never on individuals."[32] Yoke adds, "In fact, celestial events and state affairs were believed to bear a mutual influence on each other."[33]

Individuals eventually received personal horoscopes (similar to the character horoscopy in the Western tradition), in the Chinese calendar and zodiacal chart that consists of twelve animals, the rat, ox, tiger, hare, dragon, snake, horse, sheep, monkey, rooster, dog, and pig. These are used in combination with the subject's birthday to profile their character and destiny. One missionary to China recorded the fate of Chinese astrology: "One reads in part: 'The events of men's lives are supposed to be under the influences of twenty-eight stars [of the lunar lodges], each of which is an object of worship. In telling fortunes by this method, a representation on paper of a man's horoscope is prepared for each individual applicant.'"[34] Today, Chinese astrology has gained a new following largely through books that translate the ancient practice into English and other world languages.

Indian Astrology

It is likely that the Chaldeans may have influenced early Indian astrology, and possible that later Greek influence (especially after the Alexandrian rule of northern

---

30. Ching, *Chinese Religions*, 29–30.
31. Smith, *Fortune-Tellers and Philosophers: Divination in Traditional Chinese Society*, 34.
32. Yoke, *Li, Qi, and Shu: An Introduction to Science and Civilization in China*, 131.
33. Yoke, *Li, Qi, and Shu*, 123.
34. Smith, *Fortune-Tellers and Philosophers*, 175.

India) had some impact as claimed by the Internet site Astrology India. "Indian Astrology, originated in ancient Greek Civilization, defines the actual traits of an individual, marital compatibility and the future. . . ."[35] If the Greek influence is accurate, as claimed, it would have had to overcome the antagonism of Hindu and Buddhist religionists, who despised the Greeks and their customs, including astrology.[36] It was not even until 160 AD that Yavanesvara translated a Greek text on casting horoscopes into Sanskrit. During the following century, Sphujidhvaja, a respected scholar, added verses to this text, entitled *Yavanajataka* (Ionian sayings).

The oldest surviving Indian text on astrology is dated at 505 AD, which has the twelve zodiacal signs translated into Sanskrit.[37] Some scholars claim, however, that Indian astrology internally developed without foreign influence "until the introduction of Islamic ideas a millennium later."[38] Vedic astrology (named for its roots in the Indian scripture *Vedas*) asserts the same ideas as its counterparts: destiny is written in the stars and can be influenced by the attitudes and actions of human beings.

> Indian astrology, the oldest system of astrology in the world, differs considerably from the western system. Indian astrology uses the actual constellations of stars as seen in the sky. This system gives a completely different chart as compared to the one used by western astrologers. The Indian astrology is based on the date, place, and time of birth.
>
> Indian Astrology also differs considerably from the Chinese horoscope, which is based on the year of birth and believes that the year of birth indicates a certain phase or aspect of a sixty-year circle of time. Therefore you may find yourself born in the year of dog, horse or rat or even a dragon.

---

35. *Indian Astrology,* http://www.vedic-astrology-prediction.com/indian-astrology.html (accessed March 5, 2007).
36. It is ludicrous that a scholar like Irvine Hexam would claim that, "astrology arises naturally from a belief in karma and rebirth," when an elementary study shows that it was introduced late to Indian religions instead of arising from them. See Hexham and Poewe, *New Religions as Global Cultures: Making the Human Sacred,* 104. Hexham's chapter on astrology is inept; it suffers from a lack of original research from which Hexham erroneously concludes that members of Scientology "commonly appeal to astrological signs" to prove Hubbard's divine mission!
37. Garratt, *The Legacy of India,* 350.
38. Pollock, *The Language of the Gods in the World of Men: Sanskrit, Culture, and Power in Premodern India,* 265.

Hence, people who are born in a particular animal year share certain common traits just like people born in common zodiac do.[39]

Although this site claims Indian astrology as the oldest form, it would be difficult to prove historically based on the number of cultural influences during its development. Twenty-first-century practitioners revived ancient Indian astrology and now promote it through books and the Internet.

Pre-Columbian New World Astrology

In the new world, the Mayan civilization (200–900 AD) had a profoundly accurate calendar system based upon their discoveries in astronomy and mathematics. Adding superstition to the scientific, they developed Mayan astrology, which is recorded in their sacred text, *Chilam Balam*. Natal astrology, for them, was a generalized characterization of the person in accordance with their birth. "Mayan religion was closely connected with the elaborate Mayan calendar and with Mayan astrology, which made much of the revolutions of the planet Venus."[40]

The Aztecs practiced astrology by forecasting life characteristics that would bring good or bad fortune upon the subject. Aztec astrology is a complex system that connects a god or goddess to the day and week of human birth. Their forecasts were lifetime destiny projections based upon how the "equilibrium of the universe affected the human body."[41] Influenced by a polytheistic religion, they also attributed and transferred animal-god characteristics to humankind.

Since the Aztec calendar was quite accurate for ancient civilization, it can be adjusted and coordinated for today's world. This has allowed New Age marketers to publish updated Mayan and Aztec astrological predictions, even though most readers have no inkling of what the Aztec gods represent.[42] The predictions are akin to a destiny chart rather than a day-to-day horoscope. Fatalism does not look only at the good nature; it allows the bad characteristics to overshadow the good, leaving little hope for the person who appears to be trapped by unalterable cosmic forces.

39. *Indian Astrology*, http://www.vedic-astrology-prediction.com/indian-astrology.html (accessed March 5, 2007).
40. De Camp, *Ancient Ruins and Archaeology*, 198.
41. Ortiz de Montellano, *Aztec Medicine, Health, and Nutrition*, 134.
42. See K. C. Tunnicliffe, *Aztec Astrology*, 1979, wherein he coordinates the Aztec calendar with ours.

Modern Astrology

What is typically meant by modern astrology is the codification of Western
European astrology, which resulted from Babylonian astrology as filtered through
Athens and Rome. With fine-tuning over the years, a standardized practice surfaced
and remained intact until two changes took place. The first change came through
popular horoscopy in daily newspapers around 1930, and the second came through
the New Age movement in the 1970s.

In Western astrology, the zodiac is an imaginary belt surrounding the earth that
has the phenomenal appearance that twelve zodiacal constellations or signs move
within it. This belt lies eight degrees on either side of the ecliptic, which is the path
that the sun appears to trace across the sky; it takes 365.25 days to complete the
ecliptic cycle. The zodiac is divided into twelve sections, one for each sign, at thirty-
degree intervals.

Casting horoscopes from the time of Ptolemy up to 1930 was based upon the
horoscope point or the ascendant or rising sign. The zodiacal house in which the
planet rises tells the forecaster how to write the horoscope in accordance with the time
of birth. A different method has been used since 1930 for casting popular horoscopes,
like those found in the popular media. These are based upon alternate methods, like
the sun-sign *loci* (the position of the rising sun at the time of birth) or sometimes, as
earlier noted from *Time*, the zodiacal signs are seen as part of a collective whole
(Jungian) for interpreting the subject's life, trends, possibilities or patterns.

Distinguishing between the *sidereal* zodiac and the *tropical* zodiac is also problematic in modern astrology. The sidereal zodiac is the classical zodiac of Ptolemy
through 1930. The tropical zodiac, also called the solar zodiac, is a modern invention and is referenced most often in Western astrological thought. The sidereal
zodiac adjusts for the shifting vernal equinox, but the tropical zodiac does not.[43] A
serious problem exists for the sidereal zodiac in that the constellations are not equal
in size. They do not make a perfectly divided belt at 30° intervals.[44] Notwithstanding
these differences, Rene Noorbergen summarizes how professional astrologers cast a
sidereal horoscope:

---

43. See later discussion of this under "The problem of the equinox precession."
44. See later discussion under "The problem of constellation length."

The moment of birth is the essential starting point. This, coupled with the latitude and longitude of the individual's birthplace, provides the initial package . . . a factor known as the 'true local time' must also be considered . . . by adding or subtracting four minutes for each degree of longitude that your birthplace lies to the east or west of the center of your time zone of birth . . . the next step is to convert this 'true' time into 'sidereal' or star time. This is done with the aid of an ephemerus, a reference book showing the positions of the planets in relationship to the earth . . . for in doing so, the theme of the individual's 'ascendant'—the astrological sign that is supposed to have been rising on the eastern horizon at the moment of birth— is revealed . . . [T]o 'chart' your horoscope . . . you align the 'ascendant' with the nine-o'clock point on the inner circle of the horoscope, and from there you are prepared to 'read' the various zodiacal 'houses' that control your life and fortune.[45]

A few astrologers have argued about whether conception or birth is used for the starting point in charting a horoscope. This, of course, would produce an entirely different horoscope, so it seems a matter of convenience that when one does not like his or her sign, then they turn to their conception as the starting point. Another variant that is often missed is the preference of Western astrology over the Chinese, Mayan, Indian, Egyptian, or Aztec. With all of these conflicting variables, astrology prevents true scientific testing, since no one can truly say which starting point, zodiac, or method is the best. The lack of standardization is problematic in astrology.

Astrologers charted thousands of incorrect horoscopes over several decades without making an adjustment for birth records in daylight savings time zones. This throws individual charts off by one hour, resulting in a false reading. Astrological computer software now adjusts for this blunder, but it does not account for the false data people relied on as true for a century.[46] These conflicting methods confuse pertinent information that, if wrong, will alter everything else from the correct charting to the correct interpretation. With this much variation,

---

45. Noorbergen, *The Soul Hustlers,* 176–77.
46. See Dean, *Recent Advances in Natal Astrology,* 19–32.

it appears that astrologers lack a true standardization and prevent correct horoscopy. These insurmountable problems are difficult enough, but things just get worse when we add the multifaceted varieties and new techniques offered by New Age astrology.

New Age Astrology

During the countercultural movement in the mid-1960s, a new branch of astrology broke away from modern astrology. This expansion did not reach its zenith until the New Age movement began in the 1970s.[47] The lack of standardization in traditional astrology is exceeded by even wider variations in New Age astrology. There are two paths of New Age astrology. The first path uses traditional zodiacal calculations along with unorthodox interpretations, colored stones for healing or energy, healing herbs, and a variety of other New Age technique associations randomly assigned to the constellations. The second path combines traditional zodiacal calculations with non-Western astrology, such as the ancient Chinese, Druid, Mayan, Aztec, Incan, Zoroastrian, Indian, Greek, Egyptian, or Roman sources. This could be seen as reinventing the wheel. The intention, it seems, is to select the best thoughts from each of the former studies, whether ancient or modern, and infuse them into one system that is validated only by self-proclamation. This second group is bolstered by a new wave of Mayan, Aztec, Incan, and Chinese astrological books—penned by novices and scholars alike.

ASTROLOGY AND LOGIC

In direct contrast to its promise of control, astrology's logical inconsistencies are numerous and reveal a pattern of chaos. The underlying premises in constructing the astrological cosmos defy reason and reality. Equally arbitrary are the methods for interpreting horoscopes.

The Problem of the Geocentric Universe

Astrologers have continued to use the geocentric universe since Ptolemy conceived it in 150 AD. Ptolemy's theory was replaced by Copernicus's heliocentric solar system; however, horoscopy has never changed. Horoscopes are still based upon the

---

47. Cooper, *Religion in the Age of Aquarius*, 22–24, 33–36.

falsified concept that the earth is the center of the solar system. Astrologers need to explain why they use a geocentric chart when our solar system is heliocentric. If an astrologer switches to a heliocentric solar system, new problems arise concerning the position of zodiacal signs, since these are positioned from the horizon of earth instead of the sun. Astrology, based upon a geocentric universe, is unscientific.

The Problem of the Exempt People

The influence of the planets must be true for *all* people, or astrologers must explain how their theory remains true if exemptions exist. The zodiacal belt that we mentioned above is eight degrees on either side of the sun's ecliptic. Certain populated northern regions like Siberia, Sweden, the artic regions, or Alaska (land of the midnight sun or alternate twenty-four-hour darkness) have no "sun plane" or "zodiacal plane," as astrologers call it, since the sun never crosses the horizon during these times. Therefore, these time periods fall completely outside of astrological charting and, quite literally, the people born in those times and places are *exempt* from astrology. This makes it impossible to calculate the planetary positions for people born above or below the latitude 66° and therefore, no horoscope can be charted. Astrologers who cheat by using the nearest latitude undermine their practice, as astrologers insist upon accurate times and places for birth. Since there are exceptions in astrology, then astrologers need to account for how these people exist quite well outside of the influence of zodiacal astrology.

The Problem of the Equinox Precession

When Alexandrian astrologers began standardizing the zodiacal calendar about 100 BC, the sun (due to the vernal equinox) entered the sign of Aries on March 21. Newtonian astronomy (1687) showed us that the equinox is moving a full 30° zodiacal sign every 2,180 years. People who are now born on March 21 through April 19 are actually born under the sign Pieces the Fish. Those who think they are born under Taurus the Bull (April 20–May 20) are actually born under Aries. Each sign now takes on its preceding sign due to the equinox shifting. Most astrologers ignore this fact, but it destroys their foundational thesis. If they cast a horoscope for a Taurus born in April, then the real sign the person was born under was Aries, so the horoscope becomes meaningless.

The Problem of Constellation Length

As observed earlier, the constellations are not divided equally in the sky at 30° intervals. The constellation Cancer is 20° across, while Virgo is 44° across. The sun does not spend equal time in each zodiacal sign. It spends six days in Scorpio, for example, and forty-seven days in Virgo. When a horoscope is cast for the beginning or end of the longer constellations, it is counted as the neighboring sign instead of the actual sign it is in. This makes the horoscope a sham.

The Problem of Multiple Births and Contrasting Character Traits

In twins, triplets, and other multiple births, astrology runs into a great deal of difficulty, since quite often one or more of the siblings has a strikingly different character than the other, yet they are born at the same time and place astrologically. In modern or contemporary astrology, this may not pose as great a problem as with a natal or birth chart.

The Bible offers a clear example of this with the birth of Esau and Jacob. The distinct difference in their characters, one choosing to serve God and the other contemptuous, presents a problem since both were born at the same time (Gen. 25–27). Some astrologers argue that four minutes or more between birth times can make a difference, although many others disagree. Still, thousands of twins are born within four minutes of each other, leaving multiple births with contrasting character traits an unsolved dilemma for natal astrology. Charting infants is more difficult for contemporary astrologers because they usually take into account the subject's personality traits when projecting their horoscope.

The Problem of New Planets

Astronomy and astrology are related studies that grew as they accommodated new discoveries and information. Predictive astrology grew from omen astrology to zodiacal astrology. The planets were limited to those seen with the naked eye, which included the sun, moon, and Mercury through Jupiter. Predictive zodiacal astrology was satisfied in casting horoscopes and interpreting character and destiny with this limited knowledge.

Galileo Galilei (1564–1642) changed astronomy by using the telescope for stargazing in 1609. The later discoveries of Uranus (1781), Neptune (1846), and Pluto (1930) gave astrologers new planets that "influence" earth and its inhabitants. Pluto was added as a planet in 1930, which was just in time for the revival of astrology in the West.

Today, most birth charts are cast using influential positioning from all of these planets—raising a host of interesting questions. Is all past horoscopy *invalid* due to the lack of knowledge of real influential planets? Contemporary astrologers attempt to answer this in that each newly discovered planet correlated with societal shifts.

To compound the problem, on August 24, 2006, the International Astronomical Union representing 424 world astronomers officially demoted Pluto and ruled that it is no longer a planet.[48] Our solar system is reduced again to eight planets. This is certain to raise more questions within astrology. Should eight or nine planets be used? Each choice will certainly change the outcome of casting horoscopes and raise the specter of the legitimacy of all past horoscopes from ancient times to the present. The problem is that the astrologers cannot prove or disprove which planets, if any, influence earth or what kind of collective energy or collective consciousness is associated with them, if any at all. In the final analysis, astrologers cannot show what kind of influence exists from the planet in our solar system or the zodiacal constellations, whether it is collective energy, collective consciousness, influential, or casual concoctions.

CASE STUDIES

The following examples of the power and powerlessness of astrology are detailed by Dr. Kurt Koch:

Ex 41 A Christian teacher in a children's home of a Home Mission read an astrological weekly column for many years. In her mind she applied herself to these prognostications, and in the course of time she found that many of them were fulfilled in her life. Gradually she developed a faith in the horoscope.

Finally, when she was faced with an important decision, she obtained an exact horoscope. Later she repeated this astrological consultation. She

---

48. Pluto is now defined as a "dwarf planet." The three new astronomical categories are "planets" (now eight planets up to Neptune), "dwarf planets" (small round bodies) and "small solar system bodies" that will account for all other objects orbiting the sun. See "Pluto: we hardly knew you" in *San Francisco Chronicle*, August 27, 2006, E-2.

fell more and more under an astrological compulsion, which finally brought her to me for a pastoral interview. She complained of a dread of living, inability to make decisions, moods of melancholia, etc.

A medical anamnesis brought little light to bear on her psychological disturbances. The only point of significance was that her mother also believed in astrology and was melancholic. When it came to an anamnesis [patient history] of occult involvement, we discovered a faith in the horoscope which exercised a decisive suggestive power. She practically refused to be convinced of the damaging influence of astromancy upon her emotional life. Finally, after a second interview, she was persuaded to give up her engagement in astrology.

Ex 42 The editor of a large daily reported that one day he did not receive the weekly astrological forecast until it was too late. In order not to annoy his readers, he simply went to his old files and inserted in the appropriate column a horoscope from long before. Not one of the 100,000 readers noticed the "deception." The editor decided that since this had worked so well, he might as well spare himself the astrologer's weekly fee. So for three months he filled the column with old horoscopes. At last a reader wrote in, remarking that the horoscope must be wrong. In order to avoid a scandal, he began once more to send for fresh astrological horoscopes. . . .

Surely the whole ludicrous nature of horoscope practice is exposed by the above examples. This still does not mean that the whole horoscope epidemic is nothing but humbug. It is not all swindle and superstition; but it is all a great danger for the spiritual life and for the genuine Christian walk of faith.[49]

BIBLICAL ASTRONOMY

Astronomy, as a science, is set apart from astrology and the art of divination. Even though today's scientific study of astronomy has advanced by quantum leaps, it does not mean that the biblical astronomers' study and tracking of stellar movement was not scientific. They may have lacked the instruments used today, but they

---

49. Data compiled by Dr. Kurt Koch. See Koch, *Christian Counselling and Occultism*, 96–98.

certainly recognized the regular and repetitive movements of celestial bodies. Studying and tracking heavenly bodies made sense in ancient times because the skies were perpetually observed.

Biblical astronomy, unlike astrology, is free from magic, divination, and superstition. The sun, moon, and stars are part of God's creation that He revealed was for the purpose of earthly time measurement and season regulation (Gen. 1:14–15). The Hebrews did not worship the planets, as did the nations around them. In biblical astronomy, the stars are recognized as God's celestial design. The Israelites understood that all of the created heavenly bodies were under God's sovereign control and therefore had no inherent power to influence the earth.

Specific stars are mentioned by name in Amos 5:8. This was written about 760 BC as a warning to Israel before their exile, and it mentions the stars Orion and Pleiades as God's creations. The mention of these stars declares Judah and Israel's service to the Creator rather than serving the stars as did their Pagan neighbors. This stands against astrology by showing the greatness of our Creator-God.

SCRIPTURAL AND LOGICAL RESPONSE

We know from history that the Egyptians, Babylonians, Chaldeans, Aztecs, and Incans were particularly interested in astrology. The Bible is replete with passages that mention astrology, astrologers, stargazers, and monthly prognosticators. These descriptions represent those who cast horoscopes and try to forecast the future. Modern professional astrologers, who claim to cast genuine natal or birth charts, have wide-ranging and complex calculations for their interpretations that go beyond the scope of this study. The mathematical often blends with the mystical, and although it is impossible to examine all of their methods, an analysis of their intent is essential and enlightening.

The first goal of astrologers is to penetrate the future. The reason astrology appeals to so many people is that they want to pierce the hidden veil of the future. Human curiosity, uncertain living conditions, and worry all grant a motive for desiring future knowledge. From this springboard of anxiety, astrology has launched a global multibillion-dollar business.

A second purpose of astrology is the attempt to bring order out of chaos. This aim appeals to the desire for something sensible in a chaotic world. The plan is to convince people to return to this ancient way of discovering what the universe says about personal destiny; the influence of the stars upon human life. Astrology emphasizes the order of the macrocosmic universe and its power to influence the disorder in the human microcosmic world.

A third objective is the art of character analysis. By interpreting the position of the planets in a zodiacal house at the point of birth and then matching it to past astrological theories, the stars may reveal character and destiny. This is a form of natal astrology, but it does not include daily horoscopes as found in popular publications (yet another branch of astrology).

A fourth goal astrologers hope to achieve is a successful appeal to people's need for purpose and self-empowerment. People want their lives to have meaning; they look for ways to tap into personal power. This power, when sought through astrology, can be used for acquiring knowledge about relationships, compatibility, or business partnerships. Armed with such information, the subject gains a sense of control and power over his or her destiny that gives confidence in the decision-making process.

A fifth and final aim of astrologers is to gain validity by appealing to antiquity or biblical authority. Serious astrologers will firmly maintain that nothing in astrology contradicts the Bible. They respond to biblical statements against astrology by claiming the writers were prejudiced. It is vital to examine these goals and put their methods to the test, in order to determine exactly how well they work in the contemporary world.

Penetration of the Future

To determine if the future truly has been penetrated, it is important to measure the success or failure of the prediction. Accuracy is everything; it distinguishes biblical prophets from all other prognosticators. A biblical prophet is a servant of God who must predict with 100 percent accuracy. To be less accurate is to be proven false, which is unacceptable in a biblical prophet. In contrast, astrologers of the past have never been 100 percent accurate, which proves them to be false prognosticators. The occasional accurate prognostication does not change their status before God, since it still falls short of His accuracy.

Can the future be known before its time? Yes, the God who knows the future can certainly communicate it to His children, and He has done so countless times. God knows the end from the beginning (Isa. 45:21). Humans do not have access to this knowledge, and those who seem able to predict future events are in reality making educated guesses based upon past knowledge of individuals or events. There are, however, times when a future event can be predicted accurately by a human being, and this occurs when Satan, the archenemy of God, provides his knowledge or educated guesses to his servants.

The question of what or how much Satan knows has been wrestled with by theologians down through the centuries. The Bible speaks of Satan as a fallen angel, a finite being who has limited knowledge. Nothing in Scripture shows that he knows anything more of the future than other created beings. He quite likely did not know the future when he fought God in heaven, for no rational being knowing that the eternal lake of fire awaits him would voluntarily go there. His limited knowledge is shown in the book of Job, since he requested permission to test Job, thinking that Job would deny God. But in the end, Job was faithful and showed that Satan's guesswork was wrong. He did not "know" what Job would do. His knowledge of the future comes either by the same kind of prophecies available to God's people or educated guesses based upon past events. If this is the same kind of "knowledge" he gives to his servants, it is no wonder they consistently miss the mark.

Only God knows the future. Satan—at his best—simply borrows God's predictive knowledge. Deuteronomy 13:5 demonstrates that prophets and dreamers will sometimes predict things that will "come to pass." The test God gives is this: what god are they promoting in their message? If it is anyone other than the true God, then they are false prophets—even if their predictions come true. How is it possible for false prophets to give true predictions? They get their information either from guesswork or from their lord, Satan.

A second test for prophets or predictions can be found in Deuteronomy 18:19–20, where the importance of accuracy is discussed. If any single prediction fails or "if the thing does not happen or come to pass," then it was not from God. These people were marked as false prophets, and they suffered serious consequences in Israel if they did not repent.

Astrologers or stargazers fall under these same guidelines. When they give predictions that are not completely fulfilled, they must be marked as false prognosticators. Unlike the biblical prophets, there has never been a completely accurate astrologer. From the standpoint of history, it is safe to say that they do not accurately penetrate the future.

Order from Chaos

Astrologers who sincerely believe in their theories desire to help humanity by demonstrating that the order of the sidereal universe can influence earthly chaos for the better. This is based upon what some astrologers call the Hermetic principle of correspondence, "as above, so below." Humans are a miniature mirrored image, a *micro*cosmic reflection of the greater planetary *macro*cosm in the universe. Is earthly life merely a microcosmic reflection of the universe?

The Hermetic principle "as above, so below," drives home the logical conclusion that astrology is a fatalistic system. Today's astrologers rebut this with new arguments in an attempt to escape fatalism, an unavoidable conclusion since there is no free will if everything is predetermined from above.

Free will is completely absent from the history of astrology. A recent attempt by astrologers to account for this dilemma is the claim that the stellar influence only "invites" responses from the subject, but nothing compels the subject to submit to astrological influence. This is not only a red-herring argument crafted to distract from the real issue, but it distorts astrological history. The question is not whether mankind feels compelled; the question is whether the stars emanate a power that influences the earth and individuals in the "as above, so below" principle. Many of today's astrologers reject fatalism and the Hermetic principle as part of their practice, so their practice steers people toward choosing the correct paths in life decisions.

The law of cause and effect better describes the historical sense of the astrological theory. The macrocosm influences the microcosm, which is why philosophers label astrology as fatalistic. If the stars truly influence earthly affairs, then the events on earth cannot be other than the result of sidereal influence. Once an astrologer admits that earthly life can be something other than influenced by the stars, then the stellar influence becomes meaningless and the astrological theory dissolves. Christian theologian and philosopher R. C. Sproul once said, "Fatalism finds its most popular expression in astrology."[50] If the affairs of men are controlled by the influence of the stars, astrology is one of the most enduring examples of fatalism. To escape this difficulty, modern astrologers apply flexibility to their practice so that it does not become ironclad, as fatalism would require.

---

50. Sproul, *Chosen by God*, 194.

Astrologers inevitably find themselves trapped in a web of sticky issues: they cannot simply dismiss the problem of fundamental helplessness because they do not like its philosophic outcome. An astrologer cannot say that the stars cause nothing, since such an assertion annihilates the foundation of their practice. To practice astrology they must necessarily say that the stars do something. The claim that the sidereal universe influences earthly affairs is the admission that it is something, and if something, then it is back to square one: astrological cause and effect concedes earth and its inhabitants to fatalism.

Some astrologers see the flaw in astrology's fatalistic foundation. It does not consider man's free will and thus undermines the entire practice. If human will is more powerful than the power of the sidereal influence, then this weakness renders the influence as meaningless; humans could will to oppose it at any time. Due to the various branches of astrology, the fatalism argument works best in discussion about astrological history and traditional astrology. New Age and most modern astrologers avoid the fatalistic trap by basing their astrology upon items like trends, character, and personality.

Astrological Successes and Failures

Astrology claims a succession of successful predictions, but what is largely ignored is the number of failures. One of the most popular astrologers in recent years was the psychic Jeane Dixon, but even she had one failed prediction after another.[51] Until astrologers who use their art for predictions can show that something exists other than guesswork, then their statistics for success are strongly countered by their larger failure statistic. The claim that the planetary position in one's zodiacal sign holds influence, trends, or any other characteristic must first be validated prior to stating that successes emanate from it.

Astrologers need to account for the source of the power or influence from the stars and planets. If it is a natural force, then it should be subject to detection and study like other natural forces, and it should have a high (not low) degree of predictability. Instead, it appears to be completely random and devoid of consistency, which is the opposite of other natural forces. If the influence is a supernatural power, then it should have a remarkably high success rate, which it lacks. This is

---

51. See the discussion on Jeane Dixon in chapter 2.

not an argument against astrology because it is difficult to explain; it is an argument against silence. These kinds of astrologers offer no explanation or definition and so avoid outside study and testing.

This avoidance at all costs is quite unlike the God of the Bible, who opens Himself to testing.[52] The Scripture details precise predictions, given hundreds of years in advance of the event—and they always occur on schedule. A number of incidents attest to this, from King Cyrus (Isa. 45:1) who was predicted by name two hundred years before he was born, to the Messiah's birth in Bethlehem (Mic. 5:2) to the seventy weeks of Daniel (9:20–27) when the Messiah would be cut off. A Davidic psalm (Ps. 22) described the Roman method of crucifixion six hundred years before it was invented and twelve hundred years before Christ endured it.[53] A reasonable person who studies how biblical prophecy was given, with details that go far beyond vague predictions, would conclude that an intelligent mind was behind it. This mind belongs to God, and He is declaring the future and fulfilling it. Astrology lacks both detail and success.

Character Analysis

The analysis of personal character, abilities, and destiny has been part of natal astrology from its inception. This was originally reserved exclusively for ancient royalty, but over the centuries, it filtered down to common people. This unscientific analysis claims that planetary movements (the cause) at the time of birth have a direct effect on the personal character traits of the newborn (the effect).

The controversial Mars Effect study (1955) has been used by some to bolster the power of astrological character traits. This study of 2088 athletes by the French

---

52. Just because God as Spirit is not a three-dimensional being, it does not follow that He is somehow prevented from acting in our three-dimensional existence. If God exists, as what we find described in the Bible, then we would expect His actions to exceed the limitations of a three-dimensional world, rather than being restricted by it. God gave certain tests through biblical history to assure us of His reality, like the ten plagues in Pharaoh's court, where each was an "if-then" proposition and they occurred as predicted (Exodus 7–12). The ultimate test of God's reality is the resurrection of Jesus Christ, which had "many infallible proofs" (Acts 1:3). Had Jesus not risen from the dead, then all that we believe and preach is in vain (1 Corinthians 15:14). One cannot arbitrarily call these tests faulty when we have examples like John 20, where Thomas, who was a skeptic and did not believe in the resurrection, was invited to touch Jesus' nail prints. That was a three-dimensional test in the real world that was also seen by others who were present.

53. Several Messianic prophecies are defended in Josh McDowell, *The New Evidence That Demands A Verdict*, 164–202.

psychologist Michel Gauquelin claimed that a measurable percentage of champion athletes had the planet Mars rising at their time of birth. His theory, although well publicized, was later debunked as a biased test.[54] Another psychologist, Hans J. Eysenck (who promoted Gauquelin's studies), also claimed verification of astrological character traits. But further studies by other researchers under the same test conditions, revealed biases in Eysenck's subject selection—much like Gauquelin before him.[55]

According to *Time Magazine*, psychologist Carl Jung had many horoscopes cast for his patients. His purpose in doing this was to try and discover hidden personality characteristics—not to forecast events in their lives.[56] For Jung, two unrelated coincidental events may be meaningful, and this curiosity led him to explore astrology and other occult phenomena. Astrological character traits especially interested him, since they might be "meaningful coincidences"; for example, a planet rises and a superathlete is born. His biographer wrote, "Jung believed that astronomical data did 'correspond to individual traits of character,' and therefore could 'serve as a basis for character study or for an interpretation of a given situation.'"[57] Jung's daughter, Gret Baumann-Jung (an accomplished astrologer), greatly influenced his study of astrology. She assisted Jung in a two-year study of a volunteer group of astrologers designed to compliment his research (1950–1952). In the end, however, Jung's research proved nothing conclusive and only offered subjective meaning to isolated incidents.[58]

Do planets determine or reflect character traits? In 1985, a double-blind study was done on astrology and character traits, and the results found it completely lacking substantiation. Shawn Carlson, a doctoral candidate at UCLA, led a study of twenty-eight astrologers selected by their peers as gifted. Three additionally

54. See particularly the study by Jan Willem Nienhuys, "The Mars Effect in Retrospect" in *Skeptical Inquirer* 21, No. 6 (1997):24–29, where he reviews Gauquelin's research methods and points out a strong bias. Nienhuys looked for the "Mars Effect" first before selecting his athletic subjects. Gauquelin committed a fallacy of "confirmation bias" to produce favorable results.
55. See Veno and Pammunt, "Astrological Factors and Personality: A Southern Hemisphere Replication" in *Journal of Psychology 101* (1979): 73–77.
56. "Astrology: Fad and Phenomena" in *Time*, March 21, 1969, 56.
57. Bair, *Jung: A Biography*, 549. This book is the only biographical work authorized by Jung's family.
58. A new trend that is credited as an extension of Jung's work is "therapeutic astrology," where horoscopes are used to boost self-esteem or self-confidence, although our biblical analysis remains the same.

astrologers were selected as advisers for the experiment in order to ensure an equitable assessment. The conclusions arrived at during the course of this study were published in the British journal *Nature*. In the final analysis, the astrologers tested were only able to match the character traits with natal horoscopes to the same degree as *random chance* (a 1 in 3 chance of a correct guess); the astrologer's results came in the same at 1 in 3 correct. They showed no special gift for horoscopy.[59]

Purpose and Power

Astrology appeals to the human need for purpose and power. Stephanie Clement, a thirty-year astrologer, explains the truth behind astrology in her book *What Astrology Can Do for You*. "This book opens the door to the real purpose and power of astrology: understanding yourself, your path, and your future."[60] Astrologers recognize the human pursuit of purpose and power.

In direct contrast to the placebo of astrology, the Bible offers genuine truth: life's purpose comes from the Creator, and life's power has its source in His Spirit. The life of an individual can be altered by the power of God. It is quite significant that those who are absorbed in astrology are seldom absorbed in Scripture. Great astrologers do not worship at the throne of God and of His Son, Jesus Christ.

Appeal to the Bible

Although the failure of astrological predictions could be taken lightly, it must be considered as an influence or force that demands attention and understanding. Its history shows that the power it wields does not dissipate with time; astrology gains strength and generations of followers as time passes.

Practitioners of astrology often argue for the antiquity of their craft and attempt to gain validity through biblical sanction. But exactly what does the Bible have to say about astrology? Several portions of Scripture significantly reveal God's mind on the subject, so the Church is not left in darkness. In Isaiah 47:13–15, the Lord speaks clearly to those involved in astrology:

---

59. Carlson, "A Double-Blind Test of Astrology," *Nature*, 318 (1985): 419.
60. Clement, *What Astrology Can Do for You*, ii.

You are wearied in the multitude of your counsels;
Let now the astrologers, the stargazers,
And the monthly prognosticators
Stand up and save you
From what shall come upon you.
Behold, they shall be as stubble,
The fire shall burn them;
They shall not deliver themselves
From the power of the flame;
It shall not be a coal to be warmed by,
Nor a fire to sit before! Thus shall they be to you
With whom you have labored,
Your merchants from your youth;
They shall wander each one to his quarter.
No one shall save you.

God warns those in Israel who wander from His covenant, *You are not paying any attention to Me—so let them save you!* Let the astrologers cast the horoscopes and study the stars. God has told us what their end will be: they will be as stubble (dry grass) themselves. The fire of God's judgment will burn them up, and they will not be able to deliver themselves. If they are not able to deliver themselves, they are certainly not going to be able to deliver anyone else! It is dangerous to trust in the stars. The only wisdom worth trusting is the good news of God's grace as revealed in the Lord Jesus Christ.

In the first book of the Bible, God initiates His warnings against astrology. Genesis 11 tells the fascinating story of the tower of Babel. People often believe the tower of Babel was a tower intended to reach heaven. But that is not what the text says. The correct translation indicates that ancient man was actually building a platform to worship the hosts of heaven.[61] This was quite likely a Babylonian star platform that was never meant to touch heaven itself. God did not want people reaching out to the stars, so He confused their languages and disrupted their communication. His condemnation of their work is crystal clear.

---

61. See Clarke, *Adam Clarke's Commentaries*, s.v., Gen. 11:4, Biblesoft.

Jeremiah 10:2–3 offers another warning about heavenly signs delivered through the prophet Jeremiah. "Thus says the LORD: Do not learn the way of the Gentiles; do not be dismayed at the signs of heaven, for the Gentiles are dismayed at them. For the customs of the peoples are futile." It is important to note that the balance of this chapter links astrology with idol worship. Jeremiah pleaded with Israel to stop following Gentile teachings based upon heavenly signs.

In ancient Mesopotamian religions, astrology itself was religious and used as a means of worshiping other gods. This is seen in ancient writings, where priesthoods are described as committed to the study and interpretation of the stars and their divine connections.[62] But the Bible says interpretation of the future belongs only to God (Gen. 40:8). The interpretations do not belong to priests, ancient religions, or astrologers. Humans are told not to attempt to unravel it; it is in God's hands. Astrology is crafted to attempt penetration of the future—it is a tool forbidden by God, a method contrary to His Word.

In their search for biblical support, astrologers also point to the wise men who came to visit Christ soon after His birth. Since these traveling magi clearly relied upon astronomy, astrologers insist that the New Testament endorses their work. In Matthew 2 it seems clear that the Zoroastrian magi were students of the stars and looking to understand the future. What did they learn? They learned that there was a king to be born in the east: "Now after Jesus was born in Bethlehem of Judea in the days of Herod the king, behold, wise men from the East came to Jerusalem, saying, "Where is He who has been born King of the Jews? For we have seen His star in the East and have come to worship Him" (Matt. 2:1–2).

A great light attracted the attention of the magi, and it eventually led them to believe that some momentous event was in progress, usually associated with the birth of a great personage. In this case it was a king, and they came with their gifts to worship Him. It is interesting here that astrology—at its best—led the wisest astrologers of all to Herod, the archenemy of Jesus Christ and agent of Satan. He was threatened by their message that a rival king was born and planned in his heart to kill Him. Herod told the wise men to find the baby, and report back to him so that he could come and worship Him.

This is a powerful biblical message for today's astrologers. If the best astrologers

62. Barton, *Ancient Astrology*, 23.

of all time followed the star of Christ and were led to worship Him, then all astrologers should follow their example. They must come to the feet of Jesus Christ and worship Him. If they will come with their charts, dusty books, and all the arts of antiquity, and lay them at the feet of Jesus of Nazareth; if they will bow down before Him as did the wise men and worship Him as incarnate deity, if they will give Him their gifts of their souls and their material means, then He will forgive them and call them His children.

Whoever finds the Star of David no longer needs the stars of heaven. He who has found the one who is the root and the offspring of David—the bright and morning star—does not need any astrological forecasts. He has found Him of whom Moses, the law, and the prophets did write: the King of kings and Lord of lords. Astrology should follow the example of the wise men and worship Him.

Daniel and Astrology

Daniel was an expert on astrology, so his testimony should be valued by anyone searching for the truth. In Daniel 1:12–14, you will find the names of the Hebrew children God brought to serve Him—Daniel, Shadrach, Meshach, and Abednego. These individuals were dedicated to God had an unusual request: "Please test your servants for ten days, and let them give us vegetables to eat and water to drink. Then let our appearance be examined before you, and the appearance of the young men who eat the portion of the king's delicacies; and as you see fit, so deal with your servants" (vv. 12–13).

As unappetizing as a vegetable diet may seem, after ten days Daniel and his friends looked better, healthier, and fatter than all the other men who ate at the king's table. These four young men of God increased in wisdom, skill, and learning in the understanding of visions and of dreams (Dan. 1:17). They were brought before King Nebuchadnezzar, who tested them and found none like them. "Then the king interviewed them, and among them all none was found like Daniel, Hananiah, Mishael, and Azariah; therefore they served before the king. And in all matters of wisdom and understanding about which the king examined them, he found them ten times better than all the magicians and astrologers who were in all his realm" (vv. 19–20). Daniel and his friends were ten times better than all the astrologers, because they had something the astrologers did not have: the knowledge, skill, learning, wisdom, and the understanding of visions and dreams.

God revealed the answers to them. In Daniel 2:27–30, the king had a dream he could not explain:

> Daniel answered in the presence of the king, and said, "The secret which the king has demanded, the wise men, the astrologers, the magicians, and the soothsayers cannot declare to the king. But there is a God in heaven who reveals secrets, and He has made known to King Nebuchadnezzar what will be in the latter days. Your dream, and the visions of your head upon your bed, were these: As for you, O king, thoughts came to your mind while on your bed, about what would come to pass after this; and He who reveals secrets has made known to you what will be. But as for me, this secret has not been revealed to me because I have more wisdom than anyone living, but for our sakes who make known the interpretation to the king, and that you may know the thoughts of your heart.

This verse is one of the most marvelous in the Old Testament: "There is a God in heaven who reveals secrets" (Dan. 2:28). He does not do it by horoscopes, charts, or studying the stars. "He has made known to King Nebuchadnezzar what will be in the latter days" (v. 28). God opens the understanding of men because the power to do these things resides with the living God. He reveals the future.

The king encounters the astrologers again in Daniel 4:7–8. "Then the magicians, the astrologers, the Chaldeans, and the soothsayers came in, and I told them the dream; but they did not make known to me its interpretation. But at last Daniel came before me, his name is Belteshazzar, according to the name of my god; in him is the Spirit of the Holy God." Nebuchadnezzar ran into a dead end when his astrologers struck out. Scripture points out the difference between Daniel and the astrologers: "In him is the Spirit of the Holy God" (Dan. 4:8). That was the difference—it was the Spirit of God who gave Daniel the interpretation.

Many years later, King Belteshazzar needed to know the meaning of the writing on the wall:

> The king cried aloud to bring in the astrologers, the Chaldeans, and the soothsayers. The king spoke, saying to the wise men of Babylon, "Whoever reads this writing, and tells me its interpretation shall be clothed with purple

and have a chain of gold around his neck; and he shall be the third ruler in the kingdom." Now all the king's wise men came, but they could not read the writing, or make known to the king its interpretation. Then King Belshazzar was greatly troubled, his countenance was changed, and his lords were astonished. (Dan. 5:7–9)

What happened? The Scripture keeps record: Daniel came forth and gave the interpretation:

There is a man in your kingdom in whom is the Spirit of the Holy God. And in the days of your father, light and understanding and wisdom, like the wisdom of the gods, were found in him; and King Nebuchadnezzar your father—your father the king—made him chief of the magicians, astrologers, Chaldeans, and soothsayers. In as much as an excellent spirit, knowledge, understanding, interpreting dreams, solving riddles, and explaining enigmas were found in this Daniel, whom the king named Belteshazzar, now let Daniel be called, and he will give the interpretation. (Dan. 5:11–12)

It is in the hand of God to dissolve doubts and meet anxiety. It is in the hand of God to meet needs, for He will supply all needs according to His riches in glory by Christ Jesus. It is not necessary to go to the astrologers, whom God says cannot even save themselves. Any involvement with astrologers endangers the spiritual life.

CASE STUDY

Marcia Montenegro

Spirit guides, Eastern meditation, astrology, the "higher Self," Kundalini, psychic abilities, numerology, Tarot cards, contacting the dead, hanging out with Witches, Sufis, followers of Eastern gurus—all these and more were part of my journey.

How did I get on this path? I grew up with an agnostic father and a nominal Christian mother. My mother took my sister and me to Church, although she did not always go. In high school, I thought that being good would please God and get me to heaven, but eventually Christianity seemed limited and boring. I felt something was missing, so I rejected Christianity and explored other beliefs. That exploration spanned from college to beyond, taking me to psychics and astrologers, to books about contact with the dead, and to studies of Eastern beliefs.

In an Inner Light Consciousness class, I was introduced to my "spiritual master" during a guided visualization. This guide, a spirit-being, looked kind and wise. I felt his presence with me always after that, and sometimes saw him in dreams and meditations. I also had unpleasant and bizarre experiences and visitations.

When first doing Eastern meditation, I felt an incredible peace, as though I was merging with something greater and becoming one with the universe. My studies led me to Tibetan and Zen Buddhist groups, and to practices of spirit contact, numerology, psychic development, and past life regression. Books by Edgar Cayce, Theosophists, Buddhists, and paranormal experts began to fill my shelves. My spiritual progress seemed assured, and I felt I was an "insider" in the spiritual realm.

I studied astrology and took an exam to qualify for the business license required in Atlanta, Georgia. I started practicing astrology and eventually taught astrology, gave public talks, wrote for astrological and New Age journals, and sat on the Board of Astrology Examiners that gave and graded the exams, finally becoming chairman of that board. In June, 1989, I became president of the Metropolitan Atlanta Astrological Society. My Halloween birthday and astrological skills made me popular with Witches and others.

While doing chart readings for clients, I would "tune in" to the chart in a paranormal way, and felt guided through the chart. After so many years of Eastern meditation, I was slipping without effort into an altered state of consciousness while doing astrology.

I also discovered that according to what I was following, there was no answer; it was the journey that counted, with an ultimate hazy goal of merging with the Source of all. Truth is not absolute, but is based on experience, and is flexible and fluid.

An unexplained compulsion to go to a church gripped me in 1990.

Since I was hostile to Christianity, I struggled against this, finally giving in by visiting a large church. In the opening minutes, I felt a love I had never known wash down over and through me. I knew this love was from a personal God, not from the music, the people, or place.

After several weeks, I began to feel unclean about astrology although no one in this open-minded church said anything about astrology. I then got the impression that God did not like astrology and wanted me to give it up. Give up my life's work, my identity and purpose? Not even believing what I was doing, I gave up astrology in late 1990. Thinking I should read the Bible, I started reading Matthew.

This person Jesus fascinated me. One evening I read the Matthew 8 account about Jesus stopping a storm in its tracks by rebuking the winds and the sea. That meant that Jesus has authority over nature! I saw the real Jesus for the first time, and realized I was separated from God by everything I had done in my past—I had lived my life based on my will, a will that had rejected and defied God and His Word. I realized that the only way to be forgiven was through Jesus, the God-man who suffered and died for me out of a great and unconditional love. I realized Jesus is the Savior and understood for the first time why Jesus died on the Cross. The truth and the answer were one and the same: Jesus Christ. And so I gave myself to Christ and knew I belonged to Him from that moment on.

I found out four months later that a young Christian man in an office where I worked part-time had been praying for me with a fellowship group at his church. No matter where one journeys, even as I did, no one can journey beyond God's power to save, should He choose to do so, because His mercy and grace are marvelous, and glorify Him.

CONCLUSION

It is the Bible that pronounces the final word for every Christian's life. The Bible declares a warning that should instill the Christian with godly gratitude for His deliverance from darkness. The Christian needs to face astrology with God's Word and prayer because it leads its followers into a world of deception. It is not biblical to look to the stars and planets to determine their influence in accordance with one's birth or conception. The Bible says we are chosen in Him before the foundation of the ages and, "For I am the LORD, I do not change" (Mal. 3:6), and "Even from everlasting to everlasting, You are God" (Ps. 90:2).

The God of the cosmos (Ps. 8) is the God who stretched out the heavens and the earth. The heavens declare His glory! The heavens may summon people to study them, but they do not summon people to worship them.

The first commandment is first for a reason—all people are to worship God alone. "You shall have no other gods before Me" (Ex. 20:3). Astrology leads human beings to seek information from sources other than God; therefore, it is dangerous and certainly not Christian.

Recommended Resources

1. Gruss, Edmund. *Cults and the Occult.* Philadelphia: Presbyterian and Reformed Publishing, 2002.

2. Koch, Kurt. *Occult Practices and Beliefs.* Grand Rapids: Kregel, 1971.

3. Kole, Andre and Holley Terry. *Astrology and Psychics.* Grand Rapids: Zondervan, 1996.

4. Montenegro, Marcia. http://www.christiananswersforthenewage.org/.

Quick Facts About Tools of the Occult

- The dimension of earth is surrounded by other dimensions of reality that are not subject to the five senses.

- Satan and his demons inhabit one of these dimensions called hell.[1]

- The satanic plan is to separate man from God; to deceive, damage, and destroy as many people as possible.

- These evil beings can penetrate the dimension of earth and perform things contrary to the laws that govern it, such as levitating objects, spelling words on a Ouija board, or recording voices on digital recorders.

- People can penetrate this dimension and contact evil by use of certain occult tools.

- The Bible forbids all contact with any of these evil, other-dimensional beings.

---

1. According to the Bible, hell has different levels. See Matthew 12:43 and Luke 16:23.

9

Tools of the Occult

The tools of the occult must be examined at close range and thoroughly disarmed in the light of Scripture if they are ever to be unmasked. Their history is a long and malevolent one, reaching far back to such ancient peoples as the Babylonians, Chaldeans, and Egyptians. The one sure tenet of history is this: it has a distressing tendency to repeat itself. Such is the case with the history of the occult. It is never difficult to find the source of modern occultism in the remains of ancient times. In view of their influence on modern lives, these archaic occult tools must be defined, examined, and analyzed, and the spiritual antidote to them thoroughly explored.

What exactly are the tools of the occult, and how do they operate? What must be learned in order to detect them, understand them, and combat them? And perhaps, most important of all, what is the best way to evangelize those involved with them? The heart of this analysis is, of course, *evangelism*; to bring men and women, lost in the kingdom of the occult, to a redemptive knowledge of Jesus Christ. If the Church fails in this, then it does not matter how acute and powerful our arguments may be, or how great our grasp of Scripture, or the depth of our intellectual perception. In the end, we will have failed to accomplish the task God sent His people to do. Christians are in the world as ambassadors to bring men to Christ. Therefore, it is important for the Christians to see these things in their proper perspective.

In the realm of psychic phenomena, dark forces surround the Christian on every side. The word *psychic* simply refers to the soul, and *phenomena* refer to experiences: the things we can see or comprehend. It is imperative to recognize that when strange things occur, such as flying crockery, moving furniture, or slamming doors, they are controlled by *other-dimensional* forces. These are psychic experiences or experiences of the soul, things that appeal to the spiritual nature of man. An earlier study of extrasensory perception revealed that normal ESP is latent in all

307

human beings, and a study of hypnotism exposed how a thing that is essentially good can be easily perverted to gross evil. In much the same way, an analysis of the tools of the occult will bring a clearer understanding of the workings of Satan and the concept behind the forces of darkness in their operation today.

The Church is not powerless or vulnerable in the face of this evil supernatural force; it possesses the ultimate weapons to combat all of it successfully. God has not given the spirit of bondage again to fear; He has given *power* to overcome the forces of darkness (Rom. 8:15). Drawing all of these strings together is no easy task, but the serious nature of the occult must be acknowledged and investigated before a strategy for defense can be crafted. The occult enslaves the mind and soul; therefore, it is critical for Christians to be aware of it and prepared to defend against it. With hundreds of occult tools at the disposal of the prince of darkness, this examination will focus on those more frequently encountered in the modern world by a variety of individuals.

TOOLS OF THE OCCULT

Amulet, charm, fetish	An object allegedly imbued with occultic power that protects the owner from evil.
Astral projection and astral travel	Also known as an *out-of-body experience* (OBE). In *projection,* the human spirit pulls away from the body and moves into the "astral," which consists of multiple planes of existence, such as the physical world, the universe, and/or spiritual realms. It can occur as a conscious choice or happen unpredictably. *Astral travel* occurs when the spirit projects from the body and journeys into the astral—to explore other planes of existence. Energy "cords" keep the spirit linked to the body's chakras (energy points).
Aura	A field of energy thought to surround the human body. Psychics claim aura is an emanation of the soul, visible as multicolored layers. Scientists believe aura may be

	related to electricity present in the body that produces a type of magnetic field.
Automatic writing	Random writings produced without conscious thought; "spirit-guides" often use this means to communicate their message.
Chakras and yoga	Hindu belief that multiple energy points connected to consciousness exist in different areas of the human body (possibly five to eight). These points, centered in the middle of the body from midforehead to midpelvis, draw in the universal life-force said to surround people and disperse it throughout the body, creating *balance*: physical, mental, emotional, and spiritual. The Hindu practice of *yoga* is centered on these chakras. Yoga is a carefully crafted, ancient form of Hindu worship, not a harmless set of physical exercises.
Channeling	Deliberately opening your heart and mind to spirit-beings and relating their messages to others through private sessions, books, CDs, Web sites, or seminars.
Crystals	Various rocks, such as rose quartz and black tourmaline, said to contain "energies" enabling them to draw power (energy) from outside the body into it through the chakra points in order to cause a change (usually healings) in attitude or health.
Crystal ball	A glass ball used to receive occult impressions or revelations pertaining to present circumstances and/or future events.
Dowsing	The use of a tool such as a forked stick or modern metal rods to sense the earth's vibrations and discover water, minerals, information, or anything the searcher chooses; also used to achieve contact with the spirit world in order to ask questions of spirit-beings.

Energy	An indescribable force inside and/or outside a human being that some claim can be tapped into and controlled to alter life for the better. Sometimes call *chi* (chee), a Chinese word describing the supernatural energy of the universe; also known as *prana* in Hindu beliefs.
EVP (Electronic Voice Phenomena)	Strange voices or sounds not deliberately recorded on audiotape or digital recorders. Voices often sound human and relay messages such as "Get out of here!" or "Die." Foul language and sounds similar to animal growls are also quite common.
Horoscopes (also called birth charts or natal charts)	Created by an astrologer for an individual (based on personal information, such as birth date) to help that person understand the meaning and/or purpose of his or her life and offer suggestions related to this. Horoscopes are not considered fatalistic today as in centuries past. The reading of this chart is the *forecast* an astrologer makes detailing planetary positions and their influence on an individual life.
I'Ching	Considered the oldest Chinese classic text (also called the Book of Changes), it consists of a symbol system (sixty-four abstract line figures) and rules for using them to effect life changes. It also includes detailed explanations related to the symbols, and some poetry. It has been used extensively in foretelling the future.
Magic	In an occult context, *magic* can refer to supernatural power controlled by a person through means of spells or occult tools; the source of this power is often attributed to the universe, but actually originates in the satanic realm. Scholarly definitions vary; a universally accepted meaning does not exist in that what one culture might classify as *religion,* another may classify as *science.*

Numerology	Letters are assigned numbers, and numbers are assigned meanings to form a system of divination. It is believed that a person's birth date and name reveal information about him or her. Once the numerologist has this specific information, all numbers are interpreted. This interpretation can include a character analysis based on these numbers, advice on spiritual or lifestyle changes, and/or personal predictions.
Palmistry	Foretelling the future by studying the lines on the palms of the hands; also called *chiromancy*. This was often associated with tea-leaf reading, since both could take place at the same consultation. The practice of reading tea leaves left in the dregs of a cup was yet another tool used by mediums to predict future events.
Pendulums and divining rods	Often included under *dowsing*, a pendulum is a weight (e.g., rock, crystal) suspended on a long string; a divining rod can be any type of rod. Both are used to discover secret knowledge, such as the location of water, the gender of a baby, or answers to direct questions.
Psychometry	The ability to access knowledge (visions) about a person's life or about an event after it has occurred, usually by holding an object related to a person or visiting a location related to an event (psychic knowledge). Also referred to as *scrying*, *retrocognition*, or *postcognition*.
Ouija boards	A flat, rectangular board (originally made of wood) with the alphabet printed on it along with the words *Yes, No,* and *Good-bye*. Fingertips rest on the wide end of a tear-shaped pointer (called a *planchette*), generally made of plastic. The narrow end points to letters that spell out answers to direct questions as the pointer moves around the board.

Runes	Alphabet first attributed to the Vikings but possibly evolved from Etruscan or early Germanic sources. Each symbol has an assigned meaning; the symbol would be inscribed on a stone or some type of material and then cast like dice in response to questions. May originally have been used for communication, magic spells, fortune-telling, or all three.
Séances	Meetings held to contact the dead, usually presided over by a medium.
Spirit-guides	A pseudonym for demons; spirit-guides claim to be human souls existing between earth and heaven, spirit-beings that exist multidimensionally. First contact usually consists of a plea for help (a common deception) or an offer of help. Some take on physical forms in the dimension of earth, and some simply move objects and/or cause the person who summoned them to write, speak, or act for them.
Tarot	A seventy-eight-card deck illustrated with various designs (altered over the last seven hundred years) used to foretell the future.

AMULET, CHARM, OR FETISH

Ancient civilizations had no corner on this market; amulets, charms, and fetishes can be found everywhere a shopper may look in today's fashion world. Pins and necklaces displaying the signs of the zodiac, dream catchers, the ankh (a modified cross with a tear-shaped circle on the top and the lower half of a cross beneath it), all of these and more are today's amulets, charms, and fetishes.[2] The ankh, thought to be an Egyptian symbol of life, is often associated with the gods of Egypt and

---

2. Archaeological evidence suggests that various versions of a cross existed as far back as Neolithic times. See George T. Flom, "Sun-Symbols of the Tomb-Sculptures at Loughcrew, Ireland, Illustrated by Similar Figures in Scandinavian Rock-Tracings," *American Anthropologist*, New Series 26, no. 2 (1924): 139–59, http://www.jstor.org/pss/660393.

with the afterlife; Christians consider it a symbol of ancient demon worship. Modern scholars still debate its exact origin and meaning. In the days of the apostle Paul, these amulets supposedly brought the wearer protection or good luck, and they are still believed to do so today.

In one of life's strange twists, the modern influence of Hollywood has transformed the Cross of Jesus Christ into the equivalent of a charm. People buy a cross and wear it as some kind of fashion statement, resulting in a loss of meaning for many who choose to display it. Before the eyes of the Church, the Cross has become a fetish, a charm, or an amulet. It is up to Christians to make a sincere, dedicated, and consistent effort to emphasize precisely what the meaning of the Cross is, and to let people know that whoever wears it is testifying to the resurrection of Jesus Christ, and the fact that He lives.

Astral Travel

Common in New Age teachings, astral travel is also called *remote viewing* or *scrying*. Writings on astral travel have been noted throughout history. In the twenty-first century, classes can be taken on how to successfully achieve it:

In one particular nine-week course offered online, you can learn how to:

- concentrate and be aware
- wake up in dreams
- project into the astral
- remember your dreams and interpret dream symbols
- travel in the astral and explore mystical places
- understand common obstacles when trying to project and how to overcome them
- protect yourself from negative influences and entities

The course description continues, "The astral plane is not just a destination, but a whole other dimension of life, which we can use to gain true knowledge about ourselves, our purpose, and about the world and beyond."[3]

---

3. "More About the Dreams and Out-of-Body Experiences Course," The Gnostic Movement, http://www.gnosticweb.com/node/10081.

A key point in this course description is to "protect yourself from negative influences." People involved in the occult are often the first to warn against its dangers, but they do not realize that all their charms, spells, and mystical defenses provide no protection whatsoever against "negative influences." Demonic beings fear only the power of Jesus Christ.

There are different schools of thought regarding astral travel. Some practitioners subscribe to a theory taught by the 1970s author and paranormal researcher Robert Monroe, known today as *phasing*. Monroe claimed that the body remains in this dimension, but the spirit is able to "phase" into a different one. During this phasing, the spirit does not detach completely from the body; it remains linked to it by energy cords that attach to different chakra points. According to Monroe, the astral plane, the universe—all realities exist as individual stops (along with earth) on the long road of consciousness—and human beings have the ability to reach these planes of existence with an *energy body*. His work became known for the phrase *out-of-body experience,* also known as *real-time projection.*[4]

A second perspective teaches it is possible for the spirit to actually detach from the body and visit other dimensions of reality. These realities are separate from earth, and not subject to its physical laws. Some people compare the detailed realities of astral travel to those found in dreams or visions. Also known as *etheric projection,* a good example of this can be seen in the Hollywood movie *Ghost,* where the main character dies at the beginning of the film and spends the balance of the movie in a transparent-type body (etheric body), moving from place to place in the earthly realm.

Auras

Auras have garnered more attention in recent years with the advent of computer innovations such as digital imaging and medical breakthroughs such as magnetic resonance imaging (MRI). These advances in science and medicine helped people believe in the reality and power of imagery. Photographs, taken by the method known as Kirlian photography, claim to show some type of field surrounding the human body, but the sources of these photographs seem routinely biased in favor of proving the conclusion before the experiment.

---

4. See Monroe Institute history on OBE at http://www.monroeinstitute.com/content.php?section=Out-of-Body%20Experiences.

A study on Kirlian photography and the writings of Thelma Moss, one of the main promoters of this theory, produces more questions than answers about the method of photography rather than an actual "field" surrounding a human. This does not stop occult researchers from using the controversial and inconclusive Kirlian photography to claim that an energy field surrounds the human body, but these photographs have been examined and refuted by scientists. Dr. Karl Kruszelnicki, physicist, physician, mathematician, and biomedical engineer (University of Sydney), points out that Kirlian photography does not record human "life energy"; it reveals the reaction of water vapor and electricity. "The high-voltage, high-frequency electricity [rips] the electrons off atoms . . . the air around the object becomes ionized, and if the air contains any water, you get this lovely glow."[5]

The body generates heat that can be picked up by infrared, but a scientific case has yet to be made for a legitimate photograph of any field that surrounds the body, other than heat. Nevertheless, psychic healers often claim to be able to see the auras of different people, and they use the multicolor images they see to diagnose and describe someone's personality traits and/or spiritual problems. It is believed by those involved with the occult that the aura is energy generated by the inner spirit or life-force, and this energy can be "read."

Automatic Writing

Those who dabble in the occult believe that much of the direction people seek can be found from spiritual beings that exist in another realm. Everyone has his or her own spirit-guide, and all the direction needed in life is obtainable through this guide. The ability to channel spirit messages in an understandable way makes it all possible. Automatic writing is a tool that allows this to happen; it offers unique, personal spiritual guidance.[6] The occult-based Shiprock Institute recommends the practice of automatic writing for beginners in divination, urging them to keep a file

---

5. Karl Kruszelnicki, "Kirlian Aura Photography," the Dr. Karl "Great Moments in Science" Web site, http://www.abc.net.au/science/k2/moment/s1095552.htm.

6. Automatic Writing, http://www.automaticwriting.org/about_automatic_writing.htm (accessed December 7, 2006). For a twentieth century example of automatic writing and possible demon possession, see *The New York Times*, March 16, 1992, "Ghost was a Girl," http://query.nytimes.com/mem/archive-free/pdf?_r=1&res=9E03E4D61F30EE3ABC4E52DFB5668389639EDE&oref=slogin (accessed June 11, 2008).

folder of their attempts to succeed at it and noting that it is a *preferred* way to make contact with higher entities who freely communicate messages.[7]

Chakra

Meaning "wheel" in Sanskrit, chakra are energy points (sometimes referred to as *vortexes*) believed to be the key to balancing the spirit with the mind and body (spirit-body merger). According to some occult teachers, certain foods can actually fuel an individual's chakras, purifying the transfer of energies or plugging them up, if the diet is unbalanced in some areas.

Each chakra point is named and minutely associated with every known aspect of life:

Root Chakra
- *Color:* red

- *Physical location:* base of the spine

- *Purposes:* kinesthetic feelings, movement

- *Spiritual lesson:* material world lessons

- *Physical dysfunctions:* lower back pain, sciatica, varicose veins, rectal tumors, depression, immune related disorders

- *Mental and emotional issues:* survival, self esteem, social order, security, family

- *Information stored inside root chakra:* familial beliefs, superstitions, loyalty, instincts, physical pleasure or pain, touch

- *Area of body governed:* spinal column, kidneys, legs, feet, rectum, immune system

- *Exercises that stimulate the root chakra*

- *Foods that fuel the root chakra*

---

7. Shiprock Institute Learning Group, "Occult Intuitive Guidance Methods," Shiprock Institute Natural Wellness Center, http://www.angelfire.com/biz2/metaphysician/occult.html.

- *Gemstones and flower essences that stimulate, cleanse and energize the root chakra:* gemstones—hematite, black tourmaline, onyx; flower essences—corn, clematis, rosemary[8]

This particular chakra is associated with Hindu deities Indra, Brahma, and Dakini. Each of the seven chakra points (some argue only five points) should be aligned in order to facilitate the healing energy. "The energy that was unleashed in creation, called the Kundalini, lies coiled and sleeping, and it is the purpose of a tantric yogi to arouse this energy, and cause it to rise back up through the increasingly subtler chakras, until union with god is achieved in the Sahasrara chakra at the crown of the head."[9]

The six remaining chakras are:

1. Svadhisthana (sweetness)

2. Manipura (lustrous gem)

3. Anahata (not struck)

4. Vissudha (purification)

5. Ajna (to perceive)

6. Sahasrara (thousand petaled)[10]

Yoga *asana* (positions) are designed to enhance the flow of energy from these chakra points in order to establish contact with "Supreme Spirit." The meaning of the word *yoga* is "union, yoking (with the Supreme Spirit)."[11] Yoga is Hinduism; it cannot be separated from it. Those who argue that yoga is simply good exercise do not understand or accept the history of it. Subhas Tiwari, a professor of yoga philosophy and meditation at the Hindu University of America, equates Yoga with Hinduism—they are one and the same.[12]

Today, the practice of yoga has invaded the Church to the point where some pastors actually hold yoga classes in their sanctuaries.[13] There are many problems

---

8. Phylameana lila Désy, "Chakra 1—Root Chakra: Chakra One—Exploring the Major Chakras," About.com: Holistic Healing, http://healing.about/com/cs/chakras/a/chakra1.htm.

9. Crystalinks, http://www.crystalinks.com/chakras.html.

10. Timothy Burgin and Yogabasics.com, http://www.yogabasics.com/chakras/chakra1.html.

11. The *Online Etymology Dictionary* traces the history of the word *yoga*: "1820, from Hindi *yoga*, from Skt. *yoga-s*, lit. "union, yoking" (with the Supreme Spirit)." (Douglas Harper, 2001, http://www.etymonline.com/index.php?search=yoga)

12. Lisa Takeuchi Cullen, "Stretching for Jesus," *Time*, http://www.time.com/time/magazine/article/0,9151,1098937,00.html.

13. Ibid.

with Christians engaging in this practice, not the least of which is the basic structure of yoga itself—created specifically for the worship of Hindu gods. Laurette
Willis, heavily involved in yoga and the New Age for twenty-two years, points out
the dangers of it:

> I call yoga "the missionary arm of Hinduism and the New Age movement."
> We don't often think of other religions having missionaries, but the philos-
> ophy and practice of yoga have been primary tools of Hindu "missionaries"
> to America since "Indian priest and mystic" Swami Vivekananda intro-
> duced yoga to the West at the 1893 World's Fair in Chicago. . . . Another
> Hindu missionary welcomed into elite circles was Paramahansa Yogananda
> who started the Self-Realization Fellowship in Los Angeles. He cleverly
> chose to demonstrate that yoga was completely compatible with
> Christianity. Wearing a cross, he came to America in the 1920s with the
> Hindu religious text, the *Bhagavad Gita*, in one hand and the Bible in the
> other. He reasoned that yoga was the binding force that could connect all
> religions.
>
> From experience I can say that yoga is a dangerous practice for the
> Christian and leads seekers *away* from God rather than to Him. You may
> say, "Well, I'm not doing any of the meditation stuff. I'm just following the
> exercises." It is impossible, however, to separate the subtleties of yoga the
> technique from yoga the religion. I know because I taught and practiced
> *hatha* yoga for years. *Hatha* yoga is the most popular yoga style available on
> store-bought videos and in most gyms. . . . Your yoga teacher may bow to
> her class saying, "*Namaste*" ("I bow to the divine in you."). Postures have
> names such as *Savasana* (the Corpse Pose) and *Bhujangasana* (the Cobra or
> Snake Pose). References are made to *chakras* or "power centers" in the body,
> such as the "third eye." The relaxation and visualization session at the end
> of yoga classes is skillfully designed to "empty the mind" and can open one
> up to harmful spiritual influences.
>
> As Christians, you are instructed to "be transformed by the *renewing* of
> your mind" (Romans 12:2), not the *emptying* of your mind. . . . Yoga's
> breathing techniques (pranayama) may seem stress-relieving, yet they can
> be an open door to the psychic realm—inhaling and exhaling certain "ener-

gies" for the purpose of relaxation and cleansing. (Paul refers to Satan as "the prince of the power of the air" in Ephesians 2:2, and I doubt the air to which he is referring is oxygen, but rather the psychic arena some call "the second heaven" which is certainly not a playground.) Whenever you see the words prana, ki or chi, these refer to "life force" energies.[14]

Yoga is not a substitute for aerobics, and it was never intended to be used for physical activity alone; it was created to worship deities the Bible calls *demons.* Modern Hindu leaders agree that Hinduism is the "soul" of yoga.

Channeling

Channeling is a modern word for what was commonly known as a *medium's trance.* During a séance, a medium falls into a different state of consciousness or trance. He or she then communicates messages from beings outside of the dimension of earth. Channeling gained great notoriety due to the resurgence of the New Age movement in the 1970s and the fame of demonic personalities like Seth, channeled by Jane Roberts, and Ramtha, channeled by J. Z. Knight. One occult practitioner notes, *"What are channelers channeling?* This is a difficult question to answer in that there are many responses to this. Essentially, the channeler is providing communication between any entity of another realm to the client. This entity can be from another galaxy such as an alien. This entity can be a goddess, angel, deva, other incarnated human, departed friend or family. It is basically any entity that is organized enough to group its energy in a fashion that can be understood by a channeler."[15]

Channeling is a dangerous occupation for anyone attempting it. Once a door is opened, it can be extremely difficult to close it. The Bible reveals exactly where this door is located, and exactly who is doing the talking on the other side. It is not any "goddess, angel, deva, other incarnated human, departed friend or family," and it is certainly not the God of creation.

14. Laurette Willis, "Why a Christian ALTERNATIVE to Yoga?" http://www.praisemoves.com/ChristianAlternative.htm.
15. Shiprock, "Occult Intuitive Guidance Methods," http://www.angelfire.com/biz2/metaphysician/occult.html, italics in original.

Several Old Testament passages forbid the practice of "spirits" speaking through a human vessel. In Deuteronomy 18:10–12, seeking after one who speaks with a familiar spirit is called an abomination to God. Noted Old Testament commentators Karl Keil and Friedrich Delitzsch address channeling by its King James term, "familiar spirits." In referring to Leviticus 19:31, which confirms God's judgment on mediums, they point out, "True fear of God . . . awakens confidence in the Lord and His guidance, and excludes all superstitious and idolatrous ways and methods of discovering the future. This thought prepares the way for the warning against turning to familiar spirits, or seeking after wizards. [owb] denotes a departed spirit, who was called up to make disclosures with regard to the future, hence a familiar spirit."[16]

This occult practice, whether real or pretended, is designed to draw people away from God.

Crystals

Casting the crystals (such as quartz, amethyst, citrine, agate) is promoted as "decision-making made easy" by various occult sites.[17] The claim is that a crystal's structure can actually enable it to remember whatever is "programmed" into it by the individual using it. This energy, channeled by a crystal, is believed by those involved with occult healing to facilitate wellness in all areas of life. Its history stretches back to ancient times, where the word *scrying* (fortune-telling) was often associated with crystals or rocks.

Some occultists, especially those with New Age ties, have tried to associate the "white stone" given by Jesus to overcomers in Revelation 2:17 with magical amulets or stones empowered with energies. Even though there are varied definitions offered by commentators on this verse, its meaning is far from occultic.

Adam Clarke's Commentary points to the ancient practice of using white stones to indicate pardons:

> *Mos erat antiquus, niveis atrisque lapillis,*
> *His damnare reos, illis absolvere culpa.*
> *Nunc quoque sic lata est sententia tristis.*

---

16. *Commentary on the Old Testament*, Biblesoft.
17. Holistic Shop, http://www.holisticshop.co.uk/itemdet1.php/itemprcd/CASTCRYS (accessed December 11, 2006).

"A custom was of old, and still remains,
Which life or death by suffrages ordains:
White stones and black within an urn are cast,
The first absolve, but fate is in the last."
DRYDEN[18]

It was a practice in the Roman world to reward the victors of public games with a white stone, often inscribed with their names. This white stone (called a *tessera*) granted the bearer a lifelong living at the expense of public funds.

The Roman reward seems to parallel the one Jesus offered to His overcomers in Revelation. According to Adam Clarke: "There is an allusion here to conquerors in the public games, who were not only conducted with great pomp into the city to which they belonged, but had a white stone given to them, with their name inscribed on it; which badge entitled them, during their whole life, to be maintained at the public expense. . . . These were called tesserae among the Romans, and of these there were several kinds."[19]

History does not support the interpretation of Revelation 2:17 as an endorsement of the occult, magic, or amulet powers.

Crystal Ball

The crystal ball is a common way of trying to break through the dimension of earth into the dimension of Satan and his demons. A good example of someone who used it with mixed success was the well-known psychic Jean Dixon. In the 1960s, Dixon revealed that she received impressions through her crystal ball. At one point, she looked into it and claimed to see a shadow over the White House—a shadow that symbolized the death of the Democratic president soon to be elected in 1960. She later revealed the future arrival date of Antichrist, based on information she received from her crystal ball and from a talking snake that visited her regularly at night. On several occasions, this snake slithered up the bed, wrapped itself around her, and communicated supernatural information to her. In retrospect, the history of mankind clearly shows it is unwise to listen to talking snakes.

---

18. *Adam Clarke's Commentary*
19. Ibid.

People who see things in crystal balls are experiencing occultic revelations. These are real; dreams and visions in the world of the occult are real. The devil is a magnificent magician, and he has been playing a shell game with the human race ever since the garden of Eden. Under which shell is reality? One may never find out; he is the master of illusion. Dealing with the devil is not an easy task in that it involves a life-or-death safety issue. The old saying, "He who sups with the devil has need of a long spoon," could not be closer to the truth.[20] It is not smart to get too close to the satanic realm.

Dowsing

Dowsing is associated with *pendulums* (crystal or other such items of choice), usually suspended from a rod, and *divining rods*. Most people look at dowsing and laugh, but dowsers are water Witches, and it is no laughing matter. The word *dowsing* is thought to have come from the Greek word *rhabdos,* meaning "magic wand." *Rhabdomancy* is divination by use of the wand.[21] The Greek poet Homer (850 BC) spoke of rhabdomancy, as did the great philosopher John Locke (1650 AD). From the earliest times, divining rods (usually forked sticks) were used to discover answers to all kinds of questions. Throughout classical literature, there are references to the divining rod, reaching as far back as Herodotus (484 BC) and more than likely into antiquity. Evidence of this type of divination and varying versions of it can be found in countless civilizations—ancient and modern.

Some modern dowsers claim to have a "gift" passed down to them from generations of family members. One such dowser made headlines in a national newspaper some years ago by revealing to a reporter exactly how he went about "dowsing." He recounted the story of how he took a Y-shaped, green branch and went out looking for water. When he got to where he thought there might be water (people actually witnessed this), his hands moved straight out in front of him. Each hand held one of the two ends of the Y-shaped stick, and the center shaft pointed forward. Without moving his hands or arms at all, the wood turned in his hands and pointed downward.

20. American Literature, http://www.americanliterature.com/Q1.HTML (English proverb).
21. Tufts University, *A Greek-English Lexicon,* s.v. "thabdos," http://www.perseus.tufts.edu/cgi-bin/ptext?doc=Perseus%3Atext%3A1999.04.0057%3Aentry%3D%2392041 (accessed December 26, 2006).

This man was not physically turning the stick, so the question remains: who was? Wood is not subject to magnetism. Water is not attracted to twigs unless they happen to be on tree trunks. It is therefore obvious that something extraordinary was active in this situation. This particular dowser said, "Something is operative. My technique has never been wrong—I have always found water."

How does he get this information? The spirits tell him; *they* are the ones who move the wood and locate the water. The skeptic might say, "Things like this do not happen." But the facts of history support that things like this *do* happen. These facts are checked and double-checked; the dowser repeats the experiment dozens of times, and by doing so he demonstrates the existence of some type of phenomena.[22]

And it is not just water these Witches are after. Dowsers search for gold, silver, oil, archaeological artifacts—the list is as long as a count of man's hopes, dreams, and desires. There are medical dowsers, water dowsers, mineral dowsers, and information dowsers (to locate lost children and downed airplanes). Once again, the list goes on and on. An endless variety of dowsing tools are used, from feathers to sticks, arrows, bones, and jewelry; the search for future knowledge is a powerful incentive. A dowsing rod can find water, and it can answer direct questions put to it—questions about personal plans and problems.

Who is supplying these answers? God is not in the business of locating wells for people. He sank the greatest of all wells at the Cross so that out of our innermost being may flow the rivers of living water that will bubble up to everlasting life. *That* is the well of God: His Spirit. Don't be fooled or intrigued by dowsing; it is a common tool of the occult, successfully used by demons to separate man from God. If someone goes to a water Witch to find the answers, he or she has chosen to talk to someone *other* than God (Hos. 4:12).

Moses, who struck a rock with his rod so that water would come forth, is sometimes accused of being a dowser by modern water Witches. This is not the case. Biblically, Moses' rod had nothing to do with dowsing. When he struck the rock with the rod, it was an act of disobedience to the Lord for which he was punished. In Numbers 20:8, Moses was told by God to speak to the rock, and water would

22. John Weldon, "Dowsing: Divine Gift, Human Ability, or Occult Power?" *Christian Research Journal* (Spring 1992): 8, on Christian Research Institute Web site, http://www.iclnet.org/pub/resources/text/cri/cri-jrnl/web/crj0099a.html.

come forth for Israel's needs. But Moses struck the rock instead, which even by the furthest stretch of the imagination is nothing like dowsing to find water. God already told Moses where the water was located, which shows us that Moses was not dowsing to find water.

Energy

Energy can be defined in countless ways: creative life-forces, moving power, or ley lines (energy lines said to crisscross the earth), Reiki (the energy associated with Reiki massage), Prana, polarity, chi—there are many names for occult energy—but generally it refers to the creative life-forces within human beings and/or outside of them. This energy is the power that surrounds and feeds mankind, and it is fed in return *by* mankind; it is a power that can be controlled by human beings through various means—crystals, cards, ceremonies, meditation, the correct diet, and yoga. This is the power source worshiped by the kingdom of the occult. God has revealed that this power source does not originate with Him, and that leaves only one other source: the prince of darkness—the devil. It is important to note here that the devil is *not* the polar opposite of God; he is not equal to God in nature or power. The devil is a created being, but he is a *powerful* created being. A closer identity match to the devil in angelic nature and power would be the archangel Michael. Simply put: the energy of the occult is the energy of the devil, and he is using it to destroy the children of God.

EVP (Electronic Voice Phenomena)

The twin discoveries of radio waves in the late nineteenth century along with the development of audiotape and audio machines in the early part of the twentieth century brought with them a strange, modern phenomenon: inadvertently recorded voices or sounds that came to be known as EVP. Unexpected whispers, animal cries, names—all seemed to magically appear on recordings made in front of witnesses who heard absolutely nothing during the time these audiotapes were made. Only during playback could the curious sounds be heard.

The names associated with the history of EVP are many, but it is the documented experiments of Konstantin Raudive (a Latvian psychologist and professor at the University of Uppsala, Sweden) in 1965 that focused the attention of both scientists and the media on this peculiar phenomenon. Raudive stated that he had analyzed approximately twenty-five thousand different voices, or "voice-texts," as he named them, and that each had unique characteristics. Raudive's work has not been easy for scientists or laymen to refute over the years; the best arguments tend to emphasize the power of imagination in EVP research. It stands today as a roadblock to repeated scientific endeavors to disprove the phenomenon of EVP.

The advent of the digital age brought with it the invention of the digital recorder, a device that lends itself quite well to EVP. In 2001, Dr. Katherine Ramsland, a journalist with a PhD in philosophy and master's degrees in forensic and clinical psychology, embarked on an experiment involving a supposedly haunted ring. During her investigation, she used a digital recorder to document multiple encounters with a disembodied voice. One of these encounters revealed that the being behind the voice intended to possess her:

I asked, "Well, what do you want then? Do you want to *possess* me?"
I stopped the recorder and hit the playback. The response was clear. "Yes."[23]

A growing number of people through the years have heard EVP voices, growls, whines, and assorted human and animal cries, and they continue to produce the recordings to prove it. As with the phenomenon of the Ouija board, audio technology has provided yet another doorway to a dimension of reality long forbidden by the God of the Bible.

Horoscopes

The horoscope or birth chart is a prediction (although most astrologers prefer not to consider it as such) based on a diagram of the various planetary positions and stars relative to the signs of the zodiac. Modern birth charts in Western civilization have become more consultation and advice sessions than guessing games of possible future occurrences. The word *horoscope* as it is used today refers to general predictions found in stores, newspapers, magazines, and on TV and the Internet. A birth chart or natal chart is usually done one-on-one, based on personal information.

---

23. Katherine Ramsland, *Ghost: Investigating the Other Side* (New York: Thomas Dunne, 2001), 173.

All of these quasipredictions of future events, whether individually or as a group, are rooted in the ancient practice of astrology: foretelling the future based on the positions of stars and planets. The term *astrology* has been interpreted in many different ways over thousands of years, yet its modern meaning renews its link to ancient occult practices. In discussing astrology, the *Dictionary of Gnosis and Western Esotericism* notes, "It was founded on the idea of a sympathetic coincidence of the world, heaven and earth, and the realm of the gods; and on the obedience of each one, as part of the whole, to a pre-established destiny. Thus, for example, each celestial event, precisely observed, is considered as auspicious or inauspicious for the people, or for their leaders. A great number of such predictions, recorded on tablets, have been rediscovered in the library of Assurbanipal of Nineveh."[24] In ancient times, the heavy hand of fate factored significantly into astrology, but today its position has been seriously diminished. Generally, it is now believed that people control their own destinies, and no matter what the stars say, they can change the course of fate.

People often claim that amazing things have happened to them because of astrology, and the answer to that is that some amazing things *can* happen, particularly if they put their faith in the stars themselves instead of in the God who created the stars. Astrology takes the mind off the Creator and focuses it on the *creation*, and anything that does this is in danger of condemnation. God condemned the world because they "worshiped and served the creature rather than the Creator, who is blessed forever" (Rom. 1:25). Today, millions of people's lives are governed by the stars. Astrology, with its birth signs and charts, is a common tool of the occult crafted to separate people from God, so that they become absorbed with the penetration of the future.

---

24. Hanegraaff, ed., *Dictionary of Gnosis and Western Esotericism,* 111. See also the Library of King Ashurbanipal Web page at http://web.utk.edu/~giles/ for information on Ashurbanipal of Nineveh: "King Ashurbanipal (ca. 668–627 B.C.) was the ruler of ancient Assyria at the height of Assyrian military and cultural accomplishments. He is known in Greek writings as Sardanapalus and as Asnappeer or Osnapper in the Bible. Through military conquests Ashurbannipal also expanded Assyrian territory and its number of vassal states. However, of far greater importance to posterity was Ashurbanipal's establishment of a great library in the city of Nineveh. the military and territorial gains made by this ruler barely outlived him but the Library he established has survived partially intact. A collection of 20,000 to 30,000 cuneiform tablets containing approximately 1,200 distinct texts remains for scholars to study today. Ashurbannipal's library was not the first library of its kind but it was one of the largest and one of the onew to survive to the present day. Most of it is now in the possession of the British Museum or the Iraq Department of Antiquities."

I Ching

The I Ching (pronounced *Yee Jing*) is an ancient tool (originally with yarrow sticks) used in Chinese divination. Today, three coins are tossed and their pattern recorded to produce answers to personal questions. Attributed to the great Chinese emperor Fu Hsi (2850 BC), the I Ching is thought to have developed in meaning and structure over a period of a thousand years under the influence of King Wen (founder of the Chou Dynasty in 1150 BC) and finally, under the revered philosopher Confucius (550 BC). It was after the contributions of Confucius that the I Ching came to be known as *The Book of Changes.* Today, the I Ching, also known as *The Oracle of Changes,* is viewed as fulfilling "at least two functions: book of wisdom, and oracular book."[25]

Book of wisdom—because it inspired the Chinese way of thinking and generally the whole Chinese culture, being at the same time a Ting (ritual vase) in which these currents mingled.

Oracular book—because it can be used as means of investigation and foretelling success or failure.

The book of wisdom distinguishes itself through the educational passages—undoubtedly written by Confucius' advocates and legists from whom we can quote an example at random. For many people, the book is a good manners handbook or book of cultivating the noble man, character called to play an active part in social and political state life (from here derives Confucius' influence).

The oracular book uses the 64 hexagrams as landmark of orientation regarding the evolution of the present events. Each hexagram describes a typical situation and are accompanied by oracular indication of the kind: "good fortune," "misfortune," "remorse," "humiliation." Several typical situations may be found here along with their indications, that is, the advice to be followed in the given circumstances.[26]

---

25. Way of Perfect Emptiness, "I-ching as Oracle of Changes," Taopage http://www.taopage.org/iching/oracle_of_changes.html (accessed December 28, 2006; site no longer accessible.
26. Ibid.

Developed on the Chinese belief that all life is subject to either chaos or order (yin and yang), the I Ching uses a system of coin tossing and sixty-four hexagrams to predict the future and offer advice on life choices in response to direct questions. Yin is the dark element; it represents multiple aspects such as the feminine/sadness/night and is symbolized by earth and water. Yang is the light element; it represents the masculine/joyful/day. These two elements embody the principle of yin and yang; they are in constant motion—moving and changing like currents in the ocean of life—and they influence every aspect of existence.

I Ching more than likely was influenced by the ancient Chinese religion of Taoism (founded by Lao Tzu in 550 BC), which teaches there is no personal god, only an impersonal supreme force called the *Tao*. Good and evil are opposite but complementary forces, and the goal of humanity should be to become free of selfish desires, in order to flow freely with the Tao.

Taijitu symbol represents the principle of yin and yang

Often referred to as the *Oracle*, I Ching was consulted for everything from military decisions to investments, marriage, and children—and it is still consulted today. It is a complex numerical and philosophic divination tool, and as such has not achieved the worldwide popularity of a simpler device, such as the Ouija board.

Magic

The King James Bible names magic in Acts 19:19 as "curious arts," known in the Greek as *perierga*.[27] The cultural definition of this word as *divination* or *magic arts* can be found in the literature of the time. For example, it was reported that the Roman emperor Hadrian (AD 74), practiced divination and was obsessed with the "curious arts."[28]

---

27. Periergos, NT:4021, working all around, i.e. officious (meddlesome, neuter plural magic), *New Exhaustive Strong's Numbers and Concordance*.
28. *Adam Clarke's Commentary*

Scholars have argued unsuccessfully throughout history as to the correct origin and meaning of "magic." In his landmark work, *The Origin and Growth of Religion,* Wilhelm Schmidt suggests that magic is the encounter with the extraordinary—something previously unknown.[29] He also contends, from a historical standpoint, that the belief in a moral Supreme Being preceded the development of magic. It came first in the history of man, as evidenced by the study of early religions, such as those of the Pygmies, and man chose to turn away from the worship of the Supreme Being to the practice of magic. Schmidt continues:

> In this period of personification, it is to the Supreme Being that man turns, as one person to another, with words and prayers. . . . Magic, on the other hand, is of a conspicuously and entirely impersonal character. That is to say it avoids or denies the supreme personal Cause and turns to material objects themselves, striving, by means of the secret powers latent in them, to reach its ends. These new methods were capable of finding supporters even in preanimistic days, wherever men, for one reason or another, wished to cast off their reverence for and obedience to the Supreme Being and thrust him into the background.[30]

Today, many involved in occult and New Age beliefs restructure magic in spelling, meaning, and practice. Modern-day *magick* is, in essence, psychic power manipulated to influence persons, events, or objects.

Numerology

Numerology is a system of divination based on the belief that personal information, such as birth names and birth dates, reveal individual personality characteristics and personal destiny. The names—reduced to numbers—resonate with the vibrations of the universe and reveal information about the soul and the fate of the individual. Pythagoras (580 BC) was a Turkish philosopher and mathematician often credited with influencing the development of numerology:

---

29. Schmidt, *The Origin and Growth of Religion,* 151.
30. Ibid.

The combination of mathematics and theology began with Pythagoras. It characterized the religious philosophy in Greece, in the Middle Ages, and down through Kant. In Plato, Aquinas, Descartes, Spinoza, and Kant there is a blending of religion and reason, of moral aspiration with logical admiration of what is timeless. . . . The dictum of the Pythagorean school was *All is number.* What this meant was that all things of the universe had a numerical attribute that uniquely described them. Even stronger, it means that all things which can be known or even conceived have number. Stronger still, not only do all things possess numbers, but all things *are* numbers. . . . Even qualities, states, and other aspects of nature had descriptive numbers. For example,

- The number **one** : the number of reason.
- The number **two**: the first even or female number, the number of opinion.
- The number **three**: the first true male number, the number of harmony.
- The number **four**: the number of justice or retribution.
- The number **five**: marriage.
- The number **six**: creation.[31]

Numerology has evolved into a modern system of occult divination, where charts and predictions can be made based on names, birth dates, birthplaces, and so on. It still retains the basic Pythagorean tenet, however, that *all is number.* This is quite different from the meaning of symbolic numbers used in the Hebrew and Greek cultures of the Bible. Some biblical numbers follow a significant pattern as used by God and His people, but these are never used to forecast the future. Therefore, the meanings behind numerics in the Bible cannot be carried to an extreme to hunt for knowledge not plainly present. Absent from all biblical context is the occultic belief that numbers have influence over people's lives.

Ouija Boards

Meaning "yes, yes" (*oui* in French and *ja* in German), the Ouija board came into widespread modern use in the year 1848, when Kate and Margaret Fox of

---

31. Don Allen, transl., "Pythagoras and Pythagoreans," Texas A&M University, Department of Mathematics, http://www.math.tamu.edu/~dallen/history/pythag/pythag.

Hydesville, New York, claimed they had successfully contacted a dead peddler. This possible communion with the dead created a nationwide frenzy, and public interest in talking to the dead skyrocketed. During their communication with the peddler, the Fox sisters would call out letters of the alphabet and listen for a knocking response that meant either "yes" or "no." Once this information reached the public, it was only a matter of time before human creativity took over. According to the Museum of Talking Boards, inventors tried out a number of strange creations specifically crafted to reach the dead, and a few of these eventually made it to the public marketplace.[32]

The resurgence of Spiritism led to thousands of séances, and eventually to the polishing of an occult device that came to be known as the Ouija board. The board has continued to be a popular "game" distributed by Parker Brothers, which now offers a new glow-in-the-dark game board option. Thousands of stories describing personal encounters with spirits through the use of Ouija boards are easily found on the Internet and in books, magazines, and newspapers. These encounters are real, and Ouija boards are a doorway to a dark dimension that is best left closed.

Palmistry

Also known as *chiromancy*, palm reading is perhaps the most well-known of all tools of the occult, thanks to multiple television and movie spoofs on mysterious gypsies and their powers of prediction. In palmistry, certain lines in the hands, such as the life line and median line, are said to tell a story about each individual, changing through the years as the individual changes. These lines and the angles they form can be "read" and future predictions made based on the information obtained by the medium.

Although stories of cackling, palm-reading gypsies are legendary, palmistry is not limited to the gypsies of old, and its predictions will occasionally hit the target (although general predictions are more the norm). Sometimes, a palm reader can truly be a medium, like the one who visited the famous 1940s actress Maureen O'Hara when she was just a child of five. In her autobiography, *'Tis Herself*, O'Hara recalls how her entire life was foretold by an old, cackling Romany Gypsy who appeared on her doorstep and read her palms. The Gypsy told O'Hara she would

---

32. Museum of Talking Boards, "History of the Talking Board," http://www.museumoftalking-boards.com/history.html.

leave Ireland and become famous. "You are going to make a fortune and be very, very rich. . . . But it will all slip through your fingers one day."[33] The accuracy of this prediction cannot be disputed, as the facts of O'Hara's prominent life support it. Some involved in palmistry are phonies, and others receive genuine information from sources other than God.

Palmistry is an ancient tool, often combined in history with other divination arts, such as *physiognomy* ("reading" the face and/or body) and astrology, both of which became popularly attached to palmistry during the Middle Ages. Several European texts forged the link in works such as Bartholomaeus Cocles's and John of Indagine's: "Astrological introductions to chiromancy, physiognomy, natural astrology, human complexions, and the natures of planets first published in Latin in Strasbourg, 1522, and frequently reissued."[34] Chiromancy eventually lost its tie to physiognomy, thanks to the work of Johann Lavater in the late eighteenth century, and its popularity has remained to the present day.[35]

Psychometry

Psychometry is the power to pick up an object that belongs to someone and obtain information about that individual through "vibrations" emitted from the object. These phenomena explain the various mystics who can pick up objects and tell you precisely what the person is doing, where he is, or even if he is alive or dead. Dr. Kurt Koch, an expert in the occult, has an interesting observation on the subject of psychometry:

> During a mission in Switzerland, I met a clairvoyant in my counseling who used psychometric powers, and who could make statements that were 100 percent accurate. If one were to place before him an object belonging to a patient who was unknown to him, for example a handkerchief, then he was able to identify the disease of that person. A professor in Zurich tested his ability and confirmed that his statements were reliable. This clairvoyant could do other stunts using his psychometric ability. In much the same way he could state from what diseases people had died.[36]

---

33. Maureen O'Hara, with John Nicoletti, *'Tis Herself: A Memoir* (New York: Simon & Schuster, 2004), 1.
34. Hanegraaff, *Dictionary of Gnosis and Western Esotericism*, 317.
35. Ibid.
36. Koch, *Between Christ and Satan*, 46–47.

This is psychometry: allegedly the capacity to receive a vibration from a postcard, a piece of jewelry, or whatever object is presented that reveals something about the person who owns it. It is a common tool of the occult. The real source of the information, however, is not any vibration coming out of a postcard, shoe, or ring. The real source of psychometric manifestation is a spirit that communicates information. A normal, everyday individual chooses to open himself or herself to the dimension of Satan, and information is exchanged.

People are often awed by an individual who can pick up a letter opener and say, "This belongs to Cousin Willie. He lives in Oshkosh, in the third house on Main Street. He is bald, a charter member of the Elks, and wears a big tooth on a chain." And sure enough, it does belong to Cousin Willie, and everything described is true. Instantaneously, the person jumps to the unwarranted conclusion that all of the information received came from the letter opener, which it did not. It came from outside forces influencing the individual, revealed to her because she was practicing a form of occultism. This is what the Church is up against in the world of the occult.

Today, television has opened the realm of psychometry to millions. The show *Psychic Detective* chronicles case after case in which the police and others involved marvel at the information given to them by psychics. This information is often detailed, right down to artist renderings of a murderer's face. Rationally, there can be no explanation for this, but spiritually, there is a clear answer: it is information imparted to a medium through supernatural means. The realm of the demonic is always eager for contact and even more eager for publicity.

Runes

The runes are letters from an ancient Nordic, Germanic, or possibly Etruscan alphabet, used by some to predict events in the lives of individuals. It is fortune-telling through casting objects and symbol interpretation. "Each rune not only represents a phonetic sound but also has its own distinct meaning often connected with Norse mythology."[37] Runes were the alphabet, but various other meanings were assigned to them for magic or divination. For example:

---

37. Nicole Sanderson, "Runes Through Time," Nova Online, http://www.pbs.org/wgbh/nova/vikings/runes.html.

ᚠ Fehu - cattle, gold or wealth

ᚢ Ûruz - strength or good health

ᚦ Thurisaz - mythological giants

ᚨ Ansuz - deity/supreme god Odin

ᚱ Raidô - a long journey

ᚲ Kenaz - light [38]

Runic inscriptions can be found everywhere in Scandinavian countries, much like the modern graffiti scattered across the American continent; it is not the alphabet itself that is mystical, although some involved in the occult would argue that point. Whatever its origin, the runes came to be used by some for occult purposes, as a means of fortune-telling, and they are still actively in use today.

Séances

The origin of séances is most likely quite ancient. Séances are nothing more than group meetings usually presided over by a medium and held to establish some type of communication with the dead. History portrays a long, unbroken trail of séances, but in the nineteenth century they enjoyed a great revival. Also known as "rescue circles," these séances and the information from the spirit world received at them eventually formed and solidified the theology of Spiritism. Demonic doctrine often included the following points:

- This world is the worst thing humans will ever experience.

- Preaching Christ is narrow-minded and deserving of punishment.

- The Bible is not true.

- Anyone dedicated to Christ will not see Him after death.

---

38. Adapted from ibid.

- Life after death consists of working to improve yourself in order to move on to a higher plane of existence.

- There is no devil.

Séances, or *sittings,* as many modern occult practitioners call them, often include other occult tools, such as crystal balls, tarot cards, and the Ouija board.

All forms of necromancy and modern séances are condemned in the Bible as an abomination to God. It usurps God's authority for man to seek the dead on behalf of the living (Isa. 8:19–20). God's Word is a more than sufficient guide in all areas of life, as Jesus said: "Your word is truth" (John 17:17). The dead, then, cannot improve upon truth pertaining to mortal life or eternal life.

Spirit-Guides

Spirit-guides are referred to by those involved in the occult as *guardian angels, invisible helpers,* or even *mischievous spirits.* They are often contacted through meditation, a practice that appears harmless on the surface but encourages its practitioners to clear their minds completely and "open" themselves to whatever may contact them. Those involved in the occult also teach that human beings are basically "magnets" that attract whatever they think about; crystals, incense, and other occult tools can help individuals achieve contact with whatever has been "attracted." According to New Age teachers, spirit-guides teach many positive things, such as unconditional love, and they are readily available twenty-four hours a day to help mankind succeed.

The danger of these spirit-guides cannot be overemphasized. There is simply no such thing in biblical teaching as a spirit-guide—there are only demons waiting for people to "open" themselves to their influence. Human souls do not float between heaven, hell, or any other dimension, a belief that took root from the teachings of Emanuel Swedenborg (d. 1772).[39] The Bible teaches that a person's final destination is determined by faith—a man or woman who chooses to believe in Jesus Christ as Savior and Lord will immediately be with Him in heaven after death (Luke 23:43); a nonbeliever will immediately be in hell by his own choice in reject-

---

39. For more information see Martin, *The Kingdom of the Cults* (Bloomington, Minnesota: Bethany House, 2003), Appendix C, "Swedenborgianism."

ing Jesus Christ (Luke 16:22–23). The assertions of those involved in the occult that human spirits need to be guided toward the light, or that there are good spirit-guides and bad spirit-guides, are mistaken; these practicioners have chosen to believe in a scam fostered by a deadly enemy.

It is important to note that God describes His angels as "ministering spirits sent forth to minister for those who will inherit salvation" (Heb. 1:14). It is apparent that the angels' work is exclusively for those purchased by Christ, and they are sent to minister, not as spirit-guides. Even though some occultists refer to their spirit-guide as their angel, true angels from God do not minister in realms of darkness; therefore, a spirit-guide is a counterfeit who masquerades as "an angel of light" (2 Cor. 11:14). The only guarantee someone involved with a spirit-guide has is that it will "guide" him or her far from God.

Tarot Cards

Tarot cards are common tools of the occult used by mediums and laypeople alike. According to modern occult practitioners, these cards are used to foretell the future, but their primary function is to help people understand the divine purpose in their lives. They have the power to bring together the loose threads of everyday life and provide ultimate understanding.

Divination by some type of cards is most likely ancient, and scholars claim it was probably practiced in virtually every culture, although there is little proof of this other than the nature of man and his propensity for gaming.[40] "One legend attributes them to the ancient sages of Egypt. . . . To others with occult sensibilities, however, the cards, when shuffled and arranged in patterns, brought the world's operation into microcosmic focus."[41]

The modern tarot deck is thought to have descended from an original deck developed as playing cards, with personal and political meanings, for the Italian nobility.[42] It came to be known as the Visconti Sforza deck after its creator, Filippo Maria Visconti, who ruled Milan, Italy, from 1412 to 1447. This deck is thought

---

40. Dan Burton and David Grandy, *Magic, Mystery, and Science: The Occult in Western Civilization* (Bloomington, IN: Indiana University Press, 2004), 72.
41. Ibid.
42. Ronald Decker, Thierry Depaulis, and Michael Dummett, *A Wicked Pack of Cards: The Origins of the Occult Tarot* (New York: St. Martin's Press, 1988), 27.

to have developed around 1550 into another popular Italian game called *Tarocchi*. Through the centuries, the card faces were changed more than seven hundred times until they no longer resembled their originals in either meaning or purpose. In the late 1800s, a resurgence of occult practices focused attention once again on tarot cards, and new, charismatic occult personalities reassigned designs and meanings.

Today's version is a deck of seventy-eight cards divided into two sections, called the *Minor Arcana* and the *Major Arcana*. The Minor Arcana consists of fifty-six cards, divided into four suits of fourteen cards: wands, cups, swords, and pentacles (based on the Italian influence). Each of these suits represents a certain perspective on life. For example, swords includes intellect, but intellect can be influenced by ego. Each of the four suits, when read, reveals how an individual aspect, such as intellect or ego, impacts the life of the questioner.

The Major Arcana, consisting of twenty-two cards with individual names and numbers, carries more weight in a tarot reading. These twenty-two cards are considered the heart of the deck, and each refers to things in life that hold more significance, such love or marriage. The Minor Arcana generally relate to everyday problems or situations.

Tarot has also been associated by some with the Kabbalah Tree of Life, the twenty-two cards somehow corresponding to "the twenty-two paths on the Tree of Life and, by extension, to the twenty-two letters of the Hebrew alphabet."[43] This connection has been attributed to the nineteenth-century French occultist Elias Levi, but there is little historical evidence to support it.

The person who becomes involved with tarot readings on any level is looking for a picture of the future. Whoever claims to be able to interpret the cards (very innocent looking on the surface) is saying in reality, "I can tell you something about your future that you do not know." They will point the unsuspecting toward their "inner guide" and suggest that mind, soul, and spirit be opened to its direction.

The tarot is an attempt to penetrate beyond this dimension. When people talk about tarot cards, they are discussing a specially designed card believed to hold the key to the future, and to events that influence individual lives.

---

43. Burton and Grandy, *Magic, Mystery, and Science,* 72.

Occult Elements in Modern Entertainment

In the realm of entertainment, today's world is a far cry from the one experienced by the *Leave It to Beaver* and *Brady Bunch* generations. There are thousands of different types of games, movies, cartoons, television shows, books, and magazines to choose from—a feast for the senses and a daily minefield for Christians to pick their way gingerly through. The content of entertainment has always been a source of concern, but the sheer number of choices now available is responsible for multiple parental headaches. Not to be outdone, the occult has oozed its way into all forms of "fun," and it certainly does not look as if it will get any better. It would be impossible to evaluate the myriad entertainment choices present in the modern world, so this analysis will offer an examination of occult elements, along with some examples of available entertainment.

Common sense dictates that it is important to know who or what is behind any entertainment offered in this world. The elements of the occult are often easy to spot. Some of them include:

- demons and/or demon possession

- worship of spirits or nature

- Witchcraft

- spells

- ghosts

- channeling

- vampires/monsters

- glorifying evil

- pentagram, inverted cross

- psychic powers

- tools of the occult

The Australian Family and Community Development Committee, in their research project *Inquiry into the Effects of Television and Multimedia on Children and Families*, concluded that repeated viewing of violence-themed media causes people to become accustomed to it, and to gradually assimilate it into their worldview.[44] This is supported by a similar study by University of Wisconsin psychologists Lintz and Donnerstein.[45] These studies, and others like them, simply reinforce the warning Jesus gave two thousand years ago: "The lamp of the body is the eye. If therefore your eye is good, your whole body will be full of light. But if your eye is bad, your whole body will be full of darkness. If therefore the light that is in you is darkness, how great is that darkness!" (Matt. 6:22–23).

EXAMPLES OF OCCULT-INFLUENCED MEDIA

Computer/Internet Games

Known as an MMORPG (Massive Multiplayer Online Role-playing Game), these computer games are played worldwide via the Internet. All MMORPGs immerse their players in a fantasy world.

Examples of MMORPGs include *Doom, Doom II: Hell on Earth*, and *Doom 3: Resurrection of Evil*, created by id Software. The *Doomworld* website emphasizes the meaning behind the id Software name: "id: the one of the three divisions of the psyche in psychoanalytic theory that is completely unconscious and is the source of psychic energy derived from instinctual needs and drives."[46]

Created as a science fiction/fantasy "first-person shooter" adventure, similar in theme and atmosphere to the movies *Alien* and *Resident Evil*, *Doom* includes demons and possessed humans in its assortment of monsters. *Doom 3* also bestows demonic powers on the first-person player. This game and its counterparts are dark, scary, and violent.

Another MMORPG influenced by the occult is *The World of Warcraft* by Blizzard Entertainment (successor to *Warcraft III*). Embracing the fantasy genre, *World of Warcraft* offers its players magical abilities/sorcery, spells, ghosts, quests,

44. Australian Family and Community Development Committee, Inquiry into the Effects of Television and Multimedia on Children and Families (East Melbourne, Victoria: Parliament of Victoria), chap. 3, "Television and Multimedia Violence," http://www.parliament.vic.gov.au/fcdc/ PDF%20Files/TV%20&%20MM/3%20Television@20and%20Multimedia%20Violence%20p g%2067-96.pdf.
45. See E. Donnerstein and D. Lintz, "Mass Media Sexual Violence and Male Viewers: Current Theory and Research," *American Behavioral Scientist* 29 (1986).
46. Jay Wilbur (former Doom business manager), quoted in "id History" on the Page of Doom, http://www.doomworld.com/pageofdoom/idhistory.html.

extraordinary weapons, heroes, and monsters (Orcs—think *Lord of the Rings*). This game also relies heavily on magic; it is dark, sometimes scary, and violent.

Video Game Consoles

Today's video game consoles are usually connected to a TV and require a DVD player. Microsoft's Xbox and Xbox 360 offer a large assortment of titles, such as *Barbarian, Barbie Horse Adventures, Evil Dead, Grand Theft Auto: Vice City,* and the Harry Potter series. *Doom 3* can also be played on the Xbox. Each title contains varied content. For example, occult elements in *Buffy the Vampire Slayer* include vampire themes, demons, and Witchcraft.

Cartoons

Many parents are unaware that several popular cartoons have occult-influenced content. *Yu-Gi-Oh!,* also called *Capsule Monsters,* began as a trading card game in Japan. It is produced and distributed in the United States by 4Kids Entertainment. In this show, Yugi is a young boy with magical powers who can "channel" an ancient Egyptian wise man. The more he channels him, the stronger his powers become. Asian and Egyptian ideas, such as the belief in different spirits and their ability to affect lives, influence the storyline. This cartoon features fantasy adventures, spells, summoning monsters, and battles between monsters.

Avatar is a show developed by Nickelodeon that has a fantasy-based storyline influenced by Hindu religious ideas. It is best described by the *AvatarChapters* Web site: "Water. Earth. Fire. Air. Only the Avatar was the master of all four elements. Only he could stop the ruthless Fire Nation from conquering the world. But when the world needed him most, he disappeared. Until now . . ."[47] The meaning of the word *avatar,* rooted in Hindu mythology, is "the descent of a deity to the earth in an incarnate form or some manifest shape; the incarnation of a god."[48] The avatar possesses psychic powers that help him defeat his enemies.

47. "Avatar: The Last Airbender," http://www.avatarchapters.org/plot.html.
48. Dictionary.com v. 1.1 (based on the *Random House Unabridged Dictionary* [2006]), s.v., "Avatar," http://dicionary.reference.com/browse/Avatar (accessed January 2, 2007).

Books

The Secret (a book launching turned media blitz) builds on Wallace Wattles's 1910 book, *The Science of Getting Rich.* Rhonda Byrne, the producer of *The Secret* movie and book, was influenced by Wattles.[49] Wattles (1860–1911) based his work on the Hindu principle that "One is All, and that All is One; that one Substance manifests itself as the seeming many elements of the material world."[50] Wattles pointed out that this Hindu theory has been successfully incorporated into Western thought for hundreds of years. "It is the foundation of all the Oriental philosophies, and those of Descartes, Spinoza, Leibnitz, Schopenhauer, Hegel and Emerson."[51]

The Secret focuses on the so-called law of attraction, which claims that our ideas, thoughts, feelings, words, and actions *attract* things into our lives. It's the rebirth of more New Age philosophy, nicely packaged with mysterious overtones, and disseminated worldwide by Oprah, Inc. What makes it more dangerous is that Oprah's support of Rhonda Byrne enables Byrne and other popular authors and lecturers to actively teach the principles of *The Secret.* (The "secret" is becoming aware of the power of the universe and how it affects your life.)

Another occult-influenced book, *The Da Vinci Code*, was an off-the-charts best seller. In this book, "a renowned Harvard symbologist is summoned to the Louvre Museum to examine a series of cryptic symbols relating to Da Vinci's artwork. In decrypting the code, he uncovers the key to one of the greatest mysteries of all time . . . and he becomes a hunted man."[52] The hidden "code" supposedly reveals that Jesus was married to Mary Magdalene and had a daughter with her. The Catholic Church is the villain, sending its assassins to take care of anyone who discovers the "truth" behind da Vinci's code. (Leonardo da Vinci is painted as the head of a secret organization determined to preserve this "truth.")

The problems with this book are numerous, not the least of which is its claim to be "researched" and by implication, authentic. *The Da Vinci Code* distorts the

49. This is commonly posted on sites selling *The Secret,* such as Amazon and Barnes and Noble, as well as on independent sites promoting the book.
50. Wallace Wattles, *The Science of Getting Rich,* preface, quoted on the About Wallace Wattles page (Calgary, AB: Prosperity.com, 2007) at http://www.wallacewattles.com/wallace.htm.
51. Ibid.
52. Catholic Answers, "Cracking the DaVinci Code," http://www.catholic.com/library/cracking_da_vinci_code.asp.

historical record of the life of Jesus. It is propaganda based on lies, as detailed by
the Catholic Answers website:

- Jesus is not God; he was only a man.

- Jesus was married to Mary Magdalene.

- Mary Magdalene is to be worshiped as a goddess.

- Jesus got her pregnant, and the two had a daughter.

- That daughter gave rise to a prominent family line that is still present in
  Europe today.

- The Bible was put together by a Pagan Roman emperor.

- Jesus was viewed as a man and not as God until the fourth century, when
  he was deified by the emperor Constantine.

- The Gospels have been edited to support the claims of later Christians.

- In the original Gospels, Mary Magdalene rather than Peter was directed
  to establish the Church.

- There is a secret society known as the Priory of Sion that still worships
  Mary Magdalene as a goddess and is trying to keep the truth alive.

- The Catholic Church is aware of all this and has been fighting for centuries to keep it suppressed. It often has committed murder to do so.

- The Catholic Church is willing to and often has assassinated the descen-
  dents of Christ to keep his bloodline from growing.[53]

Visualization Tools

Visualization tools are taught in books or on websites; they are usually linked to
meditation. For example, the *labyrinth (maze)* is a symbol representing the long,
winding path of life. The secret meaning of life can be found within each of us by
following the labyrinth path; this path has a purpose—a destination. At some

---

53. Ibid.

point, a person traveling the inner labyrinth arrives at his or her spiritual "center," and then travels back out again to share newly discovered inner knowledge. There is never happiness for very long or suffering for very long in life; the wheel of change is constantly in motion, affecting the journey of the labyrinth. This philosophy relies heavily on Eastern religion and New Age beliefs. It has recently become prevalent in books aimed at improving or running successful businesses.

A Christian Reponse to Occult-Influenced Media

A Christian walking with Jesus Christ will make life choices based on the Word of God and the leading of the Holy Spirit. It is not always easy to decide the correct path, but the Bible gives us some guidelines that help to clarify matters. "Finally, brethren, whatever things are true, whatever things are noble, whatever things are just, whatever things are pure, whatever things are lovely, whatever things are of good report, if there is any virtue and if there is anything praiseworthy—meditate on these things" (Phil. 4:8). A vampire movie, violent computer game, or cartoon laced with occult ideology might tend to muddy the waters of the heart, so wisdom should dictate caution when making viewing choices in these areas.

The recent furor over the Harry Potter series of books pitted one Christian against the other, generating a great deal of heat and very little light. What seemed mostly overlooked in the furor is the fact that a clever storyline cannot justify or erase a foundation of Witchcraft—an abomination to God that modern Witches have since used to their advantage. It cannot be lightly dismissed, and a search for Christian themes within these books is absurd and meaningless, since Satan regularly incorporates Christian themes into his work. The occult always wraps its shadowy message in shiny, bright paper, so the basic content of entertainment must be carefully evaluated. Many Christian parents did this with Harry Potter and decided to use Rowling's work as an effective educational tool *against* the occult. Other families chose to have nothing to do with it.

We all face choices from the time we first walk and talk, and it is often difficult to decide correctly. The apostle Paul's perspective on meat sacrificed to idols dictates wisdom and sensitivity in making these choices:

But if anyone says to you, "This was offered to idols," do not eat it for the sake of the one who told you, and for conscience' sake; for "the earth is the

LORD's, and all its fullness." "Conscience," I say, not your own, but that of the other. For why is my liberty judged by another man's conscience? But if I partake with thanks, why am I evil spoken of for the food over which I give thanks? Therefore, whether you eat or drink, or whatever you do, do all to the glory of God. (1 Cor. 10:28–31)

Some people believe that Christians must interact with the world in order to refute it, and they seem able to tolerate a careful exposure to darkness; others need to remove as much darkness from their sight as possible; still others have the responsibility to inform and warn the body of Christ against pervasive evil, and to do this, they must view things that are evil. In these circumstances, it is wise to temper judgment and remember that Paul emphasized that in some things people are different, and all temptation does *not* lead to sin. Even so, when temptation comes, wrote James, "Resist the devil and he will flee from you" (James 4:7). One thing is certain: all people will answer at the judgment throne of God for the choices made in this life, and so it is prudent to search the Scriptures, pray, and "do all to the glory of God" (1 Cor. 10:31).

CASE STUDY

Walter Martin

A Christian high school in New Jersey once invited me to come and lecture on the occult. Some of their students were dabbling with Ouija boards, Tarot cards, and other tools of the occult, so the principal felt it was a very good idea for them to find out exactly what it was all about. For almost eight hours straight, I went from class to class teaching and answering questions on the occult. There were about eight hundred students in the school, and you should have seen the looks of surprise on hundreds of faces when a few students stood up in the Question and Answer Sessions and confirmed, from their *personal* experiences, exactly what I taught in my lectures.

One student began by saying, "I don't want to spend a lot of time talking, but I was into the Ouija Board myself."

You could see this shook up some of the other kids. He was a Christian boy from a Christian family; this just didn't happen in the Christian schools of yesterday—unlike today—where it is happening in Christian schools all over this country!

He went on, "I asked the Ouija Board questions, and it began spelling out answers. It was weird because something moved my hand; *I didn't move it*, but I got messages from it with other people present. Something moved our hands. We were not doing it ourselves. Finally, I decided to ask it a religious question, so I said, 'Do you know Jesus Christ? Who is He?' The Ouija Board started shaking until the plastic spinner sailed off the board and hit the wall of my bedroom."

The room became very quiet.

"At that moment," he continued, "I decided that if I was serious about Christianity, playing with the Ouija Board made no sense, since it didn't want anything to do with Jesus. So, I burned the thing. It was a very unco-operative Ouija board when it came to Jesus Christ!"

Another young gentleman told me of an experience he had interrogating a Ouija board at length. He tried to find out who the spirit was behind the board, and this spirit was quite obliging up to a point. It gave its name as "Yes." He then asked it some biblical questions—questions the other person manipulating the board (who was not biblically oriented) couldn't *possibly* have known the answers to—but the spirit knew the answers. When they got to the subject of Jesus Christ, it was an entirely different ballgame. The Ouija board, in no uncertain terms, informed him that it did not love Jesus—it *hated* Him, and it had no respect whatsoever for the Christian gospel.

Do not play with Ouija boards, even if Parker Brothers insists it is a fun "game." Do not buy them; this is one of many doorways into the world of the occult. Remember, we are strangers and pilgrims in this world; we are aliens. Our source of supply and life comes from above. We are here as invaders of a satanic kingdom—ambassadors of an alien court—to bring the gospel of recon-ciliation to a dying age. Our home is in heaven; we seek a city whose builder and maker is God. Never forget that we have priority on the satanic list for removal because each Christian is potentially a reproducing agent for more Christians.

The next best thing to a damned soul is a sterile Christian who does not reproduce spiritually and bring people into the kingdom of God. If Satan cannot have your soul, he will do everything possible to sterilize your life.[54]

MIRACLES OR PARLOR TRICKS?

Human beings are surrounded by another dimension of reality that is not subject to the senses, but it is as real as anything material, and it is capable of penetrating this dimension (in given instances), and of doing things contrary to the laws that govern it. Table and trumpet levitations, all types of phenomena can be accomplished; Scripture tells us this dimension is under the personal control of "the prince of the power of the air, the spirit who works in the sons of disobedience" (Eph. 2:2).

It is an amazing thing to see people selling their souls for a chair that is floating six inches off the floor or a trumpet that is buzzing around a room. Yes, the devil can move objects; the devil can communicate; the devil can do unusual things. If he levitated a microphone in front of an audience, it should not come as any shock, nor should it cause anyone to put their faith in him. His parlor tricks do not match the power of God.

Satan does not open the Red Sea for people to cross onto dry land. Satan does not consume sacrifices on Mount Carmel so that the crowds proclaim, "Jehovah is God!" Satan is not involved in the business of doing things the right way. He is a very sleazy imitator of the real thing. This is part of the temptation of the occult; people become involved in it slowly until—before they know it—they are in a position where they cannot help themselves.

People who choose to penetrate the dimension of the occult in any way, whether through psychic phenomena or the Ouija board or any type of occult activity, are selling their eternal souls for cheap manifestations of power. The forces of darkness operate continually in earth's dimension, and people must recognize and accept this reality. A common mistake occurs in saying, "Isn't that amazing? It must be God!" But God does not do parlor tricks; He is interested in people's souls and in human destiny. God is not in the business of psychic phenomena. He is in the business of *revelation*, and that makes all the difference. It is a far cry from parlor tricks deliberately designed to attract the attention of the world.

An example of this kind of parlor trick, or *psychic phenomena*, as it is widely known today, occurred many years ago in New York. A story appeared one day in the local Long Island newspaper, *Newsday*, about a picture hanging on the wall of a house in Long Island that was attracting enormous interest. What was the picture

54. Walter Martin, *Exorcism* (audiotape/CD) (Walter Martin Ministries), www.waltermartin.com.

doing? Was it minding its own business, hanging on the wall? No, it was *crying* at regular intervals—real salt tears:

Icon Continues to Weep; To Be Enshrined Today

The "Panagia of the Door," Long Island's second weeping icon continued shedding tears yesterday as preparations were completed to move the icon today to a special shrine in St. Paul's Greek Orthodox Church in Hempstead. The eight-by-ten inch lithograph of the Virgin Mary holding the Christ Child brought hundreds of visitors yesterday to the home of its owner Mrs. Peter Koulis for a glimpse of the phenomenon."[55]

This weeping icon was the second of three weeping icons discovered in New York that year. According to Cynthia Blair, a reporter for *Newsday*, "On March 16, 1960, Pagona Catsounis was praying at her Island Park home when she noticed a drop of water on the cheek of an icon of the Virgin Mary."[56] Catsounis contacted her pastor at St. Paul's Greek Orthodox Cathedral in Hempstead, and the icon was removed from her home. A short time later, Antonia Koulis (the aunt of Pagona Catsounis) watched as tears leaked from the eyes of a picture of the Virgin Mary hanging on a wall in her home. Both icons were donated to the church, where several experts examined them and discovered the tears were not chemically identical to human tears. "The 'tears' were oily and did not contain sufficient nitrogen or salt to be considered human tears."[57]

Skeptics laughed over these stories and said, "Who really believes this nonsense?" But the crux of the matter is this: if the tears are real, people must believe that *something* is happening. Fluid samples were taken from these weeping icons and analyzed by scientists. The results came back from the lab, and the tears were factual, although their composition was different from that of human tears. Immediately, awed worshipers placed candles around the picture and an altar *under*

---

55. Jim Hadjin, "Icon Continues to Weep; To Be Enshrined Today," *Newsday*, April 18, 1960, reposted on Oceanside Beacon, http://www.1960sailors.net/09c-2_Beacon.htm.

56. Cynthia Blair, *Newsday*, http://newsday.p2ionlin.com/LIItHappened/popup/index.aspx?webstoryid-10507689 and http://www.visionsofjesuschrist.com/weeping416.htm (accessed January 1, 2007).

57. Ibid.

the picture, and people came from all over to see it—one weeping picture, then two weeping pictures, and finally—three of them!

Billy Graham could come to New York and preach Jesus Christ in Madison Square Garden for eighteen weeks, and newspapers would cover the crusade in section L, paragraph four, near the bottom, with a careful note that eighty people came forward to make a decision for Christ. For eighteen weeks, virtually nothing would be written about peoples' lives being changed: drug addicts, prostitutes, and people on all levels of life encountering God. But this picture, hanging on the wall, *crying*, has an altar beneath it and ends up enshrined in a church, and plastered on front pages across the state.

Why does this happen? It happens because the world is impressed by crying pictures—not crying people. This is the great callousness and dilemma of the modern age; more attention is paid to a picture than to the soul of a man. God is in the business of saving human souls and reconstructing battered lives. He loved the world enough to send Christ to accomplish that; He has no interest in parlor tricks.

Once put in its proper perspective, this crying picture can be seen for what it truly is: a trap. These pictures did not weep because God almighty decided to stage a revival on Long Island. These pictures wept to focus attention on a something *other* than the Creator of all things.

A lithograph mysteriously weeping salt tears falls into the category of psychic phenomena—a tool of the occult—and it distracts people from the person of Christ. These are not miracles; they are demonic tricks designed to look like miracles. People then focus on the *mystical* and on the *person*, in this case the Virgin Mary, and fail to realize that in contrast to Jesus Christ, it is nothing. Weeping pictures are *nothing* compared to the magnificence of the Master!

SCRIPTURAL RESPONSE

In this battle for souls, the tools of the occult are right out in front, touching the lives of people on every side. In order to successfully deal with them, we must recognize them and acknowledge the truth of their reality. The Christian Church is the army of the Lord, invading the kingdom of earth; it is only natural that it will be attacked. God has not called His people to a Sunday school picnic; He has called us to full-scale *war*.

Christian theology teaches that Jesus Christ is capable of meeting all our needs. He is sufficient. His Spirit and His power can deliver people. But the Bible also teaches that people are weak, sinful, and degenerate. The inevitable valleys can only be leveled by the power of God's Spirit.

Supernatural Warfare

God instructs Christians to put on the armor of God in order to fight against a carnal nature, against forces of darkness, and against all those things that would neutralize and destroy the Church: "Put on the whole armor of God, that you may be able to stand against the wiles of the devil. For we do not wrestle against flesh and blood, but against principalities, against powers, against the rulers of the darkness of this age, against spiritual hosts of wickedness in the heavenly places. Therefore take up the whole armor of God, that you may be able to withstand in the evil day, and having done all, to stand" (Eph. 6:11–13). The tools of the occult fit comfortably into this category, and their goal is to neutralize and annihilate the Church. They excel at deception, teaching that God is within each individual, and man can only succeed if he listens to this "inner guide."

All the Gnostic philosophies that today pervade the world and reveal themselves in the kingdom of the occult—reincarnation, Theosophy, Rosicrucianism—in all of these and hundreds more, the common denominator remains the *impersonality* of God.[58] He is anything but a Father, a personal Savior, or a Comforter. But in the midst of deception, the truth stands firm: anyone searching for the reality of unconditional love will only find that reality in the living God. It is not to be found in some circle of crystal, or in tea leaves and tarot cards, where someone hovers like a spider in a web, poised to predict the future. God—not a crystal ball or an amulet or a horoscope—is the master of the future.

The world of the occult always holds out the promise of elusive knowledge to people: a tarot reading will help you find your path in life; the crystal ball will reveal helpful information; psychometry will locate something important to you; dowsing will lead you to the essential things you are searching for. All of these methods show preoccupation with the future. Their power lies in persuading many to believe in the *force* behind the knowledge, and it is but a short step from there to a place of fascination and obsession. This present danger must compel the Church to

---

58. For more information on Theosophy and Rosicrucianism, see Martin, *Kingdom of the Cults,* chap. 8 and appendix D.

action: it must leave tolerance by the wayside and return to the Scriptures to analyze the enemy's weapons—the tools of the occult.

God's Position

People have always been interested in contacting spirits outside the dimension of
earth, and these other spirits *can* be contacted. But God has much to say on the
subject of the occult and the tools it utilizes. Isaiah 8:19, for example, is a verse that
should be underlined in every Bible. "And when they say to you, 'Seek those who
are mediums and wizards, who whisper and mutter,' should not a people seek their
God? Should they seek the dead on behalf of the living?" (Isa. 8:19–20). The world
of the occult emphasizes séances and the Ouija board as a means of contact with
forces beyond this dimension, but it is forbidden. The point Isaiah is making is to
stay away from it. This passage forbids anyone to even attempt to get this information. Should not a people seek their God for knowledge? It is in question form, but
the answer to the question is in the negative: do not do it—God is against it. The
living should not attempt to go to the dead for answers. That is *exactly* what God
is communicating.

If people play with a Ouija Board or attempt a séance, they act contrary to the
revelation of God. He warned the Jews about this in an anti-Ouija and an anti-
séance passage. God simply says, "Do not do it!" This one verse expresses the view
of God on the tools of the occult and efforts to penetrate the future. All of these
things in the Bible are given for a purpose. This purpose emphasizes that people
cannot—they *dare not*—enter into a relationship that can have great spiritual dangers for them.

Throughout the Bible, God warned the Jews not to imitate the Pagan cultures
in the land that He gave them, and if they did choose to worship Pagan gods, they
would receive the same judgment as the Pagans. In His warning to Israel, God
listed the very things we see today in the kingdom of the occult. "There shall not
be found among you anyone . . . who practices witchcraft, or a soothsayer, or one
who interprets omens, or a sorcerer, or one who conjures spells, or a medium, or a
spiritist, or one who calls up the dead. For all who do these things are an abomination to the LORD, and because of these abominations the LORD your God drives
them out from before you" (Deut. 18:10–12).

It was the occult practices of ancient Israel that brought the kingdom of

Manasseh to ruin. "And he built altars for all the host of heaven in the two courts of the house of the LORD. Also he caused his sons to pass through the fire in the Valley of the Son of Hinnom; he practiced soothsaying, used witchcraft and sorcery, and consulted mediums and spiritists. He did much evil in the sight of the LORD, to provoke Him to anger" (2 Chron. 33:5–6). And in 2 Kings 21:9, God reveals Israel's fascination with the things of the occult and their rebellion against Him. "But they paid no attention, and Manasseh seduced them to do more evil than the nations whom the LORD had destroyed before the children of Israel." God judged Manasseh for using the tools of the occult.

This is an important lesson: *stay away from the occult.* If God brought judgment on His own King because of it, then whoever becomes involved with it can expect judgment. Manasseh's downfall was the direct result of the tools of the occult.

Perhaps one of the most powerful passages dealing with the occult is found in Isaiah 47:12–14. God gives a specific warning here that simply cannot be ignored. It is a warning that anyone who prizes the word of God cannot forget:

Stand now with your enchantments
And the multitude of your sorceries,
In which you have labored from your youth—
Perhaps you will be able to profit,
Perhaps you will prevail.
You are wearied in the multitude of your counsels;
Let now the astrologers, the stargazers,
And the monthly prognosticators
Stand up and save you
From what shall come upon you.
Behold, they shall be as stubble,
The fire shall burn them;
They shall not deliver themselves
From the power of the flame.

God says that the tools of the occult cannot save the occultist, so they certainly will not save the people who consult them. The Lord God of Israel warns, "The only thing that is going to save you is *Me,* so do not be led off into these things."

It is terribly easy to wander into the world of the occult. Across this nation and around the world, Christians have been lured into the world of the occult. They are people who hang in some sort of theological and spiritual limbo—living every day outside of Christian churches and outside Christian fellowship—terrified and fruitless. Scripture consistently warns them that *nothing* involving the devil is innocent. The minute they start playing with the tools of the occult, no matter how simple they may be, they are in for a world of trouble.

The New Testament has said a number of things on the subject of the occult. Acts 16:16 tells of a young maiden possessed with the spirit of fortune-telling. She had access to supernatural knowledge until Paul exorcised the demon from her. The function of the demon that lived in the girl was to predict the future. This tool of the occult works, sometimes with remarkable accuracy, to get people interested in the future.

There are only two sources of knowledge about future events: the gift of prophecy (see 1 Corinthians 12) that comes from God the Holy Spirit, and the hit-or-miss information offered by Satan and his demons. God knows the end from the beginning, and He is usually not inclined to reveal it to people. Satan, on the other hand, does not know the end from the beginning, but he does have some knowledge; certainly enough to impress the world.

God is not interested in horoscopes or astrology, nor does He conduct séances. Acts 13:6–12 confirms this:

> Now when they had gone through the island to Paphos, they found a certain sorcerer, a false prophet, a Jew whose name was Bar-Jesus, who was with the proconsul, Sergius Paulus, an intelligent man. This man called for Barnabas and Saul and sought to hear the word of God. But Elymas the sorcerer (for so his name is translated) withstood them, seeking to turn the proconsul away from the faith. Then Saul, who also is called Paul, filled with the Holy Spirit, looked intently at him and said, "O full of all deceit and all fraud, you son of the devil, you enemy of all righteousness, will you not cease perverting the straight ways of the Lord? And now, indeed, the hand of the Lord is upon you, and you shall be blind, not seeing the sun for a time."
>
> And immediately a dark mist fell on him, and he went around seeking someone to lead him by the hand. Then the proconsul believed, when he saw what had been done, being astonished at the teaching of the Lord.

The Holy Spirit filled the apostle Paul in order to rebuke a sorcerer who practiced occultism. He would not have filled Paul with power to strike the man blind if God were behind his sorceries and his occult activities. It was to show the superiority of the power of God that the Holy Spirit brought judgment on the sorcerer of Acts 13. Therefore, it is possible to say with absolute certainty that Acts 16:16 is the best possible refutation for predicting the future. It is a tool of the occult, and it is dangerous. All occult tools, one way or another, lead people down primrose paths in an effort to win their trust in powers that have never been associated with God.

The Power of the Holy Spirit

The Christian has a mighty resource to aid him in his witness for Christ. In Daniel 4:8, God reveals that Daniel was a man filled with the Holy Spirit. In Daniel 5:11, he is called the master of the astrologers, the magicians, the soothsayers, the diviners of the future, and of all the occultists. The reason for this, according to the book of Daniel, was the Spirit of the living and holy God. Daniel's superiority was postulated upon the presence of the Holy Spirit, and he was ten times better than all the astrologers, all the soothsayers, all the sorcerers, and all the occultists (Dan. 1:20). The Spirit of the Holy God lived in him, and made him ten times better than all of them!

That was Daniel's secret, and it is the secret of the Church of Jesus Christ. If anything is to be known about the future, God will reveal it through His Holy Spirit. If anything is to be known, God is the source of that knowledge and He has given us the gift of prophecy in 1 Corinthians 12 to proclaim and to foreknow. He says this is to be *coveted* by the Christian. If we want to know something, we should ask God for it. Do not file an inquiry with the devil—file it with the Holy Spirit.

The Holy Spirit predates all denominations. He has been around since eternity, and therefore we can say with assurance that the Holy Spirit is trustworthy and reliable in providing information. In 1 Corinthians 12, we see that He gives gifts and information; He gives faith. He offers the gift of the discerning the spirits, which reveals the source behind the phenomena: God or the devil. And the Holy Spirit gives power, effects miracles, and provides healing. Yes, He gives tongues and their interpretation when it pleases Him—all of the nine gifts of the Holy Spirit are for the purpose of building up and edifying the Church, which is Jesus Christ's body, and demonstrating to the world that the gospel of Jesus Christ is indeed true.

Acts 2 teaches that the apostles preached a message, and the signs and wonders followed them in confirmation. How can the Church expect anything less from the Holy Spirit today than what He poured out upon His people so long ago? Can He give less than what is necessary in order to exist in this cosmic zoo, where we are committed as witnesses for Christ? It is said of the Lord Jesus Christ that He is the same yesterday, today, and *forever* (Heb. 13:8).

God the Holy Spirit has never changed; His power is still the same. Without the full power and equipment of the Holy Spirit, a wise person would be scared witless to face the forces of darkness. The Scripture says that whoever believes in Christ and trusts Him, out of their innermost being will flow the rivers of living water that will bubble up to eternal life (John 7:38). He spoke of the Spirit who was not yet given.

The Holy Spirit does not specialize in one spiritual gift. He does not give gifts so that they can provide status in the Church. The Holy Spirit is the dispenser of all gifts, and the command is to seek from Him what He chooses to bestow. Only He has the power to help people face the forces that today challenge the Church in every area of the world.

The Christian who is not yielded to the Holy Spirit, the Christian who does not produce in his or her life the fruit of the Holy Spirit, and the Christian who does not seek gifts from the Holy Spirit will have an *extremely* difficult time in the closing days of the age of grace.

It is because this power is available that God has said, "He who is in you is greater than he who is in the world" (1 John 4:4). To counteract the tools of the occult and the forces of Satan, God has given His Spirit, and that power is for the Church until Jesus Christ returns. The task of the Church is not an easy one, but the labor is not in vain in the Lord. Christians are to go out and make disciples, and stand against the forces of darkness, proclaiming the unsearchable riches of Christ (Matt. 28:19–20; Eph. 6:12; 3:8). We dare not do this without the Holy Spirit and His power. It was He who energized the early Church to greatness, saying, "I will pour out My Spirit on all flesh" (Joel 2:28). He will do no less for His Church today.

The great Presbyterian minister Donald Gray Barnhouse once said, "Come in the wind, come in the fire, come in the earthquake, come in the sound of stillness. Come as thou wilt, oh Spirit of God, only come, come, come."[59] *That* is the only answer to the prince of darkness—the vital energy of the power of God.

---

59. Religious Information Network, Walter Martin, *Tools of the Occult* (audio transcript) (Walter Martin Ministries, 2006), www.waltermartin.com.

Recommended Resources

1. Gasson, Raphael. *The Challenging Counterfeit: A Former Medium Exposes Spiritism.* Springfield, MO: The Assemblies of God Publishing, 1996.

2. Kail, Tony M. *A Cop's Guide to Occult Investigations.* Boulder: Paladin, 2003.

3. Koch, Kurt. *Between Christ and Satan.* Grand Rapids: Kregel, 1970.

4. Martin, Walter. *Tools of the Occult.* CD/audiotape, Walter Martin Ministries, www.waltermartin.com.

Quick Facts About UFOs

- An unidentified flying object is often referred to as a UFO.

- UFO sightings are most often explained as natural phenomena, but some remain unexplained.

- UFO cults are usually based on occult messages or occult methods.

- UFO sightings are distinct from the UFO religions that later evolved from occult experiences.

- Christians cannot test every UFO sighting, but it is prudent to test the spiritual message of UFO-based religions.

10

UFOs

Why should anyone be concerned about UFOs and the religions that evolve from them?[1] Why should unexplained sightings in the skies matter at all in the realm of the spirit? From time immemorial, mankind has tried to fill the spiritual void within his soul, and the phenomenon of UFO sightings provides ample material to draw upon. In the world of faiths and creeds, there will always be people willing to define their religion around a mysterious and often misunderstood phenomenon.

UFO study is complex, and the problem is often compounded by connecting these sightings with conspiratorial theories, hoaxes, sensationalized media reports, and additional speculative theories, such as animal mutilations, *Men in Black*, the Bermuda Triangle, Area 51 tales, interpretations of ancient drawings, interpretations of the markings in the Plain of Nazca in Peru, and an assortment of other oddities, such as interstellar astronauts as the breeders of mankind, and crop circles (a hoax that has been refuted).[2] Volumes could be written on each of these colorful and complicated subjects, so their association with serious UFO study only serves to confuse and confound. Erich Von Daniken, who along with many others jumped on the 1970s UFO bandwagon, successfully developed and popularized UFO theories such as these, based upon pure speculation.[3] His hypotheses linked

---

1. The following abbreviations are used in this chapter. A *UFO* is an "unidentified flying object." *UFOs* is the plural form. *Ufology* is the study of UFOs (pronounced yoo-fology). *RUFO* is a *residual unidentified flying object*, or one that cannot be easily explained, therefore remains residual. *IFO* is an *identified flying object*, which is usually a UFO that has been reclassified as something identified. *UFOnaut* is a being from a UFO.
2. It is interesting that ufologists, such as Jenny Randles, were among the first to disavow a connection between UFOs and the crop circle hoax. See Jenny Randles and Peter Hough, *The Complete Book of UFOS* (New York: Sterling, 1996), 230–35.
3. See Erich Von Danikin's *Chariots of the Gods?* (New York: Putnam, 1969); *Gods from Outer Space* (New York: Putnam, 1970); *Gold of the Gods* (New York: Bantam, 1973); *In Search of Ancient Gods* (New York: Putnam, 1973); *Miracles of the Gods* (New York: Dell, 1976); and *According to the Evidence: My Proof of Man's Extraterrestrial Origins* (New York: Bantam, 1978). Also see Eric Nor-

Note cont'd on next pg

unconnected items and imagined parallels, resulting in erroneous conclusions based on faulty parameters.[4] For the most part, however, ufologists disregard these peripheral phenomena and see them as unhelpful in solving the UFO puzzle.[5]

When reports are lively on UFO cults, they are spotlighted as newsworthy material, but once the excitement fades, they are inevitably forgotten until the next outrageous act brings attention their way. Marshall Applewhite was an occult practitioner who believed that he was a being from another planet.[6] Applewhite and his companion, Bonnie Lu Truesdale Nettles, founded a UFO religion and changed their names to Bo and Peep (as shepherds of God's people). The newly christened shepherds believed that extraterrestrial beings communicated and visited with them on a regular basis.[7] Over the next twenty years, their influence grew and a fluctuating number of followers gathered around them. While other UFO groups remained relatively unnoticed, Applewhite and Nettles seemed to enjoy the limelight of media attention. They traveled and lectured on and near college campuses, became the subjects of a book that identified them as the "two witnesses" in Revelation 11, and were featured on an NBC television drama.[8]

Branded as odd or perhaps fringe religious fanatics, they appeared to be entirely harmless until March 26, 1997, when thirty-nine members of Applewhite's cult,

---

3. (cont'd) man's *Gods and Devils from Outer space* (New York: Lancer Books, 1973).

4. Probably the one author who did the most to refute this was Dr. Clifford Wilson, who debated Von Daniken in *War of the Chariots* (New York: Signet, 1978), but his other books adequately asnwer the issue: *Crash Go the Chariots* (New York: Lancer, 1972); *UFOs and Their Mission Impossible* (New York: Signet, 1975); *Alien Agenda* (New York: Signet, 1975); *Close Encounters: A Better Explanation* (San Diego: Master, 1978), and *The Chariots Still Crash* (New York: Signet, 1975). In this latter book Wilson shows that Von Daniken altered photographs and "lied' about his research (10).

5. Even though Von Daniken became a household name in the 1970s and sold millions of books worldwide, he contributed nothing of value to UFO studies. Entries for his work are completely absent from books by serious ufologists, such as William J. Birnes's *UFO Encyclopedia* (New York: Pocket, 2004) or Randles and Hough's *The Complete Book of UFOS*. Ufologist Jerome Clark, in *The UFO Book* (Canton, MI: Visible Ink Press, 1997), mentions him but only in dismal terms (51).

6. Christopher Hugh Partridge, ed., *UFO Religions* (Oxford: Routledge, 2003), 104.

7. Bo and Peep later renamed themselves Do (Doe) and Ti. They were known as "The Two," but they later formalized their group and named it the "Human Individual Metamorphosis." See James R. Lewis, *Odd Gods: New Religions and the Cult Controversy* (Amherst, NY: Prometheus, 2001), 14.

8. Hayden Hughes and Brad Steiger, (ed.,), wrote *UFO Missionaries Extraordinary* (New York: Pocket, 1976), using Applewhite and Nettles's interviews as the basis for their book. The NBC movie that followed was *The Mysterious Two* (1982), which starred John Forsythe and Priscilla Pointer.

Heaven's Gate, decided to commit mass suicide in order to shed "their earthly 'container' to catch a ride on a spaceship trailing the Hale-Bopp Comet."[9] Suddenly, every branch of the news media wanted sociological, psychological, and theological answers on cultic movements in an effort to bring sanity from insanity. On May 6, 1997, the media were stunned once again to hear that two of the three surviving members attempted yet another suicide in order to join their deceased companions. One member was immediately successful, and the other ended up in a coma for a short while, until he was finally able to leave on his own, ultimately succeeding in his second suicide attempt in 1998. The media scrambled yet again to understand this unrelenting suicidal drive.

The sole surviving member of Applewhite's Heaven's Gate cult was Rio DiAngelo, the member who made the gruesome discovery of the mass suicide at the cult's rented mansion in Rancho Santa Fe, California (a suburb of San Diego). He shunned the press until the mass suicide's fifth anniversary in 2002, when he tried to sell the cult's van on the Internet. DiAngelo granted a rare interview to a San Diego reporter in 2002 that provides valuable insight into the thinking of a UFO cult member who maintained his faith in Applewhite regardless of the tragedy that ensued. What emerged from this interview (for cult and occult analysis) is the fact that personal experience takes precedence over all logical explanations: blind faith defies rationality. In spite of the mass suicide and the cult being investigated from every professional discipline, DiAngelo still believes that his former leader, Marshall Applewhite, was truly a being from another planet[10] who taught him "to be more aware, honest and sensitive to the world around him: in short, a better person."[11]

It is sad, but all too true, that the cults and the occult often provide a refuge for lunacy, their members blinded to internal faults as they insist the outside world is where the lunacy lies. Before passing intellectual judgment upon these groups, however, it is important to note that not all cult members are uneducated or intellectually inferior. Applewhite, for example, was raised as a Presbyterian minister's

9. Seth Hettena, "Five Years After Heaven's Gate Mass Suicide, Last Member Still Keeping Faith," *San Diego Union-Tribune*, March 26, 2002, http://www.signonsandiego.com/news/northcounty/20020326-0138-heavensgate.html.
10. Applewhite and Nettles claimed this in their interview with Hughes and Steiger, *Two Missionaries Extraodinary*, 68.
11. Hettena, "Five Years After Heaven's Gate Mass Suicide," http://www.signonsandiego.com/news/northcounty/20020326-0138-heavensgate.html.

son, obtained his master's degree from the University of Colorado, and became a professor at the University of St. Thomas (Houston).[12] Another UFO cult, known as the Raelians, has as one of its leaders Dr. Bridgett Boisselier, a scientist with a master's degree in biochemistry from the University of Dijon, a doctorate in physical chemistry (Dijon), and a PhD in analytical chemistry from the University of Houston. She leads a group of scientists from twelve countries, called "the Association of Raelian Scientists," who support the organization's extraterrestrial cloning theories. In light of these facts, it cannot be unequivocally stated that people who lead or join UFO cults are uneducated or lacking in intelligence. Sometimes very intelligent people join what appears to be the strangest of occult groups, sects, or cults, proving that intellectualism does not seem to satisfy the spiritual need present in the heart of every human being.

UFO cults are founded on the same weakness in man's spiritual condition that inspired him in ancient times when he "changed the glory of the incorruptible God into an image made like corruptible man—and birds and four-footed animals and creeping things" (Rom. 1:23), and this rebellion remains strong today. Ideas and events that seem mysterious or unexplained are always fertile ground for all kinds of self-proclaimed religious revelators who take advantage of natural human curiosity. They stand ready to explain the unexplained through personal revelation, using clever semantics to reformulate God's words into a recycled amalgam that resembles Christian terminology but lacks its true definition. Jesus called similar revisionists "blind guides" (Matt. 23:16), a description that unfortunately fits UFO religionists all too well.

A physical UFO sighting does not automatically translate into religious devotion; a "close encounter," viewed by a reliable witness, rarely produces religious or spiritual creeds based on contact with aliens, UFOnauts, or extraterrestrials. New faiths built upon UFO mysteries, however, elevate the unexplained to a religious level, triggering the biblical mandate to examine the occultic and religious tendencies of UFO religions and evaluate them. One phenomenon allows suspended judgment on the outcome, while the other requires an immediate verdict.[13] This

---

12. Robert W. Balch, "Waiting for the Ships: Disillusionment and the Revitalization of Faith in Bo and Peep's UFO Cult," in James R. Lewis, ed., *The Gods Have Landed: New Religions from Other Planets* (Albany: SUNY, 1995), 141.

13. A few of the scriptural reasons for exposing the errors in UFO religions can be found in 2 Corinthians 11:3–4; Galatians 1:6–9; Ephesians 5:11–123; 1 Timothy 5:20; and 2 Timothy 4:2–3.

chapter does not cast a vote to affirm or deny UFO sightings or governmental conspiracies, but only to analyze the occultic methods used in the hope of achieving contact with UFOs and extraterrestrial beings.

UFOs in History

Many books on UFOs mark the beginning of modern interest in the phenomena with a sighting reported by Kenneth Arnold (1915–1984) on June 24, 1947. Arnold was a thirty-two-year-old pilot and Washington businessman who saw nine airborne objects near Mount Rainer that were boomerang shaped and traveling at an estimated 1,200 miles per hour. Arnold's story was told to newspaper reporters the following day, and the term "flying saucers" was born. The Associated Press report, in its entirety, stated:

> PENDLETON, Ore., June 25 (AP)—Nine bright saucer-like objects flying at "incredible speed" at 10,000 feet altitude were reported here today by Kenneth Arnold, Boise, Idaho, a pilot who said he could not hazard a guess as to what they were.
>
> Arnold, a United States Forest Service employee engaged in searching for a missing plane, said he sighted the mysterious objects yesterday at three p.m. They were flying between Mount Rainier and Mount Adams, in Washington State, he said, and appeared to weave in and out in formation. Arnold said that he clocked and estimated their speed at 1,200 miles an hour.
>
> Enquiries at Yakima last night brought only blank stares, he said, but he added he talked today with an unidentified man from Ukiah, south of here, who said he had seen similar objects over the mountains near Ukiah yesterday.
>
> "It seems impossible," Arnold said, "but there it is."[14]

Ever since that day, flying saucers, also known as *unidentified flying objects* or *UFOs*, have been an international subject of debate and investigation. Whether one considers UFOs to be myth or reality, their importance is twofold for this analysis.

---

14. This Associated Press report has been republished in Curtis Peeples, *Watch the Skies!: A Chronicle of the Flying Saucer Myth* (New York: Berkley, 1994), 11; Clark, *The UFO Book: Encyclopedia of the Extraterrestrial*, 61; and Randles and Hough, *The Complete Book of UFOs*, 63.

As human beings, we should naturally be concerned with the things that happen on our planet. As Christians we view earth life as a special creation by God, who is supernatural, uncreated, infinite, and is the sovereign ruler of the universe; therefore, if UFOs exist, they are part of God's ordered universe. It is our obligation to find out where they fit in this order, and we need to consider what God's Word says on this subject. An objective study of the occult and UFOs requires careful sifting of UFO material, their alleged communications with mankind, the religious ideas that developed from these encounters, and an examination of what the Bible states on these things.

Since the time of Kenneth Arnold's sighting, there have been tens of thousands of documented UFO sightings by both reliable and unreliable sources. It is a painstaking task to separate the hoaxes, false reports, and natural explanations, from the smaller percentage of still unexplained sightings. This is necessary to arrive at sound conclusions, and several books have been published to meet this challenge.[15]

Dr. J. Allen Hynek (1910–1986), was a professor of astronomy at Northwestern University, an air force consultant on the UFO research program Project Blue Book, and a learned skeptic. He became a convert to the existence of UFOs after debunking them based on various scientific grounds and wrote *The Hynek UFO Report* in 1977, where he revealed, "There are 13,134 reports in the Air Force files."[16] Dr. Hynek, who spent twenty years studying these reports, also noted that by 1977 the Center for UFO Studies had amassed mounds of paper reports that they entered into a computer, along with more than fifty thousand additional reports from around the world. The sheer number of these sightings was staggering, but the nature of UFOs went unanswered.

Tens of thousands of new reports have been added to these numbers since 1977.[17] Before 1947, the mysterious "foo fighters" and "ghost rockets" from World

---

15. For a Christian scientific viewpoint, see Hugh Ross, Kenneth Samples, and Mark Clark, *Lights in the Sky and Little Green Men* (Colorado Springs: NavPress, 2002); Wilson, *UFOs and Their Mission Impossible,* and Wilson, *Close Encounters.* A secular scientific analysis can be found in J. Allen Hynek, *The Hynek UFO Report* (New York: Dell, 19700); and Peeples, Watch the Skies!

16. Hynek, The UFO Report, 8.

17. A great deal of research was done by the Christian Research Institute staff in Wayne, New Jersey (1960s). They spend considerable time collating some six thousand cases of sightings from bona fide sources, then culling the sources until they arrived at airline pilots, Air Force and Navy pilots, and individual observers with seemingly no ulterior motive for testifying to what they had seen.

War II must be considered, along with even earlier accounts of the airship sightings in 1896 and 1897 that were widely reported in California newspapers, sometimes accompanied by sketches from witnesses.[18] Another wave of airship sightings occurred in 1909 and 1910, but this time it was worldwide, with witnesses in New Zealand and Australia.

Cataloged sightings ranged from the fabricated to the unimpeachable. It was not long after the sightings increased in the 1950s that people also began claiming encounters with UFO occupants. During the early days of investigation, Dr. Hynek realized that classification of the various sightings would be necessary, so he devised the first standardized classification that, for the most part, remains. These are:

Relatively Distant Sightings

1. *Nocturnal Lights.* These are sightings of well-defined lights in the night sky whose appearance and/or motions are not explainable in terms of conventional light sources. The lights appear most often as red, orange, or white. They represent the largest groups of UFO reports.

2. *Daylight Disks.* Daytime sightings are generally of oval or disk-shaped metallic-appearing objects. They can appear high in the sky or close to the ground (as elsewhere) and are often reported to hover. They seem to disappear with astounding speed.

3. *Radar/Visuals.* Of especial significance are unidentified "blips" on radar screens which coincide with, and confirm, simultaneous visual sightings by the same or other witness(es).

Relatively Close Sightings (within 200 yards)

1. *Close Encounters of the First Kind (CE-I).* Though the witnesses observe a UFO nearby, there appears to be no interaction with either the witness or the environment.

2. *Close Encounters of the Second Kind (CE-II).* These encounters include details of interaction between the UFO and the environment, which may vary from interference with car ignition systems and electronic

---

18. These sightings preceded the Wright brothers' first airborne flight in 1903 by seven years. See Clark, *The UFO Book,* 27–37. Information on foo fighters and ghost rockets is available at http://www.uk-ufo.org/condign/histfoo1.htm and http://www.ufo.it/test/sweden.htm.

gear to imprints or burns on the ground and physical effects on plants, animals, and humans.

3. *Close Encounters of the Third Kind (CE-III)*. In this category, occupants from a UFO (entities of more or less humanlike appearance now referred to as "humanoids," or nonhuman creatures) have been reported. There is usually no direct contact or communication with the witness, but there have been some reports, increasing in recent years, of incidents involving very close contact with, and even temporary detainment of, the witness(es).[19]

Two other categories were later added to the Hynek classifications by people who study UFOs, sometimes called "ufologists." The *Close Encounter of the Fourth Kind* is defined as those that "include alien abduction cases," and the *Close Encounter of the Fifth Kind* is "where communication occurs between a human and an alien being."[20]

The available material on this subject is voluminous, and the legitimate claims alone would take years to sufficiently study and assimilate. Researcher Kenneth Samples noted, "Although the vast percentage of UFO reports can be explained naturally, a residual percentage remains. These are called 'RUFOs' for 'residual UFOs.' If only 1 percent of UFO reports remain unexplained, the number of RUFOs sighted over the past five decades could rage into the tens of thousands, if not many more. How are these seeming inexplicable UFO reports approached?"[21]

The phenomena of unidentified flying objects are undoubtedly real; their nature, however, has yet to be determined. Today, there exist three main analysis models used in attempts to reconcile the sightings with the credibility of the witnesses (some of whom are police officers, air force personnel, commercial airline personnel, astronauts, and other professionals who have no reason to promote UFOs except to report what they saw). Within the scientific community, there appears to be a paradox of principles: on one side stands a segment of scientists who dismiss all UFO sightings without ever investigating them, and on the other side are scientists

19. J. Allen Hynek, "Categories of UFO Reports" in *The Encyclopedia of UFOs*, ed. Ronald D. Story (Garden City, NJ: Dolphin, 1980), 65–66.
20. Birnes, *UFO Encyclopedia*, 163, includes these last two categories with Hynek's list.
21. Ross, Samples, and Clark, *Lights in the Sky and Little Green Men*, 29.

who promote the search for extraterrestrial life. The Search for Extraterrestrial Intelligence (SETI) program is an exemplary program that falls into the latter category, operated under NASA's Astrobiology Institute.[22] This program is based upon the Drake equation, which projects the existence of intelligent life elsewhere in the universe.[23] The hypothesis is that a civilization somewhere in the universe may have become technologically advanced enough to produce electromagnetic microwaves that can be detected by enormously huge listening devices on earth. The Carl Sagan Center for the Study of Life in the Universe, in Mountain View, California, is also connected with this theory and involved in continued research on the subject. Some scientists (and governmental budget analyzers) think that these programs are a complete waste of time and money, while others argue for their necessity in scientific research. Either way, it boils down to the interesting idea that a sector of the scientific community believes intelligent extraterrestrial life exists.[24]

From a biblical viewpoint, it could be granted that intelligent life exists beyond earth, thus making it extraterrestrial. The realm of God and His heavenly creation includes creatures that are nonearthly beings, which are briefly mentioned in the Bible. Since they exist beyond the earth and are intelligent beings, they can be referred to as extraterrestrial.[25] The Bible also speaks of created creatures that are demonic beings, which are also, in the real sense, nonearthly and extraterrestrial. A wide difference exists between what ufologists believe are extraterrestrial planetary beings and what the Bible describes as demonic beings, but several UFO researchers have arrived at the conclusion that demons may play a large role in some of the sightings and the apparent contacts with extraterrestrials, based upon the message content from these beings.[26]

---

22. SETI is a non-profit foundation that, in part, is funded by governmental grants. The official website for SETI is www.seti.org.

23. Named after the 1961 formula developed by Dr. Frank Drake, who is now chairman of the board of the SETI Institute.

24. For a strong challenge to the SETI program and related theories, consult David Lamb, *The Search for Extraterrestrial Intelligence: A Philosophical Inquiry* (New York: Routledge, 2001), 195–98.

25. Some of these beings are described in Psalm 103:20; 104:4; Isaiah 6:2; Ezekiel 1:5; 10:12–15; and Revelation 4:6 and 5:6.

26. See Wilson, *UFOs and Their Mission Impossible*, 210–12; John Weldon with Zola Levitt, *UFOs: What on Earth Is Happening? The Coming Invasion* (New York: Bantam, 1976), 22; William R. Goetz, *UFOs: Friend, Foe, or Fantasy?* (Camp Hill, Pennsylvania: Horizon, 1997), 141–84; and Ron Rhodes, *Alien Obsession* (Eugene, OR: Harvest House, 1998), 87–102.

UFO RELIGIONS

It is wise to distinguish between UFO sightings and UFO-based religions. Most reliable people who claim a UFO sighting never join a UFO-based religion. In contrast, some people create UFO religious beliefs without ever seeing a UFO; still others join these groups out of dire spiritual need or curiosity.[27] During the last few decades, several small religions have developed that center on UFOs and contact with their occupants.[28] A large number of these dropped by the wayside without notice, but others, such as Heaven's Gate, stayed in the news until they called an end to their drama with mass suicide.

Not all UFO cults can be judged under the microscope of Heaven's Gate, but similarities, such as the channeling of information from UFO contacts, deserve attention. This is especially true when occult methods have been used to gain this information. Long before the mid-twentieth-century UFO excitement, believers claimed contact with intergalactic beings they thought existed on Venus or Mars. The following occult-based religions were founded on this supposed contact with extraterrestrial beings.[29]

Swedenborgianism

Emanuel Swedenborg founded the first formal religion, Swedenborgianism, based largely upon space travel and contact with extraterrestrial beings. Swedenborg's first work, *Earths in the Solar World* (1758), relied on this hypothesis. In it, Swedenborg claimed to leave his body through astral projection and travel to other planets, where he gained spiritual insight from spirit-beings on Mars, Venus, Saturn, and Jupiter.[30] The astral travel that Swedenborg used for his revelatory knowledge is an occultic practice—a tool of the occult used to contact multidimensional beings.

---

27. Even the most prolific writer on UFO religious ideas, Erich Von Daniken, who sold 42 million books on the subject, said, "Unfortunately, I have never had the chance to see a UFO with my own eyes." (Story, *The Encyclopedia of UFOs*, 383).
28. See Christopher Evans, *Cults of Unreason* (New York: Dell, 1975), 164. Evans published one of the early works on "Flying Saucer Clubs."
29. The concentration here is actual religions that promote extraterrestrial contact rather than independently published books that had no formal religious following, like Thomas Blot's *The Man From Mars: His Morals, Politics, and Religion* (San Francisco: Bacon, 1891) or Theodore Flournoy's *India to the Planet Mars* (New York: Harper and Brothers, 1899).
30. For more information on Swedenborgianism, consult Martin's *The Kingdom of the Cults*, 629–41.

Theosophy

Theosophy, cofounded by Helena P. Blavatsky, was the genesis that spawned myriad occult groups in the I AM movement, an influential ideology that eventually led to the development of the New Age movement.[31] A number of these groups gravitated toward contact with UFOnauts, aliens, extraterrestrials, and "Space Brothers." In particular, Blavatsky claimed to be in contact with Venusians (beings on Venus) that she called "Lords of the Flame," described as "towering giants of godly strength and beauty."[32] These contacts resulted in new authoritative messages, revelations, and precepts that adherents faithfully followed. The occult method most often employed in Theosophy and the I AM groups is one where the human becomes a channel of communication for a spirit-being, often taking over the body of the human subject and using their voice to speak through them. In other instances, the communication comes through automatic writing, whereby the spirit dictates its thoughts using the human subject as its writing vessel.

Annie Besant, the second director of the Theosophical Society, had Venusian revelations just as Blavatsky did. In these she described the same "Lords of the Flame," whom she also addressed as "the Lords of Venus."[33] Her information came through occult spirit channeling.

Mighty I AM Movement

The Mighty I AM movement began with Guy and Edna Ballard. Mr. Ballard continued Blavatsky's theme by claiming he was visited by twelve Venusians at the Grand Teton mountain range.[34] The title of one of his chapters was, "Venus Visits the Royal Teton," and in it Ballard detailed his conversation with these Venusians, which he described as seven male and five female. He later claimed that he, along with one hundred others, met Venusians at Mount Shasta (California), where the Venusians played music from harps and violins, and brought out a mirrorlike screen from which they viewed a movie about technological advances on Venus.[35]

---

31. See chapter 6, "Eastern Mysticism and the New Age."
32. Helena P. Blavatsky, *Secret Doctrine* (London: The Theosophical Society, 1893), 181.
33. Annie Besant, *The Seven Principles of Man* (Point Loma, California: The Aryan Theosophical Press, 1907), 12.
34. Godfré Ray King, *Unveiled Mysteries* (Chicago: Saint Germain, 1934), 248. Note: Godfré Ray King was Guy W. Ballard's pseudonym in his first books.
35. James R. Lewis, *Legitimating New Religions* (New Brunswick, NJ: Rugers University Press, 2003), 98.

The Urantia Foundation

The Urantia Foundation is based on *The Urantia Book*, a written message from extraterrestrial beings that has hundreds of thousands of followers.[36] The book developed from the dictation of a psychiatric doctor, who wrote down the messages of an anonymous patient as they were dictated. This communication is simply the occult practice of trance channeling, and its contents reflect its origin. *The Urantia Book* portrays a universe of seven trillion inhabited planets and many gods. It takes a stand of superiority to the Bible and often presumes to correct it on history and theology.

FIGU Society

FIGU Society was founded by Eduard Albert Meier, known as Billy Meier. During the heyday of his movement, Meier gained a large following due to his claim of ongoing contact with extraterrestrial beings in Switzerland. Most of his works are published in German as the *Contact Notes*, but some teachings are translated into English on the FIGU website.[37] Mr. Meier's *Contact Notes* from the extraterrestrials came through personal encounters, and communication through the occult practice of telepathy. Meier is considered to be one of seven prophets, and his teaching on Jesus Christ denies the historical Jesus: "The actual flesh-and-blood human being known as Jesus Christ has, in fact, neither lived nor existed; not on Earth nor in any other location throughout the entire Universe."[38]

International Raelian Movement

The Raelian movement was created by Claude Vorilhon, who changed his name to Rael (pronounced ray-el) and developed one of the most enduring of the UFO cults. This thriving sect claims tens of thousands of international followers and has successfully gained media attention due to their scientific research into DNA and cloning. Their foundational belief centers on the idea that the earth was populated

---

36. *The Urantia Book* (Chicago: Urantia Foundation, 1955). See further comments on Urantia in chapter 15, "The Jesus of the Occult."
37. According to the FIGU Society USA website, "FIGU is an aconym from the German words meaning Free Community of Interests in the Border and Spiritual Sciences and UFOlogical Studies." See http://figu.org/portal/AboutFIGU/Membership/Overview/tabid/84/default.aspx.
38. FIGU Society, USA, "Clarification of a Defamatory Claim," http://us.figu.org/portal/Billy Meier/HisWork/ClarificationofaDefamatoryClaim/tabid/58/Default.aspx.

by DNA transported to this planet from alien beings. Rael claimed an initial contact with an extraterrestrial being in 1973, who revealed that "the Elohim" created life on earth using DNA from another planet.[39] The Raelians have no published sacred texts, although they borrow terms from the Bible and Buddhism to support their beliefs. The term *Elohim*, taken from the Hebrew Old Testament, is reinterpreted by Raelianism as "those who came from the sky," and therefore, extraterrestrial "Elohims" are the creators. The occult practice of telepathy is one of the ways that extraterrestrials communicated to Rael.[40]

The Unarius Academy of Science

The Unarius Academy of Science was founded by Ernest L. and Ruth E. Norman after Ernest received telepathic and psychic communications from extraterrestrial beings in 1954. The Normans were cosmic visionaries through whom the "Space Brothers" communicated. The Normans teach past life regression and clairvoyance—occult practices—at their Unarius Academy of Science in El Cajon, California. According to the Unarius Web site, "We teach a corrective and preventive psychotherapy based upon the physics of reincarnation . . . to awaken the individual to previous life encounters, the clairvoyant aptitude of the mind, and the reality of one's spiritual connection."[41]

The Aetherius Society

The Aetherius Society began in London, England, due to the efforts of George King, who believed that UFOs would bring the earth into the New Age. King's teachings combine a number of Theosophical tenets with world religions and New Age ideas, and he has now developed an international following. Like Blavatsky and Ballard before him, King taught that Venus is an important place for extraterrestrials. According to King, Jesus Christ lived on Venus after His resurrection. Occult channeling also played a key role in the history of this cult: "King was taught by an advanced Master from the East how to obtain telepathic rapport with the Cosmic Masters . . . he was used as a channel for the Cosmic Masters to give

39. Rael's story of this is found at http://www.rael.org/rael_content/rael_bio.php?prophet (accessed August 10, 2007).
40. Rael, *The True Face of God* (Montreal: The Raelian Religion, 1998), 16.
41. Unarius, "Introduction to Unarius," http://www.unarius.org/resume.html.

Their message to Earth. He soon was designated as Primary Terrestrial Mental Channel for the Cosmic Masters."[42] This organization also teaches its members to develop their occult power of clairvoyance.

SCRIPTURAL RESPONSE

From a Christian standpoint, those who communicate with UFOs and extraterrestrial beings have always delivered messages contrary to the Bible. This can be attributed in a large part to the occult methods that they employ when they receive their messages. Christians may not have ready answers to every question about UFO sightings, but in the face of extraterrestrial doctrine, no question remains as to the source of the messages: spiritual beings opposed to God's truth and thus, *demonic* in nature.

UFO findings have important theological implications for the Church of Jesus Christ.[43] We simply cannot ignore the possibility that something extraterrestrial or ultradimensional exists; the Church must take the time to analyze what the world has come to recognize as objective reality. If there are other civilizations, if there is life in other worlds, then we need to take a good, long look at how this impacts the theology of the New Testament and the concept of salvation. Why are these beings here? What are they doing? God would not have neglected something as important as this, and yet, there is no evidence in Scripture to back up the existence of UFOs.

Fear and confusion can easily prevail without the basic faith that God is in control of all things—even extraterrestrials. C. S. Lewis commented on these strange phenomena in his pamphlet entitled *Will We Lose God in Outer Space?*[44] In it, he says that God is the God of the cosmos, the Creator of all things; wherever we go in His creation, we will find His identity, His power, and the knowledge of Him as Creator. We need not be afraid of outer space, then, because God is the God of time and space. He made the worlds; He created all things. It is only if, in the words

---

42. The Artherius Society, "Why Dr. George King?," http://www.aetherius.org/index.cfm?app=content&SectionID=40&PageID=37.
43. This was Walter Martin's basic thesis in the 1950s and again in the 1960s as founder and director of Christian Research Institute. "The Christian church simply cannot ignore the UFO subject any longer. I said it in 1956, 1962, 1968, and now 1975, and responsible Christian theologians, including the late C.S. Lewis, [also] called attention to the fact that it had tremendous implications for the Christian church." See Walter Martin, *UFOs: Friend Foe or Fantasy* (compact disc) (Walter Martin Ministries, www.waltermartin.com).
44. This paraphrase is from an extremely rare pamphlet, C. S. Lewis, *Will We Lose God in Outer Space?* (London: SPCK 1959).

of J. B. Phillips, "your God is too small" that confusion or fear, heightened by scraps of scientific evidence and empirical data on UFOs, sets in.[45]

Dr. Christopher Evans, a noted psychologist, believed this subject was important enough to include a chapter on it in his book *Cults of Unreason*, entitled "Flying Saucer Cults." In it, he made the following sober observation: "With the old Gods dying, if not dead, and the world menaced by threat of total destruction as never before in its history, men are turning to the skies to seek their redeemers there."[46] UFO phenomena remain unexplained in many thousands of cases, and as such, a root cause of demonic powers cannot be dismissed out of hand.

William R. Goetz, author of the landmark work *UFOs: Friend, Foe or Fantasy*, had this to say in later interviews about the source of UFO phenomena:[47]

A comment made back in 1968 by the late Walter Martin, founder of the Christian Research Institute, and the radio's original "Bible Answer Man," has proven to be prophetic. During the interview I conducted with him, Martin expressed the conviction that UFOs were demonic. He did so long before such a view had gained the wide acceptance it enjoys today.

A member of NICAP and involved in UFO research, Martin said he had personally seen UFOs. He indicated that the dean of a New Jersey seminary with which he was associated as a visiting professor had photographed one in broad daylight as it buzzed the campus.

Martin's comment on the identity of UFOnauts and their messages was insightful. At the time of the interview, there had been relatively few [Close Encounter] 3 or [Close Encounter] 4 encounters, with the notable exception of the Hills incident. Nevertheless, Martin said he believed that at some point in the near future UFO occupants would begin to interact extensively with people.

Their message? "We are superior beings—advanced far beyond you earthlings. Look at our technology. But we have come to help and to guide

---

45. J. B. Phillips, *Your God Is Too Small* (London: Wyvern Books, 1952), i.
46. Evans, *Cults of Unreason,* 164.
47. Goetz also stated about this interview, "I [wrote] several articles on UFOs for Compass magazine back in the early 1960s [and] interviewed the late Dr. Walter Martin on the subject." See Goetz, *UFOs: Friend, Foe or Fantasy?*, 1.

you. The only condition is that you will be willing to forget and go beyond your outmoded religious beliefs and follow our directions."

He was right on. As will be shown, this prediction is incredibly accurate. Popular New Age author Brad Steiger, who for decades has tracked numerous messages from alleged aliens—often called "Space Brothers"—offers such messages in his book *The Fellowship* as an alternative to Christianity.[48]

The Bible does not comment on the presence or absence of extraterrestrials or flying saucers. Attempts have been made by various UFO writers to make Ezekiel's "wheel within the wheel" (Ezek. 1:16) into a dervish-type spaceship, but no evidence exists in the Hebrew or in its English translation to support this interpretation. Ezekiel 1 and Ezekiel 3 say nothing whatsoever about UFOs or flying saucers. All of the references used by Erich Von Daniken and similar writers in support of unidentified flying objects in the Bible are conjecture inserted into Scripture, and the Bible is simply not interpreted by taking current events and placing them wherever they seem to fit. Christians must reject the approach of unsupported hermeneutics and instead take a very serious look at the implications of UFOs. If UFO theology is impacting Christian theology, then Christians must deal with it—this subject cannot be swept under the rug.

What does the phenomenon of alien communication mean in the context of biblical revelation? The possibility that we may be dealing with ultradimensional beings merits honest consideration. Jesus warned us in Luke 21:25–26, "There will be signs in the sun, in the moon, and in the stars; and on the earth distress of nations, with perplexity, the sea and the waves roaring; men's hearts failing them from fear and the expectation of those things which are coming on the earth, for the powers of the heavens will be shaken." In addition to what is coming upon the earth, the book of Revelation speaks of the bottomless pit being opened (9:2). A bottomless pit does not have to be one that is down—it could very well be one that is *up*, since in space there is neither up nor down, but *out* from the earth. This could reveal that what comes upon earth is from space, and not from under the earth. The symbolic language may easily refer to the manifestation of the powers of

---

48. Ibid., 167–68.

darkness near the consummation of the age. It is biblically predicted that Antichrist will reveal himself with signs and lying wonders so that if it were possible, he would deceive even the elect (2 Thess. 2:9; Matt. 24:24).

The world is not looking for a theological Savior; the world is looking for a technological savior. It is looking for someone who will appear and solve the problems of famine, overpopulation, war, and disease. It will be someone who creates what unregenerate humans want: heaven on earth on their terms. What better way for the forces of darkness to reveal themselves on earth than to appear to be the saviors of mankind?

A vital clue to the UFO mystery is this: UFO theology—gained from these so-called close encounters—is diametrically opposed to Christianity. The world of the occult and the people involved in it speak constantly of contact with UFOs and their occupants, and the theology derived from UFO contact is most revealing. Extraterrestrials (according to those who claim to have spoken to them) do not believe God is a personal being; they do not believe Jesus Christ is the only Savior, and they do not believe the Bible alone is God's Word to the world. They do not believe in eternal punishment, and they do not believe in bodily resurrection. The reincarnation of the Hindus, Kabbalah, and New Age philosophies gains a new perspective when viewed through the eyes of extraterrestrials: it transforms into planetary reincarnation, where people evolve from planet to planet in order to reach perfection.

It would be an amazing thing, from the world's perspective, if an advanced technological civilization arrived upon the earth, claiming to be the savior of mankind and the creator of *Homo sapiens*. It is not beyond the realm of possibility that with all of the fanfare of scientific accomplishment, the ultimate deception could reveal itself at the end of the ages as our deliverer. In 2 Thessalonians 2:3–9, we are told that when Satan appears in human form, he appears as the Antichrist who leads men, through deceit, to destruction. Those who refuse the knowledge of the truth of Jesus Christ will believe him.

If UFO religions were truly the revelations of alien races, then it would be logical to expect some basic consistency from them. For example, even though there are many denominations in Christianity, they hold specific elements of the faith in common—elements that unify and solidify the faith as expressed in the Bible and later reflected in the early Church creeds. God's message is unique: it is consistent, coherent, and cohesive. The Bible is *consistent* in its creation; it had more than forty writers from different cultures, nations, continents, and ethnicity, who wrote for God over a period of fifteen hundred years, but their message testified to the same God and His story of redemption for mankind. The Bible is *coherent* in its logic; the things taught in God's Word make sense; it is *cohesive* in its truth—thoughts from the one true God support one another, they are not self-contradictory, but they, in fact, adhere to the law of noncontradiction.[49] This is not so among UFO religions.

CASE STUDY

Mark Applewhite

In the midst of the tragic mass suicide of a UFO sect, Heaven's Gate, Marshall Applewhite's eldest son, Mark, alienated from his father for twenty-five years, received the shocking news of his father's suicide (along with thirty-eight of his followers) during a television newscast. Mark Applewhite, a born-again Christian and principal of a Christian school, publicly offered biblical counsel to those who were baffled by the horrific deaths that were rooted in occultic experience of contact with alien beings:

It started the Thursday morning before Easter, 1997. As I was walking out the door to start a busy day I heard something on television about a mass suicide in California. I was only able to ponder this for a few seconds in the rush to leave. It was such a busy day, in fact, I didn't think about the story again. Little did I know that it was about to affect me personally and become the hardest thing I've ever had to face.

When I arrived home, my wife Judy said, "Hurry, sit down and watch the news." The picture of a wide-eyed man speaking with a soft voice and a big smile flashed on the TV screen. I knew that smile and I knew those eyes. After 25 years of wondering where he was and what he was doing, I was staring at the face of my father on national news. In shock, I just sat in

---

49. Laws of logic are laws that are consistent with what is known of the true God, therefore, these laws are issued from God. He is the Creator of the known laws of logic, and man only discovers them.

my recliner unable to think or move. The news report went on to say that 39 members of a cult, led by my father, had committed suicide. The gruesome video of the bodies lying in their bunk beds, each covered with a strange purple cloth, was shown, and I went deeper into shock. Not only was my father dead, but 38 others had followed him to his death.

This was the beginning of an Easter weekend unlike any I had ever experienced. For the next three days the phone rang about every 5 minutes, from 4:30 a.m. until midnight, as all manner of media sought information. From the beginning my mother, sister, and I had decided to reply "no comment" to all requests for interviews. We didn't want our words twisted out of context so as to dishonor either our heavenly Father or our earthly father. . . .

"Good Friday" morning I was awakened at 5:00 a.m. by a reporter's call. When I tried to go back to sleep after giving the "no comment" reply, God seemed to impress on my heart the need to write down a statement that could be released to the press. I sat down at my computer, prayed for the right words, and spent most of Saturday faxing the statement to TV stations, newspapers, and magazines across the country.

To: anyone hurt by the actions of Marshall Herff Applewhite
From: his son, Mark Applewhite

I must first say that I am appalled by the things that have resulted from the actions of my father and others involved in that cult. I am deeply hurt by the knowledge that people have lost their lives in connection with my father. My sympathy and prayers go out to all those who are suffering the loss of loved ones.

I would, however, like everyone to know that this strange bent that my father went off on has not been passed on to his family. By the grace of God Almighty, the creator of the heavens and the earth and author of the Bible, there is hope. By that same grace, my family and I are born-again Christians with a real ticket to heaven, faith in Jesus Christ as Savior and Lord.

When I was five my father left our family. He set up circumstances that could have become just another broken home that perpetuates itself to the next generation. But God, the One True God, intervened in our family. I have not heard or seen anything from my father in over 25 years, and I know nothing about the cult he was leading. In those intervening years I came to know a new Father, the Father in heaven who has now taken what could have been a disaster of a family and turned it into a family with a 20-year marriage and two children who love and serve Jesus.

I say this to bring glory to God for what He's done and who He is, and also to give hope to all people who might hear this. God has a way of taking things that are terrible and turning them into good. At this Easter season I am reminded of the fact that God took the terrible death of His Son Jesus on the Cross and turned it into salvation for anyone who would believe. In the same way I pray that God will take this terrible news of a mass suicide and turn it into a message of hope, the hope found only in the Bible, for all to hear.

If there is a lesson to be learned here it is to find the truth in the Bible and teach it to your family so that they cannot be swayed by false teaching. I hope and pray that those touched by this tragedy in San Diego would find comfort in the God of the Bible and come to know true life after death as a gift from God through faith in Jesus Christ. I also pray that those who are still searching for answers, as members of this cult were, would find that Jesus is the Answer. "For God so loved the world that He gave His one and only Son, that whoever believes in Him shall not perish but have eternal life. For God did not send His Son into the World to condemn the world but to save the world through Him" (John 3:16–17).

When I had a chance to search my memory, I realized I was actually seven when my father left. Even so, I knew very little about him. One thing I do remember is that he was always referred to as Herff. I also remember his fun-loving playfulness, his friendly smile, and his beautiful voice. He was a strong, caring gentle father; we used to wrestle together on the floor. When my sister and I visited him after the divorce he would always go out of his way to have lots of fun things planned. The memories I have are good and I will always cherish them.

As I was faxing my statement, my prayer was that God would use it to offer hope to the families of the suicide victims and to anyone else hurt by this tragedy. I also wanted to ease any doubts of people who knew me as an elder at my Church and as a principal of a Christian school. I knew God could turn tragedy into blessing and prayed He would use my words to do so.

Sunday afternoon I heard from a reporter who had good news. He had attended Easter services at a large Church in Rancho Santa Fe, the community devastated by this suicide. He said the pastor read my entire press release to the congregation. He continued by saying, "After the service many people were talking about how the letter had helped them to refocus on God's grace and had given them some hope in a terrible circumstance." This was the first of many calls, letters, and cards with similar stories about how God was using the statement, which greatly encouraged me. . . .

My children had been watching the news reports all weekend. . . . Monday morning meant going to school and facing their friends. This could have been difficult because children can be so hurtful. Instead, as we arrived at the Christian school where I am principal, they were met by friends who gathered into a big circle around them and prayed for them.

Knowing the students would have many questions about their principal and his father "a cult leader who had just led 38 people to commit suicide," I called an all-school assembly and talked honestly to them. Afterward I asked them to stand and pray for the families of the suicide victims. High school, junior high, and elementary students prayed together. . . . Throughout the ordeal, God, my heavenly Father, provided strength, patience, and perseverance for us to go on.

Having read articles and listened to interviews, I know much more now about my father and the cult he led. I kept seeing the same question recur: "Why would educated, intelligent, gentle people do such a thing?" In these articles and interviews I began to see some reasons.

Everyone is searching for something that is missing in this life on earth. We all have a God-shaped void in our lives but each of us chooses to search in different ways. I see my father's story in the Bible, in Romans 1. My father knew God, knew about God, about His ways, and about His Word, for he grew up as a minister's son.

"For although they knew God, they neither glorified Him as God nor gave thanks to Him, but their thinking became futile and their foolish hearts were darkened. Although they claimed to be wise, they became fools.

. . . Therefore God gave them over to the sinful desires of their hearts. . . . They exchanged the truth of God for a lie, and worshipped and served created things rather than the Creator, who is forever praised. Amen. Because of this, God gave them over to their shameful lusts . . . furthermore since they did not think it worthwhile to retain the knowledge of God, He gave them over to a depraved mind, to do what ought not to be done. They have become filled with every kind of wickedness, evil greed and depravity . . . they are senseless, faithless, heartless, ruthless. Although they know God's righteous decree that those who do such things deserve death, they not only continue to do these very things but also approve of those who practice them" (Romans 1:21–32 NIV).

My father came to a point in his life where he no longer glorified God as God or gave thanks to Him and his thinking became futile and his heart darkened. Eventually God gave him over to the sinful desires of his heart. The potential for sin to ruin our lives is great when we are allowed to go from His protective mercy to our own destructive desires.

Another fallacy was the cult's desperate attempt to earn its way to heaven through good works. My father had made up dozens of rules for the cult members to follow, rules that were meant to keep them pure, cleanse them and make them ready for Heaven. I can see how these rules stemmed from guilt my father harbored about things in his past. This kind of guilt, and the desire to do good works to earn one's way to heaven has plagued people for centuries. But God has given us the answer for this too in His Word. "For it is by grace you have been saved through faith—and this not from yourselves, it is the gift of God—not by works, so that no one can boast" (Ephesians 2:8–9 NIV). "For Christ died for sins once for all, the righteous for the unrighteous, to bring you to God" (1 Peter 3:18 NIV). "Since they did not know the righteousness that comes from God and sought to establish their own, they did not submit to God's righteousness. Christ is the end of the law so that there may be righteousness for everyone who believes" (Romans 10:3–4 NIV)

My desire now is to try to right some of the wrongs my father has done by spreading the truth about God and His forgiveness through faith in His Son. My father had been teaching his followers that by good works a righteousness could be achieved that would bring them into God's kingdom. But God teaches us in His Word that righteousness, forgiveness for sin and cleansing from all guilt, comes only by faith in what His Son did on the Cross. As the old hymn says, "Jesus paid it all, all to Him I owe; Sin had left a crimson stain, He washed it white as snow."[50]

CONCLUSION

The God of the Bible, who warned us to beware of signs in the heavens, might indeed be telling us at the end of the ages to be very careful where we place our trust. It might just be that the UFO is very real, but if it is real, it is working through the influence of Satan "with all power, signs, and lying wonders" (2 Thess. 2:9). If Satan is the god of this age, there is no reason that at the end of the age he cannot appear to be its savior. He has always wanted to be the object of worship.

God created male and female in his image and likeness, reserving their worship for Himself alone (Gen. 1:27). Jesus, when facing satanic temptation on this, quoted God the Father: "You shall worship the LORD your God, and Him only you shall serve" (Matt. 4:10). Mankind is innately rebellious when it comes to serving the true God, and seeks spiritual paths outside of Him. God forbids worship of anything in heaven above, which in our age includes the spiritual aspects of UFO religions: "You shall not make for yourself a carved image—any likeness of anything that is in heaven above, or that is in the earth beneath, or that is in the water under the earth . . ." (Ex. 20:4–6).[51]

Long before any UFO-based religion was founded, God knew that sin would drive people to look to the heavens to worship anything they see, real or imagined. These religions are described as cults because most of them misinterpret the Bible to support their beliefs.[52] Marshall Applewhite and Bonnie Nettles, of Heaven's Gate fame, did this by claiming to be the "two witnesses" of Revelation 11:3. UFO

---

50. Mark Applewhite, "Son of Heaven's Gate Cult Leader Has the Answer," *Connection Magazine,* June 1998, 1.

51. The Ten Commandments are so often abbreviated in a shortened form that it does one well to see the context and comments that God attached to them.

52. *The Kingdom of the Cults* has this definition: "A cult might also be defined as a group of people gathered about a specific person or person's *misinterpretation* of the Bible." (Martin, *The Kingdom of the Cults,* 17).

religions are occultic because their spiritual information is obtained through occult methods, whether it comes through specialized visions, dreams, trances, hypnotic regression, or imaginative sources. Messages received in this way misinterpret the Bible, God, Jesus Christ, mankind, the spiritual condition of the heart and mind, morality, and humanity's future state.

If the UFO is real, then the evidence from occultic sources is that it is hostile to Christianity. The Church must take the position that our hope is not based upon those who would deliver us from other worlds, but upon Jesus Christ, who died once for all in this world to reconcile us to God. The message of the Church must not alter in the light of all the phenomena that may be revealed around us. Jesus Christ is the same yesterday, today, and forever. He said, "You believe in God, believe also in Me. In My Father's house are many mansions; if it were not so, I would have told you. I go to prepare a place for you. And if I go and prepare a place for you, I will come again and receive you to Myself; that where I am, there you may be also" (John 14:1–3).

The Church of Jesus Christ is looking for that blessed hope—the appearing of the glory of the great God and of our Savior, Jesus Christ, who shall transform these bodies of our humiliation that they shall become like His glorious body through that power whereby He is able to subdue all things unto Himself. This is our hope, and we consider all UFO phenomena to be weighed and wanting in its light.

RECOMMENDED RESOURCES

1. Ross, Hugh, Kenneth Samples, and Mark Clark, *Lights in the Sky and Little Green Men.* Colorado Springs: NavPress, 2002.

2. Alnor, William M. *UFO Cults and the New Millenium.* Grand Rapids: Baker, 1998.

3. Goetz, William R. *UFOs, Friend, Foe or Fantasy?* Camp Hill, PA: Horizon, 1997.

4. Martin, Walter. *Chariots of the Who?* Walter Martin Ministries, www.waltermartin.com.

Quick Facts About Satanism

- Satan is the archenemy of almighty God; he is the leader of the fallen angels—a created being whose power can never equal the power of God.

- Satan is not a god: he is neither omniscient (knowing all things) nor omnipresent (everywhere at once).

- It is impossible for Satan or his demons to read minds; they cannot know the secret thoughts of human beings.

- Satanic beliefs are divided into two main categories: traditionalists, who believe Satan is a unique spirit-being, and modernists, who define all evil generally as Satan.

- Jesus Christ directly challenged and defeated Satan's power and authority during His earthly ministry; Christians need not fear Satan or Satanists, since the Holy Spirit resides within them.

11

Satanism

Satanism is separated from all other occult practices by its intentional and vocal allegiance to Satan. In essence, it is the worship, adoration, or service of Satan as an entity superior to God and deserving of spiritual authority. Rituals that center upon Satan involve praying to him, seeking things from him, bargaining with him, and following the practices, beliefs, or ceremonies centered upon him. Even the Satanists who deny his personal nature cannot escape the fact that they serve, magnify, or exalt whatever is defined as Satan.

Most Pagans do not directly address Satan or intentionally worship him (astrologers and Wiccans shudder at the idea), but ignorance does not make other forms of the occult any less detestable to God (Deut. 18:9–14). It is illusionary, then, for Pagans or anyone involved in the occult to think they exist on safe ground simply because they do not directly address Satan.

Today, secular books and articles on the devil and his human followers comprise a sizable body of information, but many authors seem either unwilling or unable to agree on a consistent definition of Satanism.[1] The root of this problem lies in the secular world's rejection of the biblical devil and his motives. Satanism cannot be accurately defined if its very nature is disputed, and people will never be able to defend themselves against it if they deny the only power that can defeat it.

It cannot be overemphasized that hatred is the center of Satanism—hatred for all mankind—not just Christians. *Satanism* has been defined by some secular scholars as "a religious or philosophical system which professes or manifests a hatred of Christianity," but this oversimplification ignores the fact that there have been many enemies of Christianity who were not Satanists.[2] There is no doubt that a good definition is essential to a good defense, and the nature of Satan dictates that a definition of him must include theological ideas.

---

1. Bruce G. Frederickson, *Satanism* (St. Louis: Concordia, 1995), 29.
2. Massimo Introvigne, "Satanism" in Hanegraaff, *Dictionary of Gnosis and Western Esotericism,* 1035.

Satan is the master of Satanism, and he is best understood from historically sound Scripture, not from experience. Reducing Satan to a metaphor does not magically negate his existence or power. Most theologians who write on the subject begin with a clear description of Satanism based on the Bible and then proceed to a discussion of it that includes sociological and psychological perspectives.

THE DISTINCTIVE PERSONA OF SATANISM

A primary, personal character trait of Satan is his need to be worshiped. "Again, the devil took Him [Jesus] up on an exceedingly high mountain, and showed Him all the kingdoms of the world and their glory. And he said to Him, 'All these things I will give You if You will fall down and worship me'" (Matt. 4:8–9). Satan, absorbed in a delusion of preposterous proportions, could offer Jesus—God Incarnate—nothing other than what Satan held by divine permission. Jesus refused this empty promise, and Satan's desire was eternally revealed: complete and absolute worship. It was not enough that all of humanity bow before him—Satan wanted God Himself to worship him. "To receive worship has been Satan's chief ambition ever since, being motivated by pride, he attempted to dethrone God, usurp God's authority, and receive the worship, the honor, and the glory that belongs to God himself (Isaiah 14:14; 2 Thessalonians 2:4)."[3] Participation in these acts of worship is the core of Satanism. It is assigning allegiance to the devil instead of to the one, true God.

In the Old Testament, it is interesting to note that Satan is mentioned eighteen times without a whisper of his desire for worship; that truth was revealed for all to see in his face-to-face confrontation with Jesus.[4] Satan's preferred method throughout history was always deception, manipulating people through occult powers and enticing them to become enchanters, Witches, soothsayers, omen interpreters, sorcerers, mediums, or Spiritists. When Satan confronted Jesus, the truth was at last revealed: his all-consuming desire for worship. The Old Testament exposed Satan as the tempter, tormenter, and deceiver of mankind, and the New Testament completed the character portrait of a twisted spiritual being consumed by hatred and the need for adoration. Satan demonstrated this intense hatred of Christianity in the first three centuries of persecution and martyrdom of Christians.

---

3. Dwight J. Pentecost, *The Words and Works of Jesus Christ: A Study of the Life of Christ* (Grand Rapids: Zondervan, 2000), 105.
4. Job 1:5–2:7 (14 times); 1 Chronicles 21:2 (1 time); and Zechariah 3:1–2 (3 times.)

This pattern of harassment is the key to understanding the enemy: the direct worship and service of Satan grew up alongside a newborn Christianity, revealing itself in heresy and violence as the nemesis of the Church before the close of the first century. There is much that can be learned from the historical revelation of satanic plans. One example of this is the direct correlation between the mainstreaming of Witchcraft and the mainstreaming of Satanism. There can be no doubt that the modern liberation of Witchcraft as a spiritual alternative paved the way for Satanists to step to the societal forefront and demand the same respect. Prior to that, Satanism was forced underground to avoid the negative attention that usually triggered persecution. The age of "live and let live" embraced the mystery of Witchcraft—a practice hated and reviled throughout history—and in accepting Witchcraft, it was a short logical step to the legalization of Satanism as a religious belief, even though the two practices are distinct and unrelated.[5]

Although today most people familiar with religious movements equate the names of Aleister Crowley, Anton LaVey, or the Church of Satan with Satanism, its origin is far older and more extensive than any of these. Two main schools of thought that emerged during the twentieth century in religious Satanism became known as *traditional Satanism* and *modern Satanism*.[6] Traditional Satanism teaches that Satan is a personal spirit-being, and modern Satanism teaches an impersonal entity or corporate evil embodied under the name of Satan.[7] Historically, traditional Satanism can be traced back to the New Testament age through the writings of the Christian Church, which defines *Satanism* as a fringe belief system that venerates Lucifer in direct contrast to the gospel portrayal of Jesus Christ as God Incarnate. The idea of an impersonal Satan was essentially unknown in past centuries—it exists today as a product of twentieth-century philosophical trends that

---

5. See chapter 12, "Goddess Worship, Witchcraft, and Wicca."
6. The analysis here of Satanism as a religion uses "traditional Satanism" and "modern Satanism" to divide theological categories. *Traditional*, in this work, refers to the first century through to the present time, as running concurrently with "modern Satanism" from the nineteenth century forward. Other scholars, such as J. Gordon Melton, use "traditional Satanism" to mean sixteenth century through the twenty-first century, but this leaves the first- to fifteenth-century Satanists in a historical limbo. Massimo Introvigne uses "organized Satanism" in reference to the sixteenth century through modern times, ignoring anything prior to that date. James R. Lewis's usage of "traditional Satanism" and "modern Satanism" corresponds to our usage.
7. Minor subsets exist, such as a dualism, where God and Satan are equal powers; other Satanists may claim that an unnamed power that they can harness permeates the universe; and some are pantheists, believing that Satan is one god among many.

redefine all biblical terms, including Satan. As a direct result of this liberal interpretation of Scripture, Satanists now have flexible definitions for who or what Satan
is, and in what manner he or it exists. In essence, however, both forms of Satanism
practice, service, or worship a general or specific entity. When someone proclaims
himself a Satanist, the logical question that should always come to mind is, "What
kind of Satanist?" This inquiry is the doorway to common ground, a place where
Christians can discuss Satan's origin, his nature, and the effects of his presence in
the world today.

THE HISTORY OF SATAN AND SATANISM

The Bible teaches that the Christian life is a journey of continuous growth in the
teachings of God, sometimes referred to as "the depths" or "the deep things of God"
(Rom. 11:33; Eph. 3:18; 1 Cor. 2:10). In direct contrast to this, Scripture also
reveals the existence of "the depths of Satan": "Now to you I say, and to the rest in
Thyatira, as many as do not have this doctrine, who have not known the depths of
Satan, as they say, I will put on you no other burden. But hold fast what you have
till I come" (Rev. 2:24). God commended the Church of Thyatira for rejecting "the
depths of Satan." In the New Testament age, brazen people flaunted the essence of
Satanism: occult practices, esoteric teachings, secret wisdom, magical arts, rituals,
and the false worship of demons. Noted Greek scholar A. T. Robertson points out
the striking similarity in the Greek language between John's phrase "the depths of
Satan" and Paul's phrase "the deep things of God" (1 Cor. 2:10). The way
Christians access the depths of God, as seen in New Testament theology, is also the
way Satanists get into the depths of Satan. Robertson discusses the ancient *Ophites*
(worshipers of the serpent) and the Gnostics, who loved "the deep things" that were
spiritually rooted in Satan's kingdom.[8] Today, Satanists still pursue their dark convictions, zealously competing against the truth of Christ. But the historical facts of
the battle against the "depths of Satan" in the early Church reveal a comforting
assurance for all who enter the conflict today: Christians have faced the worst of
the occult through the centuries and have triumphed over it through the power of
God.

---

8. A. T. Robertson, *Word Pictures of the New Testament* (1932; repr., Nashville: Broadman 1933, 1938), at Revelation 2:24.

Satan may be powerful, but he is not *all-powerful*. Christians should retain a healthy respect for the power he possesses, while embracing and using the knowledge God has given that Satan will flee in fear from the children of God. There is no need to live in fear of him or run from him; instead, the Bible teaches that it is Satan who is deeply afraid of the Church. James encouraged Christians to submit to God, resist the devil, "and he will flee from you" (James 4:7). Paul revealed this promise: "For God has not given us a spirit of fear, but of power and of love and of a sound mind" (2 Tim. 1:7). John closed his first letter with this promise of victory: "You are of God, little children, and have overcome them [evil spirits], because He who is in you is greater than he who is in the world" (1 John 4:4). God's power is superior to any created being, so no matter how difficult the spiritual battle is, we are assured of the ultimate victory in Christ.

The moment Eve first tasted the forbidden fruit and convinced Adam to do the same, the battle for human souls began. The early Church fought a terrible, bloody battle against Satanic forces—a battle that is still being fought today. No soldier goes into battle without knowing as much as possible about the enemy's tactics; in this context, Paul wrote to warn of Satan's battle plans against all Christians, "lest Satan should take advantage of us; for we are not ignorant of his devices" (2 Cor. 2:11).

The Christian Church today needs to be aware of Satan's methods and strengthened by this knowledge in the same way the apostle Paul was strengthened, so that Christians recognize Satan's tricks and devices and specifically fight against them even as Paul did. The conflict with Satan is not against flesh and blood; it is a spiritual battle against supernatural powers. "We do not wrestle against flesh and blood, but against principalities, against powers, against the rulers of the darkness of this age, against spiritual hosts of wickedness in the heavenly places" (Eph. 6:12). Had the Witch hunters of the Middle Ages understood that the battle had nothing to do with flesh and blood, they would have seen that burning a Witch or Satanist at the stake could never win the battle.[9] The fight was never against *people*; it was and is against the spiritual enemies of Christ.

---

9. The Lombard code (643 AD) spoke against harming Witches based upon the fact that Witches murdering men by night was not realistic. The greatest persecution of Witches followed the Synod of Paris (829 AD), where Old Testament passages became the justification for killing them. The birth of Jesus signaled the beginning of the New Testament or age of grace—"but grace and truth came through Jesus Christ" (John 1:17)—so we do not kill people involved in Witchcraft, since we are under grace and not under the law (just as we do not stone adulterers to death).

SATAN AS A REAL BEING

Satan has been caricaturized in various movies and television programs as a poor, misunderstood being with a twisted sense of humor, pitchfork, pointed tail, and a lingering smell of sulfur. Is it any wonder, then, when Christians portray Satan as the enemy of the soul, adversary of God, or even a person possessed of an enormous capacity for evil, that people simply do not believe it? They much prefer the unrealistic, playful image of Satan to the hardcore truth as described in Scripture.

Satan's true nature and the history of his fall from heaven can be found in Ezekiel 28:12–19:

> Thus says the Lord GOD:
> "You were the seal of perfection,
> full of wisdom and perfect in beauty.
> You were in Eden, the garden of God;
> every precious stone was your covering:
> the sardius, topaz, and diamond,
> beryl, onyx, and jasper,
> sapphire, turquoise, and emerald with gold.
> The workmanship of your timbrels and pipes
> was prepared for you on the day you were created.
> You were the anointed cherub who covers;
> I established you;
> you were on the holy mountain of God;
> you walked back and forth in the midst of fiery stones.
> You were perfect in your ways from the day you were created,
> till iniquity was found in you.
> By the abundance of your trading
> you became filled with violence within,
> and you sinned;
> therefore I cast you as a profane thing
> out of the mountain of God;
> and I destroyed you, O covering cherub,
> from the midst of the fiery stones.
> Your heart was lifted up because of your beauty;

you corrupted your wisdom for the sake of your splendor;
I cast you to the ground,
I laid you before kings,
  that they might gaze at you.
You defiled your sanctuaries
  by the multitude of your iniquities,
  by the iniquity of your trading;
therefore I brought fire from your midst;
it devoured you,
and I turned you to ashes upon the earth
  in the sight of all who saw you.
All who knew you among the peoples are astonished at you;
  you have become a horror,
and shall be no more forever."

Ezekiel is describing Satan here as the real power behind the earthly king of Tyre, a perfect example of the fact that we battle against "powers and principalities" and not against flesh and blood. Several facts noted in the preceding verses distinguish Satan from the human king: he was in heaven and in the garden of Eden, when he tempted Eve; he ruled as an anointed cherub and thus a created being (twice stated)—fashioned in perfection with beautiful features.[10]

Satan's greatest weakness is his very nature: he is finite, but God is eternal. Satan is limited by time and space—his very nature ensures that he can never be like God. Still, he should not be underestimated, since he possesses enormous supernatural powers beyond any human comprehension. This magnificent creature knew the glory of God from firsthand experience and still chose to sin against Him—only to be thrown out of heaven in the end, along with countless other angels (demons) who followed him.

The Old Testament prophet Isaiah gave valuable insight into what caused Satan to fall:

---

10. It is a mistake for Christian teachers to claim that Lucifer was the most beautiful creature God created, since that claim extends beyond this passage and is unsupported by any other passage. The text only states that he had beauty, but it does not say that he was the most beautiful creation.

How you are fallen from heaven,
O Lucifer, son of the morning!
How you are cut down to the ground,
you who weakened the nations!
For you have said in your heart:
"I will ascend into heaven,
I will exalt my throne above the stars of God;
I will also sit on the mount of the congregation
on the farthest sides of the north;
I will ascend above the heights of the clouds,
I will be like the Most High." (Isa. 14:12–14 NKJV)

The creation chose to envy the Creator—Satan longed to be God. Judgment is pronounced on Satan in verses 15–20:

Yet you shall be brought down to Sheol,
to the lowest depths of the Pit.
Those who see you will gaze at you,
and consider you, saying:
"Is this the man who made the earth tremble,
who shook kingdoms,
who made the world as a wilderness
and destroyed its cities,
who did not open the house of his prisoners?"
All the kings of the nations,
all of them, sleep in glory,
everyone in his own house;
but you are cast out of your grave
like an abominable branch,
like the garment of those who are slain,
thrust through with a sword,
who go down to the stones of the pit,
like a corpse trodden underfoot.
You will not be joined with them in burial,

because you have destroyed your land
and slain your people.
The brood of evildoers shall never be named.

The context indicates that God is not only talking to the king of Babylon, but He is also addressing the force behind the Babylonian king: Lucifer—Satan himself. Satan's specific claims stem from pride:

- "I will ascend to heaven."

- "I will exalt my throne."

- "I will sit also in the mount of the congregation in the sides of the north."

- "I ascend above the height of the clouds."

- "I will be like God himself."

Satan plummeted from the high position he occupied in heaven because he was consumed by pride—and judged accordingly by God. The Bible reveals that Satan walked in Eden among the stones of fire as the covering cherub of God; his position was high in the dimension of the spirit:

You were the anointed cherub who covers;
I established you;
you were on the holy mountain of God;
you walked back and forth in the midst of fiery stones.
You were perfect in your ways from the day you were created,
till iniquity was found in you. (Ezek. 28:14–15)

How did Lucifer fall if he was created as a perfect being? How did imperfection creep into his nature? He was created as an innocent being with the power of choice, and there was no evil until he exercised that choice contrary to the will of his Creator. Satan was exposed to infinite love, mercy, compassion, and the personal character of God on every level. When the time came to make a choice, the pride of his soul deceived him, and he chose to try to be like his Creator. The origin of evil sprang from an innocent being, Lucifer, who had the power of choice between submitting to God and rebelling. Similarly, Adam was created innocent and was given the power of choice between good and evil, but Adam's fall from his sinless state brought sin into man's domain.

SPECIFIC POWERS OF SATAN

Satan can control the physical elements of earth. He has power to afflict with disease.[11] He has the power to communicate with a human spirit—a power that Jesus illustrated in the parable of the sower: "When anyone hears the word of the kingdom, and does not understand it, then the wicked one comes and snatches away what was sown in his heart. This is he who received seed by the wayside" (Matt. 13:19). Satan, identified here as "the wicked one," comes quickly after the gospel is preached and steals it out of the souls of men who do not understand it. Notice that Jesus does not say Satan steals the gospel out of the mind; he says Satan steals it *out of the heart,* or out of the spirit. There is a biblical difference between the mind and the spirit. Satan cannot read minds, but as a spiritual being, he can communicate to a human spirit. Jesus warned that Satan comes quickly after a Christian shares the gospel seed with an unbeliever and, if the unbeliever does not understand, Satan takes the words away through distractions, confusion, lies or substitutes for the truth.

C. S. Lewis grasped the genius of Satan's devises and cleverly portrayed them in his book *The Screwtape Letters.* He described Satan's tactics in order to illustrate that we cannot afford to be "ignorant of his devices:"

MY DEAR WORMWOOD,

I note with grave displeasure that your patient has become a Christian. Do not indulge the hope that you will escape the usual penalties; indeed, in your better moments, I trust you would hardly even wish to do so. In the meantime we must make the best of the situation. There is no need to despair; hundreds of these adult converts have been reclaimed after a brief sojourn in the Enemy's camp and are now with us. All the habits of the patient, both mental and bodily, are still in our favour.

---

11. See chapter 1, "The Kingdom of the Occult," and Chapter 2, "The Occult Revolution," for more information on the powers of Satan.

One of our great allies at present is the Church itself. Do not misunderstand me. I do not mean the Church as we see her spread out through all time and space and rooted in eternity, terrible as an army with banners. That, I confess, is a spectacle which makes our boldest tempters uneasy. But fortunately, it is quite invisible to these humans. All your patient sees is the half-finished, sham Gothic erection on the new building estate. When he goes inside, he sees the local grocer with rather an oily expression on his face bustling up to offer him one shiny little book containing a liturgy which neither of them understands, and one shabby little book containing corrupt texts of a number of religious lyrics, mostly bad, and in very small print. When he gets to his pew and looks round him he sees just that selection of his neighbours whom he has hitherto avoided. You want to lean pretty heavily on those neighbours. Make his mind flit to and fro between an expression like "the body of Christ" and the actual faces in the next pew. It matters very little, of course, what kind of people that next pew really contains. You may know one of them to be a great warrior on the Enemy's side. No matter. Your patient, thanks to Our Father below, is a fool. Provided that any of those neighbours sing out of tune, or have boots that squeak, or double chins, or odd clothes, the patient will quite easily believe that their religion must therefore be somehow ridiculous. At his present stage, you see, he has an idea of "Christians" in his mind which he supposes to be spiritual but which, in fact, is largely pictorial. His mind is full of togas and sandals and armour and bare legs and the mere fact that the other people in Church wear modern clothes is a real—though of course an unconscious—difficulty to him. Never let it come to the surface; never let him ask what he expected them to look like. Keep everything hazy in his mind now, and you will have all eternity wherein to amuse yourself by producing in him the peculiar kind of clarity which Hell affords.

Work hard, then, on the disappointment or anticlimax which is certainly coming to the patient during his first few weeks as a Churchman. The Enemy allows this disappointment to occur on the threshold of every human endeavour. It occurs when the boy who has been enchanted in the nursery by Stories from the Odyssey buckles down to really learning Greek. It occurs when lovers have got married and begin the real task of learning to live together. In every department of life it marks the transition from dreaming aspiration to laborious doing. The Enemy takes this risk because He has a curious fantasy of making all these disgusting little human vermin into what He calls His "free" lovers and servants—"sons" is the word He uses, with His inveterate love of degrading the whole spiritual world by unnatural liaisons with the two-legged animals. Desiring their freedom, He therefore refuses to carry them, by their mere affections and habits, to any of the goals which He sets before them: He leaves them to "do it on their own". And there lies our opportunity. But also, remember, there lies our danger. If once they get through this initial dryness successfully, they become much less dependent on emotion and therefore much harder to tempt.

I have been writing hitherto on the assumption that the people in the next pew afford no rational ground for disappointment. Of course if they do—if the patient knows that the woman with the absurd hat is a fanatical bridge-player or the man with squeaky boots a miser and an extortioner—then your task is so much the easier. All you then have to do is to keep out of his mind the question "If I, being what I am, can consider that I am in some sense a Christian, why should the different vices of those people in the next pew prove that their religion is mere hypocrisy and convention?" You may ask whether it is possible to keep such an obvious thought from occurring even to a human mind. It is, Wormwood, it is! Handle him properly and it simply won't come into his head. He has not been anything like long enough with the Enemy to have any real humility yet. What he says, even on his knees, about his own sinfulness is all parrot talk. At bottom, he still believes he has run up a very favourable credit-balance in the Enemy's ledger by allowing himself to be converted, and thinks that he is showing great humility and condescension in going to Church with these "smug", commonplace neighbours at all. Keep him in that state of mind as long as you can.

Your affectionate uncle
SCREWTAPE[12]

---

12. Lewis, *The Screwtape Letters*, 11.

Scattered throughout the Bible is a vast field of information about this archenemy of God and man. Jesus said that he is a murderer, liar, and the father of all lies (John 8:44), the ruler of the world (John 16:11), and the wicked one (Matt. 13:38). John called him the dragon, the old serpent, and the Devil (Rev. 20:2), he is the "accuser" of the brethren both day and night (Rev. 12:10), and he is the angel of the bottomless pit (Rev. 9:11). Paul called him the prince of the power of the air (Eph. 2:2), the ruler of darkness (Eph. 6:12), the god of this world (2 Cor. 4:4), and one who masquerades as an angel of light (2 Cor. 11:14). Peter wrote that he is the adversary of the Christian (1 Peter 5:8). These things describe the person and character of Satan, a being whose goal it is to destroy as many humans as possible before his final confrontation with Jesus Christ, after which he will be cast in to the lake of eternal fire (Rev. 20:10).

Satan worked miracles in the Old Testament through occult representatives such as the magicians of Pharaoh's court, and he works them today through his modern occult followers. In 2 Thessalonians 2:9, Paul foretold the final culmination of his powers on earth that result in the rise of Antichrist: "The coming of the lawless one is according to the working of Satan, with all power, signs, and lying wonders." The Church must be prepared to "Resist him, steadfast in the faith" (1 Peter 5:9).

THE DEPERSONALIZED SATAN

We live in an age of spurious definitions and arbitrarily redefined terms. Modernists, secular humanists, and New Age thinkers, for example, have redefined many values, terms and mores all under the cloak of tolerance. Society's motto today is "live and let live," especially where evil is concerned. It is not surprising, then, that even as God was redefined as a "dead" fantasy of primitive man, Satan would also undergo extensive reconstruction and eventually emerge as a depersonalized philosophical construct—a synonym for man's shadow or collective evil. Satan is no longer viewed as a person, according to modern Satanists; he simply represents the evil in each living thing. Anton LaVey, the founder of the Church of Satan, used every media opportunity offered to him to popularize this theory.

Prior to LaVey's time, the redefined Satan can be traced to the sermons of the nineteenth-century Unitarians, Christadelphians, Universalists, and metaphysicians, such as Mary Baker Eddy and Theosophist writer Madame Blavatsky.

Blavatsky, the cofounder of the Theosophical Society, wrote, "It is regarded less impious, less infidel, to doubt the personal existence of the Holy Ghost, or the equal Godhead of Jesus, than to question the personality of the Devil."[13] Eddy's reinterpretation states, "DEVIL. EVIL; a lie; error; neither corporeality nor mind; the opposite of Truth; a belief in sin, sickness, and death."[14]

With philosophers, sect leaders, and occultists dismantling Satan's persona (and thus his power to destroy), it is inevitable that such an appealing proposition would find its way into liberal Christian theology. C. S. Lewis noted the progression of corruption in a conversation he once had with a man who "believed in a Devil, but 'not a personal Devil.'"[15] Lewis focused on better defining the terms, but people reinvent Satan to fit into their personal comfort zones. They are much more willing to turn him into humanity's super-consciousness of evil than to personify him as an enormously powerful, malevolent, supernatural enemy. All the while they forget that he is a wicked enemy bent on human destruction and the specter of eternal hellfire. There is little interest in the *person* of Satan.

THE MYTHOLOGICAL SATAN

Following a close second to the depersonalized Satan is the view that Satan is a myth, invented by man to suppress weaker minds or justify contradictions in thought. Theologians and sociologists attempt to draw parallels between the history of Satan in Christianity and other world religions, attempting to trace source material from one religion to another. This hypothesis is tainted by the presupposition that all cultures have a mythical devil. The Old and New Testaments, as historical documents, invalidate these presuppositions and contain a unique account of Satan's activity.

One rationalistic way to eliminate the devil is often presented like this: "The ability of myth to transcend rational categories is of enormous value in understanding the Devil. In rational thought good and evil appear to be mutually exclusive. . . . We can say that myth, more than rational speculation, provides the material from which the concept of the Devil is ultimately constructed."[16]

13. Helena P. Blavatsky, *Isis Unveiled* (New York: Theosophical Publishing, 1888), 2:476.
14. Eddy, *Science and Health with Keys to the Scriptures*, 584.
15. C. S. Lewis, *God in the Dock: Essays on Theology and Ethics* (Grand Rapids: Eerdmans, 1994), 255.
16. Jeffrey Burton Russell, *The Devil: Perceptions of Evil from Antiquity to Primitive Christianity* (Ithaca, NY: Cornell University Press, 1987), 52.

This rationalization is not new; it is a return to nineteenth-century cult leaders such as Helena Blavatsky and Mary Baker Eddy, who not only denied a personal devil but claimed (more than a century ago) that Satan was based on a myth.

During the twentieth century, liberal theologians tried to build a case for the existence of myths within the Bible for the express purpose of demythologizing all the myths they had carefully crafted. Those who already denied such things as the virgin birth of Christ and His miracles, for example, were quick to include the myth of Satan as one of their targets. Stripping Satan of personhood and mythology makes him as harmless as a kitten. Extracting the person of Satan from the Bible renders the biblical struggle between God and Satan meaningless. Dr. George Eldon Ladd succinctly summarized the effects of demythologizing biblical history: "The result of demythologizing the biblical teaching of a God who is the Creator and the Lord of history sacrifices an essential element in the gospel and grows out of a philosophical concept of God which is other than the biblical revelation."[17]

Some academics accused the Church of inventing the devil to suppress personal freedoms. In the 1930s, sinister accusations were made that church leadership was obsessed with controlling people, and Satan was retained in his diabolical office only to ensure the continuation of this control. It is a totally unsupported assertion, but one that others have repeated. Dr. Albig wrote:

> Although Church leaders used the myth of the personal devil as a potent means of social control and although theologians in part guided the developing concept of the devil, the essential outlines of the devil myth through the Middle Ages were the simple ruminations of the folk. Later, the record of the devil's works, ways and person were essentially the product of the great writers, especially Dante and Milton. But in the heyday of his earthly power, Satan was a folk myth.[18]

Those who wish to erase Satan from scriptural history through liberal theology have no sound basis for biblical apologetics. Christianity is not based on blind leaps of faith; it is rooted in sound, rational reasoning processes. New Testament docu-

---

17. George Eldon Ladd, *The Presence of the Future: The Eschatology of Biblical Realism* (Grand Rapids: Eerdmans, 1996), 332.
18. William Albig, *Public Opinion* (New York: McGraw-Hill, 1939), 129.

ments are historical and reliable; they have stood the test of time.[19] In light of this fact, the modern Church can confidently make the same claim as the apostle Peter when he stated that *we do not follow myths* (2 Peter 1:16). The Bible does not offer unsophisticated or unsupported claims about Satan; it presents teachings that fit uniformly together with all other known aspects of the universe under God's sovereignty.

TRADITIONAL SATANISM

Traditional Satanism recognizes Satan as a personal supernatural being either greater than God (pantheism) or equal to God (dualism). Traditional Satanists participate in worship, prayer, or Pagan rituals recognizing Satan's spiritual authority. Satanism is ancient, predating mankind's history before the fall. Lucifer's angels became the first followers of Satan—the first Satanists. There is no history of individuals or groups that directly worshiped or served Satan before the time of Christ, only the biblical injunction against worshiping idols, which is characterized by God as *demon worship* (Deut. 32:17; Lev. 17:7; 2 Chron. 11:15; Ps. 106:37).[20] In tempting mankind to worship him, Satan succeeded with man where he had failed with Jesus. This success provided a great deal of satisfaction to Satan, as evidenced by his historical tendency to repeat a successful strategy; he consistently worked down through the ages to entice those made in the image of God to bow down and worship him.

In New Testament times, individuals gave themselves to Satan for the temporary exaltation of instant power (Acts 8:9–11; 16:16). At one time, the Pharisees even accused Jesus of serving Satan:[21]

> Now when the Pharisees heard it they said, "This fellow does not cast out demons except by Beelzebub, the ruler of the demons."
>
> But Jesus knew their thoughts, and said to them: "Every kingdom divided against itself is brought to desolation, and every city or house

---

19. Suggested reading in this area: McDowell, *New Evidence That Demands a Verdict*, Norman L. Geisler, *Baker Encyclopedia of Christian Apologetics* (Grand Rapids: Baker, 1999); and Wilbur Smith, *Therefore Stand: Christian Apologetics* (Grand Rapids: Baker, 1965).

20. This chapter focuses on the direct worship and service of Satan. History is filled with indirect worship, such as idolatry, but Satan's first demand for direct worship was during the temptation of Jesus, and it revealed his personal desire.

21. Beelzebub (sometimes spelled Beelzebul) was a Jewish designation for Satan, which is why Jesus answered them by using the name Beelzebub. Disputes about the meaning of Beelzebub are resolved in the context, where Matthew gave his transliteration, "the ruler of the demons." This ruler is Satan.

divided against itself will not stand. If Satan casts out Satan, he is divided against himself. How then will his kingdom stand? And if I cast out demons by Beelzebub, by whom do your sons cast them out? Therefore they shall be your judges. But if I cast out demons by the Spirit of God, surely the kingdom of God has come upon you." (Matt. 12:24–28 NKJV)

Their charge did not stick, and later generations judged their actions. Jesus refuted such claims by telling them that He cast out demons by the Spirit of God (a different kingdom), not by Satan. He strictly warned them that attributing the work of God to the power of Satan is blasphemy of the Holy Spirit, which will not be forgiven in this age or in the age to come (Matt. 12:31–32). This discussion with the Pharisees reveals that the kingdom of God is superior to the kingdom of Satan, thus denying equal power or dualism. In essence, the Pharisees accused Jesus of serving Satan, but Jesus refuted this by claiming that the kingdom of God had come through Him.

In the book of Revelation, the apostle John depicted Satanism in two ways: as a daily experience of evil or the "depths of Satan" (Rev. 2:24) and as a futuristic event where untold multitudes of people will worship and serve him as the Antichrist (the indwelling of Satan in Revelation 13:1–10).[22] This is the pinnacle of Satanism, when the vast majority of people on earth will worship and serve him (and the false prophet and beast)—an affront to God of such magnitude that it may explain why the worship of Antichrist, the false prophet, and the beast will never be forgiven. In this sense, Satanism, as we know it, was foreseen by John to be one of the strongest battles on earth for human souls. Satanism today is essentially early Satanism; simply a taste of what will come in the last days.

The Idolatry of Satanism

As discussed earlier, Satanism is the direct worship of Satan and service to him. Idolatry is the worship of icons or statues thought to represent individual "gods" but in reality representing individual demons (Lev. 17:7; Deut. 32:17; 2 Chron.11:15; Ps. 106:37). Since Satan is the ruler of the fallen angels or demons,

---

22. On Satan indwelling the Antichrist and unraveling the difference between the Antichrist, false prophet and Beast, see Unger, *Biblical Demonology,* 190.

idolatry becomes the indirect worship of Satan, as the apostle Paul described in his letter to the Corinthian church:

> What am I saying then? That an idol is anything, or what is offered to idols is anything? Rather, that the things which the Gentiles sacrifice they sacrifice to demons and not to God, and I do not want you to have fellowship with demons. You cannot drink the cup of the Lord and the cup of demons; you cannot partake of the Lord's table and of the table of demons. Or do we provoke the Lord to jealousy? Are we stronger than He? (1 Cor. 10:19–22)

Paul's answer confirms the Old Testament assertion that demons are the power behind all idols. Worship and service to these idols is the same as worship and service to the demons that have mastery over them, and thus, to the ruler of demons, Satan.[23]

Traditional Satanism and the Early Church

The Church fathers did not write specifically on Satanism, but they revealed the early practice among Christians of renouncing Satan. Tertullian (145–230 AD) confirms that early Church members "renounced the devil and his angels."[24] Hippolytus (d. 235) and Cyprian (d. 258) also mention that Christians made a practice of renouncing the devil. We have little information about what precipitated this practice, but parallels with other things renounced by Christians seems to suggest that renunciation was linked to former sinful practices that involved Satan and his angels. Just as early Christians renounced involvement with idols, adultery, injurious passions, covetousness, foreign temples, and superstitions, they renounced any former association with the devil and his angels—an association considered just as real as the other things mentioned.[25]

---

23. Paul is in full agreement with the four verses in the Old Testament that speaks of idols having demons (always plural) behind them (Lev. 17:7; Deut. 32:17; 2 Chron. 11:15; Ps. 106:37). At best one could argue that there was indirect worship of demons, but lacking still is direct worship of Satan as a personal being.
24. Allen Menzies, ed., *The Ante-Nicene Fathers* (Grand Rapids: Eerdmans, 1978), 3:64. See also 3:81, which shows that Christians "renounced the devil and his pomp and his angels," and 3:660, where Christians "by repentence renounced His rival the devil."
25. This is implicit in anxient texts, rather than explicit.

Saint Basil the Great (329–379 AD) recounted a story about a pact with Satan, which is a form of Satanism.[26] Homilies and sermons in Church history were usually given in response to pressing issues the Church faced. The fact that the Basil story was told and retold points to the likelihood of recurring skirmishes between Christianity and the forces of Satan. Consistent historical evidence indicates that satanic attacks remained an issue of intense concern.

The Black Mass

Satanists, intent on separating themselves from Christianity, developed the Black Mass as a uniquely satanic ritual—a parody in many respects of the Catholic Mass—considered by many to be blasphemy. One reputable writer, H. T. F. Rhodes, traces the possible development of the Black Mass from a ceremony originally known as the Mass of the dead:

No one really knows anything of the early history of the Black Mass. . . . There are clues, however, which suggest that these rites are magical and, what is more significant, quite divorced from Christian or other theology. The 7th century Church Council of Toledo, for instance, denounced an office known as the Mass of the dead. This was the first recorded Black Mass, and it was no requiem. The priest performed the rite . . . to consign a living man to death.[27]

Historically, the next step in the development of the Black Mass was the Mass of Saint Secaire, performed in Gascony (in southwest France). It began with sexual intercourse between the priest and his server, and it included a form of the Catholic Mass recited backward. The mass was performed for the express purpose of killing a targeted person, not as a form of satanic worship.[28]

---

26. Even though the story was retold and embellished in church history, it still confirms an early historical date for a form of Satanism. The Basil story was told from the fourth century through the Middle Ages. A synopsis of it is found in Russell, *Witchcraft in the Middle Ages,* 84, which also discusses its presence in middle church history.
27. H. T. F. Rhodes, "Black Mass," in Cavendish, *Man, Myth, and Magic,* 2:273.
28. James George Frazer, *The Golden Bough: A Study in Magic and Religion* (New York: Macmillan, 1922), 69.

Variations of the Black Masses were practiced through the Middle Ages, as evidenced in the story told by Jean Bodin in his *Demonomanie des Sorciers* (1580). According to Bodin, a Black Mass was said at the order of Catherine de Medici, queen of France, during which a child was slain. Stories like this could have been the basis for later fabrications during the Witch-hunt trials. Enduring elements of the Black Masses of the past and present include the blasphemy of Catholicism, the use of a nude woman, "the altar of flesh"[29] as a replacement for the Church altar, and a ceremony with prayers and liturgy recited backward. As the centuries passed, historical literature maintained the dark, mysterious reputation of Satanism and the Black Mass in such works as *La-Bas* (1891), a novel by nineteenth-century French writer J. K. Huysmans that popularized the Black Mass for general readership.

Middle Eastern Satanism

The Yezidis are a Middle Eastern people group characterized by their neighbors as "devil worshipers."[30] During the twelfth century, one of their sacred texts, *Kitab Al-Jilwah* (the Manifestation), was supposedly given as a revelation from Satan (the *Melek Taus*, or Peacock King).[31] Melek Taus was said to be an evil spirit who appeared to one of their leaders (hence, the Manifestation) claiming omnipresence and eternality. He then added, "I participate in all the affairs which those who are without [outside of their religion] call evil because their nature is not such as they approve."[32] Taus identifies himself as a god for the Yezidis and the source of *evil* for all people outside of them (Jews, Christians, Muslims), which explains why these outsiders labeled the Yezidis "devil worshipers."[33]

Recently, Sean Thomas, a reporter for the *Telegraph*, interviewed some leaders of the Yezidi and confirmed their worship of Melek Taus—another name for the biblical devil. "We believe he is a proud angel, who rebelled and was thrown into Hell by God. When asked if Melek Taus is good and evil, the leaders answered, "He is both."[34]

29. Ibid., 247–48.
30. Isya Joseph, *Devil Worship: The Sacred Books and Traditions of the Yezidis* (Boston: Badger, 1919), 11.
31. The Yezidis were a small group of people that generally lived in isolation from others. They spoke Kurdish, but may have been of Assyrian descent. For an English translation and analysis see Joseph, *Devil Worship*.
32. Joseph, *Devil Worship*, 31.
33. Melek Taus was not the only spirit or god the Yezidis recognized.
34. Sean Thomas, "The Devil Worshippers of Iraq," *Telegraph*, August 20, 2007, http://www.telegraph.co.uk/news/main.jhtml?xml=/news/2007/08/19/wiraq219.xml.

Although most Yezidis avoid the dangerous title of "devil worshiper," some brave Yezidi leaders do acknowledge publicly that Melek Taus is "the Devil." Mir Hazem, known as a "hereditary leader," said recently: "I cannot say this word [Devil] out loud because it is sacred. It's the chief of angels. We believe in the chief of angels."[35]

There can be no doubt that the Yezidi name of *Melek,* for the Peacock King condemned by God to hell, has ancient roots. It is chillingly reminiscent of the biblical demon *Molech,* the idol whose superheated brass arms burned child sacrifices alive in the Valley of Hinnom outside of Jerusalem (c. 1000 BC).[36]

While some have tried to "whitewash" the Yezidis (as Anton LaVey stated),[37] it is undeniable that they worshiped the devil in antiquity and they worship him today—facts that completely contradict the majority of modern scholars who claim that Satan worship is of modern origin.[38] During the ancient Yezidi ritual honoring Melek Taus, a priest carried before the people an image of the Peacock King mounted on top of a pole.[39] Today, modern Satanists have revived this ancient Yezidi worship format and practice, cementing the link between the old and the new.[40]

European Witch Hunts

Evidence of the continued practice of Satanism throughout history can also be found in the work of Jeffery B. Russell, who provides two accounts of Witch-hunt confessions that seem to prove their continued existence. Although European history provides a large number of Middle Age confessions recorded during the period of the infamous Witch hunts, most were either falsified or extracted by torture. Still, Russell cites the stories of Anne-Marie Georgel and Catharine Delort as genuine confessions (1335), although other writers cast doubt upon their historical validity.[41] Critics who challenge the legitimacy of these stories or confessions do not

35. Ibid.
36. The biblical term for this was "pass through the fire" (2 Kings 23:10). Solomon built a high place to Molech (1 Kings 11:7) and worshiped this god and others, as did many other kings of Israel. See Leviticus 18:21; 20:2–5; 1 Kings 11:5, 7, 33; 2 Kings 23:10, 13; Jeremiah 32:35
37. Anton Szandor LaVey, *Satanic Rituals* (San Francisco: Harper Collins, 1976), 161. LaVey wrote several pages about the Yezidis.
38. Writers such as Massivo Introvige, J. Gordon Melton, and John Smulo are examples.
39. For a sketch of it, see Joseph, *Devil Worship,* 8.
40. See this chapter's section on the Black Coven of Satanas.
41. Russell, *Witchcraft of the Middle Ages,* 182. Gareth J. Medway, in *Lure of the Sinister: The Unnatural History of Satanism* (New York: New York University Press, 2001), 70–72, casts doubt upon the historicity of these confessions, claiming the earliest record is 1829.

explain why Satanism was not at least real to some degree, even though the details of what took place could have been embellished, much like an automobile accident is real, but the details leading up to it may conflict.

Russell is correct in stating that there were some true confessions, but the exact number remains a mystery.

Traditional Satanism Splits

There can be little doubt that traditional Satanism survived the Witch hunts of the Middle Ages to influence the foundation of modern Satanism, its antisocial sibling. Rebellion against Catholicism tainted even the priests, who, once expelled, began exploring the dark side of carnality and eventually the forbidden realm of Satanism. One such priest, Francois Rabelais (1494–1553), promoted liberty and self-indulgence to the extent that he fathered the modern Satanist and Wiccan principle of "Do What Thou Wilt."[42] This quote was found in Francois Rabelais's fictional *Abbey of Thélème* (1534) five hundred years before Wiccans like Gerald Gardner used it; even though some argue that they misused Rabelais. Self-indulgence later became a theoretical bridge for modern Satanism, especially the derivative school of Thelema Satanism, which takes rigid stands against Christian precepts of morality.

MODERN SATANISM

Taking its cue from the licentious priest Francois Rabelais, modern Satanism quickly developed into a seductive form of hedonism. In Satanism, the fulfillment of fleshy desires ranks supreme and once again employs the dictum "Do What Thou Wilt."

Hellfire Clubs

A forerunner of the hedonism to come was practiced among the so-called Monks of Medmenham (c. 1720s), who were actually powerful English aristocrats imperson-

---

42. This is from his work *Gargantua* (1534), which has the "Law of Thelema." *Thelema* is Greek for "will." Thelema Satanism promotes the Rabelais law for the masses, especially through Aleister Crowley. Some modern Satanists push the Thelema Law to the writings of Saint Augustine, which is absurd. Augustine's commentary on 1 John 4:8 does not support this. This error is a post hoc fallacy and argues that the modern English translation of Augustine (450 AD), which happens to be the same word order as the English translation of Rabelais's sixteenth-century-old French, makes Augustine the originator of "Do as Thou Wilt." Clearly this argues the false cause fallacy.

ating monks and performing secret Black Masses. Sir Francis Dashwood, an English nobleman who named the Prince of Wales, William Pitt, and Benjamin Franklin among his friends, rented and renovated an isolated, twelfth-century Cistercian monastery called Medmenham Abbey, located on the Thames River, six miles from his home. Dashwood then set about recruiting members for what would become one of the most notorious of all hedonistic orders. He initially named the group after himself—the Order of the Friars of St. Francis of Wycombe—but it was only a short time later that its infamous reputation forever christened it the Hellfire Club:

> There actually were several Hell Fire Clubs, but the best known was probably the one founded in England by Sir Francis Dashwood, who also was a member of a neo-Druid brotherhood. Dashwood's particular Hell Fire Club was more accurately called the Friars of St. Francis of Wycombe, and when he later purchased Medmenham (pronounced Med'nem) Abbey, they also became known as the Friars of Medmenham. Curiously, when Sir Francis was renovating the abbey, he had the workmen inscribe, "Do what you will" in Renaissance French over one of the doorways. Over a hundred years later this phrase, expressed in slightly different language, would become the motto for the most well known occult figure of modern times, Aleister Crowley.[43]

Dashwood promoted all forms of hedonism, including excessive drinking and sexual orgies, justifying all of them under Rabelais's "Do what thou wilt." The Hellfire Club, also known locally as the "Mad Monks of Medmenham," came to represent wealthy aristocrats, dressed as monks and nuns, who denied God and indulged in flagrant debauchery. As in some modern Satanist rituals and Black Masses, a nude woman was used as an altar and wine poured over her body for no particular ceremonial reason. Inverted Crosses and burned black candles became part of the secret rites.[44]

The Friars of St. Francis were known to provide their membership with orgies and sometimes performed Black Masses and other similar ceremonial acts.

---

43. James Randall Noblitt and Pamela Sue Perskin, *Cult and Ritual Abuse: Its History, Anthropology, and Recent Discovery in Contemporary America* (Westport, CT: Praeger, 2000), 138.
44. Medway, *Lure of the Sinister*, 86.

Nevertheless, some authors have interpreted their unorthodox behaviors as not genuinely Satanic, but more as a kind of organized libertinism. English aristocrats and high government officials frequented the club. For example, Sir Francis was himself a personal friend and adviser to King George III and a longtime member of Parliament who later became chancellor of the exchequer.[45]

A somewhat competitive group called the Demoniacs, who conducted themselves in a similar manner, also sprang up in England.[46]

Left-Hand Path and Right-Hand Path

One of the marks of modern Satanism is that its practicioners profess to choose the Left-Hand Path instead of the dualistic traditional counterpart of the Right-Hand Path. Examples of the dualism are darkness/light, negative/positive, black/white, goats/sheep, carnal/divine, and power/wisdom, respectively.

The Left-Hand Path was discussed by the Theosophists Helena Blavatsky and Annie Besant, who borrowed it from Hinduism. Some Satanists see the Left-Hand Path as an admission that they are the goats who are separated by Jesus Christ to be at his left hand, while the sheep (Christians) shall be at his right hand. They rely on this interpretation to support their contention that they are the opposite of Christianity—the way of the goat. This explains the use of a goat's head in Satanism, quite often pictured within the symbol of the inverted pentagram (star). The goat is central to the sign of the Baphomet (the horned goat sitting upon a throne), which is commonly used by Satanists. The left-handed sign pointing the index finger and little finger upward from a clenched fist represents the goat's horns and is an accepted sign for Satanism.[47] In modern Satanism, most followers of Crowley or LaVey claim to follow the Left-Hand Path.

Aleister Crowley

Aleister Crowley (1875–1947) was raised in a Christian household, but he rejected Christianity at an early age in favor of the occult and Rabelais's Thelemic philosophy, "Do what thou wilt." Crowley admired and learned from philosophers such as

---

45. Noblitt and Pershin, *Cult and Ritual Abuse*, 138.
46. See Thomas Yoseloff, *A Fellow of Infinite Jest* (New York: Prentice Hall, 1945), 49–50.
47. Nichols, Mather, and Schmidt, *Encyclopedic Dictionary of Cults, Sects, and World Religions*, 416, 439.

Friedrich Nietzsche, whose occult doctrine and hatred of Christianity are well-documented in his work *The AntiChrist:*

> The "kingdom of heaven" is a state of the heart—not something to come "beyond the world" or "after death." The whole idea of natural death is *absent* from the Gospels: death is not a bridge, not a passing; it is absent because it belongs to a quite different, a merely apparent world, useful only as a symbol. The "hour of death" is *not* a Christian idea—"hours," time, the physical life and its crises have no existence for the bearer of "glad tidings." . . .
>
> The "kingdom of God" is not something that men wait for: it had no yesterday and no day after tomorrow, it is not going to come at a "millennium"—it is an experience of the heart, it is everywhere and it is nowhere. . . .
>
> This "bearer of glad tidings" [Jesus] died as he lived and *taught—not* to "save mankind," but to show mankind how to live. It was a *way of life* that he bequeathed to man: his demeanour before the judges, before the officers, before his accusers—his demeanour on the Cross. He does not resist; he does not defend his rights; he makes no effort to ward off the most extreme penalty—more, *he invites* it. . . . And he prays, suffers and loves *with* those, *in* those, who do him evil. . . . *Not* to defend one's self, *not* to show anger, *not* to lay blames. . . . On the contrary, to submit even to the Evil One—to *love* him.[48]

Crowley later referred to Nietzsche as "one of our prophets."[49] He reveled in attention, publicly labeling himself "the Beast, 666," a title lifted from the book of Revelation.[50] Crowley became the first in modern times to reinvent the word *magic* by adding a *k*, as in *magick*, a spelling used to separate real magick from stage illusions. It appears from Crowley's work that he truly believed throughout his life that

48. Friedrich Nietzsche, *The Antichrist,* trans. H. L. Mencken (Friedrich Nietzsche Society, 1920), secs. 34–35, emphasis in original, http://www.fins.org.uk/ac.hgm.

49. Aleister Crowley, *Magick Without Tears* (Hampton, New Jersey: Thelema, 1954), 216. Crowley was fond of Nietzsche's philosophies, and he credited Arthur De Gobineau and Adolf Hitler with shaping his thoughts.

50. It is said that his mother, in frustration with his waywardness, called him "the Beast, 666." He liked it and decided to call himself that. (Lon Milo DuQuette, *The Magick of Aleister Crowley: A Handbook of the Rituals of Thelema* [Newburyport, MA: Weiser, 2004], 4).

he possessed genuine occult powers. It is certainly a fact that he indulged in myriad occult practices, even authoring a book supposedly dictated to him by a spirit named Aiwass. Crowley's famous *The Book of the Law (Liber al vel Legis)* materialized during his honeymoon in Cairo, Egypt, April 8–19, 1904. He claimed the spirit Aiwass dictated it to him, and assured his readers that it did not come by automatic writing but by a voice he had heard, which he initially thought was the Egyptian god Horus, but his wife (a medium) later told him that it was Aiwass, his holy guardian angel. Aleister Crowley claimed occult inspiration for his book and declared it to be the occult equivalent to the Christian Bible:

> For these reasons and many more I am certain—I the Beast, whose number is Six Hundred and Sixty and Six—that this Third Chapter of The Book of the Law is nothing less than the authentic Word, the Word of the Aeon, the Truth about Nature at this time. . . . I must be crucified. . . . But, being lifted up, I will draw the whole world unto me; and men shall worship me the Beast, Six Hundred and Sixty and Six, celebrating to Me their Midnight Mass . . . their God in man is offered to me The Beast, their God.[51]

It is interesting that Crowley, like other cult leaders before him, wrote about himself in his inspired work *The Book of the Law.*[52] "Now ye shall know that the chosen priest & apostle of infinite space is the prince-priest the Beast; and in his woman called the Scarlet Woman is all power given."[53] He is the chosen priest and apostle, the Beast, in his own inspired work. The speaker or spirit dictating *The Book of the Law* claims to be the Egyptian sky goddess Nuit (Nu or Nut), the goddess of the Thelema law, but Crowley presented a revival of Rabelais's law throughout the goddess Nuit's revelation (without giving due credit to Rabelais, since an angel dictated it), saying, "Do what thou wilt shall be the whole of the Law. The

---

51. Aleister Crowley, *Magick: Liber ABA* (Newburyport, Massachusetts: Wiser, 1997), 421–22.
52. For example, Joseph Smith, in the revelations of Mormonism, wrote about himself in his Joseph Smith's New Translation of the Bible and in the Book of Mormon. Other revelators, such as L. Ron Hubbard, Theosophists, Mary Baker Eddy, and many cult leaders, also wrote of themselves in their inspired works. The point is that they wrote an inspired work, and within the inspired work they told their audience that they were inspired!
53. Aleister Crowley, The Book of the Law (Newburyport, MA: Wiser, 1997), 1:15.

word of Sin is Restriction."⁵⁴ Crowley justified his freedom from sin and moral restrictions; he could do as he pleased guilt-free, as a follower of a higher law, the law of Thelema.

Arthur Edward Waite, a British scholar who translated the works of Eliphas Levi (also known as Alphonse Louis Constant), was a magician, Kabbalist, and occultist who reinvented the tarot card set for modern usage.⁵⁵ Levi's work greatly influenced Aleister Crowley, who seemed to master the tarot and wrote on it throughout his life.⁵⁶ Crowley gravitated to like-minded people seeking esoteric knowledge, and he joined a Rosicrucian, Kabbalist, occult group called the Hermetic Order of the Golden Dawn on November 18, 1898. He reached the order's ninth degree, Magus, on October 12, 1915, eventually founding another order he called Argenteum Astrum, or Order of the Silver Star in 1907 (after receiving *The Book of the Law*).⁵⁷

Crowley used his official publication, *The Equinox* (1909–1913), to publish secret rituals of the Order of the Golden Dawn, a move viewed by Dawn members as revenge related to his falling-out with the Golden Dawn leadership. Not long after this, the media began publishing sordid accounts of Crowley's involvement with homosexuality and other sexual escapades linked to the Argenteum Astrum, which significantly hurt membership. Crowley soon turned his attention to another fledgling organization called Ordo Templi Orientis, which mimicked elements of Freemasonry and claimed sexual magick as one of its foundational principles. He joined it and soon became the president, freely writing about his experiences in the order. He drew many members into the organization, which still exists today. Its official motto is the Thelemic law, "Do what thou wilt shall be the whole of the Law," which is a quote from Crowley's work.

Occult magick dominated Aleister Crowley's life, and his definition of it would significantly impact the future development of Witchcraft and Satanism. "Magick," Crowley wrote, "is the science and art of causing change to occur in con-

---

54. Ibid., 1:40–41.
55. See the chapter on the Kabballah, and note its variant spellings.
56. See Aleister Crowley, *The Book of Thoth: A Short Essay on the Tarot of the Egyptians* (London: O.T.O, 1944).
57. See Aleister Crowley, *The Book of Thoth: A Short Essay on the Tarot of the Egyptians, Being the Equinox*, vol. 3, no. 5 (Newburyport, MA: Red Wheel, 1974), xi. The order of the Golden Dawn split and was under Arthur Waite's direction, but seemed to disband shortly after 1915, and it split yet again.

formity with the Will."[58] Sex and drugs were predominate factors in Crowley's life and magick. His drug use began early and continued throughout his adulthood. In 1922, he published *The Diary of a Drug Fiend* (1922), a shocking novel for its day, in which he drew from his personal experience. According to one biographer, "Crowley's early belief that drugs could not harm a magician possessed of pure enough will was dashed by the example of his own life. Crowley's struggles with heroin and cocaine are legendary."[59] Another of Crowley's books, the *Enochian World of Aleister Crowley: Enochian Sex Magick* (1912), illustrates his teachings on the subject of sex magick. The Ordo Templi Orientis still promotes books today dealing with sex magick and Hindu-based tantric sex, in its three international Grand Lodges and myriad small groups (including forty-four local groups in the United States) spread over twelve countries.[60]

Crowley promoted a mixed bag of religious thought. He selected ideas from Buddhism, Hinduism, Gnosticism, polytheism, occult traditions, magick, Christianity, Judaism, and just about anything he found useful. In his world, there was no need for consistency. At times he sounded anti-Christian (his moniker "the Beast," for example), and at other times he invoked the name of Jesus Christ in his rituals.

Today, many Pagan leaders avoid the subject of Aleister Crowley and discount the role he played in the development of modern Witchcraft. Satanists, however, and a small minority of Pagans, do not seem to suffer from the same embarrassment regarding Crowley. In answer to the question "Was Aleister Crowley a Satanist," the Ordo Templi Orientis (OTO) website comments, "Aleister Crowley was a systematic and scientific explorer of religious practices, techniques, and doctrines. As such, he performed devotional exercises to Satan as well as to Jesus Christ."[61] At different times in his life, Crowley practiced whatever fit the moment, regardless of whether or not these beliefs contradicted one another. "Crowley was

58. Ibid., 40.
59. DuQuette, *The Magick of Aleister Crowley*, 8.
60. A survey of the official OTO online bookstore confirms that they still promote sex magic. See www.oto-usa.org/bookstore.html.
61. U.S. Grand Lodge, Ordo Templi Orientis, "Frequently Asked Questions," www.oto-usa.org/faq.html. Some scholars deny that Crowley was a Satanist. Marco Pasi wrote, "One of the most popular misunderstandings has led to him being labeled a Satanist . . ." (See Pasi, Aleister Crowley" in Hanegraaff, *Dictionary of Gnosis and Western Esotericism*, 284.) Pasi argues this even though Crowley's works and the official OTO website affirms Crowley's involvement in Satanism.

an Atheist, a Polytheist, a Monotheist . . . a Pantheist, a Satanist . . . a Christian, a Hindu Yogi, and Hebrew Qabalist, a Muslim Mystic, a Buddhist, and a Pagan."[62]

This hodgepodge of assorted beliefs reveals a greatly unsettled and spiritually bankrupt man who recognized no solid ground in his lifelong search for truth. It is impossible for a rational mind to accept all of the assorted doctrines of Crowley's world, since the sacred texts of one oppose the foundational principles of another.

Modern Satanism as Entertainment

It is inevitable that the flamboyant escapades of men like Crowley would draw the attention of the entertainment industry. Many small but effective books translated during the twentieth century embraced Pagan ideas and the essence of Satanism, providing a measure of forbidden excitement to the curious and ignorant.

Arthur Waite accomplished more than Aleister Crowley in this area, largely due to his scholarly background and publishing connections. Waite's contribution to the spread of Satanic theology was significant and far-reaching. He searched the world for the most obscure writings of occultism, and then translated more than eighty books on the black arts, magick, the occult, and esoteric thought into English. The year 1924 brought the hardcover release to America of *Down There*, a translation of *La-Bas* by Joris-Karl Huysmans (1848–1904)—a novel on Satanism that described the Black Mass (first published in France in 1891). The American debut of *Down There* was well received, and it went through several reprints over the years, but the press promotions for the 1958 edition topped them all. *Down There* eventually became a textbook for Satanism—especially for the dabblers in Satanic rites.

The movie industry rode the wave of interest in Satanism by promoting Satanic ideology, eventually bringing the Black Mass to the silver screen for the very first time in the 1934 film *The Black Cat* (Universal Studios). Boris Karloff, the famous actor of macabre classic movies, starred in the film, which spread the dogma of Satanism and the Black Mass across America and around the world.

In the 1950s, the Agape Lodge captured the news as the American branch of Aleister Crowley's OTO. The brilliant rocket scientist, John "Jack" Whiteside Parsons, of Pasadena, California, was its director. He was a friend of the science fiction writer and Scientology founder L. Ron Hubbard (who later married Parson's

---

62. U.S. Grand Lodge, Ordo Templi Orientis, http://oto-usa.org/faq.html.

ex-girlfriend).[63] Together, Parsons and Hubbard wrote *Liber 49—The Book of Babalon*, which claims similarity to Crowley's *Book of the Law*. Organized in verses, it blasphemes God (verse 51) and Jesus Christ by claiming that the Egyptian god Horus will kill both of them.

Parsons's Agape Lodge and Church of Thelema drew a small crowd of followers, one of whom was Anton LaVey. Neighbors complained of orgies and other unsavory acts, which only captured journalistic interest and popularized Satanic rituals. Several books have been written on Jack Parsons since his early death at age thirty-seven from an accidental explosion at his home laboratory.

Anton Szandor LaVey

Anton LaVey (born Howard Stanton Levey, 1930–1997) was raised a Catholic but rebelled against his childhood training and became the founder of the Church of Satan. Influenced by Aleister Crowley's works and the OTO during his teenage years, LaVey adopted the philosophy of a nonpersonal, corporate evil named Satan. He dismissed the reality of Satan as a malevolent spirit-being and taught instead that evil was a force present on earth that must be exercised (or utilized) within man, not *exorcised* out of him. Satanism, as redefined by LaVey, is the pursuit of worshiping Satan (all evil) or performing acts and rituals under his authority and rejecting God (the force of good).

LaVey accomplished more than any other Satanist in history; taking full advantage of the rebellious spirit of a young megageneration to popularize Satanism at a time when a social countercultural movement was already under way. Social and spiritual unrest offered Satanism—the pinnacle of rebellion—an unprecedented advantage as the premier venue for expressing individualism contrary to social norms. The frenzy of media coverage only increased LaVey's infamy and influence, as he recorded and broadcasted the Black Mass, the baptism of his daughter, Satanic weddings, Satanic funerals, and other bizarre rituals of his Church. The sensibilities of conservative Americans were shocked and outraged by a nude woman on an altar, participating in sexual escapades enjoyed in the name of religion. But this outrage was precisely what LaVey wanted. The anger of the masses

---

63. Russell Miller devotes a lengthy chapter to the Parsons and Hubbard connection in *Bare-Faced Messiah: The True Story of L. Ron Hubbard* (New York: Henry Holt, 1987), 112ff.

meant media coverage, which translated to fame, and fame popularized his movement. By the time LaVey wrote *The Satanic Bible*, his popularity had increased so much among college-age students that *Time* magazine reported, "On some campuses, the paperback Satanic Bible by Church of Satan Founder Anton La Vey is outselling The Holy Bible."[64]

LaVey died in 1997, leaving the Church of Satan in the care of his consort Magistra Blanche Barton, the mother of his third child, Satan Xerxes Carnacki LaVey. Some family members remained with the Church while others left and strongly opposed LaVey's practices. His daughter Zeena (LaVey) Schreck eventually published allegations of sexual molestation and plagiarism against her father.[65]

Church of Satan

Anton LaVey founded the Church of Satan on April 30, 1966, in San Francisco, California.[66] Their main publications include the works of LaVey and a regular newsletter, *The Cloven Hoof.* Other names associated with them over the years are the First Church of Satan, the Satanic Church, and the Satanic Church of America. At one time, LaVey allowed the development of small local Satanic centers called grottos, but he later withdrew his support when control became an issue and grottos began breaking off from the main church to start a new church. He revived the grotto idea again in the 1980s. High Priestess Magistra Blanche Barton and High Priest Peter H. Gilmore hold the current leadership of the Church of Satan.

The Satanic Church today has established specific levels of membership that offer varying degrees of commitment and authority. Initiates usually begin as registered members who agree to support the philosophy of the Church of Satan and *The Satanic Bible* but receive no degree of authority in return. They simply pay their dues (currently $200) and receive a red carrying card.

The First Degree member is an active member who is granted the degree of a Satanist. These are the people who have submitted an active membership applica-

---

64. "Raising the Devil," *Time*, March 13, 1972, www.time.com/time/magazine/article/0,9171,903361,00.html.

65. LaVey's daughter Karla left the Church of Satan and has her own church. Zeena, his second daughter, and her husband, Nikolas Schreck, left the Church of Satan and published numerous Internet articles challenging LaVey's legacy. See www.churchofsatan.org/aslv.html (accessed July 3, 2007).

66. Their administrative office has since moved to New York, New York.

tion and been formally approved and accepted into the church. They are permitted to attend and participate in rituals that are usually held in other participants' homes. The application for active membership requires forty essay answers to questions that include one's thoughts on *The Satanic Bible*, the Church of Satan, Satan, their sex lives, their attitudes toward animals, and their thoughts on childhood, parenting, music, movies, travel, tobacco, drugs, and alcohol.

The Second Degree member is designated a Witch/warlock; the Third Degree becomes a priestess/priest; the Fourth Degree is a magistra/magister; and the Fifth Degree is maga/magus. Third through Fifth Degreed members hold the priesthood of Mendes and may adopt the title Reverend. The top administrative titles are High Priestess or High Priest, which are restricted to Fourth Degree and Fifth Degree members.[67]

Throughout its short history, the Church of Satan has encountered varying and consistent troubles, including major and minor internal splits. These public disagreements often resulted in spin-off churches, including the Temple of Set, Ancient Brotherhood of Satan, and many others that are now defunct. Disgruntled ex-LaVeyan Satanists did not hesitate to voice public criticisms of Anton LaVey's church and his particular brand of Satanism (LaVeyan Satanism). The voices of the critics even came from within the ranks of his children. LaVey's eldest daughter, Karla LaVey, left her father's church to begin her own—a movement she claimed would return its followers to the essence of true LaVeyan Satanism. His second daughter, Zeena LaVey Schreck, also left the original Church of Satan and became involved in several groups before settling on the Temple of Set. She heavily criticized her father's work and his personal claims.[68]

The Satanic Bible

Anton Szandor LaVey wrote *The Satanic Bible* in 1966 and sold a million copies with the help of Avon Books. In it, he set forth his thoughts on living under the Thelemic order, a philosophy rooted in the writings of Rabelais and Crowley. *The Satanic Bible* reveals nine basic statements that form the foundation of LaVey's philosophy:

---

67. On the various degrees, see www.churchofsatan.com/home.html.
68. Zeena and Nikolas Schreck, "Anton LaVey: Legend and Reality," February 2, 1998, www.churchofsatan.org/aslv.html.

1. Satan represents indulgence instead of abstinence.

2. Satan represents vital existence instead of spiritual pipe dreams.

3. Satan represents undefiled wisdom instead of hypocritical self-deceit.

4. Satan represents kindness to those who deserve it instead of love wasted on ingrates.

5. Satan represents vengeance instead of turning the other cheek.

6. Satan represents responsibility to the responsible instead of concern for psychic vampires.

7. Satan represents man as just another animal, sometimes better, more often worse than those that walk on all fours, because of his "divine spiritual and intellectual development," has become the most vicious animal of all.

8. Satan represents all of the so-called sins, as they all lead to physical, mental, or emotional gratification.

9. Satan has been the best friend the Church has ever had, as he has kept it in business all these years.[69]

Satanism defines itself with a series of negative propositions. This is consistent with its historical predecessors, who negated the positive aspects of human life and despised Christian values. Satanism's long history as a malicious, spiritually destructive philosophy reveals a worldview that disparages opposing beliefs by malicious mockery (such as reciting the Lord's Prayer and portions of the Catholic Mass backward) and promotes what is, in essence, anarchy.

Even the positive aspects of Satanism are cloaked in negativity. LaVey wrote, "Satan represents kindness to those who deserve it instead of love wasted on ingrates." You are to love others only if they deserve it. But exactly who are the ones that deserve love? The answer cannot be anything other than narcissistic in that the Satanist alone determines who is deserving of love. The Christian concept of giving love without expecting it in return is despised by Satanists as the worst weak-

---

69. Anton Szandor LaVey, *The Satanic Bible* (New York: Avon, 1966, 1969), 25.

ness. This love—offered only by Jesus Christ within the Christian gospel—is directly attacked in *The Satanic Bible*. Still, Satanism's dark belief system continues to find acceptance from one generation to the next, and its appeal will likely continue as long as it caters to the carnal nature of mankind. The lure of a lifestyle centered on experience over authority, a metaphysical supernatural excitement and blatant immorality is a potent temptation, indeed.

Within the pages of *The Satanic Bible*, a philosophy of selfish, irresponsible sexual gratification is encouraged:

> Satanism condones any type of sexual activity which properly satisfies your individual desires—be it heterosexual, homosexual, bisexual, or even asexual, if you choose. Satanism also sanctions any fetish or deviation which will enhance your sex life. . . . Adherence to the sensible and humanistic new morality of Satanism, can—and will—evolve society, a society in which children can grow up healthy and without the devastating moral encumbrances of our existing sick society.[70]

LaVey outlined a perversion of the biblical teaching on sexuality that he happily called a deviation. It is the skilled and media savvy transformation of immorality into a *new morality* that is, in reality, as ancient as Adam and Eve. Perversion thrived in all cultures throughout history where rebellion superseded biblical righteousness. By redefining it as a new morality, LaVey inadvertently fulfilled a portion of Scripture where God spoke through the prophet Isaiah (750 BC), "Woe to those who call evil good, and good evil; who put darkness for light, and light for darkness; who put bitter for sweet, and sweet for bitter!" (Isa. 5:20). The philosophies of LaVey, Crowley, Rabelais, and all who promote "Do as thou wilt" more than fulfill Isaiah's prophecy.

Anton LaVey carefully crafted a philosophy of hedonism that celebrated every vice known to man, crowning them with the well-worn promise that a human being can indeed become a god. He wrote, "The Satanist feels . . . why not really be honest, and if you are going to create a god in your image, why not create that god as yourself. Every man is a god if he chooses to recognize himself as one."[71] This

70. Ibid., 67.
71. Ibid., 90.

paraphrase of Genesis 3 where Satan, speaking to Eve through the serpent, appealed to her ego by promising "you shall be like God" is all too familiar to students of the Bible. The ancient theme of man as god has been sold and repackaged all the way up until its present incarnation in the teachings of Joseph Smith (Mormonism), Garner Ted Armstrong (Armstrongism), Maharishi Mahesh Yogi (Transcendental Meditation), Madame Blavatsky (Theosophy), and modern Satanism. Perhaps this distortion lies at the heart of the Satanists' birthday celebrations, considered the most important holiday of the year: everyone is a god if they choose to recognize themselves as one.

The essence of Anton LaVey's "might makes right" and "the good life now" philosophy can be summed up in his egotistical rendition of Jesus' Sermon on the Mount:

> Blessed are the strong, for they shall possess the earth. Cursed are the weak, for they shall inherit the yoke. Blessed are the powerful for they shall be reverenced among men. Cursed are the feeble, for they shall be blotted out. . . . Blessed are those who believe what is best for them, for never shall their minds be terrorized. Cursed are the lambs of God, for they shall be bled whiter than the snow. Life is the great indulgence; death the great abstinence. Therefore, make the most of life here and now.[72]

The LaVeyan lifestyle is based on the authority of self. No reason is ever given for exactly why LaVey's beliefs should carry more weight than the words of someone who disagrees with him. Christianity, on the other hand, has always rested on the divine authority of Jesus Christ, upholding His words as supreme truth. The life, death, and physical resurrection of Jesus from the dead was never matched or superseded by Anton LaVey. Why, then, should anyone listen to him or accept his self-authority as the standard for living? Minimally, Anton LaVey would have to rise physically from the dead to equal Jesus in power and authority, but this cannot occur since his mortal remains were cremated and divided among his heirs.[73] Anton

---

72. Ibid., 34.
73. See Don Lattin, "Satan's Den in Great Disrepair," *San Francisco Chronicle,* January 25, 1999, A-1, http://www.sfgate.com/cgi-bin/article/article?f=/c/a/1999/01/25/MN77329.DTL.

LaVey did not rise from the dead, so his words are grounded in mere opinion and hold no weight. Christians soundly reason that the words of Jesus Christ reign supreme over LaVey's, based on the solid and reasonable evidence for Christ's physical resurrection.[74]

New insight into the life of Anton LaVey came in 1998, when LaVey's daughter Zeena (along with her husband, Nicolas) left the Church of Satan. Zeena LaVey Schreck published an Internet exposure of Anton LaVey's background shortly after her departure, wherein she charged her father with plagiarism of *The Satanic Bible*. Based on specifics outlined by the Schrecks, honesty, integrity, and trustworthiness do not seem to have been Anton LaVey's strong points. Zeena gave a detailed account of exactly how her father plagiarized *The Satanic Bible*.

> Avon approached ASL [Anton Szandor LaVey] for some kind of Satanic work to cash in on the Satanism & Witchcraft fad of the late 1960s. Pressed for material to meet Avon's deadline, ASL resorted to plagiarism, assembling extracts from an obscure 1896 tract—*Might is Right* by Ragnar Redbeard into a "Book of Satan" for the SB [*Satanic Bible*], and claiming its authorship by himself. . . . Another third of the SB consists of John Dee's "Enochian Keys", taken directly but again without attribution from Aleister Crowley's Equinox. The SB's "Nine Satanic Statements", one of the Church of Satan's central doctrines, is a paraphrase, again unacknowledged, of passages from Ayn Rand's *Atlas Shrugged*.[75]

Zeena LaVey Schreck devastated her father's claim to authorship with these charges of plagiarism, since verbatim content (line after line) was lifted by LaVey without any credit to the original author. Shortly before his death in 1997, he owned up to it in part. In a clever attempt at damage control, Anton LaVey stated in his last interview that *Might Is Right* by Ragnar Redbeard was one of the most controversial books ever written, so it was something he thought he should copy.

---

74. Numerous books argue well for Christ's bodily resurrection, but this is not our purpose here. See McDowell, *New Evidence That Demands a Verdict*.
75. Schreck and Schreck, "Anton LaVey: Legend and Reality," www.churchofsatan.org/aslv.html. All parallels of plagiarism in this section are credited to LaVey's daughter Zeena, although the commentary is ours.

"It was only natural that I excerpted a few pages of it for The Satanic Bible."[76] He cleverly avoided any mention of the financial profit he had made from claiming Redbeard's work for thirty years before giving him a small token of credit, and that involuntary, since it only happened after his daughter exposed him.

Temple of Set

Another defector from LaVey's ranks of Satanists also accused him of corruption. In 1975, Michael Aquino claimed he received a revelation, which he then turned into an inspired book intended to lead others into a better way of Satanism. Aquino returned to the ideology of traditional Satanism, where Satan is worshiped as a genuine personal being—a position flatly denied by LaVey and other modern Satanists.

The Temple of Set has proven to be the most high-profile splinter group from the Church of Satan, but it is difficult to determine which is the most successful, since membership statistics are not released. Aquino published an Internet edition of a 394-page book about the Temple of Set, which contained his revelations from all of the spirits who contacted him, the most influential of which was the Egyptian god Set.[77] Some of these revelations apparently came through automatic writing, an occult practice during which a person acts as a medium, enabling a spirit to communicate by moving the hand and writing what is dictated. The book outlines the various levels of degrees that one can reach through climbing the esoteric ladder that resembles Rosicrucian and other Gnostic-based groups. Aquino's book is brimming with gods, goddesses, daimons (demons), and perversions of the nature of God (God becomes Satan, and Satan becomes God).[78] He added the notation that his manuscript is an ongoing work, not a final version, and as such is subject to change—the essence of esotericism. Today, the Temple of Set has expanded into several study groups, most of which are located in the United States.

---

76. Anton LaVey, "Creator of the Church of Satan" in *MF Magazine*, no. 3. See Shane and Amy Bugbee's The Doctor Is In website at http://www.churchofsatan.com/Pages/MFInterview.html for an online transcript of this interview.
77. Michael A. Aquino, *The Temple of Set* (San Francisco: Xeper, 2006).
78. Ibid., 111.

SATANIC GROTTOS AND SMALLER SATANIST CULTS

Satanism is a large movement, but because of the lack of statistics, no one knows exactly how large it is. Several rock-and-roll bands are known as Satanic rock bands and have large followings, but that does not mean that all fans are Satanists. The first band that laid claim publicly to the title of Satanist was Black Widow in 1969, the same year *The Satanic Bible* was released. LaVey himself listed a few bands in his final interview. "King Diamond, The Electric Hellfire Club, Acheron, Marilyn Manson, Boyd Rice, Nine Inch Nails—the list is long. . . . Today's Satanic bands are the vehicle of choice for millions of young people. If they encourage a study of real Satanism, I'm all for them."[79] Some skeptics brush off LaVey as an authority on the spiritual practices of rock bands, but as one of the fathers of modern Satanism, LaVey was in a far better position to know the power of his philosophy and the names of its devotees.

LaVey promoted Satanism far and wide, and he did not seem care if followers actually joined his Church as long as they practiced Satanism. The *Church of Satan Youth Communiqué* told young Satanists, "There is no one way that a Satanist is 'supposed' to be. . . . All you have to do to be a real Satanist is start living like one."[80] This lack of formal membership makes it difficult to determine the exact number of practicing Satanists.

Church of Satan Grottos

The rise of the Internet provided modern Satanism with a recruiting tool unparalleled in the history of the civilized world. A simple touch of a button replaced the tedium of snail mail and threw open the door to all the people, power, and perils of Satanism. Small groups, or *grottos*, of Satanists, secretly gathering in homes around the world to practice rituals, could now communicate with the church and one another in a matter of seconds via e-mail or website discussion boards.[81]

Satanism and the dogma of the occult spread at a frenetic pace from keyboard to keyboard, resulting in an explosion of satanic sites that included the once defunct Church of Satan grottos. Professor Eugene V. Gallagher, an expert in new

---

79. LaVey as quoted on http://www.churchofsatan.com/Pages/MFInterview.html.
80. Marge Bauer, "Church of Satan Youth Communiqué," ed. Peter H. Gilmore, http://www.churchofsatan.com/Pages/Youthletter.html.
81. *Grotto* is Italian for a small cave or chamber; borrowed from Latin for a crypt.

religious movements, confirmed Anton LaVey's future plans for the growth of his Church of Satan and its grottos in his work *The New Religious Movements Experience in America.* "During his life, LaVey experimented with different organizational forms for his Church. For a time it was subdivided into local Grottos; in 1975 LaVey discontinued the Grotto system and then reinstated it in the late 1980s."[82] Grotto leadership functions primarily on a local level and does not convey a degree or rank in the Church of Satan. Leaders may be designated administrator, agent, or grotto master, and the position may be held by any degreed person in the church.

When a grotto or similar group incorporates for tax-exempt status recognition in the United States, it is safe to assume their expression of Satanism is as an organized religion. The following groups are noted here because of an influential Internet presence geared toward increasing their following. Some have incorporated for tax purposes, and some have not; some fall under the heading of modern Satanists, such as Anton LaVey, and others adhere to the beliefs of traditional Satanism and worship a personal being named Satan.

The Black Coven of Satanas (2005) was organized in Mobile, Alabama. They offer a number of books on traditional Satanism and claim to be a revival of Middle Eastern devil worship based upon a twelfth-century text, *Al-Jilwah.* They believe in the personal being of Satan called Melek Taus.

Cathedral of the Black Goat (2001). No location is listed, but the group claims to meet biweekly. They produce sermons and study texts and practice "orthodox" traditional Satanic worship of Lucifer. Their website is linked to two other "orthodox" traditional Satanist groups.

Cult of Cthulhu (2004). No location is listed. This is a LaVeyan splinter study group of modern Satanists. They claim to follow the Left-Hand Path and deny the personal nature of Satan.

First Church of Satan[83] (1994) was founded by John Allee in Salem, Massachusetts, as a splinter group from Anton LaVey's Church of Satan. The First Church of Satan promotes "free thinking Satanism," which means that Allee recommends reading materials that include neo-Nazi, communistic, and homosexual

82. Eugene V. Gallagher, The New Religious Movements Experience in America (Westport, CT: Greenwood Press, 2004), 194.
83. Note: More than one group uses the name "First Church of Satan."

man-boy organization NAMBLA (North American Man-Boy Love Association) materials. They produce an Internet radio broadcast and online videos.

Lucifer's Den, Incorporated (1999). The location is not given, but it is closely connected with Texan Satanic groups. They follow the modern LaVeyan form of Satanism.

OFS Demonolatry (Ordo Flammeus Serpens), a group focused on demon worship, holds its meetings in Colorado and Oregon. They claim to be theistic Satanists who worship Satan traditionally (as a person), but they also include pantheistic Satanism, which they define as demon worship. They have Internet forums, offer training through online seminary instruction, and publish *The Black Serpent*, a biannual OFS Demonolatry magazine.

The Order of the Nine Angels (1960s) was organized in England as an esoteric magic group that believes in dark gods, Satanism, black magic, and sinister rituals.

Ordo Sinistra Vivendi, also known as the Order of the Sinister Way, is based in New Zealand and promotes individualism as Satanism, so any Satanic ideology a person selects—whether personal or impersonal—is acceptable.

The Process Church of the Final Judgment (1965) was founded in England and based on the theories and writings of Robert and MaryAnne DeGrimston, who left Scientology and developed an eclectic combination of ideas that included Satanism. The Process gained international attention when it was falsely reported that the murderous Charles Manson Family cult was connected to it. They denied this and won a libel lawsuit against a reporter who printed a story on it. Members of The Process are dualists who worship God (Jehovah) and Satan together. The main group has splintered into several small groups over the years.

Sanctuary of Satan, also known as the Temple of Satan, claims to hold to the traditional worship of Satan as a personal being. Sanctuary of Satan is associated with the *Brother Nero Show*, an Internet-based radio talk show that is also podcast. Nero claims to be a thirty-six-year-old (2007) legally ordained minister of Satan. The Sanctuary takes financial donations on the Internet.

The Syndicate of the Five Points is a Satanic coven based in Southern California that comprises several smaller groups. They adhere to modern Satanism of the LaVeyan type. Their five-point theology is (1) self-worship, (2) social responsibility, (3) magic and ritual, (4) the wolf pack, and (5) pleasures and enchantment.

Worldwide Church of Satanic Liberation (1986) was founded in New Haven,

Connecticut, by Paul Valentine, who has since moved his organization to Michigan. Valentine is an environmentalist and occasional media guest who styles himself as an individualist Satanist, anti-Christian and iconoclastic.

Case Study

Walter Martin

Those who practice satanic rituals are looking for satanic possession, and they will find it. Satanism leads to the possession of the soul by demonic forces.

Not long ago, I received a long distance telephone call from a couple in Florida. I had lectured at Dr. D. James Kennedy's Church, Coral Ridge Presbyterian, and given a whole day seminar on the subject of the occult and Satanists, and this couple, who ran a drug rehabilitation center, had been there for the seminar. They had a case of full blown demon possession on their hands, and they did not know what to do with it. They recognized exactly what it was because of the lectures I had just given at Coral Ridge. They called me and said, "We have been praying for this girl for four hours; we're simply exhausted. Please tell us what to do."

"What has happened so far?" I asked.

"Well, she is possessed with multiple devils."

"Did you get a count?"

They said, "Yes. We asked them in Jesus Christ's name how many they were and they told us '56.'"

I said, "Well, that's a good beginning. Did you get their names?"

"Every one of them named themselves (screeching) whenever we commanded them in the name of Christ." There is power in Jesus' name.

"Good," I said, "Have you been exorcising them one at a time?"

"Yes! And quite a few have gone."

"What is the girl's background?"

"She is involved in Satanism. We found the Satanic Bible in her bureau drawer; she has been on drugs for sometime. We also found some symbols of satanic worship."

I suddenly heard this awful screeching in the background. "What is going on now?" I asked.

He said, "They're talking in tongues."

"What?!" I exclaimed.

"They are talking in tongues."

"Well, do something to stop that right away because you cannot understand them, and you must understand them if you are going to have a dialogue."

So the pastor went back into the room and commanded them in the name of Jesus Christ to speak in English. They had been talking in multiple languages, but immediately (upon command) they went back to speaking English. They were exorcised one at a time over the course of the next few hours (this went on until 2:00 a.m.) and the girl was completely exhausted. Everyone in the room was ready to collapse, but they refused to give up.

Finally they called me one last time and said, "They are all gone but one, and he will not leave. We're having an awfully hard time. What are we going to do?"

I said, "Well, there is only one thing we can do. We're just going to have to concentrate once more on prayer, and ask the Lord Jesus Christ to do it for us. I will hang up the phone, kneel here and pray. You go back in there, and we will join together in prayer for her right now."

"Ok," he said, and hung up the phone. I prayed, and immediately I had a wonderful sense of peace. I said to the Lord, "Lord, time or space does not separate us; it should not separate us from our brothers and sisters in Jesus. Lord, I am right down there in Florida beside the bed of that girl, and I am praying for her. In the name of Jesus Christ of Nazareth come out of her! Set her free." And I felt wonderful! The phone rang a few minutes later and it was them. "Dr. Martin! Dr. Martin! It's gone! It's gone!"

"Are you sure?" I asked.

"Absolutely! We don't know what happened, but as we were kneeling and praying, all of a sudden she let out this terrible scream and her body jackknifed up on the bed, and then she dropped down again and moaned, "Ohhhhh!" And then we said, "In the name of Jesus Christ of Nazareth, how many are you now?!" There was dead silence. We woke her up, and she has received the Lord Jesus as her Savior."

That girl has not only overcome drugs cold turkey, but right now she is studying to be a witness for Christ. She is sitting in a drug rehabilitation center delivered from 56 demons. You may say, "Oh well, I don't really believe something like that!"

I know it is difficult to believe, but it happened. If you ever run into a case of demon possession up close, you will never ever doubt the power of Satan; it is positively enormous.

In one of the largest Churches in the world, located in Southern California, I conducted another exorcism of demons from a girl who was over one hundred miles away. I prayed with the pastors while they prayed for this girl, and multiple demons came out of her. Since then, she received Christ as her Savior, too.

These things happen. They are real. Denying them does not make them go away, and the skepticism of modern society has no power to dismiss them; it simply amuses them. Viruses are invisible to the naked eye, but we know they exist because we developed the equipment that enabled us to see them. We may not be able to place a demon under a microscope, but God gave us the means to see them:

1. Demons speak in multiple voices and in multiple languages unknown to the person they possess

2. Demons exhibit superhuman strength

3. Demons have access to private information that a possessed person could never know

4. Demons respond to and obey the authority of the name of Jesus Christ.

This experiment has been repeated countless times and it has been proved, beyond doubt, that evil, sentient beings called demons *do* exist.

SCRIPTURAL RESPONSE

Satanism, no matter how one views it, is comprised of lost souls who do not know Jesus Christ as their Lord and Savior. The parable of the sower in Matthew 13:1–23 clearly demonstrates that only God knows where His seed will germinate; people second-guess the human heart. It is a fact that some Satanists have been saved by the grace of Christ and born again to everlasting life, so there is always hope. Jesus has the power to save even a repentant Satanist.

In the beginning, mankind was made perfectly by God (Gen. 1:26–27) just as the angels were, yet we followed the lead of Satan and his fallen angels in their sin and rebellion against God. When Satan confronted Jesus and demanded, "Worship me!" he intended for all mankind to directly and boldly worship him. But Jesus rejected Satan's scheme, saying, "Away with you, Satan! For it is written, 'You shall worship the LORD your God, and Him only you shall serve'" (Matt. 4:10). Satan, a created being, was forced to obey the Lord of all creation. "Then the devil left Him, and behold, angels came and ministered to Him" (v. 11). When Satan tempts any human being to worship him, they have but to imitate the example of Jesus and in His name say, "Away with you, Satan!" and he will flee.

The answer to Satanism is the simple fact that a creation, no matter how powerful, can never be a god. Jesus was and is *God*. "Jesus said to [the Jews], 'Most assuredly, I say to you, before Abraham was, I AM'" (John 8:58). He told His disciples, "I saw Satan fall like lightning from heaven" (Luke 10:18). The omnipotent, omnipresent Creator of all the angels watched as the devil was tossed from heaven. Jesus can never be defeated by a being who is neither omnipotent nor omnipresent deity. Satan does not know all things, he cannot read the minds and hearts of human beings, he cannot be everywhere at once, and he can never be God— because God is eternal, and he, Satan, is a creation:

> The eternal God is your refuge,
> and underneath are the everlasting arms;
> He will thrust out the enemy from before you,
> and will say, 'Destroy!' (Deut. 33:27)

In his sin and rebellion, Satan believed the Son of God could be tempted to worship a fallen creation, a fatally flawed being flung from the heights of heaven to spread his poison below. But Jesus, as the beloved Son of God, could never bow to Satan.

> In the beginning was the Word, and the Word was with God, and the Word was God. He was in the beginning with God. All things were made through Him, and without Him nothing was made that was made. In Him was life, and the life was the light of men. And the light shines in the darkness, and the darkness did not comprehend it (John 1:1–5).

The god of this age blinds the intellect of man so that the gospel cannot penetrate without direct intervention of the power of the Holy Spirit. "But even if our gospel is veiled, it is veiled to those who are perishing, whose minds the god of this age has blinded, who do not believe, lest the light of the gospel of the glory of Christ, who is the image of God, should shine on them" (2 Cor. 4:3–4). It is a powerful blindness, but it cannot prevent the God of all creation from using His children to plant the seed of the gospel in the hearts of the lost.

Christians should never fear Satan, but wisdom dictates a healthy respect for an ancient, deadly enemy. When you are dealing with Satan, do not treat him lightly; remember and respect what the Scripture says of him. "But even the archangel Michael, when he was disputing with the devil about the body of Moses, did not dare to bring a slanderous accusation against him, but said, 'The Lord rebuke you!'" (Jude 9). Christians should particularly remember the daily power of the Lord's Prayer, which includes this sentence: "And do not lead us into temptation, but deliver us from the evil one" (Matt. 6:13). Jesus Christ would not have commanded us to pray that prayer unless we needed that kind of divine protection every day.

The Son of God did not bow his knee to Satan, but millions of followers of LaVey and other forms of Satanism have enthusiastically worshiped this being who takes such delight in destroying their lives. These people may refuse to bow the knee to Jesus Christ, incarnate love, while here on earth, but they will find themselves prostrate before Him in the final judgment. The apostle Paul warns of a coming day when every knee will bow and every tongue confess that Jesus is Lord: "Therefore God also has highly exalted Him and given Him the name which is above every name, that at the name of Jesus every knee should bow, of those in heaven, and of those on earth, and of those under the earth, and that every tongue should confess that Jesus Christ is Lord, to the glory of God the Father" (Phil. 2:9–11).

Christians should never fear Satan, because they can call upon Jesus Christ, who defeated Satan on the Cross and wields all of the authority of heaven and earth. After Jesus' resurrection from the dead, He demonstrated His power over sin, death, the grave, hell, and Satan. Before His ascension into heaven, He commissioned his disciples to go into all the world and share His gospel. So often Christians read the Great Commission and miss the entire reason for evangelizing people. It is found in Matthew 28:18, the verse immediately preceding His call for evangelism: "And Jesus came and spoke to them, saying, 'All authority has been given to Me in heaven and on earth.'"

Consider the vastness of the heavens—all of the authority over them belongs to Jesus. Consider the size of the earth—all of the authority belongs to Jesus. Then His next word is "Therefore." Since all authority belongs to Jesus, we are to "go and make disciples of all the nations" (v. 19). Jesus made it clear that we should go forth to evangelize because our great Lord and Savior Jesus Christ has all authority over heaven and earth.

CASE STUDY

Jeff Harshbarger

The story of my involvement in Satanism is so classic that it's almost cliché. I was a lonely young man from a dysfunctional family. My father was an alcoholic, and things at home got worse until finally, my parents divorced. I was looking for a place to belong. I was looking for people who would pay attention to me and give me acceptance. I was looking for love, caught in the middle of a violent house that left me feeling hopeless and frightened. In response, I started looking to the supernatural for courage and for some mystic power over my early existence. I was ripe for such an experience, and for a long time I had been interested in magic and other aspects of the paranormal. Even as a young boy, I knew that there was a spirit realm, and that there had to be a way to tap into it.

My first contact with Satanism came in 1978 when a snowstorm took my hometown by surprise. I was a 17 year old high school senior, working in a local store during the storm. I was just beginning to wonder how I would get home that night when the store's assistant manager, a young man of just 18, invited me to stay at his apartment, a short walk away.

This young man seemed to have everything that I ever wanted: prestige, power. He gave every indication that he was in control of his life and acted much older than his 18 years. That night, he told me the source of his strength. I was fascinated. He showed me the magic notions and occult objects he had accumulated, and I was convinced. Later that night, we performed a ceremony and I gave my life to Satan.

After I graduated from high school, my "teacher" and I moved away to attend college. The two of us attempted to begin our own satanic coven. Our coven was to consist of thirteen disciples but we were only able to recruit six, all of them males. The six of us shared a house, where we conducted what I call "freelance" satanic rituals, creating and improvising ceremonies freely. Coven activities included casting spells and desecrating Bibles and any other Christian articles that we could get our hands on. During this time I was in contact with demons on a regular basis, though not with Satan himself. Demons were powerful underlings that were at my beck and call . . . or so I thought. Eventually the frightening and distasteful parts of Satanism overshadowed the thrilling parts. I began to worry about where the coven might be headed. I knew that I could not participate in the next step. . . . I knew there were lines that even I would not cross. I wanted out.

I thought at the time, that the only thing left to do was to kill myself. But to my dismay, I failed. I know now that only Divine intervention could have saved me from both the gun and the noose. After returning home, I tried to drink myself into oblivion, but found that the taste of beer turned my stomach. So instead, I lit a cigarette to calm my nerves . . . but it burned my lips! So finally, I, the Satanist priest in the making, went to my room, lay in my bed and began to cry. I will never in my life forget what happened next. It was late at night. The rest of the coven was out partying so the house was empty. Out of the silence I heard a voice from beside my bed

that said "Get Out!" I stopped crying and looked around the room expecting the presence of a demon. This was no demon. The voice moved to the
foot of my bed and said again. "Get Out!" I remember being so shaken at
the command that I immediately obeyed. I crawled out of the nearest window in my bedroom and onto the driveway . . . and into the presence of
God. My knees went weak and I fell on my face; there was no mistaking
who this was. Looking up at the sky I pleaded, "Jesus, just make my life
okay."

I have come a long way from those days in Satanism. I still believe in a
spiritual reality. I believe in both demons and angels, evil and good. I have
simply traded darkness for light. The Lord Jesus Christ has helped me
through complete recovery. I have been married now for 18 years. My wife
Liz and I live in South Carolina. With God's help I have earned a M.A. in
Pastoral Counseling and have launched *Refuge Ministries*. Together, we
instruct others about the dangers of the Occult, New Age beliefs and other
false teachings. We don't just work with former Satanists; I know how it
feels to be a lonely and confused person, driven to despair. We are here for
whoever the Lord would send.[84]

CONCLUSION

Satanism will continue to grow because it offers something many people are interested in: metaphysical, supernatural excitement wrapped in the shiny package of
immorality. Do not ever play games with Satan. Some people will tell you to rebuke
the devil or to stand up to the devil; there are people who might even tell you to
pronounce curses on the devil. This is the height of foolishness. Michael the
archangel did not dare to rebuke him, and neither should you. If the prince of the
angels, Michael, who led the army that expelled Satan from heaven did not *dare*
rebuke Satan even after Calvary and the resurrection, for fear of some kind of retal-
iation, what makes you think *you* have the power to do so? This encounter was

---

84. My testimony does not represent LeVeyan or Traditional Satanism. I was an eclectic of self-styled
Satanist.

recorded for the Church so we could learn something from it. Take this very good advice to heart and do not try to take Satan on in your own strength, because he is far too powerful. The only victory the Christian has in dealing with Satan is in the name of Jesus Christ.

The end of this age will be a time of trouble, evil, and unparalleled wickedness. The Bible tells us that the forces of darkness will break loose upon the earth. In the face of this horror, we must rest in the security that greater is He that is in us than he that is in the world (1 John 4:4). Memorize this passage from Ephesians 6, and put on the whole armor of God:

> Therefore take up the whole armor of God, that you may be able to withstand in the evil day, and having done all, to stand. Stand therefore, having girded your waist with truth, having put on the breastplate of righteousness, and having shod your feet with the preparation of the gospel of peace; above all, taking the shield of faith with which you will be able to quench all the fiery darts of the wicked one. And take the helmet of salvation, and the sword of the Spirit, which is the word of God. (vv. 13–17)

Only when we are protected by God's armor can we withstand any battle against the archenemy of Christ and his fallen servants. The true battle is not against flesh; it is spiritual. The armor of a warrior of God is spiritual armor, but Paul compared each piece to a physical set of armor so that you can mentally don each piece of your protection—from head to foot—and use it wisely.

Satanism and *The Satanic Bible* will yield before the Christian who kneels before the Lord praying; it *must* yield to the Christian who calls on the name of Jesus—that name which is above every name. All of Christ's enemies will one day bow at His feet. Those who denied the historical Jesus; those who thought Him a myth in Scripture; those who denied His virgin birth, sinless life, and miracles; those who lowered His status to a mere man, who called Him a magician or labeled Him an occultist; those who put their words into His mouth; and all living and dead, past, present, and future, will bow their knee to the majesty of Jesus Christ and confess that He alone is Lord, to the glory of God the Father. What a day that will be!

Remember the warning of Jesus: "Do not rejoice in this, that the spirits are subject to you, but rather rejoice because your names are written in heaven" (Luke 10:20). Let us rejoice that through Calvary, God has inscribed our names in heaven, and because of Jesus Christ, we can love the Satanists, despise Satanism, and go forth to be more than conquerors through Him who loves us.

RECOMMENDED RESOURCES

1. Frederickson, Bruce G. *Satanism*. St. Louis: Concordia, 1995.

2. Martin, Walter. *The Church of Satan*. CD/audiotape, Walter Martin Ministries, www.waltermartin.com.

3. Martin, Walter. *Witchcraft and Satanism*. CD/audiotape, Walter Martin Ministries, www.waltermartin.com.

4. Mayhue, Richard. *Unmasking Satan*. Wheaton, IL: Victor, 1988.

5. Schwarz, Ted and Duane Empey. *Satanism: Is Your Family Safe?* Grand Rapids: Zondervan, 1988.

- Pagans define Witchcraft as a practice centered on the casting of spells and working of magick; it may involve the worship of individual deities (polytheism).

- Wicca is a religion focused on the worship of the Lord and Lady, and other goddesses and gods; it is based on nature magic and Hindu/New Age thought.

- Neopaganism is the worship of ancient Pagan deities: it is an umbrella term for all Pagan beliefs, such as Goddess worship, Witchcraft, Wicca, Druidism, shamanism, and other non-Christian belief systems.

- Neopagan beliefs can be animistic (all objects—including the universe— have a soul), pantheistic (the divine is present within the life of all things), panentheistic (the divine is in all and greater than all), or all three.

- Neopaganism views the biblical God as one of many gods or as an aspect of the One universal goddess/god; Jesus is simply a wise man and possibly even a Witch.[1]

- There is no such thing as "evil" or original sin; reincarnation replaces salvation.

---

1. "I believe he [Jesus] was a Witch. He worked miracles or what we would call magic, cured people and did most things expected from a Witch. He had his coven of thirteen." (Arnold Crowther and Patricia Crowther, *The Secrets of Ancient Witchcraft with the Witches Tarot* (Secaucus, NJ: University Books, 1974), 164.

12

Goddess Worship, Witchcraft, and Wicca

There exists today no realm of the occult as infamous as Witchcraft, and yet its modern definition remains as elusive and varied as the people who practice it.[2] Today, the "craft" is multifaceted, permeating a "live and let live society" wide open to embracing it. The revival of Ancient Paganism in its modern form of Neopaganism was spearheaded by a renewed fascination with Witchcraft including spin-offs such as Wicca and the Celtic-based Druids.[3] Where once Witchcraft was anathema, its very name conjuring fear, humiliation, and the sentence of horrific death, today it wears the protective mantle of religious tolerance and the seductive garment of fantasy, an illusion skillfully woven by author J. K. Rowling and the Hollywood elite.

The *Harry Potter* juggernaut spawned a fascination with all things *magical*, transforming a mildly growing twentieth-century public interest into a twenty-first-century obsession.[4] In 1972, there were approximately twenty thousand organized coven members in the United States, with the number increasing to

---

2. Neopagans do not capitalize Witchcraft since they consider it a practice and not a religion (even though it fits easily into the etymology of religion). The Bible refers to Witchcraft in the context of polytheism, so a capital is used in every section—except the one entitled Witchcraft and Wicca—to emphasize the biblical definition.

3. Anthropologist Linda Jencson noted in *Anthropology Today* that, "Neo-Paganism refers to the revival of pre-Christian Pagan gods, goddesses and spirits, their worship and ritual manipulation. It also involves an animistic sense of spiritual power and a reverence for nature. Neopagans focus much of their spiritual practice upon practical results, the ability to affect their environment through magical means." Linda Jencson, "Neo-Paganism and the great mother goddess," *Anthropology Today* 5, No 2, (1989), JSTORStable URL http://links.jstor.org/sici?sici=0268-540X%28198904%295%3a2%3c2%3ANATGMG%3E2.0.CO%3B2-%23 (accessed June 28, 2007).

4. The spelling of the word *magical* was changed to *magickal* by famous occultist Aleister Crowley (c. 1915) to distinguish it from stage magic. It was used by students of his such as Gerald Gardner, the founder of Wicca, to refer to the specific working of spells. The online *Llewellyn Encyclopedia* defines it as follows: "Magick is the science and art of causing change (in consciousness) to occur in conformity with will, using means not currently understood by traditional Western science." More information available at http://www.llewellynencyclopedia.com/term/magick (accessed June 21, 2007).

approximately fifty thousand members by 1982.⁵ In 1990, J. Gordon Melton's *New Age Almanac* noted the difficulty in determining the exact number of practicing Witches—as each Witch or coven is autonomous—and estimated their number at one thousand to five thousand covens (or about thirteen thousand to sixty-five thousand people, based on thirteen members per coven).⁶ Today, with the popularty of the *Harry Potter* books and movies, the Covenant of the Goddess website places the number of Witches in North America alone (under the classification of Neopagans) at a conservative two hundred thousand to six hundred thousand.⁷ Worldwide estimates are likely in the millions.⁸

Although the media elite and some Christian leaders scoffed at the power of Potter to influence young lives, the fact soon became clear that devotees of Witchcraft recognized opportunity when it came knocking. Some practicing Witches saw the chance Harry Potter afforded (and the dollar signs he generated) and took advantage of it, using the Potter mystique to teach and promote the Craft (as it is commonly called) to children. An example of this is Oberon Zell-Ravenheart's successful manual of Witchcraft, *Grimoire for the Apprentice Wizard*, aimed directly at young readers. A brief look at the table of contents reveals Zell-Ravenheart's intent:

Course One: **Wizardry**
Class I: Concerning Wizards
Class II: Becoming a Wizard
Class III: Foundations of Magick
Class IV: Magickal Arts
Class V: Magickal Talents
Class VI: Perchance to Dream

5. Godwin, *Occult America,* 66; Petersen, *Those Curious New Cults in the 80s,* 72. Additional data posted on Adherents.com, Wicca, http://www.adherents.com/Na/Na_666.html#422 (accessed June 28, 2007).
6. Melton, Clark and Kelly, New Age Almanac, 340.
7. Covenant of the Goddess, "Witchcraft: Commonly-Asked Questions, Straightforward Answers," http://www.cog.org/wicca/faq.html (accessed June 14, 2007); see more Poll Results at http://www.cog.org/05poll/poll_results.html and http://web.archive.org/web/20000304090749/www.cog.org/cogpoll_prelim.html (accessed June 14, 2007). The wide numeric variation may be indicative of the number of privately practicing Witches.
8. Adherents.com, "Major Religions of the World Ranked by Number of Adherents," http://www.adherents.com/Religions_By_Adherents.html#Neo-Paganism (accessed June 16, 2007). Statistics based on multiple sources.

Class VII: Patterns of Magick

Course Two: **Nature**

Course Three: **Practice**

Course Four: **Rites**[9]

Zell-Ravenheart follows J. K. Rowling's lead in identifying male Witches as *wizards*—a term that is less threatening, but historically inaccurate. The roots of the word *wizard* can be traced to Middle English (c. 1440) where it is translated "sage" or "wise," but other European roots clearly link it to the term *Witch*. A study of the words *wizard* and *Witch* prove they are synonymous and unrelated to gender.[10] Witchcraft in all its varied forms is now a worldwide phenomenon that shows little sign of abating. Witches define the term *Witch* selectively, choosing from endlessly long Old English descriptions the meaning that most appeals to them. According to the Covenant of the Goddess website the word *Witch*, "derives from an Indo-European root word meaning to bend or change or do magic/religon (making it related to 'wicker,' 'wiggle,' and even 'vicar.')"[11]

Historically, a Witch is a male or a female who uses supernatural powers for good or evil ends, hence, the designation in some circles of a *white* or a *black* Witch. But Neopagans do not necessarily accept the existence of supernatural power, believing instead in the inherent power of the *natural* (positive energy present in all things). This redefinition of the term *supernatural* allows them to categorically reject the evil or occult aspect of power, in that they simply do not believe in Satan and so the terms *white Witchcraft* or *black Witchcraft* cannot apply to them.

The most ancient definition of the word *Witch*, however, is more than likely found in the Hebrew word *kashaph*, meaning, "to whisper a spell, i.e. to enchant or practise magic."[12] In essence, the Bible defines a *Witch* as a medium or sorcerer

---

9. Zell-Ravenheart, *Grimoire for the Apprentice Wizard*, 1.
10. Online Etymology Dictionary, "Wizard," http://www.etymonline.com/index.php?search=wizard&searchmode=none (accessed June 14, 2007).
11. Covenant of the Goddess Website, "Witchcraft: Commonly-Asked Questions, Straightforward Answers," http://www.cog.org/wicca/faq.html (accessed June 14, 2007).
12. New Exhaustive Strong's Numbers and Concordance with Expanded Greek-Hebrew Ditionary, Biblesoft.

who summons occult powers to do their bidding. This definition is supported by what appears to be the most ancient Semitic text discovered to date, a text that also happens to be Egyptian. "Come, come to my house," and "Turn aside, O my beloved" are spells carved on the chamber walls of Egyptian royal tombs, intended to protect kings and queens from desecration. This text not only demonstrates the blending of Egyptian and Canaanite cultures, but it also confirms the presence of spells, which implies the presence of Witchcraft and Witches in antiquity, and their intent to influence or change the world around them.[13]

God stated from the time of His first interaction with man that He was *not* the source of Witchcraft's power:

> When you come into the land which the LORD your God is giving you, you shall not learn to follow the abominations of those nations. There shall not be found among you anyone who makes his son or his daughter pass through the fire, or one who practices Witchcraft, or a soothsayer, or one who interprets omens, or a sorcerer, or one who conjures spells, or a medium, or a Spiritist, or one who calls up the dead. For all who do these things are an abomination to the LORD, and because of these abominations the LORD your God drives them out from before you. (Deut. 18:9–13).

God clearly indicated the extent of His loathing for anything connected with the practice of Witchcraft in Deuteronomy and also in Exodus 22:18 when He said, "You shall not permit a sorceress to live."

If Witches are not drawing power from God, then it is patently obvious they must be getting it from another source. They can call that source whatever they would like to call it—elemental forces, magic, or the universe—but they are still drawing their power from a source other than God, and He reveals the name of that source as Satan (Job 1–2; Ex. 7:10; Matt. 4:9). God is the only source of the power of goodness, and Satan is the only *other* power source—an evil one that fuels the world of the occult. In reality, there are no goddesses or gods, only demons masquerading as deities.

---

13. Excerpt from Laurie Copans, "Spell May Comprise Oldest Semitic Text, Discovery Channel, http://dsc.discovery.com/news/2007/01/25/snakespell_arc.html?category=archaeology&guid=20070 125141500 (accessed September 10, 2007).

The practice of occult rites, or secret mysteries, has no part in Judaism or in Christianity. Spells, curses, and any method used to attain personal goals is never connected with Christianity. It is never, ever authorized by the Bible unless it is wrenched out of context, and if that is the case, it cannot logically be applied in support of Witchcraft. In essence, Witchcraft itself is nothing more than the practice of occultism. It is an attempt to manipulate forces in order to accomplish personal ends, and people all over the world today are attempting it.

From a biblical perspective, the ancient religion of Witchcraft has maintained its key beliefs and practices throughout many millennia, tracing its polytheistic roots to the time when Moses first recorded God's prohibition against it (c. 1400 BC). Although modern Pagans dispute the "religious" nature of Paganism and Witchcraft (and do not capitalize these names in order to indicate a *spiritual path* instead of a *religion*), its organized belief system still fits easily into the definition of religion.[14]

Wicca is a modern derivative of ancient Witchcraft that willingly claims the actual label of "religion." It can be traced directly to the influence of famous occultist Aleister Crowley (1875–1947) and one of his followers, Gerald Gardner (1884–1964), and is centered around the worship of the *Lord* and *Lady*, although it includes many other goddesses and gods.[15] It is here, interestingly enough, that the influence of Simon Magus—the sorcerer rebuked by the apostle Peter in Acts 8:9—can be found, indicating a possible ancient source for the roots of Wicca. The

---

14. *Religion*, c.1200, "state of life bound by monastic vows," also "conduct indicating a belief in a divine power," from Anglo-Fr. religiun (11c.), from O.Fr. *religion* "religious community," from L. *religionem* (nom. *religio*) "respect for what is sacred, reverence for the gods," in L.L. "monastic life" (5c); according to Cicero, derived from *relegare* "go through again, read again," from *re-* "again" + *legere* "read" (see lecture). However, popular etymology among the later ancients (and many modern writers) connects it with *religare* "to bind fast" (see rely), via notion of "place an obligation on," or "bond between humans and gods." Another possible origin is *religiens*, "careful," opposite of *negligens*; meaning "particular system of faith" is recorded from c. 1300. [Douglas Harper, "religion," Online Etymology Dictionary, http://www.etymonline.com/index.php?search=religion&searchmode=none (accessed June 21, 2007).]

15. Aleister Crowley, who labeled himself "The Beast 666" was an occultist who in 1898 became involved with the *Hermetic Order of the Golden Dawn*, a secret society formed in England by Kabbalists, Freemasons, and some members of the Rosicrucian Fellowship. It was originally formed to continue the work of Theosophy, but became centered instead on occultism, gradually deteriorating due to inflated egos and infighting. Its most lasting achievement is the *Cipher Manuscript*, a work whose roots remain obscure. The Golden Dawn appropriated the occult text and embellished it, and it has since become an important work for many modern esoteric religions. Crowley's secretary, Israel Regardie, published the foundational work on magic entitled, *The Golden Dawn*.

Roman historian and bishop Hippolytus (c. 170 AD) described the doctrine of Magus in detail in his *Philosophumena*:

> The disciples, then, of this (Magus), celebrate magical rites, and resort to incantations. And (they profess to) transmit both love-spells and charms, and the demons said to be senders of dreams, for the purpose of distracting whomsoever they please. . . . "And they have an image of Simon (fashioned) into the figure of Jupiter, and (an image) of Helen [Simon's paramour] in the form of Minerva; and they pay adoration to these." But they call the one Lord and the other Lady. And if any one amongst them, on seeing the images of either Simon or Helen, would call them by name, he is cast off, as being ignorant of the mysteries.[16]

Wiccans usually practice herbal magic and abide by the Rede doctrine, "An it harm none, do what ye will," and the Threefold Law, which dictates that whatever Wiccans do (whether good or "evil") will return to them at three times the force.[17] This is the Wiccan version of Hindu karma.

All Wiccans do not claim to be Witches, and all Witches do not claim to be Wiccan. This is the elusive nature of Neopaganism. Some Wiccans maintain that they do not practice any magick, stating that their focus is only on the Wheel of the Year (observing the eight holidays or *sabbats*), and personal spirituality. Witches who are not Wiccan abide by the basic creed "Do what you will," minus the "harm none" clause.

EIGHT WITCHES/WICCAN/PAGAN SABBATS[18]

Winter Solstice/Yule
Northern Hemisphere: Dec 21
Southern Hemisphere: June 21

---

16. Hippolytus, *Philosophumena*, (Philosophumena.com), http://www.philosophumena.com/book_vi.htm (accessed Junes 29, 2007).
17. Gardner, *The Meaning of Witchcraft*, 108. The *Rede* was copied by Gardner from Aleister Crowley's "Do what thou wilt shall be the whole of the Law. Love is the Law, Love under Will." *Rede* is Old English for counsel or advice. See the Online Etymology Dictionary, "rede," http://www.etymonline.com/index.php?search=rede&searchmode=none (accessed June 21, 2007).
18. Spiritual.com, "Wiccan Sabbats," KTL Enterprieses Pty. Ltd., http://www.spiritualcom.au/articles/Witchcraft/wiccan-sabbats.htm (accessed June 21, 2007).

Winter Solstice, Saturnalia, Alban Arthan

The holiday of Yule was celebrated long before Christians adopted the date. Many of the Christmas traditions we see today stem from old Pagan customs. As the solstice, it is the longest night of the year. From this day forward, light begins to return and we celebrate the rebirth of the Sun God.

Traditions: lighting the Yule log, wreath making, gift giving

Correspondences: pine, holly, myrrh, cinnamon

Imbolc

Northern Hemisphere: Feb 2

Southern Hemisphere: August 1

Candlemas, Imbolg, Brigid's Day

Imbolc is a day to celebrate the first glimpses of spring, and it is also dedicated to the Celtic Goddess Brigid. Non-Pagans celebrate today as Groundhog Day. Make new starts in life, as you give your home a thorough cleaning.

Traditions: burning fires and candles, cleaning, making a bed for Brigid

Correspondences: carnation, rosemary, chamomile, milk

Ostara

Northern Hemisphere: March 21

Southern Hemisphere: Sept 21

Spring Equinox, Lady Day

This is another holiday that has been overlaid with Christian meanings (Easter). Eggs and bunnies are typical symbols, representing new birth and new life. Plant the seeds of long-term goals.

Traditions: coloring eggs, decorating with flowers

Correspondences: jasmine, daffodil, lotus, new spring flowers

Beltane

Northern Hemisphere May 1

Sothern Hemisphere: November 1

May Day, Walpurgis Night

The God born at Yule is now a man, and the sacred marriage between

God and Goddess is consummated [sic].

Beltane is a celebration of fertility, growth, love and passion. However you celebrate Beltane, do it with joy and happiness.

Traditions: dancing around the May Pole, lighting bonfires

Correspondences: rose, lilac, vanilla

Midsummer

Northern Hemisphere: June 21

Southern Hemisphere: December 21

Litha, Summer Solstice, Whitsun

Midsummer is the longest day of the year, and the strength of the Sun God begins to wane. The Goddess has left her Maiden form of Imbolc and is now in her Mother aspect. Refill your herb collection for the coming year.

Traditions: fairy magick, collecting herbs

Correspondences: orange, lemon, honeysuckle, vervain

Lammas

Northern Hemisphere: August 1

Southern Hemisphere: Feb 1

Lughnasadh

As the first of the three harvest festivals, much of the symbolism for Lammas revolves around grains and bread. Sacrifices were common, though mostly symbolic, in order to ensure the continued success of the harvest.

Traditions: Bread baking, making corn dollies

Correspondences: corn, sandalwood, heather

Mabon

Northern Hemisphere: Sept 21

Southern Hemisphere: March 21

Autumn Equinox, Cornucopia

Day and night are equal again, and the weather grows colder as winter approaches. This is the second harvest festival. Rituals of thanks at this time have brought about the modern holidays of Thanksgiving. Take some time to think about what you are thankful for.

Traditions: making and drinking of wine, share with the less fortunate

Correspondences: grapes, blackberries, cedar, patchouli

Samhain

Northern Hemisphere: Oct 31

Southern Hemisphere: April 30

Hallowe'en, All Hallows

Samhain (SOW-en) is the one Sabbat that is also widely celebrated amongst non-Pagans. The God has died, and the Goddess mourns him until his rebirth at Yule. It's the last harvest festival, and the end of the Wiccan year.

Traditions: divination, honoring the dead, carving Jack o' Lanterns

Correspondences: pumpkins, apples, sage, mugwort.

Witchcraft rituals and spells are often (but not always) performed within a circle referred to as *compass round* or *circle round*; they can be "cast" individually or by a high priestess who is usually the chief authority figure within a coven.[19] Innumerable belief systems exist within the millions of sects currently under the umbrella of Neopaganism, but the heart of their teachings is essentially goddess/god worship. They supplant the authority of the God of the Bible with the authority of goddesses and—to a lesser extent—gods, drawing from a long history of Pagan cultures, rituals, and folklore. But no matter what label they may claim, the Bible teaches they are essentially mediums invoking a power other than the power of God; sorcerers, in the classic sense of the biblical term.

WICCAN TRADITIONS

Like many other religions, Wicca is divided into different schools of thought called *traditions*. Key differences between traditions are basically related to ceremonial

---

19. The term coven is thought to derive from the word convent. It was used by Sir Walter Scott in his *Crim. Trials Scot.* III 606, 1662. Scott said, "Ther vold meit bot sometymes a Coven . . . Ther is thretteein persones in ilk Coeven." See Online Etymology Dictionary, http://www.etymonline.com/index.php?search=coven&searchmode=none (accessed June 27, 2007).

procedures and personal preference. Some Witches introduce themselves as being part of a particular tradition, and some do not. Other Witches create their own tradition based on a combination of different beliefs they accept as valid. This individuality is strongly encouraged in most Neopagan belief systems. Some of the more widely accepted Wiccan traditions or sects include the following:

Traditionalist—Teachings are usually based on folklore, literature, or history of the area they live in, such as Scottish tradition, English tradition, and so on. Ancestry plays a key role in Traditionalist Wicca.

Gardnerian—Wiccans consider themselves part of the Gardnerian tradition if their coven is either directly "descended" from Gerald Gardner's coven (the acknowledged founder of Wicca) or if they use Gardnerian rituals. Some covens use the term Neo-Gardnerian to indicate a blending of new ideas with Gardner's original teachings.

Alexandrian—This tradition is based on the teachings of English Witch Alex Sanders (1926–1988). It is very similar to the Gardnerian tradition except for the increased emphasis on ceremonial magic.

Dianic—Originally based on Margaret Murray's (1863–1963) description of Witchcraft as a "Dianic cult," this tradition is now comprised of many different ideas and beliefs. They are usually distinguished by their emphasis on the Goddess, their feminist ideology, and their intense concern for ecology. The Goddess as "Creatrix" is heavily stressed, as is the importance of actively working to preserve the environment.[20]

The New Reformed Orthodox Order of the Golden Dawn—NROOGD was founded by Aidan Kelly and is one of the more active and interactive traditions in the United States. It was "created entirely out of research, poetry, inspiration and the gathering of a small group of good friends."[21] The NROOGD runs the popular Covenant of the Goddess website.

Egyptian or Neteru (The Gods of the Black Land)—Dedicated to the worship of all the gods and goddesses of ancient Egypt; this tradition focuses on everything Egyptian, including the calendar, festivals and holidays, hieroglyphs, religions and philosophies, and ancient Egyptian magic.[22]

20. Adler, *Drawing Down the Moon*, 117–125.
21. Adler, *Drawing Down the Moon*, 120. Adapted from Wicca Traditions.
22. See Wicca.com for more details of Wiccan Traditions, http://www.wicca.com/celtic/wicca/wiccas.htm.

Not all covens who claim to be part of a particular tradition maintain contact with either the founder of the tradition and/or the current promoter of it. Foundational to all Witchcraft (and to Neopaganism as a whole) seems to be a dislike of any centralized authority, and so a "tradition" is usually a flexible belief system easily adjusted to include a diversity of thoughts and practices.

THE GODDESS: YESTERDAY AND TODAY

In dealing with the realm of the Goddess, there is much that can be learned from the teachings of the past. Neopaganism, in all its complexity, is built upon the foundation of Ancient Paganism, confirming Solomon's observation that there is very little new under the sun (Eccl. 1:9). Hippolytus established the antiquity of Goddess worship and its far-reaching influence when he discussed the Pythagoreans, followers of the philosopher and mathematician Pythagoras (570 BC), and their worship of the Goddess as Creator:

And by the Mother, they allege, were created first the four elements, which, they say, are fire, water, earth, air; and these have been projected as an image of the tetrad above; and reckoning the energies of these, for instance, as hot, cold, moist, dry. . . .[23]

The gods and goddesses worshiped by Pagans around the world today are essentially the same ones (or derivatives of those) worshiped in ancient times. Tomb carvings and paintings depicting plump fertility goddesses can be found in cultures scattered around the globe, side by side with their male counterparts. The Mystery religions of Rome reveal the influence of the goddess Cybele. Isis, goddess of ten thousand names, can be found in different forms throughout the Mesopotamian region and into India in the form of the Indian goddess, Kali.[24] A small sampling of the millions of goddesses down through the ages demonstrates that virtually every culture is able to claim the influence of some goddess or another in its long and complex history.

---

23. Hippolytus, Philosophumena, (Philosophumena.com), http://www.philosophumena.com/book_vi.htm (accessed June 29, 2007).
24. David Nelson, "THE MANY FACES OF KALI," Colorado State University, Pueblo, The Virtual Pomegranate, Issue 12, http://chass.colostate-pueblo.edu/natrel/pom/old/POM12a1.html (accessed June 20, 2007).

ANCIENT GODDESSES

Canaanite   *Asherah*—mother goddess (of Syrian and possibly Minoan origin)[25]

Celtic   *Druantia*—known as the Queen of the Druids, goddess of knowledge and fertility

Chinese   *Ch'ang O*—goddess of the moon (also known as Heng-o)

Egyptian   *Isis*—goddess of ten thousand names and goddess of all things

Etruscan   *Albina*—goddess of the dawn and guardian of unlucky lovers

Greek   *Artemis*—goddess of the night and protector of women

Indian   *Kali*—goddess of death (also the goddess over all life from conception to death)

Norse   *Astrild*—goddess of love

Persian   *Anahita*—goddess of fertility

Phoenician   *Astarte*—goddess of love, fertility[26]

Phrygian   *Cybele*—mother goddess of fertility, embraced by the Greeks and Romans[27]

Roman   *Fortuna*—goddess of fate and chance

One of the most high-profile goddesses of the ancient world is Sophia, the powerful philosophical goddess of the Alexandrian Gnostics. Sophia is a goddess who grew from an idea into an actual persona, spreading her influence over the empire of Alexander the Great (356–323 BC) and eventually throughout the Mediterranean world, due to the efforts of early Kabbalists such as Simon Magus and the writings of

---

25. See the Online Jewish Encyclopedia for more information: http://www.jewish encyclopedia.com/view.jsp?artid=1942&letter=A (accessed June 20, 2007).
26. See, Cyrus H. Gordon, *The Common Background of Greek and Hebrew Civilizations,* New York: W. W. Norton & Company, 1965.
27. *Ancient History Sourcebook,* "Lucretius (98-c.55 BCE): The Worship of Cybele," Fordham University, http://www.fordham.edu/halsall/ancient/lucretius-reruma.html (accessed June 20, 2007).

Hermes Trismegistus.[28] Named for *sophia,* the Greek word for wisdom, she came to represent secret knowledge related to the feminine aspect of God.

Widespread polytheism maintained a strong and steady influence on people groups even after the advent of Christianity, as can be seen in the early letters of Bishop Winchester to St. Boniface (d. 755 AD). In 723-724 AD, the bishop wrote to encourage Boniface in his conversion of the "heathen" and to give instructions on how to defend the faith against their beliefs. He instructs Boniface to ask, "Whence or by whom or when was the first god or goddess begotten? Do they believe that gods and goddesses still beget other gods and goddesses? If they do not, when did they cease and why? If they do, the number of gods must be infinite. In such a case, who is the most powerful among these different gods? Surely no mortal man can know. Yet man must take care not to offend this god who is more powerful than the rest."[29] This apologetic argument opens a window into a world long gone and reveals the enduring power and influence of Paganism.[30]

THE BIRTH OF NEOPAGANISM

Today, the world of Rome has returned. The advent of the New Age brought the repeal of England's 1736 Witchcraft Act and the resurgence of Goddess worship under the modern umbrella of Paganism. Witchcraft, with its single-minded dedication to Goddess worship and all its attendant rituals and rites, fits neatly under the Neopagan umbrella. Freedom of religion in the West threw open the door to polytheism, and the Internet fueled its exponential growth. Suddenly, the temple of Isis was within a computer terminal instead of walls of stone, and Cybele could be worshiped with the push of a button. The Canaanite goddess Asherah became a popular name on the Internet, and an ancient statuette of Baal could be bought for a few hundred dollars on the popular online auction site eBay. Neopaganism welcomed the "energies" of the universe to a society stifled by dry scientific formulas, offering Goddess worship as a "new" way of looking at the world.

In Neopaganism, goddesses take precedence over gods, and the focus is usually on the "Mother." The goddess (a general term) is described as having three aspects:

---

28. The same Simon who Peter rebuked in Acts 8:9.
29. Medieval Sourcebook, "The Correspondence of St. Boniface," Fordham University http://www.fordham.edu/halsall/basis/boniface-letters.html (accessed February 11, 2005).
30. See Gordon, *The Common Background of Greek and Hebrew Civilizations.*

1. *Maiden*—New moon; the young huntress with a focus on sexuality
2. *Mother*—Full moon; the nurturing one focused on fertility and supremacy of the female
3. *Crone*—Waning moon; the wise elder focused on the ending of things

The waxing, waning, and full moon phases correspond to the three aspects of the Goddess, who can be an individual deity or multiple aspects of the one Goddess.

In the 1950s, Gerald Gardner's *Book of Shadows* and his high priestess Doreen Valiente's *Mother Change* birthed and mentored a new take on the old Witchcraft traditions of goddess and nature worship that would come to be known as Wicca. The peace-loving, "harmless" philosophy of Wicca bore a striking resemblance to the core principles of Goddess worship, but its new packaging increased the resale value and took Witchcraft to a new level of acceptance—blending the basics of the Craft with goddess theology and popular New Age ideas. The twentieth century saw a resurgence of ancient Pagan beliefs, due largely to the efforts of an aggressive band of Neopagans, interconnected through personal relationships or writings.

KEY LEADERS IN THE NEOPAGAN MOVEMENT

Margot Adler (b. 1946)	Wiccan priestess, author of the definitive work on Neopaganism, *Drawing Down the Moon* (1992), and correspondent for National Public Radio (NPR).
American National Witches Council	Founded in 1974 by seventy-three practicing Witches who believed that Neopagans were misunderstood by the general public, and this misunderstanding needed to be corrected. They authored the thirteen principles of belief that attempted to define "modern Witchcraft."[31] The Council did not represent any single Witchcraft tradition, but their principles became foundational to Wicca. The ANWC disbanded in 1974.

---

31. Council of American Witches, "Principles of Wiccan Beliefs," (Internet Sacred Text Archive), http://www.sacred-texts.com/bos/bos056.htm (accessed June 25, 2007).

Raymond Buckland (b. 1934)	One of the most influential Pagan leaders; considered by some to be the "Father of American Wicca."[32] He corresponded with Gerald Gardner (considered the founder of Wicca) and became a Wiccan in the Gardnerian tradition in 1963. Buckland is credited with "mainstreaming" Wicca. He is the author of more than forty books, including *Witchcraft from the Inside* and *Buckland's Complete Book of Witchcraft*.
Arnold Crowther and Patricia Crowther (b. 1921)	Patricia Crowther is a Wiccan high priestess initiated by Gerald Gardner in 1960. Arnold Crowther, a magician deeply interested in Paganism and Witchcraft, was a longtime friend of Gardner and introduced the two. She is one of the last priestesses with a personal connection to Gardner (and considered by some to be his "spiritual heir"). The Crowthers gained media recognition for their devotion to the Craft. As authors and speakers they traveled widely, founding many covens based on the Gardnerian tradition.
Aleister Crowley (d. 1947)	Dubbed by the press of his day as the "wickedest man in the world," Crowley was the disciple of S. L. Mathers and founder of the Hermetic Order of the Golden Dawn, a secret society steeped in the occult. Crowley called himself the "Great Beast, 666." He is credited with changing the spelling of the word *magic* to *magick* in reference to Witchcraft. Crowley practiced Sex Magick (Tantra), Witchcraft, Satanism, and invented a religion he called Thelema. His most famous works are *Magick in Theory and Practice* and *Liber Legis, the Book of Law*, which includes the

32. See Ray Buckland, http://www.raybuckland.com/ (accessed June 27, 2007).

	phrase that would later become the Wiccan Rede, "Do what thou wilt shall be the whole of the Law. Love is the Law, Love under Will."[33] Modern Pagans generally distance themselves from Crowley and dismiss his considerable influence as negligible.
Phyllis Curott (b. 1954)[34]	An Ivy League lawyer, Curott was formally initiated into Wicca in 1985. Her first work, *Book of Shadows*, chronicles her spiritual journey, including her "profound" discovery of the Goddess through a Tarot reading done by a Wiccan high priestess. Curott is currently intent on redefining Wicca by disputing and refuting the Wiccan Rede and the Threefold Law in her book *Witch Crafting* (2001).[35]
Stewart Farrar (d. 2000) and Janet Farrar (b. 1970)	English Witches credited with strongly influencing the growth and spread of Wicca. The Farrars' *Eight Sabbats for Witches* (1981) and *The Witches' Way* (1984), along with Stewart Farrar's book *What Witches Do* (1971) represent the Alexandrian Witchcraft tradition (which both eventually left). Janet Farrar's recent writings are viewed as foundational to the Neo-Alexandrian Witchcraft tradition.
Dion Fortune (d. 1946)	Founder of the Society of Inner Light, Fortune was a trance medium and member of the Theosophical Society and the Hermetic Order of the Golden Dawn. Fortune is best known for her *Inner Light*

33. Hugh Urban, "Unleashing the Beast," Michigan State University, http://www.esoteric.msu.edu/VolumeV/Unleashing_the_Beast.htm#_edn15 (accessed June 27, 2007).
34. No official birth date is easily found for Ms. Curott, but a 1996 New York Times article refers to her as age 42. See http://query.nytimes.com/gst/fullpage.html?res=9500E6DD1339F933A05755C0A960958260 (accessed June 27, 2007).
35. Guy Spiro, "A Conversation with Phyllis Curott," The Monthly Aspecterian, September 2001, http://www..lightworks.com/monthlyAspectarian/2001/September/conversation2.htm (accessed June 27, 2007).

	magazine and her works, *The Mystical Qabalah* and *The Cosmic Doctrine*.
Gerald Gardner (d. 1964)	A student of Aleister Crowley and Witchcraft in general, Gardner remains a pivotal figure in the history of modern Witchcraft. More than likely influenced by the work of Dion Fortune and Margaret Murray, Gardner eventually founded the Wiccan Gardnerian Witchcraft tradition and authored perhaps the most influential book in Wicca known as *Book of Shadows* (thought to have been heavily influenced by Crowley).[36] Gardner mentored Raymond Buckland and initiated him into Wicca.
Sybil Leek (d. 1983)	Descended from a family of English Witches, Leek openly characterized herself as a "white Witch." She was an astrologer and prolific occult author whose candid public discussion of the Craft led to the intense media scrutiny focused on the rebirth of Witchcraft during the 1960s. Leek's work includes *Diary of a Witch* and *Reincarnation: The Second Chance*.
Charles G. Leland (d. 1903)	Leland was a prolific writer on folklore traditions. One of his fifty books, *Aradia, or the Gospel of the Witches*—detailing Leland's thoughts on an underground Witchcraft movement practicing in Tuscany during the 1890s—had an enormous influence upon the emerging Neopagan movement. It is thought that Gerald Gardner and Doreen Valiente studied Leland's writings.
Margaret Murray (d. 1963).	Controversial Pagan anthropologist and Egyptologist who analyzed court records made during the

---

36. Roger Dearnaley, "The Influence of Aleister Crowley upon 'Ye Bok of ye Art Magical,'" Cyprian.org, http://web.archive.org/web/20050831193708/www.cyprian.org/Articles/CrowleyBAM0.html (accessed June 25, 2007).

	"Burning Times" (referring to the Witchcraft trials held during medieval times) and published her findings in *The Witch-Cult in Western Europe* (1921) and *God of the Witches* (1933). Her conclusion that many of the accused Witches executed did not recant their belief in Witchcraft (often proudly affirming it) caused consternation within the Pagan community. In addition to this, she proposed the unpalatable notions that human sacrifice, cannibalism, and sexual orgies existed within fertility (Witchcraft) cults down through antiquity. It is thought that Gerald Gardner based portions of his work on Murray's teachings.
Israel Regardie (d. 1985)	Aleister Crowley's secretary and student. Regardie authored *The Golden Dawn*, a work that revealed the secret beliefs and practices of the clandestine society known as the Hermetic Order of the Golden Dawn. Many consider Regardie's *The Golden Dawn* to be the foundational work on magic. He is credited with engineering the rebirth of occult magic.
Starhawk (b. 1951)	Born Miriam Simos, Starhawk is the activist founder of the Reclaiming tradition of Wicca, which focuses on earth magic or *permaculture*, the healing of the soil, water, and other natural elements through magic. She is a well-known author (*The Spiral Dance* and *The Fifth Sacred Thing)* and seminar speaker.
Doreen Valiente (d. 1999)	Gardner met Doreen Valiente (sometimes called the "Mother of Modern Witchcraft")[37] and initiated her into his coven. Valiente became the high priestess and later admitted to editing Gardner's work (to diminish the Crowley influence). She is generally credited with cofounding the Gardnerian Witchcraft tradition.

37. See Doreen Valiente, http://www.doreenvaliente.com (accessed June 27, 2007).

In 1975, after the disintegration of the American National Witches Council, a second attempt was made to unify the disorganized and autonomous Neopagan movement. As Margot Adler recounts it, "A more successful attempt to form an alliance of Wiccan groups took place in northern California on the Summer Solstice in 1975. Thirteen covens and several solitary Witches ratified the Covenant of the Goddess (COG) after a number of covens in California expressed the desire to build closer bonds, in part out of a concern over harassment and persecution."[38]

The planned centralization of the Craft could not be accomplished completely, however, due to the freewheeling nature of Neopaganism. Unity in all things amongst a fiercely independent following was impossible, so leaders settled for semi-unity in the form of the following statement: "We could not define what a Witch is in words. Because there are too many differences. Our reality is intuitive. We know when we encounter someone who we feel is worshipping in the same way, who follows the same religion we do, and that's our reality, and that has to be understood, somehow, in anything we do."[39]

Aidan Kelly, one of the main leaders behind the Covenant of the Goddess, suggested Pagans base their organization on the bylaws format of congregational churches, in order to set the precedent for Wiccans as separate "autonomous congregations."[40] The COG, while bringing some semblance of order to the disorganized realm of Witchcraft, did not claim the authority to dictate either doctrine or policy, but did define a basic code of ethics:

1. An ye harm none, do as ye will.
2. No one may offer initiations for money, nor charge initiates money to learn the Craft.
3. Any Witch may charge reasonable fees to the public.
4. Witches shall respect the autonomy of other Witches.
5. All Witches shall respect the secrecy of the Craft.
6. In any public statement Witches should distinguish whether we are speaking for ourselves, our coven, or our Church.
7. All these Ethics are interwoven and derive from Craft Law.[41]

---

38. Adler, *Drawing Down the Moon*, 103.
39. Adler, *Drawing Down the Moon*, 104.
40. Adler, *Drawing Down the Moon*, 104.
41. Adler, *Drawing Down the Moon*, 105.

Today, the Goddess tradition expressed in Wicca and Witchcraft is actively studied and taught worldwide, as evidenced by the flood of literature now available in bookstores and on the Internet. New leaders have emerged on the Neopagan scene, advocating social activism in the form of ecofeminism: the linking of goddess power and the preservation of the earth. One of these leaders is a Witch self-named Starhawk, who travels the world promoting her ecofeminist Reclaiming tradition of Witchcraft. Starhawk actively seeks to promote the growth of Witchcraft through education and practice. In her training manual, *Circle Round: Raising Children in Goddess Traditions,* she offers rituals, traditions, songs, crafts, and personal stories like the following, all intended to promote the culture of Goddess worship:

> Not long ago I [Starhawk] was part of a circle of women celebrating the First Blood ritual of my Goddess-daughter Shannon. We walked a labyrinth cut into a meadow on a ridge of the coastal mountains; we strung necklaces of blessings and beads; we bathed her in a clear stream trickling through a grotto of moss-covered rocks. The ritual felt as ancient as the spirals we traced on her back and shoulders with henna paste, and at the same time as contemporary as the self-tanning cream her mother added to the paste to make the designs last longer. In that way, our ritual was a perfect expression of the old/new character of the Goddess tradition itself: primeval as the big-bellied sculptures of Paleolithic cave dwellers, modern as the thousands of Pagans linked on the Internet.[42]

Goddess worship, Witchcraft, and Wicca are different labels for very similar belief systems—like endless varieties of cereal sitting on a grocery store shelf. Their specially designed boxes may look different, taste different, and be composed of different ingredients, but they are all *cereal.* The presence of the Goddess has emerged in the twenty-first century as a power to be reckoned with in world cultures. And on this ancient foundation of polytheistic worship, the practice of Witchcraft and Wicca thrives.

---

42. Starhawk, Baker and Hill, *Circle Round: Raising Children in Goddess Traditions,* 11.

COMMON TEACHINGS IN GODDESS WORSHIP, WITCHCRAFT, AND WICCA[43]

1. Witchcraft is a *practice*; Wicca is a *religion*.[44] The worship of goddesses/gods is foundational to both Witchcraft and Wicca.

2. Multiple goddesses and gods exist as "spirit parts" of the universe. Wicca believes they are different aspects of the *One* universal goddess/god (the Mother and the Great Horned God). Witchcraft views them as individual, unique deities. All the cultures on earth have different and valid names for these deities.

3. The earth is alive—she is the Goddess. (*Pantheism*—God is in all) Everything on the earth is part of her "living body." (*Animism*—objects have souls)

4. All living things are sacred; recognize the divine. Wiccans often begin or conclude rites by saying to each other, "Thou art Goddess" or "Thou art God."

5. Experience is the most important thing; beliefs are secondary. There is no "right" way to believe. Every belief system is valid—truth is found in experience not dogma. The universe is like a puzzle and no one can say they know the right way of putting it together.

6. Goddesses and gods have supernatural powers and wisdom that can help people if they take the time to study and learn from them.

7. Human beings, as part of the divine, contain energy that can be used to effect changes in the world around them.

8. The Circle of Life consists of birth, maturity, death, and rebirth.

9. After death, the spirit goes to a place of beauty and peace called the Summerland, where it considers the things it should have learned in its previous life. When all the lessons have been pondered and assimilated, the spirit is free to be reborn into a new form.

10. The Summerland is not heaven, and not all spirits must reincarnate. They may choose to stay and act as spirit-guides for the people they love or if they do not need to reincarnate, they may be reunited with the Goddess.

11. A soul that chooses to reincarnate also chooses the lesson it needs to learn. Once back on earth, it does not remember the lesson and must discover what it is.

---

43. These are general teachings as outlined by the Witch Starhawk, and all Neo-Pagans do not necessarily subscribe to them.

44. This is the position of most Pagans, but its truth is debatable since Witchcraft fits the definition of "religion" in virtually all respects.

12.   There is no such thing as original sin, evil or Satan. People may harbor negative energies within them, but most are basically good.

13.   It is not possible to call up the dead, but they often communicate to the living in dreams.[45]

14.   Magick is a way to change things within and without. It affects the energy surrounding individuals and when that energy changes, people or circumstances change. Magick can heal and accomplish good things.

15.   Bad magick exists, but if a Pagan chooses to *send it out*, it will more than likely rebound on them.

16.   All life depends on the four sacred elements air, fire, water, and earth. All rituals rely upon their energy.

17.   A fifth element called the *spirit* is found in the *center:* the inside of a person. It is the place where love is felt.[46]

The basic beliefs of Wicca mirror Witchcraft's beliefs, which in turn mirror the principles of Goddess worship. There are endless variations within different groups of Witches, but the core values remain essentially the same.

THE DRUIDS

As early as 200 BC, Greco-Roman historians recorded fascinating and fantastic details of the priest/sorcerer sect known as the Druids.[47] The Roman emperor Julius Caesar confirmed their existence and influence in 59 BC, when he encountered them during the course of the Gallic wars. His insights are the most complete and so the most intriguing of all the historians, based on his personal observations and notes:

> Throughout Gaul there are two classes of men of some dignity and importance. . . . One of the two classes is that of the Druids, the other that of the knights. The Druids are concerned with the worship of the gods, look after public and private sacrifice, and expound religious matters. A large number

---

45. Many Neopagans would disagree with the idea that it is "impossible" to call up the dead.
46. Summerland is also called the Isle of Apples or the Land of Youth.
47. Green, *The World of the Druids,* 39.

of young men flock to them for training and hold them in high honour. For they have the right to decide nearly all public and private disputes and they also pass judgment and decide rewards and penalties in criminal and murder cases and in disputes concerning legacies and boundaries. When a private person or a tribe disobeys their ruling they ban them from attending at sacrifices. This is their harshest penalty. Men placed under this ban are treated as impious wretches; all avoid them, fleeing their company and conversation, lest their contact bring misfortune upon them; they are denied legal rights and can hold no official dignity. . . . It is thought that this [the Druidic] system of training was invented in Britain and taken over from there to Gaul, and at the present time diligent students of the matter mostly travel there to study it.

The Druids are wont to be absent from war, nor do they pay taxes like the others. . . . It is said that they commit to memory immense amounts of poetry. And so some of them continue their studies for twenty years. They consider it improper to entrust their studies to writing. . . . I think they established this practice for two reasons, because they were unwilling, first, that their system of training should be bruited abroad among the common people, and second, that the student should rely on the written word and neglect the exercise of his memory. . . . They are chiefly anxious to have men believe the following: that souls do not suffer death, but after death pass from one body to another; and they regard this as the strongest incentive to valour, since the fear of death is disregarded. They have also much knowledge of the stars and their motion, of the size of the world and of the earth, of natural philosophy, and of the powers and spheres of action of the immortal gods, which they discuss and hand down to their young students.[48]

Hippolytus recorded in the *Philosophumena* that the Druids were followers of Pythagoras and his philosophy:

The Druids among the Celts enquired with the greatest minuteness into the Pythagorean philosophy, Zamolxis, Pythagoras' slave, a Thracian by

---

48. Green, *The World of the Druids*, 10.

race, being for them the author of this discipline. He after Pythagoras'
death traveled into their country and became as far as they were concerned
the founder of this philosophy.

The Celts glorify the Druids as prophets and as knowing the future
because they foretell to them some things by the ciphers and numbers of
the Pythagoric art. On the principles of which same art we shall not be
silent, since some men have ventured to introduce heresies constructed
from them. Druids, however, also make use of magic arts."[49]

Some historians viewed the Druids as scientists, brilliant philosophers, and
administrators; others considered them barbarians who practiced human sacrifice
involving cannibalism, stabbings, and burnings in secret ceremonies held among
the oak groves.[50] It is also possible that the recently discovered evidence for giant
cage sacrifices—involving hundreds of victims who were imprisoned in giant,
wooden cages suspended from trees and then set on fire—were somehow related to
the Druids. Julius Caesar noted, "Those who are suffering from serious illness or
are in the midst of the dangers of battle, either put to death human beings as sacrificial victims or take part in these sacrifices. . . . They believe that the immortal
gods delight more in the slaughter of those taken in theft or brigandage or some
crime, but when the supply of that kind runs short they descend even to the sacrifice of the innocent."[51]

Although modern scholars submit that ritual sacrifice was rare among the
Druids, ancient historians often refute this conclusion. Diordorus Siculus, in his
Library of History, corroborates Julius Caesar's observations on Druid human sacrifice: "In matters of great concern they devote to death a human being and plunge
a dagger into him . . . and when the stricken victim has fallen they read the future
from the manner of his fall and from the twitching of his limbs, as well as from the
gushing of his blood."[52]

49. Hippolytus, *Philosophumena,* http://books.google.com/books?id=0lrDy9nn1doC&dq=hippolytus+
    philosophumena&printsec=frontcover&source=web&ots=QgPvoe03pf&sig=FkxYkSxOkDPv3Itoa
    Vm4VeBsPOU (accessed June 29, 2007).
50. Green, *The World of the Druids,* 52. "Pliny, Suetonius, Tacitus and Lucan all speak with disgust about
    the Druids, referring to them as uncouth and savage."—Miranda J. Green.
51. Green, *The World of the Druids,* 72. See also Caesar, Gallic War VI 13.
52. Green, *The World of the Druids,* 73. See also Diordorus Siculus, Library of History, V, 31, 3.

First-century historian Pliny the Elder confirmed the link between Druids and sorcery, and he pointed to the origin of the name *Druid* in his *Natural History*. "The magicians perform no rites without using the foliage of those trees [oaks] . . . it may be supposed that it is from this custom that they get their name of Druids, from the Greek word meaning 'oak.'"[53]

Druid theology consisted of the following basic beliefs:

1. There are many gods and goddesses.
2. "Powers and spheres of action of the immortal gods" exist.[54]
3. Human souls do not die; they move from one body to another body at the moment of death.
4. A silent, dark Hades exists, but humans do not go there.
5. Divination is necessary to know the will of the gods.
6. Mediators (Druids) are necessary between the gods and men (ceremonies possibly included the use of a special "language of the gods.")[55]
7. Magical arts are needed to accomplish the will of the gods.
8. Magical wands (in the form of wooden staffs) carved with symbols are integral to sacred ceremonies.[56]

The role of women in Druidism is more difficult to determine, but according to archaeologist Miranda J. Green, Druidesses more than likely existed, practicing what is best described as Witchcraft. "It is not always easy to make positive identification of female images as those of female religious officials, let alone Druidesses. But archaeological evidence does suggest that Witchcraft—representing the dark aspect of religion, perhaps more properly termed superstition—may have been practiced in Celtic Europe."[57] The link between the Druids and Witchcraft has been established historically and archaeologically. Their methods reflect the rituals of even more ancient societies, providing irrefutable proof that Paganism permeated the history of mankind.

---

53. Green, *The World of the Druids*, 9. See also Pliny the Elder, *Natural History*, XVI95.
54. Green, *The World of the Druids*, 49. See also Caesar, *Gallic War VI*, 13.
55. Green, *The World of the Druids*, 49. See also Lucan, *Pharsalia* I, 441ff.
56. Green, *The World of the Druids*, 62.
57. Green, *The World of the Druids*, 93.

In the wake of the New Age movement, the ancient cult of the Druids sprang to life in Great Britain, Wales, and Ireland, spreading like wildfire in a culture suddenly enamored with the supernatural. Inevitably, it accomplished the transition from a small, ragged, and virtually unknown group meeting near Stonehenge to a polished national religious image.

Today, the Druids and their many sects such as OBODS (Order of Bards, Ovates and Druids) and RDNA (Reformed Druids of North America) are widespread, and groves (like covens) can be found scattered around the globe. Perhaps the most famous of them is the prolific author and quirky personality Isaac Bonewits, who is considered as much of an authority on Neopaganism as it is possible to be in a realm where most authority is rejected.

In thought and practice, the Druids strongly resemble Ancient Druidism, Wicca, and some aspects of Hollywood Kabbalah.[58] Today's Druids claim they are "free of dogma and any fixed set of beliefs or practices."[59] They celebrate diversity, claiming it is natural and healthy. Their basic creed seems to be: "Mother-earth is Nature—nature is all—nature is good." Today, anyone of any faith can be a Druid:

> Since Druidry is a spiritual path—a religion to some, a way of life to others—Druids share a belief in the fundamentally spiritual nature of life. Some will favour a particular way of understanding the source of this spiritual nature, and may feel themselves to be animists, pantheists, polytheists, monotheists or duotheists. Others will avoid choosing any one conception of Deity, believing that by its very nature this is unknowable by the mind.
>
> Monotheistic druids believe there is one Deity: either a Goddess or God, or a Being who is better named Spirit or Great Spirit, to remove misleading associations to gender. But other druids are duotheists, believing that Deity exists as a pair of forces or beings, which they often characterise as the God and Goddess.
>
> Polytheistic Druids believe that many gods and goddesses exist, while animists and pantheists believe that Deity does not exist as one or more personal gods, but is instead present in all things, and is everything.

58. See Chapter 5, Kabbalah, for more information.
59. Philip Carr-Gomm, "Beliefs," Druidry.org, http://www.druidry.org/modules.php?op=modload&name=PagEd&file=index&topic_id=1&page_id=30 (accessed June 20, 2007).

Whether they have chosen to adopt a particular viewpoint or not, the greatest characteristic of most modern-day Druids lies in their tolerance of diversity: a Druid gathering can bring together people who have widely varying views about deity, or none, and they will happily participate in ceremonies together, celebrate the seasons, and enjoy each others' company—realising that none of us has the monopoly on truth, and that diversity is both healthy and natural.[60]

Druids focus on reverence: they revere nature, passionately defend it, and value the spirituality of every creature. Like Wiccans, Druids do not believe in harming others in any way. They see no conflict between their beliefs and those of Christianity, asserting that one can be a Druid and also be a Christian or member of any other faith. Their beliefs center on the Circle of Eternity—the endless cycle of birth, death, and rebirth. Reincarnation plays a central role in modern Druid tradition, as does the power of different *energies* emanating from sources such as *places* (stone circles and ley lines) and ancestors (focusing on the presence of ancestral spirits). Unlike Wicca, Druids do not cast spells or circles, although they worship within one. Although they claim not to follow the Wiccan Rede, in essence they keep its spirit of "harm none."

Today, Paganism in all its forms is very popular, and Druid or Witch—all find acceptance now as never before. Witchcraft especially enjoys a very high profile courtesy of *Harry Potter*—everyday Witchcraft for everyone—but the reality is far different from the freewheeling sales pitch. Beneath the laughter and novel rituals, danger lies in wait. When people choose to reach for the unopened door of Witchcraft and turn the knob, the only thing coming though the door is evil.

CASE STUDY

Kathi Sharpe

So many people ask, "Why would a Pagan become a Christian?" or "Kathi, you had been following Netjeru (the gods of ancient Egypt) and had been very dedicated to them. What happened? Did you have a bad experience?

---

60. Philip Carr-Gomm, "Beliefs," Druidry.org.

Did someone in the Pagan community burn you? Did a ritual go bad, or magick not work for you?"

It was nothing like that. . . .

I had been a Witch for ten years, and a leader in AOL's Pagan community for 5 or 6 years.[61] For about four years, I had been dedicated to the gods of ancient Egypt.

Despite all the magic, healing rituals, Reiki, and prayers that I and others could do, I suffered from some serious health problems, including 70% deafness in both ears. The doctors told me there was no cure, and that it was likely to get worse. They told me to get a TTY phone and other deafie-devices, and advised us to start learning sign language.

Then one night, I had a dream about Jesus. No idea then "why" . . . I chalked it up to bad pizza and told Him to go away. Two nights later, I had another dream. He said, in sign language, "Come follow Me."

So I went into denial mode, big time. I couldn't blame pizza that night. I certainly didn't want anything to do with following Him. . . . I had some pretty skewed assumptions about Christianity, and there was an awful lot about Witchcraft that I didn't want to give up!

So, in utter arrogance, I asked God to prove it. Prove He wanted me, prove He's real. I work with an Internet company. We'd purchased a piece of software months before this happened, and I could not get one of the features to work. I'd written to a user's group for assistance about 3 months before, and no one had answers. I'd given up on the thing. So I figured this would be a great test for God. I prayed on a Monday afternoon, "If you're real, God, you need to come down here and not only solve this problem, solve it in a way that I know it's you."

Tuesday right after lunchtime, I checked my email. In it was a letter from someone on that user's group with the answer to my problem. Not only was it the exact solution, the email address was from @christianity.net.

You can't deny that kind of answer, now can you? :) This person was also an AIM user, so I was able to talk to him via IM . . . fortunately his boss was very understanding, because we talked for two whole days. He

---

61. America Online (AOL).

answered my questions, cleared up my incorrect assumptions, and told me about the great love of Jesus. At the end of the two days, I gave my heart to the Lord.

Now, the very next day, my family left for a planned camping vacation at the beach. Given everything that had happened, we determined that church on Sunday morning would be a Good Thing. ;) We ended up going to a small Assemblies of God church, mainly because it was completely different from what we'd experienced before in church (I was raised Congregationalist, my husband, Baptist). I don't know if you know anything about deafness and hearing aids . . . they are useless in any kind of large room environment because they tend to amplify the closest sounds. In most situations, I could hear shuffling, coughing, and breathing better than a speaker. Most people do not move their lips well when they speak, so lip-reading is not easy. However, the pastor at this church spoke in such a way that I could lip-read almost every word. After the service, I *had* to compliment him on this. When I told him why, he asked if he could pray for my hearing to be restored. Whoa! Way out of the realm of my experience with church. But I figured it couldn't hurt, so I said yes, and he did.

I felt something (which I now know was the Holy Spirit), but I still couldn't hear. We left the church and went back to our tent. Over the course of that afternoon, I got sick . . . I mean, really really sick. I spent most of that evening and the next morning in the bathhouse, puking my guts out and hallucinating (or maybe NOT). I felt greatly burdened to tell my old gods that they had to leave me, and spent a great deal of time between vomiting, doing just that. (I think I neglected to mention that my trad was Egyptian . . . they had a deity for *everything*.)[62]

Now, I'd taken my hearing aids out the night before (you don't wear them to bed) and never put them back in. Besides, violent facial contortions, like vomiting or coughing, tend to hurt when you have them in. Anyways . . . at about 2 Monday afternoon, I started to feel better. Weak, but better. So I went back to the tent and my husband asked how I was feeling. I realized, mid-sentence, that I'd heard what he said and I wasn't wear-

---

62. "Trad" is short for *tradition*, the Witchcraft method or philosophy Kathi followed.

ing my hearing aids. I was able to hear what my kids said for the first time in a VERY long time. What a blessing!

Needless to say, now I serve God and love Him with all my heart![63]

SCRIPTURAL RESPONSE

In considering the response of the Church to the revival of Neopaganism, a few simple questions should present themselves to any thinking person: *Why Goddess worship? Why Witchcraft?* There must be some reason that people have chosen this pathway through all the ages of mankind. And what exactly does the Bible have to say on the subject?

First of all, there can be no doubt that we are in the midst of a violent revolt against reason and logic. People brutalize, maim, and kill other people on an everyday basis—just for the thrill of it. It is totally irrational and completely illogical, but they choose to do it. The prophet Jeremiah observed, "The heart is deceitful above all things, And desperately wicked; Who can know it?" (Jer. 17:9) So the nature of man finds itself at home in the darkness and yet made in the image of God, longing for a peace that the world cannot give. In a society where science has disappointed and failed, Witchcraft offers the power to succeed. It is unscientific, metaphysical, and certainly does not follow the formal laws of logic. The resurgence of Neopaganism, in all its varied and colorful expressions, is first and foremost the revolt against reason and logic, a revolt that brought on the drug culture, the absorption with alcohol, the fascination with sex, and the prurient interest in death that is rapidly gaining ground in our culture.

Second, there is a rejection of a Church divided between orthodoxy and anarchy, a Church that wants only part of the substance and part of the form of the gospel, with no real commitment to the authority of either. Contemplative prayer—with its New Age technique of emptying the mind—labyrinth walking, Goddess worship, and countless other forms of mysticism have invaded the Church in the twenty-first century as they did in the first. Deserting the defense of the faith in deference to a "seeker-sensitive" mentality has resulted in a Church divided, with

---

63. For more information and personal stories, see Ex-Witch Ministries, "Testimonies," http://www.exWitch.org/index.php?option=com_content&task=view&id=82&Itemid=47 (accessed September 10, 2007). Kathi Sharpe testimony used by permission.

a "live and let live" worldview that opens the door to the invasion of God as "mother" theology—a legacy of *Sophia*. This is anarchy.

Third, there is the terrible influence of the cults and the occult, an influence of Theosophy, Spiritism, and Eastern religions that has now penetrated our culture. Hare Krishna groups in their saffron robes, banging on their tambourines and chanting have no relation to everyday reality, but they are *here*, and they have brought with them the yeast—all of their so-called mysticism—blending it into a homogenized form of Christianity lightly sprayed with biblical terminology.

Fourth, there is a desperate need for purpose, meaning, and order in a mechanistic and technocratic world where the individual has been largely forgotten, and where corporate structure and thinking has degraded the value of an individual soul. Why are people turning to Witchcraft? They are drawn to it because it offers the freedom of individuality and the power to change the world around them. As Witches, they do not feel as if they are beating their heads and their hands bloody against power structures that appear to care very little about anything, except perpetuating themselves in power. This need for purpose, meaning, and order in a mechanistic and technocratic society is certainly one of the primary reasons for a turn toward Witchcraft.

Fifth, tremendous progress was made during the twentieth century in the study, analysis, and presentation of psychic phenomena that eventually gave parapsychology some pseudoscientific validation. ESP experiments granted status to the world of the occult and to the power of Witchcraft, evidenced by the fact that both belief systems are taught in schools today. The media fascination with the occult has given it a small measure of credibility.

Sixth, people are fascinated by the unknown and challenged by any attempt to know the future. This is why they study tarot cards; this is why they visit palm readers; and this is why astrology often gains a foothold in their lives. The power of Witchcraft fascinates because through it, people can reach out and know something about themselves, the person next to them, and about their neighbors. They can exert authority and power over other people with this knowledge, and that is what Witchcraft offers to those who come looking for it.

Finally, there is an authentic reality within the world of the Witches. Some influence is operating, and God says it is not coming from Him. Spells may work, potions may heal, and apparitions may be seen. People experience this on a regular basis and testify to the validity of their experiences. There is *genuine power* in the realm of the occult that even the most skeptical and renowned scientists such as Sir William Crookes and Dr. Charles Richet could not disprove—a very frightening reality, indeed. It is real, and it has made Witchcraft popular and very much the vogue.

In the face of all of this, what should the Christian attitude be? Do we sit on the sidelines wringing our hands, quietly quoting Bible verses? Or do we learn the biblical position and then take definitive action? It is this last response that must be our choice. We have already seen God's attitude toward mediums, psychics, and all occultists. Moses details the warning of God in Deuteronomy 18:9–14:

> When you come into the land which the LORD your God is giving you, you shall not learn to follow the abominations of those nations. There shall not be found among you anyone who makes his son or his daughter pass through the fire, or one who practices Witchcraft, or a soothsayer, or one who interprets omens, or a sorcerer, or one who conjures spells, or a medium, or a Spiritist, or one who calls up the dead. For all who do these things are an abomination to the LORD, and because of these abominations the LORD your God drives them out from before you. You shall be blameless before the LORD your God. For these nations which you will dispossess listened to soothsayers and diviners; but as for you, the LORD your God has not appointed such for you.

This is God's judgment on the people who practiced these things: He drove them out of their country. God covered the whole spectrum of Witchcraft and the occult in this passage, and He emphasized the word *abomination*; a very strong word in the Hebrew. What was God's view? He repeats it three times so we cannot possibly fail to get the message: *abomination, abomination, abomination.* Do not do it! God drove out the Canaanites, the Hittites, and the Amorites because they practiced these things, and He gave a glorious land of milk and honey to the Israelites with the instructions, "Don't you do it or out *you* go!"

Nowhere in Scripture is this more poignantly illustrated than in the life of King Solomon. God told Solomon that if he would walk in His statutes, none would arise like him. But if he departed from the statutes of the Lord, everything would leave him (1 Kings 9:4–7). And in the end, Solomon lost everything—including his wisdom.

On the plains of Megiddo, overlooking the biblical Armageddon, is the beautiful valley of Jezreel, a land restored by the power of God. In the ruins of Solomon's palace and in the center of the temple he built, there are steps to an altar that faces away from Jerusalem. It is an altar Solomon built to a Canaanite deity, in an effort to please one of his wives. The Bible reveals that King Solomon loved many strange women, and he built temples to their gods (1 Kings 11:1–4). This Canaanite sacrificial altar, with the steps still facing the wrong way, stands today as a reminder of the time when Solomon turned his steps away from God, and God finished the Solomonic kingdom.

King Solomon did not worship other gods, but he condoned it and God judged him for it. It is a terrible reminder of the high price the wisest man in the world paid when he disobeyed God and tolerated evil. Christians today must learn from Solomon's mistakes and take action in the presence of evil—we must do something about it, so the Lord does not sit in judgment on us.

Another example of God's attitude toward Witchcraft is found in Acts, when the apostle Paul encountered a male Witch:

And when they arrived in Salamis, they preached the word of God in the synagogues of the Jews. They also had John as their assistant. Now when they had gone through the island to Paphos, they found a certain sorcerer, a false prophet, a Jew whose name was Bar-Jesus, who was with the proconsul, Sergius Paulus, an intelligent man. This man called for Barnabas and Saul and sought to hear the word of God. But Elymas the sorcerer (for so his name is translated) withstood them, seeking to turn the proconsul away from the faith. Then Saul, who also is called Paul, filled with the Holy Spirit, looked intently at him and said, "O full of all deceit and all fraud, you son of the devil, you enemy of all righteousness, will you not cease perverting the straight ways of the Lord? And now, indeed, the hand of the Lord is upon you, and you shall be blind, not seeing the sun for a time. And immediately a dark mist fell on him, and he went around seeking someone to lead him by the hand. Then the proconsul believed, when he saw what had been done, being astonished at the teaching of the Lord. (Acts 13:5–12)

Witchcraft will always stand against the gospel of Jesus Christ. There is no such thing as a friendly Witch when talking about the *only* path to salvation. Some Witches may be willing to talk about Christianity and Witchcraft from the perspective that modern Christians have wronged the Witches (as did the Old Testament prophets and the early Church), but it is amazing how they suddenly become angry when it gets right down to the nitty-gritty of who Jesus Christ is and what the Christian gospel is all about. Christ stands in judgment over them. He is no medium. He is no Witch. He is sovereign Lord of all, and they must obey Him—but they refuse to do so, for the source of their power is not Jesus Christ; the source of their power is the prince of darkness. That is why Witches will always oppose the Son of God.

When this Witch withstood the gospel, Paul did not negotiate on the defense of the faith. He did not say, "I suggest we sit down and have a theological orientation on this subject. We must have an ecumenical panel drawn from all the pastors in the area to decide whether the psychic phenomena you witnessed is valid, and whether it has any redeeming social or spiritual value to it. We will then compare this with the message we received from the Lord and decide if we ought to continue the dialogue." No, the apostles did not waste their time with the nonsense that ties up the Church today. They knew precisely what to do when they were confronted with evil. They never found Jesus Christ's gospel negotiable. Never!

Notice what Paul said: "O full of all deceit and all fraud, you son of the devil, you enemy of all righteousness, will you not cease perverting the straight ways of the Lord?" This is a very direct approach to the matter. It is obvious that Paul was *orthodox* in the classical sense of the term. "And now, indeed, the hand of the Lord is upon you, and you shall be blind, not seeing the sun for a time. And immediately a dark mist fell on him, and he went around seeking someone to lead him by the hand. Then the proconsul believed, when he saw what had been done, being astonished at the teaching of the Lord."

When the Holy Spirit encounters Witches, there is only one outcome: the Witches come out on the short end of the broomstick. This happens every time, and the Christian must realize the power that is at our disposal; we must recognize the *authority* that has been conferred upon us as the children of God. "Beloved, now we are children of God; and it has not yet been revealed what we shall be, but we know that when He is revealed, we shall be like Him, for we shall see Him as He is" (1 John 3:2).

What enormous power God placed in our hands when He commanded us to go into the world and confront evil with the authority of Christ. And when we confront evil, we need not fear the demons. We need not fear the Witches. We need not fear the mediums, the sorcerers, and the necromancers. We need not fear anything in the world of the occult. "You are of God, little children, and have overcome them, because He who is in you is greater than he who is in the world" (1 John 4:4–5). The Church needs only to recognize the power God has given to us, and if you feel you do not have that power, it is not because God is unwilling to give it to you. It is because you have not gotten down on your knees and cried out to God for it! God's power is there for the asking.

Whether we are Methodist, Baptist, Congregationalists, Episcopalians, Lutherans, Quakers, or whatever we choose to be, we will only be powerful for Christ if we open our minds, hearts, and souls to Jesus Christ—He who baptizes in the Holy Spirit—and receive power from Him so that we go out into the world and turn it upside down. That is why the first-century Christians were triumphant: they had power as well as authority, and men took knowledge of those who had been with Jesus. When Paul encountered evil, he knew how to deal with it because he was filled with the Holy Spirit.

The Church needs the power of God in each and every life; His Spirit moving in us and through us to touch others. It is a pity that all of this authority is just sitting there waiting, and Christians have not learned to plug in and receive the power to illuminate a world of spiritual darkness with the *Light* of the World. Paul rebuked evil in the name of Jesus Christ and it retreated, and so must we also rebuke evil—in no uncertain terms. Never minimize the power of God when you are discussing the power of Satan. The risen Christ said, "All authority has been given to Me in heaven and on earth. Go therefore and make disciples of all the nations, baptizing them in the name of the Father and of the Son and of the Holy Spirit, teaching them to observe all things that I have commanded you; and lo, I am with you always, even to the end of the age" (Matt. 28:18–20). God said to Moses, "Go! My presence will go with you" (Ex. 33:14). The ultimate power belongs to God.

Conclusion

In Galatians 5:20, the apostle Paul listed Witchcraft as one of the works of the flesh and warned the Church not to practice it. It is no accident that God chooses to remind us that Witchcraft is forbidden. The people who play with Ouija boards and occult games and spells should take care. Witchcraft is one of the works of the flesh, listed among those things condemned by God, and those who practice them will not inherit the kingdom of heaven.

Modern Witchcraft is popular, powerful, and growing. Thirty years ago, the publications on the subject of Witchcraft in Europe were minimal. Forty years ago, these books were almost nonexistent except in occultic bookstores. Today, you can pick them up at almost any bookstore. The interest is there; people are reaching out for the unknown.

But the good news in all of this is that there is power in the blood of Christ. There is power in the gospel. There is power in the Spirit that lives within the temple of the believer—power to touch the lives of the Witches and of all Neopagans—the kind of power that they fear, their masters fear, and from which Satan himself will flee. No force of evil in the universe is equal to that of a Christian on his or her knees. The Church of Jesus Christ has the priceless privilege of exposure to the message of God's grace, and we are committed to the ministry of reconciliation. Jesus commanded us to go into all the world and preach the gospel to every creature, bringing the message of redemption to a lost age. Our task is clear; the power to accomplish it has been given to us. The opportunity to do it has arrived. The challenge and the time has been presented to us, and we must all appear before the judgment seat of Christ and render an account of ourselves to God (Rom. 14:10). May the Lord give us the wisdom and the grace to realize that the Witches, and those who are dominated by Satan, are also souls for whom Jesus Christ died. He can bring them out of the authority of darkness and into the kingdom of the Son of God's love. This is the true God. This is life eternal.

In the midst of the kingdom of the occult, the Church of Jesus Christ must present something to the world that it so desperately needs: an undivided Christ, an unchanged gospel, and a dynamic witness. The Church must present a living Redeemer who can transform the lives of men, women, and young people because He is *alive*, and because He has the power to do it.

RECOMMENDED RESOURCES

1. Baker, Tim. *DeWitched: What You Need to Know about the Dangers of Wicca and Witchcraft.* Nashville: Transit, 2004.

2. Hawkins, Craig S. *Goddess Worship, Witchcraft and Neo-Paganism.* Grand Rapids: Zondervan, 1998.

3. Martin, Walter. *Evil and Human Suffering.* CD/audiotape, Walter Martin Ministries, www.waltermartin.com.

4. Martin, Walter. *Jesus: God, Man or Myth?.* CD/audiotape, Walter Martin Ministries, www.waltermartin.com.

5. Sanders, Catherine Edwards. *Wicca's Charm.* Colorado Springs: Shaw, 2005.

QUICK FACTS ABOUT TRADITIONAL RELIGIONS

- The belief in a Supreme Being is central to traditional religions; lesser deities exist, but they serve the Supreme Being.

- Powerful forces exist in the universe, and these forces can be consulted and utilized to accomplish good or evil.

- All things—trees, rocks, rivers—are inhabited by spirits that were never human (animism); they inhabit the same spiritual plane as the spirits of deceased ancestors and all can physically influence the living.

- Religion and magic are inseparable; magic has the power to influence the gods and spirits.

- Jesus is not the *only* way to God.

- There is no devil and no original sin.

13

Traditional Religions

Traditional religions born and bred in the culture and geography of various civilizations are practiced across the globe by hundreds of millions of people. From the Yoruba Tribe of West Africa to Native Americans to the colorful Caribbean Islanders, the power of indigenous religion is a force to be reckoned with—impacting the lives of millions of individuals down to the smallest, everyday detail. In traditional religions, a goat sacrificed to the correct deity may bring good luck to the petitioner, a spell cast by a priest may ensure a plentiful harvest, and a curse placed by a sorcerer may bring long overdue revenge. Woven into this busy religious fabric of deities, ceremony, and magic is the reality and presence of the ancestors: worthy relatives imbued with the power to change the lives of family members who please them through offerings and sacrifices.

It is a world of magic, where occult power offers instant spiritual gratification, a world both intensely exhilarating and supremely terrifying, and a world far removed from Western thought and sterile religious ritual. Traditional religions comprise a global belief system clearly different in multiple details and yet remarkably similar in thought and practice. In the past, Western scholars scoffed at the supernatural elements present in traditional religions, discounting all mystical rites and experiences as "superstition." A long record of Western history reveals a pervasive tone of criticism and contempt whenever traditional religions are examined in any detail—their rites and practices relegated to the status of foolish folk tales propagated by the ignorant. But the reality of traditional religions is anything but foolish. Deeply rooted in the power of the occult, the influence of these religions, in all their varied forms, is persistent in modern culture and growing ever stronger in the fertile environment of postmodern society. Science has failed to solve the problems of the world, and now millions are drawn to the comforting sanctuary and fascinating power found in a return to tribal roots.

EXAMINING TRADITIONAL RELIGIONS

Religions deeply rooted in the cultures and histories of different people groups are legion, and as such, not easily detailed. It is vitally important, however, to examine several of the major belief systems, ancient in origin, that survived wars, slavery, and genocide to emerge today as important religious influences. Their beliefs remain unique and yet surprisingly similar.

The Yoruba of West Africa survived centuries of the slave trade, successfully transporting their religion to Europe, America, and the Caribbean. They influenced the Caribbean and South Americas, laying a fertile foundation for the birth and growth of Voodoo, in all its varied forms. Native Americans lost the land they loved, but after a brief indoctrination into Christianity, they largely shunned the religion of the white man and clung—in the face of incredible opposition—to the teachings of the elders. A wealth of Spiritist and New Age twentieth century doctrine fed a contingent of hungry disciples recently divorced from the almighty realm of science and eager to revere Native American spirituality. All of these cultures fought to the death simply to survive, and they successfully illustrate today the flexibility and staying power of traditional religions.

THE CORE OF MONOTHEISM

A belief in a Supreme Being is central to traditional religions; lesser deities exist, but they serve the Supreme Being. Though he may be called by a multitude of different names, the Supreme Being of the ancient world has always been at the center of religious belief. Most view him as a father above all and removed from all (transcendent), but some consider him approachable (immanent). He is the Creator of all things, including lesser gods and spirits.

Belief in the Supreme Being can be found culturally and historically in almost all civilizations throughout history. German scholar Wilhelm Schmidt detailed this collective recognition in his *Origin and Growth of Religion*:

- The Supreme Being is generally acknowledged as creator, and called *Father* in every primitive culture where He is addressed. He lives somewhere above the earth.

- He is a being, so his physical form cannot be accurately represented. He is described as *invisible, like the wind,* or *like fire.*

- He is eternal: He existed before any other being, and He will not die.

- He is all powerful and all knowing.

- He is Good, and all good comes from Him, including moral law. He is unalterably righteous.

- He despises evil, and it must be kept far from Him.

- He is the Just Judge. Human beings are separated from Him by past offenses, and they abandoned Him for lesser, more accessible gods; yet primitive religions retain His memory as the *Sky-God*.[1]

This "Sky-God," known today in Africa as *Pa Kurumasba* or the Supreme Creator, designed this world for the pleasure of human beings, and Africans believe they owe him reverence and thanks for his creation. Sacrifices are made to him in order to ensure his continued blessing on both the land and the people.[2] Life should be centered on pleasing the Creator by following the moral laws he introduced from the beginning. "There are many things held to be morally wrong and evil, such as: robbery, murder, rape, telling lies, stealing, being cruel, saying bad words, showing disrespect, practicing sorcery or Witchcraft, interfering with public rights, backbiting, being lazy or greedy or selfish, making promises, and so on."[3] In the African worldview, religion is life and life is religion.

In the Caribbean, the roots of Africa run deep. The belief in the Supreme Being was transported in the early sixteenth century with the slaves, eventually blending with Catholicism to produce a unique system of worship. Voodoo (or Voudon), in essence, is the worship of African deities and spirits overlaid with key elements of Catholicism. Sociologist Roland Pierre notes:

This syncretism can be observed on three levels: a) that of the pantheon; b) that of the liturgical calendar; c) that of the sacramentary cult. But this

---

1. Schmidt, *The Origin and Growth of Religion*, 264–73.
2. Gibreel M. Kamara, "Regaining Our African Aesthetics and Essence Through Our African Traditional Religion," Journal of Black Studies 30, no. 4 (March 2000): 502–14, http://links.jstor.org/sici?sici=0021-9347%28200003%2930%3A4%3C502%3AROAAAE%3E2.0.CO%3B2-C.
3. John S. Mbiti, *African Religions and Philosophy* (New York: Praeger, 1969, 177.

"civil" syncretism is not in any way a fusion nor a synthesis nor an amalgam, but only a white mask put on over black skin. The Voodoo has kept
its religious originality in spite of the catholic cloak which circumstances
have obliged it to raise in front of its cultural face and in spite of the
Christian ingredients which it uses, by reinterpreting them, so as to reinforce its magical effectiveness.[4]

The saints of the Catholic Church became a shelter of sorts, taking on the characteristics of familiar tribal spirits that enabled the slaves to worship them without
fear of punishment. A great variety of religious practices exist today under the
umbrella of Voodoo; the names of gods or specific rituals differ depending on
which culture or people practice it.

Native American traditional religion varies in detail among the different tribes,
but like African religions, it is characterized by the monotheistic belief in an
omnipotent creator called the Great Spirit or Creator. During the late nineteenth
century, the American Indians lost their battle against the European
settlers/invaders and as a defeated race faced the total extinction of their way of life.
The United States government targeted the institution of the Indian family and
thus its religious beliefs, operating on the premise that only complete assimilation
into American society would prevent Indians from continuing the fight for their
land. Susan Staiger Gooding details the legal actions of the *U.S. Government vs. the
American Indian Tribes*:

In 1883, at the request of Secretary of the Interior, Henry M. Teller, so-
called Courts of Indian Offenses were instituted on all Indian reservations
to ensure the discontinuation of what he regarded "as a great hindrance to
the civilization of the Indians, viz, the continuance of the old heathenish
dances, such as the Sundance, scalp-dance, etc."

The list of Native American practices prohibited by these federal regulations suggests this policy was aimed not at the beliefs of Indian peoples

---

4. Roland Pierre, "Caribbean Religion: The Voodoo Case," *Sociological Analysis* 38, no. 1 (Spring 1977): 29, http://www.jstor.org/pss/3709834. Example: "St. Patrick stands for Danbala; St. Peter stands for Legba; St. Ann stands for Ezili; St. James stands for Ogoun; St. Expedit stands for Agouk."

but at the networks of social and political relations produced in the context of indigenous ceremonial practices. The list of indigenous practices prohibited by federal regulations promulgated in 1883, 1892, and again in 1904 included: 1) all dances and "any similar feast," 2) all plural or polygamous marriages and those not "'solemnized" by an appointed judge, 3) all practices of medicine men and the prevention of Indian children from attending religious schools, 4) the destruction, injury, taking or carrying away of any personal property without reference to its value, particularly in the case of the death of an Indian, 5) immorality, particularly the exchange of gifts between families when negotiating marriages, 6) intoxication and, 7) the failure to "adopt habits of industry, or to engage in civilized pursuits or employments" (distilled from 1892 "Rules for Indian Courts," House Executive Doc. no. 1, 52d Cong., 2nd sess., serial 3088, pp. 28-31 as quoted in Prucha 1990, pp. 186-89). These offenses were punished by fines, withholding food rations, and imprisonment. These were not referred to as elements of Indian religions *per se*. Nevertheless, with the exception of "intoxication" and "the failure to adopt habits of industry" this list of offenses designates ceremonial and symbolic practices that were so ubiquitous as means of mediating and negotiating social relations and identity in and between indigenous communities that they could form one of the first policies written for all Indian people. As Patricia Limerick has stated, "The campaign against Indian religions was, at its core, a campaign against the Indian family," against the intergenerational and extended kinship relations that "knit tribal societies together."[5]

The best efforts of the United States government to eradicate every trace of culture, and the traditional religion that was so much a part of it, inevitably failed. Native Americans and their traditional beliefs survived. Today, the spirituality of hundreds of tribes scattered across the face of North America enjoys a freedom and respect unparalleled in American history.

---

5. Susan Staiger Gooding, "At the Boundaries of Religious Identity: Native American Religions and American Legal Culture," *Numen* 43, no. 2, Religion, Law and the Construction of Identities (May 1996): 161, http://www.jstor.org/pss/3270345.

AFRICAN TRADITIONAL RELIGION

The mystery and wonder of Africa has intrigued observers and intrepid explorers down through the centuries. It is a land of stark beauty, spectacular wildlife, and unspeakable violence, populated by thousands of different peoples practicing countless complex religions. It is a land of more than one thousand languages spread over fifty-three countries—the subject of innumerable books, endless documentaries, and Hollywood movies. It is a vast continent, vibrant, violent, and steeped in the occult.

During the eighteenth and nineteenth centuries, European Colonists, intent on conquering an immense wilderness, found a world far different from the "civilized" one they had left behind, a world they dubbed the "Dark Continent." The designation was due in part to the thick rainforests that made sections of Africa virtually inaccessible, the mystery of the land and its people, and most likely the predominant color of their skin.

Divided into two main sections by these explorers, Northern Africa and the sub-Sahara (everything beneath the brutal vista of the Saharan desert) came to represent two entirely different worlds. Northern Africa, bordering Arabia's "cradle of civilization" was home to a lighter skinned people influenced more by Mediterranean cultures, while the sub-Saharan peoples included a variety of darker skin tones and a vast array of traditional religions. Northern Africa was greatly influenced by the Roman Empire, the majority of it converting to Christianity in the wake of Constantine's Edict of Milan (313 AD), which established religious freedom throughout the empire. Three hundred years later, traders from Arabia brought the message of Mohammed (c. 615 AD) to Northern Africa and it spread across the region like wildfire, eventually making its way to different sections of the continent. It was Christianity, however, mixed with traditional African religion, that dominated most of Africa below the sub-Sahara, and this remains the case today.

In the early sixteenth century, the advent of the slave trade forever changed the history of Africa and its people. Although slaves were often taken in the course of tribal wars, localized slavery could not compare with the devastation that was to come.[6] When the European and Western slave traders honed in on Africa and

---

6. African scholars today prefer not to use the designation "tribe," but it was used historically to indicate a family, village, or regional unit.

began filling their ships with thousands of slaves, entire tribes, families, and cultures were completely decimated. This ruthless slave trade centered mostly on West African nations such as Ghana (the Gold Coast), Senegal, Angola, and others unfortunate enough to live in close proximity to the coastal beaches.

The lives of these slaves were brutally transformed when they crossed an ocean and lost forever the comfort and identity of *home*. The loss of freedom was significant, but the loss of *community* far outweighed independence. African-American writer Jim Haskins notes, "The overwhelming fact of the African's experience in the New World was the brutal severing of nearly every element basic to his identity. He was separated from his family, from his village, from his tribe, from his language, from his religion, from his entire socioeconomic experience—not to mention the separation from his land. The loss of freedom cannot be overlooked, but in the context of the African's basic identity it is not the major factor."[7] This sense of community—a vital bond between the individual and everything that surrounded him—was the essence of the African worldview, and it remains so today.

Unlike Western society's emphasis on independence, the African peoples' reliance on one another and their surrounding communities is paramount. People in African culture are inextricably linked to family (alive and dead), village and surrounding area; to nature, land and water; and to the Supreme Being, gods, spirits, and ancestors.

THE HEART OF AFRICAN RELIGIONS[8]

Although specific elements of African religion vary throughout the continent, basic, underlying characteristics unite them:

1. *Powerful forces exist in the universe, and they can be consulted and utilized.* The African people view the world as a dangerous place filled with spirits of all kinds, and in this belief they have much in common with the Sumerians and the Babylonians. At any given moment, it is possible that someone or something may cause harm, and precautions must be taken to prevent this harm from occurring. The Supreme Being allows lesser gods to intervene in the affairs of men, and the existence of lesser gods means a chance to circumvent the negative actions of others.

---

7. Jim Haskins, *Voodoo and Hoodoo: The Craft as Revealed by Traditional Practitioners* (New York: Scarborough, 1981), 47.
8. Adapted from Haskins, *Voodoo and Hoodoo,* 32.

A priest must approach the gods on behalf of an individual—a person cannot approach the gods on his or her own.

2. *Fate is one of the powerful forces, but it can be defeated by the divine trickster, another separate force.* Fate is a force separate from all gods. Africans, like many people throughout history, believe that the events in a person's lifetime are predestined. But the African solution to this dilemma remains unique: a being called the *divine trickster* can change the course of fate:

> Actually, the divine trickster was a concept rather than a single deity, for it could take several forms. Some tribes envisaged the lesser deities organized into a series of family groupings that paralleled those of men. In these, the divine trickster was often seen as the youngest child of one of the deities. One of the child's duties was to carry messages from the deity to the various divine families—messages that foretold the future. As a trickster, he could be persuaded by man to alter the orders he carried, to deliver a message different from that with which he had been entrusted. Thus, if some unhappy fate were in store for a man who was a serious worshiper, he could persuade the trickster to substitute a better one. The divine trickster could also be the ancestor who had most recently died.

3. *Natural spirits inhabit the same spiritual plane as the spirits of deceased ancestors; all spirits can physically influence the living.* Ancestors are considered essential to the well-being of any African. They act as personal intercessors for their family to the Supreme Creator and lesser gods and, as such, must be treated with the greatest respect—but only if that respect was earned during their lifetime. Not all ancestors are worthy, only those who showed concern for their family by creating descendants and living a life of honor are remembered daily by those who remain. A place for honored ancestors is set at meals, and family members may speak directly to the empty place; they know that an ancestor will always be willing to help when needed.

Although some scholars claim that Africans do not worship their ancestors, the daily behaviors they exhibit are historically connected to worship: they speak aloud to ancestors about daily problems and family matters, they organize celebrations in their ancestors' honor, and they ask their ancestors to do extraordinary things that a human being is not capable of doing. They also believe that ancestors can choose to return to life in the bodies of their children. This daily link to the invisible is another expression of the strong bond Africans feel to everything in the world around them, both seen and unseen.

4. *All things—trees, rocks rivers—are inhabited by spirits that were never human (animism).* For the African, the oxygen surrounding them is not simply air; it is a spiritual space filled with all kinds of spirit-beings. While the ancestor's body may decay, the ancestor himself has simply stepped from this world into the next, and he now occupies a physical space alongside many different kinds of spirits. The spirits he shares space with may reside in rocks or trees; they are free to move about and yet tethered to those physical objects. They can leave the rock, but probably not venture far from it.

5. *Religion and magic are almost inseparable; both work in conjunction with powerful spirit forces.* Perhaps the most influential belief at the center of African religions is the power of magic to determine the fate of human beings. Magic can influence the gods, the spirits, and the ancestors to effect tremendous changes in everyday life. It is inextricably intertwined with religion itself to the point where, at times, they are one and the same.

6. *Retribution will follow immediately for any evil acts; there is no end of the world and no judgment day.* It is believed that the gods will swiftly punish anyone who has committed evil, and the individual has only a short time to petition the gods to make things right before they are punished. This quick retribution is meant to mold character and enforce respect for the community.

THE WEST AFRICAN INFLUENCE

African religions were always the center—the heart and soul—of African society. Today, the same remains true; they are the building blocks beneath the structures of everyday life, and as such their influence affects every aspect of it. African proverbs passed down through the centuries from family to family reveal and support the importance of religion, and even the African drum, so much a part of its religious rituals, is considered today to be sacred—a "living institution."[9]

---

9. Jacob K. Olupona, ed., *African Traditional Religions in Contemporary Society* (New York: Crossroad, 2000), 2.

It is no wonder, then, that slaves transported so far from their homes would carry with them their deep-rooted beliefs. The holds of the slave ships contained not just warriors, women, and children; they held the priests as well. And in a new and hellish environment, religion was all they had left. The plunder of the West African coast brought with it the influence of West African religion, and nowhere can this be seen more clearly than in the survival of the Yoruba tribal beliefs. Within the cosmology of this people lie the roots of what would come to be known as Voodoo.

The Yoruba culture is thought to be quite ancient, dating back to at least 500 BC and encompassing the southwestern part of Nigeria (Yorubaland) and large portions of the West African coast.[10] In a world full of spirits and powers that touch every aspect of life for good or ill, ceremonies, offerings, celebrations, and divination were an integral part of Yoruba society. A remarkable culture built on a foundation of oral tradition passed from generation to generation through more than two hundred thousand poems, Yoruba history would fill volumes of books if it were ever to be written down.[11]

At the center of Yoruba religious beliefs is the Supreme Being or High God Olodumare, who rules over a pantheon of gods, spirits, and ancestors, both benevolent (called *orisa*) and malignant (*ajogun*).[12] Omnipotent and unreachable, Olodumare instructs other deities to do his bidding. Thomas Blakely notes, "Each orisa was charged with his or her own responsibilities. . . .When the four hundred orisa finished their work, they changed into mountains, hills, trees and so forth." [13]

MAJOR PRINCIPLES OF YORUBA RELIGION[14]

1. *Conflict.* There is a constant struggle in the universe between the Deus de Bem (good deities) and the Deus de Mal (bad deities). The benevolent gods wish to bless man with every good thing, and the evil deities wish to destroy him. This element of conflict and struggle is central to Yoruba thought.

---

10. Egbé Omo Yorubá (National Association of Yoruba Descendants in North America), "Who Are the Yoruba?" http://www.yorubanation.org/Yoruba.htm.
11. Thomas D. Blakely, Walter E. A. Van Beek, and Dennis L. Thomason, ed., *Religion in Africa* (London: James Curry, 1994), 102, 116.
12. Ibid., 102.
13. Ibid., 103–4. Vowel/consonant accents available in original text.
14. Adapted from ibid., 111.

2. *Predestiny and Struggle.* According to the Yoruba, humans are physical (*ara*) and spiritual (*emi* and *ori*) beings. The High God Olodumare creates or breathes soul (*emi*) into the person, but the spirit Ajala, who is a drunk and disreputable spirit (not a god), provides the *ori* or "spiritual head." Humans preexist in heaven and choose an *ori* before coming to earth. If they choose a good *ori,* their lives will be blessed. If they choose a bad one, they will need to offer sacrifices throughout their lives to avoid the suffering that results from a bad choice. Free will, however, is not completely ruled out. It is possible for someone with a bad ori to eventually succeed if he or she works hard and tries to live a good life.

3. *Sacrifice.* All problems or conflicts in life can be resolved through the act of sacrifice. The Esu (a benevolent deity or orisa that takes many different forms) is approached by an individual for help; he accepts a sacrifice in exchange for convincing an *ajogun* (a malignant deity) to overlook any wrong that might have been committed. This act of sacrifice usually includes a priest, and divination is employed to determine the omens.

4. *Good Character.* The Yoruba believe that good character is essential to living a successful life. The Deus de Bem help nurture good character within each individual—traits that will enable them to live at peace with the world around them. "Good character is the essence of religion."[15]

5. *Nature, Deities, and the Afterlife.* The Yoruba are close to nature and believe they have power over it. Secret names are given to living things, and these names enable someone to wake a plant or animal, summoning them by means of spells or enchantments. Trees, rocks, or hills—all were deities at one time who took the form they preferred after their job of creation was finished. When a person dies, they also become a deity and take whatever form they desire. All punishment takes place on earth. There is no devil and no original sin.

The Yoruba belief system is perhaps best demonstrated by one of their ancient proverbs:

> . . . the aborigines, the Igbo, became difficult, and constituted a serious threat to the survival of Ife. Thought to be survivors of the old occupants of the land before the arrival of Oduduwa, these people now turned them-

---

15. Ibid., 115. Yoruba proverb.

selves into marauders. They would come to town in costumes made of raffia with terrible and fearsome appearances, and the Ife people would flee. Then the Igbo would burn down houses and loot the markets. Then came Moremi on the scene—like Deborah of the Old Testament. When no man could dare the Igbos, Moremi asked the Esinminrin river for help and promised to give offerings if she could save her people. The orisa told her to allow herself to be captured and to understudy the Igbo people. She did, and discovered that these were not spirits; only people with raffia for dress. She escaped, and taught her people the trick. The next time that Igbo people came, they were roundly defeated. Moremi then had to go back to Esinminrin to thank the gods. Every offering she offered was refused. On divination, she was told she had to give Oluorogbo, her only son. She did. The lesson of Moremi is the lesson of patriotism and selflessness. The reward may not be reaped in one's life time. Moremi passed on and became a member of the Yoruba pantheon. The Edi festival celebrates the defeat of the Igbo and the sacrifice of Oluorogbo till today.[16]

The flexibility and tenacity of these deep-rooted beliefs is evident in their survival despite some of the worst brutality in the history of mankind. The slave trade transported to distant shores not only a people group, but an ancient worldview that adopted and adapted key religious ideology like a chameleon changes color. "As the various African cultures were scattered throughout the New World by slave trade, their religious practices were influenced by the new surroundings and the strange languages spoken in the land of their exile. Each tribe borrowed freely from the customs, the ideas, and the religious beliefs of its adopted lands. This brought great diversity into the religious ceremonies of the Black man. The rites varied with each cultural group."[17]

The Yoruba beliefs of West Africa would forever change the places and peoples they touched. From South America to Cuba to Jamaica and the Caribbean, their influence survives and thrives today. The *orisa* or spirits of the Yoruba would be reborn as the pantheon of Vodun (Voodoo) gods called the *loa*, active in and influencing every

16. "Who Are the Yoruba?"
17. Jacob U. Gordon, "Yoruba Cosmology and Culture in Brazil: A Study of African Survivals in the New World," *Journal of Black Studies*, 10, no. 2 (December 1979): 231–44, http://links.jstor.org/sici?sici=0021-9347%28197912%2910%3C231%3A&CACIB%3E2.0.CO%3B2-1.

aspect of human life. Yoruba rituals and the importance of sacrifice—a way of pleasing or persuading the gods—remains a key element of both Yoruba and Voodoo today.

CARIBBEAN RELIGIONS AND OCCULT MOVEMENTS

The isolation of the Caribbean Islands provided a unique setting for the development of religious ideas that mixed the traditions of African religions, European Catholicism, American Protestant, and folklore superstition in a unique amalgamation of beliefs.[18] Protestant and Catholic missionaries introduced the power and authority of Jesus Christ—His disciples, Mary, and various saints—that eventually became integral to occult rituals. Through this, the island groups broke stride with their European and African counterparts in that they were not truly Yoruba, Catholic, or Protestant but a distinctive blend of ideology that retained only trace elements of the original influences. This unique religious melting pot consisting of God, magic, demigods, spirit-gods, and ancestral spirit worship birthed new and influential worldviews throughout the Caribbean islands.[19]

Understanding these new religious ideas is no easy task, since misperceptions have evolved due to language and cultural barriers, misinterpretations, caricatures, prejudice, and false reports.[20] Some scholars insist that indigenous religious development was distinct in origin from the African tradition. Leaders within the Caribbean cultures who traveled to Africa were surprised to find few connections to tradition, as Stephen D. Glazier pointed out:

> Over the past ten years problems of "origin," "genuineness," and "authenticity" have become hot topics of debate within a number of Afro-Caribbean religions. The debate has intensified with regard to alleged "African,"

---

18. Diana L. Eck, professor of comparative religion and Indian studies at Harvard University, made a similar observation about the importation of these beliefs to the United States: "Immigrants from Haiti and Cuba have brought Afro-Caribbean traditions, blending both African and Catholic symbols and images." (*A New Religious America: How a "Christian Country" Has Become the World's Most Religiously Diverse Nation* [San Francisco: Harper, 1997], 4).

19. See Audley G. Reid, *Community Formation: A Study of the "Village" in Postemancipation Jamaica* (Kingston, Jamaica: Canoe, 2000), 94–100.

20. For example, Afro-Caribbean polytheism, animism, and ancestral spirits were misunderstood as Witchcraft: "Europeans wrongly applied the term to Witchcraft or sorcery and often confused Witches with Myalmen and women." (Sylvia R. Frey and Betty Wood, *Come Shouting to Zion: African American Protestantism in the American South and British Caribbean to 1830* [Chapel Hill and London: University of North Carolina Press, 1998], 57).

"Asian," and "European" elements in Afro-Caribbean ritual; especially as a number of prominent Afro-Caribbean religious leaders have traveled to Africa and found there little evidence of Caribbean ritual practice.[21]

This lack of evidence makes tracing certain occult practices to Africa a bit problematic.[22] During the twentieth century, Caribbean religious leaders attempted to restore core beliefs, but this was complicated by the ceremonial variations between Caribbean and African religions. Glazier notes that the progression of the Caribbean religions into the twentieth century marked a loss of stereotyped "religions of the oppressed" and "religions of protest," as they were known in former centuries.[23] They grew as recognizable forces in influencing Caribbean politics and economics. To compound the difficulties in religious study, many of the Caribbean groups are divided between of heterodoxy and orthodoxy.[24] This is not surprising, since part of the traditional element in some groups is more culturally oriented as opposed to others with an infrastructure of ecclesiastical authority or a written canonical scripture.

Obeah

Several Caribbean religious traditions retained belief in animism, magic, and the gods from Central and Western Africa, which is called *obeah* in the Caribbean Islands and thrives mostly in Jamaica. *Obeah* is a form of spirit control where the practitioner uses magic and spiritism to exercise power or authority over another person or event. This practice became widespread and eventually influenced Caribbean beliefs like Voodoo (Vodun), Santeria, and even the later obeah-opposing Myal practitioners, who stand out as masters of spiritual power.

---

21. Stephen D. Glazier, "Contested Rituals of the African Disapora" in Peter B. Clarke, ed., *New Trends and Developments in African Religions* (Westport, CT: Greenwood, 1998), 105.
22. Glazier, an anthropologist, argues that the reason for the polyglot of religious information is that the Yoruba slaves brought to the islands were "mostly younger men who had yet to be initiated into higher levels of understanding," and they "were often left to their own devices in attempting to reconstruct ceremonies." (Ibid., 108).
23. Stephen D. Glazier, "Prophecy and Ecstasy: Religion and Politics in the Caribbean," in Jeffrey K. Hadden and Anson Shupe, eds., *Prophetic Religions and Politics: Religion and the Political Order* (New York: Paragon, 1988), 1:430.
24. Ibid., 435.

There is no doubt that African rituals are mirrored in the West Indies and the Caribbean Island practices that survived through oral tradition among the slaves. The Caribbean interpretation of *obeah* differs from African, however, in that it uses obeah for both good and evil. The power of obeah grew until plantation owners and political powers clashed with obeah practitioners who, in their view, threatened industry and prevented European-style civilization of the Caribbean Islands. Both camps distrusted each other, which eventually drove obeah underground to form secret societies.[25]

The obeah practitioner claimed to command the spirit world, a power that engendered great fear and respect in the eyes of the community. Obeah practitioners were called upon for love potions, financial blessings (charming a coin to increase money), casting or breaking spells, healing ailments, and other controlling powers over people, places, and things.[26]

Myal

A Myal man or woman is usually a healing practitioner who uses a combination of Christian teachings, Caribbean religious traditions, herbal medicine, and dance rituals. Myal teaching strictly opposes obeah and developed its own counterrituals to free people from obeah spirits, spells, and magic.

In the eighteenth century, Baptist missionaries planted churches that were left without much guidance or experienced leadership. Literacy was low in the beginning of the missionary work, so experience-based churches gained predominance over the Bible-based churches. The local church congregants, who saw no conflict between Christian beliefs and spirit world communication, developed Myalism— an earthly hierarchy of human archangels, angels, and ministering spirits. The Myal archangels functioned as leaders who used divination, the angels spoke visions to the congregants, and the ministering spirits evangelized and protected against obeah influences.[27]

Myalism also directly attacked the Trinity. It designated the Holy Spirit as the

---

25. See Brian L. Moore and Michele A. Johnson, *Neither Led nor Driven: Contesting British Cultural Imperialism in Jamaica, 1865–1920* (Kingston, Jamaica: University of the West Indies Press, 2004), 14–16.
26. Ibid., 19–21.
27. Ibid., 54.

most prominent and active in the Trinity, and the Father as a deity who does not attend revivals. The Son does attend, however, along with archangels, spirits of the prophets and disciples, and ancestral church leaders. From these roots Myalism eventually spread into Methodist and other churches.[28]

Santeria

The Santeria, or "the way of the saints," is a blend of Yoruba and Catholic beliefs with an emphasis on the occult, demon possession, trance states used to communicate with ancestors, ritual drums and dances, and ceremonial slayings of goats, lambs, and chickens. Its largest contingent of followers is in Cuba, the West Indies, and other Caribbean islands, but its numbers grew in the United States during the twentieth century due to the arrival of Cuban refugees. Their practices gained notoriety in a United States Supreme Court decision involving a Florida town and its decision to ban the slaying of chickens within city limits. The Supreme Court decided in favor of the Santeria religious rituals in 1993 (*Church of Lukumi Babalu Aye vs. City of Hialeah*), thus upholding freedom of expression as part of religious liberties.

The court could only address the issue of religious liberty and not the question of whether animal sacrifices were acceptable. As part of their defense strategy, the Santeria attorneys argued that animal blood sacrifices were practiced by Israel up to 70 AD. But to address the biblical nature of animal sacrifice is clearly a theological question and as such *outside* the jurisdiction of the courts. Those involved in Santeria often try to use the Bible as a defense for modern sacrifices, but theologians Larry Nichols, George Mather, and Alvin Schmidt dismiss this argument as invalid in light of the final sacrifice of Jesus Christ:

> The issue of blood sacrifice has been a problem that Christian missionaries have attempted to address. Christianity believes in the absolute necessity of blood sacrifice, a doctrine that has its roots in the Old Testament. The Hebrew practice is described in detail in the book of Leviticus, where the high priest was instructed to offer up the blood of various acceptable animals (bulls, goats, turtledoves, etc.) as a sacrifice for the sins of the people.

---

28. Ibid., 51–53.

Christianity made a break with Judaism, however, not by doing away with the idea of blood sacrifice, but by advancing the doctrine of the exclusivity of Jesus Christ as the only high priest who offered himself as the ultimate sacrifice for sin by the shedding of his own blood (Heb 9:12). Furthermore, this sacrifice was offered once and is sufficient for all time (Heb. 9:25–7). Therefore, the tension between Christianity and Santeria (as well as with the other transplanted African cults) is an inevitable consequence of their coming together.[29]

The foundational principle of Santeria, according to Dr. Mary Ann Clark (who converted to Santeria along with her husband while completing her doctorate at Rice University), is based on the *ashe* or energy of the universe:

To understand the Santeria belief system, it is first necessary to define *ashe*. For practitioners, *ashe* is the energy of the universe. It is "all mystery, all secret power, all divinity" . . . For the practitioners of Santeria, the movement of *ashe*, the energy of the universe, between the visible and invisible worlds influences the environment. Part of Santeria religious practice is learning to use *ashe* for the benefit of the individual, the community, and the universe as a whole.

Santeria worship involves drumming and dancing as essential rituals. By dancing, the practitioner expresses the *ashe* of the universe and calls into presence the power of the *Orisha* (gods). . . .

There are five different levels of power in the Yoruba cosmology: *Olodumare*, the *Orisha*, human beings, human ancestors, and the lowest group (which includes plants, animals, natural entities, and manufactured items). . . .

The highest god, *Olodumare*, is not directly worshiped, but is invoked in various rituals. The *Orisha* (thousands of gods) are directly worshiped and they progressively increase in power through worship. *Orisha* guides or leads the participant to fulfill their destiny. Ancestors, called *Egun*, can progress to the level of *Orisha*, although most do not. The lowest group mentioned above contains *ashe*, the universal energy, which can be used in rituals that affect the world's visible and invisible planes.[29]

29. Nichols, Mather, and Schmidt, *Encyclopedic Dictionary of Cults, Sects, and World Religions*, 248.

In addition to healing rituals and other rites where spirits are manipulated through sacrifices, spiritism is used to contact the dead. Divination is also commonly practiced in Santeria in an effort to foretell personal destiny, and trances are induced to communicate with Olodumare or Orisha. Humans are the connection between the spirit world (invisible) and the material world, so spirits (either Orisha or ancestors) can manifest themselves through willing subjects. The reincarnation of ancestors is accepted as fact, supported by the appearance of familiar behaviors in a surviving family member similar to those of the deceased.[30]

Haitian Vodun (Voodoo)

Vodun, also spelled *Voodoo* or *vodoun*, is a syncretistic religion that is mainly associated with Haiti, even though it evolved in the West Indies and has spread to other countries in the last two centuries. It is so integrated into the lives of the Haitian people that it has produced cultural trends with Vodun music, Vodun dance, Vodun art, and a Voodoo festival (New Orleans, Louisiana) that promotes more jazz music than Vodun belief.

Haitian Vodun, as described by the Haitian scholar Gerdes Fleurant, is "a religious system and way of life of the Haitian people."[31] Vodun is practiced to maintain health and personal well-being. "To achieve this end, Vodunists establish and maintain contact with cosmic entities they call *lwa*."[32] The *lwas* or *loas* are disembodied spirits, deities that may be classified as either good or bad in practice but in Vodun basic theology, remain essentially neutral. Lwas also act as intermediary spirits that can communicate to the Vodunist, an occult experience that reinforces the reality of the existence of *lwa* and the validity of Vodun.

The West Indies branch of Vodun took root immediately upon the arrival of African slaves, brought to the island plantations in the early eighteenth century to work the vast sugar cane fields. Although forcibly baptized into the Catholic Church, the language, culture, and religious barriers preserved the basics of African tradition. Plantation owners found they could not communicate Catholicism in its

---

30. Mary Ann Clark, "Santeria" in Marc Petrowsky and William W. Zellner, Eds., *Sects, Cults, and Spiritual Communities: A Sociological Analysis* (Westport, CT: Praeger, 1998), 119–20.
31. Nichols, Mather, and Schmidt, *Encyclopedic Dictionary of Cults, Sects, and World Religions*, 247.
32. Gerdes Fleurant, *Dancing Spirits: Rhythms and Rituals of Haitian Vodun, the Rada Rite* (Westport, CT: Greenwood, 1996), 2.

fullness, and so the slaves received only fragments of doctrinal truth, pieces they used to disguise the remnants of their culture. In the end, the slaves found a measure of relief by hiding under the quasi-Catholic umbrella, secretly adapting their beliefs to fit the Catholic mold and giving birth to what would come to be known as Caribbean Vodun. In 1805, the Haitian government lent fuel to the Vodun fire when it sided with Napoleon against the pope—who promptly withdrew his support from Haiti—stripping the small island of virtually all Catholic priests for almost two generations.[34] The absence of Catholicism coincided with revolutionary times in which many slaves were freed physically and religiously, most using their newfound liberty to explore and solidify Vodun beliefs.

This syncretism of the African tradition and the Catholic faith throughout the Caribbean produced an altogether new entity. Ancestral worship and veneration ruled at the heart of it, as did the spirit-gods brought from Africa. In Caribbean Vodun, it is the family that is the loci (path) and vitality, not an institutionalized church: the family is responsible for the practice of Vodun. There is no professional, seminary-trained priesthood (as in Catholicism), so the religious authority figure is the head of the family; he or she presides over the others. The following Vodun song reflects the centralization of the family:

The family is gathered
Oh yes we are gathered
The family is assembled
He should not be alone
Serving the lwa
The family is assembled[35]

The full expression of Vodun worship comes through dance, song, and ritual drums, all of which have been routinely misinterpreted by outsiders. The dance forms a connection and communication between the participant and the spirit world, especially during rituals and ceremonies. Vodun theology contains hundreds of spirit-gods, too numerous to list, some of which represent nature (the sea,

34. See Joseph M. Murphy, *Working the Spirit: Ceremonies of the African Diaspora* (Boston: Beacon, 1995), 12–13.
35. Ibid., 8.

forest, plants, water, rainbow, storms); animals (the serpent); and departed humans.

In Vodun's union with Catholicism, the saints are represented through the *loa* (although the *loas'* inclusiveness spans a vast arena for the departed). Dreams and trances are thought to be the communication line for *loa*, which comes through the individual's soul. The soul, as an English translation of *ange*, has two parts, the greater and lesser. The division called the "big good angel" is the psyche and intelligence of the conscious mind, and the "little good angel" is the subconscious mind—the *conscience* that criticizes individual thoughts. It is the "little good angel" that communicates with *loa* in trances and dreams. "The relationship between devotees and loa is thought to be a contractual one. If one is scrupulous in the performance of offerings and ceremonies, the loa will be generous in their aid. If one neglects the loa, one cannot expect their favors and even risks their wrath. It is widely believed that neglect of one's loa will result in sickness, the death of relatives, crop failure, and other misfortunes. In this respect, Vodun is a personal religion. Relations with the loa are first and foremost an individual responsibility."[36]

The similarities present in most Vodun cults paint a picture of their basic cosmology; the complexity in various strains of Vodun creates difficulties for anyone wishing to categorize individual strains as either orthodox or divergent. Joseph M. Murphy, professor of theology at Georgetown University, points out: "While there may be informal ties among neighboring vodou communities, each congregation sets its own standards in matters of ritual and belief. . . . Practices of one congregation may be unknown in another, and what is kept rigidly separate in one community may be brought together in another."[37]

Nichols, Mather, and Schmidt summarize the problems in Christian evangelism of Vodun communities:

Christianity and Voodoo subscribe to two entirely different worldviews. Most basic to their differences is that the former is strictly a monotheistic religion while the latter is polytheistic and/or animistic. In most Voodoo cults, belief in a supreme deity is professed. This deity, however, must share

36. Glazier, "Prophecy and Ecstasy," 435.
37. Murphy, *Working the Spirit*, 15.

a place with a multitude of subservient loas within the pantheon. Where Christianity has had an impact, missionaries have encountered difficulty in conveying that the God of the Bible is Sovereign Lord of the universe and shares his deity and attributes with no other. Syncretistic in orientation, Voodoo readily absorbs Christianity into itself. Roman Catholic saints are incorporated into the cultus as well, and each is assigned a respective role in the pantheon.[38]

Vodun draws upon the power of the occult to influence every aspect of human life. Some cultures attribute great power and authority to Voodoo priests or priestesses—power that allows them to create zombies from the disobedient and mete out punishment based on sliding fee scales or simply the whim of a priest. These individuals (sometimes called sorcerers) hold the lives of communities in the palms of their hands. Modern Vodun believers often try to dismiss such stories as lurid Hollywood myth, but hard evidence has been produced by many reputable sources to support the existence of Voodoo's occult practices and the deep fear they engender.[39]

Rastafarianism

The Back to Africa movement (c. 1890) and the Black Nationalist movement grew out of the cherished dream of many American slaves to return to Africa. In 1816, Robert Findley founded the American Colonization Society, whose Northern supporters lobbied Congress for help and received a one-hundred-thousand-dollar grant. Several years later, ships set sail for Africa, and in 1821 a settlement was finally established in what is now called Liberia. During the next ten years, twenty-three hundred people arrived and succeeded in colonizing Liberia, the "Land of the Free"—an independent nation founded by freed American and Caribbean slaves.

In 1852, Martin R. Delany, a well-educated descendant of slaves, wrote *The Condition, Elevation, Emigration and Destiny of the Colored People of the United States.* In the book's appendix, entitled, "We Go to Africa," Delany published a master plan for the 4.5 million African descendants throughout the United States and Caribbean Islands to return to Africa. This was astounding in light of the fact

---

38. Nichols, Mather, and Schmidt, *Encyclopedic Dictionary of Cults, Sects, and World Religions,* 329.
39. See Haskins, *Voodoo and Hoodoo,* chap. 3, "Voodoo and Hoodoo Today," African traditional folk magic is called Hoodoo.

that 3.9 million people were still slaves and only six hundred thousand were freed-men and freedwomen living in the north. The Civil War and the Emancipation Proclamation existed only in the wildest of dreams, yet Delany envisioned a mass exodus to Africa. Delany taught from the Bible and wrote a book on the biblical history of the races (*Principa of Ethnology: The Origin of Races and Color*, 1879) to counter Charles Darwin's *Origin of the Species* (1859) and some Euro-American arguments using the evolutionary process in support of racial supremacy. Martin Delany, and others who followed him in the post-Civil War era, raised awareness for the 1890s Back to Africa movement and eventually influenced a charismatic leader by the name of Marcus Garvey.

Marcus Garvey was a Jamaican journalist and an outspoken Black Nationalist whose participation in the Back to Africa movement produced the Universal Negro Improvement Association and African Communities League (UNIA-ACL) in 1918. The UNIA-ACL was "the first Pan-African organization to attempt to attract the black masses in the United States, the Caribbean, and Africa."[40] As a result of his Pan-African call, several nationalist organizations eventually formed, some of which appealed to religious needs: the Nation of Islam, Black Muslims, and the Rastafarians, who later claimed that Garvey was one of their prophets.

In 1916, when Garvey left Jamaica to travel the world and promote his cause, he was quoted as saying, "Look to Africa for the crowning of a Black King, he shall be the Redeemer."[41] That same year, the Ethiopian King Lij Iyasu was overthrown and, eventually, Tafari Makonnen (1892–1975) was elevated to the rank of Ras (head) and gained the title Ras Tafari. He was later crowned the Ethiopian king and emperor in 1930, which Jamaican UNIA-ACL associates viewed as Garvey's prophecy fulfilled. The crowned Ethiopian king was given the name Emperor Haile Selassie I (meaning Power of the Trinity). His followers, who became known as *Rastafarians,* declared him to be the biblical Messiah, God incarnate, and part of the Holy Trinity. He was declared the Lion of Judah, the King of kings, and the Elect of God.

Ras Tafari was the unquestioned "messiah" of Rastafarianism, although he never joined the movement and had no hand in its foundation. He was a baptized mem-

---

40. Nina Mjagkij, ed., *Organizing Black America* (New York: Garland, 2001), 680.
41. This often-quoted line from Garvey is passed down through oral history. As quoted in Leonard E. Barrett, The Rastafarians (Boston: Beacon Press, 1997), 67.

ber of the Ethiopian Orthodox Church and remained so until his death. On occasions where he spoke of his faith, he told constituents that the soul is doomed without Christ.[42] The Rastafarians, however, brush off the fact that he never joined their movement, preferring to view him as the Black Messiah who would lead dispersed Africans back to the promised land (Ethiopia). Rastafarians make free use of the Bible and Christian terminology (such as *Jah, King of kings, Lord of lords, Messiah,* and *Trinity*), but each of these incorporate different meanings.

L. P. Howell, a respected Rastafarian leader, summarized the tenets of Rastafarianism as:

(1) hatred for the White race; (2) the complete superiority of the Black race; (3) revenge on Whites for their wickedness; (4) the negation, persecution, and humiliation of the government and legal bodies of Jamaica; (5) preparation to go back to Africa; and (6) acknowledging Emperor Haile Selassie as the Supreme Being and only ruler of Black people.[43]

Even though Rastafarians consider the Bible a sacred text, its message has been altered and God's promised Messiah, Jesus Christ (Matt. 16:18; Acts 4:12), denied. Scripture is clear that there is only one King of kings and Lord of lords (Eph. 4:5; Rev. 17:14; 19:16). The fact that Ras Tafari, king of Ethiopia, never joined the movement casts tremendous doubt on the idea that he considered himself anything but mortal. There are clearly defined differences between the truth of the Bible and the fabrication of Rastafarianism.

Case Study

Jim Haskins

In 1969 a 22-year-old woman dashed into the emergency room of a Baltimore hospital and hysterically begged for help. Her twenty-third birthday was only three days away and she was sure she was going to die before

---

42. See, for example, his speech "One Race, One Gospel, One Task," before the World Evangelical Congress, Berlin, October 28, 1966.

43. Barrett, *The Rastafarians,* 85.

it came. The bewildered emergency room staff calmed her down and asked her to tell them why she believed she was going to die. She had been born on a Friday the thirteenth in the area of the Okefenokee Swamp in Georgia, the young woman explained. After her birth it had been discovered that the midwife who had delivered her was a "Voodoo" and that she cursed every child born on such a fateful day. The young woman knew of two other girls born on a Friday the thirteenth in the same area whom the same midwife had cursed. The midwife had predicted that one would never live to be sixteen. That girl had died in a car accident when she was fifteen. The midwife had said that the second girl would never see twenty-one. She had been shot and killed in a gun fight in a night club on the eve of her twenty-first birthday. The third girl faced her questioners in the hospital in Baltimore and told them the midwife had said she would never live to be twenty-three.

Though skeptical, the hospital staff admitted the young woman for observation. The next morning a nurse found her dead in bed. Cause of death was listed as unknown.

In July 1973 some very strange objects were reported found in New York City's Central Park. On one occasion it was the carcass of a chicken; on another, it was a pig's head.

Ridgefield, New Jersey, police reported several eerie findings during the six-month period between October 1974 and April 1975. In the fall they found twelve white wax candles, a bag of oranges and tangerines, and several raw eggs dyed yellow in the English Neighborhood Church Cemetery. They shrugged off the incident as a youthful prank and thought nothing more of it—until February. In that month they found in the cemetery a bloody towel and several severed chickens' heads. Then on Good Friday someone reported finding a blood-stained tombstone and the carcass of a mongrel dog. Searching the area later, the police found the dog's head.

In late July 1976 James R. Rosenfield of Manhattan decided to bicycle up to the Inwood section of the island. Walking his bike along the shore of the Spuyten Duyvil creek, he was astonished to find a pile of dead animals, including three chickens, two ducks, several pigeons and fish, and a baby goat. They lay on a bed of chopped apples, oranges and carrots. On a rock about ten feet away were drawings of a stylized bird and a human figure.

Reverend Willie Maxwell was suspected of doing away with several family members. He was reportedly a practitioner of Voodoo.

In November 1977, five teenagers were arrested for breaking into crypts in two Queens, New York, cemeteries and removing skulls to sell for prices ranging up to $500.00 each to cult worshippers.

In November 1977, police found the frail and dehydrated body of six-year-old Daniel Bush in the basement apartment of a house in Indianapolis. An autopsy revealed, according to a hospital spokesman, "the highest concentration of salt in the bloodstream we have ever seen." Daniel's eight-year-old brother and seven-year-old sister were hospitalized for malnutrition, and their mother, Ms. Trula Bush, was arrested. Mrs. Willa Mayes, forty, with whom Ms. Bush and her children were staying, was arrested for allegedly neglecting her three grandchildren, aged eight, seven, and five, who were also hospitalized for malnutrition. All six children, the reports alleged, had been denied solid food and fed a salt solution in what appeared to be a religious ritual of purification (salt has long been regarded as a purifier in conjure lore).

Further investigation revealed that Mrs. Mayes was a practicing Spiritist who said she had been born with a "caul" or "veil" (remnants of the fetal membrane) over her face and claimed to be able to heal the sick, foretell the future, and administer mystic spells. In the basement where Daniel Bush's body was found were two wooden altars containing a variety of religious objects, including colored candles, a seven-branched candelabrum, pictures and statues of Christ, a number of bottles filled with powders and liquids, and other items described as "characteristic of various Voodoo rites." Mrs. Mayes reportedly had traveled frequently to nearby cities, including Louisville, Kentucky, to meet with fellow believers and other Spiritists. In Louisville, she had met Ms. Bush, who had taken her children to Indianapolis and moved in with Mrs. Mayes about a month before Daniel Bush had died.

According to neighbors in Indianapolis, chanting could be heard coming from Mrs. Mayes' apartment at night. A male neighbor said, "She told me that at will she could cast a spell . . . put a whammy on anybody." A female neighbor said she had had "spiritual visits" with Mrs. Mayes: "She said she could fix people, and she could, too. I remember one time she said somebody had something on me and we took care of it." The woman refused to elaborate on how the offender had been taken care of. A Louisville man named Frank Pollack reported that the year before Mrs. Mayes had offered to cure his mother of cancer. He and his mother had refused Mrs. Mayes' help, and when Mrs. Pollack died about six weeks later, Mrs. Mayes had told him his mother's death was due to her failure to follow directions. She then told Pollack to burn a book of poems he had that she said was evil. To get rid of her, he told her he had burned the book. Pollack was the only person interviewed who agreed to be quoted by name. Some did not wish to become involved in the legal proceedings, but some feared "hexes" or curses.

The arraignment of Ms. Bush and Mrs. Mayes was cut short when Mrs. Mayes suddenly fell to her knees with arms outstretched, creating a furor in the courtroom. Ms. Bush informed the astonished onlookers that the episode was a "spiritual reply."[44]

Occult power is real, and it influences the lives of millions of people today. Western culture produces endless excuses and explanations for any event with even a whiff of the supernatural attached to it, but those who experience the reality of Voodoo and other occult-based religions know the truth of its power and influence. There exists in the world today the supernatural power of the only living God who works for the good of mankind, and the supernatural power of an evil angel, Satan (and his followers), who work to destroy all human beings. The evil ones have nothing to lose—they are forever cast out from heaven and from the presence of God. For them, there is no love, no redemption, and no hope. Is it any wonder, then, that they virulently hate the object of God's great love and redemption? What is unseen in this world is very *real,* and it affects human lives for eternity.

---

44. As detailed by Jim Haskins, African-American author and journalist, in *Voodoo and Hoodoo,* 75–79.

Native Americans and the Occult

The history of Native Americans reveals a people resolved, resilient, and deeply religious. In the face of brutal massacres, forced marches, strict missionary schools, and isolated reservations, Native Americans initially succumbed to the culture and wishes of the white race that defeated them. Tribal chiefs and medicine men, or *shamans,* became casualties of insurrection, and religion was legislated in an effort to destroy any social connections or links to tribal history. A clear plan existed in high places to separate parents from children and reeducate the young in the *correct* way of thinking.[45]

It was a nightmarish existence for Native Americans, an all-too-familiar repeat of the terror and despair experienced by millions of occupied peoples throughout history. Gone were the sweat houses, powwows, and peyote (a cactus with hallucinogenic properties), and in their places stood the doctrines and dialogue of Christianity. Most conversions had nothing to do with the love of Jesus and everything to do with self-preservation; they were political converts, very much like the African-American slaves who used the name "Christian" to stop persecution like a child uses a bandage to stop the bleeding.

Ironically, at the same time the government worked so successfully at assimilation, American scholars and those who labeled themselves "friends of the Indians" began to document and preserve Native American heritage:

> Beyond the context of this oppressive legal discourse another shift was taking place in the US in the late 19th century—the emergence of a new kind of publicity with regard to Indian religions. From Edward S. Curtis's photographic showings, to Buffalo Bill's Wild West Show, to the 1893 Columbian Exposition, the 1904 St. Louis World's Fair, and city and county fairs held annually across the United States, the display of indigenous Americans proliferated and their otherwise legally prohibited ceremonial practices were embraced as an integral part of the heritage of America. . . .
>
> Thus, just as the passing of tradition was being outlawed among Indians, its passing to the American public was pursued with a penchant.[46]

---

45. Gooding, "At the Boundaries of Religious Identity," 161.
46. Ibid.

In the face of planned extermination, Native American culture survived and remained resilient: the old ways never died out, they simply reformatted into a unique blend of Christianity and Native American traditions. The twentieth century brought the culmination of all efforts to restore respect to the Indian nations with the passage of the American Indian Religious Freedom Act (1978), a law written to ensure the fair practice of traditional religion by a people categorized as "domesticated dependant nations . . . [whose] relation to the United States resembles that of a ward to his guardian."[47] The arrival of New Age spirituality during the mid-twentieth century paved the way to a wider study and acceptance of the mystical, ecofriendly Native American tradition. Sweat houses, peyote, powwows, and Sundances became accepted and encouraged among the hundreds of tribes in America totaling almost 2.5 million people.[48] Vision seekers or healers (labeled *shaman* by Western scholars) returned to their position of influence, mixing Bible verses and Christian prayers with divination and chants to the great Creator; directing people from all walks of life in their quests for spirit-guides.

Native American Religious Beliefs

In many ways, Native American traditional religion has much in common with African traditional religion: both are ancient in origin and practice, and both struggled against seemingly insurmountable odds to emerge in the twentieth century as powerful spiritual influences. The influence of Christianity impacted both traditions to the point where they adopted its language and creeds in the interest of self-preservation, assimilating them into indigenous belief systems. Both African and Native American religons also profess:

The same monotheistic belief in one Creator or Great Spirit

The idea that every material thing has a spirit (animism)

The acceptance of nature as sacred

The integral blending of spirituality with the mundane of everyday life.[49]

---

47. As quoted in Robert S. Michaelsen, "The Significance of the American Indian Religious Freedom Act of 1978," Journal of the American Academy of Religion 52, no. 1 (1984): 93–115, http://links.jstor.org/sici?sici=0002-7189%28198403%2952%3A1%3C93%3ATSOTAI%3E2.0.CO%3B2-C.
48. U.S. Census Bureau, "Census 2000 PHC-T-18. American Indian and Alaska Native Tribes in the United States: 2000," updated June 30, 2004, http://www.census.gov/population/cen2000/phc-t18/tab001.pdf 9 (accessed July 30, 2007).

Today, Native Americans believe that every aspect of their lives reflects their religion, so they would rather not be limited to the label "Christian." Even tribal political governments are so deeply rooted in religious practices that they cannot be divorced from them and survive. On modern reservations, the word *Christian* is disliked and steadfastly avoided as a suitable religious descriptor, even if someone agrees with all the tenets of Christianity. Should an Indian adopt it, he or she would likely be labeled an "apple Indian"—white on the *inside* and Indian on the *outside*.

Although the religious details of Native American tribes are as plentiful as their numbers, many share similar core beliefs:

1. *The Great Creator.* An all-powerful, benevolent Creator exists. He created human beings and everything else in the world (although some tribes believe he distributed his creative power to lesser deities), and he watches over his creation. The Iroquois Nation, the largest segment of the North American Indian tribes (designated *Iroquois Nation* based on similar language patterns), calls him "Great Spirit" or *Hawenneyu.* The Apache call him "Creator of All" or "Sky Man."[50] Humans are not capable of understanding the Creator's nature or plan. Totem poles often told creation stories about the great Creator through carved and painted images.

2. The power of *The Sacred Tree.* A myth taught to many tribes to illustrate the powerful connection between people, nature, and the Divine. "For all the people of the earth, the Creator has planted a *Sacred Tree* under which they may gather, and there find healing, power, wisdom and security. . . . The ancient ones taught us that the life of the tree is the life of the people."[51]

49. For a detailed historical analysis of Native American religion, see Charles Alexander Eastman, The Soul of the Indian, http://www.sacred-texts.com/nam/eassoul.htm.
50. Edward S. Curtis, *The North American Indian* (Project Gutenberg, 2006), http://www.gutenberg.org/files/19449/19449-0.txt. See "Mythology—Creation Myth" under the heading "The Apache": "There was a time when nothing existed to form the universe, no earth, no sky, and no sun or moon to break the monotony of the illimitable darkness. But as time rolled on, a spot, a thin circular disc no larger than the hand, yellow on one side and white on the other, appeared in midair. Inside the disc sat a bearded man but little larger than a frog, upon whom was to fall the task of creating all things. KAtÄrastan, The One Who Lives Above, is the name by which he is now known, though some call him YAAdÄstan, Sky Man."
51. Judie Bopp, Michael Bopp, Lee Brown, and Phil Lane Jr., *The Sacred Tree* (Twin Lakes, WI: Lotus Light Publications, 1985), 7.

3. *Spirit-beings, inferior to the Creator, exist to carry out his will.* Some Native Americans are monotheists, acknowledging the existence of many lesser spirits who are not deities; others are polytheists, believing in the Creator and multiple lesser deities; still others are panentheists, believing the Divine is in all things and all things are encompassed by the Divine. The Iroquois call the lesser spirits "invisible agents" or *Honochenokeh*; they surround the Creator (Hahgwehdiyu, called the Right-Handed Twin) and fulfill his wishes.

The Apache spent a great deal of time trying to placate all of these spirits they considered lesser deities. Edward Curtis (d. 1952), the brilliant photographer and explorer who interviewed and photographed thousands of American Indians at the end of the nineteenth century, wrote:

> There is scarcely an act in the Indian's life that does not involve some cere-
> monial performance or is not in itself a religious act, sometimes so compli-
> cated that much time and study are required to grasp even a part of its real
> meaning, for his myriad deities must all be propitiated lest some dire disas-
> ter befall him. The Apache is inherently devoutly religious; his life is com-
> pletely moulded by his religious beliefs. From his morning prayer to the
> rising sun, through the hours, the days, and months throughout life itself
> every act has some religious significance. Animals, elements, every observ-
> able thing of the solar system, all natural phenomena, are deified and
> revered. Like all primitive people, not understanding the laws of nature, the
> Apache ascribe to the supernatural all things passing their understanding.
> The medicine-men consider disease evil, hence why try to treat evil with
> drugs? Disease is of divine origin, so to the beneficent and healing gods the
> Apache naturally make supplication for cure.[52]

4. *These spirits or gods directly interact with and affect human lives.* The medicine man or holy man of each tribe carried the responsibility of interceding between the gods and the people through powwows (where the Sundance is performed), rituals, amulets/fetishes, and herbal magic designed to placate and prevent disaster or pun-

---

52. Curtis, *The North American Indian.* This commentary by noted frontier photographer and explorer Edward Curtis is an invaluable eyewitness account. He notes that his work was "Field Research Conducted Under the Patronage of J. Pierpont Morgan."

ishment. The Sundance focuses on the central importance of the sun to the existence of Plains Indians like the Lakota. "[It] was their major communal religious ceremony. . . . The rite celebrates renewal, spiritual rebirth, and regeneration of the living Earth with all its components."[53] The importance of the circle within Native American cultures is also directly related to rituals. Medicine wheels of various sizes, thought to have been integral to different Indian societies, are scattered throughout North America. Their exact meaning and purpose is still a mystery today.[54]

5. *Humans are capable of evil, and some spirits are evil.* Evil spirits are supernatural entities that coexist with humans and have the power to shape individual lives. They are a simple—if deadly—fact of life, but they can be placated through ceremonies, amulets, and magic.

6. *Divination and quests for spirit-guides are necessary for determining life pathways and personal goals.* These quests are usually accomplished in a sweat house, which is a small, separate structure made of many different types of objects such as wood poles, blankets, or any convenient materials. Professor Ron Englash examined divination and noted:

> Many of the divination practices of indigenous North American cultures involved a vision quest, typically in something like a trance state. It is therefore difficult to assess in terms of a formal or mathematical description. However there were also Native American divination techniques that utilized random movement. One example was the Zuni shuttlecock. Looking a bit like European badminton shuttlecocks, with feathers attached to a weight, the Zuni version was used for both gambling purposes as well as in divination rituals. Another case of random movement in divination was the

---

53. "Native American Cultural Connections" (© 1996–2007 by the Stanford SOLAR Center, Solar Observatories Group, Stanford University, CA), http://solar-center.stanford.edu/AO/connection.html.

54. Photo available at http://medicinewheel.vcsu.edu/. For more information see http://solar-center.stanford.edu/AO/connections.html; http://www.native-languates.org/composition/native-american-medicine-wheel.html, which states, "The Native American medicine wheel was probably built for ritual and spiritual reasons"; and http://www.support-native-american-art.com/Native-American-Medicine-Wheels.html: "There have been between 70 to possibly 150 medicine wheels discovered."

Ojibway "shaking tent," which was a small covered framework which a medicine man would enter, followed by shaking motions of the entire structure. Trembling movements of the hand are used in Navajo divination. Olbrects (1930) describes the use of random movements of a stone suspended by a string in Cherokee divination. Patterns in flowing water and the crackling of a fire were also used in certain Native American divination rituals.

Of course the point of these rituals is not that the movements of tents, stones, fire, and water are simply random, but rather that—given the proper conditions—information emerges out of the randomness.[55]

7. *Philosophy, literature, science and religion are one.* In direct contrast to Western thought, all aspects of Native American life are one. Religion cannot be separated from science or science from religion:

American Indian Philosophy is concerned with the right road for humans to walk in relation to what is around them . . . what is right is true, and what is true is right; the universe is moral. It is in this way that stories, ceremonies and prayer speak the truth. All aspects of human expression have something to tell us about the best way for us to live. In this way, they are all philosophy. And just as American Indian medicine is best described in Western terms as magic, philosophy is, perhaps, best described as poetry. The knowledge of the earth and her capacity to grow plants and nourish humans takes the form of the story of the three sisters. This story is an expression of the knowledge of the earth that was acquired through many years of observation, much like a poem can be an expression of one's experience of a particular landscape. Because philosophy, literature, science and religion are one in American Indian thought; we cannot truly separate the medicine from the magic, nor the philosophy from the poem.[56]

---

55. Ron Eglash, "An Ethnomathematics Comparison of African and Native American Divination Systems" (paper presented at Realities Re-viewed/Revealed: Divination in Sub-Saharan Africa, National Museum of Ethnology, Leiden on July 4–5), http://www.ccd.rpi.edu/eglash/papers/eglash_div_paper.doc.
56. Anne Waters and John H. Dufour, ed., *American Indian thought: A Philosophy Reader* (Oxford: Blackwell, 2003), 23.

8. *Knowledge is essential to life.* Narrowly defined, three basic types of knowledge are deeply valued within the general Native American community: knowledge of the community's traditions and belief systems, knowledge of the environment for the purpose of survival, and sacred knowledge—the understanding of secrets related to spiritual traditions.[57] In this respect also, Native Americans have much in common with the African worldview.

9. *The existence of an afterlife is relative.* Belief in the afterlife varies among Native Americans, with some believing that humans will be judged for the good or evil they do on this earth, and some paying scant attention at all to the afterlife (Navajo). It is also difficult to determine to what extent Christianity influenced the formation of ideas within individual tribes. Some believe in reincarnation, and others in the fact that the universe as a whole is moral, and so life should be lived with the knowledge that punishment after death will take place.

Shamanism

The title *shaman* is not well received or even accepted as a legitimate description in the Native American community today. It is, in fact, a designation most consider derogatory, preferring instead to call healers *holy people, herbalists, wise people, vision seekers,* or just about any term other than *shaman.*[58] This attitude is based on the argument that *shaman* is a label used by the white man, and as such it has little meaning in Native American cultures. In reality, the word *shaman* originates with the seventeenth-century German word *schamane,* more than likely referring to priests of different cultures.[59] These cultures were likely global, since terms closely related to shaman are found in Asia, Africa, and multiple ancient cultures. The word *powwow* more accurately reflects Native American etymological roots as it can be traced directly to the Algonquian Nations. It is generally translated "priest, sorcerer; magical ceremony" or "to use divination, to dream."[60]

The modern use of *shaman* has much more to do with New Age healing practices than it does with any Native American rituals. This has recently become more

---

57. Jerry H. Gill, *Native American Worldviews: An Introduction* (New York: Prometheus, 2003), 154.
58. Jack D. Forbes, "Shamanism: New and Old," University of California, Davis, http://nas.ucdavis.edu/Forbes/shamanism.html.
59. Douglas Harper, *Online Etymology Dictionary,* s.v., "shaman," http://www.etymonline.com/index.php?search=shaman&searchmode=none (accessed August 3, 2007).
60. Ibid.

of a sore point between Native American leaders and freewheeling New Agers, likely due to the latter's drive for personal profit based on pilfered sacred tradition. Native American professor Jack D. Forbes points out, "'Shaman' has been pretty much of a dividing line word: those who use it are non-Native and/or anthropological, or are ignorant of Native Americans' feelings."[61] He goes on to say, "There is no such religion as 'shamanism,' since all of the religions of the world make use —perhaps equally—of the tools of the 'shaman.'"[62]

As it has done with so many ancient rites and practices, the New Age movement has randomly appropriated the methods of the medicine man, portraying scream therapy (where a blanket is placed over the face of a reclining individual who is encouraged to scream to release negative energy), crystals, dream catchers, and assorted paraphernalia as the legitimate tools of a shaman.

Historically, Native American holy men were primarily concerned with the good of the tribe, not personal psychological therapy. They used fasting, psychotropic drugs (peyote), isolation, and other physical deprivation to induce a trance state and initiate contact with the spirit world. During these peyote-induced visions, contact with spirit animals often occurred, and secret wisdom pertaining to daily life was offered and accepted; some medicine men even believed they could shape-shift into their spirit-animals at will to absorb whatever power or knowledge they might possess in order to bring good to the tribe. Animal skins or masks were often worn as a part of these ceremonies to encourage belief and to facilitate the transformation.[63] The frequency of these visions, the similarity of their content, and the spiritual power they yielded to participants all point to consistent access to occult powers.

In practice, true Native American holy men have little in common with New Age shamans, but in spirit they share an ongoing quest for supernatural power:

> The New Age tends to be a catchall for those people who practice a series of techniques taken from Native Americans, Eastern philosophies, and the Western occult tradition that are aimed at enhancing the individual's con-

---

61. Forbes, "Shamanism: New and Old."
62. Ibid.
63. Michael Webster, "Shamans and Shamanism," Grand Valley State University, http://faculty. gvsu.edu/websterm/Shamans.htm.

sciousness. Many of the same techniques that are practiced by members of the New Age, such as astral projection, meditation, sending healing energy, are also practiced by Witches, Neopagans, and Shamans. Although there are important overlaps, there are, nonetheless, differences among these groups. The most important difference lies in how each group defines its activities. For most Neopagans and Witches, the focus of their practices is on the celebration of nature. Magic is viewed as part of that celebration and as a form of self-empowerment. Non-Native American Shamans are more concerned with techniques of power and control, and less with the larger spiritual system from which these techniques are taken. The New Age is in some ways the most diverse group. Some members are minimally involved; others view their practices as part of a larger spiritual path and lifestyle.[64]

Skinwalkers and Witches

The dark side of Native American spirituality is witchcraft, also known as "bad medicine." Though its practice is kept secret from outside observers, it is well-known and feared within Native American circles, especially those of the Navajo:

"Witches train extensively—in their own very isolated and secure settings. By Navajo traditional law, a known witch, one who has thus forfeited its status as human, can be killed and this certainly applies to a kind of witch much involved in these endeavours: the Skinwalkers. These are obviously profoundly deviant Navajo who travel at night for nefarious purposes and who are believed to have the ability to turn themselves into various animals. They certainly are garbed in the skins of respective animals. These Witches and the closely related Skinwalkers are not the sorts of things about which one should talk much at all."[65]

---

64. Helen A. Berger, ed., Witchcraft and Magic: Contemporary North America (Philadelphia: University of Pennsylvania Press, 2005), 3.

65. University of Utah Economics, Marxism Archive, "Witchcraft: Skinwalkers and Witches," http://archives.econ.utah.edu/archives/marxism/2004w32/msg00262.htm. For more information on Navajo Skinwalkers see Clyde Kluckhohn, *Navajo Witchcraft* (Boston: Beacon Press, 1963).

Many Navajo believe that people can take the form of animals in order to inflict harm. It is the darkest side of Navajo witchcraft, so dark very few will talk about it and most will not even speak the Navajo name for Skinwalker. Eyewitness accounts of threatening encounters with Skinwalkers are common, whispered in the dark and posted anonymously on the Internet. In view of the demonic materialization described by Daniel D. Home and other physical mediums, these accounts cannot be completely dismissed as tall tales or myth.[66] Paranormal phenomena occur in this world whether our culture acknowledges it or not, but just how far this power can affect the human surrendered to it is unknown. The world of the occult is powerful, and it offers this power to those who seek it. But we as Christians need not fear it. Our victory is secure in the death and resurrection of Jesus—we are co-heirs with Christ and we will judge the angels (Romans 8:17; 1 Cor. 6:3).

One thing is certain: the God of the Bible has made it clear that He has nothing to do with occult rites, divination, and magic, so there can only be one other source of this supernatural power—and it is not interested in human self-empowerment. It is only interested in human self-destruction.

SCRIPTURAL RESPONSE

There exists today the divine spirit of truth and its potent counterpart, the spirit of error. Christianity, founded on the Word of God, and traditional religions, steeped in the occult, cannot both be right; someone is wrong, and Christians had better be prepared to demonstrate reasons for their faith. The Church has been deluded for many years into believing that all we must do to discharge our obligation as Christians is to go out into the world and tell people that Jesus loves them. Once we have done that, we think we have accomplished our task. But this is not New Testament theology, and it did not originate from the Holy Spirit. If you read the New Testament, you will discover the amazing fact that almost half of it is an *apologetic* document—the men speaking were speaking in defense of the faith, giving reasons for their belief in Jesus Christ.

---

66. There is no scientific proof that a Skinwalker can physically transform; what has been demonstrated by Dr. Charles Richet and Sir William Crookes is the power of spiritual beings (demons) to transform themselves into semi-physical beings with specific characteristics for short periods of time. See chapter 9, "Tools of the Occult."

When our Lord was questioned by the Pharisees, by the Sadducees, by the Herodians, and by other people who were constantly trying to entrap Him, Jesus did not turn around and say, "God loves you. The Lord bless you; depart in peace. Everything is going to be all right. Remember, love one another." You will not find that theology in the New Testament. Jesus took the time to answer their questions; He took the time to reprove and rebuke their words because they were distorting the truth of God. Some of the most scathing words ever heard on this planet were uttered by the man who said, "Let the little children come to Me, and do not forbid them; for such is the kingdom of heaven" (Matt. 19:14–15).

The world is always ready to accept the Jesus with the light beard, long hair, Nordic features, and milksop theology. It will always welcome this Jesus, but it will never stand for the Jesus who said, "Depart from Me, you cursed, into the everlasting fire prepared for the devil and his angels" (Matt. 25:41–42). The world will tolerate the love of God, but it wants nothing to do with the justice of God.

It is a strange distortion that when Christians stand up for their faith, they are accused of attacking the world. The truth of the matter is that when Christians stand up, they are *emulating* their Master. They are doing precisely what Christ and His apostles did. People say this is very narrow and dogmatic; they insist we must be more *loving.* Yet Jesus Christ, who was incarnate love—a fact no one will deny— said to the Pharisees, "Serpents, brood of vipers! How can you escape the condemnation of hell?" (Matt. 23:33). Incarnate love could invoke divine judgment, and if we emulate Jesus, so can *we.* Incarnate love spoke of divine justice, and so must we. We cannot have a schizophrenic gospel that tells people how much God loves them, and deliberately ignores the terrible price they will pay if they turn away from that love.

The goliath many Christians face today, when dealing with the challenge of traditional religions, is the specter of political correctness. The prevailing worldview of "live and let live" repeatedly rears its ugly head (even among some members of the Church)—taunting believers even as Goliath's arrogance taunted the Israelites—with the constant spiritual mantra, "All beliefs are valid." This is the foundation of the kingdom of the occult: all beliefs are legitimate and worthy of respect. All religions are valid, and who are we to say they are not? In our society, it is the height of intolerance to attack someone else's religion; what works for you may not work for others and vice versa, so we must live and let live.

Unfortunately for the world (and for some people who think they are Christians), Jesus has this to say in response: "I am the way, the truth, and the life. No one comes to the Father except through Me" (John 14:6). He also said, "I am the door of the sheep. All who ever came before Me are thieves and robbers," (John 10:7–8), and "I and My Father are one" (John 10:30).

There is only one eternal God, revealed in His Word as three persons: the Father, the Son and Savior Jesus Christ, and the Holy Spirit. In these short statements, Jesus destroys the legitimacy of every religion in this world other than Christianity. In claiming to be God, Jesus in essence exhibited the same authority and demanded the same respect as the Lord God Jehovah, Elohim—Creator of all things.

The Trinity in Scripture

There are no other gods, there are no goddesses and all ancestors of the human race are either in heaven or hell. They have no influence on the lives of human beings. Everything and everyone other than the one, eternal God is a counterfeit, specifically contrived to distract and destroy. The God of the Bible is the only God, and He reveals Himself to mankind as the Father, Son, and Holy Spirit. The Christian doctrine of the Trinity did not "begin" at the Council of Nicaea, nor was it derived from "Pagan influences." While Egyptian, Chaldean, Hindu, and other Pagan religions do incorporate so-called trinities, these have no resemblance to the Christian doctrine, which is unique and free from any heathen cultural vagaries. According to Christianity, the doctrine of the Trinity teaches that within the unity of the one Deity there are three separate Persons who are coequal in power, nature, and eternity. This teaching is derived from the clear teaching of Scripture beginning in the first chapter of the first book. In Genesis, at the dawn of creation, an interesting conversation took place: "Let *Us* make man in *Our* image, according to *Our* likeness" (Gen. 1:26).

The significance of the plural "us" and "our" is no small issue. Either God was talking to Himself (a conjecture which even Jewish commentators reject), to the angels, or to other Persons, deliberately unidentified. That He would not have been talking to angels is clear because the next verse, referring to the creation of man, declares, "in the image of God He created him" (v. 27). God never created man in the image of angels, but in the *divine* image. In Genesis 1:26, the Father was addressing His Son and the Holy Spirit. No other explanation fits the context.

In Genesis 3:22, after Adam had sinned, God declared, "The man has become like one of Us". Later, concerning the Tower of Babel, God said, "Let Us go down and there confuse their language" (Gen. 11:7). In both instances the mysterious plurality again emerges. Later, the Old Testament prophets implied this same mysterious relationship within the Deity. In recounting his call to the prophetic office, Isaiah records that God asked, "Whom shall I send? Who will go for Us?" (Isa. 6:8). Why does God say *Us* instead of *Me?* The answer is self-evident: God wished to testify of His threefold existence and nature.

In Zechariah, Jehovah spoke prophetically of the crucifixion and the second advent of the Messiah with these words: "And I will pour on the house of David and on the inhabitants of Jerusalem the Spirit of grace and supplication; then they will look on Me whom they pierced. Yes, they will mourn for Him as one mourns for his only son, and grieve for Him as one grieves for a firstborn" (Zech. 12:10). Do not miss the importance of the *Me* and *Him.* Clearly the Lord God is speaking, yet He Himself changes the usage of *I* and *me* to *Him,* and He speaks about being "pierced." There can be little room for question. God the Father is speaking of His beloved Son, the second person of the Trinity, the One who shares the Divine nature, the One who was to be made sin for us.

Quite often the question is asked, "How can God be one and yet three?" or "How can three added together produce one?" To understand this, we must realize that God is not triplex but *triune.* He is beyond the laws of finite mathematics. The word *one* itself has different meanings in the Old Testament. In Deuteronomy 6:4, Moses declared to Israel, "Hear, O Israel: The LORD our God, the LORD is one!" Many persons seize upon this text as an allegedly "unanswerable" argument against the doctrine of the Trinity. They say, "Here the Bible says that God is one. If He is one, how can He also be three, or three in One?"

The One God

But what does the word *one* mean? Does it always indicate solitary existence? Genesis 2:24 recounts that God spoke of Adam and Eve becoming: "one flesh." God did not mean that Adam became Eve, or vice versa; rather, He meant that in the marriage union, the two persons became as *one* before Him. So we see that unity of a *composite* character was recognized by God Himself as existing within the world He had created. The Lord Jesus Christ Himself recognized composite unity when He declared about people joined in marriage, "the two shall become one flesh" (Mark 10:8).

Further use of the term *one* is found in Numbers 13:23–24, where the spies returning from the land of Canaan spoke of "one cluster of grapes," which could only mean that many grapes clung from *one* stem, although all drew their life from the same source. We can see, then, that the word "one" may refer to a composite unity rather than merely to a solitary "one."

If the United States should be attacked by a foreign power, Americans would "rise as one" to the defense of the country. Yet no one would say that everyone had instantaneously become "one person." Rather, we would be one in a composite unity, one in purpose or will to work toward a common goal. Scripture, however, indicates that the doctrine of the Trinity of God is far above the idea of mere agreement of will or goal; it is a unity of the basic scriptural nature of substance, and Deity is that substance (John 4:24; Heb. 1:3). When we speak of being "one in faith and doctrine" or of "standing as one" in a time of crisis, we do not violate the sense of the word. Why then should we not accept composite unity where the nature of God is concerned? Certainly the Scriptures do not prohibit such a view.

The doctrine of the Trinity emerges from the New Testament Scriptures in several places.

1. *The Incarnation*—The birth of the Lord Jesus Christ as described in the accounts in Matthew and Luke show that the doctrine of the Trinity was not a later invention of theologians. Luke records, "*The Holy Spirit* will come upon you, and the power of *the Highest* will overshadow you; therefore, also, that Holy One who is to be born will be called *the Son* of God" (Luke 1:35; emphasis added).

Since other passages of Scripture reveal that the term "Highest" refers to God the Father, we have in Luke a concrete instance of the Holy Spirit, the Father, and the Son all being mentioned together in the supernatural event of the Incarnation.

2. *The Baptism of Our Lord*—When Jesus Christ was baptized, the heavens opened and "the *Holy Spirit* descended in bodily form like a dove upon Him, and a voice came from heaven which said, "You are *My beloved Son*; in You *I am* well pleased" (Luke 3:21–22; emphasis added).

In these verses we see the Son being baptized, the Spirit descending upon Him, and the Father bearing testimony.

3. *Discourses of Christ*—In John 14 and 15, Christ told His disciples about the

preeminence of the nature of God and the unity of Triune composition. Jesus declared, "And I will pray *the Father*, and He will give you another *Helper*, that He may abide with you forever—the *Spirit of truth*, whom the world cannot receive, because it neither sees Him nor knows Him; but you know Him, for He dwells with you and will be in you" (John 14:16–17). Our Lord here prays to the Father for the Spirit, and His awareness of the Trinity is quite apparent. In John 14:26 and 15:26, Christ uses the same formula, mentioning the three persons of the deity and indicating their unity, not only of purpose and will but of basic nature.

4. *Paul's Letters*—The apostle Paul was definitely aware of the triune nature of God. He wrote, "The grace of the Lord Jesus Christ, and the love of God, and the communion of the Holy Spirit be with you all. Amen" (2 Cor. 13:14). It would have been difficult for Paul to give this benediction if the Father, Son, and Holy Spirit were not equal. Paul also describes Christ as, "For in Him dwells all the fullness of the Godhead bodily" (Col. 2:9; literal translation) and as possessing God's very nature (Phil. 2:10; Isa. 45:23).

5. *The Great Commission*—In Matthew 28:18–20 the Lord Jesus commissions the disciples to go out and preach the gospel and to make disciples of all people. He commands them also to baptize: "Go therefore and make disciples of all the nations, baptizing them in the name of the Father and of the Son and of the Holy Spirit". Taken with the other passages bearing on the subject, this statement from Jesus is an extremely powerful argument for the Christian doctrine of the Trinity.

6. *Creation*—Although the Bible does not explain to us how the three persons of the Trinity are the one God, it tells us most emphatically that the Spirit of God created the world (Gen. 1:2), the Father created the world (Heb. 1:2), and the Son created the world (Col. 1:16). If you check the creation references in the New Testament, you will see that these particular references are bolstered by several others teaching the same things.

The apostle Paul declared in Acts 17:24, "God, who made the world and everything in it, since He is Lord of heaven and earth, does not dwell in temples made with hands." This forces us to an irresistible conclusion: as creation has been attributed to the Father, the Son, and the Holy Spirit singly and collectively, *they are the one God.* There cannot be three gods. The Scripture declares, "Look to Me, and be saved, All you ends of the earth! For I am God, and there is no other" (Isa. 45:22). There is unity in Trinity and Trinity in unity.

7. The Resurrection of Christ—A final instance of trinitarian emphasis is that of the resurrection of our Lord. In John 2, Christ declared to the Jews, "Destroy this temple, and in three days I will raise it up" (v. 19). John hastens to tell us that Jesus was speaking of the resurrection of His earthly body (v. 21). Other scriptures state that Christ was raised by the agency of the Holy Spirit (Rom. 8:11), and Peter says the Father raised the Son (Acts 3:26), so again God's Word affirms the triune existence.

Some, however, who believe in the personality of the Father and the Son have doubts about the personality of the Holy Spirit. They need not remain in doubt. The Bible clearly indicates that the work the Holy Spirit does can only be done by a personality. For example, in John 16:13–15, the Spirit is called the Guide who will lead us into all truth. In Romans 8:27, He *intercedes* for the saints; in Ephesians 4:30, He *grieves*; in Acts 21, He *commands* and *prophesies*; and in Acts 5:3-4, Peter calls Him *God*. Certainly His claim to equality and personality is as real as that of the Father and Son.

We may not fully understand the great truth of the Trinity. However, we can see the rays of light that emanate from God's Word and teach us that, in a mysterious sense beyond the comprehension of man's finite mind, God is *one* in nature but three in person and manifestation. God is capable of being and doing what the mind of man cannot fathom. But in reverence, man is still privileged to adore.

In the world of chemistry, it is possible for a substance to exist *simultaneously* in three separate and distinct forms yet remain basically one in structure or nature. Water, for example, under pressure and in a vacuum at a given temperature below freezing exists simultaneously as liquid, gas, and ice; yet it is identifiable always as water (H_2O), its basic nature. This is called in physics "the triple point of water" and is associated with the study of thermodynamics.

Those who cry "impossible" where the Trinity of God or a similar event of the supernatural is concerned must compare its chemical counterpart in the natural world. Why can they not conceive of the Author of "the triple point" being supernaturally triune in His nature? If something is true of God's creation, can it not also be true of the Creator? If our Creator can design a "triple point of water," He can surely be a triune God Himself, and He can surely live within us and care about us.

The Bible assure us that this is so, and we accede to this teaching, for "he who comes to God must believe that He is, and that He is a rewarder of those who diligently seek Him" (Heb. 11:6). From the Church fathers, through the reformers, and on to the present day, historic Christianity continues to echo the testimony of the prophets and the apostles of old.

No man can fully explain the Trinity, though in every age scholars have propounded theories and advanced hypotheses to explore this mysterious biblical teaching. But despite the worthy efforts of these scholars, the Trinity is still largely incomprehensible to the mind of man.

Perhaps the chief reason for this is that the Trinity is a-logical, or beyond logic. It, therefore, cannot be made subject to human reason or logic. Because of this, opponents of the doctrine argue that the idea of the Trinity must be rejected as untenable. Such thinking, however, makes man's corrupted human reason the sole criterion for determining the truth of Divine revelation. God cannot be judged by man, nor can God's revelation be replaced by man's reason, and it is in God's revelation that we find the remarkable evidence for the Trinity in the Christian faith.

Traditional religions originated with a belief in the one Creator until polytheism crept in, the result of sin and the activity of Satan. It corrupted the truth of the one God and His unchangeable love into a world overseen by an isolated and unreachable God; a world of fear controlled by ruthless spirit-beings appeased only through sacrifice, divination, and magic. There is power in the world of the occult—satanic power—but it can never match the awesome power of the one, true God.

CONCLUSION

Where does the occult get its zeal and power? Who energizes the kingdom of the occult? Paul tells us in Romans 10 that there is such a thing as zeal without knowledge, so we do not have to go too far to find an explanation for the sincere enthusiasm of people lost in the occult. The Jews had it, the cults have it—all kinds of people have zeal without knowledge. The problem that must be explained is *power*. What energy drives these systems throughout the world?

The apostle Paul reveals exactly what we need to know about the energy operative in the world today: he speaks of the other Jesus, the other spirit, and the other gospel, and he warns of false apostles, and deceitful workmen. "For such are false apostles, deceitful workers, transforming themselves into apostles of Christ. And no wonder! For Satan himself transforms himself into an angel of light. Therefore it is no great thing if his ministers also transform themselves into ministers of righteous-

ness, whose end will be according to their works" (2 Cor. 11:13–15). Note the progression of Divine revelation in this chapter: There is another Jesus. There is
another spirit. There is another gospel. There are false apostles. The source of their
power is Satan himself, transformer of that which is evil so that it appears to be
good (v. 13). The apostle Paul anticipated this (v. 15). It is no great surprise that
Satan causes his people to look like us, for the purpose of deceiving the world.

It is vital that Christians become *authorities* on Jesus Christ, so they will never
be fooled by anyone. It is the people who are uninformed who willingly step into
the world of the occult, and it happens to Christians and non-Christians alike.
There are Baptists, Methodists, Lutherans, and Episcopalians—every shade and
variety of born-again people—who became immersed in the occult until the Lord
graciously brought them out again, but not without times of suffering and great
spiritual anguish. Second Corinthians 11:3 is true today as when it was when Paul
first said it: "But I fear, lest somehow, as the serpent deceived Eve by his craftiness,
so your minds may be corrupted from the simplicity that is in Christ."

As believers in Christ, we have a great responsibility. Our responsibility is to
communicate Christ to the world. You may never meet an Aborigine, a Zulu, or a
Yoruba in your lifetime, even though your church may support missionaries all over
the world. But Aborigines, Zulus, and Yoruba litter the United States in the form
of Pagans and Spiritists—whatever you may call them—they are lost in the same
darkness as any of these people scattered throughout the world.

It is not vicious, unkind, or intolerant to speak of this darkness. This is what
God calls it. The task of the Christian is to remember that God loved the world
and sent Christ into it to save man out of it. Our task is to communicate Christ
and Christ's love to the world. If we must, in telling the truth, offend them, then
let us remember that Jesus Christ is the greatest offense of all.

The book of Hebrews tells us that Jesus went outside the gate, and we ought to
go outside with Him (13:12–13). He went outside the established religious structure. He went outside the power structure of politics. He went outside all of the
values of His society and His culture, and He died as a common criminal. The
Hebrew writer says we must go with Him bearing the stigmata, bearing the mark
or the reproach of the Cross. It is going to cost something to walk with Jesus Christ.
It is going to cost something to tell the world that rejects Him—a world living in
spiritual darkness—that they are lost without Him.

Paul speaks very clearly of this in a passage of Scripture most Christians seldom, if ever, stop to consider. "But even if our gospel is veiled, it is veiled to those who are perishing, whose minds the god of this age has blinded, who do not believe, lest the light of the gospel of the glory of Christ, who is the image of God, should shine on them" (2 Cor. 4:3–4). The kingdom of the occult is in darkness because the god of this world has blinded them. These people are not responsible for what Satan has done to them: *they are responsible for not responding to the grace of God.* Our task is to bring that grace into the lives of those who are bound in darkness. Where there is no vision, the people perish (Prov. 29:18). The Church must have the vision, the compassion, and the love for those lost in the dark labyrinth of traditional religions—people living in fear and anxiety—dependent and desperate before merciless false gods. "You are the light of the world. A city that is set on a hill cannot be hidden" (Matt. 5:14–15).

RECOMMENDED RESOURCES

1. Bowden, Henry Warner. *American Indians and Christian Missions: Studies in Cultural Conflict.* Chicago: University of Chicago Press, 1985.

2. Olupona, Jacob K., ed. *African Spirituality: Forms, Meanings and Expressions.* New York: Crossroad, 2000.

3. Nichols, Larry, George Mather, and Alvin Schmidt. *Encyclopedic Dictionary of Cults, Sects, and World Religions.* Grand Rapids: Zondervan, 2006.

4. *Blue Letter Bible,* http://www.blueletterbible.org/.

QUICK FACTS ABOUT DEMON POSSESSION AND EXORCISM

- Satan is the power behind all occult psychic phenomena; his purpose is to deceive mankind and lead people away from God.

- The Bible teaches that demon possession is a common occurrence, not a rare phenomenon.

- Exorcism, used with care and concern, delivers people from evil and promotes healing.

- Jesus taught exorcism by example, and the Church must follow His lead.

- One should never enter into battle against the world of the occult without prayer.

14

Demon Possession and Exorcism

I t is important to understand the nature of Satan before entering into the domain of darkness. He is the adversary of the Church of Jesus Christ and the spirit that controls this realm—the prince of the power of the air. The Bible describes him as a proud spirit, an entity created in another dimension by an all-powerful being: the God of the Bible, the God and Father of the Lord Jesus Christ, the God of the prophets and of Moses, and the God of biblical revelation. Satan was created to serve the Lord, but he was also given free will. Satan exercised that will by his own choice *against* the sovereignty of God, and because of this rebellion, he fell from his position of glory.[1]

Satan, a created being and a marvelous messenger of light (Ezek. 28), was once called Lucifer, meaning "light bearer." He occupied a remarkable position of responsibility in the kingdom of heaven until he, and a large segment of his followers, rebelled against the throne of God. He sought not to be God but to be *like* God, to share the characteristics and the power of God. The gospel of Luke recounts Ezekiel's declaration that he was hurled from heaven, driven out by Michael the archangel (the first of the angelic hosts).

Lucifer, renamed Satan, or "adversary," by God, conquered earth by penetrating the Eden paradise and causing Adam and Eve to sin. He conquered our first parents, corrupted the earth, and caused evil to penetrate the human race and the entire cosmic structure. A simple study of the history of mankind reveals that Satan is alive and well; thriving and powerful on planet earth. He is the enemy that must be confronted in the light of Scripture, and by the power that God has given the Church of Jesus Christ.

Satanic activity is not corporate evil but *personal* evil: violent, subtle, deceitful, and malignant. Satan is not an illusion or a projection of human evil. He is an

---

1. See chapter 1, "The Kingdom of the Occult" and chapter 2, "The Occult Revolution."

entity, an ego, an "I" that was encountered by Jesus Christ, and totally and absolutely defeated at the Cross. The actuality of Satan's defeat will conclude when he is hurled into a lake that the Bible describes as burning for all eternity (Rev. 20:10). He and those who followed him, worshiped him, and acknowledged him as their god, those who refused to acknowledge God himself, and those who denied God's Messiah, will then find God's judgment a reality.

THE POWERS OF DARKNESS

The Bible reveals that Satan has the power to work miracles. According to Exodus 7:10–12, he is able to transform matter. "And Aaron cast down his rod before Pharaoh and before his servants, and it became a serpent. But Pharaoh also called the wise men and the sorcerers; so the magicians of Egypt, they also did in like manner with their enchantments. For every man threw down his rod, and they became serpents. But Aaron's rod swallowed up their rods." God made short work of Satan's snakes, but it is interesting to see exactly what Satan accomplished here: the *transmutation of matter.*[2] There is no doubt that the power of Satan extends to the realm of the material.

The book of Job adds details to the knowledge of Satan's power. He has the authority to manipulate the elements, such as whirlwinds and lightning, and to influence nations so that they rise up and battle against those he desires (Job 1). It is possible for Satan to reveal, in a moment of time, things that exist at great distances—and to reveal it in complete detail. The temptation of Jesus Christ is an excellent example of this. "Again, the devil took Him up on an exceedingly high mountain, and showed Him all the kingdoms of the world and their glory. And he said to Him, 'All these things I will give You if You will fall down and worship me'" (Matt. 4:9). Satan showed Jesus all the kingdoms of the world and all their glory, in just a moment of time.

Job also reveals that Satan has the power to affect the lives of men. He goes before God and accuses people (Job 1:6–9; 2:1–4). His power can affect finances (Job 1:14–17); he can harass with illness, inflict pain and suffering, and even cause death (Job 1:18–19; 2:7; 1 Cor. 5:5). He has the power to influence world events

---

2. For more information, see chapter 7, "Psychic Phenomena."

(Dan. 10:13); political events (Ex. 1; Matt. 2; Rev. 12); and personal relationships, such as friendships and marriage (Job 1–2; John 7). People can certainly make choices in life, but they are vulnerable to outside influences manipulated by the great deceiver, and so these choices may not always be the best, leaving the door wide open for even more satanic attacks.

The good news in all of this is that God has the final word on the subject. "Blessed be the name of God forever and ever, for wisdom and might are His. And He changes the times and the seasons; He removes kings and raises up kings" (Dan. 2:20–21). God is in control; He may allow Satan to do evil in human lives that good may come, but God will only allow him to go so far (Gen. 50:20). The power of Satan is formidable and should never be taken lightly, but God has provided the weapons the Church needs for combat (Eph. 6), and Jesus won the ultimate victory on the Cross.

THE SPIRIT OF THIS AGE

The supernatural war that began in the heavenlies has been fought on earth since the day God expelled Adam and Eve from the garden of Eden, and nowhere is the manifestation of its power seen more clearly than in the mysterious kingdom of the occult. Satan's power is revealed in this world of secrecy and darkness, a power that exercises a destructive influence upon the lives of men and women.

People become preoccupied with and ensnared by the occult for many reasons. In this modern age of scientific and technological wonders, the world is not looking for a messiah to redeem the soul; the world is looking for a technological savior who will solve the problems of economic expansion. They want a savior who will solve the problem of famine, war, and cancer. They desire to prolong the life of man. The world is not looking for a savior of the soul; it is looking for a deliverer of the body and a preserver of a world utopia yet to come.

The postmodernist mind-set of freewheeling spirituality has produced a revolt against science and technology rooted in the utter failure of both to meet the spiritual and physical needs of mankind. People need to know *why* science and technology have not been able to bring into being world peace or cures for the incurable. Why has this not been accomplished? They certainly have been at it long enough. Instead, all there seems to be today is a continuous denigrating of personality. People are depersonalized; they are not human beings anymore—just numbers from birth, sequenced within a matrixlike computer program. Computerization has taken over the cultures of the world, and the backlash from progress itself has produced a tremendous fascination with the mysterious and the unknown.

The modern age, with its wealth of occult material, is proof positive of this fascination. People on the lookout for something *real* no longer pause at the brink of satanic reality—they plunge into the depths of it, secure in their mantra: *If it's real, it's right.* People are enthralled by evil, and this false sense of security is the catalyst that propels them right over the edge of the abyss. Satan has always offered *real* experiences with evil spirits, and they are not only wrong but lethal to the soul. The only thing new about the power of the occult is its modern-day audience, a fresh hunting ground at the mercy of a seasoned hunter.

Today, a balance of terror exists that sends us searching for some kind of alternate reality. People become frightened by these things, and they seek a panacea. Technology has failed, and its failure has led to fears of a mushroom cloud, terrorist attacks, and global warming disasters. Millions of frightened people are caught within a spiritual vacuum, desperately searching for a different truth—the kind that can be found in the mysterious occult reality from another dimension.

The influence of Eastern religions, cults, and Parapsychology has given a stamp of approval to the world of the occult. Scientific experiments, like those conducted by Sir William Crookes in the late nineteenth century, and by modern-day universities and governments in the realm of the occult continue to intrigue and influence the minds of a great many individuals. This type of pseudoscientific Parapsychology research paves the way for interest in the occult and the powers behind it.

Finally, the Bible has been replaced as the authority in the world today, and only Scripture can provide a rock-solid place of safety when people are threatened by invisible, other-dimensional forces. In abandoning the Bible and pushing God aside, not only on the subjects of life, morality, ethics, and salvation, but also on the world of darkness and demons, they have stepped outside the safety zone. The terrifying result of this rejection is that every man, woman, and child now becomes prey to the powers of darkness. In rejecting God, they have rejected their only defense, and they have no authority to resist Satan and his demons.

DEMON POSSESSION: YESTERDAY AND TODAY

There is no doubt that the supernatural has played a significant role throughout man's long and varied history. Wilhelm Schmidt's *The Origin and Growth of Religion* minutely details the progression of religion from monotheistic to polytheistic, supporting the Old Testament's assessment of polytheism as a later form of spirituality. Schmidt's conclusion is lent credibility by the arguments of Ninian Smart in *The Religious Experience of Mankind*:

> In most, if not all of the indigenous cultures of Africa there is a belief in a supreme spirit ruling over or informing the lesser spirits and gods. He governs natural forces, dwells on high, is inexplicable, creates souls, men, and all things. If the lower spirits and deities are more familiar and intimate . . . yet for many Africans such a God exists and is not altogether neglected in worship and prayer.
>
> Thus, ruling over the world which teems with divinities and sacred forces, there is—high above in the sky, but not *of* the sky—some kind of supreme Being. Among many primitive peoples outside Africa a similar belief is attested.[3]

Originally monotheistic, man wandered from God and worshiped idols the Scripture identified as demons. "They shall no more offer their sacrifices to demons, after whom they have played the harlot" (Lev. 17:7). Centuries of archaeological evidence confirm an assortment of religious artifacts pointing to either the fear or veneration of spirit-beings. Mesopotamian carvings (c. 2000 BC) depicting Shutu, demon of the southwest wind, and ancient Etruscan cave drawings of evil spirit-beings in the Tomb of the Blue Demons (Italy c. 400 BC) are but two examples of thousands that reflect ancient civilizations' fear of malignant spirit beings.

3. Ninian Smart, *The Religious Experience of Mankind* (New York: Scribner, 1976), 53.

Italian demons, Chinese demons, Indian demons, and depictions of spirit creatures or deities worldwide throughout ancient history—all seem to point to man's innate recognition of a power far superior to his own. E. R. Dodds discusses the underlying power of what he called the "Irrational" in his classic work *The Greeks and the Irrationa*:

> The men who created the first European rationalism were never—until the Hellenistic Age—"mere" rationalists: that is to say, they were deeply and imaginatively aware of the power, the wonder, and the peril of the Irrational. But they could describe what went on below the threshold of consciousness only in mythological or symbolic language; they had no instrument for understanding it, still less for controlling it; and in the Hellenistic Age too many of them made the fatal mistake of thinking they could ignore it.[4]

This fatal mistake is still being made today in the assessment of the reality and interaction of spirit-beings. The denial of thousands of years of human history, simply because it does not fit into a personal worldview, seems prejudicial. Yet Dr. Kurt Koch, a Lutheran minister with more than forty years' experience battling successfully in the realm of the occult, notes that in the worlds of science and medicine, the supernatural is *impossible*—and if there are no demons, there is no such thing as possession. "Possession does not exist—and cannot exist! So much for scientific objectiveness!"[5]

The Early Church

The early Church considered demon possession a dangerous reality. They dealt with it consistently and effectively, and their efforts remain for posterity. Justin Martyr (c. 150 AD) said in his *Dialogue with Trypho, a Jew*: "For we call Him (Jesus) Helper and Redeemer, the power of whose name even the demons do fear; and at this day, when they are exorcised in the name of Jesus Christ, crucified under Pontius Pilate, governor of Judaea, they are overcome."[6] Irenaeus (c. 190 AD)

---

4. Dodds, *The Greeks and the Irrational*, 254.
5. Kurt Koch, *Occult Bondage and Deliverance* (Grand Rapids: Kregel, 1970), 11.
6. Justin Martyr, *Dialogue with Trypho, a Jew* (Christian Classic Ethereal Library, 2006) chap. 30, http://www.ccel.org/fathers2/ANF-01/anf01-48.htm#P4288_866334.

recorded this concerning Christians: "For some do certainly and truly drive out devils, so that those who have thus been cleansed from evil spirits frequently both believe [in Christ], and join themselves to the Church."[7] Tertullian (c. 200 AD) discussed the well-known conflict of Christians and demons with Scapula, proconsul of Africa. "As for daemons, we not only abhor them, but we overcome and draw them forth daily, and we drive them out of men, as is known unto very many of yourselves."[8]

Demon worship was rampant in the ancient world, the wealth of deities available for adoration in the Greco-Roman sphere, mind-boggling. In addition to the official Roman pantheon of gods and goddesses, there were divine infiltrators from any number of cultures, conquered under the rule of Rome. The Church answered the threat of these religions by calling them what they were: the organized worship of demons. One example of this is Justin Martyr's criticism of the cult of Mithras, whose secret rites included the perversion of the Christian Last Supper:

> For the apostles, in the memoirs composed by them, which are called Gospels, have thus delivered unto us what was enjoined upon them; that Jesus took bread, and when He had given thanks, said, "This do ye in remembrance of Me, this is My body;" and that, after the same manner, having taken the cup and given thanks, He said, "This is My blood;" and gave it to them alone. Which the wicked devils have imitated in the mysteries of Mithras, commanding the same thing to be done. For, that bread and a cup of water are placed with certain incantations in the mystic rites of one who is being initiated, you either know or can learn.[9]

History reveals a widespread belief in supernatural powers and supernatural beings. It details real and constant battles against the forces of darkness, battles that resulted in consistent victories.

---

7. Irenaeus, *Irenaeus Against Heresies* (Christian Classic Ethereal Library, 2007), Book II, 32:4; see also Book II, 31:2, http://www.ccel.org/ccel/schaff/anf01.ix.i.html.

18. David Dalrymple, trans. *The Address of Tertullian of Carthage to Scapula, Proconsul of Africa* (Edinburgh: Murray & Cochrane, 1790), http://www.tertullian.org/articles/dalrymple_scapula.htm.

9. Justin Martyr, *First Apology* (Early Christian Writings, 2006), http://www.earlychristianwritings.com/text/justinmartyr-firstapolog.html.

The Modern Church

In the twentieth-century Western world, the majority of individuals were raised from childhood to view any supernatural phenomena as absurd, relegating the reality of demons and demonic possession to the broom closet of superstitious ignorance. The non-Christian world simply could not wrap its scientific mind around the notion that spirit-beings of any kind could possibly exist. Even a significant percentage of Christians balked at the idea that demon possession was real (let alone a noteworthy problem) in the modern world.

Poised upon the pinnacle of absolute authority, God became the target of scientists, physicians, philosophers, and liberal theologians who worked to systematically erase Him, steadfastly relying on the false premise that science *negates* the spiritual. And if people dared to dismantle God, it was inevitable they would also apply this same methodology of arrogance and ignorance to the devil, eventually relegating him to the fairy-tale realm. If there is no devil, there can be no demon possession, and therefore its symptoms must be explained away. "For the non-Christian psychiatrist, possession just does not exist. At most, it is only an advanced form of hysteria."[10] As the twentieth century progressed, however, a new wave of thinking infiltrated the intellectual scene, forever impacting Western culture by its steady assault upon the citadels of scientific power and influence.

The late 1960s and early 1970s saw the birth of the New Age movement and the slow but resolute rejection by millions of the ironclad scientific mantra: *Science above all else.* This postmodernist era of permissive spirituality evolved to fill the spiritual vacuum left by a cold, unfeeling, and regimented scientific mind-set. Suddenly, *astral projection, chakras* and *energy* became household words. Actress Shirley MacLaine's riveting personal story, *Out on a Limb*, introduced reincarnation into living rooms across America and around the world.[11] Past-life regression became the subject of television documentaries and books such as *The Search for Bridey Murphy.*[12] Famous Hollywood actors such as Glenn Ford proclaimed the reality of their past lives for all to hear and contemplate. William Peter Blatty's *The Exorcist* swept across America and around the world with the force of a tsunami,

---

10. Koch, *Occult Bondage and Deliverance*, 57.
11. Shirley MacLaine, *Out on a Limb* (New York: Bantam, 1983).
12. Morey Bernstein, *The Search for Bridey Murphy* (New York: Doubleday, 1956).

forging the way for movies such as *Poltergeist* and *The Blair Witch Project*.[13] Though incorrect theologically on many points, Blatty's book contained a few nuggets of truth, perhaps because it was based upon a true story.[14]

ENCOUNTERING THE IMPOSSIBLE

The Ouija board is characterized by author William Peter Blatty as a perfectly normal form of entertainment: a lark. But after a fourteen-year-old girl named Regan plays with it and meets a spirit by the name of Captain Howdy, her life suddenly changes. It is the spirit of this board—Captain Howdy—that invades the house and eventually invades the girl.

Here, then, is the first important lesson to be learned from *The Exorcist*: the evil spirit responds as a direct result of the child's initial contact. She penetrated the dimension of darkness using a simple tool—the Ouija board—and encountered evil. Proponents of New Age thinking often argue that good spirits exist as well as bad, and it is possible to encounter either in the quest for contact. This viewpoint flatly contradicts Scripture, which teaches that immediately upon death a person is either in heaven or hades (Luke 16:23; 23:43). Although New Age leaders warn people of the dangers inherent in trying to communicate with "the other side," they offer no guarantee that their rituals of protection hold any power whatsoever over evil spirits. The name of Jesus, however, has a long historical legacy of recorded power.

New Personalities, New Voices, New Languages

A second truth that can be found in the demonic manifestations depicted in *The Exorcist* is that someone possessed by a demonic spirit will exhibit a new personality. This personality (or personalities) may reveal itself in multiple voices—sometimes in different languages. The change in vocal patterns and in facial expressions as the girl passed deeper into possession are perfectly consistent with biblical demonology, and the foul language—used primarily for shock effect—is also consistent with the same ancient demonic powers that have exercised their authority over people from Tibet to the United States. These symptoms should always evoke concern and elicit investigation. A psychiatrist in *The Exorcist* movie (and in real

---

13. William Peter Blatty, *The Exorcist* (New York: Harper and Row, 1971).
14. See Mark Opasnick, *The Real Story Behind the Exorcist* (Philadelphia: Xlibris, 2006).

life) tried to persuade the family that this was a case of schizophrenia, until the supernatural power displayed by the girl convinced them that they could not rely upon psychiatry. They turned instead to the very ancient ritual of exorcism.

Blasphemy and Superhuman Strength

The blasphemy of God and of Jesus Christ often reveals the presence of a spirit from the realm of the demonic, as does the phenomenon of superhuman strength, and they are accurately portrayed here by an entertainment industry of unbelievers. Blasphemy can include outright fury, or it can manifest itself in mockery or in a quiet spirit of rebellion—a reluctance to pray or read the Word of God.[15]

In *The Exorcist*, the young girl attacks one of the brain surgeons who is trying to prove that she has some type of affectation in the temporal lobe of the brain. When a doctor arrives to give her an injection, this fourteen-year-old girl hits him across the face with such force that he flies ten feet across the room. This type of physical strength is a common factor in demon possession, often requiring a number of men to participate in a single exorcism. This strength, combined with the fury of blasphemy, has turned many a skeptic into a believer.

Levitation

One scene in the movie is particularly powerful, and it does Christian theology a great service. In this scene, Regan's mother enters the bedroom to check on her child, and her daughter hits her and then transforms the room into a sea of flying objects: records, bedclothes, and all kinds of floating bits and pieces. It is a fantastic special effect that succeeds in emphasizing another important truth: demonic power is real, and it can manipulate and move matter. There is also a graphic presentation of levitation where the young girl's body is raised by the power of Satan from the bed, and she only returns to normal when the name of the Lord Jesus is invoked. These things happen in the modern world, and they are consistent with biblical theology.

---

15. This is not a "stand alone" symptom, since many people blaspheme and show reluctance to pray and read the Bible. It should be considered an indication of possession only if it is found in combination with the symptoms described here.

Foul Smells and Self-Destructive Behavior

Another signal of demonic influence is the presence of foul smells emanating from or surrounding the body. Classic histories of demonic possession support this type of manifestation. Desecration of sacred objects, such as statues, with sexual symbols is also a demonic calling card.

Once Regan picked up the Ouija board and turned the knob on the dimensional door, the destructive forces of darkness flooded into her life. The child's attempts to disfigure and destroy herself are a horrifying reality portrayed by Hollywood with chilling accuracy. Quite often, scarring and destruction are the aim of demonic forces. By the end of the film, the young girl appears to be totally dominated by Satan.

The danger of the film *The Exorcist* (and many others like it) is that people may believe the inaccurate things it portrays, and in believing these things, may not see Christ as victor and conqueror. Instead, it may foster a fascination with, or fear of, evil. Although this danger exists, and *The Exorcist* has impacted people in many negative ways, it is important to note that it also contributed something positive and powerful: it educated the masses and made them aware of the presence of Satan, the reality of possession, and the fact that the name of Jesus Christ is synonymous with *victory*. When Christ exorcises, the demons *leave*, because He is Lord of all. In Mark 1:24, the demons cried out to Him, "Let us alone! What have we to do with You, Jesus of Nazareth? Did You come to destroy us? I know who You are—the Holy One of God!" Demons cannot stand before the power of Jesus Christ. He is greater than any power of darkness, and through Him, the Church has already overcome them. This is God's victory.

Demon possession is a spiritual disease that invades the body much like an invisible, lethal virus; it is the attack of an unseen entity *not of this world.* If it is never recognized as such, there is no hope for the victim. Dr. Kurt Koch details the symptoms of demon possession, drawn from the ministry of Jesus:

Eight Marks of Demon Possession

In Luke 8:26–33, 38, 39 we find the story of the possessed Gadarene. If we examine the account to discover if there are any characteristics which are typical of possession, we find eight marks or symptoms which distinguish demon possession from mental and nervous diseases.

A. The first fact we are faced with is that in demon possession demons are actually resident in the person concerned. Mark describes them as evil spirits. The phenomenon is the counterpart of the indwelling of the Holy Spirit in a believer.

B. The second sign of possession is the unusual strength exhibited by the possessed person. The Gadarene demoniac was able to break the ropes and chains which bound him.

C. The third sign is the visible conflict within the possessed person. . . . In the case of the Gadarene, on the one hand we see him coming to Jesus apparently for help, and on the other hand he suddenly reacts in fear and begs him not to torment him.

D. Next we have the phenomenon of resistance, an opposition to the things of God. "What have you to do with me?" the Gadarene cried out.

E. The fifth sign is clairvoyance. The Gadarene knew who Jesus was immediately as he saw him, although they had never met before. He recognized, too, that Jesus had the power to deliver him and to drive the demons out.

F. The next mark of possession is the ability of the person to speak with voices not his own. . . . No mentally ill or hysterical person can suddenly start speaking in a foreign language which he has never learned.

G. The seventh mark or sign that a person is demon possessed is the sudden deliverance which is possible. . . . Possessed people . . . can be delivered almost instantaneously when they come into contact with the Lord Jesus Christ.

H. The last characteristic . . . is transference. When the Gadarene was delivered, some 2,000 pigs went berserk and rushed headlong into the sea. Events like this don't occur in medicine.[16]

The Specter of Skepticism

Evil is fascinating, and people naturally find themselves drawn to it. Once someone accepts the reality of supernatural beings, the pursuit of communication with them becomes intriguing. This is why séances are invoked today as never

---

16. Kurt Koch, *Demonology Past and Present* (Grand Rapids: Kregel, 1973), 136–40.

before, and why hundreds of millions of people worldwide are involved in some type of Spiritist religion.[17] The rise of occultism in the United States during the decades of the 1960s and 1970s fostered a tremendous interest in all aspects of Spiritism, including clairvoyance and telekinesis. It was an interest harbored by millions, and as such, it demanded some investigation.

In the wake of this wave of New Age thinking, the scientific elite suddenly found themselves on a battleground of ideologies. Surrounded by persuasive New Age philosophy and experiential evidence, and under siege for failure to provide the world with much-needed answers to war, famine, poverty, and brutality, they could not explain the strange phenomena associated with the supernatural and their occasional end result: possession. Simple investigation of personal stories provided mounting evidence for the reality of spirit-beings and their possible oppression of humans. It was an observable phenomenon—a repeatable experiment—and as such, not easily dismissed.

Today, New Age proponents of spirit encounters insist that it is far more likely most spirits are friendly. Even so, the general rule is to proceed with caution when seeking contact with any supernatural beings. New Agers understand what science does not: sentient, spirit-beings exist, and they powerfully impact individual lives.

Dr. Stafford Betty, professor of religious studies at California State University Bakersfield, offers a solution to the scientific dilemma of possession in a recent article entitled "The Growing Evidence for Demonic Possession: What Should Psychiatry's Response Be?" He proposes that psychiatrists set aside any prejudicial religious definition of demonic possession, and entertain the possibility (based on growing evidence) of the existence of malignant, nonhuman beings that oppress and possess "the unwary, the weak, the unprepared, the unlucky, or the targeted."[18] Dr. Betty does not believe these evil spirits are in any way related to biblical demons. He defines them as "intelligent beings, insensible to us, with a will of their own who seem to bother or oppress us or, in rare cases, possess our bodies outright."[19]

17. Central Intelligence Agency, The World Factbook, "indigenous, eclectic, Voodoo and other," https://www.cia.gov/cia/publications/factbook/fields/2122.html.
18. Stafford Betty, "The Growing Evidence for Demonic Possession: What Should Psychiatry's Response Be?" *Journal of Religion and Health* 44 (2005): 13–30.
19. Ibid.

Dr. Betty correctly confirms the existence of these spirits, while denying any biblical or religious assessment of them. In essence, he reaches a hand across the aisle to the denizens of the scientific world, and offers a compromise on the pretext of compassion: *consider this without religion for the sake of the suffering.* If religion is removed from the equation, perhaps the reality of ethereal beings may become more palatable. It is an interesting position, and as such may eventually impact some in the scientific realm. Betty concludes his argument by suggesting people fight against the automatic assumption by psychiatrists that mental illness can only be a result of "faulty brain chemistry."[20] Instead, we should evaluate evidence related to paranormal phenomena, "to determine whether the tools and techniques of the exorcist and deliverance minister work better than the drugs and therapies of the psychiatrist."[21]

The results of such a study would be startling, especially if the power of the name of Jesus Christ were recorded clinically, as it has been recorded historically over a period of two thousand years. The biblical record on the existence, power, and purpose of these evil spirits is quite clear: malignant supernatural beings exist, and they work to destroy individual lives.

THE PROCESS OF POSSESSION

The end result of demonic attack is life changing, and it is usually the major focus of attention when it comes to the subject of possession. But the onset of possession is just as vitally important, as familiarity with it may help prevent these life-changing episodes.

Exactly what symptoms signal the dangerous beginning of possession? One of the most fascinating patterns of this can be traced in the life of Daniel D. Home (1833–1866), perhaps the most powerful physical medium in recent history. Home exhibited a formidable and consistent power at his séances, and the following is his account of how this power began.

---

20. Ibid., 30.
21. Ibid.

CASE STUDY

Daniel D. Home

My mother was a seer throughout her life. She passed from earth in the year 1850, at the age of forty-two. She had what is known in Scotland as the second sight, and in many instances she saw things which were afterwards found to have occurred at a distance, just as she had described them. She also foresaw many events which occurred in the family, and foretold the passing away of relatives, and lastly, she foretold her own four months previously. . . .

A few months after my mother had passed from earth, one night on going to bed, I heard three loud blows on the head of my bed, as if struck by a hammer. My first impression was that some one must be concealed in my room to frighten me. They were again repeated, and as they were sounding in my ears, the impression first came on me that they were something not of earth. After a few moments' silence they were again heard, and although I spent a sleepless night, I no longer felt or heard any repetition of them. My aunt was a member of the Kirk of Scotland, and I had some two years previously, to her great disapprobation, become a member of the Wesleyan body—but her opposition was so violent that I left them to join the Congregationalists. On going down to breakfast in the morning, she noticed my wan appearance, and taunted me with having been agitated by some of my prayer meetings. I was about to seat myself at the breakfast table, when our ears were assailed by a perfect shower of raps all over the table. I stopped almost terror-stricken to hear again such sounds coming with no visible cause; but I was soon brought back to the realities of life by my aunt's exclamation of horror, "So you've brought the devil to my house, have you?" I ought here to state that there had then been some talk of the so-called Rochester knockings through the Fox family, but apart from casually hearing of them, I had paid no attention to them; I did not know even what they meant. My aunt, on the contrary, had heard of them from some of the neighbors, and considered them as some of the works of the Evil One. In her uncontrollable anger, she seized a chair and threw it at me. Knowing how entirely innocent I was of the cause of her unfortunate anger, my feelings were deeply injured by her violence, and at the same time I was strengthened in a determination to find out what might be the cause of these disturbances of our morning meal.

There were in the village three ministers, one a Congregationalist, one a Baptist, and the other a Wesleyan. In the afternoon, my aunt, her anger at me having for the moment caused her to lose sight of her prejudices against these rival persuasions, sent for them to consult with her, and to pray for me, that I might be freed from such visitations. The Baptist minister, Mr. Mussey, came first, and after having questioned me as to how I had brought these things about me, and finding that I could give him no explanation, he desired that we might pray together for a cessation of them. Whilst we were thus engaged in prayer, at every mention of the Holy names of God and Jesus, there came gentle taps on his chair, and in different parts of the room; whilst at every expression of a wish for God's loving mercy to be shown to us and our fellow-creatures, there were loud rappings, as if joining in our heartfelt prayers. I was so struck, and so impressed by this, that there and then, upon my knees, I resolved to place myself entirely at God's disposal, and to follow the leadings of that which I then felt must be only good and true, else why should it have signified its joy at those special portions of the prayer? This was, in fact, the turning point of my life, and I have never had cause to regret for one instant my determination, though I have been called on for many years to suffer deeply in carrying it out. My honor has been called in question, my pride wounded, my early prospects blighted, and I was turned out of house and home at the age of eighteen, though still a child in body from the delicacy of my health, without a friend, and with three younger children dependent on me for support. Of the other two clergymen, the Congregationalist would not enter into the subject, saying that he saw no reason why a pure-minded boy should be persecuted for what he was not responsible to prevent or cause, and the Methodist was so unkind, attributing it to the devil, that I derived no comfort from him.

Notwithstanding the visits of these ministers, and the continued horror of my aunt, which only increased as each manifestation was developed, the rappings continued, and the furniture now began to be moved about without any visible agency. The first time this occurred I was in my room, and was brushing my hair before the looking-glass. In the glass I saw a chair that stood between me and the door, moving slowly towards me. My first feeling was one of intense fear, and I looked round to see if there were no escape; but there was the chair between me and the door, and still it moved towards me as I continued looking at it. When within about a foot of me it stopped, whereupon I jumped past it, rushed down stairs, seized my hat in the hall, and went out to wonder on this wonderful phenomenon.

After this, when sitting quietly in the room with my aunt and uncle, the table, and sometimes the chairs, and other furniture, were moved about by themselves in a singular way, to the great disgust and surprise of my relations. Upon one occasion, as the table was being thus moved about of itself, my aunt brought the family Bible, and placing it on the table, said, "There, that will soon drive the devils away;" but to her astonishment the table only moved in a more lively manner, as if pleased to bear such a burden. Seeing this, she was greatly incensed, and determining to stop it, she angrily placed her whole weight on the table, and was actually lifted up with it, bodily from the floor. My only consolation at this time was from another aunt, a widow, who lived near, whose heartfelt sympathy did much to cheer and console me. At her house, when I visited her, the same phenomena occurred; and we there first began to ask questions, to which we received intelligent replies—The spirit of my mother at her house in this way communicated the following: "Daniel, fear not, my child. God is with you, and who shall be against you? Seek to do good: be truthful and truth-loving, and you will prosper, my child. Yours is a glorious mission—you will convince the infidel, cure the sick, and console the weeping." This was the first communication I ever received, and it came within the first week of these visitations. I remember it well. I have never forgotten it, and can never forget it while reason and life shall last. I have reason to remember it too, because this was the last week I passed in the house of the aunt who had adopted me, for she was unable to bear the continuance of the phenomena, which so distressed her religious convictions, and she felt it a duty that I should leave her house, which I did. . . .

I go into these particulars not to revive or to cause painful recollections to any one, but merely to show the history of my mediumship, and the mysterious working of Providence in thus throwing me before the public. Had it not been for this chain of circumstances, these truths might have remained unknown so widely as they now are.[22]

Deception

Daniel Home was deceived into believing that his power came from God. This is a common occurrence in the world of the occult, where the demons do everything within their power to fool people into thinking that God is the source of occult phenomena. It is not uncommon for demons at séances to play hymns on different instruments and physically open the Bible with corporeal hands, fingers pointing to specific verses as proof of divine influence. This is clearly illustrated in another Home séance:

> A few evenings afterwards the table was near the window. It was twilight. Songs were heard on the accordion. The tune was new to us, and we were told that it was the "Song of the Angels to the Mourners." It was followed by a hymn which had been frequently played before. It was spelt out by sounds on the table, *some will show you their hands to-night.* The table was gently raised and lifted up several times, a hand appeared above the table, and took from the dress of one of the party a miniature brooch, and handed it to several at the table. Hands and arms were then distinctly seen by all at the table of different forms and sizes—sometimes crossed as in prayer, and at others pointing upwards. . . . A spirit hand took up a Bible which was on the table, and opened it. This was seen by all, and a leaf was folded down, the hand took a pencil and marked the two verses sixteen and seventeen of the thirteenth chapter of St. Matthew—"But blessed are your eyes, for they see: and your ears, for they hear. For I say unto you that many prophets and righteous men have desired to see things which ye see, and have not seen them; and to hear these things which ye hear, and have not heard them."

---

22. Home, *Incidents in My Life*, 20–27.

At this time hands and arms were frequently seen and they were repeat-edly felt by all at the table as distinctly as though they were the hands and arms of living mortals, and frequently they shook hands with them as really and substantially as one man shakes hands with another.[23]

The process of possession involves direct contact with demons; at times this contact can proceed to full possession, as it did in the case of Daniel Home, and at other times possession does not take place. The overwhelming evidence faithfully recorded by those who attended séance after séance reveals that demons cloak their true nature in the trappings of religion or spirituality, depending on the century, carefully crafting a facade of positive spirituality in order to gain the trust of the tar-geted individuals.

Strategy

Satan and his demons are ancient creatures quite familiar with the nature of Adam and Eve. They have the experience of millions of years behind them: experience in fighting God, His angels, and His most beloved creation—human beings. It is only to be expected that such ancient, fierce fighters would craft a strategy against the enemy based on detailed knowledge.

In light of this fact, it is vital that Christians recognize the enemy and his meth-ods *before* entering into spiritual warfare. The greatest generals in history planned their battles in minute detail, based on a thorough knowledge of their enemies. If the Church does not focus on exactly who the enemy is—his strategies, his meth-ods, his past successes and failures—we will never be able to combat him effectively.

Without a doubt, individuals are targeted for deception. Spiritual warfare, as taught in the Bible, is *personal* warfare (Eph. 6:12). It is always wise to know the enemy, and in their contact with human beings, demons have revealed a great deal about themselves. It is obvious, from multiple historical accounts of séances (recorded by credible sources), that demons keep track of details. All aspects of individual human lives are noted by the enemy and preserved for the time when they are needed to deceive.

---

23. Ibid., 105–6

The demonic database includes:

- names

- family members

- birth dates

- physical descriptions (DVD quality)

- geographical locations

- clothing (DVD quality)

- voice patterns (stereo quality)

- conversations

- personal mannerisms (DVD quality)

- personal preferences: perfumes/colognes, tobacco, and alcohol (including the physical smell of these items)

- daily activities (including locations and dates)

- life experiences (births, romances, sins, marriages, deaths)

These elements of the demonic database can be seen in several other examples described by Daniel Home.

I went to Springfield, Massachusetts, an entire stranger, but having heard of Mr. Henry Gordon, a medium there, I asked for and was directed to his house. He received me most kindly, and said that he was almost to have a séance that evening, requesting me to join them. . . . Those who were there had to leave at an early hour, and Mr. Gordon accompanied them, leaving me with five or six of his friends who had come in in the meantime. Among these were Mr. and Mrs. Elmer, the former being a believer, but Mrs. Elmer having violently opposed it. I was thrown into a trance, made to sit near her, telling her the names of her mother, father, brothers, and sisters; then of her children, all of whom were in the spirit world; and I repeated to her the last words of two of her children. Turning to an older lady in the room, I did the same and so on through all those who were present. Mr. and Mrs. Elmer have since been my friends, and at their house some most remarkable manifestations occurred.[24]

Dr. Hallock related some remarkable personal descriptions of spirits through Mr. Home, occurring on the same evening. One spirit was described as having been known here by the name of "Elizabeth." Her person was described, and her prominent traits of character as well as the disease of which she died, with such accuracy, that a gentleman present knew her at once from the description. The only inaccuracy that he could point out, being the color of her hair, which had been described as brown, when in fact it was rather a light auburn. In explanation of which Mr. Home said, "When I look at the forehead, which is very white, (which was the fact,) the hair looks brown to me."[25]

In August, I went on a visit to Mr. Cheney, at South Manchester, Connecticut, and it was at his house that I was first lifted in the air, a manifestation which has since frequently occurred to me both in England and France.

The following is the description of the evening, in the words of a gentleman who was present.

"On the 8th instant, in company with three gentlemen from this city, the writer paid a visit to Ward Cheney, residing in Manchester, at whose house Mr. Daniel D. Home was temporarily stopping. A circle was formed, and well-known vibrations on the table were soon loud and distinct. . . . Among others [messages] . . . came a message from two sailors lost at sea, relatives of one of the company—a stranger to most of the company. These spirits announced themselves, somewhat unexpectedly, by canting over the solid and ponderous table, and rolling it in the manner of a violent tem-

---

24. Ibid., 43.
25. Ibid., 56.

pest. Accompanying this demonstration came a violent *creaking* as of the cables of a ship in a storm at sea—and the creaking of the timbers and masts as the vessel surged to one side or the other, was distinctly heard by all. Next came the regular, sullen shocks of the waves as they struck the bows of the doomed vessel. All this time the table kept up the rocking motion. And now the large table was capsized on the floor! All this was done with no one touching the table, as a close and constant scrutiny was kept up by two, at least, of our party. These two sailors, whose names and ages were given, it seems lost their lives by the capsizing of a vessel as represented, although this fact, I have the best of reasons for knowing, could not previously be known to Mr. Home, or to any of the company excepting myself."[26]

I well remember a poor man being present one evening, and the spirit of a little girl coming with the following message. "Father, dear, your little Mary was present last Wednesday, and God gave her power to prevent you from doing what you wished. If you were ever to do that, you could not come to where your own Mary and her mother are. Promise me you will never think of such an awful thing again." We all looked astonished, but could not understand to what she alluded. Still it was evident the poor father knew too well, for throwing himself on his knees, he said, as the tears rolled down his cheeks, "Indeed, it is but too true, that on Wednesday last I decided to cut my throat; but as I took the razor to do it, I felt that had my child been alive, she would have shrunk from me with horror, and this very thought was the saving of me."[27]

CASE STUDY

Sir Arthur Conan Doyle

Dr. Guthrie gave the following . . . with Mrs. Blake [the medium] where the information supplied was not known to the sitters, and could not have been known to the medium.

---

26. Ibid., 62–64.
27. Ibid., 84.

"An acquaintance of mine, of prominent family in this end of the State, whose grandfather had been found at the foot of a high bridge with his skull smashed and life extinct, called on Mrs. Blake a few years ago and was not thinking of her grandfather at the time. She was very much surprised to have the "spirit" of her grandfather tell her that he had not fallen off the bridge while intoxicated, as had been presumed at the time, but that he had been murdered by two men who met him in a buggy and had proceeded to sandbag him, relieve him of his valuables, and throw him over the bridge. The "spirit" then proceeded to describe minutely the appearance of the two men who had murdered him, and gave such other information that led to the arrest and conviction of one or both of these individuals."[28]

Scriptural Response

The greatest authority on demon possession and exorcism is Jesus Christ. Though His ministry lasted only three years and was recorded in just four New Testament books, these eyewitness gospels include twenty-seven passages detailing Jesus' teaching on demons, demon possession, and exorcism. The number of passages discussing the same incidents emphasizes Jesus' interaction with demons: an interaction that was both frequent and confrontational.

Demons, Possession, and Exorcism in the Ministry of Jesus Christ

Matt 8:28–9:1	Mark 1:23–28	Luke 4:31–37
Matt 9:32–34	Mark 1:32–34	Luke 4:40–41
Matt 10:8	Mark 1:39	Luke 8:1–3
Matt 12:22–30	Mark 3:13–19	Luke 8:26–39
Matt 12:43–45	Mark 5:1–20	Luke 9:1–2
Matt 17:14–21	Mark 6:12–13	Luke 9:37–45
Mark 7:24–30	Luke 9:49–50	

---

28. Arthur Conan Doyle, *The History of Spiritism* (New York: Arno, 1975), 163–64.

Mark 9:14–29	Luke 10:17–20
Mark 9:38–41	Luke 11:14–26
Mark 16:9–11	Luke 13:31–33
Mark 16:17–18	

God determined that a great deal of biblical space should be devoted to the existence, intent, and strategy of intelligent evil beings, and His example confirms that demon possession is not a rare phenomenon but a common occurrence. Jesus taught exorcism by example; He confronted evil on a regular basis, revealing key information about the enemy and demonstrating His authority and power over them.

One passage in particular discloses remarkable details about demons and their relationship to human beings. "When an unclean spirit goes out of a man, he goes through dry places, seeking rest, and finds none. Then he says, 'I will return to my house from which I came.' And when he comes, he finds it empty, swept, and put in order. Then he goes and takes with him seven other spirits more wicked than himself, and they enter and dwell there; and the last state of that man is worse than the first. So shall it also be with this wicked generation" (Matt. 12:43–45). Jesus taught these things from a place of authority: He was the only man in the position to *know* the facts. His words form the foundation for spiritual warfare, and as such, they must be analyzed and assimilated.

Scripture	Strategic Information
When an unclean spirit goes out of a man	Demons have the ability to occupy or share space (like a parasite) within a human body.
he goes through dry places	Demons are multidimensional travelers; when they leave someone, they leave this dimension and enter a dimension whose atmosphere (by implication) is not welcoming; *dry places* (waterless).

Scripture	Strategic Information
seeking rest	The Greek translates, "intermission; by implication, recreation."[29] The demonic nature requires some form of *rest*—an intermission from the dry places.
and finds none	Demons cannot find any rest in the dry places, so they enter the dimension of earth to seek rest within human beings; they find an intermission from their wanderings and a form of recreation in occupying an individual.
Then he says, "I will return to my house from which I came."	Demons are rational creatures in search of *rest* and *a home*; finding no rest in the dry places, they reason it is better to return to the person they left; a human life can be a *home*. Demons are possessive of their home: *"I will return to my house"*—they consider the person they left to be their *home*.
And when he comes, he finds it empty	The Greek translates the word *empty* as "devoted to leisure; vacant."[30] Humans are *vacant*—empty without the Holy Spirit living in them.
swept	The human life can be "cleaned up"; as one would take a broom and *sweep up* the dirt in a home, humans can "sweep clean" the dirt that pollutes a life.

---

29. Greek—*anapausis*, NT:372, *New Exhaustive Strong's Numbers and Concordance*.
30. Greek—*scholazo*—NT:4980 from NT:4981; to take a holiday, i.e. be at leisure (by implication, devote oneself wholly to); figuratively, to be vacant (of a house), ibid.

Scripture	Strategic Information
and put in order	The Greek translates this as *garnished or* "set in order and decorated."[31] Everything looks perfectly beautiful from the outside, but the home is empty.
Then he goes and takes with him seven spirits more wicked than himself and they enter and dwell there[32]	An empty home is always defenseless and as such, vulnerable, but it is more difficult for a single demon to possess or repossess a home set in order—he needs to seek help. Humans whose lives are damaged (by themselves or by others) are more vulnerable than people who keep their lives "swept and put in order;" when necessary, demons will join forces and work together to defeat human beings. There are levels of evil in the demonic realm—some demons are more wicked than others. The more evil a demon is, the more *powerful* he is; life activities and beautification of the body/spirit offer no protection against the invasion of malignant beings. Multiple demons can live within one human being.
and the last state of that man is worse than the first	Once multiple demons return to the empty house, the individual becomes more evil than ever before.

31. Greek—*Kosmeo*—NT:2885; to put in proper order, i.e. decorate (literally or figuratively), ibid.
32. This "seven-fold" return of an exorcised demon refers only to the human body, not to any building or place.

A Christian Cannot Be Demon Possessed

Possession is a difficult subject, both from the standpoint of perceived threat and the actual acceptance of it as reality. Some people shudder at the mention of demons; others laugh them off as myth. But the biblical record teaches that demons exist, and the threat to an individual who is not a Christian remains a dangerous reality.

There is a place inside a human being that is meant to be filled with something outside of him—something *supernatural.* Anyone who accepts Christ into his or her heart is immediately filled or indwelt by the Holy Spirit, and anyone rejecting God remains *vacant,* prey for malignant supernatural beings known as demons. It follows then that if you are indwelt by the Holy Spirit—God Himself—you cannot also be possessed by a demon. Some argue that the human spirit is like an apartment complex, with different spirits occupying different floors (leaving Christians vulnerable to possession), but this reasoning only leads to confusion and the erroneous conclusion that God is not all-powerful. The Bible does not mention anything about individual "levels" within the human spirit. And if the human psyche has different "levels," how many *floors* are there within each individual? Is it a uniform number, or does it vary from person to person? The confusion generated by this unsupported analogy can only harm the faith of believers by producing an unwarranted fear. God is omnipotent and all-powerful. If He cannot "clean house" and instantly banish the presence of evil beings, He is not who He claims to be. The argument for Christians becoming possessed is seriously flawed in many areas, as a simple examination of Jesus' life and ministry demonstrates. Demons live in utter terror of Jesus Christ, and with a few simple words, will *always* submit to Him. There is no room for cohabitation.

The Bible does not teach that a person who is truly the servant of Jesus Christ may ever be possessed by demons. Possession by demonic forces—even if someone were able to say, "Come into me"—would be the antithesis of biblical theology. This could never happen in biblical demonology for many reasons. In 1 Corinthians 6:19–20 we are told that our bodies are the temple of the Holy Spirit. Whatever attempts to defile the temple of God, He will destroy.

God has given His children His *protection.* "Do you not know that your body is the temple of the Holy Spirit who is in you, whom you have from God, and you are not your own? For you were bought at a price; therefore, glorify God in your body and in your spirit, which are God's." The Christian is possessed by the Holy Spirit; we are not our own. We belong to God. If you are God's property, you cannot be invaded by demons because the Lord is the tenant, and He is not going to let the apartment become a duplex! He is not living on the top floor with the demons living on the bottom. That is not biblical theology.

God is very clear about what He has done for us in Jesus Christ:

Do not be unequally yoked together with unbelievers. For what fellowship has righteousness with lawlessness? And what communion has light with darkness? And what accord has Christ with Belial? Or what part has a believer with an unbeliever? And what agreement has the temple of God with idols? For you are the temple of the living God. As God has said:

"I will dwell in them
and walk among them.
I will be their God,
and they shall be My people."

Therefore

"Come out from among them
and be separate, says the Lord.
Do not touch what is unclean,
and I will receive you."
"I will be a Father to you,
and you shall be My sons and daughters,
says the LORD Almighty." (2 Cor. 6:14–22)

Scripture is adamant: Christ has no accord with Satan. The temple of God has no accord with the temple of idols, and we are commanded to remember that the believer has no fellowship with the unbeliever; neither does righteousness with unrighteousness. It is obvious in reading the Word of God that if we are God's temples, then our temples make no truce in any way with idols. We must accept God's Word as true when it says that the Gentiles sacrifice to demons (1 Cor. 10:20). So the unbelievers' prayers and the unbelievers' sacrifices are directed to demons, not to God. God must be worshiped in spirit and in truth—through the Holy Spirit and in truth—and a person must be reborn spiritually before one can worship God in spirit and in truth (John 4:24).

Some who are in the ministry of "deliverance" often argue that they have seen many Christians delivered of demons. The answer to this is simple: what they have seen are the *tares* in the wheat field. These people look like Christians; they act like Christians; they know all the vocabulary of people walking with Christ, but in their heart of hearts, they have not yielded their lives to the Holy Spirit. If a pastor is praying for someone like this, and voices manifest that do not belong to the individual, it is a good indication of a tare, since it is biblically impossible for true children of God to be possessed.[33]

It is also possible in some cases that a vulnerable Christian might respond to the prompting of a pastor or counselor and react to please him or her by crying out or claiming to be fighting "Jezebel, the demon of control."[34] This can be a difficult problem to diagnose, and that is why a strong network of leadership is needed—not just in individual denominations—but throughout the Church. Communication between Church leaders and laymen is essential for wise evaluation of difficult cases.

Christians are the temple of God. If you are a Christian, God's Spirit dwells in you. You are possessed by the Holy Spirit, and you can never become the temple of idols or the temple of demons. "You are of God, little children, and have overcome them, because He who is in you is greater than he who is in the world" (1 John 4:4). The Church has overcome the forces of Satan in the world through the sacrifice of the Lord Jesus Christ on the Cross. Our protection lies in the authority of Jesus Christ in the life of the believer. "We know that whoever is born of God does not sin; but he who has been born of God keeps himself, and the wicked one does not touch him" (1 John 5:18). According to the Greek, it is Christ who is "keeping," and the wicked one cannot touch you. "For He Himself has said, 'I will never leave you nor forsake you.' So we may boldly say: 'The LORD is my helper; I will not fear. What can man do to me?'" (Heb. 13:5–6).

---

33. It is also possible the individual is dealing with mental illness or responding out of spiritual immaturity to the doctrinal error taught by some involved in "deliverance" ministries.

34. For more information on the "Jezebel spirit" see chapter 17, "Christian Counseling and the Occult."

Battling Demonic Oppression

The Christian cannot be possessed, but he or she can be *oppressed* by the powers of darkness. The difference is that possession manifests from *within*, and oppression manifests from *without*. This is the reality of spiritual warfare: Satan will use every weapon at his disposal to wound, weaken, confuse, and paralyze a Christian. The next best thing to an unbeliever is a wounded Christian, lying around on the spiritual battlefield, *paralyzed* by past sins, failures, and insecurities. This paralysis is the result of *oppression*, which often manifests itself as a spirit of continual heaviness, despair or depression.[35] It can lead to a sense of hopelessness and an attitude of apathy. It can be rooted in sin: a wrong choice exacerbated by guilt. It can be the consequences of rebellion. It can be the result of failing to *obey* God by studying His Word and spending time in prayer. If Christians do not care enough to put on their spiritual armor daily, they cannot stand against the *daily* attacks of Satan and his demons.

Oppression is best dealt with by repentance, prayer, and sometimes, fasting. Rededicating your life to Jesus and obeying Him is the first step to the defeat and banishment of oppression. The fellowship of believers also provides enormous protection to those who stand firmly within its circle. Constant prayer offered by brothers and sisters in Christ provides powerful protection. "Confess your trespasses to one another, and pray for one another, that you may be healed. The effective, fervent prayer of a righteous man avails much" (James 5:16).

Jesus promised that He would be with us to the consummation of the ages (Matt. 28:20), and He told the Church that the gates of hell would not prevail against us (Matt. 16:18). The Lord Jesus Christ has given His word, and we know that the Son of God has come and given us understanding that we may know Him who is true (Heb. 13:20). He has delivered us from the powers of darkness. We are in Him who is true, even in His Son, Jesus Christ. This is the true God; this is eternal life.

Battling Possession

What are Christians to do in the face of demonic possession? Scripture teaches it is imperative to put on the whole armor of God and resist the devil (Eph. 6:11; James

---

35. There are some forms of depression that are medically related, and medication is sometimes necessary to live a balanced, productive life. This decision can only be reached after consultation with your physician and pastor.

4:7). Resist him! James says if you resist, the devil will flee from you—not walk away, but *flee*. The apostle Paul warned that our adversary the devil stalks about like a roaring lion, seeking someone to devour (1 Peter 5:8), but Jesus Christ encountered Satan and vanquished him by using the Word of God: "Get behind Me, Satan! For it is written, 'You shall worship the LORD your God, and Him only you shall serve'" (Luke 4:8). It is the power of God's Holy Spirit, manifested with great authority, that conquers Satan (Heb. 2:4, 14). Jesus Christ was manifested to *ruin* the works of the devil (1 John 3:8). And when Jesus entered the world, died for our sins, and rose from the dead, He became the victor over Satan. Scripture reveals that Jesus took from Satan the power of death, and He liberated those who feared death. Death was swallowed up in resurrection life; fear was conquered with eternal love. Fear has torment, but perfect love casts out fear (1 John 4:18).

Evaluating the Possibility of Possession

Demon possession is almost always related to exposure to some type of occult activity. Whether it is personal experimentation with the Ouija board, or a family member or friend involved in Witchcraft, the consequences of exploring the world of the occult can be far-reaching and quite toxic.

Whenever demon possession is suspected by family or friends, based on symptoms evident in the person's life, it is imperative that a trusted minister or ministry be asked to evaluate the situation.[36] Often, schizophrenia is associated with demon possession, and in these instances, medication will be of little help to the individual. This is a clear sign that something else is involved in the mix. It is possible to have a mental illness and be demon possessed, and it is also possible to *appear* to have a mental illness as a result of demon possession. A simple way to determine the difference is to use the name and authority of Jesus Christ. His ultimate power strips away what some have called the "pretense" stage of possession, where the individual is able to hide the presence of the demon. It is common for someone who is demon possessed to exhibit arrogance and contempt for anything related to God, Jesus Christ, or Christianity. Some also have difficulty praying and refuse to have anything to do with the Church. If possession is suspected, a short question-and-answer session involving the name of Jesus Christ is usually enlightening.

---

36. For more information on counseling, see chapter 17, "Christian Counseling and the Occult."

Once a counselor has been chosen, and the fact of demon possession has been determined and accepted, Dr. Kurt Koch offers the following steps to deliverance:

1. Deliverance is only possible through Christ

2. Every object of sorcery must be destroyed

3. Mediumistic contacts and friendships must be broken

4. Confession [of sin]

5. The prayer of renunciation [asking forgiveness for any personal or family contact with the occult)

6. The forgiveness of sins

7. Loosing from the powers of darkness [commanding the demons to leave]

8. The prayer group [can take place during and after the exorcism]

9. Prayer and fasting [again, can take place during or after the exorcism]

10. The protection of the blood of Christ

11. Commanding in the name of Jesus

12. The means of Grace

13. The return of evil spirits [a biblical warning explaining what can happen if a person rejects Jesus Christ]

14. The weapons of this warfare

15. Realizing the victory

16. Complete surrender[37]

Exorcism is a process of deliverance and healing, demonstrated by Jesus Christ throughout His ministry and practiced regularly by the early Church. In light of

---

37. Koch, *Occult Bondage and Deliverance*, 89–127. For a more detailed discussion of the process of exorcism, see chapter 17, "Christian Counseling and the Occult."

the biblical example, it should never be avoided or discounted based on fear or skepticism. Demonic forces respect and dread the Cross of Christ, and they are subject to it. When you invoke the name of Jesus Christ of Nazareth and say, "Be silent!" they are silent and remain so. There may be times when Christians encounter demonic forces that will not respond to normal exorcism, as Jesus revealed in Matthew 17:16; these are demons that will only come out by prayer and by fasting. But if this proves to be the case, it is important to remember that when the disciples encountered demons and when Paul encountered demons, Christ's authority inevitably conquered (Acts 16:16–18). Satan has been overcome by the Cross and the glory of the resurrection.

The Bible clearly teaches that the demons believe and tremble. "And suddenly they cried out, saying, 'What have we to do with You, Jesus, You Son of God? Have You come here to torment us before the time?'" (Matt. 8:29). When Christ encountered Satan in Luke 4, Satan believed Jesus was the Christ, the Son of God. Even Satan recognized Jesus' authority and met Him with authority, "Again, the devil took Him up on an exceedingly high mountain, and showed Him all the kingdoms of the world and their glory. And he said to Him, 'All these things I will give You if You will fall down and worship me'" (Matt. 4:8–9). The powers of darkness should always engender a healthy respect in any encounter, but they remain in subjection to the Church through the power of Christ.

CONCLUSION

Biblical demonology gives the Christian a very strong position in the realm of spiritual warfare. The Scripture reveals that when the disciples of our Lord encountered demonic forces, they had authority over them, and cast them out. The children of God have been given enormous power, but with it comes a warning: "Nevertheless do not rejoice in this, that the spirits are subject to you, but rather rejoice because your names are written in heaven" (Luke 10:20).

Do not be afraid of demonic oppression. Jesus Christ is the great deliverer; call on Him. If you know Jesus Christ as your Savior, you are the temple of God and do not need to be afraid of demonic possession. If you are not a believer in the Lord Jesus and do not rest in the authority of God's Word, then hear the word of the Lord: "Whoever calls on the name of the LORD shall be saved" (Acts 2:21). Victory over the forces of darkness is victory sustained by God's Holy Spirit. "'Not by might nor by power, but by My Spirit,' says the LORD of hosts" (Zech. 4:6).

This world is under the dominion of the prince of darkness. The apostle John reminds us the whole world languishes in the lap of the evil one. Never forget the power of the enemy, and never underestimate him. Demons keep track of details— there is a reason the Bible calls them "familiar spirits." The world of the occult offers mystery and power in thousands of different forms, but whether it is tarot cards, the Black Mass, or the daily horoscope, it is the same force. When dealing with these things, we must learn the nature of the adversary and beware.

The apostle John warned the Church to guard their hearts and keep themselves from idols (1 John 5:21). An idol is a representation of a *demon;* a dangerous deception some may fall into if not prepared. The word *keep* is from the Greek word *phulasso* meaning "be on guard."[38] *Children, be on guard.* Guard against the demons by keeping away from idols, recognizing the place you have in Jesus Christ, and by putting on the whole armor of God. "Put on the whole armor of God, that you may be able to stand against the wiles of the devil. For we do not wrestle against flesh and blood, but against principalities, against powers, against the rulers of the darkness of this age, against spiritual hosts of wickedness in the heavenly places" (Eph. 6:11–12).

Jesus knew the difficulty of this struggle, and He prayed for the Church. "I do not pray that You should take them out of the world, but that You should keep them from the evil one" (John 17:15). God has placed His Church in this world for a purpose, and that purpose is to resist the forces of darkness through the power of the Lord Jesus Christ.

---

38. NT:5442, probably from NT:5443 through the idea of isolation; to watch, i.e. be on guard (literally or figuratively); by implication, to preserve, obey, avoid. *(New Exhaustive Strong's Numbers and Concordance)*

RECOMMENDED RESOURCES

1. Koch, Kurt. *Occult Bondage and Deliverance.* Grand Rapids: Kregel, 1970.

2. Koch, Kurt. *Occult Practices and Beliefs.* Grand Rapids: Kregel, 1971.

3. Martin, Walter. *Evil and Human Suffering.* CD/audiotape, Walter Martin Ministries, www.waltermartin.com.

4. Martin, Walter. *Growing in the Spirit.* CD/audiotape, Walter Martin Ministries, www.waltermartin.com.

QUICK FACTS ABOUT THE JESUS OF THE OCCULT

- People involved in the occult deny the true history and person of Jesus Christ; He is generally added to occult practices for credibility.

- The "Christ" of the occult is not a unique Being; He is not the only Christ.

- Jesus is a great man who discovered principles that can be imitated.

- The name of Jesus may be invoked in some occult practices for added power or authority.

15

The Jesus of the Occult

God has identified the Bible as the standard for measuring truth; it reveals everything essential about the person, nature, and work of His Son, Jesus Christ. Yet in spite of biblical warnings forbidding any alteration or manipulation of God's Word, invariably there are those who cross the line and create a false image of Jesus.[1] This redefinition of Jesus Christ, crafted to suit personal ends, is nothing more than a repackaging of the same complex lies created and circulated by the Gnostics during the time of the early Church.

Throughout his lifetime, the apostle John watched false teachings about Jesus infiltrate the Church, and he responded strongly to the Gnostic heresy by offering proof of his eyewitness testimony to the true person of Jesus Christ:

> That which was from the beginning, which we have heard, which we have seen with our eyes, which we have looked upon, and our hands have handled, concerning the Word of life—the life was manifested, and we have seen, and bear witness, and declare to you that eternal life which was with the Father and was manifested to us. (1 John 1:1–2)

In closing his gospel, he pointed out that the world could not contain the books written truthfully about Jesus, so it is probable he knew the world would make every effort to record the lies. "And there are also many other things that Jesus did, which if they were written one by one, I suppose that even the world itself could not contain the books that would be written" (John 21:25). It is no coincidence, then, that Theosophy and other occult-based beliefs speak in glowing terms of the ancient cult of Gnosticism, which thrived in the first three centuries of the Christian era and almost succeeded in doing irreparable damage to the historic

---

1. "Do not add to His words" (Prov. 30:6).

Christian faith. Paul's epistle to the Colossians and the epistle of 1 John are recognized by biblical scholars as direct apologetic thrusts against the teachings that spawned this cult: spiritualizing (by metaphor) the Old Testament, redefining contemporary Christian terminology, substituting an impersonal god for the God of revelation, and reducing Jesus Christ to a demigod or a pantheistic emanation from the unknowable divine essence.[2] Unfortunately, these early heretics wrote many false things about Jesus that managed to survive two thousand years of tumultuous history. Today, the Church battles the same cultic and occultic opposition that the apostles fought in ancient times. It is true that Jesus' followers left innumerable books written to Christ's glory, but the writings of the enemy still manage to confuse and overwhelm the unwary.

THE IDENTITY OF JESUS

Jesus taught His disciples that deceivers always alter His identity, so He asked them, "Who do men say that I, the Son of Man, am?" The disciples' answer reveals how unregenerate men desperately tried to explain Jesus Christ: "Some say John the Baptist, some Elijah, and others Jeremiah or one of the prophets." Jesus then asked His disciples for their understanding: "Who do you say that I am?" Peter's answer glowed with revelation: "You are the Christ, the Son of the living God" (Matt. 16:13–16).

The unsatisfied curiosity of mankind's soul, in its lost condition, demands an explanation of Jesus. Even those who had access to Christ's earthly ministry falsely concluded that he was John the Baptist, Elijah, Jeremiah, or one of the prophets. One person who did this was Herod. In Matthew 14:1–2, we find: "At that time Herod the tetrarch heard the report about Jesus and said to his servants, 'This is John the Baptist; he is risen from the dead, and therefore these powers are at work in him.'" It is astounding that those who had access to Jesus Christ and His work did not know His true identity. These people only had to listen to Jesus and believe what He said when He called Himself the Son of God (John 10:36). It is no surprise, then, that others since that time would try to palm off a distorted image of Christ. This is the nature of the occult—it is what occultists do to Christ's person, nature, work, and history.

---

2. Martin, *Kingdom of the Cults* (1965), 222.

World literature overflows with speculative texts about Jesus Christ. His enemies span the ages and include secular philosophers, religionists, and occultists. These volumes deride the biblical Christ and reinvent Him so that the person presented as Jesus is unrecognizable and is indeed a false christ. This coincides perfectly with what the apostle Paul wrote in 2 Corinthians 11:4 about those who preach another Jesus: "For if someone comes and proclaims another Jesus than the one we proclaimed, or if you receive a different spirit from the one you received, or if you accept a different gospel from the one you accepted, you put up with it readily enough." He admonished the Church that others will use Jesus' name, but the Jesus they preach is not the Jesus he preached. Words have meaning, and we cannot allow people to redefine Jesus and Christianity on a whim. We must demonstrate the same faithfulness to the true Jesus of the Bible in the same way His disciples did. The antithesis of the apostles' teaching is markedly a false Jesus.

Some may wonder why anyone who denies Christ's true biblical person would bother to write about Him or include His name in their works. For cultists and occultists, however, connecting Jesus' name to their beliefs and practices gives the illusion of credibility, since so many people have heard of Him. But when Scripture tests their Jesus, he falls miserably short of God's truth; he is never truly their central figure, and he is not core to their beliefs. Jesus is incidental—remaining on the fringe—and inserted wherever they find Him beneficial or acceptable. Their system of self-exaltation exists without Him.

Nonbelievers often treat Jesus as a myth or a mystical figure, and their view of the historical Jesus influences their spiritual direction. There are those who deny the trustworthiness of New Testament history and approach Him as a myth in the same way they would approach Krishna, Thor, or Neptune. To them, the name Jesus has nothing to do with a personal Savior. Instead, Jesus is a means to an end: cosmic personal power needed to accomplish a task. By relegating Jesus to myth, they can rewrite and reinvent His life to fit comfortably within their worldview. They are minimalists when it comes to accepting the historical Jesus, giving a tacit nod to His existence while denying any certainty of it. This opens wide the door to the deconstruction of truth and the invention of error.

To complicate matters, the last century of occult writers digested a steady diet of denials concerning Christ from those who claimed to represent Christianity—liberal theologians dating from the nineteenth century. Leading the way in modern times was the demythologizing of the Gospels by the liberal Lutheran theologian Rudolf Bultmann, whose premise assumed a gospel myth. Bultmann's form criticism culminated in the infamous Jesus Seminar debacle of the 1990s, during which every word of Christ was challenged by yea and nay votes of the scholars. This backdrop encouraged occult writers to reinterpret Christ's history at will, thus producing a vastly different persona for Jesus than that portrayed by Scripture: a Jesus composed of myth and mysticism, existing somewhere beyond history. It was a reinvention that elevated all who contrived it far above dry historical studies. This is the Jesus of the occult. Many try to justify this worldview by claiming Jesus taught theories similar to theirs—accepting the illusion of a historical Jesus even as they alter Him to fit their theory or perceptions.

An example of this is found among the followers of Scientology, who claim without evidence that "Jesus was a member of the cult of the Essenes, who believed in reincarnation," thus implying that Jesus, like them, believed in reincarnation.[3] L. Ron Hubbard, the founder of Scientology, touted his connection to occultists such as Aleister Crowley and Jack Parsons, and he mingled occult practices with his theories.[4] Even though he sometimes treated Jesus as a historical figure, Hubbard wrote at other times about Christ in mythological terms, calling Him a legend: "You will find . . . the Christ legend as an implant in preclears a million years ago."[5] In Scientology, there is only the illusion of the historical Jesus, not one based upon the historical New Testament documents.

Hubbard's comment upon mythology and prayer is revealing: "The curse of the past has been a pretense of knowledge. We have had a worship of a fable. We have had prayers sent up to a myth."[6] Christianity has a long history of distinguishing between fables or myths and historically verifiable *truth*. Ironically, the apostle Peter used the Greek word *moothos* for "myths" to refute folly like this in the first century: "For we did not follow cunningly devised fables [myths] when we made known to you the power and coming of our Lord Jesus Christ, but were eyewitnesses of His

3. See *Scientology: A World Religion Emerges in the Space Age* (Los Angeles: Church of Scientology of California, 1979), 15.
4. Details on this can be found in Martin, *Kingdom of the Cults* (2003), 350.
5. L. Ron Hubbard, *Professional Auditor's Bulletin 31*, quoted by Kevin Anderson, *Report of the Board of Inquiry into Scientology* (Melbourne: Australia Parliament Government Printer, 1965), 150.
6. L. Ron Hubbard, *A New Slant on Life* (Los Angeles: Publications Organization, 1952), 59.

majesty" (2 Peter 1:16). Peter emphasized the historical and factual foundation for Christianity.

Some occult writers accept Jesus' historical existence yet treat Him as a mystical figure, a man who learned how to use the latent powers that they desire. By transforming Jesus into a Jewish mystic, they change His character, arbitrarily adding false attributes that fit their purpose. The fluidity of mysticism allows them to *form* Jesus in their personal image as opposed to *conforming* to His biblical image.

It is hard for people like this to believe they are doing anything immoral or harmful by changing the image of Jesus, since they see no future retribution for their actions. Elizabeth Clare Prophet, an occult mystic, uses this type of *creative* reasoning in her teachings on discovering the inner "Self." Most of her followers only have a cursory knowledge of Jesus, so she is able to use Him as a catalyst in her writings, urging her followers to do what she claims Jesus did: learn the Self is Christ.[7] Contrary to this, the Bible teaches that Jesus did not discover the self to be the Christ; He is the one and only Christ—a unique Being. According to the apostle John, anyone who denies that Jesus is the Christ is a liar (1 John 2:22).

Mrs. Prophet tries to separate *Jesus* from *the Christ*—an error many occult writers make concerning Jesus Christ, and an old Gnostic heresy that John faced two thousand years ago. Occult teachers maintain that Jesus exercised the Christ consciousness, discovered the Christ, was baptized with the Christ, or manifested the Christ—anything to differentiate Him from *the Christ*. To occult writers, Jesus cannot be *the* Christ, since "Christ" is an invisible ethereal entity that anyone can exhibit; Jesus simply discovered how to demonstrate it more successfully than others had been able to do up to that point.

The Aquarian Gospel of Jesus Christ is a book that portrays Jesus as one attracted to the occult, and it teaches the Gnostic heresy that the Jesus is not the Christ. Furthermore, it maintains that Jesus supposedly revealed this: "'Men call me Christ, and God has recognized the name; but Christ is not a man. . . . Look to the Christ within who shall be formed in every one of you, as he is formed in me.'"[8] This common thread denying Jesus as the Christ runs rampant in occult literature.

---

7. Elizabeth Clare Prophet, *Inner Perspectives* (Livingston, MT: Summit University Press, 2003), 2.

8. Levi H. Dowling, *The Aquarian Gospel of Jesus, the Christ of the Piscean Age* (Santa Monica, CA: DeVorss, 1907), 8.

In the face of this heresy, Christians cannot settle for less than Peter's confession: "You are the Christ, the Son of the living God" (Matt. 16:16).

<h2 style="text-align:center">REDEFINING JESUS</h2>

Occultists alter Jesus' nature in multiple ways, since there is no organizational superstructure and no requirement for uniformity. It does not seem to concern them that Jesus differs in nature from one group to another or from one book to another. However, the precedent has been set throughout all history that words must have specific meaning. Definitions exist to clarify and prevent confusion. A kidney cannot be redefined as a heart or a heart as a kidney simply because one group of people insists upon it. In the same way, Jesus cannot be redefined as an idea instead of a person simply to accommodate an individual belief system.

In the defense of the faith, it is important to track, identify, and refute this kind of error wherever it occurs. The biblical Jesus must be defended; His identity cannot be supplanted by any writer's preconceived ideas based on cosmology, epistemology, philosophy, theology, and psychology. The apostle Paul warned about this error: "Beware lest anyone cheat you through philosophy and empty deceit, according to the tradition of men, according to the basic principles of the world, and not according to Christ" (Col. 2:8). The biblical Jesus is the standard against which all worldly philosophies or principles must be measured—not the reverse.

The name *Jesus* is the only similarity between the biblical Jesus and the *other* Jesus as redefined in occult teachings. For example, the Jesus preached by Spiritism—an occult group with séances, spirit-channeling, and assorted methods for contacting the dead—is an advanced medium in the sixth sphere of the astral plane.[9] Spiritualists, or Spiritists, are mediums who contact the dead, so their view of Jesus is a medium who also contacted the dead. They also replace heaven with six spheres of astral projection, so Jesus, too, dwells in the sixth sphere of astral projection.

This is the world of the cults and the occult: they ultimately blend Jesus into any and all mixtures of false doctrine. What separates Christianity from them is one theological term: *Christology,* the person, nature, and work of Jesus Christ. The most important question we must ask of someone lost in the occult is this: "What do you think of Christ?" Do not argue with the Spiritists about phenomena and

---

9. For a thorough analysis of Spiritism, see Martin, *Kingdom of the Cults* (2003), 261.

extrasensory perception or with New Age groups and Christian Scientists about how matter exists. Forget arguing with liberal theologians and Unitarians about the historicity of the gospel and the Dead Sea scrolls. Instead, get down to the only important question: who is Jesus of Nazareth? If He is the eternal God in human form, the foundation of the kingdom of the occult disintegrates, because it is all based on one premise: Jesus is not truly God in human form.

The biblical Jesus revealed His true identity when He said, "For if you do not believe that I am He, you will die in your sins" (John 8:24). The Jesus of the occult is not the Jesus of the Bible.

OCCULT WRITERS AND JESUS[10]

During the nineteenth century, the American Spiritism movement created intense public interest in the occult through the sensationalized story of the Fox sisters of Rochester, New York (1848). The Theosophical Society, openly occultic, followed closely behind in revelations of spiritual contact from the other side (1875). Theosophy splinter groups and new organizations under the labels of mind science, New Thought, and psychic research groups sprang up quickly and spread prolifically, providing a host of authors writing about do-it-yourself occultism that would lay the foundation for the New Age groups of the 1980s. These movements and the writings of their leaders would have a profound impact on the world around them:

The Ancient Magick Jesus

Johannes Trithemius (1462–1516)—an esoteric occult magician and a mentor to Heinrich Cornelius Agrippa. He devoted himself to writing on angelic magic and integrated Jesus into his magical invocations. This invocation, taken from his book *The Art of Drawing Spirits into Crystals*, uses the Trinity and the name of Jesus for magical rites: "Taking your ring and pentacle, put the ring on the little finger of your right hand; hang the pentacle round thy neck . . . then take your black ebony wand, with the gilt characters on it, and trace the circle, saying, 'In the name of the blessed Trinity, I consecrate

---

10. Each quotation includes a synopsis of the group or writer staking the claim, so that the Christian can speak more intelligently in evangelism. Each writer is selected specifically for stating something aobut Jesus that is either a representative statement of an occult group or something that was obtained through an occultic means, such as spirit channeling.

this piece of ground . . . through Jesus Christ our Lord.'"[11] Jesus, then, became part of a magick invocation, which is contrary to His holiness and righteousness.

Arbatel of Magick (1655)—a book, written anonymously, that was published in Latin in 1575 and translated into English in 1655. It contained, as the subtitle states, "the Spiritual Wisdom of the Ancients." Jesus Christ is presented in the opening paragraphs as one who blesses magic and magical invocations. "In the Name of the Creator of all things . . . who revealeth his Mysteries out of his Treasures to them that call upon him; and . . . bestoweth his Secrets upon us without measure. May he grant unto us, through his only-begotten Son Jesus Christ our Lord, his ministering spirits, the revealers of his secrets, that we may write this *Book of Arbatel*, concerning the greatest Secrets which are lawful for man to know."[12]

The Mystical Kabbalist Jesus

Heinrich (Henry) Cornelius Agrippa (1486–1535)—an influential German philosopher, writer, and university lecturer on magic, the occult, and Cabala. His Catholic training enabled him to sound quite orthodox on the Trinity and Jesus Christ, but he departed from orthodoxy by claiming that there was particular magic in the name of Jesus, especially the Cabalistic four letters for Jehovah that he transforms into Jesus or *Jesu*.

Agrippa wrote:

> In the Church, over which the name of the Lamb hath influence, that is, the name of Jesus, in which is all the vertue (*sic*) of the four lettered name; seeing that *Jehovah* the Father hath given him all things. Therefore the Heavens receive from the Angels, that which they dart down; but the Angels from the great name of God and *Jesu*, the vertue whereof is first in God . . . being translated into the name of Jesus, in which only miracles are

11. Trithemius, *The Art of Drawing Spirits into Crystals,* as quoted in Francis Barrett, trans., The Magus, book II, (London: N.P., 1801), 135ff. Internet edition: www.esotericarchives.com/ tritheim/trchryst.htm.

12. Robert Turner, trans. *Arbatel of Magick* (London, 1655). Digital edition with foreword by Joseph H. Peterson (1997), www.esotericarchives.com/solomon/arbatel.htm.

done. . . . Hence at this time no favour can be drawn from the heavens, unless the authority, favor and consent of the name *Jesu* intervene.[13]

The Jupiter and Mars Jesus

Emanuel Swedenborg (1688–1772)—the founder of the Church of the New Jerusalem, who claimed revelation through astral projection, spirit contact, and other occultic means. In Swedenborg's revelations, he left his body and traveled the solar system, communicating with spirit-inhabitants of Venus through Jupiter, about which he wrote voluminous works. He taught that Jesus governs spirit communication with man: "Man is quite ignorant that he is governed by the Lord through angels and spirits, and that there are at least two spirits with a man and two angels. Through the spirits a communication of the man with the world of spirits is effected; and through the angels, with heaven."[14]

In Swedenborg's *Earths in the Universe*, we read that Jesus appeared on Jupiter, "The spirits and angels who are from the earth Jupiter . . . acknowledge our Lord. . . . They were asked, whether they know that the only Lord is a Man. They replied that they all know that He is a Man, because in their world He has been seen by many as a Man."[15] Jesus is adored on Mars: "The spirits of Mars are among those who are the best of all from the earths of this solar system, for they are mostly celestial men . . . they acknowledge and adore our Lord . . . that the Lord rules both heaven and the universe is a truth known also to Christians in this earth."[16]

The Ascended Master Jesus

Helena Petrovna Blavatsky (1831–1891)—the cofounder of Theosophy, which became the mother organization for many occultic, esoteric, and New Age groups.

13. Henry Cornelius Agrippa, *Three Books of Occult Philosophy or Magic, Book Three—Ceremonial Magic* (London: Gregory Moule, 1651), chap. 4. Digital edition by Joseph H. Peterson (2000) available at www.esotericarchives.com/agrippa/agrippa3.htm.

14. Emanuel Swedenborg, *Arcana Coelestia*, n. 50, quoted in Julian K. Smyth and William F. Wunsch, comps., *The Gist of Swedenborg* (Philadelphia: Iungerich Publication Fund, 1920), http://www.sacred-texts.com/chr/swe/gos.htm.

15. Emanuel Swedenborg, *Earths in the Universe*, trans. John Whitehead (1892), www.sacred-texts.com/swd/eiu/eiu02.htm (accessed June 2, 2007).

16. Swedenborg, *Arcana Coelestia*, 745–78.

Blavatsky, the author of *Isis Unveiled* (1877), *The Secret Doctrine* (1888), and numerous Theosophical publications, taught the existence of a Hierarchy of Ascended Masters in heaven. Jesus is one of them. They teach the law of Karma and reincarnation that they claim Jesus taught and was also subject to. In true Gnostic fashion, Blavatsky stated that Jesus is not the Christ: "For Christ—the true esoteric Saviour—is no man but the DIVINE PRINCIPLE in every human being."[17]

The Aquarian Part-Time Christ

Levi H. Dowling (1844–1911)—a preacher who became a physician. He had a recurring vision to "build a white city" that led him on esoteric and occult paths. The city he sought became the "translation" of a book from his occult visions of the Akashic Records from the Aquarian Masters, *The Aquarian Gospel of Jesus, the Christ of the Piscean Age* (1907). He imitated ancient Gnostics by separating Jesus from the Christ. Dowling taught that there are many christs and that one is sent to "every world and star and moon and sun."[18]

The book reveals the lost eighteen years of Jesus' life, where Dowling puts Him in India, Tibet, Persia, Assyria, Greece, and Egypt. The *Aquarian Gospel* states, "When we say 'Jesus the Christ' we refer to the man and to his office; just as we do when we say Edward, the King, or Lincoln, the President. Edward was not always king, Lincoln was not always president, and Jesus was not always Christ. Jesus won his Christship by a strenuous life."[19] Dowling apparently missed Luke 2:11, where Jesus "is" Christ at his birth. "For there is born to you this day in the city of David a Savior, who is Christ the Lord."

The Full Moon Jesus

Alice Bailey (1880–1949)—a Theosophist who, through the occultic means of automatic writing and mediumship contacted a spirit named Djwhal Khul, also known as *the Tibetan*. She wrote twenty-six books with the Tibetan's revelations and founded the Lucis Trust, the Arcane School, and World Goodwill. Her first revelation of the Christ came in June 1945, during "the Full Moon of the Christ,

---

17. Helena Blavatsky, *Studies in Occultism* (Pasadena: Theosophical University Press, 1973), 134.
18. Dowling, *Aquarian Gospel,* 12.
19. Ibid., 14.

just as the Full Moon of May is that of the Buddha."[20] She received an invocation (prayer) that her followers recite daily, and she informed them that Jesus Christ and the Hierarchy of the Ascended Masters also recite it daily.[21] In the Hierarchy, Buddha and Christ will be exalted together: "Buddha and the Christ will together pass before the Father . . . and eventually pass to higher service of a nature and a caliber unknown to us."[22] On reincarnation, she wrote that "Christ will teach the law of rebirth" at his reappearance.[23]

The Masonic Jesus

Freemasonry—lodges of several orders exist worldwide. As members of a secret lodge, Masons are oathbound not to reveal ceremonial rites on penalty of death, but numerous books written by former highly degreed Masons still remain the best source of information. Many of the Freemasonry rituals are considered occultic (secret or hidden), and they integrate Gnostic ideas, the Zodiac, and other beliefs with the Bible and Jesus Christ.

Masons teach that they can become Christs: "It is far more important that men should strive to become Christs than that they should believe that Jesus was Christ. . . . Jesus is no less Divine because all men may reach the same Divine perfection."[24] Albert Pike, Confederate officer and 33rd Degree Mason, revealed that Jesus was considered coequal with other religious leaders: "It reverences all the great reformers. It sees in Moses, the lawgiver of the Jews, in Confucius and Zoroaster, in Jesus of Nazareth, and in the Arabian Iconoclast, Great Teachers of Morality, and Eminent Reformers, if no more: and allows every brother of the order to assign to each such higher and even Divine Character as his Creed and Truth require."[25] He also questioned whether Jesus was the only redeemer: "He will redeem and regenerate the world, and the Principle, the Power, and the existence of Evil will then cease; that this will be brought about by such means and instruments as He chooses to employ; whether by the merits of a Redeemer that has already appeared, or a

20. Alice Bailey, *The Reappearance of the Christ* (New York: Lucis Trust, 1979), 31.
21. Ibid., 34.
22. Ibid., 40.
23. Ibid., 115.
24. Jirah Dewey Buck, *Mystic Masonry* (Chicago: Regan Publishing Corporation, 1925), 62.
25. Albert Pike, *Morals and Dogma of the Ancient and Accepted Rite of Freemasonry* (Richmond, VA: L. H. Jenkins Book, 1958), 525.

Messiah that is yet waited for, by an incarnation of Himself, or by an inspired prophet, it does not belong to us as Masons to decide."[26]

The Great White Brotherhood Jesus

Guy Ballard (1878–1939) and *Edna Ballard* (1886–1971)—founded a popular Ascended Masters organization outside of the Theosophical Society, called the I AM movement and the Saint Germain Foundation.[27] Guy believed he was Richard the Lionhearted, King Henry V, and George Washington reincarnated. Edna believed she was Benjamin Franklin and Joan of Arc. Steeped in occultism, the Ballards made Jesus Christ one of the members of the Great White Brotherhood of Ascended Masters, which is a hierarchy of heavenly beings (much like Theosophy). The Hierarchy, as it is called, is also known as the White Lodge, the Great White Lodge, and the Brotherhood. Writing under the pen name Godfré Ray King, Guy Ballard described how to receive the esoteric Christ: "The next step is the acknowledgment: 'I now joyously accept the Fullness of the Mighty God Presence, the Pure Christ.' Feel the Great Brilliancy of the 'Light' and intensify It in every cell of your body for at least ten minutes longer."[28]

The Mystical Rosicrucian Jesus

Harvey Spencer Lewis (1883–1939) and *Max Heindel* (1865–1919)—Lewis was the founder of the Ancient and Mystical Order Rosae Crucis (AMORC) and Heindel founded the rival order, the Rosicrucian Fellowship. These American groups widely popularized Rosicrucianism, but others trace its history to small followings from the fourteenth century.[29] Lewis claimed that Jesus was not Jewish— "Jesus was born of Gentile parents through whose veins flowed Aryan blood"[30]—and he did not die on the Cross—"Jesus was not dead. The blood flowing from the wounds proved that this body was not lifeless."[31] Instead, Jesus "retired

26. Ibid., 308. Similarly, on page 525, Pike stated, "Nor whether the Redeemer, looked and longed for by all nations, hath appeared in Judea, or is yet to come."
27. The St. Germain Foundation has thirty-four sub-entity names, the most common being the Mighty I AM and the I AM Activity.
28. King, *Unveiled Mysteries,* 11.
29. In fact, several eighteenth-century Rosicrucian organizations sprang up in Europe but were often limited to Freemason membership, as was Wenworth Little's society, Societas Rosicruciana (1866).
30. Harvey Spencer Lewis, *The Mystical Life of Jesus* (San Jose, CA: Rosicrucian, 1948), 53.
31. Ibid., 265

to the monastery at Carmel [where] He lived for many years, and carried on secret missions with His Apostles."[32]

Heindel claimed occult mysticism for Jesus: "The founder of the Christian Religion stated an occult maxim [in] (Mark 10:15). All occultists recognize the far-reaching importance of this teaching of Christ."[33] In Gnostic terms, Heindel wrote, "The Christ spirit which entered the body of Jesus when Jesus Himself vacated it, was a ray from the cosmic Christ. We may follow Jesus back in His previous incarnations and trace His growth to the present day."[34]

The Sleeping Prophet's Jesus

Edgar Cayce (1877–1945)—was known as the "sleeping prophet" because he appeared to be sleeping while giving "readings" in a trance state. His following is worldwide, and he founded the organization Association for Research and Enlightenment (ARE). From his fourteen thousand readings, he often spoke of God and Jesus Christ, since he was once a Protestant Sunday school teacher who read the Bible through some fifty times, but his teachings embraced a mixture of Theosophy and the occult.[35]

Cayce taught that Jesus and Christ are distinct entities: "Christ is not a man! Jesus was the man! Christ was the Messenger! . . . Christ in all ages!"[36] Jesus was a man who had been reincarnated as "Amilius, as Adam, as Melchizedek, as Zend, as Ur, as Asaph, as Jeshuah—Joseph—(Joshua)—Jesus."[37] As Adam, then, the future Jesus is also the one who sinned in Eden, "Q: When did the knowledge come to Jesus that He was to be the Savior of the world? A: When He fell, in Eden."[38] In his early years, Jesus was taught the "tenets of the [Great White] Brotherhood," he studied astrology, and was educated in Essene, India, Persia, and Egypt.[39]

32. Ibid., 289.
33. Max Heindel, *The Rosicrucian Cosmo-conception or Mystic Christianity* (Oceanside, CA: Rosicrucian Fellowship, 1937), 5.
34. Max Heindel, *The Rosicrucian Philosophy in Questions and Answers* (Oceanside, CA: Rosicrucian Fellowship, 1941), 181.
35. See Noel Langley and Hugh Lynn Cayce, *Edgar Cayce on Reincarnation* (New York: Paperback Library, 1967), 51–52 and 364–65 for examples on the Akasha Records, astrology, and the Great White Brotherhood spirits that guided Cayce.
36. Ibid., 157.
37. Jeffrey Furst, *Edgar Cayce's Story of Jesus* (New York: Berkley, 1968), 39–40. Enoch is also added to the incarnation of Jesus, 71.
38. Ibid., 47.
39. Ibid., 188–91.

The Pure Energy Jesus

Dolores Ashcroft-Nowicki (b. 1929)—director of the Servants of the Light School, a European New Age group. Ashcroft-Nowicki has seventeen books to her credit that include a redefinition of Jesus' resurrection as a supercharged occult form of energy and not a resurrected human body. She interpreted Jesus' statement in John 20:17, "Touch me not; for I am not yet ascended to my Father" (KJV), as meaning that he had a body of proto matter that consisted of pure energy. She further indicated that Mary may have been killed by an energy wave had she touched Him, since it would have destabilized His body's thought form.[40]

The Christ Who Is Now Here

Benjamin Creme (b. 1922)—a New Age student of Theosophy, who surprised the world with the 1982 announcement placed in seventeen of the world's largest newspapers that "the Christ Is Now Here." When asked how he knew this, Creme revealed that he received telepathic psychic messages from a Tibetan (similar to Alice Bailey) whom he had never seen nor met. He founded the TARA Center, a New Age organization. Creme taught:

> God always works through agents. . . . The Christ is an agent. The Christ is not God. . . . The Christ is the Master of all the Masters, but He is not God, and never claimed to be God. He is a Son of God, but then so are we. . . . To me, God is the sum total of all that exists in the whole of the manifested and unmanifested universe. . . . That energy—because it is an energy (there isn't anything else)—is not a man, but manifests through men. Maitreya, the Christ, is the embodiment of That Principle on this planet.[41]

The Astrologer's Jesus, Christ, and Son

Linda Goodman, born *Mary Alice Kemrey* (1925–1995)—a sun-sign astrologer whose popular books maintain her strong influence long after her death.

---

40. Dolores Ashcroft-Nowicki and J. H. Brennan, *Magical Use of Thought Forms: A Proven System of Mental and Spiritual Empowerment* (Woodbury, MN: Llewellyn, 2001), 137.
41. Creme, *The Reappearance of the Christ and the Masters of Wisdom,* 115.

Astrologers today carry a variety of New Age ideas with varying degrees of flexibility, including karma, reincarnation, twin souls, soul mates, and God as an impersonal vibration permeating the universe (perhaps Brahma), although some astrologists, like Jeane Dixon, personalized God.

Goodman claimed to be a Christian, but she wrote that Jesus was a married man and had a "Twin Soul."[42] Everybody can be "the Christ" as Jesus was, since "Christ is simply another term for the Holy Ghost or the Holy Spirit, which can enter into anyone."[43] On Jesus and the Trinity, she wrote, "Pluto's vibratory Zero also contains the secret mystery of Christianity's Holy Trinity. 'Father-Son-Holy Ghost.' The 'son' (humans of both sexes) is *masculine energy*. The 'Holy Ghost' (Christ's spirit) is the *feminine energy*."[44] Goodman claimed to be a Christian, as many occult writers do, but the test of truth is whether their words align with God's Word. She completely changed the nature of the Trinity into something unrecognizable in Scripture.

Jesus on the Wrong Course

Helen Schucman (1909–1981)—a Columbia University professor and medical psychologist who took the country by storm with her runaway best seller, *A Course in Miracles* (1975), channeled by an inner voice she claimed was Jesus Christ. Through these occult medium experiences, Schucman's book aimed to correct errors in orthodox Christianity, which resulted in redefining many aspects of Christianity. The book has three parts. The first part represents Jesus speaking a new revelation where the apostles misunderstood the crucifixion: "The message of the crucifixion is perfectly clear. . . . Teach only love. . . . If you interpret the crucifixion in any other way, you are using it as a weapon for assault rather than as the call for peace for which it was intended. The Apostles often misunderstood it."[45]

Schucman presented a Gnostic Christ, stating, "The name of Jesus is the name of one who was a man but saw the face of Christ . . . he became identified with Christ, a man no longer. . . . The man was an illusion. . . . Is he the Christ? O yes, along with you."[46]

---

42. Linda Goodman, *Linda Goodman's Love Signs* (New York: Fawcett Columbine, 1978), 7.
43. Ibid.
44. Ibid., 17.
45. Helen Schucman, *A Course in Miracles* (New York: Foundation for Inner Peace, 1975), 1:87.
46. Ibid., 3:83

Spangler's Awakened Jesus

David Spangler (b. 1945)—widely known among New Age adherents as an enthusiastic promoter of his paranormal and occult experiences. Encounters with out-of-body experiences, spirit-beings, channeling, and UFOs led Spangler to embrace esoteric writings and education, which is reflected in his comments on separating Jesus from the Christ: "The true birth of the Christ was not the birth of Jesus. Jesus was an individual who himself had to recapitulate certain stages. He built upon the pattern the Buddha had established. . . . He himself had to become awakened. He had to, in his consciousness, touch this Christ pattern."[47]

The Out-of-Body Psychic Christ

Jane Roberts (1929–1984)—a trance medium channeler for a spirit named Seth. Roberts wrote a series of books called *The Seth Material*, based on her encounters with this entity. Her spirit communications came through out-of-body experiences, the Ouija board, trance channeling, and automatic writing. In Roberts's view, the Christ is not Jesus alone, but is a group of people, chiefly Jesus, John, and Paul, the last of whom she stated, "The third personality of Christ will indeed be known as a great psychic."[48] She questioned whether Jesus was crucified, and referred to the crucifixion as a "psychic event."[49]

The Cosmic Jesus Mantra

Elizabeth Clare Prophet (b. 1939)—a Theosophist and New Age occultist who leads Summit Lighthouse and the Church Universal and Triumphant. A prolific author of more than seventy-five books, she has been the trance medium for several Ascended Masters who speak through her. Prophet has amassed a large following by merging the major tenets of world faiths into her system. "Students who come to Summit Lighthouse find on our altar a statue of the Buddha, a statue of Mother Mary, a magnificent painting of the Lord Jesus Christ and a painting of Saint Germain, the master of the Aquarian Age. Thus the blending of our spirits in

47. David Spangler, *Reflections on the Christ* (Moray, Scotland: Findhorn, 1978), 6.
48. Jane Roberts, *Seth Speaks: The Eternal Validity of the Soul* (San Rafael, CA: Amber-Allen, 1994), 329. Roberts also stated that Jesus, John, and Paul are collectively called "the Christ entity," 339.
49. Ibid., 206

East and West has produced a meditation upon the Mother, the Christ and the Buddha."[50] On mantras and meditation, Prophet wrote, "Jesus used mantras and he taught them to his disciples in the Upper Room, but much of this is not recorded in Scripture."[51] In their prayers, Prophet's followers call for the Cosmic Christ: "I call for the great light of understanding of the Cosmic Christ, Lord Maitreya; of Jesus Christ and Kuthumi, the World Teachers; of Gautama Buddha and all who are serving with the evolutions of the earth for the advancement of consciousness."[52]

The Soul-Traveling Jesus

Paul Twitchell (1918–1971)—an occultist who founded Eckankar, a religious organization that practices esoteric soul-travel, where the subject leaves his body to travel the spiritual planes taught by Eckankar. Twitchell's theological perspective replaced the word *God* with the sacred name *Sugmad,* whom he described as the divinity in all life forms. *ECK* is the Divine Spirit. ECK Masters have emerged at times in history, of which the 971st is Twitchell. As an ECK Master, the reincarnated Jesus Christ soul-traveled and helped others do the same. Christ is actually an ECK Master from 3000 BC. "A Christian tends to clothe himself with feelings and thoughts of the Christ, and everything is seen in that context. Years later these particular individuals found that it wasn't Jesus at all; it was the ECK Master Gopal Das."[53] Gopal Das, who is identified as Jesus Christ here, is also called the founder of the mystery cults of Osiris and Isis.

The UFO Jesus

Charles Boyd Gentzel "El-Morya" (1922–1981) and *Pauline Sharpe* "Nada-Yolanda" (1925–2005)—founders of Mark-Age, Inc., an occult group that mixes UFOs with Theosophical ideas. Gentzel and Sharpe received messages from UFO aliens and "etheric teachers" via automatic writing, and they taught that Jesus was the Christ or *Sananda*, orbiting the earth in a UFO as the commander of a fleet of UFOs that occasionally landed to demonstrate their reality to earthlings.[54]

---

50. Prophet, *Inner Perspectives,* 32.
51. Ibid., 10.
52. Ibid., 44.
53. Sri Harold Klemp, "Paul Twitchell's Spiritual Search," www.eckankar.org/Masters/Peddar/hisSearch.html. Klemp, the 973rd ECK Master, replaced Darwin Gross, who replaced Twitchell.
54. Nada-Yolanda, *Visitors from Other Planets* (Miami: Mark-Age, 1974), 1ff.

Claude Vorilhon (b.1946)—also known as Rael, is the founder of the UFO cult the Raelian movement (1987). They surfaced in international news in 2002 by claiming to clone the first human baby. This gained international media attention and investigation, but Rael stonewalled media questions with silence. Rael, who openly calls himself the Messiah, God's last prophet, and the fulfillment of the return of Christ, has medium communication with alien beings he believes are extraterrestrial human scientists, our creators, who reveal esoteric secrets.[55] Their Internet "message" states that these extraterrestrial creators were misunderstood as "gods" and that they originated our main religions, namely that, "Jesus, whose father was Eloha, was given the task of spreading these messages [the Rael messages] throughout the world."[56] It was further stated that Jesus, Moses, Buddha, and Mohammed were alive on the extraterrestrials' planet through an advanced cloning technique, which they claim is "the secret of eternal life."[57]

Jesus as Michael

William S. Sadler (1897–1969)—a medical doctor who was instrumental in the founding of the Urantia Foundation (1955) and the transcribing and publishing of *The Urantia Book*. The foundation has an estimated 250,000 followers who believe *The Urantia Book* is sacred scripture. The book claims to be a revelation from intergalactic superhuman beings that call the earth Urantia (one of the ten million inhabited planets in our local universe, and six other universes exist). These superbeings gave a history of the universe to two scribes as dictated from an anonymous person in a sleep state, similar to occult methods employed by channelers. The book corrects several supposed errors in the Bible and fills in missing data on Jesus Christ.

In *The Urantia Book*, the Paradise Trinity consists of "the Universal Father, the Eternal Son, and the Infinite Spirit."[58] They created "Creator Sons" called "Michaels."[59] The Creator Michaels created some 7 trillion inhabited planets (including earth),[60] where "they are as Creators and Gods."[61] Michael of Nebadon

55. International Raelian Movement, http://rael.org/rael_content/intro.php?elan=English.
56. www.rael.org/rael_content/rael_summary.php.
57. http://www.rael.org/e107_plugins/vstore/showpic.php?id=1&cat=1.
58. *The Urantia Book*, 1141.
59. Ibid., 335. Jesus is also called the "Christ Michael" in several places (341).
60. Ibid., 164, 167.
61. Ibid., 241.

is the creator of Urantia (earth). Jesus' incarnation is described as follows: "The Eternal Son did come to mortal man on Urantia when the divine personality of his Son, Michael of Nebadon, incarnated into the human nature of Jesus of Nazareth."[62] Denying Jesus' bodily resurrection, the book states, "His material or physical body was not a part of the resurrected personality. When Jesus came forth form the tomb, his body of flesh remained undisturbed in the sepulcher."[63]

The Ouija Board and Jesus the Occult Master

Chelsea Quinn Yarbro (b. 1942)—the author of four books about Ouija board contact with a spirit named Michael: *Messages from Michael* (1979), *More Messages from Michael* (1986), *Michael's People* (1988), and *Michael for the Millennium* (1995). Yarbro popularized the Michael Teaching groups, and subsequent authors have published more than a dozen additional books containing "Michael Teachings" from various Michael groups in America. The premise of Michael's spiritual teaching is New Age and claims that we are reincarnated beings. Michael, through the Ouija board, said, "Greek thought had much influence upon the man Jesus, particularly Epicurius. . . . Jesus was an occult master. . . . The man you call Jesus did not die on the Cross but died later."[64] Michael went on to reveal that Jesus was not virgin born and that he was a married man.

Jesus the Witch

Witchcraft, as a loosely knit belief system, still has its representative teachers and teachings. *Patricia Crowther* (b. 1927)—a Witch high priestess and spokesperson for Witchcraft, said this about Jesus: "I believe he was a Witch. He worked miracles or what we would call magic, cured people and did most things expected from a Witch. He had his coven of thirteen."[65]

Jesus the Psychic

Jeane Dixon (1904–1997)—a world-famous psychic and astrologer who claimed to

62. Ibid., 86.
63. Ibid., 2021.
64. Chelsea Quinn Yarbro, Messages from Michael (New York: Berkeley, 1980), 176–77.
65. Crowther and Crowther, *The Secrets of Ancient Witchcraft*, 164.
66. See the discussion on Jeane Dixon's predictions in chapter 9, under the heading "Crystal Ball."

predict the assassination of the United States president John F. Kennedy through psychic powers.[66] Dixon claimed that her psychic gifts came from the Lord, saying, "It is an awesome and inspiring feeling to be a worker for the Lord," and, "I have been given certain psychic gifts which I have been working to develop and use in accordance with God's will."[67]

Mary T. Browne (n.d.)—a New York–based psychic and best-selling author who has more than five thousand clients from Wall Street and other upper-class professionals dependent upon her psychic abilities for their careers. Browne said of Christ, "Jesus was psychic. He told Thomas, 'Before the cock crows, you will betray me three times.' Tell me, is that not a psychic prediction?"[68] Somehow, the *psychic* Browne missed the fact that it was *Peter* to whom Jesus said this, not Thomas.

Jesus the Powerless Mad Redeemer

Anton Szandor LaVey, born **Howard Stanton Levey** (1930–1997)—the author of *The Satanic Bible* (1969) and the founder of the Church of Satan (1966). Even though skeptics spoofed his mockery of Christianity, his longevity and steadfast followers demand serious attention. *The Satanic Bible* says little about Jesus Christ, since that is not the subject; however, the following lines call Jesus a powerless "mad redeemer" and mock his crucifixion. LaVey wrote, "I dip my forefinger in the watery blood of your impotent mad redeemer, and write over his thorn-torn brow; The TRUE prince of evil—the king of the slaves!"[69]

Ramtha's Jesus Who Saved Himself

Judy Zebra Knight (J. Z. Knight), born **Judith Darlene Hampton** (b. 1946)— a deep trance channeler for a thirty-five-thousand-year-old spirit named Ramtha; she is the founder of Ramtha's School of Enlightenment (1987). J. Z. Knight is a popular and sought-after New Age medium with a worldwide following. Knight wrote that Jesus was a God, just as other humans are, which places him in the status of a brother and not a savior. She also claimed that Jesus became a Christ, just as other

67. Rene Noorbergen, *Jeane Dixon: My Life and Prophecies* (New York: William Morrow, 1969), 57, 65.
68. "Confessions of a Psychic," *Psychology Today* (November/December 1994), http://psychologytoday.com/articles/pto-19941101-000020.html.
69. LaVey, *The Satanic Bible*, 30.

humans have done, and that Jesus is not responsible for our salvation, because he was saving himself through the realization that he was God.[70]

SCRIPTURAL RESPONSE

Jesus Christ, in the true essence of His being, cannot be changed by man's whimsical or capricious desires. The doctrine of Christ's immutability, which refutes all of man's changes to his nature, is clearly laid out in Hebrews 1:8–12:

But to the Son He says:

"Your throne, O God, is forever and ever;
a scepter of righteousness is the scepter of Your kingdom.
You have loved righteousness and hated lawlessness;
therefore God, Your God, has anointed You
with the oil of gladness more than Your companions."

And:

"You, LORD, in the beginning laid the foundation of the earth,
and the heavens are the work of Your hands.
They will perish, but You remain;
and they will all grow old like a garment;
like a cloak You will fold them up,
and they will be changed.
But You are the same,
and Your years will not fail."

The Father addressed these statements to Jesus Christ. He quoted Psalm 102:25–27, directly applying these words to Jesus Christ. He was saying that Jesus created the heavens and earth, He remains, He is the same, and His years will not fail. These facts, coupled with Hebrews 13:8, "Jesus Christ is the same yesterday, today, and forever," give ample support to the immutability of Christ's nature.

---

70. Judy Zebra Knight, *Ramtha: The White Book* (Yelm, WA: JZK, 2005), 63z–64.

When those within the cults, the occult, or world religions reinterpret Jesus, they directly contradict Scripture.

A Christian who understands Christology, as grounded in the New Testament texts, should have no difficulty exposing the errors of man's twisted Jesus. There is only one true Jesus, so any "other Jesus" must be labeled false. In crafting their corrupted image of Him, these false teachers betray themselves and reveal that they know nothing of the Lord Jesus Christ.

The following Christian doctrines stand to refute all forces that rise up against our Savior:

- One God exists, and no others.

- Jesus Christ preexisted as God, second Person of the Trinity, coequal with the Father and Holy Spirit.

- He became God incarnate on earth through the miraculous conception of the Virgin Mary and was declared Lord and Christ at His birth.

- Jesus is Christ, and no others can be "a Christ." He lived a sinless life. He vicariously atoned for our sins through His death upon the Cross. He rose from the dead in the same body as was crucified, yet it rose as a glorified immortal body. He ascended into heaven to sit at the right hand of the glory of God. He will personally return for His Church in the same manner in which He left.

Only One God

The Bible explicitly teaches that no gods exist except the true and living God. Deuteronomy 6:4 states, "Hear, O Israel: The LORD our God, the LORD is one!" Isaiah added that no God existed before or after Him, "Before Me there was no God formed, nor shall there be after Me" (43:10). The psalmist expressed the same doctrine: "You alone are God" (Ps. 86:10).[71] Since occultists often portray Jesus as one among many gods, then we can rest assured in the biblical testimony that there is only one God.

---

71. Other verses to consult are Deuteronomy 4:39; Isaiah 44:8; Mark 12:32; and James 2:19.

God Is a Trinity of Persons

God is personal, which means that He has all of the characteristics of what makes a person, and He communicates that way throughout Scripture.[72] The fact that the Father, Son, and Holy Spirit communicate with one another as Persons goes further to demonstrate their personal distinction. All three Persons have eternally coexisted in perfect unity, harmony, and love in their nature as God.

It is important to note that the word *one* does not necessarily indicate a *solitary* existence. God referred to Adam and Eve as becoming "one flesh" in Genesis 2:24—the union of two people who became as one before Him. The unity of a composite character was recognized by God Himself as existing within the world He created.[73]

God is a person called the Father. This is easily proven from many biblical passages, such as Romans 1:7: "Grace to you and peace from God our Father and the Lord Jesus Christ." There is no doubt the Father is a person, and He is God.

God is a person called the Son. Hebrews 1:8 makes this clear: "But unto the Son, He says, 'Your throne, O God, is forever and ever.'" God the Father spoke to another person, the Son, addressing Him as God. It is clear from Scripture that only one God exists, but we now see two persons as God.

God is a person called the Holy Spirit. In 2 Samuel 23:2–3, David wrote (as the introduction to his last prophecy), "The Spirit of the LORD spoke by me. . . . The God of Israel said . . ." (NKJV). David's introduction shows the Holy Spirit is a speaker, a person, and that the same person is the God of Israel.

When the biblical evidence is examined, it reveals three divine persons as one triune God.[74] Hundreds of verses provide a strong biblical foundation for the doctrine of the Trinity. Occult writers often deny that God is a personal Being, let alone a tripersonal Being, opting instead for a pantheistic, impersonal, all-permeating entity that is as much a rock as it is water or air. Some occult writers liken their god to an

---

72. Norman Geisler put it this way: Each individual member of the Trinity is a person, since each is referred to as a person (I, Who). Each has all the basic elements or powers of personhood: mind, will, and feeling." (Geisler, *Systematic Theology,* 2:287).
73. Walter Martin, *Essential Christianity* (eBook), 25, www.waltermartin.com.
74. The power of Matthew 28:19 should never be underestimated in demonstrating the Trinity in Jesus' teachings: "baptizing them in the name of the Father and of the Son and of the Holy Spirit." Norman Geisler states, "Another helpful illustration is that God is like one to the third power (1 X 1 X 1 = 1). God is three ones in One; He is not 1+1+1=3. That is the heresy of tritheism, which holds three different gods, not just one God." (Geisler, *Systematic Theology,* 2:294).

impersonal energy force akin to monism—*all is one*—sometimes called Mind, Force, consciousness, or universal energy. In any case, the personal nature of God, even the tripersonal nature of God as taught in the Scripture, corrects their error. Jesus' nature as God is that of the true eternal person of God, the second person of the Trinity. When occult teachers alter Jesus' deity and make Him less than true God, they have breeched a forbidden barrier and perverted the nature of the Son of God.

Jesus Is God Incarnate

Christians speak of the incarnation of Jesus Christ with the confidence of direct testimony in the Old and New Testaments. Becoming man did not change Jesus' nature as God, and His nature as God incarnate did not alter His humanity. Neither His deity nor His humanity suffered change in the union of two natures as the unique person of Jesus Christ. One particular statement Paul made clearly illustrates this:

> Who [Christ Jesus], being in the form of God, did not consider it robbery to be equal with God, but made Himself of no reputation, taking the form of a bondservant, and coming in the likeness of men. And being found in appearance as a man, He humbled Himself and became obedient to the point of death, even the death of the cross. (Phil. 2:6–8)

In this remarkable passage, we find that Jesus preexisted in the "form of God." The noted Greek scholar A. T. Robertson amplifies the Greek meaning: "In the form of God *en morphei theou. Morphe* means the essential attributes as shown in the form. In his preincarnate state Christ possessed the attributes of God and so appeared to those in heaven who saw him. Here is a clear statement by Paul of the deity of Christ."[75] The verb translasted "being" is a present active participle (*huparchon*), which demonstrates continuous action.[76] Jesus was always and is continuously in the form (attributes) of God. He did not consider it "robbery" to be equal with God, since He existed as the eternal Word of God (John 1:1) prior to His incarnation (John 1:14) and as such fully shared all the Father's prerogatives and attributes. Jesus had no desire and no need to strive for what was His by nature and inheritance.[77]

---

75. Robertson, *Word Pictures of the New Testament*, 4:444.
76. From Walter Martin's live classroom lectures, as noted by Kurt Van Gorden.
77. Martin, *Kingdom of the Cults* (2003), 89.

Paul tells us that Jesus, as God, became man by taking upon himself another "form" (same Greek word, *morphe*), the "form of a bondservant . . . in the likeness of men" (Phil. 2:7). This Scripture gives Christians every solid reason to teach that Jesus Christ is fully God and fully man united uniquely in one person. Other passages that directly demonstrate Christ's deity are Isaiah 9:6; Matthew 1:23; John 1:1–14; 5:18; 8:58; 20:28; Acts 20:28; Colossians 2:9; Hebrews 1:8–12; and 1 John 5:20.

Jesus Is the Christ

A common thread that runs through occult writing is the Gnostic heresy that separates Jesus from the Christ. To them, the Christ is a spiritual idea, mind, principle, essence, consciousness, spark, energy, force, or some other "christ spirit" entity that either indwelled or came upon Jesus and can likewise indwell or come upon any other person.

Biblically, the word *Christ* is simply the Greek translation of the Hebrew term *Messiah*. The New Testament writers followed the Hebrew translators of the Septuagint and consistently replaced the Hebrew word "Messiah" for the Greek *christos* (Christ), which is from the word *chrio*, meaning *to anoint*. This is the equivalent of *Messiah* or *anointed one* in Hebrew. The apostle John understood this and stated that those who deny that Jesus is "the Christ" are liars. He wrote, "Who is a liar but he who denies that Jesus is the Christ?" (1 John 2:22). John pointedly said that believing in Jesus as "the Christ" is the reason he wrote his gospel: "These are written that you may believe that Jesus is the Christ, the Son of God, and that believing you may have life in His name" (John 20:31).

It is interesting to note that nowhere in the New Testament do we find Jesus as "*a* Christ," as if there are many, but Jesus is always called "the Christ"[78] or simply "Christ," "Jesus Christ," and "Christ Jesus." No one else has that title. No christ spirit, consciousness, or any other entity came upon Jesus during his life—He was already Christ and Lord at his birth. "There is born to you this day in the city of David a Savior, who is Christ the Lord" (Luke 2:11).

Jesus singled Himself out as the only Christ. In His teaching on the warning signs that will occur before His return, He said, "Many will come in My name, saying, 'I am the Christ,' and will deceive many" (Matt. 24:5). It cannot be emphasized enough that in the last days there will be many who will claim to be "the Christ," but Jesus

---

78. Other examples in John's writings are John 1:41; 4:42; 6:69; 11:27; and 1 John 5:1.

called them deceivers, and so they are. This stands as a strong indictment against Theosophists, New Agers, Kabbalists, mind-science groups, and all occultists who call themselves christs or who make christhood a goal to be achieved.

Occult believers claim the *christ* power for many—precisely what Jesus said we should not do. "Then if anyone says to you, 'Look, here is the Christ!' or 'There!' do not believe it" (Matt. 24:23). In the world of the occult, there is a christ here, there, and everywhere. A christ spirit or consciousness indwells them; they make becoming a christ one of their goals. Any group centered on the occult can point to one of their followers and say, "Here is the Christ" or "There is a christ." Elizabeth Clare Prophet, Helena Blavatsky, Alice Bailey, Anne Besant, Charles Filmore, and L. Ron Hubbard are but a few of the many who have done so in print, *fulfilling* Jesus' words—to their own destruction. Jesus clearly said, "Do not believe it!" Yet millions of their followers believe in vain. Jesus made it quite clear that He is the only Christ. The first sign of an imposter is when he or she claims to be a christ or teaches that every human being is christ. *Do not believe it.*

Finally, in Matthew 24:24, Jesus stated, "For false christs and false prophets will rise and show great signs and wonders to deceive, if possible, even the elect." Do not be amazed or persuaded when occultists and New Agers claim signs and wonders. It is only to be expected that this will occur before Jesus returns, and Scripture warns the Church to be on the lookout for it. Jesus singled Himself out as the true Christ because His signs and wonders were genuine hallmarks testifying to His person, nature, and work. False christs and false prophets display their signs and wonders by deception and for deception, but Jesus—by His nature as God incarnate—did so to glorify God.

Jesus as the Sinless Miracle Worker

Several occult writers present Jesus as merely a man who discovered a higher consciousness, implying that the miracles Jesus performed were the result of universal powers available to anyone who discovers the same secrets Jesus discovered. However, the Christian doctrine of Jesus' sinless life effectively refutes this. If Jesus did not do the specific miracles attributed to Him, then He lied to the people. If Jesus lied, He would not be a righteous person, only a deceiver and liar. In direct contrast, the New Testament shows that Jesus is sinless, and therefore, He cannot be a liar. The authority of Scripture enables Christians to trust that the miracles of Jesus happened exactly as He said they happened.

The sinlessness of Jesus is found in His own testimony and from those who knew Him. Jesus said that He had no unrighteousness (John 17:18). He also offered the opportunity to anyone listening to point out a sin in Him: "Which of you convicts Me of sin?" (John 8:46). No one answered Jesus' challenge because they could not find any sin in Him. A mere man would have demonstrated sin just like the rest of humanity. But Paul stated that Jesus "knew no sin" (2 Cor. 5:21); Peter said He "committed no sin" (1 Peter 2:22); and John's testimony is that "in Him there is no sin" (1 John 3:5). The writer of Hebrews confirmed this with: "We do not have a High Priest who cannot sympathize with our weaknesses, but was in all points tempted as we are, yet without sin" (Heb. 4:15). Jesus' righteousness was not something that He worked hard to obtain; it was inherent in Him from His conception as the true Son of God.

The miracles of Jesus are not the result of discovering a christ consciousness and pulling off magick or the illusion of supernaturalism to mask natural laws. Jesus truly performed the supernatural because he was God incarnate, and He superseded the natural laws with miracles.[79] Not one single occult leader or follower has ever come close to the caliber of Jesus' life. He is truly the *incomparable Christ.*

Jesus, Resurrected, Ascended, and Returning, but Not Reincarnated

Jesus became man only once (the Incarnation). Philippians 2:5–8 confirms this and denies that He was anyone other than God:

> Christ Jesus . . . being in the form of God, did not consider it robbery to be equal with God, but made Himself of no reputation, taking the form of a bondservant, and coming in the likeness of men. And being found in appearance as a man, He humbled Himself and became obedient to the point of death, even the death of the cross.

Jesus was not a reincarnated Adam, Moses, Buddha, or any other person; He was God, the second person of the Holy Trinity. Jesus made it clear that He alone

---

79. Feeding seven thousand and five thousand from a few loaves of bread, walking on water, raising people from the dead (after four days), and raising Himself from the dead are a few examples that defy natural explanation without labeling Jesus a deceiver.

came from above, and everyone else came from this world. "You are from beneath; I am from above. You are of this world; I am not of this world" (John 8:23). Notice that Jesus is not from this earth, and therefore was not reincarnated from formerly living human beings. He was God, who became incarnate in man, but not man who came back as a man.[80]

Jesus did not teach reincarnation. There is no evidence that He ever associated with the Essenes, much less was taught by them. Everything we read of His life in the New Testament denies reincarnation and supports His bodily resurrection. Luke recorded Jesus' response to those who claim that He was raised from the dead as an ethereal body, a Light body, a spirit-body, or anything other than a truly glorified immortalized human body: "Behold My hands and My feet, that it is I Myself. Handle Me and see, for a spirit does not have flesh and bones as you see I have" (Luke 24:39). Jesus offered the same body that they saw crucified as proof; a body with the print of the nails remaining—yet glorified as immortal and resurrected in flesh and bones.

Jesus refutes reincarnation and so-called Ascended Masters in John 3:13: "No one has ascended to heaven but He who came down from heaven, that is, the Son of Man who is in heaven." *No one has ascended*, therefore all Theosophy-related groups that claim a host of Ascended Masters are proved false by the words of Christ. Jesus, after His resurrection, is the only one who ascended. The singular "He" is used—not the plural "they"—as if there were others. Jesus made an *exclusive* claim in this category. There is no reincarnation, according to the words of Christ, and no ascended masters.

Jesus is returning to earth in His resurrected flesh-and-bones body—the same body He left the earth in: "Men of Galilee, why do you stand gazing up into heaven? This *same* Jesus, who was taken up from you into heaven, will so come in like manner as you saw Him go into heaven" (Acts 1:11). Some occult writers claim that Jesus will be born on earth as a baby once again, only to be revealed later as a Maitreya, Buddha, or a world teacher. But Scripture promises it will be the *incomparable Jesus* who returns in the clouds; He will not be known by any other name.

---

80. Hebrews 9:27 also stands contrary to reincarnation, stating, "It is appointed for men to die once, but after this the judgment."

CASE STUDY

Walter Martin

One Sunday a lady came up to me after my Bible study, handed me a thick stack of papers and asked if I had ever seen her metaphysical poetry.

I smiled and said, "No, I don't believe I ever have."

She replied, "I spent eleven or twelve years of my life composing this junk. I was a member of one of the mind-science groups. I thought I was on a higher plane than the poor average Christian. I was so proud of what I found out in my cult that I just looked down my spiritual nose at everyone else. I was enraptured by writing my poetry, 'The Music of the Celestial Spheres.'

"And then," she said, "Jesus came and ruined the whole thing. After I was born again I started reading this stuff, and I thought, 'Oh, dear God, how did you ever put up with me? How could I have written garbage like this?' As soon as the light of the Gospel entered my life I couldn't think the same way, and I knew that what I had been doing was the grossest evil. But if you had told me that the day before, I would never have believed it."

This is the perfect illustration of one important fact: the people you will be talking to are incapable of understanding the truth of the gospel apart from God the Holy Spirit operating through you and upon them, to open their eyes. You should be constantly in prayer, "Lord, open their eyes. Lord, let them see. Lord, give them just a brief glimpse of yourself. Lord, keep me out of the way. Lord, let Jesus Christ be seen." Do you know what happens [when you do this]? Remarkable and wonderful things begin to occur.

When we started in this ministry that the Lord gave to me almost thirty years ago, all of my colleagues in the Christian world told me that it was extremely negative. You should never go out and defend Christianity. Truth is like a lion. "Turn it loose," they said, "and it will defend itself." Well, I have seen truth turned into a pussycat so fast that you would not even know what happened. Truth without the knowledge to defend it, without the Spirit of God to guide and apply it, will not go far with a cultist or occultist.[81]

---

81. Walter Martin, *Evangelizing the Cults and Occult*, www.waltermartin.com.

CONCLUSION

In sharing the good news of the gospel, it is of paramount importance that Christians *define terms*. It is never safe to assume that the name Jesus, spoken by someone lost in the occult, is the same Jesus spoken of in Scripture. As we have seen, there are many false concepts of Jesus preached in the occult, but only one true Jesus Christ. The kingdom of the occult grows daily in numbers, a terrible fact that gives us every reason to present Jesus Christ's gospel with a compelling relevancy. We must make the message of Jesus significant to them by distinguishing between the false Christ and the true; we must eloquently reveal Him as the one and only way, planting the seed of the gospel in accordance with God's will.

An examination of the *other Jesus* should stimulate an innate awareness inextricably linked with the name of Jesus Christ. The apostles stressed the fact that not every image of Jesus or Christ is equal. The Jesus of the occult falls terribly short of God's truth as found in His Word. We must view the lost through the eyes of Jesus, when He asked His disciples, "Who do you say that I am?" The correct answer comes only through knowing the correct Jesus. Every branch of the occult offers a false Jesus that condemns the soul to eternal damnation by replacing the true Jesus and Christ with a counterfeit. Love compels us to tell the world of the occult about the true Jesus; it is a love that God puts in our hearts—a gracious, patient love that must swell to overflowing, seeking every opportunity to lead lost souls to the true Master and Savior, Jesus Christ.

Recommended Resources

1. Green, Michael. *Who Is This Jesus?* Grand Rapids: Baker, 2005.

2. Gomes, Alan. *Truth and Error.* Grand Rapids: Zondervan, 1995.

3. Martin, Walter. *Essential Christianity* (eBook) www.waltermartin.com.

4. Martin, Walter. *Kingdom of the Cults.* Minneapolis: Bethany House, 2005.

5. McGrath, Alister. *Understanding Jesus: Who Jesus Christ Is and Why He Matters.* Grand Rapids: Academe, 1987.

Quick Facts About Spiritual Warfare

- The supernatural realm of the occult is centered upon Satan's kingdom, and its power is directly dispensed through him and his demonic servants to the limits of his domain.

- The human realm of the occult is centered upon mankind's sinful nature, which seeks power over self, other beings and circumstances.

- Christians face two spiritual war fronts: one is directly against the powers of Satan, and the other is against the power of sin.

- God has provided authority, power, and victory for Christians over Satan and his representatives, whether demonic or human.

16

Spiritual Warfare

The diversity of world religions, sects, cults, spiritualities, and occult practitioners all demonstrate mankind's attempts to deal with evil, sin, suffering, and the quest to explain our existence.[1] New Testament Christianity teaches that one plan of personal salvation is offered to humanity. It is offered by God's grace through faith and belief only in the person and work of Jesus Christ, in His shed blood as the appeasement of God's wrath against our sins, and in His victorious bodily resurrection that conquered death, hell, and the power of sin. Jesus taught that His followers must be "born from above," commonly translated as "born again" in order to see the kingdom of God (John 3:3). When a person enters the kingdom of God, the prince of darkness incurs an immediate loss, and he then makes it his goal to trouble the new Christian at every opportunity. This engagement of Satan, his power, his works, or his demons is called spiritual warfare.[2]

Two conflicting elements define this warfare in individual Christian living: one consists of the wonderful benefits of the abundant life promised by Jesus in John 10:10, replete with miracles, healings, power, signs, wonders, and seemingly unlimited blessings and joy; the other element brings tribulation, trials, temptations, hardships, frustrations, afflictions, illnesses, and spiritual war. Most Christians experience both sides of this conflict, though some endure more of one than the other. The how and why of this division in individual lives is best left to the wisdom of God, whose power it is to change all circumstances. Jesus said, "With God

---

1. Arguments for the superiority of Jesus Christ and Christianity to other religions fall outside of this writing, but we recommend Walter Martin's messages entitled "Seven Campus Curses," "Reasons for Faith," and "Existence of God" (cassettes), available at http://www.waltermartin.com/prodserv.html. We recommend the apologetic works of Walter R. Martin, Josh McDowell, Norman Geisler, Alvin Plantinga, Ravi Zacharias, Francis A. Schaffer, Os Guiness, A. B. Bruce, and Wilbur Smith.

2. Two books that powerfully provide insight into how Satan and the demons scheme against Christians are C. S. Lewis's *The Screwtape Letters: A Devil's Diabolical Advice for the Capturing of the Human Heart* and Walter R. Martin's *Screwtape Writes Again* (Santa Ana, CA: Vision House, 1975).

all things are possible" (Matt. 19:26), but we bow at His throne in humble acceptance of the life that He has given to each of us. Jesus taught that life will always
have its troubles: "Do not worry about tomorrow, for tomorrow will worry about
its own things. Sufficient for the day is its own trouble" (Matt. 6:34).

On the upside of life's difficulties, we also know that God will not allow more
trouble or temptation than what we can endure. "No temptation has overtaken you
except such as is common to man; but God is faithful, who will not allow you to
be tempted beyond what you are able, but with the temptation will also make the
way of escape, that you may be able to bear it" (1 Cor. 10:13). The way of escape
spoken of here is only a glimpse of the power available to Christians in spiritual
warfare, but the sad truth is that this power is not exercised enough to the glory of
God in our individual lives. Too often, people become absorbed in self-pity and
forget to call upon the Holy Spirit—the *Comforter*. Many have not been taught to
properly exercise their faith in times of need, and Satan delights in weak Christians
who have not schooled themselves in the powerful Word of God—a sword
intended for daily use by Christians. "For the word of God is living and powerful,
and sharper than any two-edged sword, piercing even to the division of soul and
spirit, and of joints and marrow, and is a discerner of the thoughts and intents of
the heart" (Heb. 4:12)

Jesus used the power of God's written Word to defeat Satan's temptations during His time of trial in the wilderness (Luke 4:1–13). This is one of many examples found in the New Testament that reveal exactly how the Christian can emerge
victorious in spiritual warfare. The glorious end of this story is that Jesus defeated
Satan's wilderness trials. "Now when the devil had ended every temptation, he
departed from Him until an opportune time" (Luke 4:13). Satan will flee when
confronted by the power of God's Word, but it is only to await another opportunity for attack.

This is a point Christians would do well to remember, because it demonstrates
the strategy of the enemy: Satan may withdraw for a time, but he always returns.
This is why the apostle Peter warned the body of Christ that our enemy stalks
about "like a roaring lion, seeking whom he may devour" (1 Peter 5:8). We dare
not soften our view of a prowling enemy. He is always seeking *whom he may devour*.
He is always accusing the brethren, both day and night (Rev. 12:10). He is no
friend of Christ, no friend of Christians, and no friend of the Church. Christians

battle not one, but a *host* of enemies in the invisible world, who sometimes manifest themselves or their works in the visible world, and they all delight in seeing Christians distressed and defeated.

The Church is not subject to their bidding, since the power of God is greater than all of the works of darkness, but they are an enemy to be reckoned with. The apostle John offered this great encouragement in the fight: "You are of God, little children, and have overcome them, because He who is in you is greater than he who is in the world" (1 John 4:4).

SPIRITUAL WARFARE: YESTERDAY AND TODAY

Spiritual warfare did not begin with the human race; it began with the rebellion of the angels. These powerful and magnificent created beings possess an intellect and will similar to human beings but different from them in one vital respect: man is uniquely made in the image and likeness of God. Angels are special creatures, since they dwell in heaven and were created as ministering spirits, but human beings are exclusively God's children, since we bear His image (Heb. 1:7). People are important to God, or He would have abandoned us to the destruction we so richly deserved as a punishment for our rebellion. But instead of destroying man, God provided a way of escape.

A vast number of angels rebelled against God, but even as important as angels are in God's universe, He provided no redemption for them. They are judged and condemned to eternal torment for their sinful rebellion. "God did not spare the angels who sinned, but cast them down to hell and delivered them into chains of darkness, to be reserved for judgment" (2 Peter 2:4). Jude notes, "And the angels who did not keep their proper domain, but left their own abode, He has reserved in everlasting chains under darkness for the judgment of the great day" (v. 6). This insight into the destiny of the fallen angels gives no indication that redemption was offered to them. But in God's love for the human race, we should be ever grateful for His mercy and grace, a grace that purchased the Church "with His own blood" (Acts 20:28).

Heavenly Rebellion and Judgment

The first account of the creation of the angels is found in Genesis 2:1: "Thus the heavens and the earth, and all the host of them, were finished." At some time in the six days of creation, God made the angels who are included in the reference "all the host of them," meaning all the host of the realm of the heavens, just as animals, fish, fowl, and humans are included in all the host of the earth.

Ezekiel 28:12–19 compares Lucifer to the king of Tyre, and through this association we have a glimpse of Lucifer's creation. He was full of wisdom, beauty, power, and holiness until the corruption of pride and the defilement of sin destroyed his perfection and transformed him into a "horror":

Son of man, take up a lamentation for the king of Tyre, and say to him, "Thus says the Lord GOD:

'You were the seal of perfection,
full of wisdom and perfect in beauty.
You were in Eden, the garden of God;
every precious stone was your covering:
the sardius, topaz, and diamond,
beryl, onyx, and jasper,
sapphire, turquoise, and emerald with gold.
The workmanship of your timbrels and pipes
was prepared for you on the day you were created.
'You were the anointed cherub who covers;
I established you;
you were on the holy mountain of God;
you walked back and forth in the midst of fiery stones.
You were perfect in your ways from the day you were created,
till iniquity was found in you.
'By the abundance of your trading
you became filled with violence within,
and you sinned;
therefore I cast you as a profane thing
out of the mountain of God;
and I destroyed you, O covering cherub,
from the midst of the fiery stones.
'Your heart was lifted up because of your beauty;

you corrupted your wisdom for the sake of your splendor;
I cast you to the ground,
I laid you before kings,
that they might gaze at you.
'You defiled your sanctuaries
by the multitude of your iniquities,
by the iniquity of your trading;
therefore I brought fire from your midst;
it devoured you,
and I turned you to ashes upon the earth
in the sight of all who saw you.
All who knew you among the peoples are astonished at you;
you have become a horror,
and shall be no more forever.'"

Isaiah 14:12–15 speaks further of the fall of Lucifer, which is the only biblical passage that calls him by this name. Here, he lifted up his will and pride against God and attempted to usurp God's throne and power, but God cast him out of heaven for this:

How you are fallen from heaven,
O Lucifer, son of the morning!
How you are cut down to the ground,
You who weakened the nations!
For you have said in your heart:
"I will ascend into heaven,
I will exalt my throne above the stars of God;
I will also sit on the mount of the congregation
on the farthest sides of the north;
I will ascend above the heights of the clouds,
I will be like the Most High."
Yet you shall be brought down to Sheol,
to the lowest depths of the Pit.

These two Scripture passages provide important information on Lucifer's origin, his fall, and his corruption of the nations. Jesus confirmed His dealings with Satan before His incarnation. "I saw Satan fall like lightning from heaven" (Luke 10:18). Exactly when this took place, we do not know, but enough information is provided to assure us it occurred.

When Lucifer fell into sin, a vast number of angels sided with him in battle against Michael the archangel and his angels. In Michael's victory, the rebellious angels were also cast out of heaven along with Satan. Revelation 12:7–9 states:

And war broke out in heaven: Michael and his angels fought with the dragon; and the dragon and his angels fought, but they did not prevail, nor was a place found for them in heaven any longer. So the great dragon was cast out, that serpent of old, called the Devil and Satan, who deceives the whole world; he was cast to the earth, and his angels were cast out with him.

The exact number of angels that rebelled and were cast out is unknown, but the apostle John reveals that it was one-third of all the angels in heaven (Rev. 12:4). The Bible teaches that these fallen angels are the enemies of both God and man. God created holy beings that chose to rebel against him, and the righteous angels that still exist provide proof positive that they could have chosen to remain righteous. Lucifer and the fallen angels were not created as evil beings, but became evil through an act of their own volition. God, therefore, is not the author of evil, as some philosophers have suggested, and He did not create evil. Evil in the universe is not a dualistic part of God's being, as presented in some cultures and false religions.

The rebellion that Satan began in heaven is still ongoing against both God and the human race. The force we battle in spiritual warfare is a powerful, invisible enemy that often chooses to manifest its power on a physical level. We are hated and despised by Satan because we are the redeemed of the Lord. Bought with the precious blood of the Lamb, we escaped the wrath of God only to encounter and endure the wrath of Satan, who passionately hates God's children. It is Paul who reveals, in his first letter to the Corinthians, exactly why this hatred exists: "Do you not know that we shall judge angels?" (6:3). God, out of His great love, not only redeemed men and women, but He *elevated* them to the position of judge over every fallen angel, since the righteous angels need no judgment. Rebellious angels sinned, and God reserved part of the honor of their judgment to the redeemed of the Lord. Why would God bestow such an awesome duty upon His children? One reason might be that we will be judging the very demons that tempted, troubled, and tormented us during times of weakness. Our strength will be fully triumphant in the end, when God grants us the heavenly privilege of judging these fallen angels.

Earthly Rebellion and Judgment

Spiritual warfare on earth began in the garden of Eden. Satan, who appeared to Eve as a serpent, presented the first temptation to her and, according to the apostle Paul, deceived Eve in her mind: "But I fear, lest somehow, as the serpent deceived Eve by his craftiness, so your minds may be corrupted from the simplicity that is in Christ" (2 Cor. 11:3). The weapon in this first spiritual battle was Satan's intellect. Though once full of wisdom, he chose to envy God and exchanged his wisdom for lies. Jesus said, "He was a murderer from the beginning, and does not stand in the truth, because there is no truth in him. When he speaks a lie, he speaks from his own resources, for he is a liar and the father of it" (John 8:44). Satan's carefully crafted lies caused the first human beings on earth to lose their standing with God. Spiritual warfare commenced at this separation of the first humans, Adam and Eve, from their Creator.

Throughout Israel's history, there were battles that occurred in the flesh and the spirit; Satan was behind the scenes, stirring up trouble. In their exodus through the wilderness, demons were connected to Israel's idolatry (Lev. 17:7). An evil spirit entered King Saul as he led the nation, causing trouble for David and Israel (1 Sam. 16:14–23). In the New Testament, we find people in various locations causing trouble, only to discover in the end that each had a demon. Three examples of this can be found in Scripture: the two men of the Gergesenes, the man at the tombs with a legion of demons, and the girl possessed of the spirit of divination (Mark 5:2–20; Matt. 8:28–32; Acts 16:16). Spiritual warfare is never against the possessed person, but against the forces in the spiritual realm that possess them. In each of these biblical cases, the evil spirits possessing the individuals were properly dealt with in a spiritual battle, in order that generation after generation would see the victories over evil in the natural realm.

Demons cannot stand before the power of God. They believe in one God (monotheism) and shudder at the thought of Him. James tells us, "You believe that there is one God. You do well. Even the demons believe—and tremble!" (James 2:19). It is because of this knowledge of the true nature of God that demons do everything within their power to lead mankind into the false doctrines that often embrace many gods (polytheism). Scripture points out that these idols, gods, and goddesses represent *demons*. Moses clearly stated that sacrifices to any god other than Jehovah God are sacrifices made to demons. "They sacrificed to demons, not to God, to gods they did not know, to new gods, new arrivals that your fathers did not fear" (Deut. 32:17). Paul carried this same truth through to the New Testament world. "The things which the Gentiles sacrifice they sacrifice to demons and not to God, and I do not want you to have fellowship with demons" (1 Cor. 10:20).

Polytheistic false doctrines originate with demons, but man's rebellion against God provides the perfect conduit for disseminating their dogma. The battles fought on earth are often fueled from the spiritual realm. Man's evil nature is always a factor to be reckoned with in assessing the situation, but to discount the dimension of darkness is to court disaster. Demons were once a part of the heavenly host of angels, and they know for a fact that only one God exists, yet they actively work to deceive the world into believing in *any* god other than Elohim—Lord of all Creation. They know they will not escape judgment for this, and they tremble in fear before the awesome God who redeemed mankind through the blood of His Son, and by His grace, before His children, who will ultimately judge them.

The Doctrine of the Demons

The doctrine of demons is any doctrine that opposes God's truth. Among these are the world religions, each one built upon man's efforts to please a god through a series of human works. But people do not need to bow to an idol to be involved in false doctrine or a false religion, for some religions that shun idols, such as Baha'i or Islam, are just as false as idolatry. They reject the Bible as God's final Word to mankind, they reject Jesus as God's solution to sin and personal salvation, and they reject God's exclusivity that no other way of salvation is available except through Jesus Christ.[3]

---

3. This biblical position, while called offensive by non-Christians, is one that cannot be extracted from the Bible without mangling the entire plan of salvation. Aside from its implicit intertwining with Christ's sinless life, His atonement, and His bodily resurrection, there are explicit, direct statements on this by Jesus and His Apostles (John 8:24; John 14:6; and Acts 4:12).

The doctrine of the demons is prevalent among these sects, the New Age, and the cults. The soundest way to detect a heretical position (that would bar the holder from true salvation) is to be thoroughly acquainted with biblical doctrine. Early Church councils distinguished heresy from genuine Christianity by forbidding fellowship with those who held contrary doctrines on the Trinity (one God who eternally exists as Father, Son, and Holy Spirit), the resurrection, atonement, justification, and salvation by grace.[4] These doctrines are not arbitrarily chosen, but derived from several statements within Scripture that set them apart as essential to the plan of salvation.

Demonic doctrines attack these biblical positions head-on, always changing or obliterating them by outright denial or subtle, yet significant, alterations. Occult groups and practitioners embrace false doctrine and rituals that find no parallel in the Bible, but they are no less demonically inspired. These practices—involving occult symbols, pentagram circle rituals, chants, enchantments, spells, potions, and charms—draw their authority from the doctrines of the demons and are carefully crafted to keep people interested in the occult and *away* from the true and living God.

Satan and his demons have centuries of experience in tempting billions of people, so we are simply no match for them without the Father, Son, and Holy Spirit. It is only with God and through God that Christians can understand their enemy and see victory in their personal lives. Paul's personal victory came through an awareness of Satan's schemes: "We are not ignorant of his devices" (2 Cor. 2:11).

Biblical Examples of the Doctine of Demons

The Bible provides many examples of the strategy of Satan and his demons—examples that should raise our awareness level and help us understand the kind of devices he uses.

1 Timothy 4:1: "Now the Spirit expressly says that in latter times some will depart from the faith, giving heed to deceiving spirits and doctrines of demons." This verse speaks of two works of the demons: seducing or deceiving spirits, and the initiation of false doctrines among men. Both of these works are directly linked to the occult. All occultic practices are deceptive, and all of their doctrines are false.

---

4. Most of these are discussed by systematic theologians, but for general reading, see Martin, *Essential Christianity.*

Sometimes the most deceptive occult products come in the most innocent-looking packages, such as games like the the Ouija board, Dungeons & Dragons, and other fantasy role-playing games that invoke powers, enchantments, or spells. Attractive and popular books abound teaching the how-to of vampirism, Wicca, Satanism, demonology, divination, Witchcraft, the Kabbalah, ESP, horoscopy, astrology, séances, spirit channeling, New Age, UFOs and many more. Parents give these items as gifts to their children; friends share them with other friends—all without a moment's thought to the power (or consequences) of spiritual deceit. The spirit behind these items has been working on the human race from its conception, and the New Testament warns us to steer clear of its influence.

2 Thessalonians 2:9–10: "The coming of the lawless one is according to the working of Satan, with all power, signs, and lying wonders, and with all unrighteous deception among those who perish." The strength of this passage lies in its warning against Satan's works, as revealed by John in Revelation 13: there will be a false prophet, the one who works for Satan by deceiving most of the world through great signs and wonders, such as calling fire down from heaven. Satan is able to produce powerful signs and lying wonders. Moses boldly stood against this in his encounter with the magicians of Pharaoh's court, who counterfeited God's miracles through Moses. Pharaoh's attack against God's power is detailed in Exodus 7:11: "But Pharaoh also called the wise men and the sorcerers; so the magicians of Egypt, they also did in like manner with their enchantments." The fact that Aaron's rod, which God turned into a snake, swallowed the snakes of Pharaoh's magicians should have sent a clear message that God will not be mocked, and He will always have the last word. The clear difference between Moses and the magicians is that the latter worked with "enchantments," while God worked through Moses.

Deuteronomy 18:10–11: "There shall not be found among you anyone who makes his son or his daughter pass through the fire, or one who practices witchcraft, or a soothsayer, or one who interprets omens, or a sorcerer, or one who conjures spells, or a medium, or a spiritist, or one who calls up the dead." Each of these nine occult practices is actively pursued by people today, some thirty-five hundred years after Moses penned Deuteronomy, yet people still consider themselves extremely advanced in their thinking, technology, and wisdom. These occult practices are real, and they remain the legacy of the billions of people who practiced them for thousands of years and passed them on to their children—all the way down to our modern age.

- *"pass through the fire"*: This was directly tied to the Canaanite worship of the god Molech, but three viable occult rituals may be intended.[5] Today there are fire rituals practiced by occultists on various levels. New Age writer Tony Robbins was one of many who had a fire-walking initiation ritual for his personal awareness seminars. The belief that engaging in such rituals releases personal power is where the occult begins. Several fire rituals exist within occult groups, from naked dancers before bonfires to The Burning Man festival in Nevada to Witch coven rites to Satanism, where Satan is represented by fire.[6]

- *"one who practices witchcraft"*: The word witchcraft is otherwise translated "divination" (NASB, NIV). Divination is the practice of divining knowledge or information concerning the past, present, or future. The occult methods are numerous and sometimes vary by culture, but the most commonly known are fortune-telling by means of tarot cards, palmistry (palm reading), scrying (tea leaf reading, coffee ground reading, crystal balls, mirror gazing, water gazing, glass gazing, wax reading), ESP, precognition, telepathy, clairvoyance, Ouija boards, pendulum swinging, dowsing rods, dream interpretation, table tipping, numerology, I Ching oracles, casting runes, and psychometry (impressionists who read objects belonging to a subject).

- *"a soothsayer"*: one who forecasts the future for an individual or nation, which is also translated as an "observer of times" (KJV). This is found among occult practitioners in the modern world as astrology, horoscopes, and conjuring rituals in accordance with certain times and seasons.

- "one who interprets omens": The occult practice of gaining power or knowledge through various omens and signs. These signs may be read in

---

5. Duane L. Christensen briefly discusses three plausible positions, see Christensen, *Word Biblical Commentary: Deuteronomy* (CD-ROM) (Nashville: Thomas Nelson, 2001), s.v. "Deuteronomy 18:10–11."
6. Nichols, Mather, and Schmidt, *Encyclopedic Dictionary of Cults, Sects, and World Religions*, 395.

the sky, as a passing comet, or they may be read in nature, as when a certain animal crosses the reader's path. Many ancient societies, including the Romans, also practiced animal sacrifice, during which the entrails or organs of the animals were read in search of omens.

- *"a sorcerer"*: This is one who practices the induction of formulas, potions, or incantations to assist in gaining power over a person or an event. In the New Testament, this is referenced by Paul in Galatians 5:22 by the Greek word pharmakia, which includes illicit drugs for spiritual awareness, promoted by the infamous Timothy Leary and others. Richard N. Longnecker points out that pharmakia "also acquired two negative connotations: the use of drugs to poison people and the use of drugs in sorcery or Witchcraft."[7]

- *"one who conjures spells"*: refers to occultists, Witches, and Satanists, who believe that they can change events through casting spells. This description also includes the usage of amulets, talismans, charms, and "good luck pieces," all of which can be used for good or bad.

- *"a medium [and/or] spiritist"*: someone who claims to make contact with spirit-beings, whether deceased, extraterrestrial beings (UFOs), spirit guides, angels, or demons, often through external manifestations such as table tipping, table rapping, ectoplasm, psychometric (impressionists), or the moving of objects, as by a poltergeist attributed to the deceased. Trance channeling and spirit channeling in the New Age fall into this category.

- *"one who calls up the dead"*: a medium, a necromancer; one who makes contact with departed human beings and allows them to speak through his or her body as their mouthpiece, sometimes manifested through automatic writing, automatic typing (as in the Ruth Montgomery books), or channeling the spirit's voice through the voice of the necromancer. "Calling up the dead" is most often displayed during modern séances, where contact is sought for a specifically named individual who is deceased.

---

7. Richard N. Longnecker, *Word Biblical Commentary: Galatians* (CD-ROM) (Nashville: Word, 1990), s.v. "Galatians 5:22."

God forbids all of these practices, and they are called an abomination in His sight. The occult is a vast subject with many far-reaching tentacles, but the list we gain through this biblical passage serves as a reminder against participation in any of these or their related practices.

In spiritual warfare, our knowledge of how Satan and his demons work is vital to properly identifying and dealing with these works when we encounter them. Knowing what the Bible says on this subject fosters recognition of the enemy's weapons and aids in disarming him and his minions. Every Christian should be involved in prayer, biblical counsel, defending the gospel, and working to bring victory in the lives of people entrapped by the occult. Paul counsels the Church well on the condition of those who live in such bondage, "that they may come to their senses and escape the snare of the devil, having been taken captive by him to do his will" (2 Tim. 2:26).

CASE STUDY

Merrill F. Unger

Dr. Merril F. Unger, the noted professor of Old Testament studies at Dallas Theological Seminary, recorded the following case on occultic demon possession and deliverance in his book *Demons in the World Today:*

> It must be remembered that demonic powers seek to keep the occult victim from believing God and trusting Christ who they know (Romans 10:9–10) will liberate him from their slavery (James 4:7; 1 Peter 5:9), bringing the light and power of God's salvation. Sometimes, when the patient is severely oppressed and definitely indwelt by one or more demons, prolonged prayer will be a prelude to any deliverance. The efficacy of the blood of Jesus must be pleaded, and the battle waged incessantly before the victim will be able to frame a confession of faith with his lips and have faith generated in his heart.
>
> The Rev. J. A. MacMillan gives an account of a present-day deliverance from very severe demon oppression, or actually demon possession, since the patient suffered periods of unconsciousness (coma) in which her senses were bound, and the resident evil spir-

its took charge of her, actually speaking out of her body. . . . Upon the fairly recent death of her mother [she] had sought the services of a Spiritistic medium. She naively believed that this was good and could help her communicate with her departed loved one. Little did she realize how directly she was breaking God's commands (Exodus 20:3–5; Leviticus 19:31; 20:6; Deuteronomy 18:10, 11) and opening herself to occult enslavement.

The medium quickly discovered that her visitor was highly psychic. Before long she asked her to unite with her in certain trance experiences, and later obtained her cooperation in her Spiritistic séances, inducing her to yield to the will of the spirits. It was then that the woman found herself occultly bound and in serious psychic trouble. She sought spiritual help from her pastor, who called together a group of Christians to pray for the deliverance of this woman.

The struggle lasted for several months, with seven nights spent in prayer. The sufferer was unable to claim the Lord's help for herself, intense fear paralyzing her mind. At intervals, when the struggle in prayer was being waged, she would come briefly out of the coma in which her senses were bound. When she was urged to confess the name of Jesus and praise God, she would try to do so but immediately the spirits would use the victim's own hands in a fierce endeavor to strangle her. Two strong Christian men were constantly alert at her side to hold her when she became violent. At other moments, she would attempt to bite those around her, as an angry dog might do.

During the various prayer battles, more than a score of unclean spirits came out of this woman, each identifying himself by name as he made his exit. This is a well-known phenomenon of disposition, and not a fantastic oddity in the history of demon manifestations. Finally the woman was completely and joyfully delivered. All attempts of the spirits to regain possession were thwarted by steadfast prayer and resistance. The woman's tongue was loosed to confess and praise the name of Jesus Christ as Savior and Deliverer.[8]

---

8. Merrill F. Unger, *Demons in the World Today* (Wheaton, IL: Tyndale, 1972), 193–95.

Scriptural Response

Spiritual warfare, from the Christian believer's position, is best studied by examining the spiritual armor found in Ephesians 6:10–12. Paul painted a powerful picture here of spiritual warfare and its impact on the Christian life, a warfare that begins at the threshold of a born-again experience and runs continuously throughout life:

> Finally, my brethren, be strong in the Lord and in the power of His might. Put on the whole armor of God that you may be able to stand against the methods of the devil; for we are not fighting against flesh and blood, but against the rulers of the spiritual darkness of this age, against spiritual wickedness in heavenly or high places of authority.

Spiritual warfare is a fact of Christian living, but unfortunately, some Christians do their utmost to ignore it, thinking it will have no effect upon them. Adverse conditions are usually treated as a common occurrence or brushed off indifferently and treated as anything other than a demonic attack. But spiritual conflict is one method God uses to catch our attention: it is real, and Christians must properly deal with it. The Bible clearly warns us about the reality of spiritual war. We are in conflict against the world, in conflict against our carnal natures, and in conflict against the devil, and we will live in that conflict and die in that conflict, unless Jesus Christ returns in our lifetime.

Take Up Arms

The weapons of our warfare are not fleshly (2 Cor. 10:4–5), so the reality of spiritual war is biblical: "For the weapons of our warfare are not carnal but mighty in God for pulling down strongholds, casting down arguments and every high thing that exalts itself against the knowledge of God, bringing every thought into captivity to the obedience of Christ." Notice that it is the weapons of *our* warfare—indeed, it is *our* warfare—it is a personal war.

These weapons have divine power to tear down strongholds, to demolish arguments, and to literally decimate every proud thought that exalts itself against the throne of God, to bring every thought into captivity to the Lord Jesus Christ. The spiritual war against Christianity is going on here and now, and it will not go away simply by ignoring it. This is the fact of spiritual war: our true enemy is not the human being who opposes Christ but the rulers of the darkness of this age that manipulate people as on a great chessboard, and the forces are arrayed against the Christian Church. In 1 Timothy 1:18, Paul wrote, "This charge I commit to you, son Timothy, according to the prophecies previously made concerning you, that by them you may wage the good warfare." Another way of translating this last phrase is "war the warfare."[9] Paul used the strongest word imaginable, *strateian*, which is the Greek word for "strategy." The strategy: the logistics of combat, polemics, *war.* On this, William D. Mounce wrote, "The terminology is military, describing a soldier at war."[10] It is an inescapable fact that the Christian is committed to spiritual warfare.

Avoid Distractions

Anyone chosen by God to be a soldier does not get entangled or encumbered with civilian pursuits. "No one engaged in warfare entangles himself with the affairs of this life, that he may please him who enlisted him as a soldier" (2 Tim. 2:4). In other words, when God called you into the Church of Jesus Christ, you enlisted in the army of God. You can truthfully agree with the nineteenth-century hymn that goes, "Onward, Christian soldiers, marching as to war," because you are at war. In Paul's battle analogy, he emphasized the danger of distractions. Do not let anything get in the way of your concentration and focus, or it will impact your survival.

In the heat of battle, it is a deadly mistake to become preoccupied with anything other than the battle itself. Distractions cause injury, and different levels of injury cause different levels of pain. To avoid pain, it is necessary to pay attention to the battle—pleasing the Lord means keeping your eyes on the prize.

Acknowledge the Battle

One of Satan's best tricks is to neutralize Christians by making them think there is no spiritual war or no battles. In *Screwtape Writes Again,* we find valuable insight into how Christians are sometimes deceived. The book portrays a master demon,

---

9. See also Robertson, *Word Pictures of the New Testament,* at 1 Timothy 1:18, where he translates this as "war the good warfare."
10. William D. Mounce, *Word Biblical Commentary: Pastoral Epistles* (CD-ROM) (Nashville: Word, 2002), s.v. "1 Timothy 1:18."

Screwtape, who is writing to his nephew demon, Wormwood, advising him, "If you can't convince them, then confuse them—the next best thing to a damned soul is a neutralized Christian."[11] Some Christians have been erroneously taught to believe in the positive things of life to the exclusion of anything negative, through which they sometimes deny the existence of Satan, demons, or hell. They seem so prone toward possibility thinking that they deny the existence of spiritual battles or even the fact that a spiritual war is taking place. Wishful thinking or simple denial does not change the biblical facts about the existence of spiritual war. The entire world is in disarray, and there is no room for the pretense that all is well and nothing is happening. It is here and it will continue, because the moment you enlist in the army of God, you personally become a target of God's enemies: Satan and his demons. You are on the satanic hit list whether you're willing to admit it or not, and if you are really a Christian living and walking with Jesus Christ, they are coming after you.

Guard Against Residual Evil

Jesus said, "I will no longer talk much with you, for the ruler of this world is coming, and he has nothing in Me" (John 14:30). Satan here is called the ruler of this world or age. Paul called him the "god of this age" (2 Cor. 4:4). In John's gospel, Jesus said that when Satan comes, he will find nothing in Him. Unfortunately, the same cannot be said of the rest of the human race. Dr. Donald Barnhouse put it this way: "The ruler of this age is coming and he finds *plenty* in us."[12] There is residual evil in all of us that Satan can appeal to, and he then uses that evil to manipulate and use us against each other, and even against the Church of Christ. Christians do some of the worst damage to the Christian Church by yielding themselves to Satan—often without recognizing it.[13] The direct result of this is the disruption of the body of Christ. These people are everywhere today, disrupting the kingdom of God and resisting those who stand for the kingdom of God.

---

11. Martin, *Screwtape Writes Again,* 10.
12. Dr. Barnhouse was Walter Martin's teacher and mentor.
13. This yielding is not possession—the Bible teaches that a Christian cannot be possessed (1 Cor. 6:19).

Seek Healing

Spiritual warfare is a fact of life when you enlist in the army of God. If you will not fight in the army of God, then the Lord will discipline you until you get to the place where you will fight, because you will get so many attacks that eventually you will have to do something. That is a warning, and it is also biblical theology. You are in the middle of a spiritual war. People who walk around in the middle of war, acting as if there is no war, are called *casualties*. There are people scattered all over the landscape who are ineffective in their Christian lives, neutralized in their Christian witness, and paralyzed in their Christian activities simply because they do not realize that they are casualties. They must be restored by God so they can get back into the battle.

Face Facts

It is no accident that the fact of spiritual warfare is biblical theology. People learn to engage the opposition in every facet of life, from contact sports to military training. It is necessary to engage it in spiritual combat as well. Christians were never meant to lie around the battlefield like so much litter; they were designed to get up and fight the good fight of faith. The fact that we are in a spiritual war is not going to disappear. The Church is the army of God, and every Christian is designated to fight in it with the weapons of spiritual warfare, the arguments of God, the texts of Scripture, and the power of the Spirit.

Who are we fighting? The Bible states very clearly that we are fighting satanic power. We are fighting worldly dominion, and we are fighting our carnal nature. "For we do not wrestle against flesh and blood, but against principalities, against powers, against the rulers of the darkness of this age, against spiritual hosts of wickedness in the heavenly places" (Eph. 6:12). This verse describes the devil and his demons.

Peter also reminds us to "be sober, be vigilant; because your adversary the devil walks about like a roaring lion, seeking whom he may devour. Resist him, steadfast in the faith" (1 Peter 5:8–9). Peter painted a perfect picture of our enemy as a roaring lion hunting its prey. He does not sleep. He is always stalking Christians, seeking to devour us, but Peter and James tell us we are able to resist him, steadfast in the faith. "Therefore submit to God. Resist the devil and he will flee from you" (James 4:7). James also keys us in to God's plan of victory. First submit to God, and then resist the devil, and he will turn and flee. The only way to resist him is by prayer, supplication, thanksgiving, and getting dressed for combat.

Assess the Enemy

The first foe of Christianity is *Satan,* along with the *demonic powers,* but these are not the only enemies of the Church. Another foe to be wary of in spiritual battle is the *world system,* as taught in James 4:1–4:

> Where do wars and fights come from among you? Do they not come from your desires for pleasure that war in your members? You lust and do not have. You murder and covet and cannot obtain. You fight and war. Yet you do not have because you do not ask. You ask and do not receive, because you ask amiss, that you may spend it on your pleasures. Adulterers and adulteresses! Do you not know that friendship with the world is enmity with God? Whoever therefore wants to be a friend of the world makes himself an enemy of God.

James made it abundantly clear that the world and its pleasures are our enemy. Part of our spiritual warfare is against the world system in which we dwell.

Yet another enemy, according to 1 Peter 4:1–4, is our own flesh:

> Therefore, since Christ suffered for us in the flesh, arm yourselves also with the same mind, for he who has suffered in the flesh has ceased from sin, that he no longer should live the rest of his time in the flesh for the lusts of men, but for the will of God. For we have spent enough of our past life-time in doing the will of the Gentiles—when we walked in lewdness, lusts, drunkenness, revelries, drinking parties, and abominable idolatries. In regard to these, they think it strange that you do not run with them in the same flood of dissipation, speaking evil of you.

Our foes are the devil, demonic power, the pressure of the world, and the desires of the flesh. Soldiers cannot fight a war if they do not know who their enemy is, and, likewise, Christians cannot fight spiritual battles if we do not recognize our enemies. To be properly fit for spiritual battle, we must know the tactics of the enemy. If you do not know the strategy of the enemy, then you cannot successfully combat him. It is only when you realize what you are up against that you can effectively stand against it.

Paul instructed the Church at Ephesus to fight the good fight of faith. Ephesians 6:18 provides one of our *secret weapons* in battle: "praying always . . . in the Spirit." It is wise to ask the Spirit of God to enable you to effectively recognize your enemies and deal with them.

Get in Shape

A Christian must get into the best possible spiritual condition to fight the battle. "You therefore must endure hardship as a good soldier of Jesus Christ" (2 Tim. 2:3). If you are going to be a soldier, then get in shape. The only way to fight hand-to-hand combat is to be in the best of physical conditioning. An out-of-shape, lazy person will be defeated by the enemy every time. Just as a soldier goes through training to get in good, enduring physical shape, Christians must be trained biblically to withstand the enemy. Being battle-ready requires the ability to stand and fight at any moment, but a Christian who is not in fighting condition will quickly become a casualty on the battlefield. It is that simple. One must either respond in spiritual combat or become spiritually wounded, moaning and groaning about all the bad things that have happened in life.

Put on the Whole Armor of God

God wants his people to endure these hardships and, according to the apostle Peter, to be sober and vigilant (1 Peter 5:8). The word *sober* means alert. There is no such thing as a sleepy, successful soldier. A sleepy soldier is *unsuccessful.* God tells us to be alert, because we are fighting a spiritual war.

Peter also reminds us to be vigilant because our adversary, the devil, stalks about as a roaring lion, seeking whom he may devour. There is only one way to turn that lion into a pussycat, and that is to resist him, steadfast in the faith of Christ. Those who do not are unsuccessful soldiers, and this is why there are so many Christians who are weak and ineffective. They have not combated the enemy. They have not fought back as servants of God.

Effective Christians recognize the *fact* of spiritual warfare. Effective Christians are conditioned and ready for battle. The ultimate part of training is getting properly dressed for combat, secure in the strength of your weapons. Ephesians 6 demonstrates that no one goes out to war unclothed. A trained soldier carries about thirty or forty pounds of equipment once he is dressed for combat. But there are Christians running around today unfit and unclothed, trying to conduct spiritual warfare against the enemy, and they do not understand why the flaming arrows of the wicked one consistently wound them. The solution is to be properly equipped for battle, to "present yourself approved to God, a worker who does not need to be ashamed, rightly dividing the word of truth" (2 Tim. 2:15). Ignorance of the Bible is ignorance of the Lord Jesus Christ. Ignorance of Christ is ignorance of your own defense. You cannot protect yourself unless you are walking in the light with Him (1 John 1:7). Paul's advice in Ephesians 6:10–12 still stands today. *Put on the whole armor of God,* that you may be able to stand against the methods of the devil. You *can* stand against Satan. You *can* be victorious. You *can* know the final conquest, and the final conquest in spiritual warfare is something God has promised us in the Lord Jesus.

Fight Victoriously

The victorious Christian must have God's power to conquer his foes. The conquering power of God is derived from a simple biblical truth that many Christians consider simplistic, and therefore they overlook it or ignore it. The power behind the final conquest is seen in 1 John 5:4: "This is the victory that overcomes the world." The word *overcome* means conquer, so: "This is the victory that *conquers* the world—our faith." This is not something new and startling. John gave it to the first-century Church. What is faith? Faith, according to Hebrews 11:1, is being sure of what you hope for and *absolutely certain* of what you cannot see. The hope and absolute certainty of what is unseen can only come through God, who gives each Christian a measure of faith (Rom. 12:3). It is not in proportion to the efforts of the Christian, but it is God who gives the measure of faith to every person as it pleases Him. The Lord Jesus Christ gave us the ultimate foundation of faith, and this is the key: "Be of good cheer; I have conquered the world" (John 16:33).

The promise of God is the simplest thing in the world to accept but one of the most difficult for mankind to accomplish. People struggle to do everything *alone* instead of allowing God to fight the battles through us. Christians cannot win conflicts in the strength of the flesh; we must bend our knee to the Savior and in so doing discover that spiritual warfare, and ultimate victory, is easily accomplished.

CASE STUDY

Walter Martin

When I first became a Christian, I didn't know anything about the Bible. I knew my catechism; I knew my religion. I didn't know much at all about Scripture, but I knew Jesus Christ as my Savior. I used to wake up every morning in prep school, a new Christian with a brand new Bible, not knowing one end of the book from the other. The first thing that would come out of my mouth in the morning was a hymn:

> When morning gilds the skies my heart awaking cries:
> May Jesus Christ be praised!
> Alike at work and prayer, to Jesus I repair:
> May Jesus Christ be praised!
>
> Be this, while life is mine, my canticle divine:
> May Jesus Christ be praised!
> Sing this eternal song through all the ages long:
> May Jesus Christ be praised![14]

The victory is in the One being praised. "Cheer up," Jesus said, "I have conquered the world." That is our victory over spiritual warfare. Face the fact that it is there; face the foes that represent it. Face the need to get yourself in spiritual condition by the study of the Word of God in submission to the Holy Spirit, and by believing Jesus Christ.

I've been fighting this spiritual battle since 1944, and I can tell you with absolute certainty that the key to spiritual conquest is the acknowledgement that Jesus Christ is Lord to the glory of God the Father. And now how do you do that? Put on the whole armor of God. Put on the helmet of salvation—it is a gift. Put on the breastplate of righteousness—it is a gift. Put on

---

14. Edward Caswall, trans., "When Morning Gilds the Sky," in Formby's *Catholic Hymns* (London: 1854), from the Katholisches Gesangbuch (Würzburg, German: c. 1744). Music by Joseph Barnby. See http://www.cyberhymnal.org/htm/w/h/e/whenmgts.htm.

the belt of truth—it is a gift. Put on the readiness to preach the gospel—it is a gift. Take the shield of faith—it is a gift. Take the sword of the Spirit, which is the Word of God—it is a gift. Take God's gifts for God's conquests, and then get dressed for battle. Every single piece of armor in Ephesians 6 is for the front of your body. There is not one single piece for your backside. Soldiers do not turn around in the middle of combat; they go forward.

The reason why Christians have become ineffective, weak and drained; the reason why they litter the battlefield and get in everyone's way is because in the midst of conflict and combat, they did not trust in Jesus Christ. They turned around and ran away, the flaming arrows of the wicked one firmly lodged in their spiritual behinds. If you see yourself in this scenario, there is only one way to get your strength back: get down on your knees, confess your sins and ask Jesus Christ to pull the arrows out! Affirm what Christ told you: "Be of good cheer; I have conquered the world!" And this is the victory; this is your conquest. Seize this promise with faith, and God will open the windows of heaven and bless you. He will give you victory, and He will lead you in paths of righteousness for His name's sake.

The victory is ours. The final conquest is your recognition that Jesus Christ is the source of faith—the author and finisher of your faith. He is "the Alpha and Omega, the beginning and the end, the first and the last" (Revelation 1:8). *Cheer up, I have conquered the world* (John 16:33). "This is the victory that overcomes the world, even our faith" (1 John 5:4).

CONCLUSION

Christ defeated Satan on the Cross. He defeated him in the glory of the resurrection, and He imparts that capacity of conquest to our lives every day that we are willing to believe Him. Christians can rise in the morning and say with confidence, "Lord Jesus, I believe You have conquered the world; conquer today through me. I believe You—give me victory. Take away my doubts; take away my fears. Give me the measure of faith that is necessary for me to survive today. Give me the faith to trust You to overcome Satan today. Give me the faith to triumph over the forces of darkness. Give me the victory over the world—a victory that is a gift from You." The key to spiritual conquest is the acknowledgment that Jesus Christ is Lord, to the glory of God the Father (Phil. 2:11).

RECOMMENDED RESOURCES

1. Barnhouse, Donald G. *The Invisible War.* Grand Rapids: Zondervan, 1980.

2. DeWaay, Bob. *Critical Issues Commentary,* www.cicministry.org.

3. Lewis, C. S. *The Screwtape Letters: A Devil's Diabolical Advice for the Capturing of the Human Heart.* New York: Bantam, 1982.

4. Martin, Walter R. *Screwtape Writes Again.* Santa Ana, CA: Vision House, 1975.

5. Unger, Merrill F. *Demons in the World Today.* Wheaton, IL: Tyndale, 1972.

QUICK FACTS ABOUT CHRISTIAN COUNSELING AND THE OCCULT

- Exploring the world of the occult will expose an individual to malevolent supernatural beings.

- Non-Christians involved in the occult become vulnerable to demonic oppression and possession.

- Christians *cannot* be possessed by any type of demon, but they can be harassed or oppressed.

- The name of Jesus and the power of His Holy Spirit are the only authorities on earth that demons fear and obey; Jesus can deliver all people from possession or oppression.

- Counseling and deliverance ministries, based on solid biblical principles, are desperately needed in the Church today.

Christian Counseling and the Occult

The world of the occult is a dangerous reality, but God has promised in His Word that Christians are well equipped to fight it. Today, there is a desperate need in the Church for trained counselors who understand and accept the reality of demon possession and oppression, and who are prepared to battle zealously against it. The rational worldview so prevalent in our time seeks to deny and deride any phenomena outside the five senses, but the Church recognizes the reality of the supernatural power of Jesus Christ, and thus the undeniable existence of His supernatural enemy—Satan. Any Christian or non-Christian who denies these facts contradicts Jesus Christ Himself.

God chose to include select events in the New Testament for a reason, and He placed great emphasis on demon possession and deliverance. The ministry of Jesus lasted only three years and was recorded in just four New Testament books, but these eyewitness accounts include *twenty-seven* separate passages detailing Jesus' teaching on the subject of demons, demon possession, and exorcism. The Church must follow the example of Jesus Christ; it must resist the spirit of this age—the spirit of doubt—and offer disciplined, biblical alternatives to those in need of them.

The resurgence of New Age ideas has heightened natural human curiosity and increased substantially the desire for supernatural power, so it is inevitable that the entertainment industry would gravitate toward the source of the money, producing films, television shows, and books on Witchcraft, sorcery, and demon possession that reflect people's interests. The audience exists, it is hungry for knowledge, and the experience that knowledge produces has eternal consequences.

REQUIREMENTS OF A COUNSELOR

Counseling those who are involved in the occult is intense and dangerous spiritual warfare. In order to succeed in aiding these individuals without risking harm to the helpers, it is important to follow the biblical guidelines for battling the enemy. Demons are not behind every evil event (man has enough residual evil within him to commit endless horrors), but the Bible specifically teaches that demons exist, and they regularly interfere in human lives. Possession may not be an everyday occurrence, but it is always a possibility.

Christian counseling directly related to the occult is a perilous task, and as such it should never be undertaken by anyone without the following qualifications:

1. A personal relationship with Jesus Christ (John 15)

2. Spiritual maturity as evidenced by a consistent display of the fruits of the Spirit in his or her life; a serious commitment to reading the Scripture and prayer; regular attendance and fellowship at a doctrinally sound, Christian church (Gal. 5:16–22; Heb. 10:25)[1]

3. Acknowledgment of the power of the Holy Spirit (1 Cor. 2:14)

4. A calling to serve (John 17:18).

5. Knowledge, training, and experience in the biblical method, analysis, and resolution of occult phenomena (2 Peter 1:5; Col. 1:10; 2 Tim. 2:15).[2]

CASE STUDIES

Counselors trained to assess and deal with the occult are few and far between, so true case histories, along with the counsel given in them, are invaluable to those in need. As in any learning situation, reliable studies are essential and offer the most expeditious way to evaluate a method of assessment and apply it. The following case studies are based on true stories with names and circumstances altered to protect individual privacy.

---

1. According to Dr. Kurt Koch, a pastor with forty years of experience in dealing with the occult, those who are young *physically* and young spiritually should not become involved in occult counseling.
2. See chapter 14 for chart detailing "Demons, Possession, and Exorcism in the Ministry of Jesus Christ."

Dungeons and Dragons

Example: A young Christian woman named Lisa, backslidden in her faith, married a non-Christian man named Craig. Several years after their marriage, Craig became involved in a role-playing game steeped in the occult called Dungeons & Dragons, and it was not long before the game began to consume large amounts of his time. Lisa's daughters, ages five and three, became more withdrawn during this time, repeatedly saying strange things to their mother, such as, "The people in my room are really nice, Mommy. One is beautiful, and one is ugly, but I like talking to them," and "Mommy, why do the people in the basement hate you?" Concerned and frightened by the changes she could see taking place in her children, Lisa confronted Craig and told him the playing of Dungeons & Dragons had to stop. Craig refused. Lisa went to her pastor and asked for prayer, but nothing seemed to change. She became more and more upset by her husband's involvement in this game, and on a day when he wasn't home, she walked through the house and prayed in each and every room, asking for God's protection on her home and family. Toward the end of her prayers, the windows in the living room began rattling loudly, and terrified, she took her children and left. Lisa is now discouraged, depressed, and very frightened. She feels powerless to change the situation.

Analysis: First, there does not seem to be any indication here of mental illness in Lisa, Craig, or their two young daughters. No one is on any regular medications, and parents and children all respond normally to everyday situations. Second, there is clearly an exposure here to the occult. The game Dungeons & Dragons includes demonic characters, sorcerers, spells, and a myriad of other occultic creatures and practices, so it is a fact that this home has been opened to the world of the occult. Third, in clear violation of Scripture, Lisa married a non-Christian. Paul warned the Church against this in 2 Corinthians 6:14–18:

Do not be unequally yoked together with unbelievers. For what fellowship has righteousness with lawlessness? And what communion has light with darkness? And what accord has Christ with Belial? Or what part has a believer with an unbeliever? And what agreement has the temple of God with idols? For you are the temple of the living God. As God has said:

"I will dwell in them
and walk among them.
I will be their God,
and they shall be My people."

Therefore

"Come out from among them
and be separate, says the Lord.
Do not touch what is unclean,
and I will receive you.
"I will be a Father to you,
and you shall be My sons and daughters,
says the LORD Almighty."

Contrary to the apathetic attitude prevalent in the Christian Church today, God does not wish for His children to be bound together with unbelievers—whether in marriage, business partnerships, or religious events. There is nothing wrong with friendship, but our dating relationships, marriages, and other formal commitments should be carefully considered before we enter into them. Lisa disobeyed Scripture and became vulnerable to spiritual attack. This does not mean God abandoned her; it simply means she damaged a vital piece of spiritual armor—the breastplate of righteousness (Eph. 6:14)—and chose not to repair it. To be righteous before God is to obey Him and walk with Him.[3] Satan is quick to spot a Christian in trouble, and he takes full advantage of it. Fourth, Lisa's young children

---

3. Albert Barnes describes *righteousness* as "Integrity, holiness, purity of life, sincerity of piety. The breastplate defended the vital parts of the body; and the idea here may be that the integrity of life, and righteousness of character, is as necessary to defend us from the assaults of Satan, as the coat of mail was to preserve the heart from the arrows of an enemy." *Breastplate*—"The word rendered here as 'breastplate' *thoorax* (NT:2382) denoted the "cuirass,' Lat.: *lorica*, or coat of mail; i.e., the armor that covered the body from the neck to the thighs, and consisted of two parts, one covering the front and the other the back. It was made of rings, or in the form of scales, or of plates, so fastened together that they would be flexible, and yet guard the body from a sword, spear, or arrow." *(Barnes' Notes)*

are describing a classic pattern of demonic contact. Something *not of this world* is talking to them, and one thing is certain: it will not stop. According to the children, it hates Lisa, the only adult Christian in the home. Fifth, an actual physical phenomenon has been observed that does not have a rational explanation. Windows do not rattle uncontrollably in response to prayer unless something makes them rattle, and in this case, it was not the wind.

Resolution: First, Lisa can correct her personal relationship with Jesus Christ by simply asking His forgiveness. "If we confess our sins, He is faithful and just to forgive us our sins and to cleanse us from all unrighteousness" (1 John 1:9). The breastplate of righteousness can be mended by the power of the Holy Spirit. Second, Lisa must take a stand to protect herself and her children from further harm. If Craig were lighting fires around the house, she would not allow him to continue doing so. In this case, he is lighting spiritual fires that will hurt all of them. Lisa needs to seek counsel from her pastor and then confront her husband with her fears. Third, Lisa is not powerless; she is extremely *powerful.* She is authorized by Scripture to use the name of Jesus Christ to cleanse her home and free her family. Lisa should seek support from other Christians and continue praying over her home and family in the name of Jesus, commanding any demons to leave. Whenever possible, she should rid the house of anything related to the occult. Sometimes, it might be necessary to fast and pray over a period of time, but the demons *must* eventually obey. Lisa can ask the Lord to protect and deliver her entire family, "for the unbelieving husband is sanctified by the wife, and the unbelieving wife is sanctified by the husband; otherwise your children would be unclean, but now they are holy" (1 Cor. 7:14). The demons Lisa fears are in reality utterly terrified of *her,* and they will run from all Christians because, "you are of God, little children, and have overcome them, because He who is in you is greater than he who is in the world" (1 John 4:4). Lisa has the enormous power available through Jesus Christ to defend her home.

Demon Possession

Example: A young man named Kyle worshiped Satan during his teen years. He listened day in and day out to heavy metal music, took part in satanic ceremonies, and spent all his time with friends who were also Satanists.

Once he became an adult, Kyle lost interest in Satanism and even began attending church, although he did not profess to be a Christian. Shortly after Kyle's twenty-first birthday, his family began noticing a marked change in his personality. Depression set in, along with a strange hostility toward his father and sister, both strong Christians. Any mention of God or things related to Him would result in a vicious, mocking response—usually in a voice sounding nothing like Kyle's voice—that often included blasphemy. Soon, a "new" personality seemed to overshadow the old Kyle, and he began threatening the lives of his father and sister. He agreed to see a psychiatrist, who diagnosed him as bipolar. Kyle immediately began taking medication, but it made little difference in his demeanor. His father, devastated and deeply grieved over the "loss" of his son, began to suspect demon possession.

Analysis: First, a diagnosis of mental illness was made. Medication was prescribed and taken for it on a daily basis. Kyle is being seen regularly by a doctor, and his medicine is adjusted accordingly. Still, there has been little discernible change in his behavior or demeanor. Second, there is a history of exposure to the occult. In worshiping Satan, Kyle opened his life to the power and presence of evil supernatural beings. Third, Kyle worshiped Satan—the thing Satan most desires from humans—and he never renounced his commitment. He then tried to *withdraw* his worship of the prince of the power of the air without ever accepting the only Person able to deliver him from Satan: Jesus Christ. Fourth, Kyle displays the classic behavior of a person possessed. His attitudes and even his physical voice have changed, and he hates anyone or anything related to God.

Resolution: First, it was imperative for Kyle's father to find a local pastor who would pray with them and perform an assessment and exorcism, if necessary. He tried to do this but was met on every side by skepticism. It wasn't that these men didn't believe in demon possession; they just didn't see it happening much today. Even some Christian apologetic ministries, formed for the defense of the faith, doubted the common occurrence of possession in the twenty-first century. Biblically, they believed it could happen, but practically, they considered it a "rare phenomenon" and so did not wish to be involved in either assessment or deliverance. In desperation, Kyle's father finally tracked down someone in another well-known ministry and pleaded for help. This ministry referred him to another ministry in his area with difficulty, since so few reputable ones exist. Second, a case assessment needed to be done, in order to determine if Kyle needed an exorcism. Fortunately, both of these steps were successful and an exorcism was performed, and today, Kyle is a brand-new person committed to Jesus Christ. He is still on medication, but it now seems to be helping him cope with life.

Ouija Board Encounter

Example: A young girl named Rose received a Ouija board for her fifteenth birthday. At first she laughed about it, but it wasn't long before things got weird and the board began communicating with her and a group of her friends. Sometimes, the words were spelled out so quickly that they couldn't keep up with the pointer (technically known as a planchette). Another friend, Renee, who happened to be a Christian, came over one night while they were playing with the board. She knew it was wrong to participate, but she was so curious that she decided to give it a try. She wanted to make sure no one was pushing the pointer across the board, so she placed her fingers lightly on it, and to her amazement, the pointer moved without any effort from her or the friend sitting across from her. The spirit told them:

- His name was Jared Peterson, and he died in 1974 (from something too obscene to quote).

- He knew secret things about people in the room, and proceeded to prove it.

- He was their friend and wanted to help them.

Renee decided she would test the spirit of this Ouija board to show her friends it was a demon and not the spirit of someone who had died. She asked the board, "In the name of Jesus, are you a demon?" The spirit answered, "Yes."

In the name of Jesus, is Jesus Christ the Son of God?" The demon answered, "Yes!"

"In the name of Jesus, were you at the crucifixion?"

THE KINGDOM OF THE OCCULT

"Yes!"

"What did you feel?"

"Fear."

The speed of the pointer had increased so much that it seemed the demon was very agitated. Renee decided it was time for it to leave.

"We know what you are. In the name of Jesus Christ, I command you to leave and not come back!"

The demon answered, "No!"

Three times Renee commanded it to leave in the name of Jesus, and on the third time, the demon answered, "—— you!" And the pointer flew off the board and onto the floor. It was gone. The next day, Rose burned the Ouija board.

Analysis: First, a Ouija board is not a toy; it is a communication device specifically designed to contact spirits. It may not always work for everyone, but it does work for some. These teenagers who decided to use it ended up dabbling in the occult. Second, Rose's parents, who are Catholics, were ignorant of the biblical warning and oblivious to the fact that by giving their daughter this board, they had exposed her and their entire family to the world of the occult. They did not even know the board had actually worked. Their involvement in their daughter's life was minimal, and it could have been disastrous. Third, although Renee disobeyed Scripture by using a Ouija board, she quickly recognized the danger of the situation, stopped playing with it, and started defending herself and her friends against it.

Resolution: It was clear to all present in the room with the Ouija board that something nonhuman was using the board to communicate. The absence of any parental discernment left their child and their child's friends vulnerable. Fortunately, a young girl familiar with the reality of spiritual warfare assessed the situation and followed a biblical method of confrontation. The demon was forced to answer Renee repeatedly and truthfully, in the name of Jesus. In a matter of a few moments, the carefully crafted persona the demon hid behind was demolished. An evil spirit so ancient that he was present when Lucifer fell from heaven, could do *nothing* against a fifteen-year-old girl filled with the power of the Holy Spirit. He *had* to obey her. This is our heritage in Christ. "Do you not know that we shall judge angels?" (1 Cor. 6:3)

Demon Harassment

Example #1: Robert, a student at the local university, was lying in bed one night, alone in his family home. The son of a pastor, he'd heard about the reality of spiritual warfare, but seldom experienced it. It was close to midnight when he first heard the loud knocking on his closet door: *Tap Tap Ta-Tap Tap—Tap Tap.* It sounded exactly like a cartoon knock, *very loud* and with a deliberate pattern, yet he knew the house was empty.

Example #2: A young woman named Lani was home alone one night, getting ready for bed, when she heard loud footsteps downstairs and the sound of cabinets opening and closing in the kitchen. Shaken, she crept out of the bathroom to the top of the open staircase and peered through the rails down into the kitchen below. To her shock and dismay, all of the cabinet doors in the kitchen were randomly opening and closing without any human help! As she watched from above, the doors finally slammed shut, and loud footsteps crossed the kitchen floor to the entryway below her, but no human body stood where the footsteps stopped.

Example #3: Danny, a thirty-year-old man, woke with a start in the middle of the night and found himself staring at a figure sitting on the end of his bed. He'd been woken up before by a suffocating feeling of pressure on his chest and the sense of something very bad in the room, but this time he could actually see a human form in the bedroom with him. As he watched, heart pounding, the figure sitting on the end of the bed turned toward him, and in the moonlight he saw its face. It was extraordinarily beautiful, but the hair on the back of his neck stood up, and he was suddenly afraid.

Example #4: Lynn, a mother of two, has come to the end of her rope. For several weeks now, her youngest daughter has been having terrible nightmares—dreams that seem to be so much more than just "bad." Her eight-year-old daughter woke up from a sound sleep, utterly terrified, shaking so hard her teeth chattered, and ran down the hall to tell her there were lights flying around her room. A few nights later the same thing happened, only this time it was some kind of large creature with red eyes, sitting by the dresser, talking to her. She is scared to be in her room alone.

Example #5: Desirée, a six-year-old girl, has been complaining for months to her parents that "the black sheep" is in her room at night. At first, they wrote it off as a typical "monster under the bed" syndrome, but as the months went by and Desirée became more and more afraid to go to bed, her parents began to wonder what was going on. One day, Desirée innocently turned to her mother and said, "Mommy, the black sheep is talking to me, and he has red eyes." Frozen in midstep, she turned to her little girl and asked, "What does the black sheep say to you, sweetie?" Desirée looked at her mom and said, "He tells me to kill my parents."

Analysis: All of these examples are true, and they all happened to Christians. First, there is no history of mental illness in any of these cases. Second, it is important to emphasize that there is not a demon behind every lamppost, nor are demons responsible for every bad thing in life, but they do have a long historical track record of harassing human beings. The quickest way to distinguish between a human phenomenon and a demonic one is to use the name of Jesus. If it is demonic, you will notice an immediate improvement or change in circumstances. Third, all of the people involved in these encounters recognized the signs of demonic harassment: knocking or banging sounds, severe and repetitive nightmares, colored lights moving across the room, red eyes, apparitions and objects moving without any human help. Fourth, as soon as they recognized the source of the problems, every single one of them prayed and commanded the presence to leave, in the name of Jesus Christ. In the final example, it is interesting and sad to note that four years after this incident, the house was sold to another family, and shortly afterward, a fire swept through it and destroyed this family of four: two adults and one eight-year-old child were killed; the only survivor was a twelve-year-old boy. The police suspected it was a homicide but were unable to prove it. The question of whether or not these terrible events were related to anything demonic will always remain, but the violence attached to the deaths is a strange coincidence, and fires are known to occur in homes troubled by demonic activity.

Resolution: Despite the skepticism of our Western culture, walls do not knock on themselves, cabinet doors do not open and close on their own, footsteps do not happen without feet, and apparitions with red eyes do not appear and say terrible things unless something *supernatural* is involved. And that particular type of *some-*

thing has an interest in making life difficult for human beings. Sometimes, demonic harassment is a direct result of unresolved sin, sometimes it comes because a Christian (or another family member) is involved in spiritual warfare or *will be* involved at some time in the future (this is the case with two of the above examples), and sometimes the harassment is due to either former or current involvement with some type of occultic activity. The latter was not the case in the above examples, but it happens all too frequently. In all of these instances of demon harassment, the Christians involved assessed the situation, recognized the extraordinary circumstances, and moved immediately to confront the invisible enemy. The name of Jesus quite effectively halted all harassment. In some cases, it reoccurred weeks or months later, but finally stopped for good after continual prayer.

Psychic Healing

Example: Mary Ettie V. Smith (1841)

When I was ten years of age, [my father] . . . bought a large tract of land and soon after, was killed accidentally while drawing a log to a saw-mill. He left his business in a very unsettled condition, and my mother with nine children then living—two of whom were younger than me. A terrible series of misfortunes began at his death in January, 1841, a history of which will form the subject matter of the following pages.

About this time, a Mormon elder called upon my mother. He had been holding meetings in this neighborhood and he told her that the Latter Day Saints claimed to be able to heal the sick. If she would consent to be baptized, the deafness that afflicted her (and which had become a great annoyance to her) would in a very short time be removed, and she would hear again. Willing to try the experiment, she was baptized. The water was very cold and immediately after the baptism her hearing improved, and soon was entirely restored.

---

4. Mary Ettie V. Smith, *Fifteen Years Among the Mormons* (New York: Charles Scribner, 1858), 18–19.

> I feel it my duty to do my mother the justice of stating this very remarkable circumstance—as it was the real foundation of her conversion to Mormonism, and the basis of her implicit faith in Joseph Smith as a prophet of God. This faith was never shaken until years after when she found herself shut up in Utah, a prisoner, and an unwilling witness of abominations that in the States had been disguised.[4]

Analysis: First, was there a genuine issue of deafness? This seems to be the case based on the profound effect the cure had on everyone in the family. Second, since hearing was restored, what was the source of the power that healed Mary Ettie's mother? Mormon doctrine teaches that the Jesus of the Mormons was conceived by physical sex between God the Father, an exalted man, and the Virgin Mary.[5] Both Joseph Smith and Brigham Young taught that Jesus was not conceived by the Holy Spirit.[6] Mormonism, then, is a different spirit and a different gospel, so the power behind it is not the God of the Bible. Third, Satan has the power to heal. Wherever there is an original, you will find a counterfeit, and this is certainly the case with healing. It was common knowledge that Mary's mother could not hear very well before the Mormon baptism, and eyewitness testimony confirmed she regained her hearing after this baptism. God does not heal when the person praying believes in a different Jesus, so there can only be one other source of this healing power. There is no doubt that the deafness of Mary Ettie's mother was cured for a reason, as her entire family became Mormons after that event.

Resolution: God heals for His own purposes, and He allows Satan to accomplish healings for unknown reasons. What is certain is that this healing was so extraordinary that it influenced Mary's mother, a wealthy woman, to give everything to the Mormon Church and become dependent upon them for charity. A trusted friend of Brigham Young's family, Mary was in a position to learn the dark

---

5. See Young, Brigham and G. D. Watt, *Journal of Discourses by Brigham Young V8, His Two Counsellors, the Twelve Apostles, and Others* (Whitefish, MT: Kessinger, 2006), 8:116, 8:211, 8:115; and Bruce R. McConkie, *Mormon Doctrine* (n.p., 1966), 546–47.
6. Young and Watt, *Journal of Discourses*, 1:50–51. According to Brigham Young, "The question has been, and is often asked, who it was that begat the Son of the Virgin Mary. . . . When the Virgin Mary conceived the child Jesus, the Father had begotten him in his own likeness. He was *not* begotten by the Holy Ghost. . . . Now, remember from this time forth, and forever, that Jesus Christ was not begotten by the Holy Ghost."

side of Mormonism. It wasn't until years later that she and her family realized exactly what Mormonism was, and by then they were virtual prisoners in Salt Lake City. Psychic healing like this usually impacts lives for years after it occurs. It can lead to oppression and depression that only ends when a commitment to Jesus Christ occurs. Years after this healing, and after a painful struggle with polygamy, Mary Ettie escaped Salt Lake City with some of her family and came to realize the difference between the Mormon Jesus and the Jesus of the Bible.

Demonic Oppression

Example (As documented by Dr. Kurt Koch):

A well-known pastor and evangelist told me of a peculiar experience, which he has allowed me to make public. As a young pastor, our reporter was assigned to an irreligious parish. The villagers had little respect for the word of God. Rather, all manner of superstitious customs were carried out. The charmer was esteemed more highly than the vet. The magnetizer had more work to do than the doctor. The village card layer was visited more often than the council house or the parsonage. At first the young pastor did not feel happy in his new field of work. In the parsonage several remarkable things were to be seen, which could not be accounted for rationally. Repeatedly the pastor's wife would say to her husband that there was some-thing uncanny about the house. The husband would brush this off with a laugh: "There is no such thing. It is all humbug and swindle. Either our senses are playing some trick on us, or a special 'friend' of the pastor is play-ing a practical joke." This thoroughly sober, intelligent man of sharp judge-ment gave no further attention to the happenings in the parsonage. But one night he was compelled by a remarkable incident to take note of the unusual occurrences. Their baby, which slept in the adjoining room to its parents, suddenly set up a most horrible cry. The young wife hurried through the open door into the adjoining chamber to comfort the child. But she started back in astonishment, and called her husband. Both parents saw how the child had been drawn out of its bedclothes and had been turned round in its cot. On its body there were blood-smeared fingerprints. The man first thought it must be some brazen trick. He carefully checked the window catches and the doors into the corridor, and then searched the whole room with a torch. The child's clothes and nappy were then carefully checked for a cause of the injuries to the child. But the parents could not find the slightest clue to explain this painful occurrence.

The mother settled the child again in its cot and quieted it. Then they went back to bed again. But almost immediately the terrible cries and moans broke out again. The parents together hurried into the room. The baby was again unwrapped, drawn out of the clothes, and turned round in the cot. The little body showed new traces of having been violently seized, with the typical marks of a human hand. The couple now had a distinctly uncanny feeling. They took the baby into their bed, and the husband said to his wife, "Something mysterious seems to be going on after all. Come, let us pray." The couple earnestly prayed for God's protection and in faith committed themselves consciously to His care. Then they lay down quietly to rest, and were troubled no more in their sleep.

Early in the morning there was another surprise. The pastor noticed flames shooting out of the window of the farm-house next door. He hurried over with his wife to lend a hand in dealing with the fire. How surprised they were, when they found everything quiet in the neighbour's house! The appearance of fire had vanished. Shaking their heads, they went home. For a little while all was quiet. Then there was a new alarm. The farmer, deeply disturbed, came to the pastor to tell him that his daughter had an attack of mania, was beating about wildly, and had gone out of her mind. The pastor accompanied the troubled man to his home and saw the maniacal girl. Now, he was almost convinced that something was wrong with the parsonage and with the farm-house. What it might be, however, he had no idea.

A few months passed by. Everything in the parsonage and in the farm-house was quiet once more, although the farmer's daughter had unfortunately had to be taken to a mental hospital. The pastor had consciously avoided speaking in the village about these strange events. But secretly he continued to search for some explanation of the mysterious happenings. Then one day, an old elder of the church shed some light on the problem. The old man told him confidentially that the previous pastor, who had been the village's spiritual guide for almost a lifetime, had for twenty-eight years maintained a Spiritist group in the parsonage and experimented in occult things. At first no light dawned in the mind of the young pastor concerning a connexion (*sic*) between these experiments in the field of the occult and the strange events which he had experienced in his house. He was, like so many other people, a man of academic training who did not accept these superstitious things at their face value but regarded them at most as an interesting hocus-pocus. In the course of his ministry, however, and as he was invited to conduct various evangelistic campaigns, he gained an insight into this mysterious realm.[7]

Analysis(as assessed by Dr. Kurt Koch):

This experience, which is guaranteed by the reporter's truthfulness and soundness of judgement, certainly makes great demands on the rational mind. We thus have here the question of how we should evaluate the occurrences in these two houses. In connexion with this case, the following questions need to be considered:

Was the pastor's family victim of a gross sense delusion? Was the observation of flames from the farm-house window merely an hallucination? Were the ten blood-smeared finger-marks merely insect bites?

Had the baby only kicked itself loose and twisted round because of the pain of insect bites? Were the flames coming out of the farm-house window perhaps a reflection of the sunrise, or the flickering of a fire in the farmer's grate? The layout of the buildings and rooms makes this suggestion untenable. . . .

Was there any connexion between the occurrences in the parsonage and the mania of the farmer's daughter? Is there in the sphere of the occult such a thing as transference from one person to another? Do spook activities leap from place to place?

Can people be physically or psychically attacked by powers unknown to us? Is there such a thing as psychic or magic persecution?

Were the occult practices of the old pastor the cause of the strange events in the parsonage?

Do experiments in occult activities leave behind them peculiar effects after the death of the one who practised them?

---

7. Koch, *Christian Counselling and Occultism,* 174–78.

Are there actually haunted houses?

Must we not dismiss all such apparitions as mere humbug, or is a rational explanation of all these phenomena possible?

Do all occult apparitions involve simply an activation of mental powers present in man, or are there invasions by powers from the beyond? In other words, which is valid, the animistic or the Spiritistic hypothesis, or some other view?

Can the disturbances in the parsonage be explained as a dissociation of certain psychic powers, which lead a mysterious separated existence? This would involve the problem of depersonalization or psychic dissociation. The possibility is here excluded, because the young family were emotionally stable, balanced people.

If we are to give these occult apparitions a genuine validity, is there then any safeguard or deliverance in this area?

To the psychologically and para-psychologically trained observer it will be clear from such spook experiences that these phenomena cannot be forced into a mould before the forum of rationality.[8]

Resolution (as summarized by Dr. Kurt Koch):

From the *pastoral* standpoint it is clear that this experience constituted a severe trial for the pastor's family, which they could not readily explain. But out of the welter of questions one thing stands out clearly, that faith in Jesus Christ brought them help in their affliction. In this fact of experienced deliverance from the mysterious occurrences, we have in clear lines a New Testament truth. It is the message which Matthew reports as the words of the Lord (Matt. 28:18): "All authority in heaven and earth has been given to me." Christ has the final dominion in all the areas of the cosmos. He is Lord over all the power of darkness.[9]

Commentary: Demonic oppression and harassment exhibits the same phenomena in thousands upon thousands of different cases: strange noises, cold air, foul smells, fire, moving objects, red eyes, apparitions, moving colored lights, intense feelings of fear, prolonged depression, and visible marks on persons or

---

8. Ibid.
9. Ibid.

objects (scratches, a cloven hoof appearing on a wall) are some, but not all of the phenomena. Western culture ridicules these case studies for any number of different reasons, but all the skepticism in the world does not prevent them from reoccurring. The Bible teaches that we battle against the invisible—not the visible. Throughout Dr. Koch's forty-year ministry, he kept meticulous records documenting his encounters with occult phenomena. Such records, replete with names, dates, and witnesses, remain difficult to refute.

Jezebel Spirit

Example: A young mother named Kate decided to go to a large local church for spiritual counseling. She came from a long line of mediums, and as a new Christian, felt her family's past history was causing problems in her new relationship to Christ. She felt burdened and sad, and hoped to pinpoint exactly why nothing seemed to be going right in her life. The Christian counselor, an older gentleman, began his meeting with Kate by listening quietly as she recounted all the difficult circumstances of her life and then asked if Kate would pray with him. During this prayer, the counselor rebuked the spirit of Jezebel in Kate's life and then asked her to renounce it. Confused (and wondering, *Who is Jezebel?*), Kate did as she was asked to do but did not feel a peace about it in her spirit. She left after her session and did not return to that church again for counseling.

Analysis: People in search of genuine biblical counseling are being warned by some believers that a demon named Jezebel, a so-called spirit of rebellion, roams the earth, harassing people. This demon—exhibiting the same character traits as the ancient biblical queen Jezebel—can supposedly inhabit anyone, including Christians. But the Jezebel spirit is a false teaching, a product of Latter Rain or Dominion theology (also known as Kingdom Now theology), a heresy rejected by the Assemblies of God Church more than fifty years ago.[10] Latter Rain theology

---

10. The Latter Rain movement takes its name from Joel 2:23, believing that in the latter days God will once again "rain" His power on certain key individuals. Their teaching on Jezebel can be found at http://latter-rain.com/eschae/jezebel.htm. For a Christian examination of the Latter Rain movement see Apologetics Index, "An Examination of Kingdom Theology—Part 1/3," http://www.apologeticsindex.org/105.html; and Robert Bowman, "The Faulty Foundation of the Five-Fold Ministry," http://www.apologeticsindex.org/f09.html.

also produced the Manifest Sons of God heresy that promotes the elevation of a select group of Christians in the last days who may (among other things) become divine and judge apostates. These Christians, somehow superior to other Christians, will allegedly be able to produce amazing signs. Today, a revival of Latter Rain theology has produced the Jezebel demon trend, and many churches are embracing it instead of examining the Scriptures to ascertain its truth. There is no biblical evidence whatsoever for the existence of a demon named Jezebel; it is a lie born in the realm of false doctrine. Christians cannot be possessed by any demon, because the Holy Spirit resides within them.[11] A human soul is not an apartment complex; there is no biblical foundation for the existence of multiple levels within the human soul and no teaching that the Holy Spirit will tolerate demons—*ever.* On the contrary, every biblical example proves that demons are terrified of and flee from the power of God.[12] Still, this false teaching has invaded churches all across America.

Resolution: The behaviors that some Christian counselors label as "Jezebel" are caused by a sin nature (although mental illness can at times be a factor). They could also be related to occult influence, but if any possession (in the case of a non-Christian) or any oppression is diagnosed, it would have nothing to do with a demon named Jezebel. Christians can stand firm and secure in the fact that they belong to their Savior, Jesus Christ, and He successfully defended people against demons throughout His entire ministry. Jesus only had to say, "Go!" and all demons fled in terror from Him. Counselors who give names to demons and teach that Christians can be demon possessed are in error; they may have the best interests of the person they are counseling at heart, but there is no biblical precedent for their teachings. In this case scenario, it is best to avoid any further interaction with them and seek counseling elsewhere.

---

11. For a detailed, biblical argument in support of this, see Bob DeWaay, "The Bondage Makers: How Deliverance Ministries Lead People to Bondage," *Critical Issues Commentary,* September/October 2003, http://cicministry.org/commentary/issue78.pdf.
12. For more details on this, see chapter 14, "Demon Possession and Exorcism," and chapter 17, "Christian Counseling and the Occult."

Cursed to the Third or Fourth Generation

Example (as documented by Dr. Kurt Koch):

It was in Hesse in 1938 that I had one of my most memorable counselling experiences. We were holding a mission there when a young man came to me and unburdened himself. His case was so typical that I told him at once that either he or his family had been engaging in occult practices. He admitted this freely and what he went on to confess left a deep impression on my mind. . . .

Even as a child the young man had suffered from depression and had had thoughts of suicide and other psychic disorders. From his early years, he had heard noises during the night and had sometimes witnessed ghost-like appearances, which had caused rustling and whistling noises. A psychiatrist would perhaps diagnose these experiences as psychoneurosis, but this would not explain the cause of the disturbances. However, when one went into the family history the source became clear.

The young man's great-grandmother had been a magic charmer. She had healed both animals and people by means of her charms. In addition to this she had also belonged to a Spiritistic circle which practised communication with departed spirits. It was her involvement with occult phenomena that brought about the tragic downfall of the family.

The magic practices of the great-grandmother had been passed down to her son and daughter, who in turn had charmed both animals and people, using the 6th and 7th book of Moses as an aid. They had also carried on communication with the dead, and had practised the use of a pendulum and the laying of cards as a means of fortune-telling. They both died in a terrible way. The woman had at night seen ghosts in her room, and she had had the feeling that evil spirits were for ever trying to keep her mouth and nose shut. This continued for many years and finally she had been committed to an asylum. Since she was not really mentally ill though, she was released after six months. Her brother later died in terrible agony in spite of the fact that he had asked that all his magic books be burned or thrown out of the house. He had even asked for a Bible to read, but he was not able to understand it. When he finally died in great pain an obnoxious stench spread throughout the house.

The grandchildren were no better off. One granddaughter used to have fits of frenzy in which she threw furniture around or sometimes lay down in the street screaming almost unbearably. She too was committed to an asylum. Another granddaughter heard the already mentioned sound of knocking during the night, and she was so emotionally disturbed that one day she killed both herself and her two children by jumping with them off a cliff. A grandson became a medium for a Spiritistic séance, and he too suffered from a persecution mania and finally ended up in a mental home.

Among the great-grandchildren, one girl continued the card-laying and charming tradition and later died when she was quite young. Her family asserts that she still haunts the house in which they live in the form of a poltergeist.[13]

Analysis (as assessed by Dr. Kurt Koch): It was one of the brothers of this girl who had come to me for counselling. He told me that he was utterly convinced that all the terrible psychic disorders in his family history could be traced back to their contact with occultism. We see evidenced here the punishment for sin mentioned in the second commandment, ". . . visiting the iniquity of the fathers upon the children to the third and the fourth generation of those who hate me." And this is not an isolated case. In my missionary work I have heard many similar family histories while counselling people. It is distressing to note how little is known of the powers of Satan among psychiatrists and Christian counsellors. The present atmosphere of rationalistic thought has caused these things to be regarded lightly as if they did not exist. But if it is our desire to help people then we must take these satanic forces seriously. Man stands in the midst of a battle between Christ and Satan. When people think of Satan merely as a man with a tail and horns, and just mock at the idea of a real devil, they make a terrible mistake and thus enable Satan to ensnare and attack his victims without hindrance. The most dangerous area of satanic seduction is magic, for it is here that people consciously participate in Satan's work even though he hides behind a camouflage of pious ceremonies.[14]

Resolution (as summarized by Dr. Kurt Koch): Thank God that Satan has not got the last word in this matter. Jesus Christ came to destroy the works of the

---

13. Koch, *Between Christ and Satan*, 157–60.
14. Ibid.

devil (1 John 3:8). We have a mighty enemy but an almighty Friend, as the late German evangelist, Ernst Modersohn, used to say. The right hand of the Lord does valiantly in all circumstances, even in the case where a person has been driven into direct dependence upon the devil through occupation with occult things. This fact was revealed in the case of the young man whose story I have just recounted. Christ gave him both joy and freedom. The bulwarks of darkness yielded to the almighty hand of the Victor of Calvary. Jesus Christ remains today the Saviour of the world.[15]

Commentary: It is important to note here that many "deliverance" counselors ignore the last half of Exodus 20:5–6: "For I, the LORD your God, am a jealous God, visiting the iniquity of the fathers upon the children to the third and fourth generations of those who hate Me, *but showing mercy to thousands, to those who love Me and keep My commandments*" (emphasis added). God promised *immediate* mercy to all those who love Him. This mercy is given the moment salvation by grace takes place and the Holy Spirit enters the heart of the believer. Jeremiah 32:18–19, which refers to a generational curse, does *not* apply to Christians. The Hebrew emphasizes God's mercy, not His wrath, and it refers to *individual accountability*; only those who choose to continue in the sin of their ancestors will be punished. Dr. Koch documented many cases where psychic abilities were passed down from generation to generation, inflicting awful penalties on those who practiced them, but these people were not Christians. When a person turns his or her life wholly and truly over to the Lord Jesus Christ, he or she is immediately forgiven all sin and given mercy in regard to any punishment relating to that sin or preceding sins. "Therefore if the Son makes you free, you shall be free indeed" (John 8:36). The idea that Christians need to be released from generational curses has no foundation in Scripture.[16]

---

15. Ibid.
16. For a detailed, biblical argument in support of this, see Bob DeWaay, "Generational Curses," *Critical Issues Commentary*, January/February 2002, http://cicministry.org/commentary/issue68.pdf.

Demonic Influence

Example: A recent article shed some light on the life of actress Sharon Tate, shortly before she died. It is revealing (although speculative) and points to the possibility of some type of occult activity or demonic influence in her life.

Actor Christopher Jones claims he had an affair with Sharon Tate in 1969 after she was married to Roman Polanski for just one year. During their affair, Jones recalls how Tate talked about her belief in reincarnation and how she was sure she had lived previously as a nine-year-old child who died tragically in a fire. Jones remembers, "The second she said that, the doors to the restaurant blew open even though there wasn't any wind, and she looked really shocked."[17] He went on to say that one time when he was with her, he suddenly had the strongest feeling she was going to die. Another time, he asked her what she was thinking, and she said, "The Devil is beautiful. Most people think he's ugly, but he's not."[18] Christopher Jones eventually asked Sharon Tate to stop talking about things like this because it made him nervous.

Analysis: First, mental illness does not seem to be an issue here in regard to the credibility of the witness. Although Jones claims that drugs were part of Tate's lifestyle, he does not admit to taking them. Second, if his memory is basically correct, Christopher Jones's candid conversations with Sharon Tate reveal a young woman influenced by occult beliefs. At the very least, her participation in movies featuring Witchcraft and Satanism, her belief in reincarnation, and her attitude toward the devil all point to someone in serious rebellion against God. Third, it is certainly out of the ordinary for a twenty-six-year-old woman to consider the devil beautiful, and it is unusual for any door to blow open without wind (especially during a discussion on occult reincarnation).

Resolution: Perhaps it is not so surprising after all that Sharon Tate would be influenced by occult ideology, considering she had been very involved in her hus-

---

17. Lina Das, "The Final Affair of Roman Polanski's Murdered Wife Sharon Tate," *Daily Mail*, August 31, 2007, http://www.dailymail.co.uk/pages/live/femail/article.html?in_article_id=478867&in_page_id=1879.
18. Ibid.

band's occult films, *Dance of the Vampires* and *Rosemary's Baby*—a movie about Witchcraft and Satan worship that ended with the devil impregnating a young woman.[19] A link to the occult cannot be ruled out in the life of Sharon Tate, but what part it played in her death is unknown.[20] What is certain is the fact that for this young woman, there was no resolution.

CASE STUDY

Kurt Van Gorden

In 1979, I was Walter Martin's Teaching Assistant for his seminary and Bible classes, and people would occasionally ask for counsel following the class. One Sunday, a man approached me and asked if Dr. Martin would see him about demon possession and doing an exorcism. I asked him who it was that had the demon. He said it was he himself—that he had a demon.

My experience with demon possession was very little at that time, so I asked the man to step aside and talk so that I could ask him a few questions before bringing the matter to Dr. Martin. Routinely, Dr. Martin taught us that some marks of demon possession, as taken from Scripture, are that a person will either attempt to maim himself or commit suicide. This is drawn from Matthew 17:15, where a demonized young man threw himself into water or fire, and Mark 5:4–5, where the man in the tombs became violent, fierce, excessively strong, crying out at night, and cutting and maiming himself with stones. I asked the man if he was a born again Christian, and about maiming or suicidal tendencies. He acknowledged that he had accepted Jesus as his Savior, but he also had attempted suicide.

I took this to Dr. Martin and he said that he would see the man. He then asked me if I had ever been involved in an exorcism, and I answered,

---

19. Sharon Tate was married to Roman Polanski. The film *Eye of the Devil* featured Tate as a one-thousand-year-old, evil Witch. Rumors circulated involving her initiation by Alex Sanders into an actual coven while working on Polanski's *Dance of the Vampires* (also called *The Fearless Vampire Hunters*), but this remains unproven. Sanders, called "King of the Witches," was a major influence in British Witchcraft.

20. See investigative reporter Maura Terry's work, *The Ultimate Evil* (Los Angeles: Grafton, 1988), for speculation on Tate's involvement in the occult.

"No."

"Well," he said, "Start praying, because you're about to enter your first one."

Dr. Martin said that since this man proclaimed Christ as his Savior, he either had a false testimony of salvation and only mimicked the words someone asked him to repeat or he was genuinely saved, and was a troubled Christian, who only thinks he has a demon since, as Dr. Martin put it, "a demon cannot possess a true Christian who is the property of the Holy Spirit."

He continued, "There is one more thing, Kurt. If he has no demon, then we may recommend him to the counseling center here at the Church. He may be a Christian in need of spiritual or psychological counseling. If he has a demon, get ready to hold him if he lashes out at me. Now, let's pray together before you bring him in."

I was nervous with uncertainty and yet excited to see what would happen. My hands were clammy, but I gathered my calmness by praying on my way back to tell him that Dr. Martin would be glad to see him in a few moments. During that time together, I asked him a couple of other questions that Dr. Martin gave to me: "Did someone tell you that you have a demon or was it by self-awareness?" And, "Have you ever been through demon deliverance before?" These questions were asked because most people who are demon possessed do not admit it, and in that case, we might be dealing with a disturbed Christian. If someone told the man that he had a demon, then it may be that he believed their cruel remarks and was troubled by it. The last question was to find out if the man had a habit of going to demon deliverance sessions where it is believed that Christians can be demon possessed. The man told me that the demon was "a demon of lust."

We went into a room and I apprised Dr. Martin of the new information as I introduced them. Dr. Martin asked him the same questions and only said, "I see. Please bow your head in prayer."

We bowed our heads, but I admit to keeping one eye open as Dr. Martin led the prayer to first cleanse himself before the Lord before entering into battle. Then he grabbed my hand and placed it upon the man's head along with his and he simply said in a strong voice, "I command you in the name of Jesus Christ, if there is a demon in this man, then speak forth."

Nothing happened except that my eyes were wide open and I was praying and trying not to shake. Again, Dr. Martin repeated the same line just as forcefully, but again nothing happened. We waited a few seconds and Dr. Martin spoke to the man, "I'm glad to tell you, my brother, that you do not have a demon." The man looked up and said, "What?"

Dr. Martin went on to say that if he was a Christian, then a demon could not live in him at the same time. "You are not a duplex, with God in the upstairs of your heart and the devil in the downstairs. You either belong to God or you do not."

The man protested that he knew he had a demon. Then Dr. Martin counseled him further by saying that not all lust is generated from Satan, there is a lust of the flesh and a lust of the eyes, both of which are from man (1 John 2:16). Dr. Martin's next line has stuck with me all of these years, "Young man, I know that you do not have a demon because I prayed first and then I commanded the demon to speak, and nothing spoke. Under God's authority, when a servant of God commands a demon to speak, they must speak. Nothing answered when I commanded it to speak, so you do not have a demon. What you have is a fleshy struggle with lust and I am recommending that you get counseling for it. I cannot cast out your flesh, and it is your flesh that you are struggling with instead of a demon." Dr. Martin continued to talk with the man about the problem of lust, and he cited several Bible passages to assure the man that what he faced was his flesh and not a demon.

The most important thing I learned that day was the fact that this man wanted to exorcize a demon that was not there. I have preached this as part of a sermon several times since, "The Demon that Was Not There." I have also applied this lesson in my ministry ever since that day. Dr. Martin told the man that he did not believe in a long, drawn out exorcism. Our time in prayer with that man probably lasted twenty to thirty seconds, and it was over. He had no demon in spite of his protest, and in the end, he took Dr. Martin's advice and got counseling. When I saw him several times afterward, he was doing quite well.

SCRIPTURAL RESPONSE

In dealing with the world of the occult, there is no substitute for the power of the Holy Spirit. It is a vital, indispensable tool in the spiritual warfare connected to occult counseling. D. L. Moody, in his book *Secret Power*, details the ministry, the fullness, and the anointing of the secret power of the Holy Spirit. Kurt Koch points out:

> Only the Holy Spirit can bring us to the ultimate understanding of man and of his mental disorders. . . . Charismatic equipment is the heart of the matter in Christian counselling. This means that Christian counselling cannot in its essence be learned. . . . The charisma is a Spirit-gift which comes from Him who Himself bestows the Spirit. There is only one door which opens the way to this: "Ask, and it shall be given unto you." For this prayer we have the promise of Luke 11:13, "How much more will *your* heavenly Father give the Holy Spirit to those who ask Him!"[21]

The New Testament speaks of certain "gifts" bestowed by God the Holy Spirit upon the Church of Jesus Christ—gifts meant to aid in spiritual warfare. In Romans 12:6, the apostle Paul taught that each member of the Church or body of Christ possesses different gifts "according to the grace that is given to us." In Ephesians 4:8, Paul further wrote that God "gave gifts to men," and in 1 Corinthians 12:1 he added, "Now concerning spiritual gifts, brethren, I do not want you to be ignorant."

Throughout Church history, Christians recognized these gifts in one manner or another, and beyond a reasonable doubt they believed that they are a definite part of the spiritual inheritance of all true Christians. Certainly, these gifts existed in the early Church, and there is no logical, historical, or exegetical reason to suppose that they were *not* intended to exist in either greater or lesser measure so long as that Church would endure on the earth.

The apostle Paul stressed quite heavily the importance of spiritual gifts, particularly those known as charismatic gifts or *the gifts of grace.*

> To one is given the word of wisdom through the Spirit, to another the word of knowledge through the same Spirit, to another faith by the same Spirit,

---

21. Koch, *Christian Counselling and Occultism,* 303–4.

to another gifts of healings by the same Spirit, to another the working of miracles, to another prophecy, to another discerning of spirits, to another different kinds of tongues, to another the interpretation of tongues. But one and the same Spirit works all these things, distributing to each one individually as He wills. (1 Cor. 12:8–11).

Paul not only announced that there are spiritual gifts manifested by the Holy Spirit, but he also taught that there are varieties of gifts (v. 4), varieties of service (v. 5), and varieties of operation concerning these gifts (v. 6), and that the manifestation of the Spirit is given to profit the entire church or body (v. 7). Paul went on to declare that all of these manifestations are from the same Spirit and are manifested through the one body, the Church.

Of course, there have been and still are abuses of spiritual gifts by some believers, even as there is neglect of these gifts by other believers. However, neither neglect nor abuse negates the Spirit's moving, for by virtue of His omnipotence He can do anything today that He has done in the past.

That these gifts may be neglected is clear from 1 Timothy 4:14, "Do not neglect the gift that is in you, which was given to you by prophecy with the laying on of the hands of the eldership," and 2 Timothy 1:6: "Therefore I remind you to stir up the gift of God which is in you through the laying on of my hands." But neglect is *not* denial, and it is with denial that we are primarily concerned.

Fruit and Gifts

In order to avoid a confusion of terminology, we must understand the difference between "the fruit of the Spirit" and "the gifts of the Spirit." In Galatians 5, Paul carefully differentiated between the fruit of the Spirit and the gifts of the Spirit for a very important reason: "But the fruit of the Spirit is love, joy, peace, longsuffering, gentleness, goodness, faith, meekness, temperance" (vv. 22–23 KJV); but he also commented that "the fruit of the Spirit is in all goodness and righteousness and truth" (Eph. 5:9–10).

The "fruit of the Spirit" is to be evidenced in the life of *every* believer as proof of the transforming power of the new birth. On the other hand, the gifts of the Spirit are bestowed as the Spirit wills, and not all believers receive the same gifts. This distinction is carefully maintained throughout the New Testament references relevant to the subject.

Since 1 Corinthians 12, in conjunction with Romans 11:29, teaches the perpetuity of God's gifts, some Christian groups maintain that they have the right to claim these gifts on what unfortunately amounts to an exclusive basis. While we cannot rightfully challenge the possibility of the manifestation of gifts such as *prophecy*, we must clearly understand what the word translated "prophecy" means in the Greek. Its primary meaning is that of foretelling a given event as a result of knowledge imparted from God. Consider, for example, the Old Testament prophecies concerning the birth, death, and resurrection of our Lord. But the word also means proclaiming or reiterating something God has said in the past, with a contemporary application as the Spirit leads. This thought we find running through the entire Bible in line with the clear revelation of God. Although the people have the right to accept the "gift of prophecy," the Church as a whole should not be required to accept anything without testing it and holding firmly to the truth.

The power of God is needed in order to accomplish the successful counseling of those involved in the world of the occult. We should test both the gifts and those who profess to possess them by the biblical standards of sound doctrine and fruit. We ought never to forget the apostle's injunction to seek for spiritual gifts as a means of power in the Christian life (1 Cor. 14:1) so that God may minister to us through the Spirit to the fullest extent attainable: "But one and the same Spirit works all these things, distributing to each one individually as He wills. . . . For in fact the body is not one member but many. . . . But now God has set the members, each one of them, in the body just as He pleased. . . . That there should be no schism in the body, but that the members should have the same care one for another. . . . Now you are the body of Christ, and members individually" (1 Cor. 12:11, 14, 18, 25, 27).

Certainly, great confusion can result from the abuse of the gifts of the Spirit, but we ought to keep an open and balanced mind on this subject of the "charismata," or spiritual gifts, remembering, of course, the supreme imperative of love (1 Cor. 13:13). It is this that compels us, as our primary duty, to love one another as Christ loved us and to preserve the unity of the body, "that there should be no schism in the body; but that the members should have the same care one for another" (1 Cor. 12:25). This, we believe, is the key to understanding the relationship of the Christian to all of the gifts of the Spirit.

The world of the occult is a real dimension, it is powerful, and it *can* get through that door to you if you let it; it can disrupt your life, and if you are not a believer, it can possess you so that you are not your own anymore, and you must be delivered by the power of God. The man with an experience is way ahead of the man with a theory. You can have a theory about the occult, but many have the experience; many men of God have been there throughout all of church history— with lots of witnesses to prove it.[22]

God's perspective on the occult is this:

> When you come into the land which the LORD your God is giving you, you shall not learn to follow the abominations of those nations. There shall not be found among you anyone who makes his son or his daughter pass through the fire, or one who practices witchcraft, or a soothsayer, or one who interprets omens, or a sorcerer, or one who conjures spells, or a medium, or a spiritist, or one who calls up the dead. For all who do these things are an abomination to the LORD, and because of these abominations the LORD your God drives them out from before you. (Deut. 18:9–12).

In Leviticus 19:31, God said, "Give no regard to mediums and familiar spirits; do not seek after them, to be defiled by them: I am the LORD your God." The word translated "defiled" in this verse is one of the strongest possible words in the Hebrew. In the Old Testament, if you were a family member, and one of your family died, you were forbidden by God to touch the body after the death had occurred. To touch the body was to be defiled by it, and if you did this, you had to go and make an offering to the Lord before you would be considered acceptable to enter the tabernacle for worship. That is the usage of the word here: corrupted or defiled.

Once again, in Leviticus 20:26–27, God spoke on the same subject, warning Israel, "I the LORD am holy, and have separated you from the peoples, that you should be Mine. A man or a woman who is a medium, or who has familiar spirits, shall surely be put to death; they shall stone them with stones. Their blood shall be upon them." In other words, touching the occult is a capital offense: whoever does so is considered by God to have defiled himself, and the penalty is death.

---

22. Some of these witnesses were very competent medical men. See Walter R. Martin, *Revival of the Occult* (CD/audiotape), Walter Martin Ministries, www.waltermartin.com.

In Leviticus 20:6, God said, "And the person who turns to mediums and familiar spirits, to prostitute himself with them, I will set My face against that person and cut him off from his people." God used sexual relations with a prostitute as the equivalent of touching the world of the occult. You are defiled by the body of a prostitute, and you are defiled by touching Witchcraft or any aspect of the occult; every single one of them is a capital offense to God.

There are many other passages throughout Scripture that clearly reveal God's position on the occult, and yet there are always some who argue, "Well, yes, but that is all the Old Testament. We are not under law; we are under grace." It is amazing how people run for grace when they have been condemned by law. God has not changed His mind one bit. He is just as upset now as He was thousands of years ago. In the book of Acts, Paul commanded a demon to leave a young girl, in the name of Jesus Christ, and the young girl was delivered as a result of it (16:16–18). After Paul preached at Ephesus, the people brought all of their occultic works to him and burned them—books worth fifty thousand pieces of silver. "Many of those who had practiced magic brought their books together and burned them in the sight of all. And they counted up the value of them, and it totaled fifty thousand pieces of silver" (Acts 19:19–20). Today, that adds up to about twelve thousand dollars. They burned them all for the glory of God, and the Word of God grew and prospered.

Jesus Christ dealt with the occult repeatedly, and throughout the Bible there are many examples of God's attitude toward it. Jesus commanded the demons, and they obeyed Him, and He gave the same power to His Church. You can command the demons in the name of Jesus, and they will obey you, but you had better be walking with God if you do so. You had better not have any unconfessed sin in your life, because demons will loudly recite all your sins to you. A lot of men trying to perform exorcisms have been embarrassed by demons who told them to stop calling on them to come out of those bodies when they themselves were sinning. So, if you go into an exorcism as a Christian, be sure there is no unconfessed sin in your life, and be sure you are walking with the Lord. You do not want to be called a hypocrite in front of witnesses.

Women should not be involved in exorcism because they are not elders and they do not have the physical strength necessary to control a possessed individual.[23] Do not fool around with demons; they have lots of information. They know a great deal about you—things you think no one else could possibly know. They know these details because Satan knows them.

In Acts 13, Paul and Barnabas were sent out to preach the gospel by the Holy Spirit. And being sent forth by the Holy Spirit (v. 4), they went and preached in the island of Cyprus. They preached in the synagogue of the Jews, and then they went to the capital of Cyprus, which was then Paphos (v. 6). When they arrived at the center of Roman power on that island (that is where the occult generally is— at the center of political power), they found a certain occultist, a false prophet and a Jew whose name was Bar-Jesus, or "Son of Jesus." He was in the company of the proconsul of the country, Sergius Paulus, a prudent man who summoned Barnabas and Saul, desiring to hear the Word of God. Here was a man looking for the Word of God, but the sorcerer Elymas Bar-Jesus withstood them—he resisted them— seeking to turn the proconsul away from the faith.

All at once, Paul was filled up to overflowing with the Holy Spirit (a beautiful phrase in the Greek). He fixed his eyes on Bar-Jesus and said, "O full of all deceit and all fraud, you son of the devil, you enemy of all righteousness, will you not cease perverting the straight ways of the Lord? And now, indeed, the hand of the Lord is upon you, and you shall be blind, not seeing the sun for a time" (Acts 13:10–11). And that is exactly what occurred. Elymas Bar-Jesus was immediately struck blind.

The Holy Spirit defines the methodology of the occult quite specifically in this passage of Scripture, and it is something that should never be forgotten:

1. The occult always withstands or opposes the gospel.

2. The occult always seeks to turn people away from faith in Jesus Christ, never toward the faith.

3. The occult is full of all deceit or subtlety.

4. The occult is a child of the devil.

---

23. There is no biblical injunction against women participating in exorcisms. The question is : *In what capacity should they participate?* Walter Martin believed that women could not hold the office of Elder, so as deaconesses and teachers under the authority of pastors and elders in the church, they should not direct an exorcism. Many women participate in exorcisms today as intercessors, praying for all involved in the exorcism. There is also the question of safety that must be considered during an exorcism, since just one demon has a tremendous amount of strength, and *many* demons often possess an individual.

5. The occult is the enemy of all righteousness.

6. The occult is a perverter (or a changer) of the right ways of the Lord.

CONCLUSION

The early Christians preached the gospel and demonstrated the supernatural power of the Holy Spirit—gifts given according to the will of God (Heb. 2:4). It was not just the Word that went forth; it was the power that went forth, and that is as true today as it was in the first century. God not only saves people, but God also manifests Himself in power. He heals minds, bodies, lives, marriages, and memories. He saves to the uttermost. It is our history—our heritage—and we should lay claim to it.

Christians cannot grow on the same power they received from the Holy Spirit the day they became Christians. They need more power, more grace, more gifts, and more fruit; they need more from the Spirit every day of their lives. A person who is filled with the Holy Spirit need never fear the occult. The demons know when a person walks with God; the demons recognize the presence of the Sprit of God.

Put on the whole armor of God and stand against the methods of the devil (Eph. 6). God does not send you into combat in your underwear; He sends you in *equipped* for combat. God says that if your Christian life is all together, you are armed and ready, but if your Christian life is weak, you are vulnerable. Study, pray, be filled with the Spirit, and preach the Word. The Lord knows those who are His. He is a stronghold in the day of trouble.

Speak up. Speak out. Confront evil. Resist the devil; he will flee from you. Put on the armor of God, a godly Christian life, and remember—all the armor is for the front of your body; none of it fits your derriere. A soldier always moves forward; he does not turn around and run. Some Christians have run away from combat, and the flaming arrows of the wicked one have been sapping their strength ever since. The Holy Spirit is able to remove these arrows that are causing you so much pain—all you need do is ask.

Claim the joy of your salvation; put on the whole armor of God, and stand against the methods of the devil. We are not fighting flesh and blood, but the spiritual rulers of the darkness of this age. You have overcome them, little children. Greater is he that is in you than he that is in the world (see 1 John 4:4).

He that has ears to hear—*hear* what the Spirit says to the Church, and obey Him.

RECOMMENDED RESOURCES

1. Koch, Kurt. *Christian Counseling and Occultism*. Grand Rapids: Kregel, 1981.

2. Korem, Danny and Paul Meier. *The Fakers*. Grand Rapids: Baker, 1980.

3. Unger, Merrill. *Biblical Demonology: A Study of Spiritual Forces at Work Today*. New York: Kregel, 1994.

COUNSELING RESOURCE LIST

Kevin and Jill Rische
Walter Martin Ministries
http://www.waltermartin.com

Kurt Van Gorden
Utah Gospel Mission
http://www.jude3missions.org

The following ministries are currently counseling people involved in or troubled by the occult. *

Jeff Harshbarger
Refuge Ministries
http://www.refugeministries.cc/main.asp

Vince McCann
Spotlight Ministries
http://www.spotlightministries.org.uk/index.htm
Ex Occultists for Christ Blogspot
http://exoccultistsforchrist.blogspot.com/

Jay Howard
The Religious Research Project

http://www.dwaddle.com/focus/Pages/home.shtml

Anton and Janet Hein-Hudson
Apologetics Index
http://www.apologeticsindex.org/about02.html

Rafael Martinez
Spiritwatch Ministries
http://spiritwatch.org/
E-mail: joy@spiritwatch.org

Kathi Sharpe
http://iamhealed.net

E-mail: kathi.sharpe@gmail.com

Jonna Sutherland
Living Lamb Ministries
http://livinglamb.com/

The views and opinions of these ministries are not necessarily those of the authors or Thomas Nelson Publishers.

Quick Facts About Evangelism

- People lost in the world of the occult are precious souls for whom Jesus Christ offered Himself; they are human beings who have homes, families, and friends.[1]

- Evangelism in the true biblical sense of the term means a return to the content of the gospel and to the *methods* of the New Testament church—a fiercely personal, door-to-door and neighbor-to-neighbor effort.[2]

- Evangelism and apologetics work hand in hand to accomplish the same goal: the salvation of souls.

- A definition of terms is vital to successful communication.

- Biblical love risks hatred, in order to tell people the truth.

---

1. Martin, *The Kingdom of the Cults,* 478.
2. Ibid. See also page 484. Etymology of *Evangel*—"from Gk. *evangelistes* "preacher of the gospel," lit. "bringer of good news," from *evangelizesthai* "bring good news," from *eu-* "good" + *angellein* "announce," from *angelos* "messenger." In early Gk. Christian texts, the word was used of the four supposed authors of the narrative gospels. Meaning "itinerant preacher" was another early Church usage, revived in M. E. (1382)," Douglas Harper, *Online Etymology Dictionary,* s.v., "evangel," http://www.etymonline.com/index.php?search=evangel&searchmode=nl (accessed September 11, 2007).

18

Evangelism:
Reaching the Hearts of People

The great dilemma the Church of Jesus Christ faces today is how to communicate the gospel without turning people away from the truth. If the heart of evangelism is communication, how do we confront people with a gospel that is essentially *confrontational*? How do we communicate the truth without alienating them?

When the subject of evangelism comes up, people frequently discover that the message gets bogged down. Often Christians who are trying to emphasize a point find their words misinterpreted—a confusing situation that happens regularly to laypeople, pastors, apologists, and teachers. When you begin comparing and contrasting views, particularly with someone involved in the kingdom of the occult, people tend to get a bit edgy, and it may even come down to a shouting match.

The most important thing to recognize at the start is this fact: confrontation is basically biblical (2 Tim. 2:25). The Church in the modern era has forgotten that. We think that if we tell people about Jesus and spell it out in terms of the historic gospel, then we have accomplished what we set out to do. But apologetics is the partner of evangelism. After you tell someone the truth of Jesus Christ, he or she will expect some answers, and rightfully so. The Bible instructs Christians to give to every man an answer, a reason for the hope within us (1 Peter 3:15). In our day, the Church has largely avoided giving answers to the hard questions because it involves confrontation. All too often Peter's "meekness and fear" cancels out Jude's "contend earnestly for the faith" or Paul's correction of those in opposition (1 Peter 3:15; Jude 1:3; 2 Tim. 2:24). Yet each apostolic commission is equally true and authoritative without conflict. The Christian's duty, then, is to contend for the faith and to correct those in opposition by giving answers for the inward hope, in personal humility and reverence toward God.[3]

     See Note 3 on following page

Across America and around the world today, talk radio is still popular because people keep asking the tough questions, and that means they are not getting the answers to those questions from their church, pastor, or friends. Tough questions inevitably bring debate, but it is necessary to have controversy—not for the sake of controversy—but for the sake of truth. Benjamin Rush, the great physician, and signer of the Declaration of Independence once said, "Controversy is only dreaded by the advocates of error."[4]

In his compelling work, *Hell's Best Kept Secret,* Ray Comfort pointed out an inescapable truth: "The way we present the gospel determines the kind of response the sinner makes."[5] On the day of Pentecost, Peter did not give a sermon on the unity of all religions, the fatherhood of God, and the brotherhood of man. There were no soft lights, soft music, and even softer sermons. He began with, "There is no other name under heaven given among men by which we must be saved" (Acts 4:12). How offensive was *this* to the scribes, the Pharisees, and the Sadducees? Confrontation, by its very nature, will become offensive.

3. Dr. Bryce A. Pettit, a student of Dr. Martin's at Melodyland School of Theology (1976–1979), contributed research on Armstrongism to Walter R. Martin's *Rise of the Cults.* Dr. Pettit, a mission specialist for cult and occult adherents, wrote on mission work among the New Religious Movements (NRMs) and emphasized the early pioneering work of Walter R. Martin in information gathering on cultic and occultic material:

> The current interest in the effect NRMs have on missionary activities began in 1958 when Walter Martin, an evangelical critic of the "cults," was asked to be part of the Pastor's Conference Team of World Vision Incorporated. He traveled over 25,000 miles throughout Africa and Asia speaking to thousands of Christian workers and gathering information on the impact NRMs were having on their missionary efforts. Over the next few years he visited other countries and continued to gather information relevant to the threat these groups posed to world missions. His Christian Research Institute became the model for dozens, and eventually hundreds, of other counter-cult organizations worldwide over the next four decades. (See Pettit, "New Religious Movements and Missions," 125–34.)

Dr. Pettit summarized, under the New Religious Movements, what we lay out in a historical timeline in chapter 6, "Eastern Mysticism and the New Age": Spiritism, occultism, mysticism, humanism, New Thought, mind-science groups, and the Human Potential Movement, all culminated in the New Age Movement. The importance of this kind of research in reaching the lost for Jesus Christ, beginning with the *Kingdom of the Cults* and all subsequent works, should not be underestimated for evangelism.

4. ThinkExist, "Benjamin Rush Quotes," http://thinkexist.com/quotes/benjamin_rush/.
5. Ray Comfort, *Hell's Best Kept Secret* (New Kensington, PA: Whitaker, 2002), 12.

The people who believe that talking forever on the same subject will bring everyone to the same place in the end have led us down the primrose path to possibility thinking. If we never depart from common ground discussions, we will never be able to warn the lost of an eternity in hell. The New Age movement has so infiltrated the structure of the Church with its philosophy of religious equality, that if you speak out against evil, you become the bad guy. In God's eyes, all religions are not created equal, and we do not need to pretend that they are.

Scripture offers an excellent example of this kind of thinking. King Ahab, married to Jezebel, priestess of Baal and devil worshiper, offended God so deeply that He closed the heavens for three years in response to Elijah's prayer. The minute Ahab met Elijah after three years of drought, he said, "Is that you, O troubler of Israel?" (1 Kings 18:17). Here is Elijah—a prophet of God—standing before him, and the devil worshiper says, "Aha! This is all your fault!" It is this attitude of blame that so many come up against today in the defense of the faith.

The first five centuries of the Christian era are known as the age of the Church fathers. These men spent their time writing magnificent apologetics and excellent theology, and today we benefit from their hard work. If Augustine had not inspired Luther to go back to the core of the gospel, "The just shall live by faith" (Rom. 1:17), the Church would not be where it is today. Luther was committed to a reformation faith—a faith based upon the teachings of the Church fathers.

This history lesson exists to teach us something. If the early history of the Church rests on providing reasons for faith and answers to questions, then the Church today must continue in the same tradition in order to survive and be successful. The early Church took on every issue they possibly could; they never shied away from controversy for the sake of truth. But today, we have lapsed into a false line of reasoning that if we confront someone forcefully with the truth, we are unloving. This is a lie, and you should mark it very carefully. For if it is true, Jesus Christ was the most unloving man who ever lived, and His apostles Paul and Peter were the most unloving people who ever wrote, because they certainly confronted the world.

A perfect example of this Christlike confrontation is found in Matthew 15:12–14, where Jesus' disciples asked, "Do You know that the Pharisees were offended when they heard this saying?" Rather than apologizing, Jesus answered, "Every plant which My heavenly Father has not planted will be uprooted. Let them alone. They are blind leaders of the blind. And if the blind leads the blind, both will fall into a ditch." If that explanation were offered today to counter those offended by Christ's gospel, then the evangelist or apologist would be labeled as insensitive, intolerant, mean-spirited, and uncharitable, when in reality Jesus provided this example.

Offenses will occur because of unmitigated truth, but that is the fault of the *listener* rather than the speaker. Otherwise, today's anti-apologetics critics must equally condemn our Lord and Master Jesus Christ for His actions in this text.

DEFINITION OF TERMS

We are surrounded on every side by the forces of darkness, and it is only a fool who does not analyze the nature of the enemy in order to become effective in dealing with him. Jesus Christ warned us, "Beware of false prophets, who come to you in sheep's clothing, but inwardly they are ravenous wolves. You will know them by their fruits" (Matt. 7:15–16 NASB). Anytime Christians enter into the defense of the faith in the world of the occult, it is vital to *define terms*, so we do not end up talking into a vacuum.

What is evangelism? Is it merely mass rallies, where so-called wholesale decisions for Christ are made? Is it, on the other hand, just the task of the local church to shoulder the responsibility of having a week or two of meetings for revival each year? By evangelism, do we mean massive emphasis on radio, television, and the Internet to communicate the good news of redemption? Or is evangelism somehow or other bound up with *all* of these forms of expression, and yet, in essence, none of them? To answer these questions, and to place evangelism in its proper perspective where the challenge of the occult is concerned, we must consider carefully the pattern laid out for us in the New Testament.[6]

Evangelism involves tact. Apologetics involves sanctified tact: *how to effectively destroy the altars of Baal while carefully erecting the altar of Jehovah.* It must be a practiced art, and it is practiced all through the New Testament. The word *evangelism* is derived from the Greek word *euangelizomai,* generally translated "to announce good news." The term *apologetics* is derived from the Greek word *apologia,* which simply means to give a reasonable defense for your faith. Apologetics is the partner

---

6. Martin, *The Kingdom of the Cults,* 480.

of evangelism; it is the defense of the faith in order to secure its *survival* so that it may proclaim the good news of Christ. The defense of the faith is something meant to help, not harm, the process of evangelism. The apostle Peter spelled it out in terms that very few people can misunderstand, if they are willing to listen to him. "But sanctify the Lord God in your hearts, and always be ready to give a defense to everyone who asks you a reason for the hope that is in you, with meekness and fear" (1 Peter 3:15). Evangelism and apologetics are inseparable—for hope is bound to reason, and reason to hope.

But in the last days, we see all around us the defense of the faith sacrificed on the altar of ego. They are here; we are living in them right now. "For men will be lovers of themselves, lovers of money, boasters, proud, blasphemers, disobedient to parents, unthankful, unholy, unloving, unforgiving, slanderers, without self-control, brutal, despisers of good, traitors, headstrong, haughty, lovers of pleasure rather than lovers of God, having a form of godliness but denying its power. And from such people turn away" (2 Tim. 3:2–5). This is the exterior of religiosity—people whose lives are living contradictions. Religion surrounds us on every side, but there is a vast difference between religion and a true experience grounded in revelation. The latter produces *eternal* fruit, staunch proclaimers of the Word and defenders of the faith.

Today, the Church knows what we believe, but quite frequently we do not know *why*—and *why* is what the world wants to know. This is a tremendously important point. The world wants to know if what you believe is something passed on to you by relatives or friends. Have you ever accepted something without examining it? The world does not want the faith of your relatives; they do not want the faith of your friends. They do not want the faith of your pastor. They want to know what *you* believe. And you may say, "Well, I have had an experience with Jesus Christ. He came into my life, and He touched me. I was into drugs, I was into alcohol, I was into sex, and Jesus came and He delivered me. Hallelujah! I want you to have the same experience." And the fellow with a shaven head and a saffron robe looks at us as he hops up and down chanting, "Hare Krishna, Hare Krishna. I want to tell you what Hare Krishna did for me. I was into drugs, I was into sex, I had an experience with Hare Krishna, and now my whole life has been changed!"

Do you see what has happened? You rested your case upon experiential reasoning, and it will disintegrate on experiential reasoning alone. Christianity rests upon objective, demonstrable, *empirical* authority; if it is not there, you are finished. This is precisely what we face today. It does no good to share an experience with someone unless that experience is grounded in the historicity of the person of the risen Christ. You had better know how to move in the direction of demonstrating these things, because without it, you will not communicate.

CASE STUDY

Walter Martin

A few years ago, I was flying back from Miami Beach, and my assigned seat placed me next to a very nice, elderly gentleman. At the time I remember thinking, *This fellow won't bother me too much.* I wasn't thinking about a single thing except resting. I settled into my seat and after a few minutes, I began to notice this fellow was terribly tense. He told me he hadn't flown very much, and this poor guy was trying to explain his fears to me. He turned out to be a medical doctor—afraid of flying! So I decided I'd take ten minutes before going to sleep, and set his mind at ease.

I described the safety features of the plane; I told him all the positive aspects of it—it was the Norman Vincent Peale approach to aerodynamics—the power of positive flight. After we finished discussing it, he said, "I am very grateful sir. Thank you so much."

I leaned back in my seat, ready to go to sleep, but he wanted to talk a bit more. So we started talking again, and he turned out to be a semi-retired Jewish doctor, living in New York, and commuting to his vacation home in Florida.

He finally asked me, "What do you do for a living?"

I said, "I am a minister."

"Oh!" he said, "I want to ask you some questions." That was the end of my sleep. "Why is the world in such terrible condition today? I see it all the time in my practice. People aren't people anymore; they're animals!" And he went on to give me a bird's eye view of the Bronx, and what his life was like.

I listened for a few minutes, then said, "Doc, I agree with you 100 percent. I'm a Brooklyn boy myself. I know what it's all about; I've been there, and it's miserable. I agree with you—the world is going to hell on a down-hill pull."

He said, "Yes, but *why?*"

I replied, "You wouldn't believe it if I told you."

"I want to know!" he insisted. "Someone has to tell me. I don't know what's going on anymore."

I said, "All right, let me tell you. There's a little three-letter word called *sin,* and it has infected the human race. You are capable of diagnosing it, but you are not capable of treating it."

"Oh," he replied.

I went into the Scriptures: the prophecies of the Old Testament and the Messianic teachings. We looked at verse after verse, line upon line, precept after precept.

"You're trying to convert me," he said.

"You've got the message!" I smiled.

"I never talked to anybody like you before."

"Cheer up!" I said, "There are a lot more where I came from. Do you want to know the answer to all of this? Christ is *your* answer to *your* problems."

I started telling this doctor about Christ: how He could change his life, and what the gospel had to say. I talked about prophecy and the restoration of Israel, about biblical archaeological facts and data. I drew on all my memory banks for the last twenty years, and I let him have it broadside. I figured I only had him for two hours. I had to give him everything I had in two hours.

Our dinner arrived, and he ate without ever taking his eyes off me—he could barely get his food down he was asking me so many questions.

Finally, he said, "Listen, you know what they call the route you're talking about in the synagogue?"

"What?" I asked.

"The chicken route. If I go the Jesus route, it's the chicken route. I'm chickening out—but I want to ask you a question."

"What is it?"

He said, "You really believe this, don't you?"

I said, "I believe it because I believe Moses and the Prophets. Don't you?"

"Yes!"

"Then you must believe Jesus is the Christ. Who is Isaiah 53 talking about?" And I read it to him.

"That sounds like Jesus," he said.

"You've got it right, Doc! It's not chicken to come to Jesus. It takes a lot of courage."

I told him about a friend of mine who was a rabbi. He founded the Hebrew Christian Fellowship in Baltimore, Maryland. He had a successful medical practice as a podiatrist, a lovely wife, a closet full of clothes, a beautiful apartment, and a good job in the synagogue. One day, he was reading Isaiah 53 in the Hebrew, and the Holy Spirit tapped him on the shoulder and said, "Over here, Stupid." (That's the way he tells it.)

He read Isaiah and said, "Who is this?"

The Spirit spoke to him, "It is Jesus Christ!"

My friend, Jack Buckler, got down on his knees in that moment and received Jesus Christ as his Savior. There were no evangelists to be found— it was the power of the Word of God! The Word of the Lord cut through him like a sword and he came to Christ.

He went home to his wife and told her, "I have the most wonderful news for you. I found the Messiah!"

She said, "You're crazy, Jack!" and divorced him.

They kicked him out of the synagogue. His podiatrist practice was 97 percent Jewish, so naturally, that disappeared. They held a funeral for him.

He lost everything.

He said "I count it all dung." And he went to seminary and graduated two years later.

He began preaching in Hebrew and Yiddish in Baltimore, and built one of the greatest congregations Baltimore ever saw—out of the *synagogue* there. He would go to the synagogue and talk to people about Jesus Christ. They threw him down the steps a couple of times but he always said, "As long as I can get up and walk, I'll tell them about Christ."

Jack was obsessed with the person of the Master. He had found Him of whom Moses, the Law, and the Prophets had written.

This Jewish doctor looked at me for a minute and said, "He had guts!"

I said, "You're right. How much have you got?"

"You don't know what they'll do to me. You don't know what they'll say to me."

I said, "If Jesus of Nazareth is the Messiah of God, He is worth it."

He said, "You're right. If He is the Messiah, it is worth anything."

"He is the Messiah, and He is worth it."

I gave him my card before we left, and he said, "You don't give up, do you?"

"No, I don't give up. I love you for the sake of Jesus Christ. It is because you rejected your Messiah that I, a gentile, have come to life in Christ. I want you to know the same life."

He said, "I will think about it."

"Pray about it!" I said.

"I will pray about it," he smiled.

This is a classic illustration of the hunger of the world. Here is a professional man who has seen life and death up close, and he *knows* there is more to it than red and white corpuscles, hemoglobin, and the beat of the heart. There is something in man that animates him, and this man was hungry to find out what it was all about.

We have something powerful in our favor when it comes to apologetics. God has inscribed two things on the nature of man that cannot be erased: the knowledge of His existence and the certainty of His judgment (Rom. 1). Those two things can never be eradicated, so they can be appealed to, and people respond to them.

CRISIS IN THE CHURCH

The current crisis in the Church exists today for two basic reasons: first, a segment of Christians have attempted to divorce themselves from apologetics and elevate the more lucrative philosophy of evangelism far above it—when in reality these two ministries (not philosophies) are inextricably intertwined. It seems the distorted perception is that evangelism produces financial gain, and apologetics engenders financial loss.

The reverence for God and the defense of His name now take second place to the frenzy of evangelism. Numbers mean money—always a tempting goal—and the megachurch, seeker-sensitive, emergent philosophy has infected Christian leadership to the point where reverence for God now takes second place to the entertainment antics designed to draw a money-producing crowd. "The fear of the LORD is the beginning of wisdom" (Prov. 9:10), but that fear is missing in many churches today—and so is the wisdom. Where is the fear of God? Where is the humility in His holy presence? And if the kingdom of God is not sacred, then why bother to defend it at all? The end result of the seeker-sensitive movement is the *rejection* of the defense of the faith, discarded by thousands of Christians as confrontational and divisive. In the end, megachurches produce five morning services, ten thousand fringe participants, and very few *disciples* of Jesus Christ. The rush to the bank has dumped discipleship by the suburban wayside. Rev. Bill Hull presents a fresh perspective on this crisis in his work, *New Century Disciplemaking*

> God's primary plan for the Church is for disciples of Jesus to develop other men and women into disciples!
>
> There is probably no other primary matter of negligence in the Church today than our failure to follow the Lord's command to develop disciples. Because of this gross neglect, many Christians think of themselves as an audience to be entertained rather than an army ready to march. The first century Church, composed of a tiny band of committed people, brought the mighty Roman world to its knees. In the twentieth century, however, it often seems that we who are many in the Church have allowed the worldly culture to disciple us into its way of thinking.[7]

Evangelism as a means to a financial end produces temporary fruit and the elevation of man. Disciplemaking as a result of obedience to God produces eternal fruit and the elevation of Jesus Christ.

---

7. Bill Hull, *New Century Disciplemaking: Applying Jesus' Ideas for the Future* (Grand Rapids: Revell, 2000), 10.

A second but no less important reason for the current crisis is the specter of *culture,* rising like the phantom of political correctness to become a guiding force for some former staunch defenders of the faith. Christian apologetics has split into two distinct camps: *biblical apologetics* and *cultural apologetics.* Biblical apologists pair tact and sensitivity with the truth of the gospel, regardless of whether that truth will offend; cultural apologists pair tact and sensitivity with the spirit of this age— *tolerance.* They absorb this spirit and apply it to the defense of the faith so that biblical truth is now *subject* to cultural sensitivity. If it will offend, *do not say it.* Worse than this, they ally themselves with the enemies of Jesus Christ in a misguided attempt to persuade them without ever offending them. "Missionary dating" has now infiltrated the defense of the faith.

For example, let's say you are sharing your faith with a Mormon, and he tells you his young Mormon wife died in childbirth. He asks if he will see her again if he accepts the Jesus you are preaching. As an apologist, what do you say?

A *biblical apologist* expresses genuine sorrow at this man's terrible loss, and then tells him the truth—there is a difference between Joseph Smith's Jesus and the Jesus of the Bible. This difference impacts eternity.

The *cultural apologist* expresses genuine sorrow and then *avoids* the truth in order to be culturally sensitive to this Mormon's feelings about Joseph Smith, his religious leader. He uses *the only time he will ever have to speak to this man on earth* to reassure him that he might see his wife again someday.[8]

Cultural apologists reason that if the gospel is not culturally sensitive, it will not persuade. They argue that the gospel of Jesus Christ can be presented in an appealing way. It is here that error is born and grows at a rapid pace, for Jesus Christ said He did not come to bring peace, but a sword. "Do not think that I came to bring peace on earth. I did not come to bring peace but a sword. For I have come to 'set a man against his father, a daughter against her mother, and a daughter-in-law against her mother-in-law'; and 'a man's enemies will be those of his own household'" (Matt. 10:34–36). Not only does Scripture contradict this error in the logic of cultural apologists, but it has been refuted by two thousand years of Church history. The great Church fathers did not mince words, and many came to a saving knowledge of Christ. The gospel of Jesus Christ is offensive to the world. Biblical

---

8. Based on an actual encounter between a respected Christian apologist and a young Mormon.

apologetics, by its very nature, is offensive. Cultural sensitivity can be a considera-tion in outreach, but it should never be the guiding force behind it.

The Church stepped off the path of biblical evangelism the minute it con-demned biblical apologetics in favor of the spirit of tolerance so prevalent in the occult: *the spirit of this age.* We are not in the world for a popularity contest: we are in the world to bring men and women to Christ. But if the Church does not rec-ognize the fact that attendance *numbers* are meaningless without true commitment and spiritual growth, it will have no line of defense before the inevitable assault of the kingdom of the occult. The seeker-sensitive philosophy is just that—a philoso-phy, not a ministry. It stifles personal growth and maturity by condemning the earnest defense of the faith, offering a lifetime of kindergarten to a Church fight-ing for its very existence.

Christians must accept the unpalatable truth that we will never be able to please everyone. The great error of the seeker-sensitives and the cultural apologists is this invasive attitude of *appeasement.* The attempted divorce of evangelism from its apologetics counterpart has orchestrated a disaster of epic proportions. Suddenly, *numbers* have become synonymous with *success,* and anything controversial is suspect and divisive. Pleasing people is the name of the game—no matter what the cost.

Scripture instructs us to run from the numbers game; it warns us that pleasing man is impossible. The Word of God tells the Church that there are people who are always learning and never able to come to knowledge of the truth (2 Tim. 3:7). Some people will never believe, no matter what we do. Coffee shops in the lobbies may lure them to your church, and financial planning sermons may intrigue them—but in the end, they will not listen, so stop trying to please the world. If they would not believe Jesus Christ, if they would not believe John the Baptist, if they would not believe the prophets, they certainly will not believe you. You cannot please everyone. John the Baptist came neither eating nor drinking and they said, "He is a lunatic!" Jesus came eating and drinking and they said "He is possessed by the devil" (Matt. 11:18–19). John could not please them by abstinence, and Jesus could not please them by participation. You and I are not going to please them either way.

THE MARRIAGE OF EVANGELISM AND APOLOGETICS

A passage of Scripture that illustrates the ideal melding of evangelism and apolo-getics is Acts 17:16. When Paul appeared in Athens, he was appalled to see the city given over to idolatry. The Bible says "his spirit was provoked within him."[9] The apostle was provoked in his spirit when he saw evil openly displayed.

What is the reaction of *your* spirit in the presence of evil? Does it provoke you?

If the Church stands in the presence of evil and accommodates it, if it has no sense of provocation to stand up and say, "This is not the truth!" then how much zeal for evangelism truly exists? The Scripture instructs us to *abhor* what is evil and cleave tenaciously to what is good (Rom. 12:9). How can you cleave tenaciously to good without a corresponding abhorrence for evil? Paul was provoked by what he saw, and he acted upon it. Paul *disputed* in the synagogue with the Jews, and in the marketplace with the devout, every single day. The Greek word translated "dispute" is *dielégeto,* meaning "to strongly argue." Paul argued the truth of the gospel right in the middle of the marketplace of Athens. What was his reaction to provocation? He was compelled to go out and tell them the truth.

Paul practiced evangelism *at the same time* he offered an apologetic dialogue. This is an important biblical point. He must have been successful in his argument, since the philosophers, the Epicureans, the Stoics, and all the rest of the people surrounded him and tried to silence him. They made fun of him—a man who was a student of Gamaliel and a master of philosophy himself—but Paul did not flaunt his credentials. He simply declared his case and answered their questions. They finally were forced to take him to Areopagus, which was the Greek Supreme Court, in order to determine the validity of his words and his right to speak them.[10]

Paul would never have made it to Areopagus, and he would never have preached on Mars Hill, and we would have no Acts 17 at all, if Paul had not *first* become provoked in his spirit to go out into the marketplace and dispute for the gospel. He got to Mars Hill by standing up for Jesus, and I do not mean singing the song—I mean *living* it. When he got there, he stood in the midst of Mars Hill and evangelized.

---

9. The Greek word is *parooxúneto,* meaning "provoked."
10. Areo-pagus or *Hill of Mars*—"The Areopagus was a hill not far from the Acropolis, already described, where the supreme court of justice was held; one of the most sacred and reputable courts that had ever existed in the Gentile world. . . . The justice administered in this court was so strict and impartial, that, it was generally allowed, both the plaintiff and defendant departed satisfied with the decision. "Innocence, when summoned before it, appeared without apprehension; and the guilty, convicted and condemned, retired without daring to murmur." *(Clarke's Commentary)*

Evangelism and apologetics come together biblically in this clear illustration taken from the life of the apostle Paul. Paul stood on Mars Hill and told the world, both ancient and modern, that the God who made the world—and all the things within it—is the Lord of heaven and earth who does not dwell in temples made by hands. Here is the heart of evangelism: the only living and true God. The presence of apologetics is revealed in the same verse. Paul said there that God does not live in temples, and he was directly referring to the temples that lined the hillside. He told anyone who would listen that they wasted their time building them, because there is only one true and living God. He then pointed to an altar engraved with the words "TO THE UNKNOWN GOD" (Acts 17:23), and told them he (Paul) was God's *personal representative* sent to proclaim everything He wanted them to know. "God, who made the world and everything in it, since He is Lord of heaven and earth, does not dwell in temples made with hands. Nor is He worshiped with men's hands, as though He needed anything, since He gives to all life, breath, and all things" (Acts 17:24–25). Paul argued for the truth, and this argument opened the door to evangelism.

Paul displayed tact in his evangelism, commending the people for being religious so they could not assault him for being unkind, and yet *in the same breath* he cut out the foundations of all their temples by saying the living and true God does not live in houses. He is the Creator of the universe. Finally, Paul went on to describe point by point the gospel of Jesus Christ. He said that God has not abandoned mankind, and that He gives life and health to all things (Acts 17:25). He then went on to say that God has placed us here that we should seek after Him, feel for Him, and find Him. The word *feel* in the Greek is *pseelafeéseian*, meaning "to grope"; we are blind men groping around in the darkness, trying to find Him. The good news is that He is not far from us.

A REASON FOR THE HOPE

The wonder of Christian evangelism is that God has blessed us despite our ignorance, certainly not because of it. Christians have a tremendous opportunity today to do *something*, because the world is hungry. There is a vacuum of the spirit—a great emptiness—and people are looking for something to fill it. If they do not find Jesus Christ in terms that are meaningful to them, if you and I cannot communicate, then it will be filled by the cults and the occult so that the last estate of a man is worse than the first.

In the face of this direct attack against biblical truth, Christians must be ready to present *reasons* for faith. The problem is spread out before the Church in terms that we cannot fail to grasp. We must know more than just *what* we believe; we must have reasons for faith. Why does Christianity stand out among all the religions of mankind? The answer to this is vital, and it must be successfully communicated to others. Exactly *why* do we believe what we believe?

History reveals that in two very important aspects, Christianity stood apart from every known religion: the *salvation of mankind* and the *revolutionary doctrine of unconditional love.* Historian Michael Grant noted that Christianity, from its very conception, was unique among religions of the Roman Empire: "This transcendent doctrine of redemptive suffering—of life given to man originally, lost by man, and restored to him by the Redemption—was a concept unknown to the Pagan Mysteries."[11] Also unknown in the Roman Empire was the concept of selfless, unconditional love; love that extended to all human beings, regardless of sex, age, social status, or race. It was a revolutionary idea: a love that embraced everyone, even those rejected by society.

And then there was the promise of eternal life offered by Jesus Christ: a gift that was vibrantly alive and full of promise—everlasting paradise with God. It was a type of eternal life that had never been available to mankind, and Christ was the only one who could provide it. "The Savior, too, was no created being endowed with human shape as intermediary between God and man, but God himself incarnate in man."[12] Christ offered the people of the Roman Empire something they simply could not find anywhere else—a promise of love, redemption, resurrection, and eternal life in a paradise far beyond anything they could ever imagine. This promise endures to the present day, and it is the foundation of evangelism and apologetics.

Study to Show Yourself Approved

When you proclaim Jesus Christ as Lord, the next thing that happens to you after a discussion of John 3:16, Acts 16:31, and the four spiritual laws (and whatever else

11. Grant, *The World of Rome,* 209.
12. Ibid. For more details on the Savior myth, see chapter 4, "Ancient Paganism."

you can lay your hands on) is the challenge, "But what about cultural relativism?" And the average Christian says, "Cultural *what?*" Cultural relativism teaches that individual societies should not be judged by a single standard. In other words, there are no absolutes. What is right for the pygmies of Africa may not be correct for Europeans. The great fallacy in these philosophies is that they transform Hitler from a cold-blooded killer to a man simply living by the standards of his people group, the Nazis. This is an argument Christians must be prepared to answer, and the answer is only found through study.

The Bible commands us to give a reason for the hope that lies within us (1 Peter 3:15). Scripture must be studied, and authoritative sources *outside* of the Bible must be studied if we are ever to provide the answers people so desperately need. "Be diligent to present yourself approved to God, a worker who does not need to be ashamed, rightly dividing the word of truth" (2 Tim. 2:15).

The apostle Paul, trained under Gamaliel, emphasized his education and was not averse to quoting academic sources to make a point (Acts 17:28). Christians will never acquire an education by osmosis. There is no shortcut for study—you must acquire *discipline* in order to be able to communicate with an undisciplined and rebellious age. If you do not have the kind of discipline that drives you to study, to work, and to doggedly pursue the answers so that you do not rest until you find them, you will not successfully communicate.

The modern age is a scientifically oriented society, and the name of the game is factual, empirical data. The only way to get through to these people is to provide them with evidence—facts and information—to point out reasonable things that will cause them to stop and think. Remember, if a person gets a little shock therapy and takes a moment to stop and think, you have a great opportunity to communicate. God honors you when you boldly stand up for the gospel.

Put on the Whole Armor of God

Pray before you communicate. Pray when you defend the faith. He who inspired Holy Scripture can illuminate your mind. He can give you the right words, the right context. You will be surprised what a great warrior the Holy Spirit is—just give Him the chance to make you into a warrior too: "For we do not wrestle against flesh and blood, but against principalities, against powers, against the rulers of the darkness of this age, against spiritual hosts of wickedness in the heavenly places"

(Eph. 6:12). In light of this biblical warning, the Church *must* prepare for spiritual warfare. "Put on the whole armor of God, that you may be able to stand against the wiles of the devil" (Eph. 6:11). The word is translated "wiles," but the Greek word is actually *methodeias*, meaning the methods of Satan. In this world, we encounter the methodical strategy of the devil, and we must be prepared to use the sword of the Spirit against him. The Scripture specifically commands us in numerous places that the gospel must be defended. The apostle Paul said, "I am appointed for the defense of the gospel" (Phil. 1:17). It is obvious that Paul was talking positively; it is not negative to defend the gospel.

CASE STUDY

Walter Martin

I will never forget my teacher, Dr. Donald Gray Barnhouse, told me of a luncheon he had with Norman Vincent Peale, who was then riding the crest of the wave on the power of positive thinking. Dr. Barnhouse chatted with him for a few minutes, and Dr. Peale said, "I would like a candid answer, Dr. Barnhouse. I know you will give me one. What do you really think of what I've written on the power of positive thought?"

Dr. Barnhouse said, "Well, I can only tell you what a great many clergymen have said to me."

"And what is that?" asked Dr. Peale.

Barnhouse replied, "Paul is appealing, but Peale is *appalling*."

Dr. Peale just stopped in the middle of his soup and said, *"What?"*

"You have forgotten the most important thing," Barnhouse continued, "Before anyone can think positively, they must think negatively."

"What do you mean?" asked Peale.

"Look," said Barnhouse, "I am a sinner—negative or positive?"

"Negative," said Peale.

"I am a lost sinner—negative or positive?"

"Negative."

"I am going to eternal judgment—negative or positive?"

"Negative," Peale repeated for the third time.

Barnhouse said, "Here are three negative propositions without which you *cannot* think positively. 'Believe on the Lord Jesus Christ and you will be saved' (Acts 16:31). But if you do not think the first three, you will never get to the fourth."

"I never thought of it that way before," Peale replied.

Dr. Barnhouse said, "You must write a new book: *The Power of Negative Thinking!*

"I couldn't do that—it would ruin me!" said Peale.

"Get out the truth," replied Dr. Barnhouse, "and the Lord will take care of it."

Peale never wrote the book, but he was told what he should do. The truth of the matter is this: whatever the cost, *tell the truth*. Speak the truth in love, but for the sake of Christ, we must speak it.[13]

Put Up a Stiff Fight

Another verse in the Bible that is greatly neglected in the ministry of evangelism is the third verse of Jude: "When I wrote to you brothers concerning the common salvation, it was necessary for me to urge you to put up a stiff fight for the faith, once for all, delivered to the saints." The Supreme Commander of the universe has ordered us to take up arms and *defend* the faith. It is no accident that the apostle Paul wrote, "Both in my chains and in the defense and confirmation of the gospel, you all are partakers with me of grace" (Phil. 1:7). He was talking about the defense of the gospel. Evangelism is not the only ministry the Church has been called to cultivate.

Today, Christians fight on two fronts: the battle against the kingdom of darkness and the battle against the forces of compromise within the Church. We have been sucked into tolerating a totally alien philosophy—the idea that it is positive only to *preach* Christ and negative to *defend* Him. That is simply not the truth. Jesus Christ not only preached and taught, but He entered into dialogue, confrontation, and disagreements with his enemies, and they regretted engaging Him in arguments. He encountered the scribes, Pharisees, Herodians, and the Sadducees, and He silenced them. The apostle Paul was a man who did not hesitate to go into the mar-

---

13. Walter R. Martin, *Evangelism and Apologetics* (CD/audiotape), Walter Martin Ministries, www.waltermartin.com.

ketplace of Athens and do battle for the Lord. He once said, "I wrestled with the beasts at Ephesus" (1 Cor. 15:32). In other words, he fought for the gospel.

We should never become belligerent in this fight. Contrary to the charges laid against us by the cultural apologists, the object is to argue boldly for the truth, not to alienate people—for the weapons of our warfare are spiritual. We should never attack people; we should attack spiritual error.

TECHNIQUES OF OCCULT EVANGELISM

In approaching the problem of occult evangelism, one central goal can never be forgotten: we are trying to reach the hearts of people. Close, personal, caring evangelism is a powerful force that will lead to the salvation of souls. There are Christians in the world today who cannot count even one non-Christian among their friends. How can we expect to influence people if we refuse to talk to them? The heart of evangelism and apologetics is *communication,* and it is impossible to communicate if you are miles away from the person you need to reach. You must first make the effort to get to know someone, and then share your worldview from the context of caring.

In dealing with occult beliefs, it is important to remember that some people acknowledge a need for a type of salvation, and some do not. Those who do are involved in their respective systems of theology, dependent upon forms, ceremonies, rituals, good works, right living, or self-sacrifice as a means of obtaining whatever justification they may feel is necessary. It is completely subjective, with an absence of absolute truth, and an eternity dependent upon individual efforts. Fundamentally, then, occult theology is a form of *self-salvation.*

The Christian must point out, from Scripture and from history, the danger of the loss of absolute truth and the weakness of human effort as a means to obtaining spiritual redemption. We should always remember that repentance, atonement, regeneration, resurrection, and retribution in the biblical sense is seldom part of the vocabulary of someone lost in the occult, and *never* part of his personal experience. The Christian must *define, apply,* and *defend* the historical meanings of these terms before it is possible to effectively proclaim the gospel. In a word, one must begin at the beginning, repeat, emphasize, and repeat. This is the sowing of seed that one day, by God's grace alone, will bear fruit to eternal life.[14]

---

14. Adapted from Martin, *The Kingdom of the Cults,* 486–487.

FIND A COMMON GROUND

The importance of a common ground cannot be overemphasized. The agreement that Jesus is a great teacher can become the common ground that leads to a debate over *why* He is the greatest of all teachers, and much more. Your argument should always support your points, and there is never any room for *ad hominem* or personal attacks. As writer Kathy Duffin points out, Argument 101 requires reason. "Argument implies tension but not combative fireworks. This tension comes from the fundamental asymmetry between the one who wishes to persuade and those who must be persuaded. The common ground they share is reason. Your objective is to make a case so that any reasonable person would be convinced of the reasonableness of your thesis."[15] The common ground of reason itself is a powerful arena.

You will encounter antagonism, but it is not toward you personally; the antagonism is toward what you are saying. The hatred is not for you; it is for the gospel. If you are the ambassador for Christ, you present your credentials and search for a common ground of conversation. If someone throws your credentials back in your face, it is not your problem, it is his problem. You must tell that individual the truth.

Define and Apply Your Terms

Common ground offers Christians a chance to define terms and *apply* their theological and historical meanings, consistently, and repetitively. Whenever faith is shared, it is vital to define your terms and then repeat, emphasize, and repeat the definitions. In the occult perspective, God is cosmic oneness, Jesus is a great teacher, and evil is often nonexistent. If Christians do not discuss *definitions* before proceeding into the discussion of different worldviews, then they become the blind leading the blind.

In order to define your terms, you must know what you believe and why you believe it. Scripture should be at your fingertips, and you should be well aware of basic occult beliefs. The world of the occult is built on this foundation: *there is no single truth.* All truth is subject to personal experience, and there is no one reality. If reality is different for every person, how do you share your faith in Jesus Christ? Why is your faith more valid than any other?

---

15. Kathy Duffin, "Overview of the Academic Essay," Writing Center at Harvard University, http://www.fas.harvard.edu/~wricntr/documents/Overvu.html.

It is at this point that Christians can offer the truth of the *uniqueness* of Christ. Christ offered the people of the Roman Empire something they simply could not find anywhere else—and He offers the same hope today: a promise of love, redemption, resurrection, and eternal life in a paradise far beyond anything they could ever imagine.

The one great weakness of occult theology is this: it promises *nothing* to its followers after a lifetime of believing it. The best reward someone in the occult can hope for throughout eternity is to lose every unique thing he cherishes about himself in order to become one with the cosmic consciousness. This *oneness* means *nothingness;* individual personality vanishes in the final absorption. It is a troubling and frightening end to life as we know it, and cause for concern to those who commit their entire lives to this so-called path of love. In contrast, Jesus Christ cherishes us as His children. He created distinctive individuals and died to save them. In the respectful definition of terms and discussion of key differences, Christians will be able to communicate eternal truth.

Debate Key Issues

It is important to debate all kinds of people: occultists, atheists, agnostics, skeptics, New Agers—everything that pops up and challenges the gospel of Jesus Christ. If we do not confront them head-on, they will take our silence as a sign of agreement. Many Christians forget it is possible to offend God by doing absolutely nothing! It is called the sin of *omission.* Humans can go to hell as fast for this as for any sin of *commission* they might ever commit. God made it quite clear in Ezekiel 33–34 that if you are silent when you should speak, God will judge you for it. "When I say to the wicked, 'O wicked man, you shall surely die!' and you do not speak to warn the wicked from his way, that wicked man shall die in his iniquity; but his blood I will require at your hand" (Ezek. 33:8). Today, the Church is guilty of exactly that. Christian media is sinking into a sea of censorship where if you say something confrontational or controversial, everyone comes after you.

The answer to this is simple: do not sell out your integrity to anyone. If you avoid confrontation for the sake of communication, you have lost your integrity. The question remains, then: what price will you pay for that integrity? Controversial voices stir up interest. They get the adrenaline flowing and stimulate thought.

If you believe something is right, then say it or write it the way you believe it, and express it in such a way that people can understand it. Stand up for the cause of Christ, and do it in a spirit of Christian love, but for His sake, do not sell yourself out. If you do, you will not have anything to say to anyone that means *anything*. Shakespeare phrased it poetically: "This above all: to thine own self be true."[16] Stand by your convictions, and defend the faith against all comers.

SCRIPTURAL RESPONSE

The apostle Paul's approach to communicating the gospel, known as Pauline methodology, is perfectly consistent with Christ and with all of New Testament teaching. Paul was incarnate love when he wrote to the Corinthians and told them how he cared for them, and how they should live. But he did not hesitate, in the midst of his love, to rebuke them sharply for the evils and excesses they were practicing. He said, "This does not become saints." He loved them, but he told them the truth, and he did not have any inhibitions in doing it. He certainly was one of the most successful writers of all time. Christians can learn a great deal from his words.

In both evangelism and apologetics, you must communicate a biblical sense of selflessness. Paul did it. He said, "I took nothing from you. I did not exploit you. I did not try to get something out of you. I worked among you as a tentmaker; I paid my own way. All I want you to learn is that God wants you to follow *me* as an example of how you should treat each other. If you do not have any money at all, and you cannot work, the church should help you. But if you feel that you are too spiritual to work—so filled with the Holy Spirit that you remain unemployed and spend your time running around witnessing to everyone—living off the hard work of other people, you do not have any part in the Christian ministry. You are, in fact, a hindrance to it."[17]

Paul exemplified altruism. He outlined his perils, recalled his persecution, and shared his care of the churches. He told them what he went through to be a servant of God. He said, "You see, I have nothing to gain by all this" (See 2 Corinthians 11:22–12:1).

---

16. William Shakespeare, *Hamlet*, quoted in Literature Network, "Act 1, Scene III," http://www.online-literature.com/shakespeare/hamlet/4/.
17. For more on these teachings of Paul, see 1 Thessalonians 2 and 2 Corinthians 11.

We should not hesitate to become biographical and anecdotal in our witnessing and defense of the faith. Be very careful how you do it; season with salt, and sprinkle with humor. Do not be afraid to make a joke at your own expense, and let the people who are hearing and reading you understand that you do not take yourself too seriously. The only difference between you and them is that you happen to have the opportunity and the privilege of knowing Christ first, and they may come to know Him at a later date. Paul used his writings to communicate his altruistic spirit. If a person perceives that you have an ax to grind, you can forget the message. In that case, any intelligent person will not listen to you, and rightly so. And if people do listen to you, it is because they are not thinking. Donald Barnhouse once said, "Whenever two people think exactly alike, one of them is not thinking!"

Be *you*, and communicate what you have to say in your words. Incorporate concepts and documentation from other people into your approach. Do your homework, and express yourself; let it be you and not someone else. Your faith is *your* faith, not your father's or your mother's faith. The experiences you have are yours: the pain, the joy—whatever it is—it is yours! Show them you have walked the same path. Just because you are a Christian does not mean that you have not been down in the valley where they may be. Let them identify with you, and if your experiences are meaningful, spiritually uplifting, and edifying, then they will be blessed.

Finally, you must do something quite difficult. In confrontational speaking and writing you must learn to *do* what Paul said in practice—and there is a risk involved. *Reprove, rebuke, exhort.* "For the time will come when they will not endure sound doctrine, but according to their own desires, because they have itching ears, they will heap up for themselves teachers; and they will turn their ears away from the truth, and be turned aside to fables" (2 Tim. 4:3–4). What is Paul telling the Church? "I charge you therefore before God and the Lord Jesus Christ, who will judge the living and the dead at His appearing and His kingdom: Preach the word! Be ready in season and out of season. Convince, rebuke, exhort, with all longsuffering and teaching" (2 Tim. 4:1–2).

The choice you have is this: you can exhort people so that they pull out the torches, ready to burn you alive—or you can reprove, rebuke, and exhort them in a godly, love-centered way. If you choose this method, they will see you are teaching them something that can be beneficial to them because it has been beneficial to you. When Paul reproved, rebuked, and exhorted people, he always balanced it by emphasizing his concern for them, his motivation behind it. Spell out your motives. People do not automatically understand motivation. Temper clarity with patience, since some will only hear what they *want* to hear based on their own motivation. It is very important to check your facts and be honest in presenting *context*. If you practice this when you reprove, rebuke, and exhort, you will be doing it from a position of authority and love.

A good grounding in the Scriptures is fundamental so that you do not open your mouth to exchange feet. Always remember that someone listening to you will be influenced by what you say. If you are not careful, someday you may have your own words returned to you parboiled because you would not say it clearly enough or forcefully enough.

Tough love is telling people the truth. They may not like it, but you are telling them the truth. Jesus gave a magnificent example of tough love when He spoke to the woman at the well, as recorded in John 4. His approach to her was not to consider her an immoral woman, which she was. That was love. His approach was "I am going to teach you something." He then led her into a dialogue and explained things to her. He answered her questions in a loving, patient way. And finally, He confronted her. He said very casually, "Go call your husband." What could be more disarming than that? He was being nice to her.

She said, "I do not have a husband."

And Jesus answered, "Now, we have arrived at the core of the matter. You have had *five* husbands, and the one you have now is not your husband. In that, you have told the truth." That poor woman did not know what to say. "We know that when the Messiah comes, He will tell us everything." Here is confrontation for you: "I who speak to you am He!" And she ran to town and came back with a mob of people.

Jesus is the perfect illustration of love that can be tough. Right in the middle of their conversation, He stopped her cold. When you share Jesus Christ and defend Him, you must give people a reason for why they should believe you. Your words and actions should show that you have done your homework. You must be articulate and expressive, and communicate your convictions. People will respect you if *you* have that kind of respect for yourself, and even though they may not like you or even like what you say or write, they will listen to you.

CASE STUDY

Walter Martin

I experienced the truth of this firsthand, when I tried to have my book *Jehovah the Watchtower* published. It was the first in-depth book ever written on Jehovah's Witnesses dealing with their history, their theology, and key answers to their arguments. I finished the work when I was a junior in college, and then made the rounds trying to get it published for three years. Christian publisher after Christian publisher, fearless in their approach to the defense of Christianity, all said the same thing to me, "It is too controversial."

One publisher, I will never forget, had a big sign over his door. It said, "If God is your partner, make your plans big."

He told me, "I cannot print your book because it might upset someone."

I said, "God is not your partner. He's mine, but He isn't yours. You will not come out in the open. You will not say the truth."

He said, "Well, people would not buy it."

Jehovah of the Watchtower just passed its twenty-fifth year in print, thank God, and it has been translated into many languages. It is still being used. And every once in a while, I sit back and think I ought to send this publisher a card that says: "Surprise! Silver anniversary!"

In the end, I went to Wilbur Smith to ask for his help in publishing my book. He'd already read the manuscript and was waiting to talk to me about how we needed to get this in print right away. He put up his own money and was willing to spend five hundred dollars, a considerable amount of money at the time. Robert Van Kampen had the courage to publish it through Van Kampen Press. It was then picked up by Zondervan and Bethany, and the rest of it is history.

The good news here is this: there *are* men of courage who see confrontation as a command from God. They were my mentors—Wilbur M. Smith, professor of English Bible at Fuller Theological Seminary; Frank Gaebelein of Stonybrook School; and Donald Gray Barnhouse, my teacher. All of them taught me the same principle: say it articulately, say it forcefully, but *say it*. Do not sit on it—say it.

Wilbur Smith said, "We have to speak!" Therefore, *stand*.

Do not change your thoughts to meet anyone else's thoughts or you will lose your integrity. What price will you pay for that integrity? You have a right to your own thoughts and the expression of them. Never change what you said under pressure or you will lose *you*, and that is the only thing you have. Your words are you, unless they are dollar signs. If you are writing for dollar signs, you do not have any place in the defense of the faith.[18]

CONCLUSION

The motivation of the Church must always be to get to people, confront them, and give them the facts. The Holy Spirit must breathe on your communication. He has to breathe through you and in you; He has to help you. Remember this—anything the Holy Spirit did two thousand years ago, He can do today, because He is God, the Holy Spirit!

The most important thing in the world is the communication of the ultimate truth that Christ died for the ungodly. He rose from the dead, He ascended into heaven, and He will come again. Salvation is by grace through faith. That is the message of the gospel: the unchanging, infallible Word.

In dealing with religions steeped in the occult, Christians ought to have a working knowledge of what the doctrines of these religions are in relation to the historical Christian revelation. It is foolish to attempt to discuss Christian doctrines with those who do not accept the authority of the Scriptures. At the same time, evangelism aimed at the realm of the occult must never fail to emphasize that Christ and the disciples taught certain irrevocable doctrines as well as consistent ethics and morality.[19]

Knowledge is power, but when you evangelize and defend the faith, you must also communicate your concern; you must show your love. It should be translated into *daily life*. This is what the Church desperately needs! We have the sound doctrine, but love is the translation of doctrine into experience—and if love is not there, why should anyone believe your doctrine? If you do not love as Christ said,

18. Walter R. Martin, *Advice to Writers* (CD/audiotape), Walter Martin Ministries, www.walter martin.com.
19. Martin, *The Kingdom of the Cults*, 491.

what difference does it make if you understand the Trinity, the deity of Christ, the virgin birth, the atonement, the resurrection, the Second Coming? That is all straw compared to the essence of the Incarnation—God appearing in human flesh. He makes all the rest alive, meaningful, and true. It becomes straw when it becomes everything to you. You must show people that you are sound in what you believe, and you love the person you are trying to reach. Otherwise, why should people believe you? I would not believe me, apart from divine love.

Do what Paul did: encourage your listeners without insulting their intelligence. Love them, and let them see the real you. "What you see is what you get" should be our creed in terms of communication. We are not hiding things, and we do not have any hidden agenda. We are just out there to minister, and we want God to help us.

People will disagree with you, but your grounding in the Word of God and your knowledge of the subject will stand you in good stead. You should always know exactly what you are talking about. If anyone communicates a message from the perspective of *teacher*, he must know more than the people he's trying to reach. Research, study, and communicate with accuracy.

Finally, do not be afraid to resort to biblical sarcasm, when necessary. *Reproof* is a term you find all through Scripture. Jesus was a master at the turn of a phrase. He should be—He invented it. Jesus got into a conversation with the Pharisees, Sadducees, and the scribes, and they were not a friendly audience.

He told them, "Blind guides, who strain out a gnat and swallow a camel!" (Matt. 23:24). That was not only humor; that was sarcasm. The Pharisees strained out the gnats—tiny points of theology that meant nothing in the scheme of eternity—but they swallowed the camel of their own ignorance and blindness.

Or consider the account of Elijah on Mount Carmel. Few are able to read it in the Hebrew, but if you do, it is devastating. Elijah confronted the prophets of Baal and mocked them, saying, "Cry aloud, for he is a god; either he is meditating, or he is busy, or he is on a journey, or perhaps he is sleeping and must be awakened" (1 Kings 18:27).

This is sarcasm, pure and simple. And then Elijah called on the fire of God, and it burned everything, including the water and the rocks! He executed the prophets of Baal because they were devil worshipers. Elijah used pure sarcasm—for what purpose? Communication. He was doing it for the benefit of the Jews, not the prophets of Baal. He knew what was going to happen; God would answer, and they would die. He was, in essence, telling the Jews, "What are you afraid of? There is no Baal. There is no Pagan religion. There is only one God! I can say anything I want to say." And he proved it.

The apostle Paul became so sarcastic in 2 Corinthians 9–11 that it is hard to believe this is the same man speaking with such love in Philemon. When Paul talked about the false apostles misrepresenting themselves in the Church, he mocked them: "For you put up with fools gladly, since you yourselves are wise!" (2 Cor. 11:19). Reproof sometimes involves biblical principles, and Paul could say and do it in such a way that people learned from it. Sarcasm can sometimes teach something that will be received positively by people and foster maturity in their service to God.

There are times when you must say things that are difficult to say. Readers of Jonathan Edwards's sermon "Sinners in the Hands of an Angry God" know that he could never preach in the Crystal Cathedral today. Reproof is hard to take, but the person who turns away from reproof hardens his neck and should be cut off suddenly without remedy; he will not submit. In the days of the apostles, there were people exactly like this. They refused to believe in the resurrection of Jesus Christ, even though the evidence was all around them. Jesus was actually *there*, and it did not matter. This is why He said that some will not believe, even "though one rise from the dead" (Luke 16:31).

It is a hard grind to become productive and communicative in the midst of confrontation. It has to be done in the spirit of Christian love that is grounded in biblical authority. You must encourage people whenever necessary and emphasize that your motivation is altruistic. It is wise to give example after example. One good illustration is worth a thousand words.

And finally, you must be willing to use whatever tools are necessary to reprove, rebuke, and exhort those who will not listen, keeping in mind that it is God who will apply the truth to their hearts. You must exhort people to arrive at a biblically centered conclusion; something that can be practically utilized in their lives. Exhortation calls forth *action*.

In the words of perhaps the greatest illustrative Bible teacher in the history of the Church, Dr. Donald Barnhouse, "If you are ever going to be a success, get the hay down out of the loft, onto the barn floor, where the cows can get at it." Do not speak or write to impress people about yourself, your scholarship, and what you know. Lift up the Lord Jesus Christ, and let them see Him. That is all that is necessary to success. You must communicate who you are and what you believe, and put it in terms that a person can grasp, appreciate, apply, and use.

Today, young people around the world still ask for the same thing in multiple languages: "Tell me what life really means. I want to know. I don't want a lot of garbage; I want the real meat of it." They are searching for spiritual reality. It is at this juncture that the gospel of Jesus Christ stands ready where no other power on earth is ready, since Jesus is ultimate reality. He is not just one of many equally good ways, an aspect of the truth, or a fragment of the life. He is the way, the truth, and the life (John 14:6), and He will not share His glory or His authority with anyone. Men try to put Jesus on panels alongside Zoroaster, Confucius, and Muhammad—a nice little ecumenical homogenization where everyone agrees, out of the abundance of their ignorance, on *truth*. As the Creator of the universe, Savior, and Lord, Jesus Christ sits on no such panels.

Controversy for the sake of controversy is sin—controversy for the sake of truth is a divine command. Truth should hold forth. It should evoke response. It should be Christ-centered. It should be honoring to the Lord. It should be within the context of Christian morality and ethics, but it must include the capacity for tough love. It must include in it your personal willingness to be vulnerable and to let people know you as you truly are, not just as a name, a book, an article, or something else.

Hermeneutics is not a song or some crazy rock group brought in for special performances. It is knowledge, and knowledge is power. Ignorance is not bliss with eternity in the balance. So many people today are totally in conflict with the history of the Church primarily because they do not know what the history of the Church is! They teach heresy, blasphemy, evil, and error, and in the next breath sing, "All Hail the Power of Jesus' Name." This is the conflict. Informed Christians have a chance to do something about this if they see the issues and have a desire to communicate. It is vital to know what you believe and why you believe it, and then you must *tell people*.

Scripture teaches that the consummation of the ages is to be marked by specific events, and we are living in the acceleration of those events. There are many people who talk a great deal about how we are approaching the time of the end, when Jesus Christ will return to earth. It may come as a terrible shock to these people to find out that 1 John 2 reveals that we have been in the last days for almost two thousand years. They are not sneaking up on the Church right now; we are living in them—and the entire history of the Church has been *written in the last days* up until the present day.

Peter says that we are supposed to set apart the Lord God in our hearts and be ready always to give to everyone that asks of us an answer; a reason for the hope that lies within us (1 Peter 3:15). But the problem of the Church today in witnessing and communication is that we have forgotten that evangelism has as its natural adjunct, *apologetics.* Unless Christians embrace the defense of the faith as eagerly as they embrace its proclamation, there will be no one ready to guard against the attacks of the kingdom of the occult.

RECOMMENDED RESOURCES

1. Comfort, Ray. *Hell's Best Kept Secret.* New Kensington, PA: Whitaker, 2002.

2. DeWaay, Bob. *Redefining Christianity—Understanding the Purpose Driven Movement.* Springfield, MO: 21st Century Press, 2006, www.cicministry.org.

3. Green, Michael. *Evangelism in the Early Church.* Grand Rapids: Eerdmans, 2004.

4. Hull, Bill. *New Century Disciplemaking: Applying Jesus' Ideas for the Future.* Grand Rapids: Revell, 2000.

5. Litz, Dwayna. *Lighting the Way Worldwide,* www.lightingthewayworldwide. org/.

6. Martin, Walter. *The Spirit of the Age.* CD/audiotape, Walter Martin Ministries, www.waltermartin.com

Appendix A

Questions and Answers on the Occult

Walter Martin

Question #1: What should I do if I have a teacher in my school who is into the occult and gets kids at school to come to the séances she holds every Saturday night?

Answer: You should go to the school, with your parents and with a group of pastors from the community, and specifically point out that he or she is proselytizing for a religion. Witchcraft and Satanism are religions, and séances represent Spiritism, which is also a religion. I suggest that you react strongly—face it, and make no bones about it—and that will stop her from recruiting kids for her séances. The authorities must be made aware. This is a definite violation of Church and state; it simply has to be dealt with on that level. The reason why evil sometimes multiplies so successfully is because we don't do anything about it. So, get up and do something about it, and it will stop.

Question #2: If you are involved in the occult, will God accept you if you give it up?

Answer: Oh, most definitely. I was at Explo '72 and had a remarkable experience there.[1] A young man took me aside and said, "Man, I have got to tell you something."

I said, "What is it?"

He said, "It is all words. I can't get through to God; He won't listen to me. I can't get through." He sat down and started to cry. He was a handsome boy, and his whole

---

1. Called "the Jesus Woodstock" by *Time* magazine, Explo '72 was, "an International Student Congress on Evangelism" sponsored by Campus Crusade for Christ that drew seventy-five thousand people. For more information on Explo '72, see "The Jesus Woodstock," *Time*, June 26, 1972, http://www.time.com/time/magazine/article/0,9171,906107,00.html.

body just shook. There were about twenty or thirty kids sitting nearby praying for him the entire time I talked to him at the back of the tent. After a moment, I said to him, "Well, let's have a word of prayer, and we'll see what the Lord will do."

"I can't pray," he said.

The Lord spoke to my heart, and I said to him, "Then there's something wrong that you're not telling me; you don't want me to know. But if you don't come clean with God, you're not going to get anywhere."

He looked at me for a moment and just dissolved into tears again. "Yes," he said, "There is something. I was a Satan worshiper. I got mixed up with a girl, and she used sex to bring me into Satan worship. I was in it up to my eyeballs. Now I just can't pray; I can't use the name of Jesus. I don't know what to do—I can't talk to God!"

I said, "Well, if that's your only problem, it's solved."

"It is?"

"Of course, why didn't you tell me this at the beginning? Here's how we get rid of this in a minute. Bow your head and repeat after me: I renounce you, Satan, and all your works—all my pledges, all my sins and everything I've done wrong, in the name of Jesus Christ of Nazareth."

He slowly repeated it after me, and all of a sudden he cried, "Ohhhhhh!" and put his head down and started to cry even harder. He said, "I can pray!"

I said, "I know you can pray. How can you reach for God with one hand and hang on to the devil with the other? You can't do that; you've got to cut him loose and hang on to Jesus. Now, do you want to accept Jesus as your Savior?"

"Man, do I!"

"Good," I said. He got right down on his knees and gave his heart to Christ.

You see, people don't always tell the truth, and that's part of the problem we're dealing with in the occult. It is dangerous, but if you're willing to renounce evil, accept Christ, and commit to Him completely, God says He will wash you as white as snow. So, there is forgiveness and there is restoration. Satan has no power in the presence of Jesus Christ. Never forget that.

Listen—this is an important point—the demons are afraid of *you*; don't you be afraid of them. You are the temple of the living God, and you have within you the Spirit of God Himself. Whatever will defile the temple of God, God will destroy, says the apostle Paul (1 Cor. 3:17). They do not want any part of you; you are plain poison to them. They want the unbeliever, so do not be afraid of them, and do not go hunting them up either. There are enough of them around, but don't be afraid of them. "You are of God, little children, and have overcome them, because He who is in you is greater than he who is in the world" (1 John 4:4–5).

Question #3: Is the casting out of demons valid today?

Answer: It most certainly is valid, because they're still around. Don't go out of your way to hunt them up, and don't be afraid of them, but it is certainly a valid exercise today. I have practiced it myself.

Question #4: If we're not supposed to be afraid and we have more power than these demons, why was a young Christian girl just murdered by people involved in a satanic cult?

Answer: There is absolutely no guarantee in the Scripture that you or I will not be a martyr; we've certainly had all kinds of martyrs before us. The fear I'm talking about is the fear of spiritual possession, fear of demons being able to *do* something to you. The people that murdered the girl were not demons; human hands committed the act. We are not talking about that—human hands may well kill all of us, because there is no guarantee you and I will survive this earth. After all, our ancestors were all thrown to the lions, boiled in oil, and crucified upside down—so you hope to get to heaven on flowery beds of ease? No way! It may just happen that someone is going to come looking for us someday. There is no guarantee that you're going to get out of this world alive!

Question #5: Is it true that a Scientologist can create matter out of nothing?

Answer: If they were into the occult, they could do some peculiar things with matter, such as moving it, or possibly apportation. But to create matter? No, there is no evidence of that at all.

Question #6: Do demons speak through people at séances?

Answer: Yes, demons *do* speak through people. This can happen and does happen at séances when a person becomes possessed. The symptoms of demon possession often include the manifestation of different voices. They can also parallel a form of mental illness, so you must go beyond normal investigation. There are more activities of demonic nature abroad today on our campuses and throughout this world than anybody could ever dream up. I'm not telling you there's a devil under every chair or behind every post, but we must face the reality of their existence and deal with them.

Question #7: Is it possible to exorcise someone without their permission?

Answer: Absolutely. Acts 16 is a classic illustration. There was a young girl following the apostle Paul, and he turned around and exorcised the demon within her—without her permission. It can be done.

Question #8: Does demon possession cause some mental illnesses?

Answer: I have friends who are psychiatrists, and they think so. In fact, I have one psychologist I worked with here in Southern California who was present during an exorcism. He can testify that the symptoms were those of mental illness. It turned out that the girl was possessed by multiple demons.

Question #9: When demons are exorcised from a person in the name of Christ, are Christians in danger of being possessed by those demons?

Answer: There is not the slightest shred of biblical evidence that any believer can ever be possessed by demons; not the slightest. Some Christian writers today are doing a lot of harm by the things they're writing on this subject, but the word of God is flatly against this. The Holy Spirit lives within you; you are the temple of God. He is not going to share a duplex apartment with demons! The Scripture flatly contradicts this, and there is not a verse in the Bible that teaches it. It is inferential, it is argumentative, it is deductive, and it is drawn from what I like to call the great well of human experience.

For example, someone will come to me and say, "I know of a case . . . ," and they spin this tale for me. You can take all your cases and drop them in the garbage if they contradict Holy Scripture. The Bible judges all experience—never the reverse. Some people talk about examples of Christians being possessed by demons, but the Bible is absolutely opposed to the idea that you can be possessed by the devil. What an awful thing to tell Christians that, as representatives of Jesus Christ, they still have to worry for the rest of their lives that somehow or other, in the carrying on of their Christian ministry, Satan might possess *them*. What kind of theology is this? It is a theology of experience; it is not a theology of revelation. I am violently opposed to it, and the people who are writing on it most of the time are people who have not had training or experience. They've *heard* about it from someone else, and I'm suspicious of that.

Question #10: Can you sell your soul to the devil, and if so, is it possible for you to get it back again?

Answer: There is not a bit of evidence in the Bible that anyone ever sold their soul to the devil. You can *give* him your soul by worshiping him; you can ignore God's method of saving men—Jesus Christ's redemption—and lose your soul, but there is no evidence that Satan is in the pawn broker business. This makes a marvelous fiction theme in stories like *The Devil and Daniel Webster* and Faust's legendary struggles, but it is not a biblical theme at all, and I wouldn't waste time with it.

Question #11: In Matthew 16:22, Jesus rebuked Peter: "Get behind Me, Satan! You are an offense to Me, for you are not mindful of the things of God, but the things of men." Why did he rebuke Peter, and what does this mean?

Answer: Jesus revealed here that Satan is capable of communicating with our minds. Exactly how he puts some ideas into our heads, as in the case of Peter, we don't know. We do know that Satan is a spirit, and he communicates on a spiritual level. When Jesus said He was going to Jerusalem to die, Peter responded by saying, "Far be it from You, Lord; this shall not happen to You!" Jesus immediately recognized a different voice *behind* the voice of Peter. He did not say, "Get thee behind me, Peter." He said, "Get behind me, Satan!" This is a very important point. The origin of Peter's idea was a direct communication to the mind of Peter by Satan, and Jesus confirmed this by addressing Satan, not Peter. How did Peter receive that message? It was not audible. If Satan is a spirit, and he is, he must communicate on different levels than you and I communicate on as men. For example, if you blow a high-pitched whistle near a Doberman pinscher that has been trained by the army canine core, he will come to you either to lick your hand or take it off. The dog is trained by pitch.

I am convinced that Satan, as a spirit, communicates on the level of the spirit, and that the mind and the spirit are interlocked because man is a unit. He does not audibly whisper in our ear; his communications come on a plain higher than the natural senses. Just as the dog can hear the whistle that humans cannot hear, your spirit and your mind can hear satanic suggestions. Satan cannot read what is in your mind, but he can plant suggestions.

Therefore, when Jesus taught us to pray, He deliberately included the phrase, "Do not lead us into temptation, But deliver us from the evil one" (Matt. 6:13). This should be your constant prayer. If you don't pray the Lord's Prayer every day, you are neglecting your own defense. Deliver us from whom? The evil one! The Greek said the *evil one*. Jesus told you to pray to be delivered from Satan and from temptation. I pray that prayer every day.

Satan communicates on another level, so look out for it. Martin Luther once said, "I am not responsible for the birds that circle my head. I am only responsible for the ones that build their nest in my hair."[2] So if you have evil thoughts and desires, they may originate with your carnal nature, or Satan may make the appeal on another level. Be on guard for influences like this, and the next time something hits your mind or your spirit and you know that it is alien to your thinking, at that moment, say, "Lord Jesus, deliver me from this thing, from Satan, and from everything connected with him." I have done this, and it disappears as if it had never been there.

I am convinced that evil communicates with us every day of our lives. Remember the dog whistle—Satan is the source of a great many of our temptations. You may not audibly hear their suggestions, but they are there.

Question #12: Just as Hitler was equated with the devil as a personification of evil, do you think Communism is a personification of Satan?

Answer: I think that all of these things are anti-Christ. There is only one great Antichrist to come, but these are *anti-Christs*, and we should recognize them for what they are. Adolf Hitler certainly was possessed. His physicians' accounts of his life indicate he had every classic symptom of demon possession.

Joseph Stalin's daughter, Svetlana Alliluyeva, gives an account of his death that is particularly chilling. He had been in a coma and all at once, came totally out of it. "[He] cast a glance over everyone in the room. It was a terrible glance, insane or perhaps angry and full of the fear of death."[3]

---

2. Martin Luther, *Vitae Paltrum, Patrologia, Series Latina*, LXXIII, 940, *Logos.*
3. Svetlana Alliluyeva, *Twenty Letters to a Friend* (New York: HarperCollins, 1967), 10.

She said in that last moment her father regained consciousness, his whole face changed. That is one of the classic indications of demon possession—the person's countenance changes. It is a strange thing to see, and if you took a picture of them at that moment, you could not identify that person positively fifteen minutes later. If ever there was a case of possession, it was Stalin.

Question #13: Can the devil imitate speaking in tongues?

Answer: Most definitely. In fact, I have recorded cases of it. I have an instance of a girl in Florida in a dope addiction reclamation center—a Satan worshiper possessed by multiple demons. I insisted they tell us their names and how many there were, and we wrote them all down. Finally, to circumvent answering the questions, the demons began to speak in *multiple* languages! A person in the room with us recognized one of the languages. I told them to tell the demons in the name of Jesus Christ of Nazareth to speak English—and they did. The demons were exorcised, and today that girl is a born-again Christian.

Satan can imitate any of the gifts of the Holy Spirit. He would not be so busy counterfeiting the gift of tongues if the original did not exist today. Paul specifically says in Romans that the *gifts of grace* (charisma) and the calling of God are irrevocable. Anything God wants to do with the power of His Holy Spirit, God will do, but there is a danger in taking any one gift and making it a *test* of the presence of the Spirit. The gifts of the Spirit were given to unify and build up the Church, not to divide us. Therefore, let's be extremely careful. The apostle Paul warned not to prohibit speaking in tongues, but it must all be done decently and in order. People should not be considered second-class citizens in the Church of Jesus Christ because they do not have a specific gift or experience. That is a dangerous form of Phariseeism that must be immediately rebuked as divisive to the body of Christ.[4]

---

4. Walter R. Martin, *Questions and Answers from Walter Martin, Evangelism and Apologetics.* (CD/audiotape), available at Walter Martin Ministries, www.waltermartin.com. Walter Martin: "I have investigated the Charismatic movement for seven years and I know what is going through your mind. *Does he speak in tongues?! Is he one of them?!* OK, I am a charismatic Baptist—just like Calvin, Luther, Zwingli, Knox—all the reformers. I believe the gifts of the Spirit are here until Jesus Christ returns. I am a true Charismatic. I am not a Pentecostal Charismatic. I have never spoken in tongues but I am willing to receive from the Holy Spirit any gift He wants to give me, and anybody that is not, is an extremely foolish Christian." For more information on this see Walter R. Martin, *Charisma: Cultic, Occultic or Christian?* (CD/audiotape), available at www.waltermartin.com.

Appendix B

Counseling Assessment Sheet

1. Date:

2. Name of Person:

3. Name of Contact:

4. Location:

5. Phone Number:

6. E-mail:

7. Has this person been prayed for by a pastor or elders?

8. Is this person willing to seek Christian counseling?

9. What is his or her religious background?

10. Has a medical doctor made a diagnosis of mental illness?

11. Is this person currently seeing a physician or psychologist?

12. Is this person taking any prescription medications?

13. Has there been any kind of hallucinogenic drug use? If so, what drugs were used and when were they last taken?

14. Did this person ever seek alcohol or drug counseling?

15. Does he or she have a criminal record?

16. Has this person ever been involved in any occult activities? Has a relative or close friend been involved in the occult? If so, what and when?

17. What paranormal phenomena have been experienced and/or observed?

   _____   Strange lights in the room

   _____   Taps or banging on walls

   _____   Nightmares

   _____   Strange voices or visible presence

   _____   Cold spots and/or strange smells

   _____   Use of a previously unknown foreign language

   _____   Personality changes

   _____   Other

18. Is it still occurring? Frequency?

19. Does it seem to be centered on one particular person?

20. Has this person experienced a noticeable personality change (for example, hostile and/or threatening attitude including but not limited to foul insults or death threats)?

21. Has this person ever practiced self-mutilation or tried to commit suicide?

22. Does he or she have an obvious aversion to and/or contempt for God, Jesus, Christian family members, pastors, or friends?

23. Has this person ever requested an exorcism?

24. Will he or she be willing to participate in follow-up counseling if an exorcism is performed?

Bibliography

Abelson, J. *Jewish Mysticism*. New York: Dover, 2001.

Adare, Viscount. *Experiences in Spiritism with Mr. D. D. Home*. New York: Arno, 1976.

The Age. "Faith or Fad?" August 12, 2004, http://www.rickross.com/reference/kabbalah/kabbalah92.html.

Agrippa, Hienrich Cornelius. *Three Books of Occult Philosophy or Magic, Book Three — Ceremonial Magic*. London: Gregory Moule, 1651, http://www.esotericarchives.com/agrippa/agrippa3.htm.

Albanese, Catherine L. "Physic and Metaphysic in Nineteenth-Century America: Medical Sectarians and Religious Healing." *Church History* 55 (1986): 493–94.

Albig, William. *Public Opinion*. New York: McGraw-Hill, 1939.

Alliluyeva, Svetlana. *Twenty Letters to a Friend*. New York: HarperCollins, 1967.

Anderson, Kevin. *Report of the Board of Inquiry into Scientology*. Melbourne: Australia Parliament Government Printer, 1965.

Ankerberg, John and John Weldon. *The Encyclopedia of New Age Beliefs*. Portland: Harvest House, 1996.

Applewhite, Mark. "Son of Heaven's Gate Cult Leader Has the Answer." *Connection Magazine*, June 1998.

Aquino, Michael A. *The Temple of Set*. San Francisco: Xeper, 2006.

Arbatel of Magick. Translated by Robert Turner. London: 1655. Digitial edition, with foreword by Joseph H. Petersen (1997), http://www.esotericarchives.com/solomon/arbatel.htm.

Archer, Gleason. *A Survey of Old Testament Introduction*. Chicago: Moody Press, 1964.

Ashcroft-Nowicki, Dolores and J. H. Brennan. *Magical Use of Thought Forms: A Proven System of Mental and Spiritual Empowerment*. Woodbury, MN: Llewellyn, 2001.

Australian Family and Community Development Committee. *Inquiry into the Effects of Television and Multimedia on Children and Families* (East Melbourne, Victoria: Parliament of Victoria), chap. 3, "Television and Multimedia Violence," http://www.parliament.vic.gov.au/fcdc/PDF%20Files/TV%20&%20MM/3%20-%20Television%20and%20Multimedia%20Violence%20pg%2067-96.pdf.

Bach, Marcus. *They Have Found a Faith.* New York: Bobbs-Merrill, 1946.

Bahrani, Zainab. *The Graven Image: Representation in Babylonia and Assyria.* Philadelphia: University of Pennsylvania Press, 2003.

Bailey, Alice A. *The Externalisation of the Hierarchy.* New York: Lucis Trust, 1943.

———. *The Reappearance of the Christ.* New York: Lucis Trust, 1979.

———. *The Unfinished Autobiography.* New York: Lucis Trust, 1951.

Bair, Deirdre. *Jung: A Biography.* New York: Bay Back, 2003.

Balch, Robert W. "Waiting for the Ships: Disillusionment and the Revitalization of Faith in Bo and Peep's UFO Cult." In *The Gods Have Landed: New Religions from Other Planets.* Edited by James R. Lewis. Albany: SUNY, 1995, 141–42.

Barrett, Leonard E. *The Rastafarians.* Boston: Beacon, 1997.

Barton, Tamsyn. *Ancient Astrology.* London: Routledge, 1994.

Behar, Richard. "The Thriving Cult of Greed and Power." *Time,* May 6, 1991.

Benski, Claude, Dominique Caudron, Yves Galifret, Jean-Paul Krivine, Jean-Claude Pecker, Michel Rouzé, and Evry Schatzman. *The "Mars Effect," A French Test of Over 1,000 Sports Champions.* Buffalo, New York: Prometheus, 1996.

Berg, P. S. *The Essential Zohar.* New York: Harmony/Bell Tower, 2004.

———. *Immortality: The Inevitability of Eternal Life.* Los Angeles: Kabbalah, 2000.

———. *Wheels of a Soul: Reincarnation and Kabbalah.* Los Angeles: Kabbalah, 2005.

Berg, Yehuda. *The Power of Kabbalah.* New York: Kabbalah Centre International, 2004.

Berger, Helen A., ed. *Witchcraft and Magic: Contemporary North America.* Philadelphia: University of Pennsylvania Press, 2005.

Besant, Annie. *The Seven Principles of Man.* Point Loma, CA: Aryan Theosophical Press, 1907.

Betty, Stafford. "The Growing Evidence for Demonic Possession: What Should Psychiatry's Response Be?" *Journal of Religion and Health* 44 (2005): 13–30.

Bjornstad, James. *Twentieth Century Prophecy, Jeane Dixon, Edgar Cayce.* Minneapolis: Dimension Books, 1969.

Blakely, Thomas D., Walter E. A. van Beek, and Dennis L. Thomson, ed. *Religion in Africa.* London: James Curry, 1994.

Blavatsky, Helena P. *Isis Unveiled.* Vol. 2. New York: Theosophical Publishing, 1888.

———. *Secret Doctrine*. London: The Theosophical Society, 1893.

———. *Studies in Occultism*. Pasadena: Theosophical University Press, 1973.

Blot, Thomas. *The Man from Mars: His Morals, Politics, and Religion*. San Francisco, Bacon, 1891.

Bock, Barbara. "An Esoteric Babylonian Commentary Revisited," *The Journal of the American Oriental Society* 120 (2000).

Boeft, J. Den. *Calcidius on Demons*, W. J. Verdenius and J. C. M. Van Winden, eds. Vol. XXXIII. Leiden, the Netherlands: E. J. Brill, 1977.

Bok, Bart J., Lawrence E. Jerome. *Objections to Astrology*. Buffalo: Prometheus, 1975.

Bopp, Judie, Michel Bopp, Lee Brown, and Phil Lane Jr. *The Sacred Tree*. Twin Lakes, WI: Lotus Light Publications, 1985.

Boyce, Mary. "On Mithra's Part in Zoroastrianism." *Bulletin of the School of Oriental and African Studies, University of London* 32, no. 1. (1969): 10–34, http://links.jstor.org/sici?sici=0041-977X%281969%2932%3A1%3C10%3AOMPIZ%3E2.0.CO%3B2-A.

———. *Textual Sources for the Study of Zoroastrianism: Textual Sources for the Study of Religion*. Chicago: University of Chicago Press, 1984.

———. *Zoroastrians: Their Religious Beliefs and Practices*. London: Routledge, 1979.

Braden, Charles. *These Also Believe*. New York: Macmillan, 1949.

Branham, William. *Conduct, Order, Doctrine of the Church*. Jeffersonville, IN: Voice of God Recordings, 1991.

Bromiley, Geoffrey W., ed. *The International Standard Bible Encyclopedia*. Grand Rapids: Eerdmans, 1979.

Brown, Brian. *The Wisdom of the Egyptians*. New York: Brentano's, 1923, chap. 2, 43, http://www.sacred-texts.com/egy/woe/index.htm.

Bruce, Robert and C. E. Lindgren. *Astral Dynamics: A New Approach to Out-of-Body Experiences*. Charlottesville, VA: Hampton Roads, 1999.

Buck, Jirah Dewey. *Mystic Masonry*. Chicago: Regan Publishing Corporation, 1925.

Budge, E. A. Wallace. *Amulets and Talismans*. New York: University Books, 1961.

Carey, Benedict. "A Princeton Lab on ESP Plans to Close Its Doors," *New York Times*, February 10, 2007, http://www.nytimes.com/2007/02/10/science/10princeton.html?ex=1328763600&en=2f8f7bdba3ac59f1&ei=5090&partner=rssuserland&emc=rss.

The Catholic Encyclopedia. New York: The Encyclopedia Press. 1917.

Cavendish, Richard. ed., *Man, Myth and Magic.* New York: Marshall Cavendish Corporation, 1970.

Cayce, Edgar and Jeffrey Furst. *Edgar Cayce's Story of Jesus.* New York: Berkley, 1976.

Chopra, Deepak. *The Path to Love: Spiritual Strategies for Healing.* New York: Three Rivers Press, 1998.

Christensen, Duane L. *Word Biblical Commentary: Deuteronomy.* CD-ROM, Thomas Nelson, 2001.

Clark, Jerome. *The UFO Book: Encyclopedia of the Extraterrestrial.* New York: Visible Ink, 1998.

Clarke, Peter B., ed. *New Trends and Developments in African Religions.* Westport, CT: Greenwood, 1998.

Ching, Julia. *Chinese Religions.* London: Macmillan, 1993.

Clarke, Adam. *Clarke's Commentary.* Nashville: Abington, 1977.

Clement, Stephanie J. *What Astrology Can Do for You.* Woodbury, MN: Llewellyn Worldwide, 2004.

Comfort, Ray. *Hell's Best Kept Secret.* New Kensington, PA: Whitaker House, 2002.

"Confessions of a Psychic." *Psychology Today* (November/December 1994), http://psychologytoday.com/articles/pto-19941101-000020.html.

Cooper, John Charles. *Religion in the Age of Aquarius.* Philadelphia: Westminster, 1971.

Copans, Laurie. "Spell May Comprise Oldest Semitic Text." Associated Press. January 23, 2007, http://news.yahoo.com/s/ap/20070123/ap_on_sc/israel_ancient_spell_1.

Crawford, Michael and David Whitehead. *Archaic and Classical Greece: A Collection of Ancient Stories.* Cambridge: Cambridge University Press, 1983.

Creme, Benjamin. "The Christ Is Now Here," *Los Angeles Times*, April 25, 1982, 31; and *London Times*, April 25, 1982, 5.

———. *The Reappearance of the Christ and the Masters of Wisdom.* North Hollywood, CA: Tara Center, 1980.

Crowley, Aleister. *The Book of the Law.* Newburyport, MA: Wiser, 1997. Internet Sacred Text Archive, 2006. http://www.sacred-texts.com/oto/engccxx.htm.

———. *The Book of Thoth. A Short Essay on the Tarot of the Egyptians.* London: O. T. O., 1944.

————. *The Book of Thoth: A Short Essay on the Tarot of the Egyptians, Being the Equinox*, Vol. 3, no. 5. Newburyport, MA: Red Wheel, 1974.

————. *Magick: Liber ABA.* Newburyport, MA: Wiser, 1997.

————. *Magick Without Tears.* Hampton, NJ: Thelema, 1954.

Crowther, Arnold, and Patricia Crowther. *The Secrets of Ancient Witchcraft with the Witches Tarot.* Secaucus, NJ: University Books, 1974.

Cullen, Lisa Takeuchi. "Stretching for Jesus." *Time Magazine*, August 29, 2005, http://www.time.com/time/magazine/article/0,9171,1098937,00.html.

Cumont, Franz. *Astrology and Religion among the Greeks and Romans.* New York: Dover, 1960.

————. *The Mysteries of Mithra.* Internet Sacred Text Archive, 2007. http://www.sacred-texts.com/cla/mom/index.htm.

Curtis, Edward S. *The North American Indian; Being a Series of Volumes Picturing and Describing the Indians of the United States, and Alaska.* Project Gutenberg, http://www.gutenberg.org/files/19449/19449-0.txt, 2006.

Dahood, Michael. *Are the Ebla Tablets Relevant to Biblical Research?* Biblical Archaeological Society, http://members.bib-arch.org/nph-proxy.pl/000000A /httpl/www.basarchive.org/bswbSearch.asp=3fPubID=3dBSBA&Volume=3d6 &Issue=3d5&ArticleID=3d6&UserID=3d0&.

Dalrymple, Sir David, trans. *The Address of Tertullian of Carthage to Scapula, Proconsul of Africa*, (1790). Tertullian.org, http://www.tertullian.org/articles/ dalrymple_scapula.htm.

Dean, Geoffrey. *Recent Advances in Natal Astrology: A Critical Review 1900–1976.* Subiaco, Australia: Analogic, 1977.

De Camp, Lyon Sprague, and Catherine Crook De Camp. *Ancient Ruins and Archaeology.* New York: Doubleday, 1964.

Dickie, Matt. W. *Magic and Magicians in the Greco-Roman World.* London: Routledge, 2001.

Dodds, E. R. *The Greeks and the Irrational.* Berkeley: University of California Press, 1951.

Donnerstein E. & Lintz, D. "Mass Media Sexual Violence and Male Viewers: Current Theory and Research." *American Behavioral Scientist,* 29 (1986): 601–18.

Dowling, Levi H. *The Aquarian Gospel of Jesus, the Christ of the Piscean Age.* Santa Monica, CA: DeVorss, 1907.

Doyle, Arthur Conan. *The History of Spiritism.* New York: Arno, 1975.

————. *Wanderings of a Spiritist.* New York: George H. Doran, 1921.

DuQuette, Lon Milo. *The Magick of Aleister Crowley: A Handbook of the Rituals of Thelema.* Newburyport, MA: Weiser, 2004.

Eck, Diane L. *A New Religious America: How a "Christian Country" Has Become the World's Most Religiously Diverse Nation.* San Francisco: Harper, 1997.

Eddy, Mary Baker. *Science and Health with Key to the Scriptures.* Boston: Trustees Under the Will of Mary Baker Eddy, 1934 (rep. 1975).

Eglash, Ron. "An Ethnomathematics Comparison of African and Native American Divination Systems," paper presented at Realities Re-viewed/Revealed: Divination in Sub-Saharan Africa, National Museum of Ethnology, Leiden on July 4–5. Center for Cultural Design, Rensselaer Polytechnic Institute, http://www.ccd.rpi.edu/eglash/papers/eglash_div_paper.doc.

Elwell, Walter A., ed. *Baker Encyclopedia of the Bible.* Grand Rapids: Baker, 1988. Two volumes.

Encyclopaedia Britannica 2007 Deluxe Edition. Chicago: Encyclopaedia Britannica, 2007.

Eshman, Richard. "Center of Controversy," http://www.rickross.com/reference/kabbalah/kabbalah10.html.

Evans, Christopher. *Cults of Unreason.* New York: Dell, 1975.

Ewell, Walter A., ed. *Baker's Evangelical Dictionary of Biblical Theology.* Grand Rapids: Baker, 2006.

Fenton, John. *"Biographical Myths; Illustrated from the Lives of Buddha and Muhammad.* London: Taylor & Francis, 1880.

The Folk-Lore Record," vol. 3, no. 1. (1880), http://links.jstor.org/sici?sici=17441994%281880%293%3A1%3C26%3ABMIFTL%3E2.0.CO%3B2-P.

Fillmore, Charles. *Jesus Christ Heals.* Lee Summit, MO: Unity School of Christianity, 1944.

Fishbein, Aynat. "The Cabal of the Kabbalah Centre Exposed: New Relations," Tel Aviv Magazine, September 1994, http://www.rickross.com/reference/kabbalah/Kabbalah1.html.

Fleurant, Gerdes. *Dancing Spirits: Rhythms and Rituals of Haitian Vodun, the Rada Rite.* Westport, CT: Greenwood, 1996.

Flom, George T. "Sun-Symbols of the Tomb-Sculptures at Loughcrew, Ireland, Illustrated by Similar Figures in Scandinavian Rock-Tracings." *American Anthropologist* 26, no. 2. (April–June 1924), http://www.jstor.org/pss/660393.

Flournoy, Theodore. *India to the Planet Mars*. New York: Harper and Brothers, 1899.

Fordham University, *Medieval Sourcebook*. "The Correspondence of St. Boniface," http://www.fordham.edu/halsall/basis/boniface-letters.html.

Forsyth, J. S. *Demonologia or Natural Knowledge Revealed*. London: A. K. Newman and Co., 1831.

Frazer, James George. *The Golden Bough: A Study in Magic and Religion*. New York: Macmillian, 1922.

Frederickson, Bruce G. *Satanism*. St. Louis: Concordia, 1995.

Freedland, Nat. *The Occult Explosion: From Magic to ESP—The People Who Made the New Occultism*. New York: G. P. Putnam's Sons, 1972.

Frey, Sylvia R., and Betty Wood. *Come Shouting to Zion: African American Protestantism in the American South and British Caribbean to 1830*. Chapel Hill and London: University of North Carolina Press, 1998.

Fritscher, Jack. "STRAIGHT FROM THE WITCH'S MOUTH: An Interview with Anton Szandor LaVey, High Priest and Founder of The Church of Satan." http://www.jackfritscher.com/Non-Fiction/Witchcraft/Straight%20Witches%20Mouth.html.

Furst, Jeffrey. *Edgar Cayce's Story of Jesus*. New York: Berkley, 1968.

Gabel, W. Creighton. "European Secondary Neolithic Cultures: A Study of Prehistoric Culture Contact." *The Journal of the Royal Anthropological Institute of Great Britain and Ireland* 88, no. 1. (January–June, 1958). http://links.jstor.org/sici?sici=0307-3114%218 95801% 2F06%2988%3A1%3C97%3AESNCAS %3E2.0.C0%3B2-2.

Gager, John G., ed. *Curse Tablets and Binding Spells from the Ancient World*. New York: Oxford University Press, 1992.

Gallagher, Ann-Marie. *The Wicca Bible*. New York: Octopus, 2005.

Gallagher, Eugene V. *The New Religious Movements Experience in America*. Westport, CT: Greenwood Press, 2004.

Gardner, Gerald, *The Meaning of Witchcraft*. Newburyport, MA: Red Wheel, 2004.

Gardner, Martin. *The New Age: Notes of a Fringe Watcher*. Buffalo, NY: Prometheus, 1991.

Garratt, G. T. *The Legacy of India*. Oxford: Clarendon, 1937.

Geisler, Norman L. *Baker Encyclopedia of Christian Apologetics*. Grand Rapids: Baker, 1999.

————. "Primitive Monotheism." *Christian Apologetics Journal* 1, no. 1, (1998).

————. *Systematic Theology,* Vol. 2. Minneapolis: Bethany House, 2003.

Geisler, Norman L. *Systematic Theology,* Vol. 3. Minneapolis: Bethany House, 2004.

Gill, Jerry H. *Native American Worldview: An Introduction.* New York: Prometheus, 2003.

Giller, Rabbi Pinchas. "God in Kabbalah." American Jewish University, Ziegler School of Rabbinic Studies, n.d., http://www.ajula.edu/content/html/other/god.unit%207.pdf.

Glotzer, Leonard R. *The Fundamentals of Jewish Mysticism: The Book of Creation and Its Commentaries.* Amsterdam: Aronson, 1992.

Glover, T. R. *The Conflict of Religions in the Early Roman Empire.* Boston: Beacon, 1960.

Godwin, John. *Occult America.* Garden City, NY: Doubleday, 1972.

Goetz, William R. *UFOs: Friend, Foe or Fantasy?* Camp Hill, PA: Horizon, 1997.

Golb, Norman. *The Origins of the Dead Sea Scrolls: The Search for the Secret of Qumran.* New York: Scribner, 1995.

Gooding, Susan Staiger. "At the Boundaries of Religious Identity: Native American Religions and American Legal Culture." *Numen* 43, no. 2 (May, 1996). http://www.jstor.org/pss/3270345.

Goodman, Linda. *Linda Goodman's Love Signs.* New York: Fawcett Columbine, 1978.

————. *Linda Goodman's Sun Signs.* New York: Bantam, 1968.

Gordon, Cyrus H. *The Common Background of Greek and Hebrew Civilizations.* New York: Norton, 1965.

Gordon, Jacob U. "Yoruba Cosmology and Culture in Brazil: A Study of African Survivals in the New World." *Journal of Black Studies* 10, no. 2 (December 1979), JSTOR Stable URL: http://links.jstor.org/sici?sici=0021-9347%28197912%2910%3A2%3C231%3AYCACIB%3E2.0.CO%3B2-I.

Grant, Michael. *Eros in Pompeii: The Secret Rooms of the National Museum of Naples.* New York: William Morrow, 1975.

————. *The World of Rome.* New York: World, 1960.

Green, Miranda J. *The World of the Druids.* London: Thames and Hudson, 1997.

Guinness, Os. *The Dust of Death.* Downers Grove, IL: InterVarsity, 1973.

Hadden, Jeffrey K., and Anson Shupe, eds., *Prophetic Religions and Politics: Religion and the Political Order*, Vol. 1. New York: Paragon, 1988.

Hale, George Ellery. *Beyond the Milky Way*. New York: Charles Scribner's Sons, 1926.

Hall, Elvina M., "Jesus Paid It All," n.p., 1865.

Hames, Harvey J. *Exotericism and Esotericism in Thirteenth Century Kabbalah*, Ben Gurion University, http://www.esoteric.msu.edu/VolumeVI/KabbalahHames.htm.

Haskins, Jim. *Voodoo and Hoodoo*. New York: Scarborough, 1981.

Hanegraaff, Wouter J., ed., Antoine Faivre, Roelof van den Brock, and Jean-Pierre Brach. *Dictionary of Gnosis and Western Esotericism*. Leiden: Brill, 2006.

Heathcote-James, Emma. *They Walk Among Us*. London: Metro, 2004.

Hecker, Raquel. "Give Me Back My Old Madonna." *Observer*. October 31, 2004, http://arts.guardian.co.uk/features/story/0,,1340389,00.html.

Heindel, Max. *The Rosicrucian Cosmo-conception or Mystic Christianity*. Oceanside, CA: Rosicrucian Fellowship, 1937.

———. *The Rosicrucian Philosophy in Questions and Answers*. Oceanside, CA: Rosicrucian Fellowship, 1941.

Herodotus, *Histories*, Vol. 1.

Hettena, Seth. "Five years after heaven's gate mass suicide, last member still keeping faith." *San Diego Union-Tribune*, March 26, 2002, http://www.signon-sandiego.com/news/northcounty/20020326-0138-heavensgate.html.

Hexham, Irving, and Karla Poewe. *New Religions as Global Cultures: Making the Human Sacred*. Boulder, CO: Westview, 1997.

Hippolytus, *Philosophumena*, vol. 1 (c. 1921). Translated by F. Legge. Harvard College Library.

Holzer, Hans. *Ghosts: True Encounters with the World Beyond*. New York: Black Dog & Leventhal, 2004.

Home, D. D. *Incidents in My Life*. New York: Carleton, 1863.

Hooke, S. H. *Babylonian and Assyrian Religion*. Tulsa: University of Oklahoma Press, 1963.

Hornung, Eric. David Lorton, trans. *The Secret Lore of Egypt: Its Impact on the West*. Ithaca, NY: Cornell University Press, 2002.

Houdini, Harry, and Joseph Dunninger. *Magic and Mystery*. New York: Weathervane, 1967.

Hubbard, L. Ron. *A New Slant on Life*. Los Angeles: Publications Organization, 1952.

Hughes, Hayden, and Brad Steiger, ed. *UFO Missionaries Extraordinary*. New York: Pocket, 1976.

Hull, Bill. *New Century Disciplemaking: Applying Jesus' Ideas for the Future*. Grand Rapids: Revell, 2000.

Hutton, Ronald. "Paganism and Polemic: The Debate over the Origins of Modern Pagan Witchcraft." *Folklore Journal* 111 (2000).

Hutton, Ronald. *The Pagan Religions of the Ancient British Isles*. Oxford: Blackwell, 1991.

———. *The Triumph of the Moon: A History of Modern Pagan Witchcraft*. New York: Oxford University Press, 2001.

Hynek, J. Allen. "Categories of UFO Reports." *The Encyclopedia of UFOs*. Edited by Ronald D. Story. Garden City, NJ: Dolphin, 1980.

———. *The Hynek UFO Report*. New York: Dell, 1977.

International Raelian Movement, http://rael.org/rael_content/intro.php?elan=English.

Irenaeus, *Irenaeus Against Heresies*. Christian Classics Ethereal Library, 2007. http://www.ccel.org/ccel/schaff/anf01.ix.i.html.

Israel Insider Staff and Partners, "Kabbalist Rabbi Yitzhak Kaduri Dies in Jerusalem." *Israel Insider*. http://web.israelinsider.com/Articles/Culture/ 7665.htm, Israel Insider staff and partners, January 28, 2006.

Jencson, Linda. "Neopaganism and the Great Mother Goddess." *Anthropology Today* 5, no. 2 (1989), http://links.jstor.org/sici?sici=0268-540X%28198904% 295%3A2%3C2%3ANATGMG%3E2.0.CO%3B2-%23.

Jones, Prudence, and Nigel Pennick. *A History of Pagan Europe*. London: Routledge, 1995.

Jordan, Michael. *Witches: An Encyclopedia of Paganism and Magic*. London: Kyle Cathie Limited, 1996.

Joseph, Isya. *Devil Worship: The Sacred Books and Traditions of the Yezidis*. Boston: Badger, 1919.

Kahaner, Larry. *Cults That Kill*. New York: Warner, 1988.

Kamara, Gibreel M. "Regaining Our African Aesthetics and Essence Through Our African Traditional Religion." *Journal of Black Studies* 30, No. 4 (March, 2000), http://links.jstor.org/sici?sici=0021-9347%28200003%2930%3A4% 3C502%3AROAAAE%3E2.0.CO%3B2-C.

Karade, Baba Ifa. *The Handbook of Yoruba Religious Concepts.* Newburyport, MA: Weiser, 1994.

Katz, Morris. *The Journey.* Victoria, BC: Trafford Publishing, 2004.

Kawasaki, Guy. *Selling the Dream.* New York: HarperCollins, 1991.

Kelley, David Humiston, Anthony F. Aveni, and Eugene F. Milone. *Exploring Ancient Skies: an Encyclopedic Survey of Archaeoastronomy.* New York: Springer, 2005.

King, Godfré Ray. *Unveiled Mysteries.* Chicago: Saint Germain, 1934.

Kippenberg, Hans G. "Comparing Ancient Religions." *Numen* 39, no. 2. (December 1992): 221.

Klemp, Sri Harold. "Paul Twitchell's Spiritual Search." http://www.eckankar.org/Masters/Peddar/hisSearch.html.

Knight, Judy Zebra. *Ramtha: The White Book.* Yelm, WA: JZK, 2005.

Koch, Kurt. *Between Christ and Satan.* Grand Rapids: Kregel, 1970.

———. *Christian Counseling and Occultism.* Grand Rapids: Kregel, 1981

———. *Demonology Past and Present.* Grand Rapids: Kregel, 1973.

———. *Occult ABC.* Germany: Literature Mission Aglasterhausen, 1978.

———. *Occult ABC: Exposing Occult Practices and Ideologies.* Grand Rapids: Kregel, 1986.

———. *Occult Bondage and Deliverance.* Grand Rapids: Kregel, 1973.

Ladd, George Eldon. *The Presence of the Future: The Eschatology of Biblical Realism.* Grand Rapids: Eerdmans, 1996.

Laing, Gordon J. *Survivals of Roman Religion.* New York: Longmans, Green and Co., 1951.

Lamb, David. *The Search for Extraterrestrial Intelligence: A Philosophical Inquiry.* New York: Routledge, 2001.

Langley, Noel, and Cayce, Hugh Lynn. *Edgar Cayce on Reincarnation.* New York: Paperback Library, 1967.

Lattin, Don. "Satan's Den in Great Disrepair," *San Francisco Chronicle,* January 25, 1999.

LaVey, Anton Szandor. "Creator of the Church of Satan." (interview). *MF Magazine,* no. 3, on Shane and Amy Bugbee's The Doctor Is In Web site, http://www.churchofsatan.com/Pages/MFInterview.html.

————. *The Satanic Bible*. New York: Avon, 1966, 1969.

————. Anton Szandor. *Satanic Rituals*. San Francisco: Harper Collins, 1976.

Lewis, C. S. *God in the Dock: Essays on Theology and Ethics*. Grand Rapids: Eerdmans, 1994.

————. *The Screwtape Letters*. London: Geoffrey Bles, 1948.

————. *Shall We Lose God in Outer Space?* London: SPCK, 1959.

Lewis, Harvey Spencer, *The Mystical Life of Jesus*. San Jose, CA: Rosicrucian, 1948.

Lewis, James R. "Diabolical Authority: Anton LaVey, The Satanic Bible, and the Satanist 'Tradition.'" *Marburg Journal of Religion* 7, no. 1 (September 2002).

Lewis, James R., ed. *The Gods Have Landed: New Religions from Other Planets*. Albany: SUNY, 1995.

Lewis, James R. *Legitimating New Religions*. New Brunswick, NJ: Rutgers University Press, 2003.

————. *Odd Gods: New Religions and the Cult Controversy*. Amherst, NY: Prometheus, 2001.

Longnecker, Richard N. *Word Biblical Commentary: Galatians*. CD-ROM. Word, 1990.

Luck, Georg. *Arcana Mundi: Magic and the Occult in the Greek and Roman Worlds*. Baltimore: Johns Hopkins University Press, 1985.

Lundberg, Zaid. *Lights of Irfan: Papers Presented at the 'Irfán Colloquia and Seminars*. Wilmette, IL: Irfan Colloquia, 2000.

Luria, Isaac ben Solomon, *Kabbalah of Creation: The Mysticism of Isaac Luria, Founder of Modern Kabbalah*. Translated and edited by Eliahu Klein. Berkeley, CA: Atlantic Books, 2005.

Luther, Martin. *Vitae Patrum, Patrologia, Series Latina*, LXXIII, 940. CD-ROM. *Logos*, 2006.

Lyons, Delphine C. *Everyday Witchcraft: Love Magic, Charms, and Spells, Fortunetelling: Everything You Need to Know to Enjoy Occult Power*. New York: Dell, 1972.

McDowell, Josh. *The New Evidence That Demands a Verdict*. Nashville: Thomas Nelson, 1999.

McDowell, Josh, Don Stewart, assisted by Kurt Van Gorden. *The Occult: The Authority of the Believer over the Powers of Darkness*. Nashville: Thomas Nelson, 1992.

MacDonald-Baine, M. *Beyond the Himalayas.* London: Fowler and Co., n.d. http://www.soilandhealth.org/03sov/0304spiritpsych/030418.beyond.himalayas.pdf.

Mackenzie, Donald A. *Myths of Babylonia and Assyria.* Project Gutenberg, 2005. http://www.gutenberg.org/files/16653/16653-h/16653-h.htm.

Makkai, Ellen. "Harry the Wiz Is the Wrong Biz." *WorldNet Daily* (November 26, 2001), http://www.wnd.com/news/article.asp?ARTICLE_ID=25446.

Martin, Walter R. *Advice to Writers.* CD/audiotape, Walter Martin Ministries, www.waltermartin.com.

———. *Astrology.* CD/audiotape, Walter Martin Ministries, www.waltermartin.com.

———. *Chariots of the Who?* CD/audiotape, Walter Martin Ministries. www.waltermartin.com

———. *Church of Satan.* CD/audiotape, Walter Martin Ministries, www.waltermartin.com.

———. *Doctrine of the Demons.* CD/audiotape, Walter Martin Ministries, www.waltermartin.com.

———. *ESP and Parapsychology.* CD/audiotape, Walter Martin Ministries, www.waltermartin.com.

———. *Essential Christianity.* Walter Martin Ministries, Walter Martin Ministries e-Book, 2000.

———. *Evangelism and Apologetics.* CD/audiotape, Walter Martin Ministries, www.waltermartin.com.

———. *Evangelizing People in the Cults and Occult.* Audiotape. Melodyland Christian Center, Anaheim, California, 1978.

———. *Evil and Human Suffering.* CD/audiotape, Walter Martin Ministries, www.waltermartin.com.

———. *Exorcism.* CD/audiotape, Walter Martin Ministries, www.waltermartin.com.

———. *Growing in the Spirit.* CD/audiotape, Walter Martin Ministries, www.waltermartin.com.

———. *Hermeneutics. Pt. 1-6,* CD/audiotape, Walter Martin Ministries, www.waltermartin.com.

———. *Hypnotism.* CD/audiotape, Walter Martin Ministries, www.waltermartin.com.

————. *Inspiration of Scripture.* CD/audiotape, Walter Martin Ministries, www.waltermartin.com.

————. *Introduction to the Cults.* CD/audiotape, Walter Martin Ministries, www.waltermartin.com.

————. *Jeane Dixon and Edgar Cayce: 20th Century Prophets.* CD/audiotape, Walter Martin Ministries, www.waltermartin.com.

————. *Jesus: God, Man or Myth?* CD/audiotape, Walter Martin Ministries, www.waltermartin.com.

————. *The Kingdom of the Cults.* Minneapolis: Bethany House, 1965 (rep. 2003).

————. *Martin Library Tapes 1-20.* CD/audiotape, Walter Martin Ministries, www.waltermartin.com.

————. *Modern Scribes and Pharisees.* CD/audiotape, Walter Martin Ministries, www.waltermartin.com.

————. *The New Age Cult.* Minneapolis: Bethany House, 1989.

————. *New Age Movement.* CD/audiotape, Walter Martin Ministries, www.waltermartin.com.

————. *The New Cults.* Santa Ana, CA: Vision House, 1980.

————. *Occult Revolution.* CD/audiotape, Walter Martin Ministries, www.waltermartin.com.

————. *Psychic Phenomena.* CD/audiotape, Walter Martin Ministries, www.waltermartin.com.

————. *Reasons for Faith.* CD/audiotape, Walter Martin Ministries, www.waltermartin.com.

————. *Revival of the Occult.* CD/audiotape, Walter Martin Ministries, www.waltermartin.com.

————. *Riddle of Reincarnation.* CD/audiotape, Walter Martin Ministries, www.waltermartin.com.

————. *Robert Schuller and the Cult of Self-Esteem.* CD/audiotape, Walter Martin Ministries, www.waltermartin.com.

————. *Rosicrucians and Theosophy.* CD/audiotape, Walter Martin Ministries, www.waltermartin.com.

————. *Screwtape Writes Again.* Santa Ana, CA: Vision House, 1980.

————. *Secret of Apologetics.* DVD/audiotape, Walter Martin Ministries, www.waltermartin.com.

————. *Spiritism*. CD/audiotape, Walter Martin Ministries, www.waltermartin.com.

————. *Spirit of the Age*. CD/audiotape, Walter Martin Ministries, www.waltermartin.com.

————. *Spiritual Warfare*. CD/audiotape, Walter Martin Ministries, www.waltermartin.com.

————. *Tools of the Occult*. CD/audiotape, Walter Martin Ministries, www.waltermartin.com.

————. *UFOs: Friend, Foe or Fantasy?* CD/audiotape, Walter Martin Ministries, www.waltermartin.com.

————. *Witchcraft and Satanism*. CD/audiotape, Walter Martin Ministries, www.waltermartin.com.

Martyr, Justin. *Apology I*. Christian Classics Ethereal Library, 2007. http://www.ccel.org/fathers2/ANF-01/anf01-46.htm#P3935_744654.

————. *Dialogue with Trypho, a Jew*. Christian Classics Ethereal Library, 2007. http://www.ccel.org/fathers2/ANF-01/anf01-48.htm#P4288_866334.

————. *First Apology*. Early Christian Writings, 2006. http://www.earlychristian-writings.com/text/justinmartyr-firstapology.html.

May, Edwin C., and Larissa Vilenskaya. "Overview of Current Parapsychology Research in the Former Soviet Union." *Laboratories for Fundamental Research*, http://www.lfr.org/LFR/csl/library/Fsu1.pdf.

Mbiti, John S. *African Religions and Philosophy*. New York: Praeger, 1969.

Medway, Gareth J. *Lure of the Sinister: The Unnatural History of Satanism*. New York: New York University Press, 2001.

Meier, Samuel A. *Baker's Evangelical Dictionary of Biblical Theology*. Grand Rapids: Baker, 1996.

Melton, J. Gordon. *Encyclopedic Handbook of Cults in America*. New York: Garland, 1992.

Melton, J. Gordon, Jerome Clark and Aidan A. Kelly. *New Age Almanac*. New York: Visible Ink, 1991.

Menzies, Allen., ed. *The Ante-Nicene Fathers,* Vol. 3. Grand Rapids: Eerdmans, 1978.

Mettinger, Tryggve N.D. *Riddle of Resurrection: "Dying and Rising Gods" in the Ancient Near East*. Philadelphia: Coronet Books, 2001.

Michaelson, Johanna. *The Beautiful Side of Evil*. Eugene, OR: Harvest House, 1982.

Michaelsen, Robert S. "Cherokee Nation: 17. The Significance of the American Indian Religious Freedom Act of 1978." *Journal of the American Academy of Religion* 52, no. 1. (March, 1984), http://links.jstor.org/sici?sici=0002 7189%28198403%2952%3A1%3C93%3ATSOTAI%3E2.0.CO%3B2-C.

Miracle Distribution Center. *A Course in Miracles: Combined Volume.* Glen Ellen, CA: Foundation for Inner Peace, 1987.

Miller, Russell. *Bare-Faced Messiah: The True Story of L. Ron Hubbard.* New York: Henry Holt, 1987.

Mjagkij, Nina., ed. *Organizing Black America.* New York: Garland, 2001.

Montgomery, Ruth. *A Gift of Prophecy: The Phenomenal Jeane Dixon.* New York: William Morrow, 1965.

Moore, Brian L., and Michele A. Johnson. *Neither Led nor Driven: Contesting British Cultural Imperialism in Jamaica,* 1865–1920. Kingston, Jamaica: University of the West Indies Press, 2004.

Moore, David W. "Three in Four Americans Believe in Paranormal," Gallup, June 16, 2005, http://www.gallup.com/poll/16915/Three-Four-Americans-Believe-Paranormal.aspx.

Mounce, William D. *Word Biblical Commentary: Pastoral Epistles.* CD-ROM. Word, 2002.

Muller-Ebeling, Claudia, Christian Ratsch and Wolf-Dieter Storl. *Witchcraft Medicine: Healing Arts, Shamanic Practices, and Forbidden Plants.* Rochester: Inner Traditions, 1998.

Murphy, Joseph M. *Working the Spirit: Ceremonies of the African Diaspora.* Boston: Beacon, 1995.

Nada-Yolanda, *Visitors from Other Planets.* Miami: Mark-Age, 1974.

Nelson's Complete Book of Bible Maps & Charts: Old and New Testaments. Rev. and updated ed. CD-ROM. Thomas Nelson. 1996.

Nichols, Larry A., George A. Mather, and Alvin J. Schmidt, with Kurt Van Gorden, *Encyclopedic Dictionary of Cults, Sects, and World Religions.* Grand Rapids: Zondervan, 2006.

Nietzsche, Friedrich. *The Antichrist.* Translated by H. L. Mencken, section 35. Friedrich Nietzsche Society, http://www.fns.org.uk/ac.htm, 1920.

Nigosian, S. A. *The Zoroastrian Faith: Tradition and Modern Research.* Montreal: McGill-Queens University Press, 1993.

Noblitt, James Randall, and Pamela Sue Perskin. *Cult and Ritual Abuse: Its History, Anthropology, and Recent Discovery in Contemporary America.* Westport, CT: Praeger, 2000.

Noorbergen, Rene. *Jeane Dixon: My Life and Prophecies.* New York: William Morrow, 1969.

———. *The Soul Hustlers.* Grand Rapids: Zondervan, 1976.

Norman, Eric. *Gods and Devils from Outer Space.* New York: Lancer, 1973.

O'Hara, Maureen, with John Nicoletti. *'Tis Herself: A Memoir.* New York: Simon & Schuster, 2004.

Olupona, Jacob K., ed. *African Spirituality: Forms, Meanings and Expressions.* New York: The Crossroad Publishing Company, 2000.

———. *African Traditional Religions in Contemporary Society.* New York: Paragon, 1991.

Orr, James, ed. *International Standard Bible Encyclopedia.* Chicago: Howard-Severence, 1915.

Ortiz de Montellano, Bernard R. *Aztec Medicine, Health, and Nutrition.* New Brunswick, NJ: Rutgers University Press, 1990.

Partridge, Christopher Hugh, ed. *UFO Religions.* Oxford: Routledge, 2003.

Peck, M. Scott. *People of the Lie.* New York: Simon & Schuster, 1983.

Peeples, Curtis. *Watch the Skies! A Chronicle of the Flying Saucer Myth.* New York: Berkley, 1994.

Pentecost, J. Dwight. *The Words and Works of Jesus Christ: A Study of the Life of Christ.* Grand Rapids: Zondervan, 2000.

Petersen, William J. *Those Curious New Cults in the 80s,* New Canaan, CT: Keats, 1982.

Petrie, W. M. Flinders. *Personal Religion in Egypt Before Christianity.* London: Harper and Brothers, 1912.

Petrowsky, Marc and William W. Zellner, eds. *Sects, Cults, and Spiritual Communities: A Sociological Analysis.* Westport, CT: Praeger, 1998.

Pettit, Bryce A. "New Religious Movements and Missions." *International Journal of Frontier Missions* 15 (1998): 125–34.

Phillips, J. B. *Your God Is Too Small.* London: Wyvern, 1952.

Phillips, Rebecca. "Kabbalah for Everyone." Beliefnet (2007), http://www.beliefnet.com/story/158/story_15886_1.html.

Pierre, Roland. "Caribbean Religion: The Voodoo Case." *Sociological Analysis* 38, no. 1 (Spring 1977), http://www.jstor.org/pss/3709834.

Pike, Albert. *Morals and Dogma of the Ancient and Accepted Rite of Freemasonry.* Richmond, VA: L. H. Jenkins Book, 1958.

Pollock, Sheldon I. *The Language of the Gods in the World of Men: Sanskrit, Culture, and Power in Premodern India.* Berkeley, CA: University of California Press, 2006.

Prophet, Elizabeth Clare. *Inner Perspectives.* Livingston, MT: Summit University Press, 2003.

Rabinovitch, Dina, "Fallen Idol," *The Guardian*, June 22, 2005, http://books.guardian.co.uk/news/articles/0,6109,1511663,00.html.

Radar Online, "The Kabbalah Chronicles: Inside Hollywood's Hottest Cult," June 17, 2005, http://www.radaronline.com/web-only/the-kabbalah-chronicles/2005/06/inside-hollywoods-hottest-cult-ii.php.

Radin, D. I., and R. D. Nelson. "Evidence for Consciousness-Related Anomalies in Random Physical Systems." *Foundations of Physics* 19, no. 12 (December 1989), http://www.springerlink.com/content/n0576p6352g84158/.

Rael. *The True Face of God.* Montreal: The Raelian Religion, 1998.

"Raising the Devil." *Time Magazine*, March 13, 1972, www.time.com/time/magazine/article/0,9171,903361,00.html.

Ramsland, Katherine. *Ghost: Investigating the Other Side.* New York: Thomas Dunne, 2001.

Randles, Jenny and Peter Hough. *The Complete Book of UFOs.* New York: Sterling, 1996.

Reid, Audley G. *Community Formation: A Study of the "Village" in Postemancipation Jamaica.* Kingston, Jamaica: Canoe, 2000.

Regardie, Israel. *The Tree of Life: A Study in Magic.* York Beach, Maine: Weiser, 2000.

Reuchlin, Johann. *On the Art of the Kabbalah.* Lincoln, NE: University of Nebraska Press, 1993.

Reynolds, John Lawrence. *Secret Societies: Inside the World's Most Notorious Organizations.* New York: Arcade Publishing, 2006.

Rhodes, Ron. *Alien Obsession.* Eugene, OR: Harvest House, 1998.

Richet, Charles, and Stanley Debrath. *Thirty Years of Psychical Research.* Whitefish, MO: Kessinger, 2003.

Roberts, Alexander, and James Donaldson, eds. *Ante-Nicene Fathers, Volume 7: Fathers of the Third and Fourth Centuries.* Grand Rapids: Eerdmans, 1886.

Roberts, Jane. *Seth Speaks: The Eternal Validity of the Soul.* San Rafael, CA: Amber-Allen, 1994.

Roberts, Jane, and Susan M. Watkins. *The God of Jane: A Psychic Manifesto.* Needham, MA: Moment Point Press, 2000.

Robertson, A. T. *Word Pictures of the New Testament.* Nashville: Broadman, 1932 (repr. 1933, 1938).

Ross, Hugh, Kenneth Samples, and Mark Clark. *Lights in the Sky and Little Green Men.* Colorado Springs: NavPress, 2002.

Ross, Rick A. Official Web site of the Rick A. Ross Institute for the Study of Destructive Cults, Controversial Groups and Movements, http://www.rickross.com/.

Russell, Jeffrey B., and Brooks Alexander. *A History of Witchcraft: Sorcerers, Heretics and Pagans.* London: Thames & Hudson, 2007.

Russell, Jeffrey Burton. *The Devil: Perceptions of Evil from Antiquity to Primitive Christianity.* Ithaca, NY: Cornell University Press, 1987.

———. *Witchcraft in the Middle Ages.* Ithaca, New York: Cornwell University Press, 1984 (rep. 1995).

Schneider, Lisa. "Spirituality in a Material World." Beliefnet, http://www.beliefnet.com/story/154/story_15474_2.html.

Scholem, Gershom. *Kabbalah.* New York: Penguin Group, 1978.

———. *Major Trends in Jewish Mysticism.* New York: Schocken, 1961.

Schreck, Zeena, and Nikolas Schreck. *Anton LaVey: Legend and Reality.* www.churchofsatan.org/aslv.html.

Schucman, Hellen. *A Course in Miracles.* New York: Foundation for Inner Peace, 1975.

Scientology: A World Religion Emerges in the Space Age. Los Angeles: Church of Scientology of California, 1979.

Seznac, Jean. *The Survival of the Pagan Gods.* New York: Pantheon, 1953.

Smart, Ninian. *The Religious Experience of Mankind.* New York: Scribner, 1976.

Smith, Henry Goodwin. "Persian Dualism." *The American Journal of Theology* 8, no. 3. (July 1904), http://links.jstor.org/sici?sici=15503283%28190407%298%3A3%3C487%3APD%3E2.0.CO%3B2-Y.

Smith, Mary Ettie V. *Fifteen Years Among the Mormons.* New York: Charles Scribner, 1858.

Smith, Robert J. *Fortune-Tellers and Philosophers: Divination in Traditional Chinese Society.* Boulder, CO: Westview, 1991.

Smith, Wilbur. *Therefore Stand: Christian Apologetics.* Grand Rapids: Baker, 1965.

Snodgrass, Mary Ellen. *Signs of the Zodiac: A Reference Guide to Historical, Mythological, and Cultural Associations.* Westport, CT: Greenwood, 1997.

Spangler, David. *Reflections on the Christ.* Moray, Scotland: Findhorn, 1978.

Sproul, R. C. *Chosen by God.* Carol Stream, IL: Tyndale, 1986.

Starhawk, Diane Baker, Anne Hill, and Sara Ceres Boore. *Circle Round: Raising Children in Goddess Traditions.* New York: Bantam, 1998.

Stavish, Mark. "Kabbalah and the Hermetic Tradition," http://www.hermetic.com/ stavish/essays/kabbalah-hermetic.html.

Steiner, Rudolf. *Goddess: From Natura to the Divine Sophia.* London: Rudolf Steiner, 2002.

Story, Ronald D. ed. *The Encyclopedia of UFOs.* Garden City, NJ: Dolphin, 1980.

Swedenborg, Emanuel. *Arcana Coelestia* n. 50, quoted in Smyth, Julian K., and William F. Wunsch, comps., *The Gist of Swedenborg.* Philadelphia: Iungerich Publication Fund, 1920, http://www.sacred-texts.com/chr/swe/gos.htm, http://www.sacred-texts.com/swd/ac/index.htm.

———. *Earths in the Universe.* Translated by John Whitehead. Internet Sacred Text Archive, 2007. www.sacred-texts.com/swd/eiu/eiu02.htm.

Tacitus. *Histories.* The Internet Classics Archive, 2000. http://classics.mit.edu/ Tacitus/histories.1.i.html.

Taylor, Robert Jonathan. *An Analysis of Celestial Omina in the Light of Mesopotamian Cosmology and Mythos.* Nashville: Vanderbuilt, 2006.

Tenney, Merril C., ed. *The Zondervan Pictorial Encyclopdia of the Bible.* Grand Rapids: Zondervan, 1976.

Trithemius. *The Magus*, book II. Translated by Francis Barrett. London, N. P., 1801, http://www.esotericarchives.com/tritheim/trchryst.htm.

Trobe, Kala. *Magic of Qabalah.* St. Paul: Llewellyn, 2001.

Tunnicliffe, K. C. *Aztec Astrology.* Essex, Great Britain: L. N. Fowler, 1979.

Unger, Merrill F. *Biblical Demonology.* Wheaton: Scripture Press, 1952.

———. *Biblical Demonology: A Study of Spiritual Forces at Work Today.* Grand Rapids: Kregel, 1994.

———. *Demons in the World Today.* Carol Stream, IL: Tyndale, 1972.

The Urantia Book. Chicago: Urantia Foundation, 1955.

USA Today, Talk Today, May 27, 2007, http://cgi1.usatoday.com/mchat/20040526006/tscript.htm.

Valantasis, Richard., ed. *Religions of Late Antiquity in Practice.* Princeton: Princeton University Press, 2000.

Varner, William. "The Christian Use of Jewish Numerology." *The Master's Seminary Journal* (1TMSJ 8/1), http://www.tms.edu/tmsj/tmsj8c.pdf.

Veno, A., and P. Pammunt. "Astrological Factors and Personality: A Southern Hemisphere Replication." *Journal of Psychology* 101 (1979).

Von Daniken, Erich. *According to the Evidence: My Proof of Man's Extraterrestrial Origins.* New York: Bantam, 1978.

———. *Chariots of the Gods?* New York: Putnam, 1969.

———. *Gods from Outer Space.* New York: Putnam, 1970.

———. *Gold of the God.* New York: Bantam, 1973.

———. *In Search of Ancient Gods.* New York: Putnam, 1973.

———. *Miracles of the Gods.* New York: Dell, 1976.

Ward, Charles A. *Oracles of Nostradamus.* Internet Sacred Text Archive, 2007. http://www.sacred-texts.com/nos/oon/oon05.htm.

Warren, Ed, and Lorraine Warren. *Ghost Hunters: True Stories from the World's Most Famous Demonologists.* New York: St. Martin's, 1989.

Waters, Anne, and John H. Dufour, eds. *American Indian Thought: A Philosophy Reader.* Oxford: Blackwell, 2003.

Weldon, John. "Dowsing: Divine Gift, Human Ability, or Occult Power?" *Christian Research Journal Article* 8 (Spring, 1992), http://www.iclnet.org/pub/resources/text/cri/cri-jrnl/web/crj0099a.html.

Weldon, John, with Zola Levitt. *UFOs: What on Earth is Happening? The Coming Invasion.* New York: Bantam, 1976.

Wilson, Clifford. *Alien Agenda.* New York: Signet, 1975.

———. *The Chariots Still Crash.* New York: Signet, 1975.

————. *Close Encounters: A Better Explanation.* San Diego: Master, 1978.

————. *Crash Go the Chariots.* New York: Lancer, 1972.

————. *UFOs and Their Mission Impossible.* New York: Signet, 1975.

————. *War of the Chariots.* New York: Signet, 1978.

Wineman, Aryeh, ed. *Mystic Tales from the Zohar.* Philadelphia: Jewish Publishing Society, 1997.

Wolfe, Tom. *Mauve Gloves & Madmen, Clutter & Vine.* New York: Farrar Straus Giroux, 1976.

Wolpe, Rabbi David. "False Promises in Berg's 'Becoming.'" *Jewish Journal* (December 17, 2004), http://www.jewishjournal.com/home/preview.php?id=13394.

Yarbro, Chelsea Quinn. *Messages from Michael.* New York: Berkeley, 1980.

Yoke, Ho Peng. *Li, Qi, and Shu: An Introduction to Science and Civilization in China.* Hong Kong: Hong Kong University Press, 1985.

Yoseloff, Thomas. *A Fellow of Infinite Jest.* New York: Prentice Hall, 1945.

Zaehner, R. C. *The Dawn and Twilight of Zoroastrianism.* New York: Putnam, 1961.

Zell-Ravenheart, Oberon. *Grimoire for the Apprentice Wizard.* Franklin Lakes: New Page, 2004.

Index

astral projection, 197, 203, 245, 256, 259–60, 263, 308, 366, 507, 526, 560, 563
astral travel, 308, 313–14, 366. *See also* scrying
astrology, 14, 24, 26, 146, 191, 195, 239, 268–305, 326, 352, 465, 597:
    ancient, 272–81:
        Aztec, 281
        Babylonian, 273–77, 282, 289
        Chinese, 279
        Egyptian, 276–77, 278
        Elysian, 195
        Greco-Roman, 277–78
        Greek (*also* Hellenistic), 277–78
        Indian, 279–82
        Mayan, 281
        Mesopotamian, 272–75
        omen, 274–75, 286
        Pre-Columbian New World, 281
        Zoroastrian, 275–76
    contrasted with astronomy, 271
    Daniel and, 14, 45, 274, 299–301, 353
    modern, 284–84
    problems with, 284–87: constellation length, 282, 286; equinox precession, 282, 285; exempt people, 285; geocentric universe, 284–85; multiple births and contrasting character traits, 286; new planets, 286–87
    New Age, 284
    Western, 277, 278
astronomy, 70, 91, 271–72, 276–77, 279, 281, 285, 286, 298: biblical, 288–89
auras, 195, 244, 308–9, 314–15
automatic writing, 192, 195–96, 244, 255–56, 309, 315–16, 367, 419, 564, 570, 571, 598
avatar(s), 73, 117, 200, 208, 209, 215, 220, 340

Avatar (cartoon), 340
Avebury (stone circle), 19, 70

B

Baal, 117, 122, 447, 651, 675–75
Babylon, 70–71, 102, 121, 274, 275, 391
Babylonian:
    astrology, 272–77, 282, 289
    captivity of the Jews, 71
    concepts, 274, 479
    deities, 115,
    history and conquests, 71, 101, 289
    king (Lucifer), 391
    influence on dualism, 104
    origins for present-day customs, 121
    portrayal of Satan, 4
    text, 274, 277
Bacchus (Roman god), 51, 84, 88–90, 95, 114, 120–21. *See also* Dionysus
Bach, Marcus, 29–33, 42–43, 194
Back to Africa movement, 493–94
Bailey, Alice, 192, 195, 203–4, 207, 564–65, 568, 580
balance, 209–10, 212, 219, 309
Ballard, Edna, 191, 204, 367, 566
Ballard, Guy, 191, 204, 367, 369, 566
Bar-Jesus, 11–12, 352–53, 467, 643
Barnhouse, Donald Grey, 7–8, 354, 603, 665–66, 671, 673, 676
Barr, Roseanne, 153, 161
Barton, Magistra Blanche, 413
Barton, Tamsyn, 270, 278
Basil the Great, Saint, 401
BC (dating), 70
BCE (dating), 70
Beelzebub. *See* Satan, other names for
Belial, 5, 546, 615. *See also* Satan, other names for
Berg, Michael, 152, 158, 167–69, 173